THE PORTABLE WORLD

A

COMPLETE POCKET ATLAS

EDITED BY

B.M. WILLETT
AND DAVID GAYLARD

AVON BOOKS ◢ NEW YORK

CONTENTS

WORLD

8-9   **World: Northern part**

10-11   **World: Southern part**

12-13   **Arctic**

14-15   **Antarctic**

EUROPE

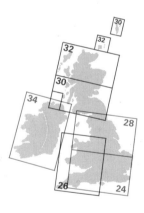

16-17   **Europe: Physical**

18-19   **Europe: Political**

20-21   **British Isles: South**

22-23   **British Isles: North**

24-25   **Southern England**

26-27   **Wales and South West England**

28-29   **Northern England**

30-31   **Southern Scotland**

32-33   **Northern Scotland**

34-35   **Ireland**

Published in Great Britain in 1996 as
Philip's Essential World Atlas

Cartography by Philip's
81 Fulham Road, London SW3 6RB, England

AVON BOOKS
A division of
The Hearst Corporation
1350 Avenue of the Americas
New York, New York 10019

Printed in Hong Kong

© 1992, 1994, 1996 Reed International Books Ltd
All Rights Reserved
Published by arrangement with George Philip Ltd,
London

ISBN 0–380–77329–5

Third Avon Books Trade Printing:
August 1996 — Reprinted 1997

AVON TRADEMARK REG. U.S. PAT. OFF. AND IN
OTHER COUNTRIES, MARCA REGISTRADA.

10 9 8 7 6 5 4 3

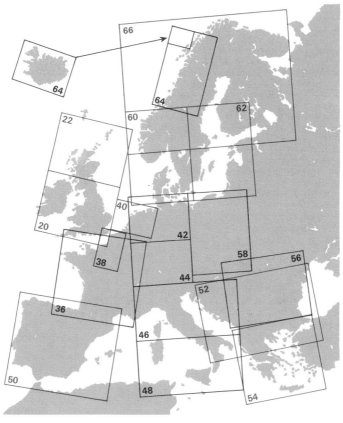

36-37 France
38-39 Northern France
40-41 Netherlands
42-43 Germany and the Low
       Countries
44-45 Alpine Lands
46-47 Northern Italy and
       Corsica
48-49 Southern Italy and
       Sardinia

50-51 Spain and Portugal
52-53 Danube Lands
54-55 Greece and Albania
56-57 Romania
58-59 Central Europe
60-61 Southern Scandinavia
62-63 Baltic Lands
64-65 North West Scandinavia
       and Iceland
66-67 Northern Scandinavia

ASIA

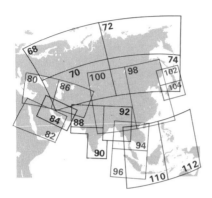

76-77   Asia: Physical
78-79   Asia: Political

80-81   Turkey and the Middle East
82-83   Arabian Peninsula
84-85   The Gulf
86-87   Central Asia and Afghanistan
88-89   Pakistan and North West India
90-91   Central and Southern India, Sri Lanka
92-93   Eastern India, Bangladesh and Burma
94-95   Mainland South East Asia
96-97   The Malay Peninsula
98-99   China: East
100-101   China: West

68-69   Eastern Europe
70-71   Kazakstan and Central Asia
72-73   North East Russia
74-75   South East Russia and Mongolia

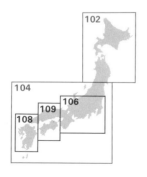

102-103   Japan: North
104-105   Japan: South
106-107   Japan: Tokyo, Kyoto, Osaka
108-109   Japan: Kyushu, West Honshu and Shikoku

110-111   Indonesia: West
112-113   Indonesia: East

AUSTRALASIA

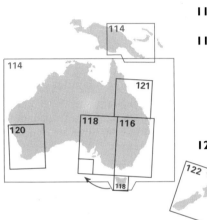

114-115 Australia, New Zealand
         and Papua New Guinea
116-117 Australia: Brisbane,
         Sydney and Melbourne
118-119 Australia: Adelaide,
         Melbourne and Tasmania
    120 Australia: Perth
    121 Australia: North East
         Queensland

122-123 New Zealand, Central and
         South West Pacific

AFRICA

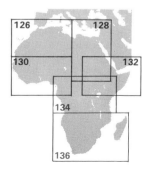

124 Africa: Physical
125 Africa: Political

126-127 Africa: North West
128-129 Africa: North East
130-131 Africa: West
132-133 Africa: East
134-135 Africa: Central
136-137 Africa: South

NORTH AMERICA

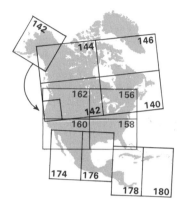

138   North America: Physical
139   North America: Political

140-141   Canada: South East
142-143   Canada: South West and Alaska
144-145   Canada: North West
146-147   Canada: North East
148-149   Canada: Saint Lawrence Estuary
150-151   Canada: The Great Lakes
152-153   Canada: Southern Saskatchewan and Manitoba
154-155   Canada: Southern British Columbia and Alberta

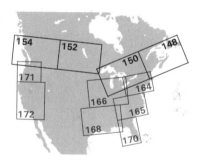

156-157   USA: North East
158-159   USA: South East
160-161   USA: South West
162-163   USA: North West
      164   USA: Boston, New York, Washington
      165   USA: Washington, Atlanta
166-167   USA: Upper Mississippi
168-169   USA: Lower Mississippi and Gulf Coast
      170   USA: Florida
      171   USA: Columbia Basin
172-173   USA: California

174-175   Mexico: West
176-177   Mexico: East
178-179   Caribbean: West
180-181   Caribbean: East

SOUTH AMERICA

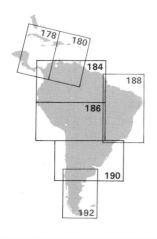

182 South America: Physical
183 South America: Political

184-185 South America: North West
186-187 South America: West
188-189 South America: East
190-191 South America: Central
192 South America: South

INDEX

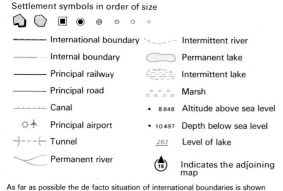

MAP SYMBOLS

Settlement symbols in order of size

⬠ ⬡ ■ ● ◎ ○ ○ ○

———— International boundary
········· Internal boundary
———— Principal railway
———— Principal road
+++++ Canal
☼✈ Principal airport
-)---(- Tunnel
∿ Permanent river

`-~-_-` Intermittent river
⬭ Permanent lake
⬭ Intermittent lake
۰۰۰ Marsh
▲ 8848 Altitude above sea level
▼ 10497 Depth below sea level
263 Level of lake
(18) Indicates the adjoining map

As far as possible the de facto situation of international boundaries is shown

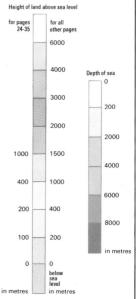

Height and depth colours

Height of land above sea level

for pages 24-35	for all other pages
	6000
	4000
	3000
1000	2000
	1500
400	1000
200	400
100	200
0	0
in metres	below sea level
	in metres

Depth of sea
0
200
2000
4000
6000
8000
in metres

Scale note
To the right of each map title there is a number representing the scale of the map for example, 1 : 2 000 000. This means that one centimetre on the map represents 2 million centimetres or 20 kilometres on the ground. Or, if the number is 1 : 40 000 000, one centimetre represents 40 million centimetres or 400 kilometres.

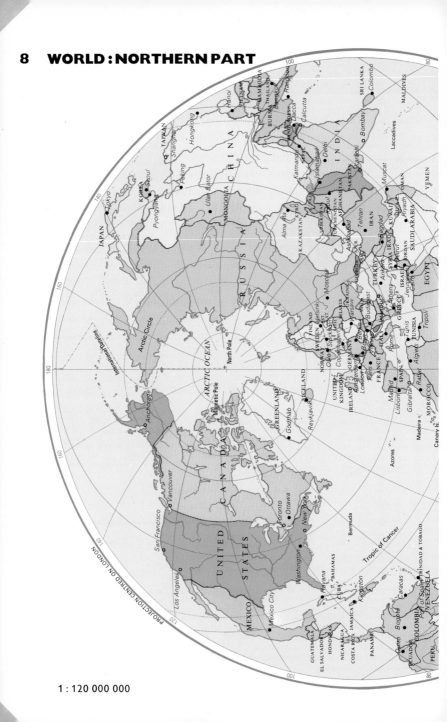

1 : 120 000 000

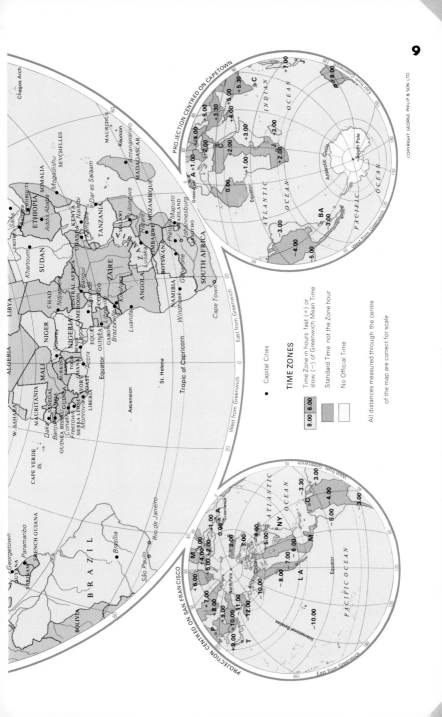

9

Chagos Arch.

SEYCHELLES

MAURITIUS
Réunion

MADAGASCAR
Antananarivo

W. SAHARA
ALGERIA
LIBYA
Saha

ERITREA
Djibouti
SOMALIA
Mogadishu
ETHIOPIA
Addis Ababa

Khartoum
SUDAN
UGANDA
KENYA
Kampala
Nairobi
RWANDA
Dar es Salaam
TANZANIA

MAURITANIA
MALI
NIGER
CHAD
CENTRAL AFRICA
N'djaména
Bangui
ZAIRE
MALAWI
Lilongwe
Lusaka
ZAMBIA
Harare
ZIMBABWE
MOZAMBIQUE
Maputo

Dakar
SENEGAL
GAMBIA
GUINEA BISSAU
GUINEA
Banjul
Conakry
Freetown
SIERRA LEONE
Monrovia
LIBERIA
IVORY COAST
BURKINA
GHANA
Accra
TOGO
BENIN
NIGERIA
CAMEROON
Abuja
Porto Novo
Lomé
Yaoundé
EQUAT. GUINEA
GABON
CONGO
Libreville
Brazzaville
Kinshasa
ANGOLA
Luanda

NAMIBIA
Windhoek
BOTSWANA
Gaborone
Pretoria
Johannesburg
Maputo
SWAZILAND
LESOTHO
SOUTH AFRICA

CAPE VERDE IS.

St. Helena

Ascension

Tropic of Capricorn

Cape Town

Equator

GUYANA
Georgetown
SURINAM
Paramaribo
FRENCH GUIANA

B R A Z I L

BOLIVIA

Rio de Janeiro
São Paulo
Brasília

West from Greenwich   East from Greenwich

• Capital Cities

TIME ZONES

| 9.00 | 6.00 |

Time Zone in hours fast (+) or
slow (−) of Greenwich Mean Time

Standard Time not the Zone hour

No Official Time

All distances measured through the centre
of the map are correct for scale

PROJECTION CENTRED ON CAPETOWN

Greenwich
A +1.00
+2.00
+3.00
+4.00
+5.00
+5.30
+4.00
+3.00
+2.00
+1.00
0.00
C
J
INDIAN OCEAN
ATLANTIC OCEAN
PACIFIC OCEAN
−3.00
−3.00
−4.00
−5.00
BA
Equator
Antarctic Circle
South Pole
East from Greenwich
West from Greenwich
+8.00
+7.00
P

PROJECTION CENTRED ON SAN FRANCISCO

West from Greenwich
East from Greenwich
Greenwich
0.00
A
+1.00
+2.00
+3.00
+4.00
M
+4.00
+5.00
+6.00
+7.00
+8.00
P
+9.00 +10.00
−11.00
−12.00
T
−10.00
−9.00
−8.00
−7.00
−6.00
LA
−5.00
−4.00
C
−3.00
−3.30
O
NY
ATLANTIC OCEAN
PACIFIC OCEAN
Equator
North Pole
International Date Line

PROJECTION CENTRED ON THE ANTIPODES OF LONDON

100

80

120

140

Galapagos Is.

Easter I.

PACIFIC OCEAN

Marquesas Is.

Tuamotu Arch.

Pitcairn I.

Tropic of Capricorn

FRENCH POLYNESIA

Tahiti

160

Hawaiian Is.

PACIFIC OCEAN

Tropic of Cancer

Kiritimati

Cook Is.

SAMOA

180 West from Greenwich

Midway I.

Equator

Antipodes I.

Antarctic Circle

Victoria Land

International Dateline

East from Greenwich

KIRIBATI

TONGA

FIJI

Wellington

Auckland

NEW ZEALAND

Marshall Is.

Wake I.

TUVALU

Auckland I.

Macquarie I.

Adélie Land

160

Bonin I.

Northern Marianas

Guam

Caroline Is.

SOLOMON IS.

VANUATU

New Caledonia

Sydney

Canberra

140

PAPUA NEW GUINEA

Port Moresby

AUSTRALIA

Perth

120

PHILIPPINES

Manila

INDONESIA

INDIAN OCEAN

VIETNAM

BRUNEI

Ho Chi Minh City

MALAYSIA

Singapore

Kuala Lumpur

Jakarta

100

80

1 : 120 000 000

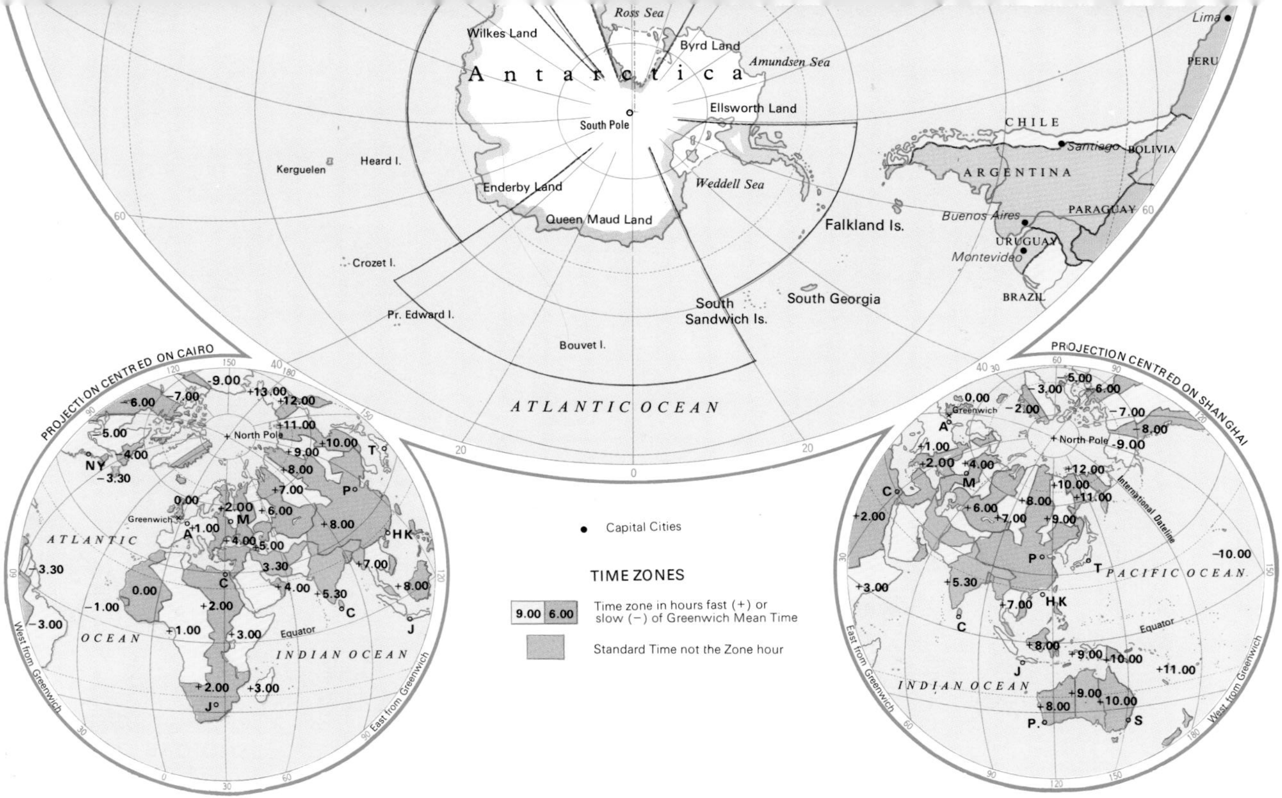

PROJECTION CENTRED ON SHANGHAI

Lima
PERU

BOLIVIA
Santiago
CHILE
ARGENTINA
PARAGUAY 60
Buenos Aires
URUGUAY
Montevideo
BRAZIL

Falkland Is.

South Georgia

South
Sandwich Is.

ATLANTIC OCEAN

Ross Sea
Byrd Land
Amundsen Sea
Ellsworth Land
Wilkes Land
Antarctica
Weddell Sea
South Pole
Queen Maud Land
Enderby Land
Bouvet I.

Heard I.
Kerguelen
Crozet I.
Pr. Edward I.

INDIAN OCEAN

PROJECTION CENTRED ON CAIRO

West from Greenwich
East from Greenwich

TIME ZONES

• Capital Cities

9.00 | 6.00   Time zone in hours fast (+) or
slow (−) of Greenwich Mean Time

Standard Time not the Zone hour

PROJECTION CENTRED ON SHANGHAI

International Dateline
PACIFIC OCEAN
North Pole
−10.00
−9.00
−8.00
−7.00
−6.00
−5.00
−3.00
−2.00
+11.00
+10.00
+12.00
+9.00
+8.00
+7.00
+6.00
+5.30
+4.00
+3.00
+2.00
0.00
Greenwich
A°
M°
C°
P°
HK
J
S
P.
Equator
INDIAN OCEAN
−1.00

West from Greenwich
East from Greenwich

PROJECTION CENTRED ON CAIRO

North Pole
ATLANTIC OCEAN
INDIAN OCEAN
Equator
+13.00
+12.00
+11.00
+10.00
+9.00
+8.00
+7.00
+6.00
+5.30
+4.00
+3.30
+3.00
+2.00
+1.00
0.00
Greenwich
−1.00
−3.00
−3.30
−4.00
−5.00
−6.00
−7.00
−9.00
NY
A°
M°
C°
P°
HK
J°
T°
Greenwich

West from Greenwich

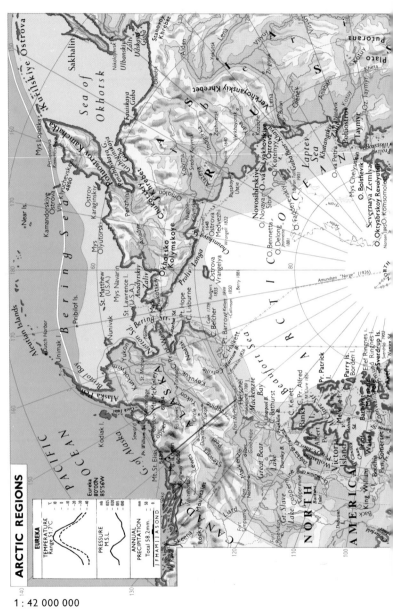

ARCTIC REGIONS

EUREKA
80°00'N
85°56'W

TEMPERATURE
Range 51.7°C

PRESSURE
M.S.L.

ANNUAL
PRECIPITATION
Total 58.2mm.

J F M A M J J A S O N D

1 : 42 000 000

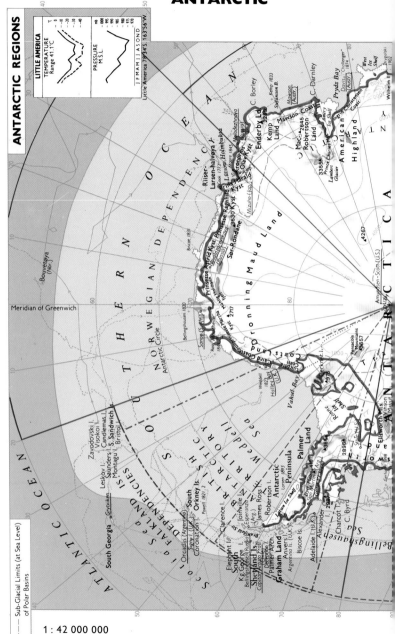

ANTARCTIC REGIONS

LITTLE AMERICA

TEMPERATURE
Range 41.1°C

°F	°C
	0
	-10
	-20
	-30
	-40

PRESSURE
M.S.L.

mb
1000
995
990
985
980
975
970

J F M A M J J A S O N D

Little America 78°34'S. 163°56'W.

SOUTHERN OCEAN

NORWEGIAN DEPENDENCY

Dronning Maud Land

Coats Land

ANTARCTIC

Palmer Land

Antarctic Peninsula

Graham Land

ATLANTIC OCEAN

PACIFIC OCEAN

Meridian of Greenwich

Antarctic Circle

Enderby Ld.

Kemp Land

Mac. Robertson Land

American Highland

Mawson Coast

C. Darnley

Prydz Bay

Wilhelm II

West Ice Shelf

Amery Ice Shelf

Prince Charles Mts.

Lambert Glacier

Riiser-Larsen halvøya

Prinsesse Astrid Kyst

Prinsesse Ragnhild Kyst

Sør-Rondane

C. Borley

Kemp 1833

Stefansson B.

Mawson (Austr.)

Davis (Austr.)

Challenger

Bouvetøya (Nor.)

Bellingshausen 1820

Biscoe 1831

Weddell Sea

Filchner Ice Shelf

Ronne Ice Shelf

Vahsel Bay

Pensacola Mountains

Ellsworth Land

Ellsworth Mts.

Vinson Massif

Bellingshausen Sea

C. Byrd

Charcot Is.

Alexander I.

Adelaide I. (U.K.)

Biscoe Is.

Anvers I.

Argentine Is. (U.K.)

Deception I.

Brabant I.

Trinity Pen.

Joinville I.

James Ross I.

Robertson I.

Snow Hill (Arg.)

Seymour I.

Marambio (Arg.)

Clarence I.

Elephant I.

Shetland Is. (U.K.)

Esperanza (Arg.)

King George I.

Bellingshausen (Russ.)

Capitán Arturo Prat (Chile)

Scotia Sea

South Orkney Is.

Orcadas (Argentine)

Signy I. (U.K.)

Coronation I.

Powell 1821/2

Laurie I.

South Georgia

Grytviken

South Sandwich Is.

Zavodovski I.

Visokoi I.

Leskov I.

Candlemas I.

Saunders I.

Montagu I.

Bristol I.

FALKLAND ISLANDS DEPENDENCIES

Scotia Sea

NORWEGIAN DEPENDENCY

Amundsen-Scott (U.S.)

Holmbukta

Utsteinen

Løvstakken B.

Mizuho (Japan-Syowa)

Syowa (Japan)

Borg Massif

Kraul Mts.

Vestfjella

Heimefrontfjella

Maudheim 1950/2

Halley Bay (U.K.)

Ahlmannryggen

2630 Kyst

2717 Kyst

3355

4267

4267

3657

3864

2899

2996

1957

1062

ATLANTIC OCEAN

PACIFIC OCEAN

---- Sub-Glacial Limits (at Sea Level)
      of Polar Basins

1 : 42 000 000

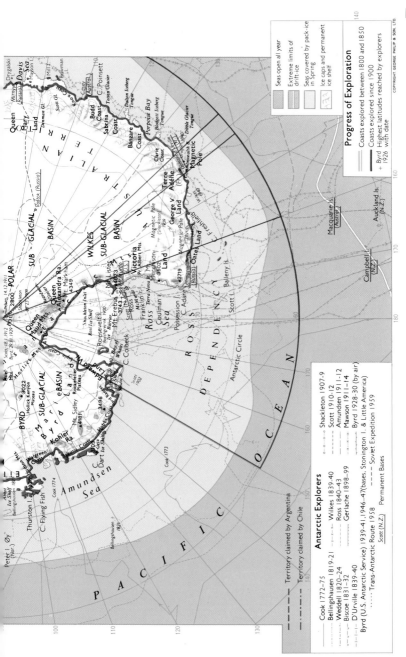

15

Seas open all year

Extreme limits of drift-ice

Seas covered by pack-ice in Spring

Ice caps and permanent ice shelf

Progress of Exploration

———— Coasts explored between 1800 and 1850

———— Coasts explored since 1900

+ Byrd Highest latitudes reached by explorers
1926 with date

COPYRIGHT GEORGE PHILIP & SON, LTD.

— · — · — Territory claimed by Argentina

— ·· — ·· — Territory claimed by Chile

Antarctic Explorers

———— Cook 1772–75
— · — · — Bellingshausen 1819–21
— ·· — ·· — Weddell 1820–24
———— Biscoe 1831–32
— · — · — D'Urville 1839–40

— — — — Wilkes 1839–40
———— Ross 1840–43
———— Gerlache 1898–99

Byrd (U.S. Antarctic Service) 1939-41, 1946-47(bases, Stonington I. & Little America)
·········· Trans-Antarctic Route 1958
Scott (N.Z.) — — — Permanent Bases

○—○—○ Shackleton 1907-9
———— Scott 1910-12
— — — Amundsen 1911-12
———— Mawson 1911-14
———— Byrd 1928-30 (by air)
— — — Soviet Expedition 1959

1 : 24 000 000

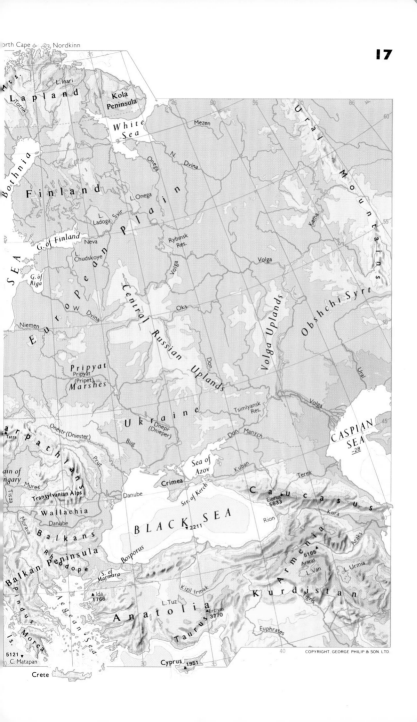

North Cape · Nordkinn

Mts.
Lapland
L. Inari
Jorma
Kola
Peninsula

White
Sea

Mezen

Ural Mountains

60

Bothnia

Finland

Onega
N. Dvina

L. Onega

European Plain

55

L. Ladoga
Svir
Rybinsk.
Res.
Kama

G. of Finland
Neva

Volga

Volga

SEA

Chudskoye

Central Russian

Oka

Volga Uplands

Obshchi Syrt

G. of
Riga

Niemen

W. Dvina

Uplands

Don

Ural

Pripyat
Pripyat
(Pripet)
Marshes

Ukraine

Dnepr
(Dnieper)

Tsimlyansk
Res.

Volga

CASPIAN
SEA
-28

45

arpathians
Tatra

Onestr (Dniester)

Bug

Don
Manych

ain of
ngary
Tisza
Mures

Sea of
Azov

K. Kuban

Terek

Elbruz
5633

C a u c a s u s

Kura

Transylvanian Alps

Crimea

Str. of Kerch

Rion

40

Wallachia
Danube

Morava

Danube

BLACK SEA
·2211

Aras

Balkans

Bosporus

5166·
Ararat

Armenia

Rhodope

Balkan Peninsula

S. of
Marmara

L. Van
L. Urmia

Pindus

Ida
·1766

Kizil Irmak

Kurdistan

ls.

5121·
C. Matapan

Morea

Aegean Sea

Anatolia

L. Tuz

Ercyas
3770

Taurus

Euphrates

40

Crete

Cyprus ·1951

30

35

COPYRIGHT. GEORGE PHILIP & SON. LTD.

1 : 24 000 000

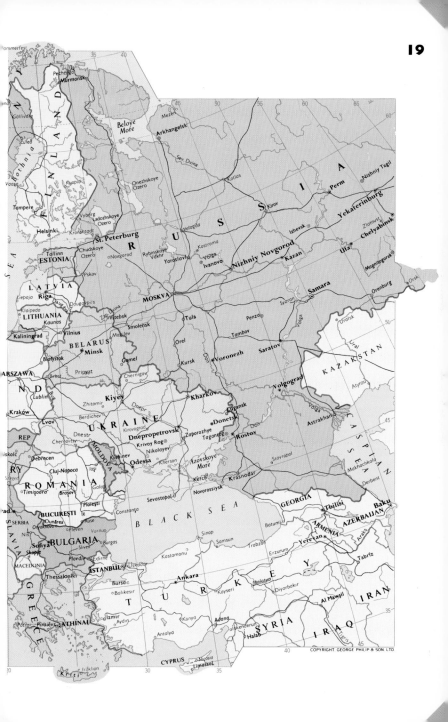

Hammerfest
Pechenga
Murmansk
Gällivare
Beloye More
Arkhangelsk
Mezen
Luleå
Onezhskoye Ozero
Sev. Dvina
Kotlas
Nizhniy Tagil
Perm
Vaasa
Kuopio
FINLAND
Ladozhskoye Ozero
Vologda
Kirov
Izhevsk
Yekaterinburg
Zlatoust
Chelyabinsk
Tampere
Vyborg
R U S S I A
Helsinki
Kronstadt
St. Peterburg
Chudskoye Ozero
Novgorod
Rybinskoye Vdkhr.
Kostroma
Volga
Nizhniy Novgorod
Kazan
Ufa
Magnitogorsk
Tallinn
ESTONIA
Pskov
Yaroslavl
Ivanovo
Orsk
L A T V I A
Riga
Liepaja
Daugavpils
Zap. Dvina
MOSKVA
Syzran
Samara
Orenburg
Klaipeda
Daugava
LITHUANIA
Kaunas
Vitebsk
Tula
Penza
Volga
Uralsk
Ural
Kaliningrad
Vilnius
Smolensk
Orel
Tambov
K A Z A K S T A N
BELARUS
Mogilev
Voronezh
Saratov
ARSZAWA
Bialystok
Minsk
Gomel
Kursk
Don
Atyrau
N D
Brest
Pripyat
Chernigov
Volgograd
Volga
Lublin
Zhitomir
Kiyev
Dnepr
Kharkov
Astrakhan
C A S P I A N
Kraków
Berdichev
UKRAINE
Lugansk
Lvov
Kirovograd
Donetsk
Dnepropetrovsk
Zaporozhye
Don
REP
Dnestr
Krivoy Rog
Taganrog
Rostov
Chernovtsy
MOLDOVA
Nikolayev
Makhachkala
iskolc
Kishinev
Odessa
Kherson
Azovskoye More
Stavropol
Debrecen
Kerch
Krasnodar
Derbent
RY
Cluj-Napoca
Iasi
S E A
Sevastopol
Novorossiysk
ROMANIA
Galati
GEORGIA
Timişoara
Brasov
Ploiesti
Tbilisi
Baku
ad
BUCURESTI
Constanta
B L A C K   S E A
Batumi
ARMENIA
AZERBAIJAN
SERBIA
Dunarea
Ruse
Araks
Pleven
Varna
Sinop
Trabzon
Yerevan
LAVIA
Sofiya
Burgas
Samsun
Erzurum
Tabriz
Skopje
BULGARIA
Sliven
Kastamonu
MACEDONIA
Plovdiv
Edirne
ISTANBUL
Üsküdar
T U R K E Y
Al Mawsil
Thessaloniki
Bursa
Ankara
Malatya
IRAN
GREECE
Balikesir
Kayseri
Diyarbakir
Izmir
Konya
Adana
SYRIA
Aydin
Iskenderun
Halab
IRAQ
Patrai
Piraievs
ATHINAI
Antalya
Tigris
Kriti
Iraklion
CYPRUS
Nicosia
Limassol

I. Tory C. Malin North Channel

Aran I. Derryveagh Mts. Coleraine Antrim Mts. 22

Letterkenny Londonderry Larne Stranraer Wigtown

Lifford Ballymena

Donegal Antrim Bangor

Donegal Bay NORTHERN IRELAND Belfast Mull of Galloway

Erris Hd. Bundoran Omagh L. Neagh Lisburn

Killala Bay Erne Blackwater ISLE OF MAN

Ballina Sligo Enniskillen Armagh Downpatrick Dundrum

Achill I. L. Conn Upper Clones Monaghan Newry Mourne Mts. Douglas

Clare I. Castlebar Leitrim Cavan Greenore

Westport Carrick-on-Shannon Dundalk

L. Mask Roscommon Longford Ceanannus An Uaimh Drogheda I R I S H S

Connemara L. Corrib Ree Mor Boyne Balbriggan

Galway IRELAND Athlone Mullingar

Galway Bay Athenry Tullamore Liffey Dublin Anglesey

Birr Kildare (Baile Atha Cliath) Holyhead

Loop Ennis Port Laoise Naas Bray Dun Laoghaire Llandu

Hd. Kilrush L. Derg Athy Wicklow Mts. Wicklow Caernarfon Bay

Shannon Nenagh Carlow Pwllheli

Listowel Limerick Thurles Kilkenny Arklow

Golden Vale Tipperary Enniscorthy Cardigan Bay

Tralee Rath Luirc Clonmel Carrick-on-Suir New Ross

Mallow Blackwater Wexford Rosslare

Macgillycuddy's Killarney Fermoy Dungarvan Waterford Carnsore Pt. Fishguard Cardigan

Reeks 1040 Youghal St. David's Hd.

Cahirciveen Blarney Cork Carmarthen

Castletown Bantry Bandon Kinsale Cork Harbour St. George's Channel Haverfordwest Llanelli

Bere Lee Cobh Milford Haven Pembroke

C. Clear Bristol C

Lundy I.

Hartland Point

Bude

St. Austell Devonport

Truro Camborne

Penzance Falmouth

Land's Lizard

Scilly Is. End

1 : 4 000 000

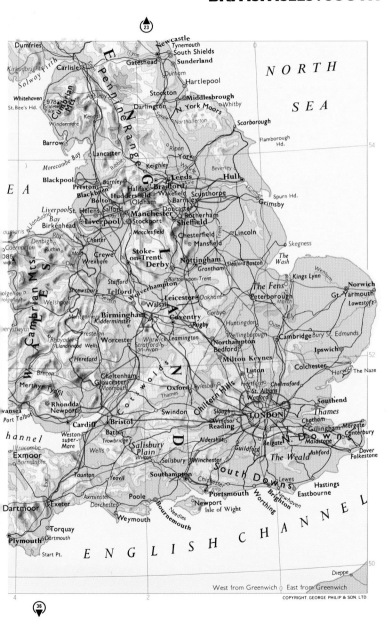

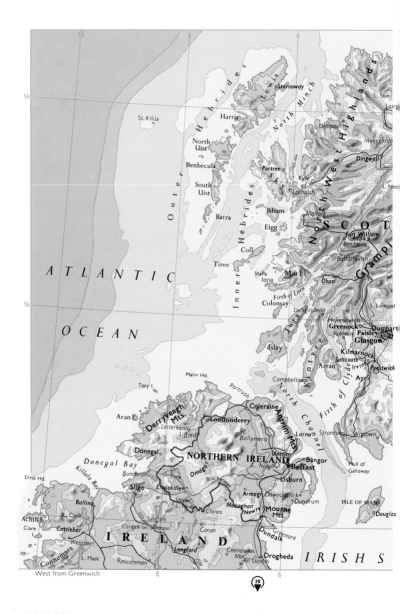

1 : 4 000 000

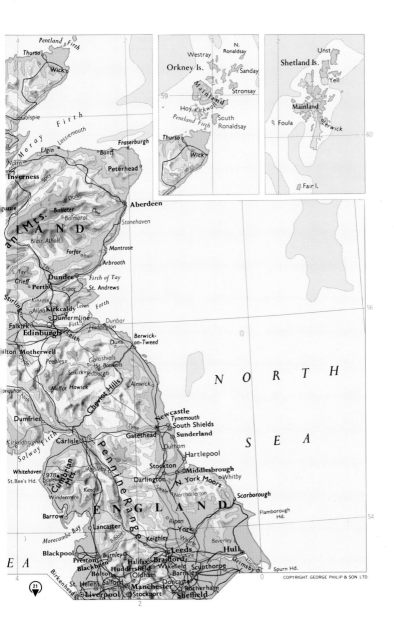

Pentland Firth
Thurso
Wick
Golspie
Moray Firth
Elgin
Nairn
Lossiemouth
Banff
Fraserburgh
Inverness
Peterhead
Spey
Aberdeen
HIGHLANDS
Ballater
Balmoral
Stonehaven
Blair Atholl
Dee
Forfar
Montrose
Arbroath
L. Tay
Tay
Dundee
Crieff
Firth of Tay
Perth
St. Andrews
Cupar
Leven
Forth
Kinross
Kirkcaldy
Alloa
Stirling
Dunfermline
Falkirk
Firth
Dunbar
Edinburgh
Leith
Haddington
Motherwell
Peebles
Galashiels
St. Boswells
Berwick-on-Tweed
Duns
Selkirk
Jedburgh
Sanquhar
Moffat
Hawick
Cheviot Hills
Alnwick
Dumfries
Nith
Newcastle
Tynemouth
Kirkcudbright
Solway Firth
Carlisle
Tyne
South Shields
Gateshead
Sunderland
Durham
Pennine Range
Hartlepool
Whitehaven
Cumbrian Mts.
Appleby
Stockton
St. Bee's Hd.
978
Scafell Pike
Kendal
Darlington
Middlesbrough
Whitby
N. York Moors
Windermere
Swale
Northallerton
Scarborough
Barrow
ENGLAND
Flamborough Hd.
Morecambe Bay
Lancaster
Ripon
York
Beverley
Ribble
Keighley
Wharfe
Blackpool
Preston
Burnley
Halifax
Bradford
Leeds
Hull
Blackburn
Huddersfield
Wakefield
Scunthorpe
Grimsby
Bolton
Oldham
Barnsley
Spurn Hd.
St. Helens
Salford
Manchester
Doncaster
Birkenhead
Liverpool
Stockport
Rotherham
Sheffield

N O R T H   S E A

Pentland Firth
Thurso
Wick
Orkney Is.
Westray
N. Ronaldsay
Sanday
Stronsay
Mainland
Hoy
Kirkwall
South Ronaldsay
Pentland Firth

Shetland Is.
Unst
Yell
Mainland
Foula
Lerwick
Fair I.

COPYRIGHT GEORGE PHILIP & SON. LTD.

21

1 : 2 000 000

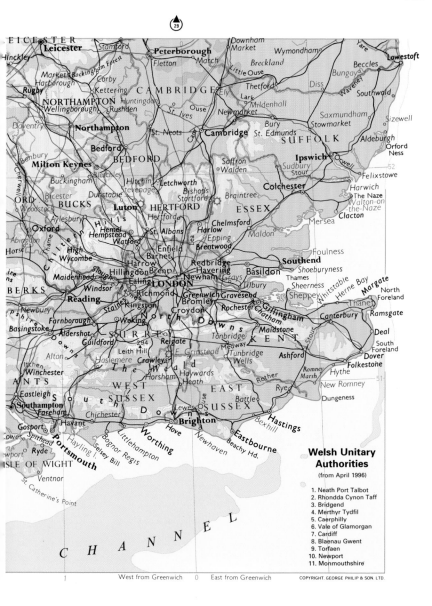

LEICESTER
Leicester Stamford
Hinckley Peterborough Downham Wymondham Yare
Fletton Market Lowestoft
Rugby Market Rockingham Forest Corby Little Ouse Breckland Beccles
Harborough Kettering Thetford Diss Bungay Waveney Southwold
NORTHAMPTON Huntingdon CAMBRIDGE Ely Lark Mildenhall Saxmundham Sizewell
Wellingborough Rushden St Ives Newmarket
Daventry Northampton St. Neots Cambridge Bury Stowmarket SUFFOLK Aldeburgh
Banbury Bedford St. Edmunds Orford
Milton Keynes BEDFORD Ipswich Ness
Buckingham Bletchley Saffron Sudbury Orwell
ORD Bicester Dunstable Hitchin Letchworth Walden Stour Felixstowe
Woodstock BUCKS Stevenage Bishop's Colchester Harwich
Aylesbury Luton HERTFORD Stortford Braintree ESSEX The Naze
Oxford Hemel St. Albans Hertford Mersea Walton-on-the-Naze
Abingdon Hempstead Watford Harlow Chelmsford Clacton
Horsp High Enfield Epping Maldon
Wycombe Barnet Brentwood Foulness
BERKS Maidenhead Harrow Brent Redbridge Southend
Slough Hillingdon Havering Shoeburyness
Windsor Ealing LONDON Newham Basildon Thames
Reading Richmond Greenwich Grays Tilbury Sheerness Sheppey Whitstable Herne Bay Margate
Newbury Kingston Bromley Gravesend Rochester North Foreland
Farnborough Woking Croydon Chatham Gillingham Canterbury Thanet Ramsgate
Basingstoke North Downs Maidstone KENT Stour Deal
Aldershot Guildford Reigate South Foreland
Alton 294 Leith Hill Tonbridge Medway Ashford Dover
SURREY E. Grinstead Tunbridge Folkestone
Itchen Haslemere Crawley Wells Romney Hythe
Winchester The Weald Horsham Heath Rother Marsh New Romney
HANTS WEST Haywards EAST Rye
Eastleigh South SUSSEX Downs SUSSEX Battle Dungeness
Southampton Lewes Ouse Hastings
Fareham Chichester Brighton Bexhill
Gosport Havant Hove Eastbourne
owes Spithead Hayling I. Worthing Newhaven Beachy Hd.
wport Ryde Portsmouth Bognor Regis Littlehampton
ISLE OF WIGHT Selsey Bill
Ventnor
St. Catherine's Point

**Welsh Unitary
Authorities**

(from April 1996)

1. Neath Port Talbot
2. Rhondda Cynon Taff
3. Bridgend
4. Merthyr Tydfil
5. Caerphilly
6. Vale of Glamorgan
7. Cardiff
8. Blaenau Gwent
9. Torfaen
10. Newport
11. Monmouthshire

C H A N N E L

West from Greenwich 0 East from Greenwich COPYRIGHT GEORGE PHILIP & SON. LTD.

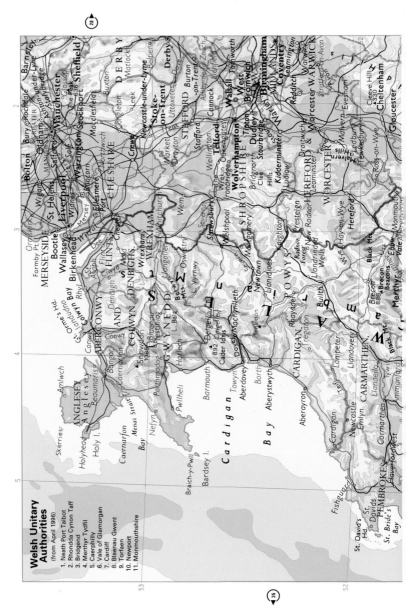

Welsh Unitary Authorities
(from April 1996)

1. Neath Port Talbot
2. Rhondda Cynon Taff
3. Bridgend
4. Merthyr Tydfil
5. Caerphilly
6. Vale of Glamorgan
7. Cardiff
8. Blaenau Gwent
9. Torfaen
10. Newport
11. Monmouthshire

1 : 2 000 000

NORTHUMBERLAND · Ashing
Morpeth
N. Tyne · Blyth
Dumfries · Gretna Green · Wall · Tyne mout
Annan · Tyne · Blaydon · Newcastle
Hexham · Gateshead · TYN
Newton Stewart · Carlisle · Sunderland
Castle Douglas · Dalbeattie · Consett · Hough
Kirkcudbright · Silloth · Eden · S. Alston · Durham · le-Sp
Wigtown · Cross Fell · Wear
Solway Firth · Maryport · 893 · DURHAM
Wigtown Bay · Penrith · Bishop Auckland
Workington · Derwent · Skiddaw · Barnard
Whithorn · Derwentwater · 931 · CUMBRIA · Castle
Keswick · Helvellyn · Appleby
Whitehaven · Ullswater · Darlington
St. Bee's Hd. · 950 · Shap · Brough
Pt. of Ayre · Cumbrian Mts. · Richmond
Sca Fell · Northallerton
Ramsey · 978 · Ambleside
Seascale · Windermere · Kendal · Wensleydale · Swale
Snaefell · ISLE OF · Windermere · Ure
Peel · 620 · MAN · Millom · Ulverston · Lune · Whernside
Port · 737 · Pen-y-Ghent · NORTH
Erin · Douglas · Barrow- · Furness · 693 · 704 · Ripon
Castletown · in-Furness · Ingleborough · Gt. · YORKSH
Walney I. · 723 · Whernside · Knaresborough
Morecambe B. · Settle · Harrogate
IRISH · Morecambe · Lancaster
Heysham · Forest of · Keighley
Fleetwood · Bowland · Skipton
SEA · Ribble · Nelson · Colne
Cleveleys · Fylde · LANCASHIRE · Bradford · Lee
Blackpool · Preston · Burnley · Accrington · W. YORKSHIRE
Lytham-St. Annes · Blackburn · Halifax · Wakef
Ribble · Chorley · Rochdale · Dewsbury
Southport · Bolton · Bury · GREATER · Huddersfield
Ormskirk · Wigan · Oldham · Ashton-under-Lyne · SOU
Formby Pt. · MANCHESTER · Stalybridge · Barnsley · YORK
MERSEYSIDE · St. Helens · Salford · Manchester
Skerries · Amlwch · Bootle · Glossop
Gt. Orme's Hd. · Wallasey · Liverpool · Sale · 636 · Sheffield
Holyhead · Llandudno · Birkenhead · Widnes · Warrington · Stockport
Holy I. · Conwy · Colwyn Bay · Rhyl · Runcorn · Macclesfield · Chesterfield
ANGLESEY · Ellesmere · Northwich · Buxton
Anglesey · St. · Port · CHESHIRE · DERBY
Beaumaris · Asaph · Mersey · Congleton
Caernarfon · Bangor · Flint · Chester · Leek · Matlock
Menai Strait · ABERCONWY · Denbigh · Mold · DERBY
Bay · Caernarfon · AND · FLINTS · Crewe · Belper
Nefyn · COLWYN · DENBIGHS · Newcastle-under-Lyme
Snowdon · Wrexham · Stoke- · Derby
Porthmadog · 1085 · WREXHAM · Whitchurch · on-Trent · Dove
Blaenau · Uttoxeter
Pwllheli · GWYNEDD · Ffestiniog · Llangollen · Market · STAFFORD · Burton
Harlech · L. Bala · Berwyn · Wem · Drayton · -on-Trent · Ash
Bardsey I. · Mts. · Oswestry · Stafford · la
Barmouth · L. Vyrnwy · Cannock · Lichfield
Dolgellau · Severn · Shrewsbury · Wellington · Telford · Walsall · Tamwort
892 · (Dolgelley) · WALES · The · Oakengates · Nuneaton
Cader Idris · Wrekin · Cannock · West
Towyn · Welshpool · Ironbridge · Wolverhampshire · Bromwich
Aberdovey · Dovey · Machynlleth · Bridgnorth · Dudley · Birmingha
Montgomery · SHROPSHIRE · Stourbridge · Tipton · MIDLANDS
Newtown · Coventry

4   West from Greenwich   3   2

1 : 2 000 000

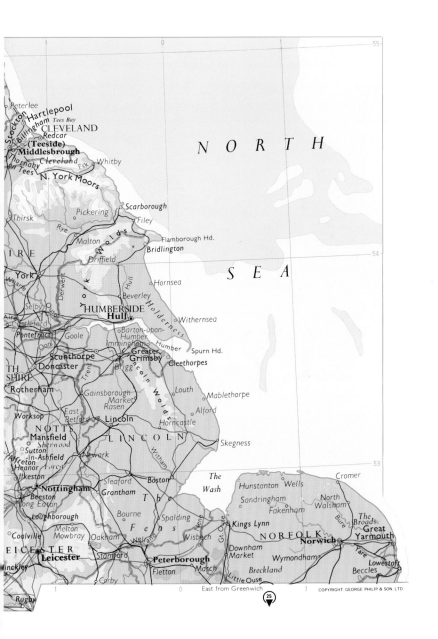

Peterlee

Stockton Hartlepool
Billingham *Tees Bay*
CLEVELAND
Redcar
(Teeside)
Middlesbrough
Cleveland Whitby
Thornaby
on Tees
N. York Moors

N O R T H

Thirsk
Pickering Scarborough
Rye Filey
Malton W o l d s
Flamborough Hd.
Driffield **Bridlington**

I R E

S E A

York
Wharfe Hornsea
Selby Ouse Beverley
Derwent Hull
Aire **HUMBERSIDE**
Castleford **Hull** Holderness
Pontefract Goole Withernsea
Don Barton-upon-
TH Humber
SHIRE Scunthorpe Immingham Humber Spurn Hd.
Doncaster Greater
Trent Brigg Grimsby
Rotherham Cleethorpes

Worksop Gainsborough L o u t h
Market Mablethorpe
East Rasen
Retford Alford
NOTTS Lincoln Horncastle
Mansfield L I N C O L N
Sutton
-in-Ashfield Newark Skegness
Alfreton
Heanor F o r e s t Sherwood
Ilkeston
Sleaford Boston *The*
Nottingham Grantham *Wash* Hunstanton Wells Cromer
Beeston North
Long Eaton Sandringham Walsham
T h e Fakenham
Loughborough Bourne Spalding The
F e n s Nene Kings Lynn Bure Broads
Melton Great
Coalville Mowbray Oakham Nelson Wisbech **NORFOLK** Yare Yarmouth
EICESTER Downham **Norwich**
Leicester Stamford Market Wymondham
Hinckley **Peterborough** Lowestoft
Corby Fletton March Breckland Beccles
Rugby *Little Ouse*

East from Greenwich COPYRIGHT GEORGE PHILIP & SON. LTD.

Scottish Local Authorities
(from April 1996)

1. City of Aberdeen
2. City of Dundee
3. Dumbarton & Clydebank
4. East Dunbartonshire
5. City of Glasgow
6. Inverclyde
7. Renfrewshire
8. East Renfrewshire
9. North Lanarkshire
10. Falkirk
11. Clackmannan
12. West Lothian
13. City of Edinburgh
14. Midlothian

SHETLAND IS.
On same scale

West from Greenwich

1 : 2 000 000

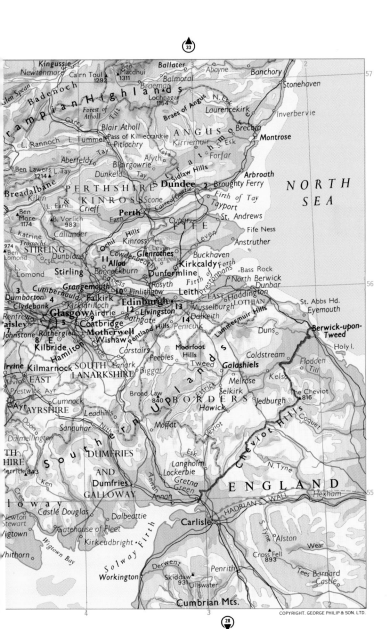

NORTH SEA

ENGLAND

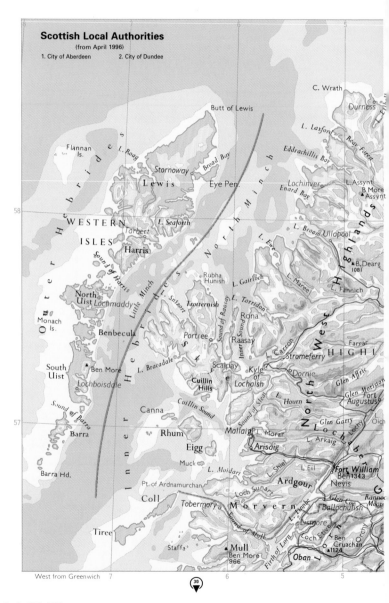

Scottish Local Authorities
(from April 1996)
1. City of Aberdeen   2. City of Dundee

West from Greenwich   7   6   5

1 : 2 000 000

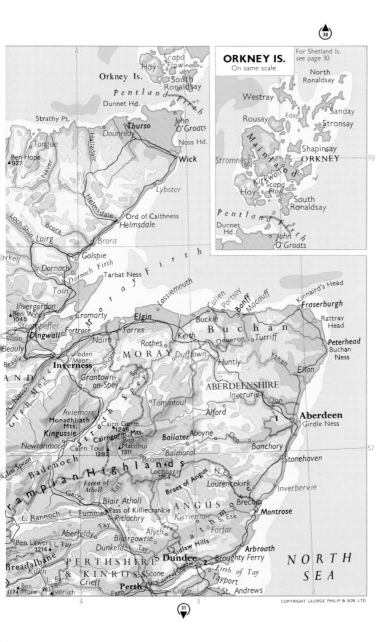

ORKNEY IS.
On same scale
For Shetland Is.
see page 30

North
Ronaldsay

Westray
Rousay   Eday   Sanday
Stronsay
Shapinsay
Stromness   Maps   ORKNEY

Kirkwall
Scapa
Hoy   Flow
South
Ronaldsay

Pentland   Firth
Dunnet
Hd.   John
O'Groats

Orkney Is.
Hoy
Scapa
Flow
South
Ronaldsay

Pentland   Firth
Dunnet Hd.
Strathy Pt.
Thurso   John
O'Groats
Dounreay   Noss Hd.
Tongue
Halladale   **Wick**
Ben Hope
▲927
Naver
Lybster

Loch Shin
Brora   Ord of Caithness
Lairg   Helmsdale
▲ykell   Brora
Golspie
Dornoch
Dornoch Firth
Tarbat Ness   Firth
Tain

Invergordon
Ben Wyvis   Cromarty
1045   Lossiemouth
Strathpeffer   Cullen Portsoy   Banff Macduff   Kinnaird's Head
▲non   Dingwall   Fortrose   **Elgin**   **Fraserburgh**
Beauly   Nairn   Forres   **Buckie**   B u c h a n   Rattray Head
Be▲ly   Rothes   Keith   Deveron   Turriff   Peterhead
Culloden   Dufftown   Buchan
Moor   M O R A Y   Ness
Inverness   Findhorn   Huntly
Grantown-   Ythan   Ellon
on-Spey
Spey   A B E R D E E N S H I R E
Aviemore   Inverurie
Tomintoul   Don
Monadhliath   Alford   **Aberdeen**
Mts.   Cairn Gorm   Girdle Ness
Kingussie   1246
Newtonmore   Cairngorm Mts.   Ballater   Aboyne
Cairn Toul   Ben   Dee   Banchory
1292   Macdhui
1311   Braemar   Stonehaven
Braemar
Glen Spean   Lochnagar
B a d e n o c h   1156   N.Esk
Forest of   Braes of Angus   Laurencekirk   Inverbervie
Atholl
▲rampian Highlands   Brechin
Tilt   A N G U S   ▲sm   **Montrose**
L. Rannoch   Tummel   Blair Atholl   Kirriemuir   Esk
Pass of Killiecrankie   ▲sm
Pitlochry   Forfar
Aberfeldy   Tay   Alyth   Sidlaw Hills   **Arbroath**
Ben Lawers   L. Tay   Blairgowrie   **Dundee**   Broughty Ferry   N O R T H
1214▲   Dunkeld   Tay
Breadalbane   P E R T H S H I R E   Scone   Firth of Tay   S E A
Killin   &   K I N R O S S   Tayport
Ben   Earn   Crieff   **Perth**   St. Andrews
1174 More   983▲   Earn   Cupar
Vorlich

COPYRIGHT GEORGE PHILIP & SON. LTD.

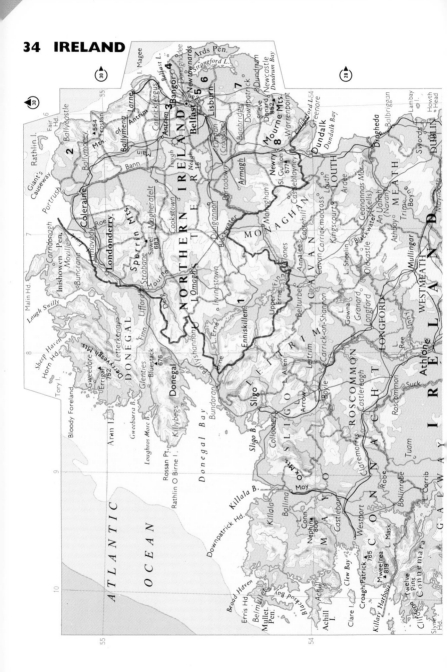

1 : 2 000 000

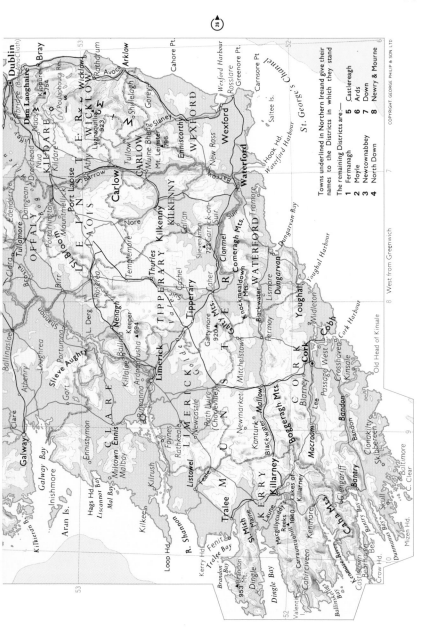

Towns underlined in Northern Ireland give their names to the Districts in which they stand

The remaining Districts are:—

1 Fermanagh   5 Castlereagh
2 Moyle   6 Ards
3 Newtownabbey   7 Down
4 North Down   8 Newry & Mourne

COPYRIGHT GEORGE PHILIP & SON LTD

Cap Gris-Nez
Boulogne-sur-Mer
Étaples
Berck-Plage
Le Tréport
Dieppe
50
Neufchâtel-en-Bray

E N G L I S H

Alderney
Cap de la Hague   Pointe de Barfleur
Cherbourg
Fécamp
Bolbec

Guernsey
St. Peter Port
Valognes
Le Havre
Deauville-Trouville
Elbeuf
Louviers
Rouen
Seine

Channel Is.
(Br.)
Jersey
St. Helier
Carentan
Bayeux
Bernay
Vernon
Évreux
Mantes-la-Jolie

C H A N N E L

St-Lô
Caen
Lisieux
Dreux

Ile d'Ouessant
Brest
Lannion
Granville
Vire
Falaise
Argentan
417
Alençon
Verneuil-sur-Avre
Chartres

Landerneau
Morlaix
Guingamp
St-Malo
Avranches
Flers
Nogent-le-Rotrou

B   391   R
Châteaulin
St-Brieuc
Dinan
St-Servan-sur-Mer
Fougères
Châteaudun
BEAUCE

Crozon
Douarnenez
326
E   T
Loudéac
Vitré
Laval
ORL

Pointe du Raz
48
Quimper
Pontivy
Rennes
Le Mans
Vendôme
Loir

Pointe de Penmarch
Concarneau
Quimperlé
Hennebont
Ploërmel
Vilaine
Châteaubriant
Sarthe
La Flèche
Château-Renault
Blois

Lorient
Auray
Vannes
Redon
Angers
ANJOU
Saumur
Amboise
Tours
Cher

Ile de Groix
Belle-Ile
St-Nazaire
La Baule
Nantes
Loire
Cholet
Chinon
Vienne
TOURAINE
Indre

Ile de Noirmoutier
Les Herbiers
Bressuire
FRA
Châtellerault

Ile d'Yeu
La Roche-sur-Yon
Chantonnay
Parthenay
POITOU
Le Blanc

Les-Sables-d'Olonne
Fontenay-le-Comte
Poitiers
MAR

46
Ile de Ré
AUNIS
Niort
Bellac
Confolens

La Rochelle
Rochefort
St-Jean-d'Angély
Vienne
Limoges
LIMOUS

Ile d'Oleron
Saintes
ANGOUMOIS
St-Junien
La Perche

Royan
SAINTONGE
Cognac
Angoulême

Pointe de Grave
Le Verdon-sur-Mer

Bay of
Biscay
Pauillac
Dronne
St-Yrieix
Brive-la-Ga

Médoc
Riberac
Périgueux

42
Libourne
Coutras
Dordogne
Gourdon

Bordeaux
Bergerac

Cap Ferret
La Teste
Arcachon
Langon
GUYENNE

Garonne
Marmande
Tonneins
Villeneuve-sur-Lot
Cahors

Mimizan
Nérac
Moissac
Lot
Aveyron
Montauban

44
Morcenx
Castets
GASCOGNE
Agen
Castelsarrasin

Mont-de-Marsan
Lot

Santander
Dax
Adour
Toul

Santoña
Aire
Muret

Torrelavega
Gueicho
San Sebastián
St-Jean-de-Luz
Biarritz
Bayonne
Orthez
BÉARN
Mourenx-Ville-Nouvelle
Garonne
St-Gaudens

Portugalete
Sestao
Eibar
Irún
Oloron-Ste-Marie
Pau
Tarbes
Tarbes
Lannemezan

Bilbao
Lourdes
S   P
A   I   N
West from Greenwich
2504
3298
Pic d'Aneto
3404
ANDORRA

1 : 5 000 000
2355
Mt. Perdido
Jaca

Inset — Corse:

C. Corsa
Bastia
Calvi
Mt. Cinto
2710
Haute-Corse
Mte. Rotondo
2625
Corse
Ajaccio
Corse du Sud
Porto-Vecchio
Bonifacio
Bouches de Bonifacio

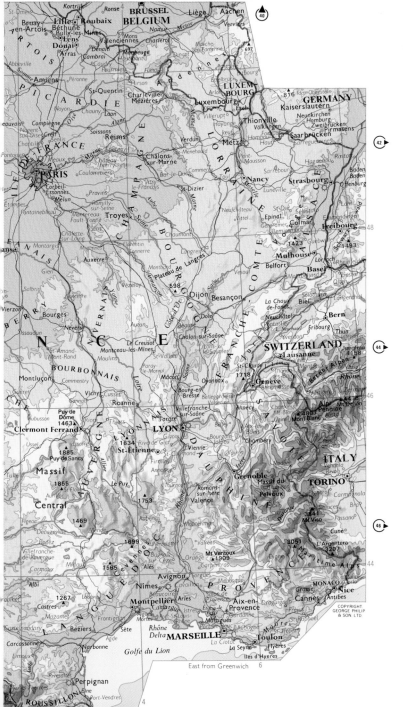

East from Greenwich   6

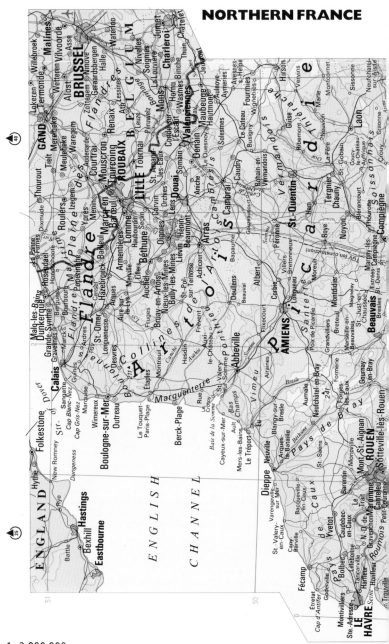

1 : 2 000 000

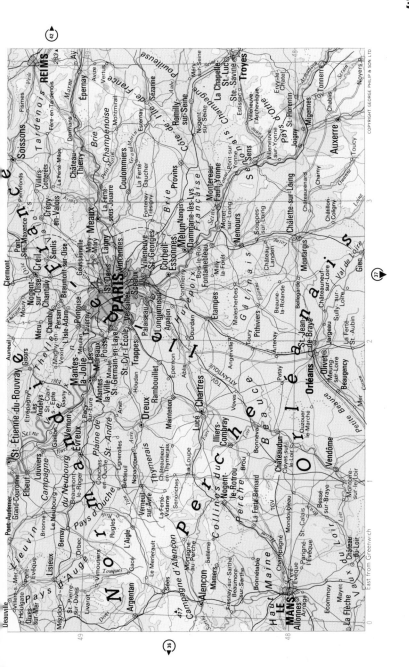

WESTFRIESCHE

Terschell

Vlieland

Texel

Den Burgo

Den Helder

Den Oever

Staveren

Middenmeer

IJssel

N O R T H

S E A

Bergen-Binnen

Alkmaar

Heiloo

Enkhuizen

Castricum

Hoorn

Wormer

Purmerend

Edam

Beverwijk

Volendam

IJmuiden

Velsen

Marken

Zaanstad

AMSTERDAM

Haarlem

Zandvoort

Amstelveen

Weesp

Huizen

Heemstede

Bussum

Loren

Hillegom

Aalsmeer

Lisse

Hilversum

Baar

Noordwijk-aan-Zee

Katwijk-aan-Zee

Leiden

Soes

Wassenaar

Oude

Alphen

Scheveningen

Voorburg

Rijn

Zeist

s'GRAVENHAGE

Waddinx

UTRECHT

(The Hague)

Rijswijk

Gouda

Hoek van Holland

Delft

IJsselstein

Europoort

Naaldwijk

Lek

Maassluis

Vlaardingen

ROTTERDAM

Schiedam

Sliedrecht

Leer

Tiel

Helvoetsluis

Gorinchem

Gelder

Goeree

Ouddorp

Overflakkee

Dordrecht

Hardinx

malse

Schouwen

Brouwershaven

Middelharnis

veld

Waalwijk

Noord Beveland

Zierikzee

Madeo

's Her

Oosterschelde

Dongen

Vught

Walcheren

Oudenbosch

Breda

Boxtel

Middelburg

Goes

Roosendaal

Oosterhout

Vlissingen

Bergen-op-Zoom

Goirle

Tilburg

(Flushing)

Westerschelde

Baarle

Nassau

Knokke

Essen

Blankenberge

Zeebrugge

Kalmthout

Oostende

Terneuzen

Brasschaat

Rijkevorsel

Turnhout

(Ostend)

Hulst

Schoten

Arendonk

Brugge

Merksem

ANTWERPEN

Lommel

(Bruges)

Maldegem

Beveren

Antwerpen

Mol

Nieuwpoort

Eeklo

Deurne

Geel

Leopoldsbu

Eernegem

Zelzate

St-Niklaas

Hoboken

Lier

Berlaar

Veurne

Torhout

Lokeren

Boom

Duffel

Nethe

Tessenderlo

Diksmuide

St-Amandsberg

Willebroek

Hetentals

Loo

Ruiselede

Ledeberg

Gent (Gand)

Mechelen

Diest

Hoogleede

Tielt

Wetteren

Lebbeke

Aarschot

Demer

Poperinge

Deinze

B

Hassel

Roeselare

Ongelmunster

Asse

Vilvoorde

Kessel-Lo

Diepenbeek

Izegem

Harel-beke

Zottegem

Jette

Leuven

Ieper

Menen

Oudenaarde

Ninove

BRUSSEL

Kortrijk

(Bruxelles)

East from Greenwich

38

1 : 2 000 000

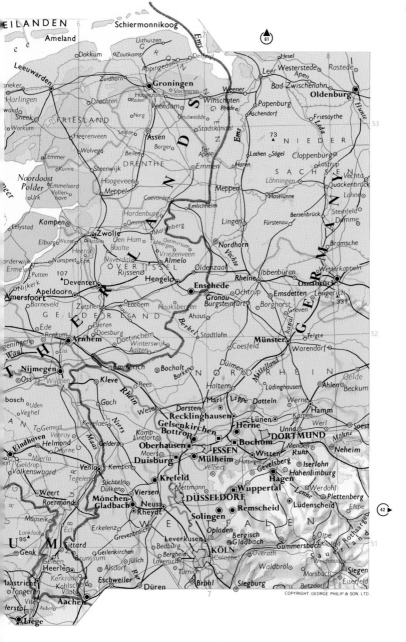

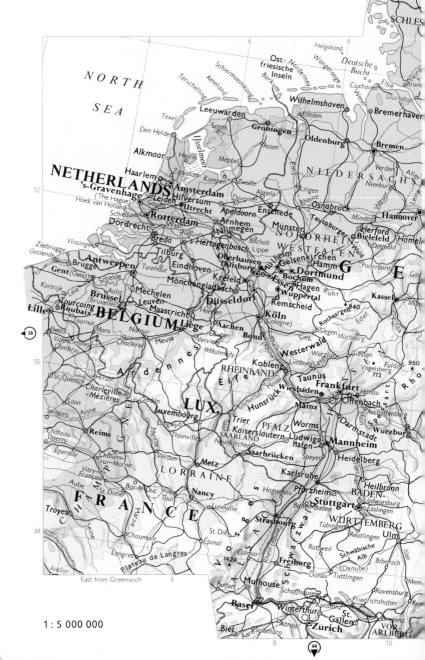

Flensburg
SCHLES-WIG
Kiel
HOLSTEIN
Neumünster
Lübeck
ona
Hamburg
burg
Lüneburg
Lüneburger
Heide
Celle
Hildesheim
Braunschweig
Salzgitter
Goslar
Halberstadt
Brocken
1142
Nordhausen
Harz
Halle
Mühlhausen
Merseburg
Naumburg
Eisenach
Erfurt
Gotha
Weimar
Jena
Gera
Thüringer
Wald
Coburg
Schweinfurt
Reichenbach
Zwickau
Plauen
Hof
Bamberg
Erlangen
Fürth
Nürnberg
Amberg
BAYERN
Regensburg
Ingolstadt
Augsburg
Landshut
München
(Munich)
Rosenheim
Salzburg
Kufstein
AUSTRIA

Puttgarden
Fehmarn
Mecklenburger
Bucht
Warnemünde
Stralsund
Greifswald
Wismar
Rostock
Güstrow
Schwerin
Parchim
Müritz
See
Neustrelitz
Neuruppin
Oranienburg
Spandau
Charlottenburg
BERLIN
Brandenburg
Potsdam
Magdeburg
Luckenwalde
Zerbst
Dessau
Bernburg
Wittenberg
Torgau
GERMANY
Leipzig
Zeitz
Meissen
Dresden
Chemnitz
(Karl-Marx-Stadt)
Erzgebirge
Teplice
Most
Chomutov
Karlovy
Vary
Cheb
Fichtel-
geb.
1051
Bayreuth
Böhmerwald
1457
Deggendorf
1378
Passau
Freising
Isar
Ried
Welser
Steyr
Gmunden
Bad Ischl

BALTIC SEA
Sassnitz
Rügen
Darłowo
Słupsk
Koszalin
Kołobrzeg
Usedom
winoujście
Wolin
Szczecinek
Oder Haff
Goleniów
Szczecin (Stettin)
Dobie
Stargard
Choszczno
Piła
POLAND
Gorzów
Noteć (Netze)
Skwierzyna
Warta
Warthe
Kostrzyn
Międzychód
Poznań
Nowy Tomyśl
Grodzisk
Świebodzin
Kościan
Gubin
Zielona
Góra
Leszno
Forst
Żary
Zagań
Głogów
Sprembergo
Lauchhammer
Großenhain
Bautzen
Görlitz
Bolesławiec
Legnica
Wrocław
Silesia
Liberec
Jelenia Góra
Świdnica
Riesengebirge
1602
Wałbrzych
Jablonec
Sněžka
Trutnov
Sudety
Mladá
Boleslav
Hradec
Kralové
Kłodzko
1492
Praha
(Prague)
Beroun
Kolín
Labe (Elbe)
Pardubice
Šumperk
CZECH REPUBLIC
Příbram
Sázava
Vrchovina
Havlíčkuv Brod
Olomouc
Plzeň
(Pilsen)
Klatovy
Písek
Tábor
Jihlava
Třebíč
Prastějov
Brno
(Brünn)
Slavkov
(Austerlitz)
Hodonín
České
Budějovice
Třeboň
Českomoravská
Gmünd
Zwettl
Znojmo
Jihlava
Morava
Malé Karpaty
Horn
OBER-
Linz
NIEDER-
ÖSTERREICH
Stockerau
Urfahr
ÖSTERREICH

COPYRIGHT GEORGE PHILIP & SON LTD

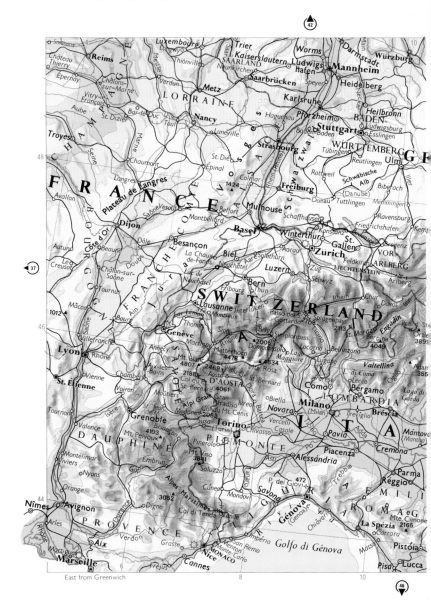

East from Greenwich

1 : 5 000 000

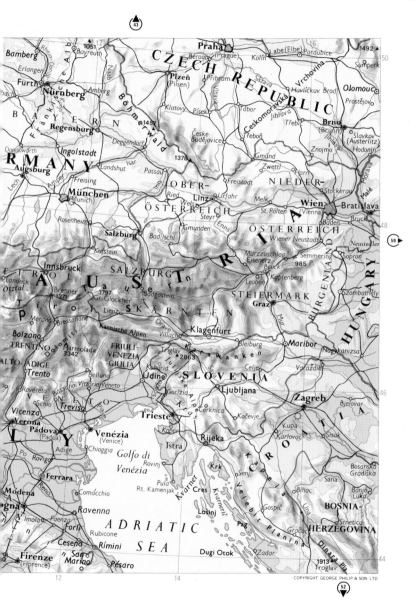

Bamberg
1051
Bayreuth
Erlangen
Fürth
Nürnberg Amberg
Regensburg
CZECH REPUBLIC
Praha (Prague)
Beroun
Kolín
Pardubice
1492
Šumperk
50
Plzeň (Pilsen)
Příbram
Sázava
Vrchovina
Huvličkuv Brod
Olomouc
Prostějov
Klatovy
Písek
Tábor
Jihlava
Třebíč
Brno (Brünn)
Slavkov (Austerlitz)
Hodonín
B A Y E R N
Böhmerwald
1457
Deggendorf
České Budějovice
Třeboň
Gmünd
Znojmo
Morava
RMANY
Augsburg
Ingolstadt
Landshut
Isar
Passau
1378
Zwettl
Horn
Freistadt
N I E D E R -
Stockerau
Male
Donauwörth
Lech
Amper
Freising
Ried
Wels
Urfahr
OBER-
Linz
Melk
St. Pölten
Wien Vienna
Bratislava
Bruck
Rosenheim
München (Munich)
ÖSTERREICH
Steyr
Enns
Baden
ÖSTERREICH
Wiener Neustadt
Neusiedler
59
48
Salzburg
Bad Ischl
Gmunden
Innsbruck
Kufstein
Mürzzuschlag
Eisenerz
Semmering
985 P.
Sopron
SALZBURG
Bruck
Kapfenberg
Szombathely
Landeck
Ötztal
Brenner
1371
3797
Gr. Glockner
Badgastein
Leoben
STEIERMARK
Graz
HUNGARY
Merana
Bressanone
Lienz
K Ä R N T E N
Drave
Villach
Klagenfurt
Maribor
Nagykanizsa
Bolzano
Dolomiti
TRENTINO
Marmolada 3342
FRIULI-VENEZIA GIULIA
Karnische Alpen
Triglav 2863
Karawanken
Bleiburg
Celje
Varaždin
46
ALTO-ADIGE
Trento
Belluno
Vittorio Veneto
Kobarid
S L O V E N I A
Rovereto
Schio
Bassano
V E N E T O
Udine
Gorizia
Ljubljana
Zagreb
Bjelovar
Vicenza
Treviso
Cerknica
Kočevje
Kupa
Verona
Pádova (Padua)
Venézia (Venice)
Trieste
Koper
Rijeka
Karlovac
Sisak
LY
Po
Adige
Chioggia
Golfo di Venézia
Rovinj
Istra
Krk
C R O A T I A
Bosanska Gradiška
Ferrara
Comácchio
Rt. Kamenjak
Pula
Cres
Senj
Bihać
Banja Luka
Módena
gna
Reno
Imola
Faenza
Ravenna
Losinj
Kvarnerić
Pag
Gospić
Una
BOSNIA-HERZEGOVINA
Srnetica
Forlì
Rubicone
Cesena
Rímini
A D R I A T I C   S E A
Velebit Planina
Dugi Otok
Zadar
Gračac
Dinara Pla.
Firenze (Florence)
San Marino
Pésaro
1913 Troglav
44

12
14

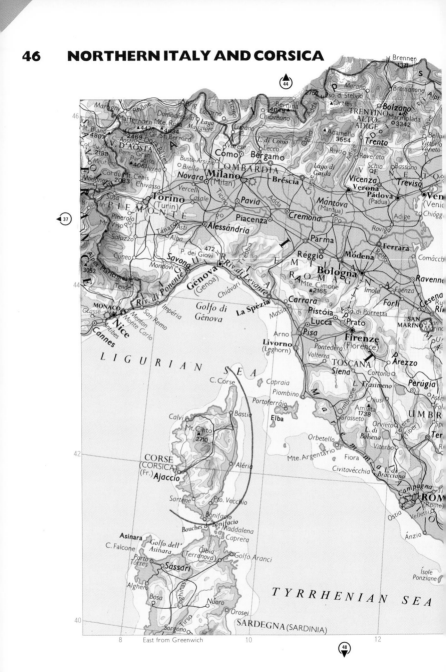

1 : 5 000 000

A USTRIA

Carniche

Drave

Villach

Tagliamento

FRIULI
VENEZIA
GIULIA

2863 Kobarid
(Caporetto)

Udine

Gorizia

Trieste

Koper

Golfo di
Venézia

Istra

Rijeka
(Fiume)

Rovinj

Pula
(Pola)

Rt. Kamenjak

Kvarner

Cres

Lošinj

Kvarnerić

A D R I A T I C

Pésaro
Fano

Senigállia

Ancona

Loreto

Macerata

Fabriano

Civitanova

Monti
Vettore
2478

Ascoli Piceno

Teramo
Gran Sasso
2914

Pescara

Chieti

A B R U Z Z I o

L'Aquila

Sauto

Ortona

Lanciano

Mt. Amaro
2795

Vasto

Térmoli

MOLISE

S. Severo

Campobasso

Frosinone

Fondi

Gaeta

racina

Garigliano

Volturno

Ischia

Caserta

Aversa

Capri

(Naples) Napoli

Torre Annunziata

Sorrento

Vesuvio
1277

Castellammare

Nocera

Salerno

Sele

Avellino

Benevento

Sannicandro

Monte Gargano
1056

Monte S. Ángelo

Fóggia

Ofanto

Eboli

Potenza

Matera

BASILICATA

G. di Manfredónia

Cerignola

Andria

Corato

Barletta

Trani

Molfetta

Bari

Spinazzola

Monópoli

Putignano

Taranto

Bríndisi

Francavilla

Lecce

Bleiburg

Klagenfurt

Karawanken

Celje

Maribor

Drava

Varaždin

Nagykanizsa

HUNGARY

Kaposvár

Szekszárd

Pécs

Mohács

Ljubljana

SLOVENIA

Cerknica

Postojna

Kočevje

Sava

Zagreb

Kupa

Bjelovar

Drava

Karlovac

Sisak

Novska

Brod

Vinkovci

Osijek

C R O A T I A

Kapela

Senj

Krk

Pag

Dugi Otok

Velebit Planina

Gospić
Kremen
1591

Gračac

Zadar

Šibenik

Bihać

Una

Banja Luka

Bosanska
Gradiška

Sava

Srnetica

Unac

Dinara Planina
1913
Troglav

Split

Brač

Hvar

Vis

Korčula

Lastovo

Palagruža
(Croatia)

Dalmacija

Odžak

Brčko

Bosna

Tešanj

Tuzla

BOSNIA-
HERZEGOVINA

Travnik

Sarajevo

Konjic

Neretva

Mostar

Stolac

Vrbas

Dubrovnik

Hercegnovi

Trebinje

S E A

1224

C O P Y R I G H T   G E O R G E   P H I L I P   &   S O N   L T D

45

52

49

14   16

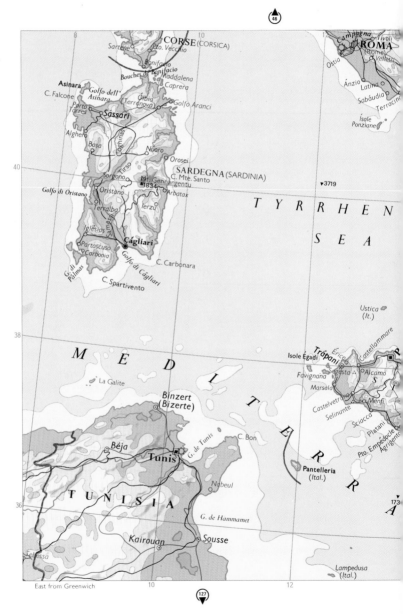

1 : 5 000 000

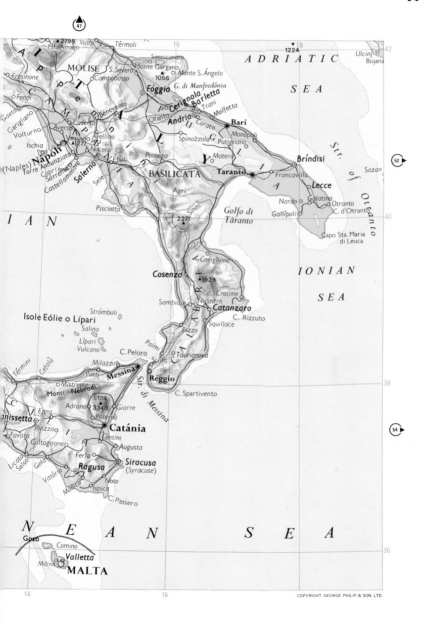

▲2795
Mt. Amaro
Vasto
Térmoli
16
▼18
1224
ADRIATIC
Ulcinj
Bojana
42

Frosinone
MOLISE
S. Severo
Sannicandro
Monte Gargano
1056
Monte S. Ángelo
SEA

Campobasso

Fondi
Benevento
Fóggia
G. di Manfredónia
Cerignola
Barletta
Trani
Molfetta

Gaeta
Garigliano
Caserta
Ofanto
Andria
Corato
Bari

Volturno
Aversa
Avellino
Spinazzola
Putignano
Monópoli

Ischia
Vesuvio
▲1277
Nocera
Potenza
Matera
Bríndisi

(Naples)
Nápoli
Torre Annunziata
Capri
Sorrento
Salerno
Éboli
BASILICATA
Taranto
Francavilla
Lecce
Sazan

Castellammare
Sele
Nardo
Galatina
Otranto
C. d'Otranto

Pisciotta
Agri
Sinni
2271▲
Golfo di
Táranto
Gallípoli
40

IAN
Capo Sta. Maria
di Leuca

Coriglicino
IONIAN

Cosenza
▲1929
SEA

Crotone

Sambiase
Nicastro
Catanzaro

Isole Eólie o Lípari
Strómboli
Pizzo
Squillace
C. Rízzuto

Salina
Palmi
Taurianova

Lípari
Vulcano
C. Peloro
Scilla
Réggio

Términi
Cefalù
Milazzo
Patti
Messina
C. Spartivento
38

Mistretta
Monti Nébrodi
Str. di Messina

nissetta
Enna
Adrano
Etna
▲3340
Giarre

Favara
Piazza
Paternò

Caltagirone
Catánia
54

Licata
Salso
Gela
Ferla
Lentini
Augusta

Vittória
Ragusa
Siracusa
(Syracuse)

Módica
Noto
Ispica

NEAN
C. Passero
SEA
36

Gozo
Comino
Valletta
Mdina
MALTA

14
16
COPYRIGHT. GEORGE PHILIP & SON. LTD.

West from Greenwich

1 : 6 000 000

San Sebastián
Biarritz
Bayonne
F R A N C E
Pau
Mont-de-Marsan
Adour
Condom
Dax
Orthez
Tarbes
Auch
Toulouse
Castres
Béziers
Montpellier
Agde
Sète
Port-St-Louis
Lourdes
Foix
Carcassonne
Narbonne
Golfe du Lion
P y r é n é e s
Perpignan
Port-Vendres
Port-Bou
C. Creus
Tolosa
Roncevaux
Puerto de
Somport 1640
ANDORRA
Seo de Urgel
Col de
Puycerda
Rosas
Golfo de
Rosas
NAVARRA
Pamplona
Tafalla
Jaca
Gállego
C A T A L U Ñ A
Vich
Ter
Gerona
Palamós
S. Feliu de Guixols
Logroño
Sádaba
Aragón
Huesca
Monzón
Cardona
Manresa
Granollers
Lloret
Calella
C O S T A   B R A V A
Calahorra
Cervera
Ebro
Balaguer
Igualada
Cervera
Tarrasa
Mataró
Sabadell
Badalona
Cervera
Almazán
Moncayo
Sa. de 2316
Moncayo
Zaragoza
Jalón
Calatayud
A R A G Ó N
Lérida
Valls
Hospitalet
Barcelona
Reus
Sitges
Llobregat
Calamocha
Alcañiz
Caspe
Tarragona
Costa Dorada
▼ 2224
Jiloca
Montalbán
Tortosa
Golfo de
San Jorge
C. de Tortosá
Sa. de Albarracín
Teruel ▲ 2019
Mts. del Maestrazgo
Morella
Vinaroz
Cuenca
Serranía de Cuenca
Cabriel
Castellón de la Plana
Villarreal
Islas
Columbretes
B A L E A R E S
Menorca
Mahón
Liria
Sagunto
Golfo de
Valencia
Sóller 1445
Inca
Manacor
Mallorca
Cala Millor
Villarrobledo
La Roda
Júcar
Algemesí
Sueca
Cullera
Valencia
Albufera de Valencia
Valencia
Magalluf
Palma
Bahía de Palma
Andraitx
I S L A S
Cabrera
Albacete
Almansa
Játiva
Alcira
Denia
C. Nao
Ibiza
S. Antonio
Ibiza
Formentera
de Alcaraz
▲ 1796
Yecla
Villena
Alcoy
Altea
Benidorm
MURCIA
Hellín
Jumilla
Cieza
Elche
Alicante
Costa Blanca
Segura
Caravaca
Cehegín
Orihuela
Torrevieja
La Sagra
▲ 2381
Murcia
Vélez
Rubio
Alhama
Mar Menor
C. de Palos
Sangonera
Lorca
Águilas
Mazarrón
Cartagena
Cuevas
de Almanzora
Almanzora
Almería
C. de Gata
▼ 2850
M E D I T E R R A N E A N   S E A
Alger (Algiers)
Thenia
Boufarik
Koléa
Ténès
Blida
A L G E R I A

2   0   East from Greenwich   2

36

East from Greenwich

1 : 6 000 000

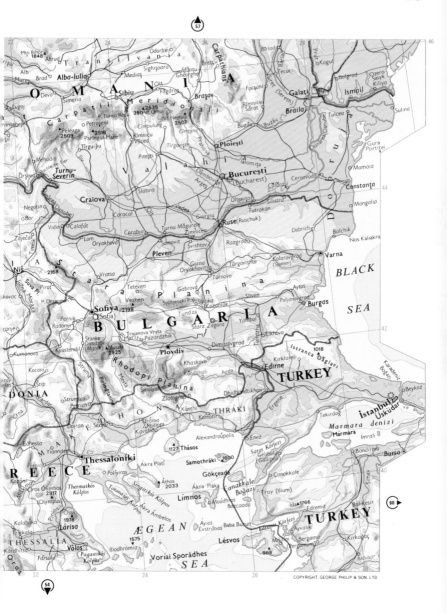

Mţii Bihor 1848
Abrud
Odorheí
Transilvania
Alba-Iulia
Bîrlad
Deva
Mediaş
Sighişoara
Sfântu-Gheorghe
Tecuci
Prut
Kagul
Alb
Brad
Murăş
ROMANIA
Olt
Focşani
Galaţi
Belgrad
Ozero Sasyk Kiliya
Simeria
Sibiu
Fǎgǎraş
Braşov
Siret (Sereth)
Ismail
Lugoj
Carpaţii Meridionali
2535 Vf Omul
Rîmnicu Sǎrat
Brǎila
Sulina
Petroşeni
350 Vf Negoiu 2507
Cîmpulung
Buzǎu
Tulcea
Peleaga 2509
2518 Parîngul-Mare
Rîmnicu Vîlcea
Cîmpina
Ploieşti
Dunǎrea Danube
Gura Portiţei
Tîrgu-Jiu
Tîrgovişte
Valahia
Prahova
Ialomiţa
Orşova Porţile de Fier
Mehadia
Piteşti
Dîmbovița
Bucureşti (Bucharest)
Cernavodǎ
Mamaia
Turnu-Severin
Slatina
Argeş
Oltenita
Silistra
Constanţa
Craiova
Olt
Vedea
Giurgiu
Tutrakan
Călăraşi
Mangalia
Negotin
Bor
Vidin
Calafát
Dunáv (Danube)
Caracal
Cerabia
Turnu Mǎgurele
Zimnica
Ruse (Ruschuk)
Dobrich
Balchik
Nos Kaliakra
Zaječar
Lom
Oryakhovo
Somovit
Svishtov
Razgrado
NIS
Stara
Pleven
Gorna Oryakhovitsa
Türgovishte
Kolarovgrad (Shumen)
Varna
2168
Vratsa
Türnovo
BLACK
Suva Pl.
Pirot
Teteven
Planina
Gabrovo
Aytos
P. Dragoman
Vezhen 2198
Shipchenski Pr. Shipka
Sliven
Poljanovgrad
Burgas
SEA
Sofiya (Sofia)
Pernik
Radomir
Tundza
Stara Zagora
Yambol
Kumanovo
BULGARIA
Stanke Dimitrov (Marek)
Trajanova Vrata
Musala 2925
Pazardzhik
Plovdiv
Dimitrovgrad
Elkhovo
Kyustendil
Rhodopi Planina
Khaskovo
Arda
Istranca Dağlari 1018
42
DONIA
Struma
Pirin Planina
Kürdzhali
Edirne
Kïrklareli
TURKEY
Karadeniz Boğazı
Kocani
Štip
Mesta
Smolyan
Dhidhimótikhon
Ergene
Beykoz
Strumica
Petrich
Zlatograd
Ergene
Tekirdağ
İstanbul
Üsküdar
Edhessa
Dojran
Serrara
Drama Philippi
Xánthi
THRÁKI
Komotiní
Marmara denizi
Marmara
İmralı
Bursa
Yiannitsá
Kavalla
Alexandroúpolis
Enez
Saroz Körfezi
Gelibolu (Gallipoli)
REECE
Thessaloníki
Polýiros
1127 Thásos
Samothráki ▲600
Gökçeada
Çanakkale
Bandirma
Simav
Kozáni
Óros Ólimbos 2917 (Olympus)
Thermaïkós Kólpos
Toronéos Kólpos
Áthos 2033
Ákra Pláka
Çanakkale Boğazı
Troy (Ilium)
Ida ▲1766
Edremit
Balikesir
80
Ossa 1978
Ákra Ámbelos
Límnos
Moúdhros
Bozcaada
Kalabáka
Larísa
THESSALIA
Voríai Sporádhes
1575
Iliodhrómia
Áyios Evstrátios
AEGEAN
Lésvos
Baba Bucun
Edremit Körfezi
Mytilíni
Bergama Pergamum
TURKEY
Kirkağaç
Tríkkala
Vólos
Pagasitikós Kólpos
SEA
96B
Ayvalik
Akhisar
Kardhítsa
Fársala
Pinos

Ákra Platí
Singitikós Kólpos

57

54

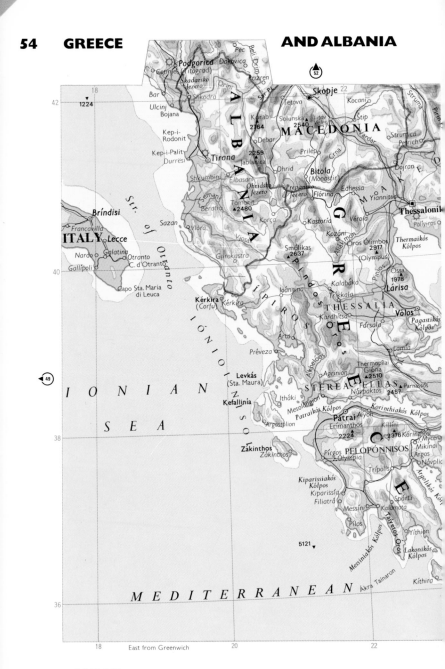

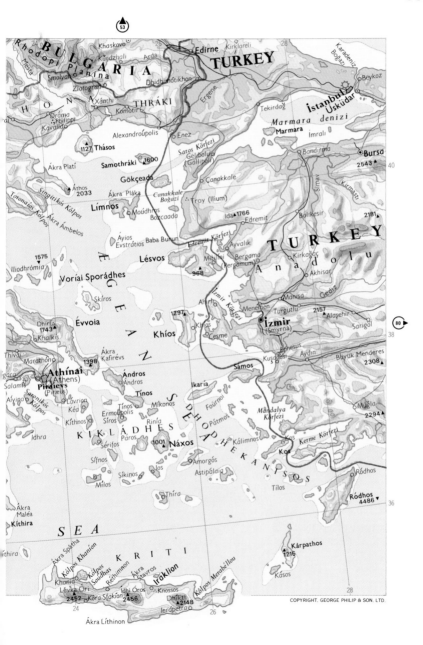

BULGARIA

Rhodopi Planina

Khaskovo

Kŭrdzhali

Arda

Edirne

Kırklareli

Karadeniz Boğazı

TURKEY

Smolyan

Zlotograd

Dhidhimótikhon

Ergene

Beykoz

Mesta

Xánthi

THRÁKI

Komotiní

Tekirdağ

İstanbul

Üsküdar

HON

Dráma

Philippi

Kaválla

Alexandroúpolis

Enez

Marmara denizi

Marmara

İmralı

Bandırma

Bursa

2543 ▲

40

1127 Thásos

Saros Körfezi

Gelibolu (Gallipoli)

Ákra Platí

Samothráki ▲1600

Gökçeada

Çanakkale

Simav

Kırmıklı

2181 ▲

Áthos 2033

Ákra Pláka

Canakkale Boğazi

∴ Troy (Ilium)

Balıkesir

Limnos

Moúdhros

Bozcaada

Ida ▲1766

Edremit

2181 ▲

Singitikós Kólpos

Toronaíos Kólpos

Ákra Ámbelos

Áyios Evstrátios

Baba Burun

Edremit Körfezi

Ayvalık

Bergama (Pergamum)

TURKEY

Anadolu

Kırkağaç

1575 ▲

Iliodhrómia

Lésvos

Mitilíni

968 ▲

Akhisar

Voríai Sporádhes

İzmir Körfezi

Ahırlı

Menemen

Manisa

Turgutlu

Gediz

2157

Alaşehir ▲

Sarıgöl

Skíros

Dhirfís 1743 ▲

Évvoia

1297 ▲

Khíos

Kınas

Çeşme

İzmir (Smyrna)

38

Khalkís

Thívai

Marathóna

1398 ▲

Ákra Kafirévs

Ephesus

Kuşadası

Aydın

Büyük Menderes

2308 ▲

80

garo

Athínai (Athens)

Piraévs (Piræus)

Salamís

Ándros

Ándros

Tínos

Míkonos

Ikaría

Foúrnoi

Sámos

Mándalya Körfezi

Muğla

2294 ▲

Aíyina

Saronikós Kólpos

Lávrion

Kéa

Ermoúpolis

Síros

Rínia

Páros

Pátmos

Kálimnos

Kerme Körfezi

Kós

Idhra

Kíthnos

KIKLÁDHES

Sérifos

Sífnos

1001 ▲ Náxos

Amorgós

Íos

Astipálaia

Kós

DHODHEKÁNISOS

Ródhos

36

Síkinos

Thíra

Tílos

Ródhos 4486 ▼

Mílos

Ákra Maléa

Kíthira

SEA

Kárpathos ▲1215

ithira

Ákra Spátha

Khaniá

KRITI

Kásos

Lévka Óri 2452 ▲

Kólpos Khaníon

Kólpos Soúdhas

Réthimnon

Ákra Stavrós

Iráklion

Knossós

Kólpos Merabéllou

28

Kóra Sfakíon

Ídhi Óros 2456 ▲

Dhíkti ▲2148

Ierápetra

26

24

Ákra Líthinon

53

80

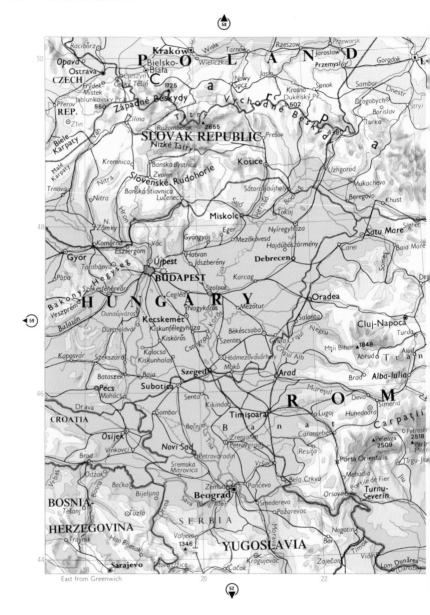

1 : 5 000 000

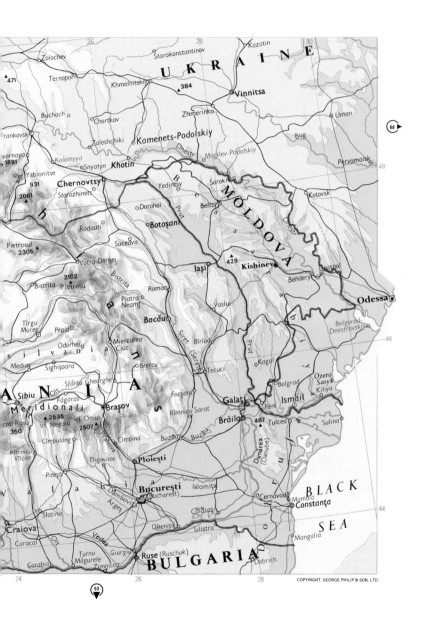

Zolochev
Starokonstantinov
Kazatin
U K R A I N E
▲471
Ternopol
Khmelnitskiy
▲384
Vinnitsa
Buchach
Chortkov
Zhmerinka
Uman
rankovsk
Zaleshchiki
Kamenets-Podolskiy
Bug
vornaya
1881
Kolomyya
Snyatyn
Khotin
Dnestr
Mogilev-Podolskiy
Pervomaisk
Perl Yablonitse
▲931
Chernovtsy
Yedintsy
Soroki
Kotovsk
48
▲2061
Storozhinets
M O L D O V A
h
Dorohoi
Beltsy
Dnestr
Pietrosul
2305
Radauti
Suceava
Botoşani
Vatra-Dornei
Bistrita
Iaşi
▲429
Kishinev
Tiraspol
▲2102
Bistrita Pietrosu
Roman
Bendery
Odessa ■
Tîrgu
Mureş
Piatra
Neamţ
Bacău
Vaslui
Belgorod-
Dnestrovskiy
46
Praid
Odorhei
Miercurea
Ciuc
Bîrlad
Medias
Sighişoara
Bretcu
Tecuci
Kagul
Ozero
Sasyk
Kiliya
A
Sibiu
Sfântu Gheorghe
Focşani
Bolgrad
N I A
Meridionali
Făgăraş
Braşov
Rîmnicu Sarat
Galaţi
Reni
Ismail
Sulina
rna Roşu
350
▲2535
Vf. Negoiu
Vf. Omul
2507▲
Cîmpulung
Cîmpina
Buzău
Brăila
▲467
Tulcea
Rîmnicu
Vîlcea
Prahova
Tîrgovişte
Ploieşti
Dunărea
(Danube)
Pitesti
Bucureşti
(Bucharest)
Ialomiţa
Cernavodă
Mamaia
Constanţa
44
a
Slatina
Dâmboviţa
Arges
Căluraşi
B L A C K
Craiova
Caracal
Olt
Oltenita
Silistra
Mangalia
S E A
Corabia
Vedea
Turnu
Măgurele
Zimnicea
Giurgiu
Ruse (Ruschuk)
B U L G A R I A
Dobrich

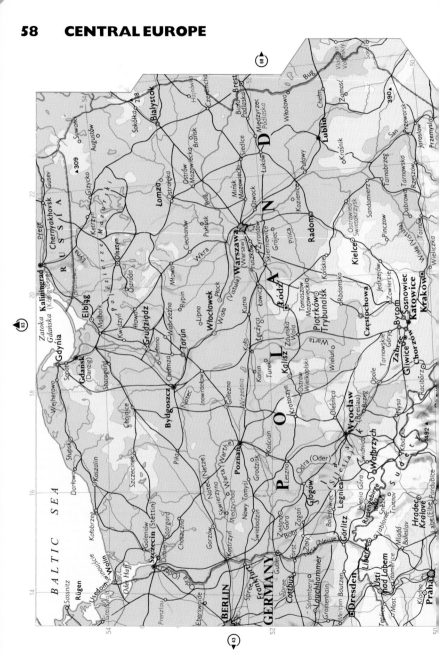

1 : 5 000 000

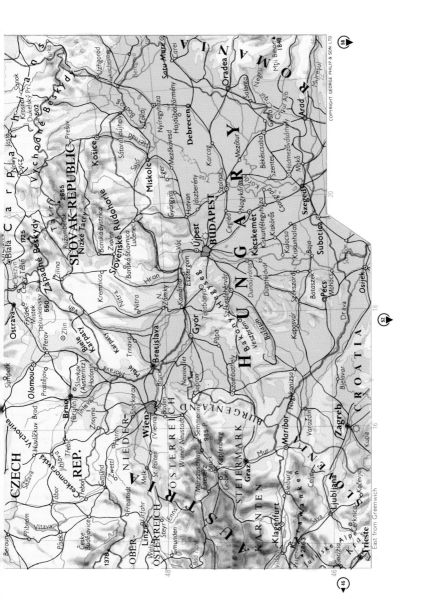

East from Greenwich

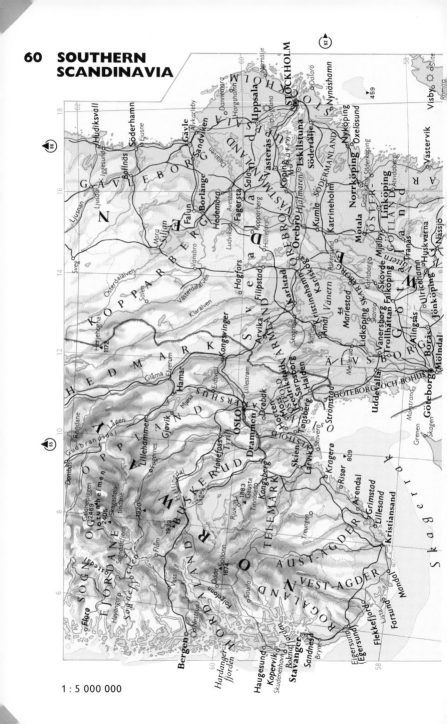

1 : 5 000 000

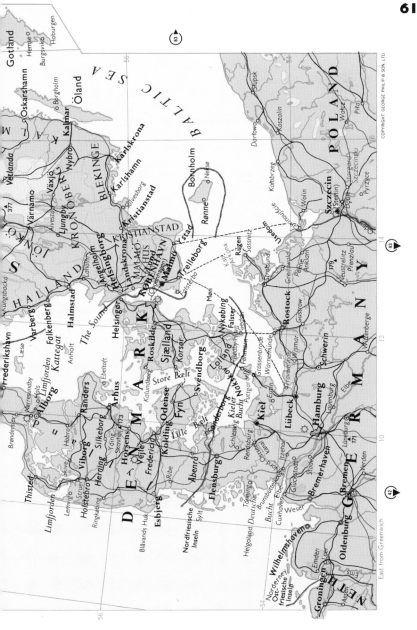

1 : 5 000 000

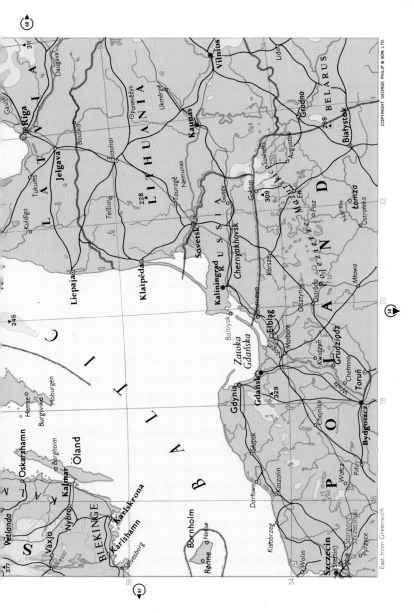

63

LATVIA

Gauja

Daugava

Riga

Tukums

Kuldiga

Jelgava

Bauska

Siauliai

Tolsiai

LITHUANIA

228

Panevėžys

Ukmergė

Vilnius

Kaunas

Nemunas

Tauragė

Grodno

Suwałki

Augustów

BELARUS

Białystok

288

54

Lida

POLAND

22

Mazurske Pojezierze

Giżycko

309

Pisz

Narew

Ostrołęka

Łomża

Ełk

Olsztyn

Ostróda

Korsze

Gusev

Chernyakhovsk

Sovetsk

RUSSIA

Klaipėda

Liepaja

Bałtiysk

Kaliningrad

Zheleznodorozhno

Elbląg

Malbork

Kwidzyn

Chełmno

Grudziądz

Toruń

Wisła

Chełmno

Chojnice

Mława

Narew

Bydgoszcz

18

20

Gdynia

Gdańsk

329

Zatoka
Gdańska

BALTIC

Słupsk

Dartowo

Koszalin

Kołobrzeg

Świnoujście

Szczecin
(Stettin)

Odra

Stargard

Szczeciński

Pyrzyce

Piła

Wałcz

16

54

SEA

Bornholm

Rønne o Neksø

245

Hemsö

Burgsvik

Hoburgen

Veltanda

377

S

Växjö

Nybro

Kalmar

Öland

Borgholm

KALMAR

Oskarshamn

BLEKINGE

Karlskrona

Karlshamn

Sölvesborg

Alsterro

68

311

58

61

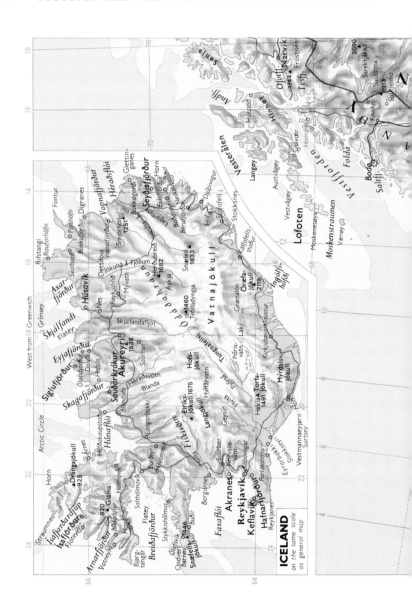

ICELAND
on the same scale
as general map

1 : 5 000 000

N O R W E G I A N

S E A

Arctic Circle

East from Greenwich

Lofoten

Svartisen
1599

Mo

Mosjøen

Vefsna

Denna

Alsten

Vega

Vega

Vikna

Folda

Namsos

Grong

Tunnsjøen

Namsen

Steinkjer

Verdalsøra

Levanger

Kallsjön

N-TRØNDELAG

R

Blåfjelle-hatten
1703

1390

Frøya

Hitra

Smøla

Kristiansund

Molde

Volda

Ålesund

Stadlandet

MØRE OG ROMSDAL

Dovrefjell

Åndalsnes

Romsdalen

Snøhetta
2286

Frohavet

SØR-TRØNDELAG

Orkla

Støren

Trondheim

Orkanger
Løkken

Gaula

Rørosfjell

Femund
1604

N

Trondheimsfjorden

VÄSTERBOTTEN

Storuman

Vojm
sjön

Malgomaj

Vilhelmina

Ångermanälven

Storsele

Sorsele

Uddjaur

1589

1915

Rosvatnet

Børge-
fjellet

Tåsjön

Flåsjön

Hoting

Ströms
vattuda

Strömsund

Holagen

J Ä M T

Åre

Storsjön

Östersund

Ljungan

Hede

Sylarna

1766

N D

S

Indals ven

Bispfors

Bräcke

Ånge

Ångermanälven

Sollefteå

Kramfors

 Å

N G E R M A N L A N D

Sundsvall

Hälsj.

60 ▲

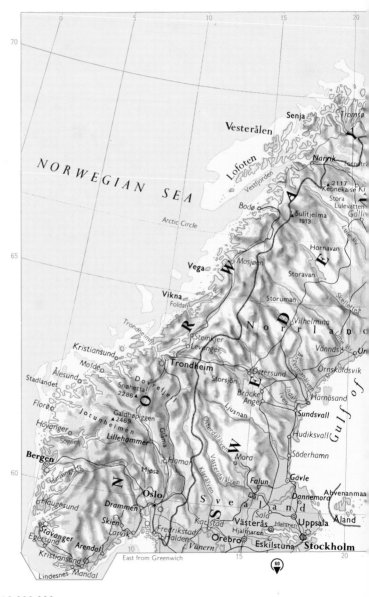

NORWEGIAN SEA

Arctic Circle

Vesterålen
Senja
Tromsø
Lofoten
Narvik
Vestfjorden
▲ 2117
Kebnekaise Kj
Stora
Lulevatten
Bodø
Sulitjelma
1913
Hornavan
Vega
Mosjøen
Storavan
Vikna
Storuman
Foldaf
Vilhelmina
Trondheim
Vännäs
Ur
Kristiansund
Steinkjer
Örnsköldsvik
Molde
Levanger
Ålesund
Trondheim
Östersund
Stadlandet
Dovrefjell
Storsjön
2286 ▲
Snøhetta
Härnösand
Florø
Bräcke
Ange
Galdhøpiggen
Jotunheimen
▲ 2469
Ljusnan
Sundsvall
Høyanger
Lillehammer
Hudiksvall
Sognefj.
Söderhamn
Bergen
Hamar
Mora
Mjøsa
Gävle
Falun
Ahvenanmaa
Haugesund
Oslo
Dannemora
Drammen
Sala
Åland
Skien
Karlstad
Västerås
Uppsala
Stavanger
Larvik
Fredrikstad
Hjälmaren
Mälaren
Egersund
Arendal
Halden
Örebro
Eskilstuna
Stockholm
Kristiansund
Vänern
Lindesnes
Mandal
East from Greenwich

NORWEGIAN
SWEDEN
Norrland
Svealand

1 : 10 000 000

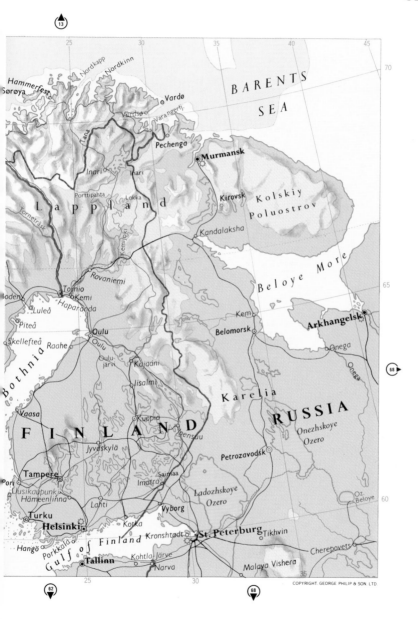

BARENTS

SEA

Hammerfest
Sørøya
Nordkapp
Nordkinn
Vardø
Vardsø
Varangerfj.
Tana
Pechenga
Inari
Inari
Murmansk
L a p p l a n d
Porttipahta
Lokka
Kirovsk
Kolskiy
Poluostrov
Torneträsk
Kandalaksha
Kemijoki
Rovaniemi
B e l o y e   M o r e
oden
Tornio
Kemi
Haparanda
Kem
Luleå
Piteå
Belomorsk
Arkhangelsk
Skellefteå
Raahe
Oulu
Oulu
Onega
Oulu-
Järvi
Kajaani
Onega
B o t h n i a
Iisalmi
K a r e l i a
Vaasa
Kuopio
RUSSIA
F I N L A N D
Joensuu
Onezhskoye
Ozero
Jyväskylä
Petrozavodsk
Tampere
Saimaa
Pori
Imatra
Uusikaupunki
Hämeenlinna
Lahti
Ladozhskoye
Ozero
Oz.
Beloye
Turku
Vyborg
Helsinki
Kotka
Kronshtadt
St. Peterburg
Tikhvin
Hangö
Porkkala
G u l f   o f   F i n l a n d
Kohtla-Järve
Cherepovets
Tallinn
Narva
Malaya Vishera

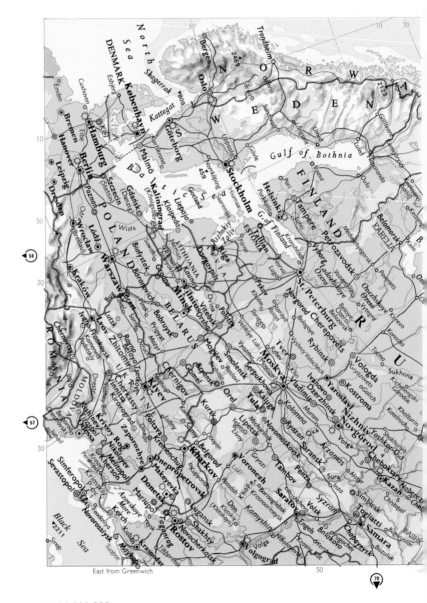

1 : 20 000 000

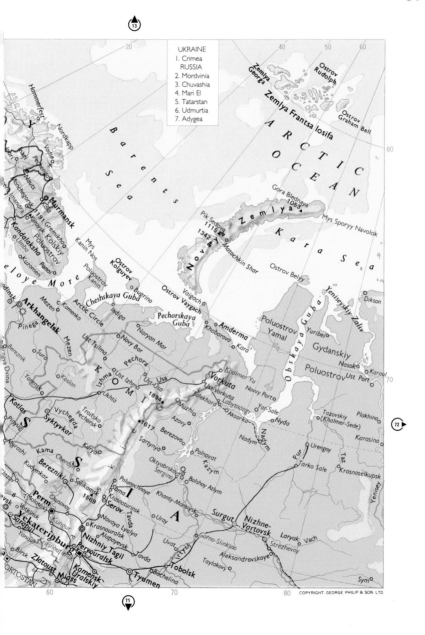

UKRAINE
1. Crimea
RUSSIA
2. Mordvinia
3. Chuvashia
4. Mari El
5. Tatarstan
6. Udmurtia
7. Adygea

Hammerfest
Nordkapp
Vardso
Vadso

Nordvik
Kolksi
Peciga

Murmansk
Kola
Gremikha
Monchegorsk
Kirovsk
Olenegorsk
Poluostrov
Kovdor
Kuzomen
Kandalaksha
Umbo
Penoy
Kolskiy

Mys
Kanin Nos

Ostrov
Kolguyev

Poluostrov
Kanin
Bugrino

Ostrov Vaygach
Indiga
Kamenka

Beloye More

Arkhangelsk
Pinega
Mezen
Suro
Bereznik
Yorensk
Koslan
Pinega
Naryan Mar

Cheshskaya Guba
Ust Tsilma
Novy Bor
Pechorskaya
Guba

Khabarovo
Kara

Amderma

Pechora

Usa

Vorkuta
Ust Usa
1894
Muzhia
Labytnangi
Salekhard
Aksarka

Khalmer Yu
Ust Vorkuta
Novvy Porto
Yar-Sale

Poluostrov
Yamal

Obskaya Guba

Gydanskiy
Poluostrov

Yenisevskiy
Zaliv

Dikson

Ostrov Belyy

Ostrov Graham Bell
Ostrov Rudolph

Zemlya Georga
Zemlya Frantsa Iosifa

ARCTIC OCEAN

Gora Blednaya
1063

Mys Sporyy Navolok

Zemlya

Pik Sedova
1115

1342

Matochkin Shar

Kara Sea

Nosok
Karaul
Yuribeo
Ust Port

Tazovskiy
(Khalmer-Sede)
Karasino

Plakhino

Syktyvkar
Katlas
Myroshi
Kotlas
Vychegda
Troitsko
Pechorsk
Ukhta
Izhma
Ust Izhma

1617

Berezovaya
Azovy

Sartynya

Polnovat
Kazym

Nadym
Nyda

Pur

Tarka Sale

Urengoy

Taz

Krasnoselkupsk

Yenisey

Kama
Cherdyn
Kudymkar
Berezniki
Solikamsk
Polunochnoye
Krasnovishersk
1569

Perm
(Molotov)
Chusovoy
Serov

Krasnoturinsk

Khanty-Mansiysk

Bolshoy Atlym

Oktyabrskoye
Sergino

Surgut
Nizhne-
Vartovsk

Laryak

Vach

Strezhevoy

Sym

Ekaterinburg
Voykutsk
Pervouralsk
Nizhniy Tagil
Novaya Lyalya
Krasnouralsk
Alapayevsk
Tavda

Uray

Gorno-Slinkino

Aleksandrovskoye

Taylakovy

Birsk
Zlatoust
Miass
Kamensk-
Uralskiy

Tobolsk

Bachelina

Tyumen

Uvat

Irtysh

BASHKORTOSTAN

Barents Sea

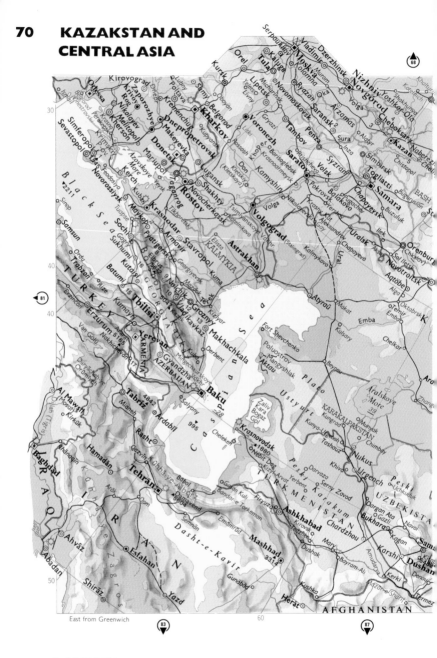

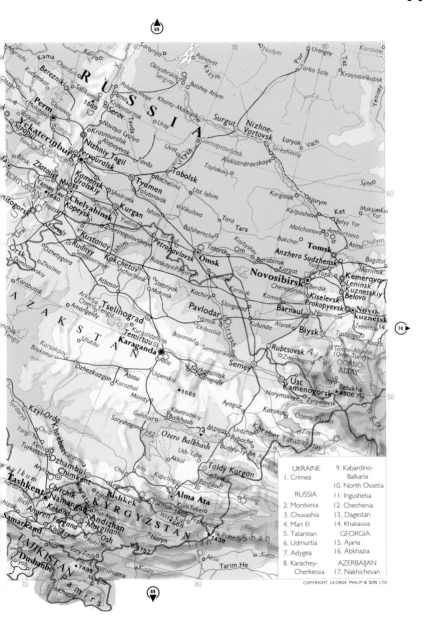

UKRAINE
1. Crimea

RUSSIA
2. Mordvinia
3. Chuvashia
4. Mari El
5. Tatarstan
6. Udmurtia
7. Adygea
8. Karachey-
   Cherkessia

9. Kabardino-
   Balkana
10. North Ossetia
11. Ingushetia
12. Chechenia
13. Dagestan
14. Khakassia

GEORGIA
15. Ajaria
16. Abkhazia

AZERBAIJAN
17. Nakhichevan

COPYRIGHT GEORGE PHILIP & SON LTD

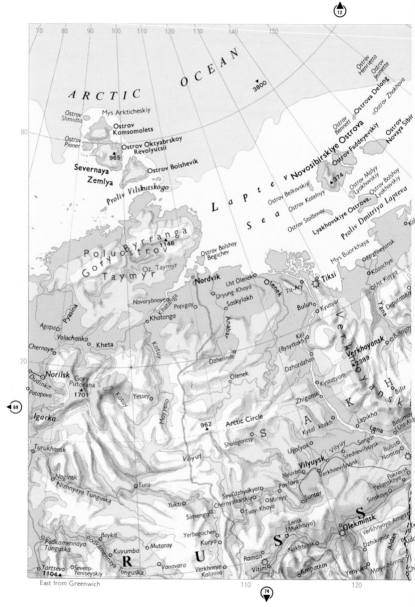

ARCTIC   OCEAN

3800

Ostrov Henrietta
Ostrov Jeanette
Ostrov Zhokhova

Ostrov Shmidta
Mys Arkticheskiy

Ostrov Komsomolets

Ostrov Pioner
Ostrov Oktyabrskoy Revolyutsii

965

Severnaya Zemlya
Ostrov Bolshevik

Proliv Vilskutskogo

Ostrov Bennett   Ostrova Delong   Ostrov Vilkitskogo
Novaya Sibir

Ostrov Faddeyevskiy

Novosibirskiye Ostrova

874   Ostrov Malyy Lyakhovskiy   Ostrov Bolshoy Lyakhovskiy

Lapte v

Ostrov Belkovskiy

Ostrov Kotelnyy

Sea

Ostrov Stolbovoy

Lyakhovskiye Ostrova

Proliv Dmitriya Lapteva

Kol

P o l u O s t r o v B y r r a n g a   1146
G o r y

T a y m y r

Oz. Taymyr

Ostrov Bolshoy Begichev

Nordvik

Ust Olenёk   Olenёk   Tit-Ary   Tiksi

Mys Buorkhaya

Nizhneyansk
Kozachye

Novorybnoye
Uryung-Khaya   Saskylakh

Popigay

Khatanga

Buluna   Kyusyur   Ust Kurga

Yana   Deputatsk

Pyasina

Agapa

Volochanka   Kheta

Khatanga

Kotuy

Anabar

Kel (Bysyttakh)

Verkhoyansk

Verkhoyansk   2389

Batagay

Chernoye

Dzhelinde

Dzhardzhan   Kystatyam

V e r k h o y a n   Bilir

Norilsk   Gory Putorana
Dudinka   1701
Potapovo

Olenёk

Zhigansk   Lepikha

Batom
Aldo

Igarka

Kotuy   Yessey

Molyero   962   Arctic Circle

Kytal Ktakh   Lena   Lusa

S   A   K   H   A

Turukhansk

Vilyuy   Shologontsy

Ugolyakh   Srednevilyuysk   Bulus   Namtay

Noginsk
Nizhnyaya Tunguska   Tura

Vilyuysk   Vilyuy   Verkhnevilyuysk

Nyurba   Pavlova   Suntar   Yelanskoye   Pokrovs   Sinaskoye

Yukti
Syurdzhyukyoro
Chernyshevskiy   Mirnyy   Tuoy-Khaya

S

Baykit

Podkamennaya Tunguska   Kuyumba   Mutaray

Simenga

Yerbogachen   Kurya

Lensk (Mukhtuya)

Olekminsk

Verkhnyaya Amega   Dzhikimde   Aldan

Vanavara

Yartsevo   1104   Severo-Yeniseyskiy   Podkamennaya Tunguska

R   U   S   Verkhnee Kalinina   Roman   Vitim   Nokhtuysk   Kropatkin   Yenyuk   Malyy Nimnyy

S

70   80   90   100   110   120   130   140   150

70

80

1 : 20 000 000

Mys Dezhneva
(East C.)

Chukotskoye More

Uelen
Lavrentiya
Providenlya
St. Lawrence I.
(U.S.A.)

Ostrov Vrangelya

East Siberian Sea

Ostrova Medvezhi

Ostrov Ayon

Anadyrskiy Zaliv

Beringovskiy

Peek
Ust Chaun

Chukotskiy Khrebet

Vankarem
Egvekinot
Kanchalan

Anyuy
Ambarchik
Chaunskaya
1853
Bilibino
Anadyr

Nizhne Kolymsk
Bolshoy Anyuy
1742

Khatyrka
Koryakskiy Khrebet
2562

Chukardakha
Indigirka
Srednekolymsk

Shamanovo
Ulyandi
(Otur-Kyuyel)
Druzhina
Oloy
Verkne
Markovo
Penzhino

Zashiversk
Khonu
Kolyma
Zyryanka

Omolon
Poren
Gizhiga
Penzhinskaya Guba
Matochkin
Tilichiki
Karaga

Ilirney
Kamenskoye

Pobeda
3147

Bering Sea

Khrebet Cherskogo
Gora Chen
2682

Balygychan
Taskan
Seymchan
Omsukchan
Oroturan
Evensk
Nayakhan

Viliga
Gizhiginskaya
Guba

Ukoi
Ust-Kamchatsk
Komandorskiye Ostrova
Nikolskoye

Alyaskitovyo
Kulu
Kyulyunken
Omsukchan
2959
Loshkalakh

Balaka
Iret
Atka

Zaliv Shelikhova

Tigil

Poluostrov
Klyuchevskaya
4750
Zhupanovo
Petropavlovsk-
Kamchatskiy
2498

Aldan
Boroganiy
Khandyga
Ytyk-Kyel

Oymyakon
Perevoz
Ust-Omchug
Songa-Talon
Susuman

Magadan

Ust-Kheyryuzovaya
Voroskoye
Sobolevo
Pushchino

Yakutsk
Allakh-Yun
Atka
Okhotsk

Kirovskiy
Opala

Maykchanskiy
Yur
Ulya

Severo-
Kurilsk

Amga
Ust Maya
Kayakhanskiy

Sea of
Okhotsk

Ostrov Paramushir

Uste-Mile
Almo
Maya

Nelkan
1790

Ostrov Onekotan

Chagda
Uchur

Chasovnya
Uchurskoye

Khrebet Dzhugdzur

Ayan

Ostrova
Kurilskiye

Ostrov
Simushir

2246
Kankunskiy

Ostrov Bolshoy
Shantar
Sakhalinskiy
Zaliv

Okha

Nemuy
Tuguro

Chumikan
2482

Nikolayevsk-
na-Am.

Selenino
Bogorodskoye

Katangli
Nekrasovsk-
G. Lopatina

Sakhalin

COPYRIGHT GEORGE PHILIP & SON LTD

130
140
160

60
180
170
50

75

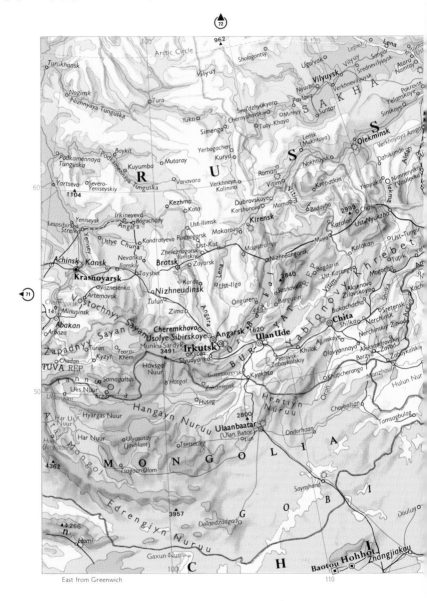

East from Greenwich

1 : 20 000 000

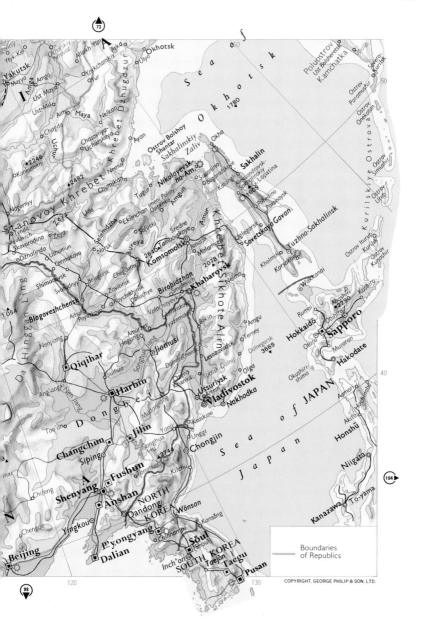

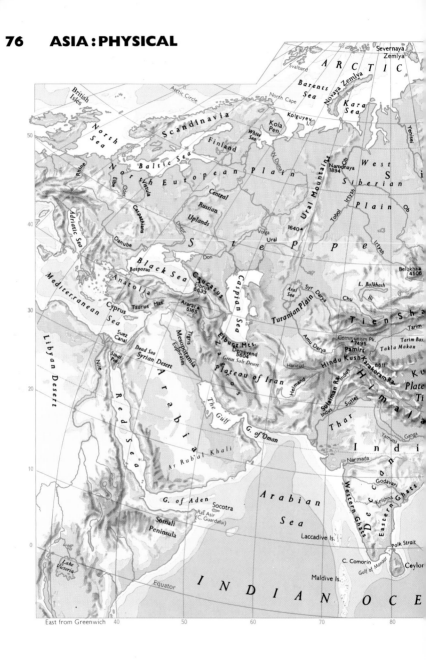

ARCTIC

Severnaya Zemlya

Svalbard

Barents Sea

Novaya Zemlya

Kara Sea

North Cape

Kolguyev I.

British Isles

Arctic Circle

North Sea

Scandinavia

Kola Pen.

White Sea

Finland

Baltic Sea

North European Plain

Rhine

Elbe

Oder

Vistula

Carpathians

Central Russian Uplands

S. Dvina

Ural Mountains

Narodnaya 1894

Ob

West Siberian Plain

Yenisei

Tobol

Irtysh

Ob

Irtysh

Danube

Volga

Don

Dnepr

Ural

1640

S t e p p e

Belukha 4506

Adriatic Sea

Black Sea

Bosporus

Caucasus

Elbrus 5633

Caspian Sea

Aral Sea

Syr Darya

Chu

Ili

L. Balkhash

Anatolia

Mediterranean Sea

Cyprus

Taurus Mts.

Ararat 5165

Turanian Plain

Tien Sha

Tarim

Suez Canal

Dead Sea

Syrian Desert

Tigris

Euphrates

Mesopotamia

Elburz Mts.

Demavend 5604

Great Salt Desert

Zagros

Plateau of Iran

Amu Darya

Harirud

Communism Pk. 7495

Pamirs

Hindu Kush

Karakoram Ra.

8611

Tarim Bas.

Takla Makan

Ku

Plate

Ti

Libyan Desert

Nile

Sinai Pen.

Red Sea

A r a b i a

The Gulf

G. of Oman

Helmand

Suleiman Ra.

Indus

Sutlej

Indus

Thar

Himala

Yamuna

Ganga

I n d i

Narmada

Ar Rub'al Khali

G. of Aden

Socotra

Ras Asir (C. Guardafui)

Somali Peninsula

A r a b i a n

S e a

Godavari

Krishna

Western Ghats

Eastern Ghats

D e c a

Laccadive Is.

Palk Strait

C. Comorin

Gulf of Mannar

Ceylon

Lake Victoria

Maldive Is.

Equator

I N D I A N   O C E

East from Greenwich   40   50   60   70   80

1 : 60 000 000

ARCTIC OCEAN
Chelyuskin
New Siberian Is.
Wrangel I.
C. Dezhneva
Bering Strait
Laptev Sea
aimyr
eninsula
Kotuy
Olenek
Lena
Verkhoyansk Range
Indigirka
Kolyma
Gydan Ra. (Kolyma)
Kamchatka Peninsula
Klyuchevsk vol. 4750
Bering Sea
Aleutian Is.
7822
Central
b
e
r
i
a
Plateau
Lena
Aldan
Stanovoy Ra.
Sea of Okhotsk
Sikhote Alin Ra.
Sakhalin
Kurils
10,542
Lower Tunguska
Siberian
Angara
Baikal
Amur
Great Khingan Mts.
Manchurian Plain
Sungari
La Pérouse Str.
Hokkaidō
Sayan Mts.
Selenga
Yablonovy Ra.
G
o
b
i
Sea of Japan
Altai
Plateau of Mongolia
Korea
Honshū
Fujisan 3776
Turfan Basin
Lop Nor
Koko Nor
Hwang
Great Plain of China
Po Hai
Yellow Sea
Korea Str.
Shikoku
Kyūshū
10,864
Bonin Is.
PACIFIC OCEAN
nlun
Shan
C
h
i
n
a
Yangtse Kiang
East China Sea
Ryūkyūs
Tropic of Cancer
au of
bet
Tsangpo
Si-kiang
Formosa
a
Brahmaputra
Salween
Mekong
Hong (Red)
G. of Tonkin
Hainan
Luzon
Guam
11,022
y
a
Irrawaddy
Menam
Philippine Is.
Caroline Is.
Bay of Bengal
Cape Johnson Deep 10,497
Pelew Is.
Andaman Is.
G. of Siam
Palawan
Sulu Sea
Mindanao
Kinabalu 4101
Celebes Sea
Halmahera
Nicobar Is.
South China Sea
Celebes
Moluccas
New Guinea
Malay Peninsula
Borneo
Makasar Strait
Ceram
A
N
Sunda Is.
Str. of Malacca
Sumatra
East
Indies
Banda Sea
Arafura Sea
Java Sea
Flores
Timor
Sunda Str.
Java
Bali
Australia

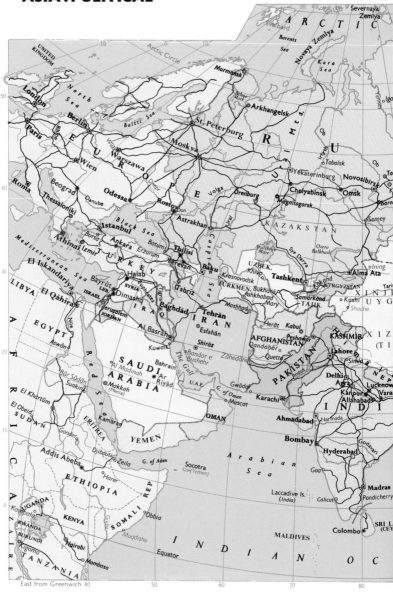

ARCTIC

Severnaya Zemlya
Svalbard
Barents Sea
Novaya Zemlya
Kara Sea

London
North Sea
Murmansk
Arkhangelsk
R U
Arctic Circle

Berlin
Paris
Baltic Sea
St. Peterburg
Ob
Tobolsk
Novosibirsk

Warszawa
Wien
Moskva
Yekaterinburg
Chelyabinsk
Omsk
Barn

Roma
Beograd
Odessa
Rostov
Orenburg
Magnitogorsk
Semey

Thessaloniki
Danube
Astrakhan
Volga
K A Z A K S T A N

Istanbul
Black Sea
Bursa
Tbilisi
Batumi
Caspian Sea
Ozero Balkhash

Athinai Izmir
Ankara
Erzurum
Yerevan
Baku
Aral'skoye More
Syr Darya
Ilning

El Iskandariya
Bayrût
Halab
Tabriz
Krasnovodsk
UZBEK.
Tashkent
Alma Ata

LIBYA
El Qâhira
ISRAEL
SYRIA
Dimashq
TURKMEN.
Bukhara
Samarkand
KYRGYZSTAN
Kashi

EGYPT
Jerusalem
JORDAN
Baghdâd
Tehrân
Ashkhabad
Mary
TAJIK.
Shache

Aswân
Al Basrah
IRAN
Mashhad
XINJ
UYG

Nile
Kuwait
Esfahân
Herât
Kabul
AFGHANISTAN
Peshawar
KASHMIR
XIZ
(TI)

SAUDI
Shîrâz
Zâhedân
Qandahâr
Quetta
Lahore
Simla

Bûr Sûdân
Al Madînah
Ar Riyâd
Bandar e Bushehr
The Gulf
Gwâdar
PAKISTAN
Delhi
NEP

El Khartûm
Makkah (Mecca)
U.A.E.
Karachi
INDIA
Agra
Lucknow
Vara

Suakin
Bahrain
G. of Oman
Muscat
Ahmadâbad
Narmada
Kânpur
Allahabad

El Obeid
Kamaran
OMAN
Bombay
Goa
Godavari

S U D A N
ERITREA
YEMEN
Hyderabad

Gondar
Addis Abeba
Djibouti
Zeila
G. of Aden
Socotra (Yemen)
Arabian Sea

Harer
Laccadive Is. (India)
Calicut
Madras
Pondicherry

ETHIOPIA
SOMALI REP.
Obbia
Colombo
SRI L (CEY)

UGANDA
RWANDA
BURUNDI
KENYA
Muqdisho
MALDIVES

Kampala
Kigoma
Nairobi
Mombasa
Equator
I N D I A N   O C

ZAIRE
TANZANIA

East from Greenwich 40   50   60   70   80

1 : 60 000 000

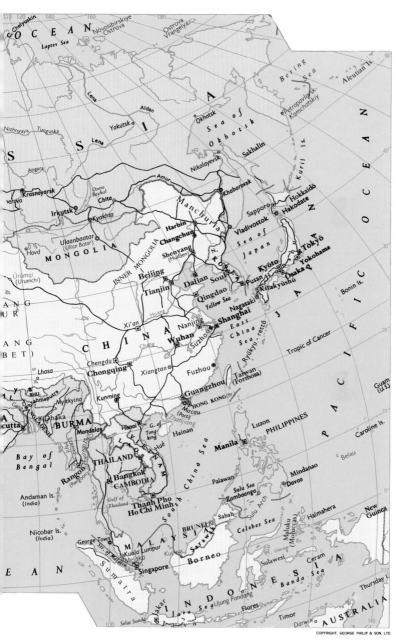

ARCTIC OCEAN
Chelyuskin
Novosibirskiye Ostrova
Ostrova Vrangelya
Laptev Sea
Nizhnyaya Tunguska
Lena
Yakutsk
Aldan
Bering Sea
Aleutian Is.
R U S S I A
Krasnoyarsk
Angara
Kemerovo
Ozero Baykal
Irkutsk
Chita
Kyakhta
Amur
Nikolayevsk
Okhotsk
Sea of Okhotsk
Sakhalin
Petropavlovsk-Kamchatskiy
Ulaanbaatar (Ulan Bator)
Hovd
MONGOLIA
Manchuria
Khabarovsk
Harbin
Changchun
Sapporo
Hokkaido
Hakodate
Vladivostok
Ürümqi (Urumchi)
INNER MONGOLIA
Shenyang (Mukden)
N. KOREA
Sea of Japan
Beijing
Dalian
Seoul
Kyōto
Tōkyō
Yokohama
Osaka
Tianjin
Pusan
Kitakyūshū
Qingdao
Yellow Sea
JAPAN
Nagasaki
SANG
(TIBET)
Lhasa
Xi'an
Huang
Nanjing
Shanghai
Suzhou
East China Sea
Bonin Is.
SANG
Chang
C H I N A
Wuhan
Ryūkyū-rettō
Chengdu
Chongqing
Xiangtan
Fuzhou
Tropic of Cancer
BHU
Brahmaputra
Ganges
Myitkyina
Kunming
Guangzhou
Taiwan (Formosa)
Guam (U.S.)
Dhaka
Mandalay
BURMA
Hanoi
HONG KONG (Br.)
Macau (Port.)
Zhanjiang
G. of Tongking
Hainan
Luzon
PHILIPPINES
Caroline Is.
Bay of Bengal
LAOS
Huế
South China Sea
Manila
Belau
Andaman Is. (India)
THAILAND
Bangkok
CAMBODIA
Palawan
Mindanao
Davao
Gulf of Thailand
Thanh Pho Ho Chi Minh
Sulu Sea
Zamboanga
Sulu Arch.
Celebes Sea
Halmahera
New Guinea
Nicobar Is. (India)
BRUNEI
Sabah
Maluku (Moluccas)
Sarawak
George Town
MALAYSIA
Kuala Lumpur
Kuching
Borneo
Sulawesi
Ceram
Banda Sea
Melaka
Singapore
I N D O N E S I A
O C E A N
Str. of Malacca
Sumatra
Jakarta
Java Sea
Ujung Pandang
Flores
Timor
Darwin
AUSTRALIA
Thursday I.
Selat Sunda
Java
PACIFIC OCEAN

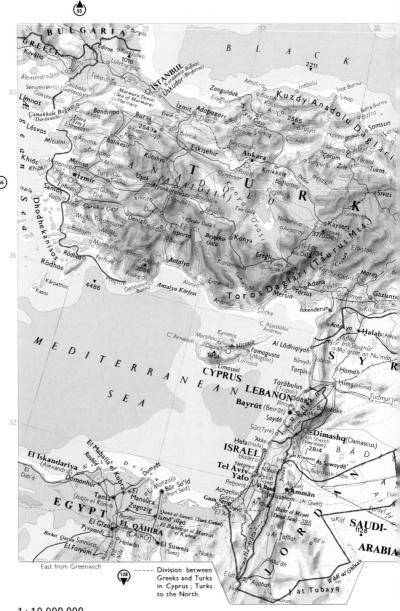

East from Greenwich

----- Division between
Greeks and Turks
in Cyprus ; Turks
to the North.

1 : 10 000 000

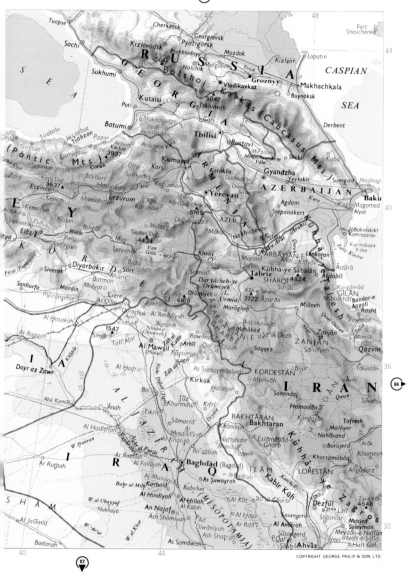

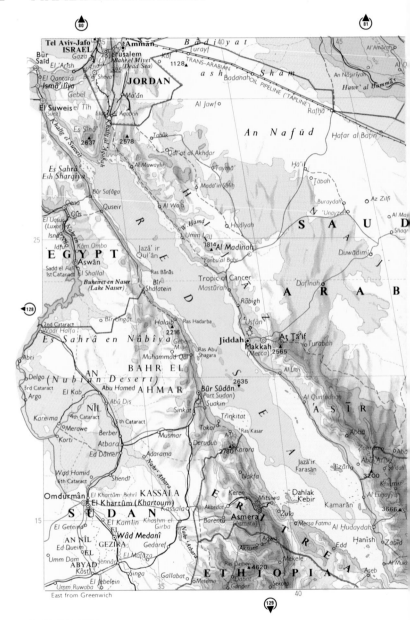

Tel Aviv-Jafo
ISRAEL
Būr Saīd
El 'Arīsh
El Qantara
Ismā'īlīya
El Suweis (Suez)
Gaza
Jerusalem
Bahr el Miyet (Dead Sea)
Be'er Sheva
Gebel
El Tih
Es Sīnā'
2637
2578
Amman
JORDAN
Ma'ān
Elat
Aqabah
Tabūk
Qal'at al Akhdar
Al Muwaylih
Taymā'
Madā'in Ṣāliḥ

Bādiyat
Ṭurayf
Kāf
1128
ash
TRANS-ARABIAN
Badanah OIL PIPELINE ('TAPLINE')
Al Jawf
Sham
An Nāṣirīyah
Hawr' al Hammar
Rafḥa
An Nafūd
Ḥafar al Bāṭin
Hā'il
Ṭābah
Az Zilfī
Buraydah
'Unayzah
Al Ma
Shaqr

Es Sahrā
Esh Sharqīya
Būr Safāga
Qena
Quseir
El Uqṣur (Luxor)
Isnā
Idfū
Kōm Ombo
Aswān
Saḍd el 'Āli
1st Cataract El Shallāl
Buḥeiret en Naser (Lake Nasser)

EGYPT
Al Wajh
Ẉ Ḥamḍ
Umm Lajj
Hadīyah
1814 Al Madīnah
Yanbu' al Baḥr
Ras Bānās
Bīr Shalatein
Tropic of Cancer
Mastūrah
Rābigh
Usfān

SAUD
'Unayzah
Duwādimī
Dafīnah
A R A B

2nd Cataract
Wadi Halfa
Abri
Delgo
3rd Cataract
Argo
El Kab
Abu Hamed
Kareima
Merawe
Korti
4th Cataract
Berber
Atbara
Ed Dāmer

Es Sahrā en Nūbīya
Bīr Ungāt
Halaib
2216 Gebel Mīṣei
Muhammad Qōl
Abu Dis
Sinkat
Ras Hadarba
Ras Abu Shagara
Jiddah
Makkah (Mecca)
2565
At Ṭā'if
Turabah

RED SEA
2635
Būr Sūdān (Port Sudan)
Suakin
Trinkitat
Tokar
Musmar
Derudub
Ras Kasar
1780 Karora
Al Līth
Al Qunfudhah

BAHR EL AHMAR
(Nubian Desert)
AN NĪL

Wād Hamid
6th Cataract
Shendī
Omdurmān
El Khartūm Baḥrī
El Khartūm (Khartoum)
SUDAN
El Geteina
El Kamlīn
AN NĪL
Ed Dueim
Umm Dam
Kōstī
ABYAD
Umm Ruwaba
El Jebelein

KASSALA
Kassala
Khashm el Girba
Barentū
Wād Medanī
EL GEZĪRA
Gedaref
El Ḥawāta
Senna
Singa
Gallabat

Jazā'ir Farasān
Jizāna
Dahlak Kebir
Keren
Mitsiwa
Akordat
Zula
Asmera (Asmara)
ERITREA
Zābona

'ASĪR
Abba
Zahrān
Kamarān
Al Ḥudaydah

ETHIOPIA
Ras Dashen 4620
Dabat
Gander
Sekoṭa
Mekele
Aksum
Adwa
Metema

Mersa Fatma
Al Ḥudaydah
Edd
Ḥanīsh
Zabīd
Aseb
Al Matāma

East from Greenwich

1 : 15 000 000

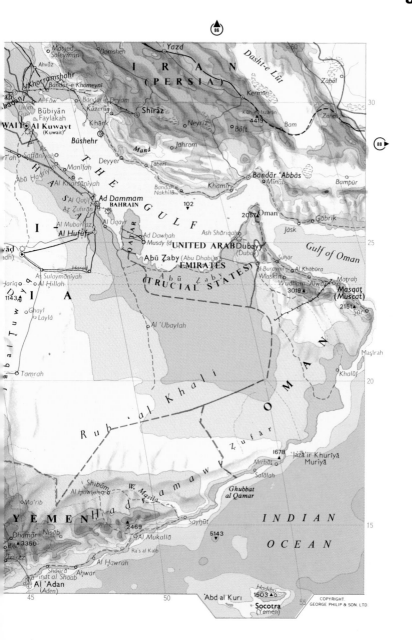

IRAN (PERSIA)

Masjed-e Soleymän
Ahvāz
Khorramshahr
Bandar-e Khomeyni
Af Fāw
Umm
Būbiyān
Faylakah
WAIT
Al Kuwayt (Kuwait)
Būshehr
Dashti-e Lūt
Yazd
Qomsheh
Kermān
Zābol
Zarand
Kazerūn
Shīrāz
Kohī–e Hazārān 4419
Bam
Khārk
Neyrīz
Bāft
Deyyer
Jahrom
Ţāheri
Mand
Bandar 'Abbās
Mīnāb
Bampūr
Saffānīyah
Maniîfah
Abū Ḥagriy
Al Kharsānīyah
Bandar
Nakhīlū
Khamīr
S Al Qaṭīf
Ad Dammam
BAHRAIN
Āz Zuhrān
Al Mubarraz
Al Uqayr
Al Hufūf
THE GULF
102
Jāsk
Gābrik
2057 Oman
Ad Dawhah
Musdy īd
QATAR
Ash Shāriqah
UNITED ARAB Dubayy (Dubai)
EMIRATES
Abū Ẓaby (Abu Dhabi)
Al Buraymī
Al Khābūra
Wašlim
Sūhar
Wudham 'Alwot
3019
Maţrah
Masqaṭ (Muscat)
2151
Šūr
yād (adh)
As Sulaymānīyah
Al Hillah
Harad
A b ū Ẓ a b y
(TRUCIAL STATES)
Jabal Tuwayq
1143
Ghayl
Laylá
Al 'Ubaylah
D I A
Tamrah
Maşīrah
Khalūf
R u b ' a l K h a l i
O M A N
Zufār
1678
Jazā'ir Khurīyā Murīyā
Mirbāt
Salālah
Ghubbat al Qamar
Ma'rib
Shibām
Al Hawtah o
W. Masila
H a d r a m a w t
Sayhūt
Nisāb
2469
Al Mukallā
5143
Ra's al Kalb
INDIAN
OCEAN
Dhamār
3350
 Taizz
Shaqra
Ahwar
Al Hawrah
Ma'inat al Shaab
Al 'Adan (Aden)
Hadibu
1503
'Abd al Kuri
Socotra (Yemen)

YEMEN

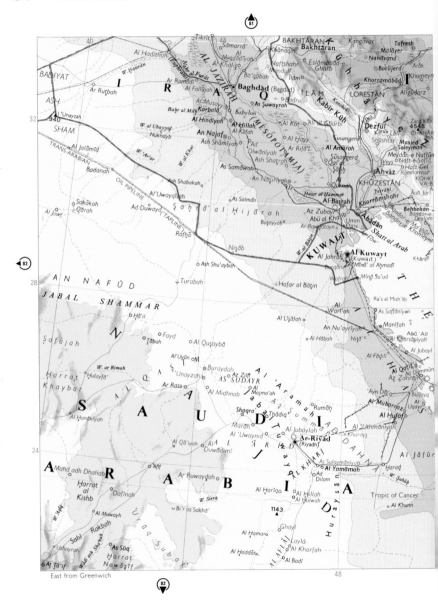

East from Greenwich

1 : 10 000 000

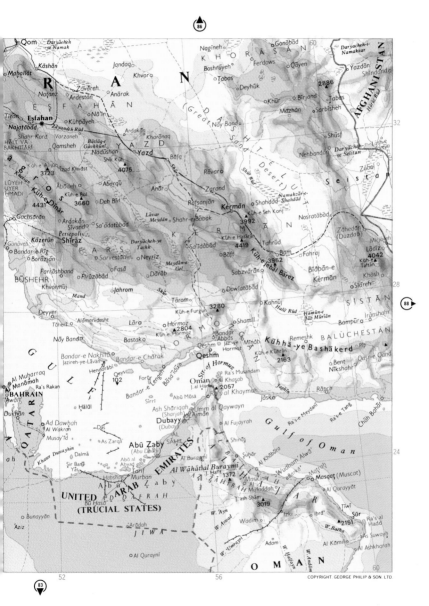

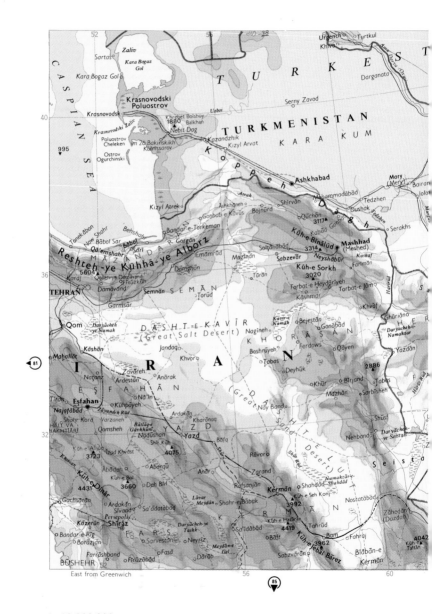

East from Greenwich

1 : 10 000 000

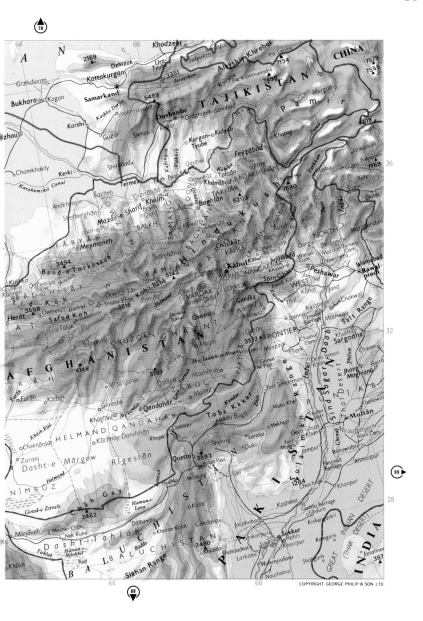

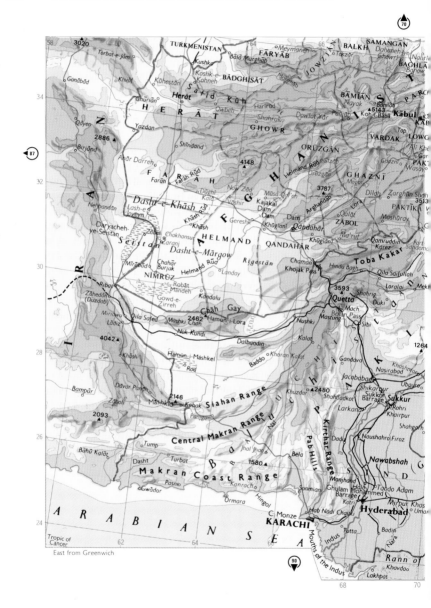

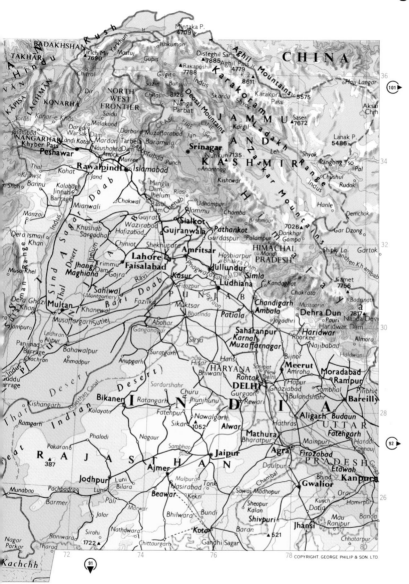

HINDU Kush

BADAKHSHAN
TAKHAR
VAN
KÁPISA
LAGHMAN
KONARHA
NANGARHAR
Jalalabad
Khyber Pass
Warsak Dam
Peshawar
Kohat
Bannu
n-Shah

Tirich Mir 7690
Mastuj
Chitral
Dir
NORTH WEST FRONTIER
Saidu
Malakond
Durband Muzaffarabad
Mardan
Naushahra Dam
Attock
Murree

Gupis
Ishkuman
Mintaka P. 4709
Disteghil Sar 7885
Rakaposhi 7788
Gilgit
Indus
Chilas
Skardu
Nanga Parbat 8126
Desai Mountains
Aghil Pass 4779
Aghil Mountains
K 2 8611
Karakoram Pass 5575
Saser 7672
Lanak P. 5486

CHINA

Haji Langar
Aksai Chin

Karakoram
JAMMU
LADAKH
Kargil
Leh
Shyok
ZANSKAR Range
KASHMIR
Srinagar
Nunkun 7135
Anantnag
Kishtwar

Rangong Tso
Pal
Chushul
Rudok
Hanle
Demchok
Gar Dzong

Kalabagh
Jinnah Barrage
Mianwali
Thal
Manzai
Dera Ismail Khan
Khushab
Sargodha
Chiniot
Sind Sagar Doab
Indus
Musa Khel
Dera Ghazi Khan

Jand
Chakwal
Mangla Dam
Jhelum
Rasul Dam
Gujrat
Gujranwala
Hafizabad
Shekhupara
Sialkot
Pathankot
Gurdaspur
Chamba

Riasi
Udhampur
Jammu
Brahmaur
Palampur
Dankhar Gompa
7026
Shipki La
Gartok
Kanchen Khambadzong

Lahore
Faisalabad
Maghiana
Trimmu Dam
Gojra
Sahiwal
Montgomery
Multan
Muzaffargarh
Khanewal

Amritsar
Hoshiarpur
Bhakra Dam
HIMACHAL PRADESH
Mandi
Simla
Kandaghat
Chakrata
Kamet 7756
Badrinath
Nanda Devi 7817

Jullundur
Ludhiana
PUNJAB
Kasur
Firozpur
Muktsar
Fazilka
Chandigarh
Ambala
Dehra Dun
Mussoorie
Haridwar Dam
Roorkee
Saharanpur
Karnal
Muzaffarnagar
Haridwar
Almora
Haldwani

Bari Doab
Ravi
Sutlej
Abohar
Bhatinda
Patiala
Jagadhri
Sirsa
Hisar
Hansi
Bhiwani
HARYANA
Rohtak
Bijnor
Meerut
Amroha
Moradabad
Rampur
Pilibhit
Bareilly

Ghaggar
Anupgarh
Sardarshahr
Churu
Jhunjhunu
Sambalka
New
Hapur
Ghaziabad
Bulandshahr
Sambhal
Budaun

Bikaner
Ratangarh
INDIA
Nawalgarh
Fatehpur
Sikar 1052
Alwar
Bharatpur
DELHI
Gurgaon
Rewari
Hathras
Aligarh
Budaun
Fatehgarh
Hardoi
Kannauj
UTTAR

Kolayato
Nagaur
Sambhar
Mathura
Mainpuri
Jaipur
Agra
Firozabad
PRADESH
Etawah
Kanpur
Pokaran 387

Phalodi
RAJASTHAN
Ajmer
Daulpur
Chambal
Gwalior
Bhind
Orai
Hamirpur

Jodhpur
Luni
Bilara
Nasirabad
Tonk
Sowai Madhopur
Etawah

Bilwara
Malpura
Kekri
Bundi
Sheopur Kalan
Datia
Mau Ranipur
Banda

Barmer
Pachpadra
Pali
Marwar
Beawar
Kota
Shivpuri
Jhansi
Chhatarpur

Jalor
Sirohi
Nathdwara
Bhilwara
Baran 521
Gandhi Sagar
80

Nagar Parkar
Tharad
Raniwara
1722
Chittaurgarh

Kachchh

COPYRIGHT GEORGE PHILIP & SON LTD

CEASE FIRE LINE

Sind Doab

Indian Desert

Thar Desert

Great Indian Desert (Thar Desert)

Gangacanal
Rajasthan Canal

Guddu Barrage
Panjnad Barrage
Bahawalpur
Ahmadpur
Chachran
Kishangarh
Ramgarh

36
34
32
30
28
26

72 74 76 78

181
92
31

Continuation Southwards
on same scale

East from Greenwich

1 : 10 000 000

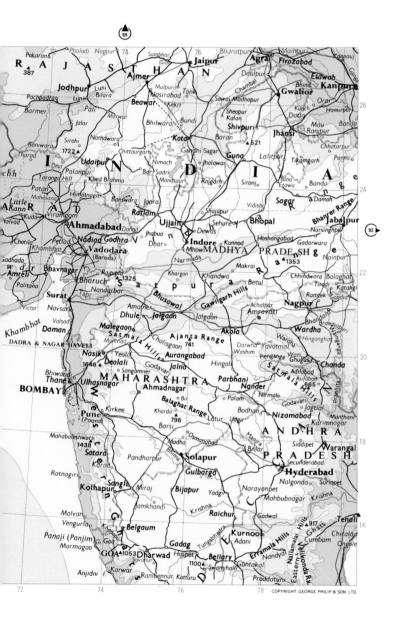

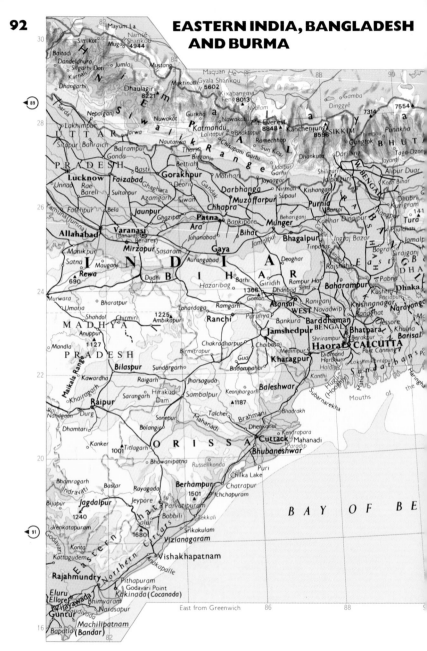

1 : 10 000 000

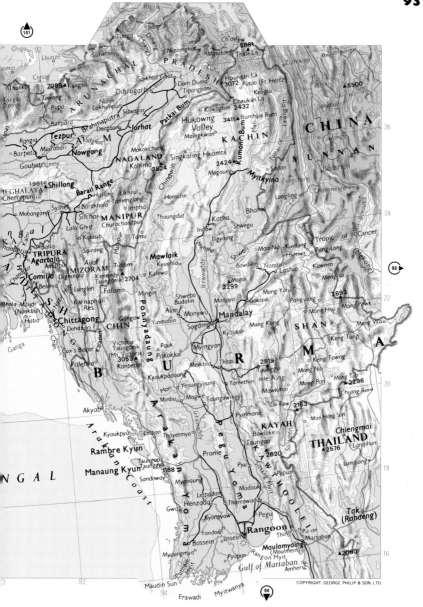

99

94

ARUNACHAL PRADESH

Tunga   Tida   Dihang   Siang   Nizamghat   Ch'ayu   5881   Minutong   Hala La   Zhongdian

Chigu   92   Lhunze   Subansiri   Luhit   Hpungan La   3072   Putao (Ft. Hertz)   Weixi   5500

Conai   Hkunkoi   2088   Kangto   Saikhod Ghat   Dam Duma   Tipongpani   Kongla   Zizhuang

Tongsa   Towang   North   Dibrugarh   Kawnglum   2432   Chaukan La   Dzong   Rupa   Lakhimpur   Sibsagar   Bumhpa Bum

Balpara   Brahmaputra   Dergaon   Jorhat   Parkai Bum   Hukawng   Valley   3411   CHINA   YUNNAN

Rangia   Tezpur   Sibsagar   Nowgong   Mokokchung   Maingkwan   Lumon Bum   Yulong   Basishan

Barpeta   Mairbari   NAGALAND   Singkaling Hkamti   2424   Myitkyina   Tengchong   Chanoning

Gauhati   MEGHALAYA   1961   Shillong   Kohima   3924   Mogaung   Sadon   Longling

Cherrapunji   Barail Range   Haflong   Chindwin   Homalin   Bhamo   Longling

Mohangani   Sylhet   Barakhola   Tamenglong   Thaungdut   Katha   Shwegu

Lala   Ghat   Ukhrul   Imphal   Wuntho   Tigyding   Inbaw   Shweli   Mon Na   Kunlong   Tropic   of   Cancer

TRIPURA   MANIPUR   Churachandpur   Shwell   Hsenwt   Pang-Long   (Mekong)

Agartala   Sairang   Tamu   Namtu   Lashio   Kawnro

Comilla   MIZORAM   Tiddim   Mawlaik   Kyunhla   Bawdwin   Mengso

Dighinala   Kennedy   Kyunhla   Mogok   Mong Yai   Pangyang   2693

Belonia   Lunglei   Taungdeik 2704   Kalewa   2299   Gokteik   Mong Pawk

Karnaphuli   Falam   Mingin   Modaya   Pangyang   Mong Hsu

Bhola Maidi   Res.   Shwebo   Budalin   Monywa   Mong Yate   Mong Wao

(Noakhali)   Chittagong   Gangaw   Alon   Yinmabin   Mandalay   SHAN

Hatia   Dohazari   CHIN   Padaung   Sogaing   Mong Kung   Keng Tung

Cox's Bazar   Victoria   Pauk   Kyaukse

Ganga   Taungdeik   Pakokku   Myingyan   Thazi   2519   Keng Tawng

Paletwa   (Mt. Victoria)   3053   Meiktila   Taunggyi   Mong Nai   Mong Ton   2296

Kanpetlet   BURMA   Kyaukpadaung   Yenangyaung   Yamethin   Inle Aing   Mong Pan   Chiang Rai

Akyab   Minbu   Mon   Magwe   Taungdwingyi   Mawkmai   Loi-kaw   2163   Mae Hong Son

Kyaukpyu   Letpan   Thayetmyo   Pyinmana   KAYAH   Chiengmai   Lamphun

Rambre Kyun   Arakan   Coast   Prome   Bawlake   2576   THAILAND

Manaung Kyun   Tounggup   1168   Pyu   Pegu   2620   Lampang

Sandoway   Myanaung   Madauk   Pepun

Gwa   Letpadan   Tharrawaddy   Tak   (Rahdeng)

BENGAL   Kyonpyaw   Henzada   Pegu   Pa-an   Martaban

Yandoon   Insein   Rangoon   Thaton

Bassein   Maulamyaing   (Moulmein)   2080

Myoungmya   Pyapon   Rangon Myit   Amherst

Maudin Sun   Erawadi   Myitwanya   Gulf of Martaban

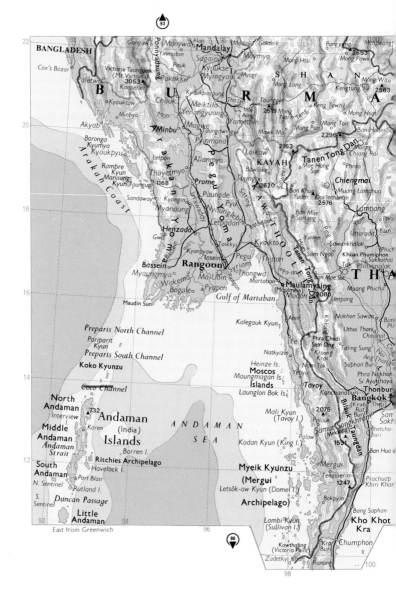

PENINSULAR MALAYSIA
AND SINGAPORE
1:6 000 000

50   0   50   100 km

East from Greenwich

1 : 10 000 000

102 · 106

1328
Nong
Khai · Pracin Buri · Phanom Dang Rek · Cheom Ksan · Phnom Thbeng Meanchey · Khong · San · Pleiku (Gia Lai) · Kontum · An Nhon (Binh Dinh) · Qui Nhon · 14

Chachoengsao · Ban Aranyaprathet Sisophon · Koulen · Srepok · Cheo Reo · Song Cau · Tuy Hoa

Samut Prakan (Paknam) · Chon Buri · Angkor Siem Reap · **C A M B O D I A** · Sandan (Sambar) · Stung-Treng · Buon Me Thuot

Si Racha · Battambang · Pursat · Kratie · Senmonorom · Cao Nguyen · 2405 · Nha Trang

Ban Lamung · Rayong · Pailin · Phnom Kravanh · 1144 · Pursat · Kompong Chhnang · Kompong Cham · Chhlong · Budop · Gia Nghia Da Lat · Di Linh · Cam Rhan · 12

Chanthaburi · Trat · 1813 · **Phnom Penh** · Prey-Veng · Loc Ninh · Djrlagnep · Phan Rang

Ko Chang · Ka Kong · Prek Thnot · Kompong · Banam · Tay Ninh · Hoa Da (Phan Ri)

of Thailand · Ko Kut · Kas Kong · Sre Umbell · Speu Takeo · Svay Rieng · Bien Hoa · Phan Thiet

I L A N D · Koh Kong · 1075 · Kampot · **Thanh Pho Ho Chi Minh** (Saigon) · Cu Lao Hon

Koh Rong · Kompong Som (Sihanoukville) · Long Xuyen · My Tho · Go Cong · Ba Ria · Vung Tau

Phu Quoc · Hon Chong · Sa Dec · Can Tho · 10

Rach Gia · Khonh Hung (Soc Trang)

Bac Lieu

Mui Ca Mau · Ca Mau · Côn Dao · 8

S O U T H   C H I N A   S E A

Pattani · Yala · Narathiwat Tumpat · Kota Baharu · 6

Betong · Kepulauan Perhentian

Gerik · 2170 · Kuala Trengganu

Taiping · 2182 · **PENINSULAR** · Laut · Telukbutun

Ipoh · Gunong Tahan · Kuala Dungun · Kepulauan Natuna Besar · 959 · 4

Cameron Highlands · 2190 · **MALAYSIA** · Binjal

Kuala Lipis

Kuala Selangor · Raub · Pahang · Kuantan · Matak · Siantan · Subj

Port Kelang · **Kuala Lumpur** · Kelang · Seremban · Tioman · Jemaja · Kuala · Midar · Kepulauan Natuna Selatan

Port Dickson · Gemas · Mersing · **Kepulauan Anambas** · 2

Melaka · Bandar Maharani · Keluang

TERA · Bandar Penggaram · Kepulauan Tambelan

ONESIA · Johor Baharu · Malacca · **SINGAPORE** · **I N D O N E S I A**

102 · 104 · 106 · 108

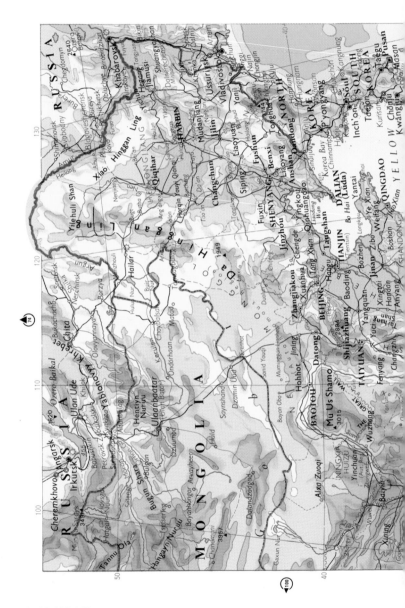

1 : 20 000 000

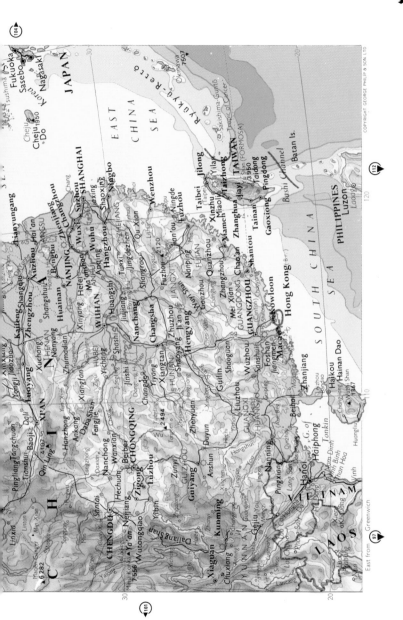

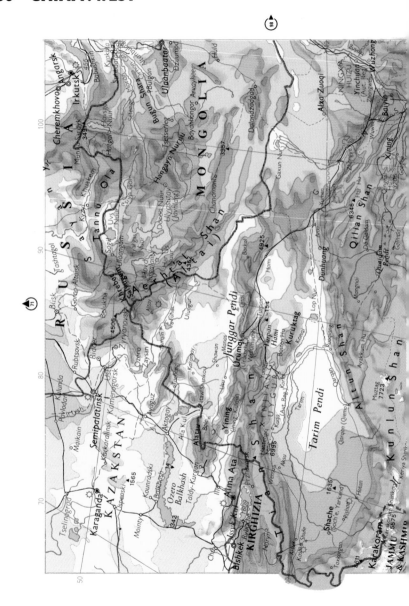

1 : 20 000 000

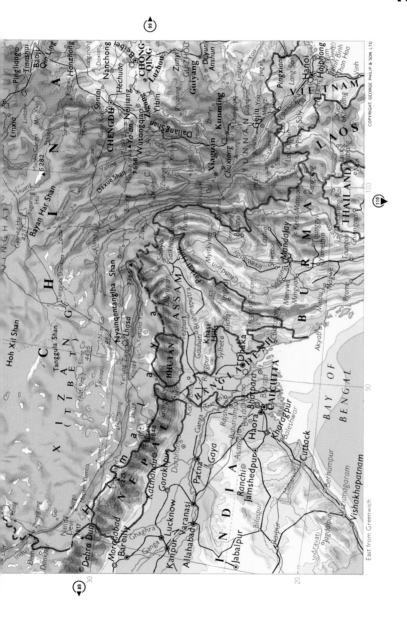

East from Greenwich

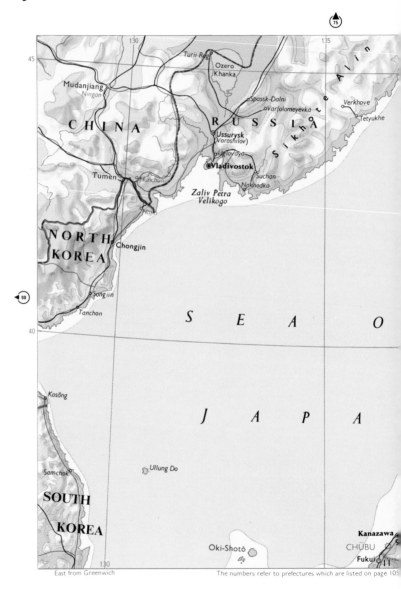

45

130 135

Turii Rog

Ozero
Khanka

Mudanjiang
Ningan

Spassk-Dalni
Varfolomeyevka

Verkhove
Tetyukhe

CHINA

RUSSIA

Ussurysk
(Voroshilov)

Sikhote Alin

Ugloyaya

Tumen
Hunchun

Vladivostok

Suchan
Nakhodka

Zaliv Petra
Velikogo

Najin

NORTH
KOREA

Chongjin

Songjin

Tanchon

40

S E A O

Kosŏng

J A P A

Samchok

Ullung Do

SOUTH
KOREA

Oki-Shotō

Kanazawa
CHŪBU
Fukui

130

East from Greenwich

The numbers refer to prefectures which are listed on page 105

1 : 7 500 000

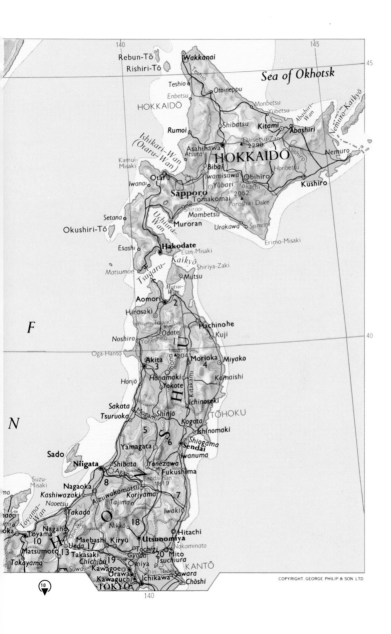

140°   145°

Rebun-Tō
Rishiri-Tō
Wakkanai
45°

Sea of Okhotsk

Teshio
Otoineppu
Enbetsu
Monbetsu
HOKKAIDŌ
Yubetsu
Shibatsu
Kitami
Rumoi
Abashiri-Wan
Abashiri
Nemuro-Kaikyō

Asahikawa
Daisetsu-Zan
2290
Nemuro
Kamui-
Misaki
Atsuta
Bibai
HOKKAIDŌ
Otaru
Iwamizawa
Obihiro
Honbetsu
Iwanai
Yūbari
Obachi
Kushiro
Sapporo
Tomakomai
2052
Poroshiri Dake

Setana
Uchiura-
Wan
Shiraoi
Mombetsu
Muroran
Urakawa
Samani

Okushiri-Tō
Esashi
Erimo-Misaki

Hakodate
Esan-Misaki
Matsumae
Kaikyō
Shiriya-Zaki

F
Mutsu

Tsugaru-
Mutsu-
Wan
Aomori
2
Hirosaki
Towada-ko
Hachinohe
Kuji

Noshiro
Odate
Yoneshiro
Iwate-San
2041
Miyako

Oga-Hantō
Akita
Morioka
3
Hanamaki
Yokote
Kitakami
Kamaishi

Honjō

Sakata
Ichinoseki
Mogami
Shinjo
Tsuruoka
TŌHOKU

5
Ishinomaki
N
Yamagata
6
Shiogama
Sendai
Iwanuma

Sado
Agano
Yonezawa
Niigata
Shibata
Fukushima
Suzu-
Misaki
Bandai-San
1819
Nagaoka
8
Aizuwakamatsu
Koriyama
Kashiwazaki
Naoetsu
Tajima
7
Iwaki
Takada
Nikkō
18
O
Hitachi
Nagano
H
Maebashi
Kiryū
Utsunomiya
Toyama
Ueda
17
Tochigi
Ndkaminato
10
13
Takasaki
19
Gyoda
20
Mito
Matsumoto
Chichibu
Omiya
Tsuchiura
Takayama
Suwa
Kawagoe
Shin-Tega
Sawara
Urawa
Kawaguchi
Ichikawa
Chōshi
KANTŌ
TOKYO

140°

SEA OF JAPAN

SOUTH KOREA

Ullung Do

Oki-Shotō

Kanazawa
CHŪBU
Fukui
Takefu
Tsuruga

Kyō-ga-Saki
Wakasa-Wan

Hi-no-Misaki
Matsue
Tottori
Toyooka
Maizuru
Ayabe 28
26
Hikon
Kuwana
Yonago 31
24
25

Pusan
CHŪGOKU
Izumo
32
Tsuyama
Okayama
Kyōto
Ōkkaichi
Kōbe
Ōsaka
Ts

KOREA STRAIT
Hamada
33
Hōkoku
Kurashiki
Himeji
Amagas
Akashi
Sakai
27
Nara
29
KINKI

Tsushima
Tsushima-Kaikyō
Masuda
Fukuyama
34
Onomichi
Mihara
Takamatsu
Kishiwada
Wakayama

Yamaguchi
Hiroshima
35
Kure
Marugame
Owase

Shimonoseki
Tokuyama
Niihama
Tokushima
36
37
30
Shingū

Iki
Ube
Suō-Nada
Seto-Naikai
Matsuyama
SHIKOKU
Kii-Suidō
Shio-no-Misaki

Nakadori-Jima
Fukuoka
40
Kitakyūshū
38
39
Kōchi
Muroto-Misaki

Karatsu 41
Nakatsu
Beppu
Kawatahama
Tosa-Wan
SHIKOKU

Sasebo
Saga
Kurume
Ōita
Uwajima

Fukue-Jima
42
Kashima
Ōmuta
Aso 44
Usuki
Saiki
Nakamura
Ashizuri-zaki

Nagasaki
Isahaya
Asō 1592
Kumamoto
Sdiki

Shimo-Jima
Shimabara
Yatsushiro
Nobeoka
Bungo-Suidō

Minamata
43
45
KYŪSHŪ

Sendai
Miyazaki

Kagoshima
46
Kobayashi
Miyakonojō

KYŪSHŪ
Kanoya
Makurazaki
Shibushi-Wan

Kagoshima-Wan
Ōsumi-Kaikyō
Nishinoomote

Ōsumi-Shotō
Tane-ga-Shima
Kuchinoerabu-Jima

Yaku-Jima

Tokara-Kaikyō

Naka-no-Shima

Suwanose-Jima

PACIFIC OCEAN

Samchok

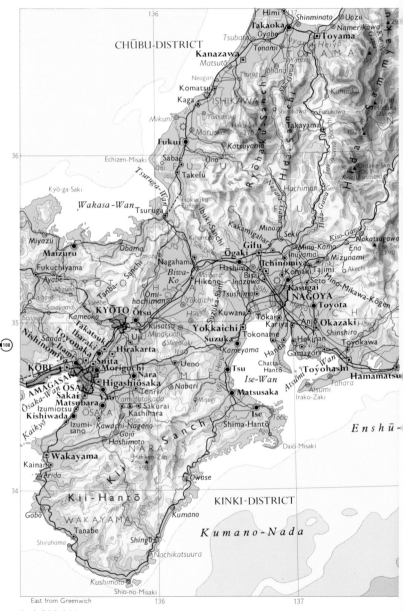

1 : 2 500 000

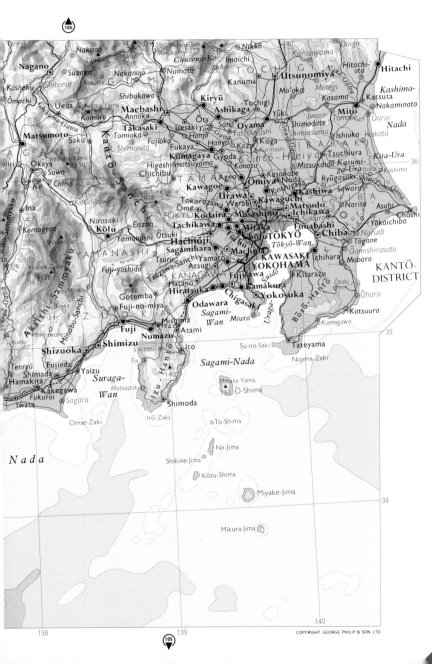

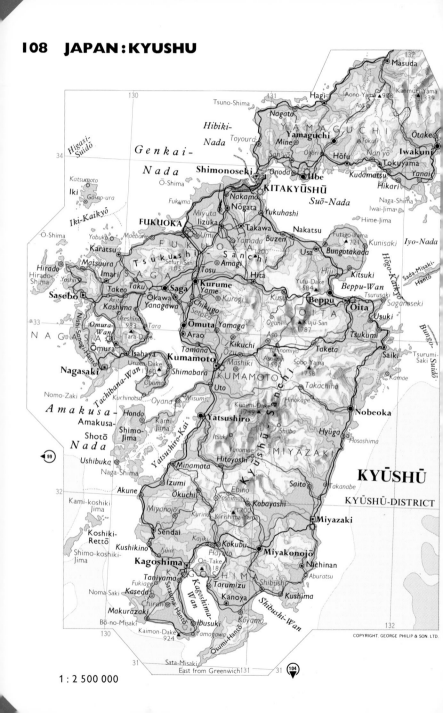

1 : 2 500 000

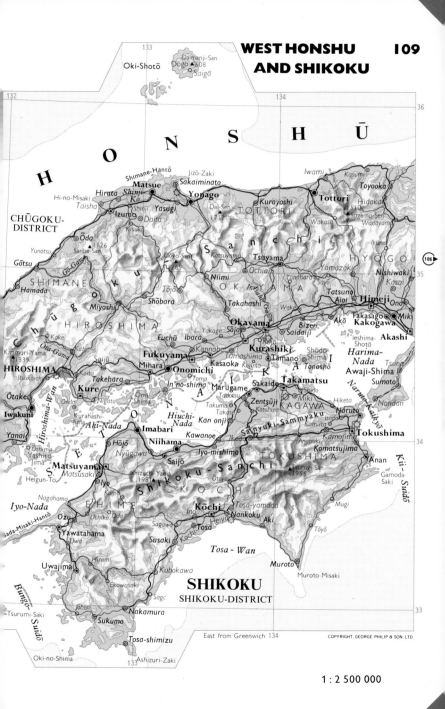

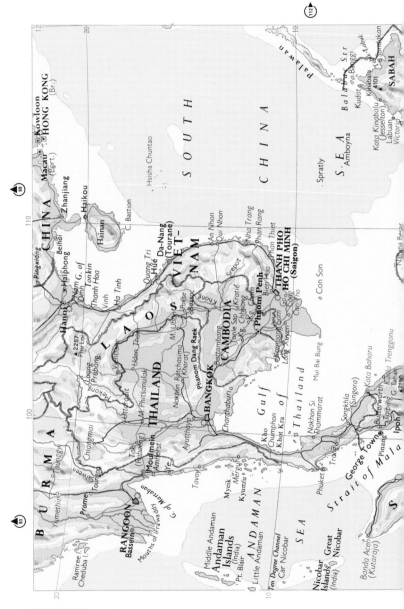

1 : 20 000 000

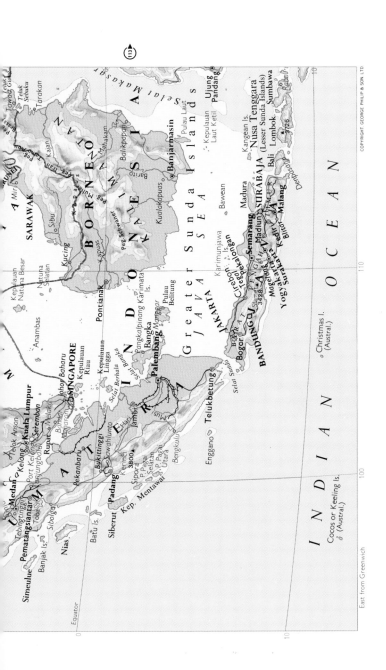

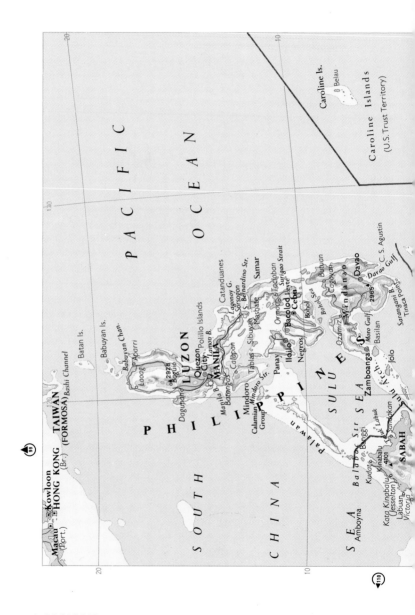

1 : 20 000 000

113

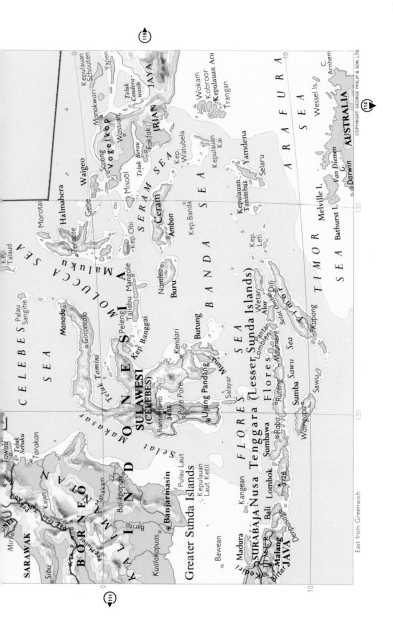

East from Greenwich

SARAWAK

Miri
Sibu
BRUNEI
Teluk
Sebuku
Tarakan

BORNEO

KALIMANTAN
Ketapang
Kajan
Mahakam
Balikpapan
Barito
Pegunungan
Kualakapuas
Banjarmasin
Pulau Laut
Kepulauan
Laut Ketil

Greater Sunda Islands

Bawean
Kangean
Madura
SURABAJA
JAVA
Malang
Kediri
Blitar
Denpasar
Bali
Lombok
3726
Sumbawa
Raba

Nusa Tenggara (Lesser Sunda Islands)

FLORES SEA

Sumba
Waingapu

Sawu

SULAWESI
(CELEBES)
Ujung Pandang
Pare Pare
Rantepao
3455
Salayar

CELEBES
SEA

Palau
Sangihe

Manado
Gorontalo
Teluk Tomini
Kep. Banggai
Selat Makasar

Kendari
Butung

Flores
Ruteng
Maumere
Selat Ombai
Wetar
Alor
Ende
Lombata
Kantar
Dili
Omin
TIMOR
Kupang

SAWU SEA

MOLUCCA
SEA

Kep.
Talaud

Morotai
Halmahera
Ternate
Tidore
Kep. Obi

MALUKU

Pelengi
Talabu
Mangole
Namleo
Buru

BANDA SEA

Kep.
Leti
Kep. Banda
Ambon

SERAM SEA

Ceram

Misool
Sorong
Gebe
Waigeo

Kep.
Watubela
Kep.
Kai

Kepulauan
Tanimbar
Yamdena
Selaru

TIMOR
SEA

Kepulauan
Schouten
Yapen

Manokwari
Waropen

IRIAN JAYA

Teluk
Cenderawasih
Vogelkop
Fakfok
Teluk Berau

Wokam
Kobroor
Kepulauan Aru
Trangan

ARAFURA

SEA

Wessel Is.
Melville I.
Bathurst I.
Van Diemen
G.
Darwin
C. Arnhem

AUSTRALIA

110
120
130
10

1 : 24 000 000

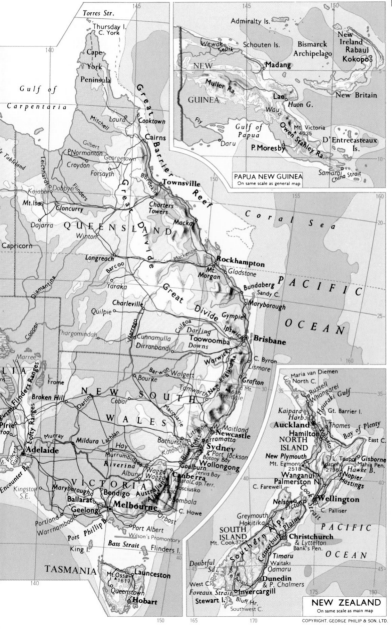

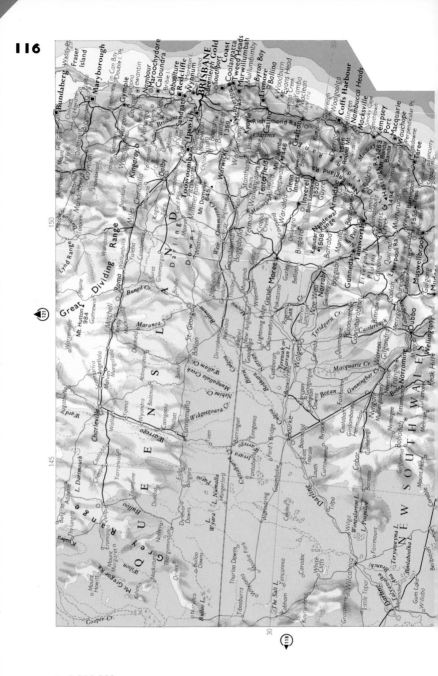

1 : 8 000 000

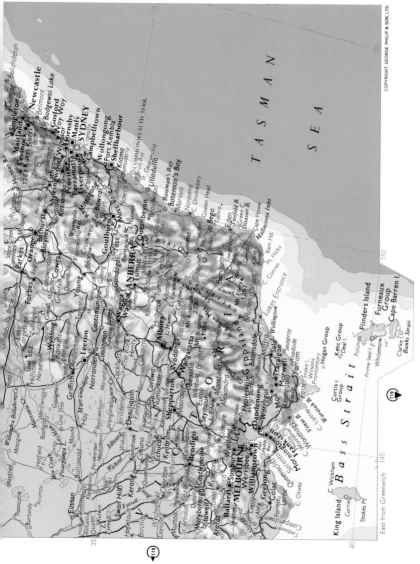

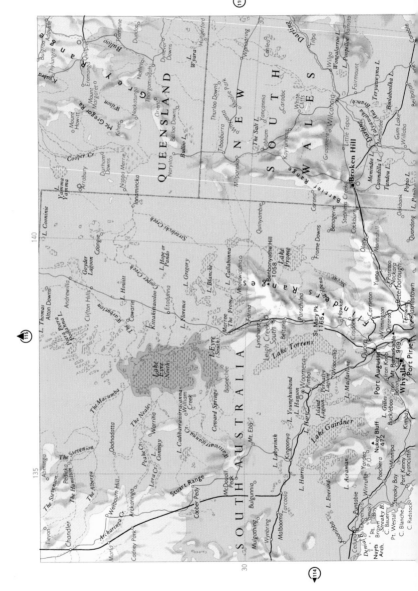

1 : 8 000 000

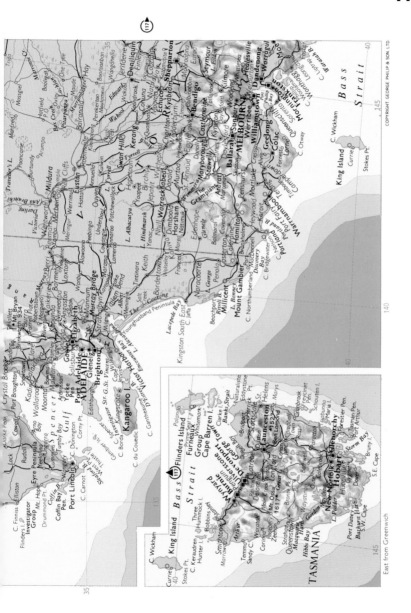

East from Greenwich

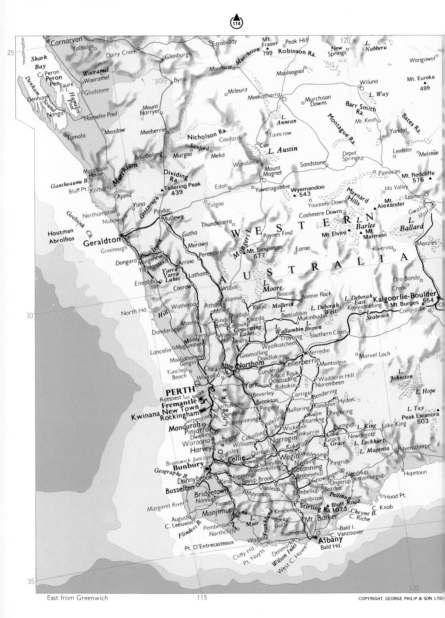

1 : 8 000 000

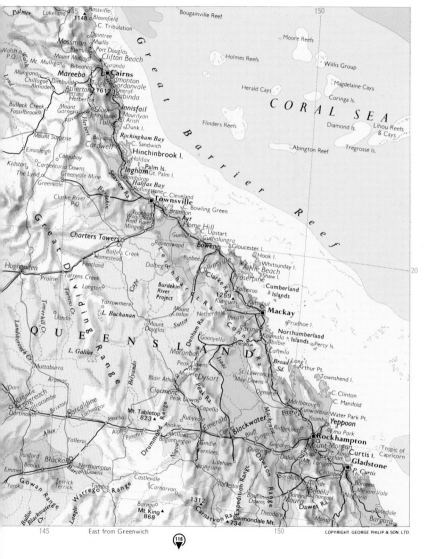

1 : 8 000 000

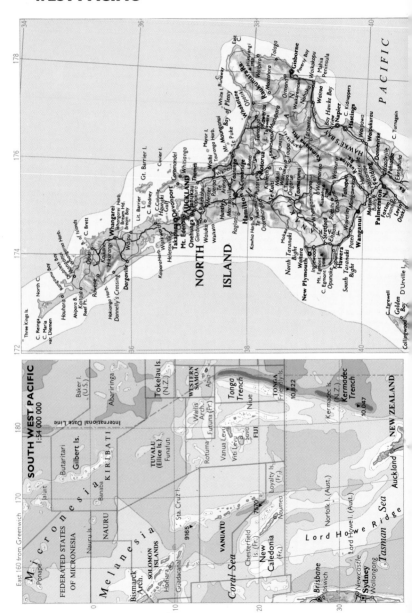

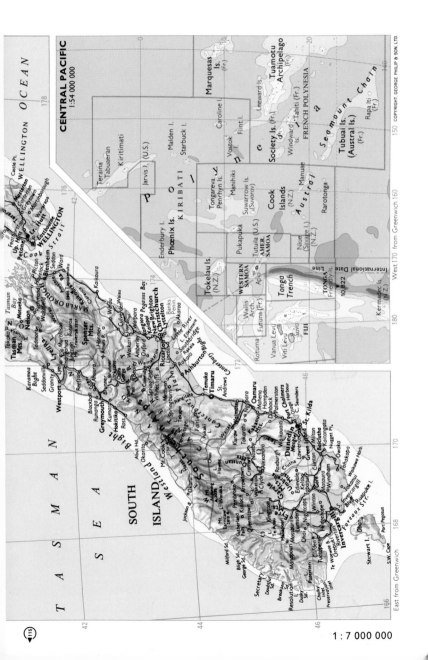

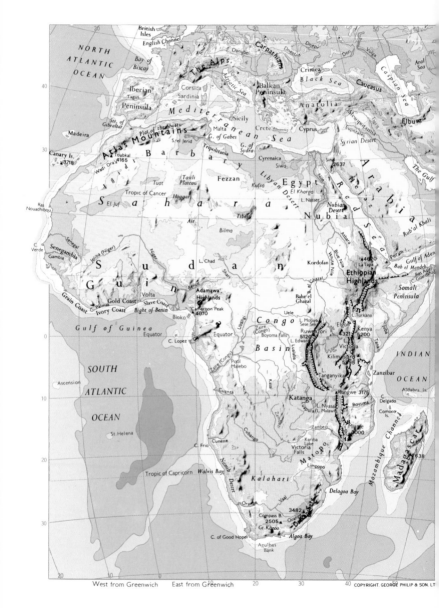

1 : 70 000 000

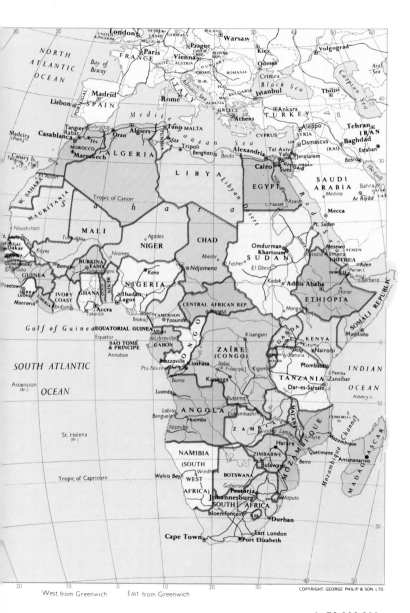

London, NETHER-LANDS, GERMANY, POLAND, Warsaw, Kiev, Volgograd, Prague, SLOVAK REP., UNITED KINGDOM, FRANCE, Paris, Vienna, CZECH REP., HUN., AUSTRIA, SWITZ.

NORTH ATLANTIC OCEAN, Bay of Biscay, ITALY, ROMANIA, Crimea, Odessa, Black Sea, Caspian Sea, Aral Sea, Tbilisi

Lisbon, Madrid, SPAIN, PORTUGAL, Rome, Mediterranean Sea, YUG., B.-H., BULGARIA, GREECE, Istanbul, Ankara, TURKEY, Tehran, IRAN, Baghdad, Esfahan

Madeira (Port.), Casablanca, Rabat, Tangier, Gibraltar, Fès, Oran, Algiers, Tunis, MALTA, Tripoli, Sfax, ALBANIA, CYPRUS, Aleppo, SYRIA, Damascus, LEB., Tel Aviv, Jaffa, Jerusalem, IRAQ, Basra, The Gulf, Bahrain, QATAR, U.A.E.

Canary Is. (Sp.), Tenerife, Ifni, MOROCCO, Marrakech, ALGERIA, Benghazi, Beida, Alexandria, Cairo, Port Said, Suez, ISRAEL, JORDAN, SAUDI ARABIA, Medina, Ar Riyâd

W. SAHARA, El Aaiún, MAURITANIA, Nouakchott, Sahara, Tropic of Cancer, LIBYA, Libyan Desert, EGYPT, Nile, L. Nasser, Red Sea, Mecca, Pt. Sudan, Mesewa

t. Louis, Dakar, SENEGAL, Kayes, MALI, Timbuktu, Agades, NIGER, Niamey, CHAD, Abeshr, SUDAN, El Fasher, Khartoum, Omdurman, Kassala, Asmera, YEMEN, Aden, ERITREA

BISSAU, GUINEA-BISSAU, Bamako, BURKINA FASO, Ouagadougou, BENIN, Kano, NIGERIA, Ndjamena, El Obeid, Kadok, Addis Ababa, Harer, DJIBOUTI, Djibouti, Berbera

Freetown, SIERRA LEONE, GUINEA, LIBERIA, Monrovia, IVORY COAST, GHANA, Abidjan, Takoradi, Accra, Ibadan, Lagos, CAMEROON, Yaoundé, CENTRAL AFRICAN REP., Bangui, Mongal, ETHIOPIA, SOMALI REPUBLIC

Gulf of Guinea, Bioko, EQUATORIAL GUINEA, Mbini, Libreville, GABON, Equator, SÃO TOMÉ & PRINCIPE, Annobon, CONGO, Brazzaville, Pte Noire, Kinshasa, ZAÏRE (CONGO), Kisangani, UGANDA, Kampala, Kisumu, Nairobi, KENYA, Mogdisho

SOUTH ATLANTIC OCEAN, Ascension (Br.), Ileba (P. Françqui), Kigoma, L. Victoria, Mombasa, INDIAN OCEAN

St. Helena (Br.), Boma, Kananga, Bukama, Dar-es-Salaam, TANZANIA, Zanzibar, Pemba, Aldabra Is.

Luanda, ANGOLA, Lobito, Benguela, Huambo, Namibe, Lubumbashi, ZAMBIA, Lusaka, MALAWI, Blantyre, Harare, COMORO IS., Mozambique Channel, MADAGASCAR

Tropic of Capricorn, Walvis Bay, NAMIBIA (SOUTH WEST AFRICA), Windhoek, BOTSWANA, Gaborone, ZIMBABWE, Bulawayo, MOZAMBIQUE, Beira, Quelimane, Antananarivo

Pretoria, Johannesburg, SOUTH AFRICA, Bloemfontein, SWAZILAND, Maputo, LES., Durban, Cape Town, East London, Port Elizabeth

1 : 70 000 000

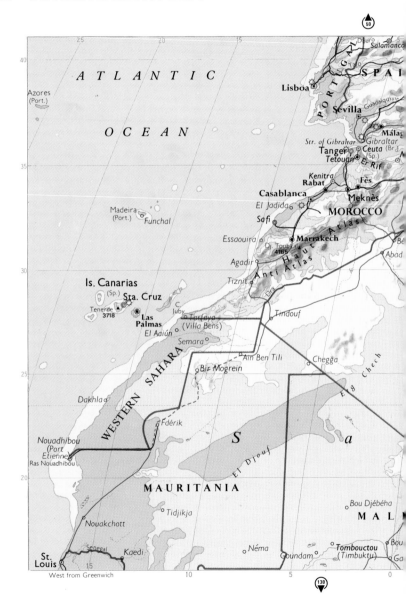

1 : 20 000 000

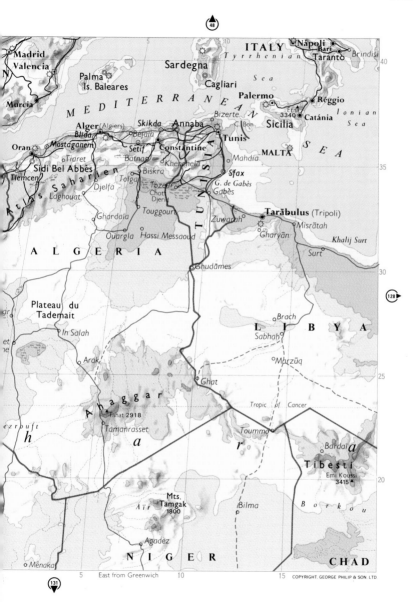

ITALY

Napoli
Bari
Taranto
Brindisi

Tyrrhenian

40

Madrid
Valencia
Palma
Is. Baleares
Murcia

Sardegna

Sea

Cagliari

Palermo

MEDITERRANEAN

Bizerte
C. Bon

Réggio
Etna 3340
Catánia

Ionian Sea

Sicilia

Alger (Algiers)
Blida
Skikda
Annaba
Bejaïa
Tunis

MALTA

SEA

Oran
Mostaganem
Setif
Constantine
Tiaret
Batna
Khenchela
Mahdia

Sidi Bel Abbès
Biskra
Sfax
G. de Gabès
Tlemcen
Djelfa
Tolga
Tozeur
Chott
Djerid
Gabès

Laghouat

Atlas Saharien

35

Ghardaïa
Touggourt
Zuwarah
Tarābulus (Tripoli)
Misrātah

T U N I S I A

Ouargla
Hassi Messaoud
Gharyān
Khalij Surt

Ghudāmes
Surt

A L G E R I A

30

128

Plateau du
Tademaït
Brach
L I B Y A
Sabhah

In Salah

Marzūq

Arak

Ghat

25

A h a g g a r
Tropic of Cancer
Tahat 2918
Tamanrasset
Toummo
Bardaï
Tibesti

ezrouft
h
a
r
Emi Koussi
3415

20

Mts.
Tamgak
1800
Aïr
Bilma
Borkou

Agadez

Mênaka
N I G E R
CHAD

5   East from Greenwich   10   15   COPYRIGHT GEORGE PHILIP & SON LTD.

131

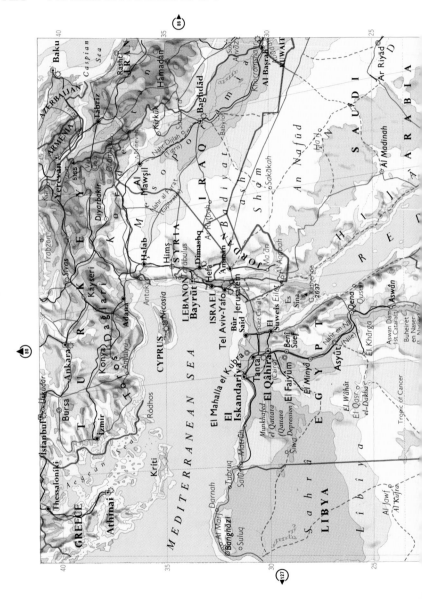

1 : 20 000 000

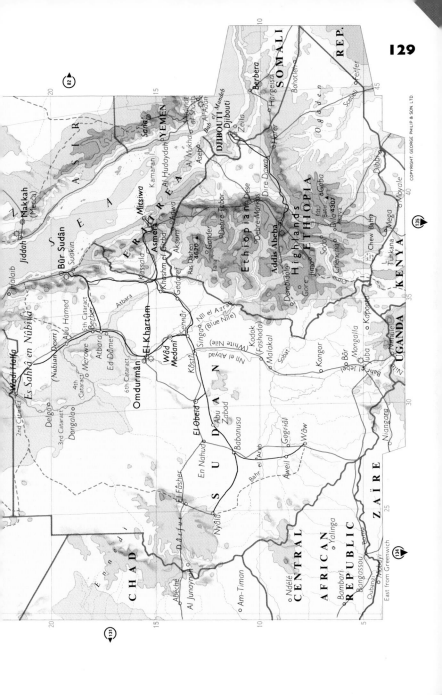

SOMALI REP.

SOMALI

Berbera

Horgeisa   Bonaatlehu

Bosaaso   Gerfer

DJIBOUTI   Zeila   'O g a d e n

Djibouti   Harer   Dibba

Bab el Mandeb   Dire Dawa   Baki   Aroba   Moyale

YEMEN   Aseb   Debre Tabor   Mega

Sanaa   Al Mukhā   of Shoa   Dire Dawa   Chew Bahir

Al Hudaydah   Mandab   Debre Markos   Sodo

Kamaran   Addis Abeba   Gimma   Chencha   KENYA

Mitsiwa   Adwa   Ethiopian   Gore   Turkana

Asmera   Aksum   Highlands   Dembidolo   Kapoeta

ERITREA   Ras Dashen   Gambela   Mongalla   UGANDA

Jiddah   4620   Gander   Sobat   Juba

Makkah   Kassala   Gedaref   T'ana   Kodok   Bahr el Jebel   Nili

(Mecca)   Khashm el Girba   (Fashoda)   Kongor   Niangara

Būr Sūdān   Singa   Malakal   Bōr

Halaib   Sudkin   Sennar   Nil el Azraq   ZAÏRE

A S I R   Atbara   (Blue Nile)   Wāw

Wadi Halfa   Abu Hamed   Atbara   Singa   Waw

Es Sahrâ en Nûbîya   4th Cataract   Berber   Nili el Abyad

(Nubian Desert)   Ed Dâmer   (White Nile)   Gogrial

2nd Cataract   Merowe   El Khartûm   Kōstī   Aweil   Bahr el Arab

Delgo   Wād   Bahr el Arab   CENTRAL

3rd Cataract   Dongala   Omdurmân   Medanî   AFRICAN

Abéché   Ennedi   El Obeid   Abu Zabad   REPUBLIC

CHAD   Babanusa   Yalinga   Bambari

Al Junaynah   En Nahud   Nyala   Ndélé   Bangassou

Am-Timan   Darfur   El Fāsher   S U D A N   Oubangi   Mongti   Bomu

East from Greenwich

COPYRIGHT GEORGE PHILIP & SON LTD

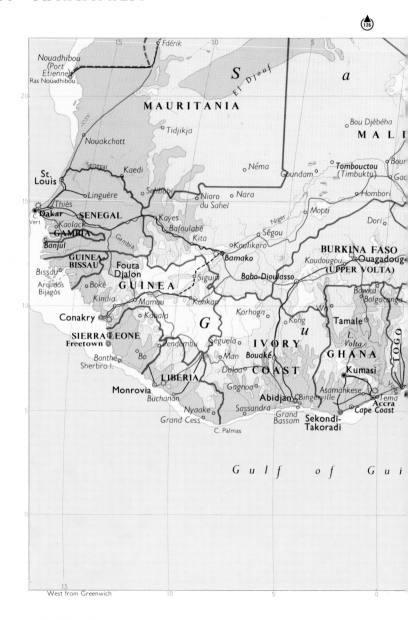

1 : 20 000 000

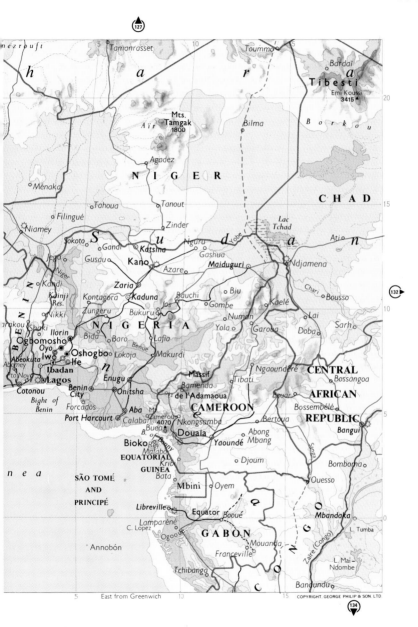

nezrouft

h *a* *r* Toummo

Tamanrasset

Bardaï

Tibesti
Emi Koussi
3415▲

20

Mts.
Tamgak
1800

Aïr

Bilma

B o r k o u

Ménaka

Agadez

N I G E R

C H A D

15

Niamey

Tahoua

Tanout

Lac
Tchad

Atin

Filingué

Zinder

Sokoto *S* Gandi Katsina Nguru *u* Yobe *d* *a*

Jega Gusau Gashua Bousso

Niger Kano Azare Maiduguri Ndjamena

Kainji
Res.

Kandi Kontagora Kaduna Bauchi Biu Chari Bousso

Zaria Kaele

Nikki Zungeru Jos Gombe

Bukuru Numan Lai Sarh

arakou Shaki N I G E R I A Yola Garoua Doba

Ilorin Bida Baro Lafia

Ogbomosho Oyo *n* Benue Makurdi

Abeokuta Iwo Oshogbo Lokoja Ngaoundéré CENTRAL

Eto Nov Ife Enugu Massif Tibati Bossangoa

Ibadan Onitsha Bamenda AFRICAN Bouar

Lagos Benin de l'Adamaoua

Cotonou City CAMEROON Bossembélé REPUBLIC

Bight of Forcados Aba Cameroun Nkongsamba Bertoua Bangui

Benin Port Harcourt Calabar 4070 Abong

Buea Douala Mbang

Bioko Yaoundé

Malabo

EQUATORIAL Djoum Bomborna

nea Bata GUINEA

SÃO TOMÉ Kribi

AND Mbini Oyem

PRINCIPÉ

Libreville Equator Booué Ouesso Mbandaka

Lambaréné L. Tumba

C. López Ogoou GABON

Annobón Mouanda L. Maï-Ndombe

Francéville

Tchibanga C Bandundu

East from Greenwich COPYRIGHT GEORGE PHILIP & SON LTD

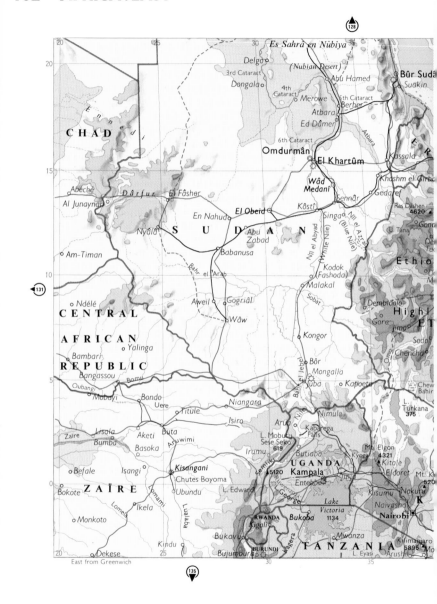

East from Greenwich

1 : 20 000 000

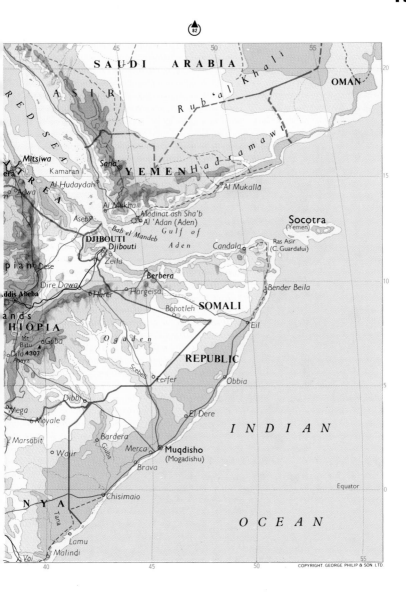

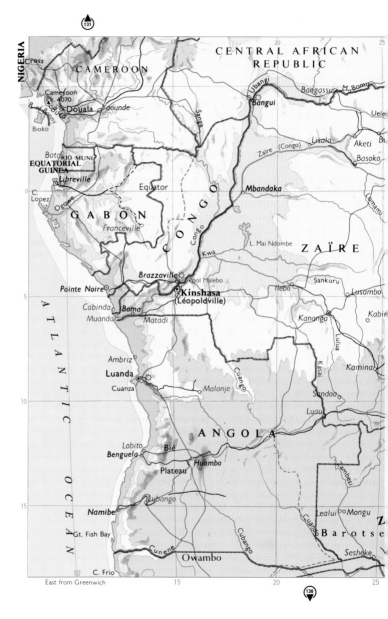

NIGERIA

CAMEROON

CENTRAL AFRICAN REPUBLIC

Cross

Cameroon Pk. 4070

Douala

Yaounde

Bioko

Bata

RIO MUNI

EQUATORIAL GUINEA

Libreville

C. Lopez

Ogowe

GABON

Franceville

Equator

Bangassuo

M. Bomu

Ubangi

Bangui

Uele

Zaïre (Congo)

Lisala

Aketi

Basoko

Mbandaka

CONGO

Kwa

L. Mai Ndombe

ZAÏRE

Lomami

Brazzaville

Pool Malebo

Kinshasa
(Léopoldville)

Pointe Noire

Cabinda

Boma

Muanda

Matadi

Itebo

Sankuru

Lusambo

Kananga

Kabir

Lulua

Kasai

Kamina

Ambriz

Luanda

Cuanza

Malanje

Cuango

Sandoa

Luau

ANGOLA

Lobito

Benguela

Bié

Plateau

Huambo

Cuanza

Lubango

Namibe

Gt. Fish Bay

Lealui

Mongu

Barotse

Cubango

Cuando

Sesheke

Z

Zambesi

Cunene

Owambo

C. Frio

ATLANTIC OCEAN

1 : 20 000 000

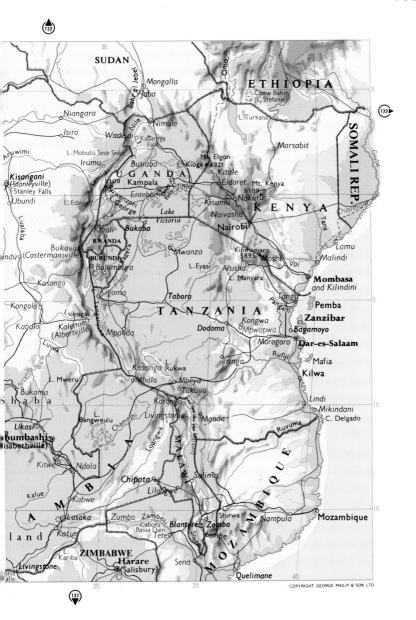

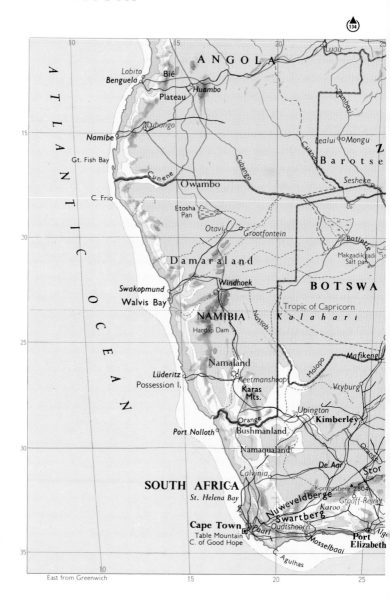

1 : 20 000 000

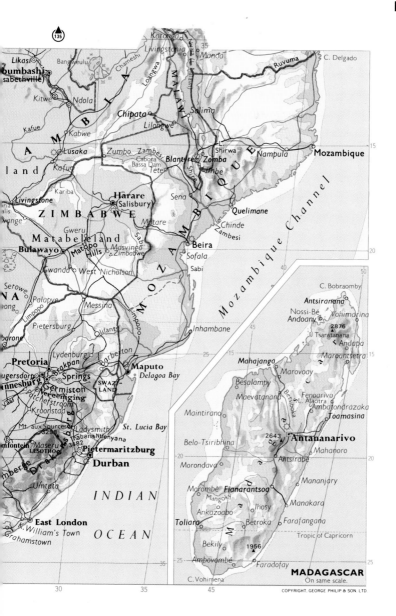

135

Likasi
bumbashi
sabethville)
Bangweulu
Kitwe
Ndola
Chameshi
Karonga
Livingstonia
Monda
C. Delgado
Ruvuma

Chipata
Lilongwe
Salima
MALAWI

A M B I A
Lusaka
Zumbo
Zambes
Cabora
Bassa Dam
Teto
Blantyre
Zomba
Shirwa
Nampula
Mozambique
15

land
Kafue
Kafue
Kabwe
Kariba
L.
Kariba
Harare
(Salisbury)
Sena
Shire
Chimbe
Quelimane

Livingstone
alls
ange
Z I M B A B W E
Gweru
Matare
Chinde
Zambesi

M a t a b e l e l a n d
Masvingo
Zimbabwe
Beira
Sofala
20

Bulawayo
Matopo
Hills
Sabi

Gwanda
West Nicholson
Sabi
40
50

Serowe
N A
Palapye
C. Bobraomby

aong
Messina
Antsiranana

barone
Limpopo
Pietersburg
Olifants
Inhambane
45
15
Nossi-Be
Andoany
Vohimarina
2876
Tsaratanana
Andapa
Maroantsetra
15

Pretoria
Lydenburg
Barberton
Maputo
Delagoa Bay
Mahajanga
Marovoay

ugersdorp
nnesburg
Springs
Germiston
Vereeniging
chefstroom
Kroonstad
SWAZI-
LAND
Besalampy
Maevatanana
Fenoarivo
L. Alaotra
Ambatondrazaka
Toamasina

Mt. aux Sources
Maseru
8298
Kabana Ntlenyana
3482
LESOTHO
Ladysmith
Pietermaritzburg
St. Lucia Bay
Maintirano
2643
Antananarivo
Mahanoro

mberg
mfontein
Durban
Belo-Tsiribihina
20
Antsirabe
Morondava
Mananjary

mberg
Umtata
I N D I A N
Marombe
Fianarantsoa
Manakara

East London
William's Town
Grahamstown
O C E A N
Toliara
Ankazoabo
Mango
Ihosy
Betroka
Farafangana
Tropic of Capricorn

Bekily
1956
Ambovombe
Faradofay

C. Vohimena
MADAGASCAR
On same scale.

30
35
45
COPYRIGHT. GEORGE PHILIP & SON. LTD.

M o z a m b i q u e   C h a n n e l

M O Z A M B I Q U E

1 : 60 000 000

West from Greenwich   100   90

COPYRIGHT. GEORGE PHILIP & SON. LT.

ASIA

ARCTIC OCEAN

Ostrov Pt. Barrow
Vrangelya

Bering Sea

Bering Str.

Beaufort Sea

Parry Is.
M'Clure Str.

Banks I.

Viscount Melville Sd.

Victoria I.

Lancaster Sd.

Ellesmere I.

GREENLAND
(Denmark)

ICELAND

Denmark Str.

Baffin Bay

Upernavik
Disko I.
Godthaab

Davis Strait
Limit of pack ice (Spring)

C. Farewell

Baffin Island

Yukon

ALASKA
Fairbanks
Anchorage
Arctic Circle
Dawson
Klondike
Whitehorse
Skagway
Juneau

Pr. Rupert

Queen Charlotte Is.

Mackenzie

Gt. Bear L.

Yellowknife
Gt. Slave L.

CANADA

Athabasca L.

Southampton I.
Chesterfield Inlet

Hudson Strait

Hudson Bay

James Bay

Labrador

Sept Iles

Corner Brook
Newfoundland
St. John's
C. Breton I.
Nova Scotia

Vancouver

Victoria
Vancouver
Seattle
Tacoma
Portland
Eugene

Fraser

Dawson Creek
Edmonton
Calgary
Lethbridge
Medicine Hat
Spokane

Prince Albert
Saskatoon
Moose Jaw
Regina

Flin Flon

Churchill

Nelson

Winnipeg

Thunder Bay

Duluth

Timmins
Sault Ste. Marie

Québec
Ottawa
Montreal
Halifax

Sacramento
Reno
San Francisco
Oakland
Fresno

Los Angeles
San Diego

Snake

Billings

Gt. Salt L.
Salt Lake City

UNITED

Missouri

St Paul
Minneapolis

Milwaukee
Chicago

Detroit
Cleveland
Toronto
Buffalo
Pittsburgh

Boston
New York
Philadelphia
Baltimore

Platte

Denver

Colorado

Omaha

STATES

Kansas City

St Louis

Cincinnati

Washington

C. Hatteras

Bermuda
(Br.)

Phoenix
Tucson

El Paso

Pueblo

Amarillo

Alburquerque

Red

Dallas

Memphis

Atlanta
Birmingham

Charlotte

Savannah

ATLANTIC

Baja

California

Hermosillo

Ciudad Juarez

Chihuahua

Mississippi

Baton Rouge
Mobile

Jacksonville

OCEAN

PACIFIC

Tropic of Cancer

Revilla Gigedo
(Mex.)

Torreón

Mazatlán

Guadalajara
León
México
Puebla
Acapulco

Monterrey

MEXICO

San Antonio
Houston
Galveston

New Orleans

Florida

Tampa

Miami

Gulf of Mexico

BAHAMAS

S. Luis Potosí
Tampico

Mérida

Veracruz

Coatzacoalcos

Salina Cruz

BELIZE

Yucatan Strait

La Habana

CUBA

Santiago de Cuba
JAMAICA
Kingston

HAITI
DOM. REP.

Prince
P. Rico
(U.S.)

Caribbean Sea

GUATEMALA
Guatemala

HONDURAS

CENTRAL

EL SALVADOR
NICARAGUA
Managua

AMERICA

COSTA RICA
San José

Cartagena

Panama

PANAMA

SOUTH AMERICA

OCEAN

COPYRIGHT. GEORGE PHILIP & SON. LTD

1 : 60 000 000

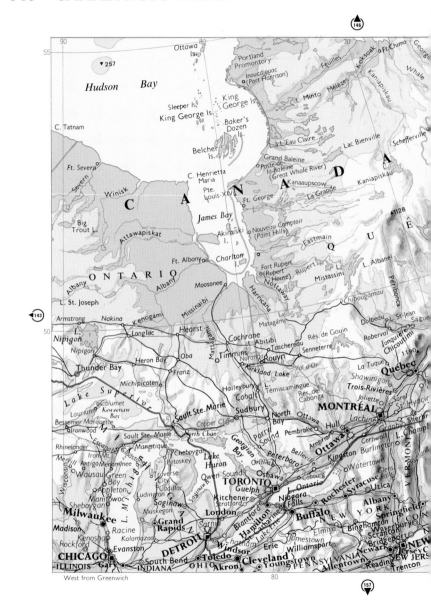

West from Greenwich

1 : 15 000 000

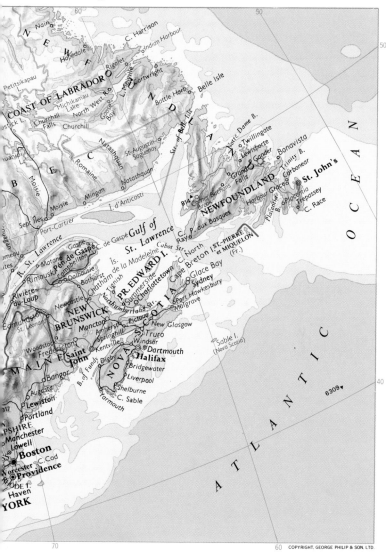

COAST OF LABRADOR

Petitsikapau L.
Michikamau Lake
Churchill Falls
Churchill
Natashquan

Nain
Hopedale
C. Harrison
Indian Harbour
Rigolet
L. Melville
Cartwright
Battle Harb.
Belle Isle

QUEBEC

Natashquan
St-Augustin
Saguenay
Natashquan
Mingan
Moisie
Romaine
Sept Iles
Port-Cartier
Moisie
R. St. Lawrence
Î. d'Anticosti

Str. of Belle Isle

NEWFOUNDLAND

Notre Dame B.
Twillingate
Lewisporte
Gander
Botwood
Corner Brook
Grand Falls
Buchans
814
Bonavista
Bonavista B.
Trinity B.
Carbonear
Harbour Grace
St. John's
Placentia B.
Placentia
Trepassey
C. Race

Gulf of St. Lawrence
Pén. de Gaspé
C. de Gaspé
Gaspé
Matane
Rimouski
Campbellton
Dalhousie
Bathurst
Chatham
Îs. de la Madeleine

P. aux Basques
Ray
C. North
Cabot Str.
Cape Breton I.
ST-PIERRE
et MIQUELON
(Fr.)

PR. EDWARD I.
Summerside
Charlottetown
Northumberland Str.
Tignish

Glace Bay
Sydney
Port Hawkesbury
Mulgrave

Riviere-du-Loup
Edmundston
St. Leonard
Woodstock
Fredericton

NEW BRUNSWICK
Newcastle
Moncton
Amherst
Springhill
Pictou
New Glasgow

NOVA SCOTIA
Truro
Windsor
Dartmouth
Halifax

MAINE
Bangor
Augusta
Lewiston
Portland

N. HAMPSHIRE
Manchester
Lowell
Boston
Worcester
Providence
RHODE I.
New Haven
NEW YORK

Saint John
Kentville
Digby
B. of Fundy
Bridgewater
Liverpool
Shelburne
C. Sable
Yarmouth

Sable I.
(Nova Scotia)

ATLANTIC OCEAN

6309

C. Cod

317

50
50
60
50
40
40
70
60

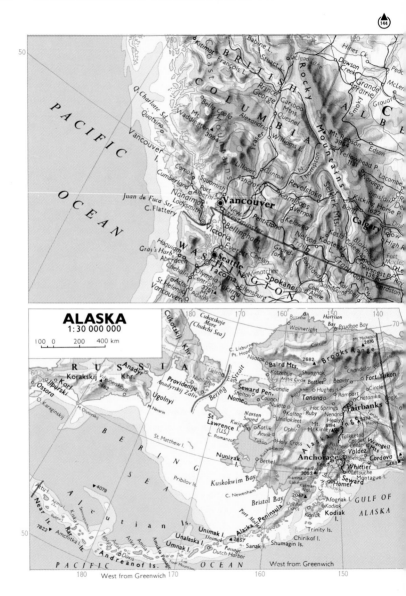

1 : 15 000 000

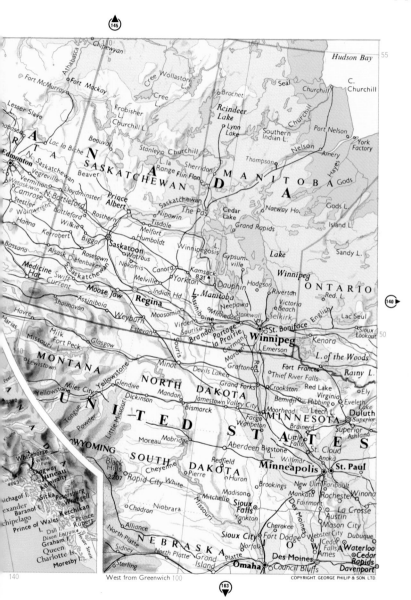

West from Greenwich 100

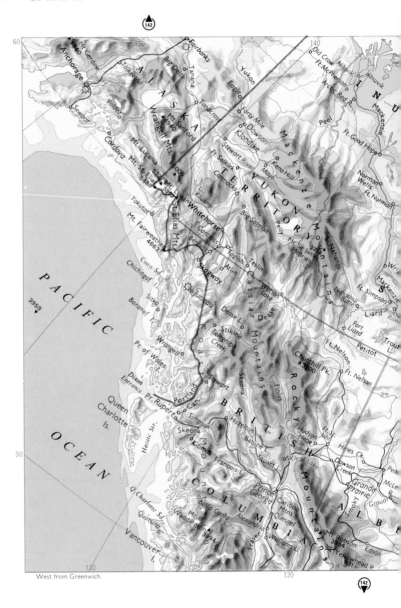

142

PACIFIC

OCEAN

West from Greenwich

1 : 15 000 000

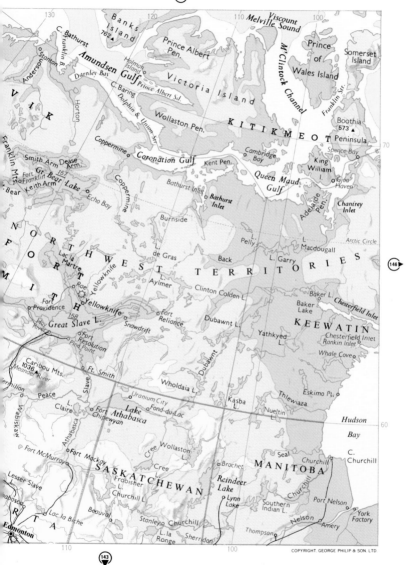

Banks Island
C. Bathurst
762▲
Prince Albert Pen.
Holman Island
C. Franklin B.
Stanton
Anderson
Amundsen Gulf
Darnley Bay
C. Baring
Prince Albert Sd.
Dolphin & Union Str.
Victoria Island
Viscount Melville Sound
M'Clintock Channel
Prince of Wales Island
Somerset Island
Franklin Str.
Horton
Wollaston Pen.
V I K
KITIKMEOT
Boothia 573▲ Peninsula
Spence Bay
Coppermine
Coronation Gulf
Kent Pen.
Cambridge Bay
King William I.
Gjoa Haven
70
Smith Arm
Dease Arm.
157
Fort Franklin
Gt. Bear Lake
Keith Arm
Echo Bay
Coppermine
Bathurst Inlet
Bathurst Inlet
Queen Maud Gulf
Adelaide Pen.
Chantrey Inlet
Franklin Mts.
Bear
Burnside
L. de Gras
L. Pelly
Back
L. Garry
L. Macdougall
Arctic Circle
N O R T H W E S T
T E R R I T O R I E S
146▶
F O R T
Lac la Martre
Roe
Yellowknife
L. Aylmer
Clinton Colden L.
Fort Reliance
Dubawnt L.
Baker L.
Baker Lake
Chesterfield Inlet
KEEWATIN
M I T H
Fort Providence
158
Yellowknife
Snowdrift
Yathkyed L.
Chesterfield Inlet
Rankin Inlet
Whale Cove
Hay River
Great Slave L.
Fort Resolution
Pine Point
Dubawnt
Caribou Mts.
1036▲
Meander River
Ft. Smith
Slave
Wholdaia L.
Thlewiaza
Eskimo Pt.
ermillion
Peace
L. Claire
Athabasca
Fort Chipewyan
Lake Athabasca
Uranium City
Fond-du-Lac
Kasba L.
Nueltin L.
Hudson Bay
60
Wabiskaw
Fort McMurray
Fort Mackay
Cree
Wollaston L.
Brochet
Seal
Churchill
C. Churchill
MANITOBA
Lesser Slave
Frobisher L.
Cree
Reindeer Lake
Lynn Lake
Southern Indian L.
Churchill
Port Nelson
York Factory
R T A
habasca
Lac la Biche
Churchill L.
Beauval
SASKATCHEWAN
Stanley Churchill
Sherridan
Nelson
Thompson
Amery
Edmonton
L. la Ronge

130   120   110   100   110   100

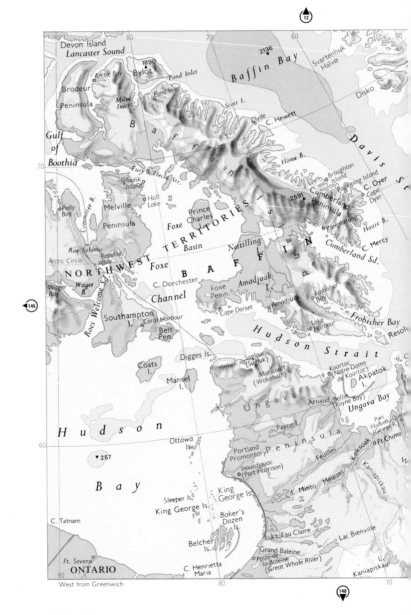

1 : 15 000 000

GREENLAND

○ Angmagssalik

○ Christianshåb

Disko
B.

teinsborg○

I a i t

Søndre Strømfjord

Sukkertoppen

▲ 2850

Kong Frederik VI's Kst.

Godthåb

○ Fiskenæsset

Frederikshåb ○
Ivigtut ○
Julianehåb ○
○ Syttprøven
Nanortalik ○

Kap Farvel

ATLANTIC

OCEAN

▼ 3809

▲ 1676

Hebron ○
Nutok ○

George

Nain ○

NEW

Hopedale ○

C. Harrison
○ Indian Harbour

Rigolet ○

COAST OF LABRADOR

Michikamau
Lake

L. Melville
Cartwright

Battle Harb.

Belle Isle

FOUNDLAND

Kapau○

L.
Lobstick

North West R.

Churchill
Falls

Goose
Bay

Churchill

Str. of Belle Isle

Notre Dame B.

○ Twillingate

St-Augustin ○

Ashuanipi

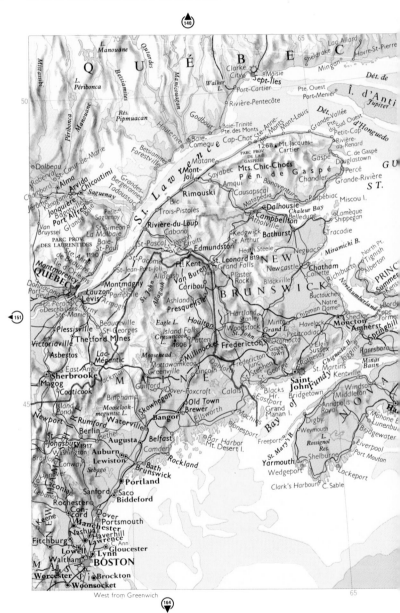

QUÉBEC

L. Manouane
L. Péribonca
Rés. Pipmuacan
Mistassini
Betsiamites
Manouane
Outardes
Manicouagan

Sheldrake
Lac Allard
Havre-St-Pierre
Mingan
Clarke City
Moisie
Sept-Îles
Port-Cartier
Pte. Ouest
Port-Menier
Î. d'Anti
Jupiter
Dét. de
Walker L.
Rivière-Pentecôte

Godbout
Baie-Trinité
Pte. des Monts
Baie-Comeau
Cap-Chat
Ste-Anne
Mont-Louis
Dét. Vallée
Grande-Vallée
Pte. Sud Ouest
Petit-Cap
Rivière-au-Renard
d'Honguedo

Dolbeau
Roberval
St-Cœur-de-Marie
Alma
Arvida
Chicoutimi
Jonquière
Kénogami
Jérôme
Port Alfred
Bagotville
Saguenay
Tadoussac
Petit-Saguenay
St-Siméon
La Malbaie
Baie-St-Paul
Forestville
Betsiamites
Mont-Joli
Matane
Sayabec
Amqui
Causapscal
Matapédia
Bonaventure
Paspébiac
Chaleur Bay
Miscou I.
Lamèque
Shippegan
Tracadie

Mts. Chic-Chocs
1268 Mt. Jacques-Cartier
PARC PROV. DE LA GASPÉSIE
Pén. de Gaspé
Gaspé
C. de Gaspé
Douglastown
Percé
Grande-Rivière
GU
ST.

Rimouski
Bic
Trois-Pistoles
Rivière-du-Loup
Cabano
St-Pascal
St-Pacôme
St-Jean-Port-Joli
Dalhousie
Campbellton
Atholville
Kedgwick
St-Arthur
Bathurst
Bellédune
Newcastle
Chatham
Collette
Blackville
BRUNSWICK
Buctouche
NEW
Heath Steele
St. Leonard 819
Grand Falls
Plaster Rock
Negua
Miramichi B.
North Pt.
Tignish
Alberton
Summer
PRINC
Former
Borde
Cape

Detroits
Edmundston
Joseph
Ft. Kent
Van Buren
Caribou
Allagash
Ashland
Presque Isle
Hartland
Woodstock
Grand L.
Minto
Havelock
Petitcodiac
Moncton
Shed
Amherst
Springh
Jog
PARC PROV. DES LAURENTIDES
1190
Île aux Coudres
Île d'Orléans
QUÉBEC
Montmorency
Donnacona
Portneuf
Lauzon
Lévis
Pamphile
Montmagny
La Pérade
Deschaillons
Ste-Marie
Cerny
St-Georges
Beauceville
Victoriaville
Plessisville
Thetford Mines
Asbestos
Lac-Mégantic
East-Angus
Sherbrooke
Magog
Coaticook
MAINE
Jackman
Bingham
Moosehead L.
Greenville
Mattawamkeag
Lincoln
Millinocket
Patten
1606
Chesuncook
Eagle L.
Island Falls
Houlton
Stanley
St. John
Gage town
Fredericton
Oromocto
McAdam
Rothesay
Sussex
Elgin
Petitcodiac
Chipman
Notre Dame
St-Pamphile

Newport
Island Pond
Mooselook-meguntic L.
Rumford
Berlin
St. Johnsbury
Washington 1917
Bradford
Conway
Hanover
Lebanon
Laconia
Keene
Fitchburg
Lowell
Lynn
Waltham
BOSTON
Worcester
Brockton
Woonsocket
MASS
Skowhegan
Waterville
Augusta
Bethel
Auburn
Lewiston
Bath
Brunswick
Sebago
Sanford
Saco
Biddeford
Portland
Rochester
Con-cord
Dover
Manchester
Nashua
Haverhill
Lawrence
C. Ann
Gloucester
Portsmouth
Bangor
Old Town
Brewer
Ellsworth
Belfast
Camden
Rockland
Bar Harbor
Mt. Desert I.
Machias
Jonesport
Eastport
Calais
Blacks Hr.
St. Stephen
St. George
St. Martins
Saint John
Bay of Fundy
Grand Manan I.
St. Mary's B.
Freeport
Weymouth
Digby
Bridgetown
Annapolis Royal
Middleton
St. Chignecto B.
Minas Basin
Kentville
Windsor
Jogg
NO
Yarmouth
Wedgeport
Clark's Harbour
C. Sable
Lockeport
Port Mouton
Shelburne
Liverpool
L. Rossignol Res.
Bridgewater
Lunenburg
Mahone B.
Ha

St. Lawrence

50

45

70

65

65

1 : 7 000 000

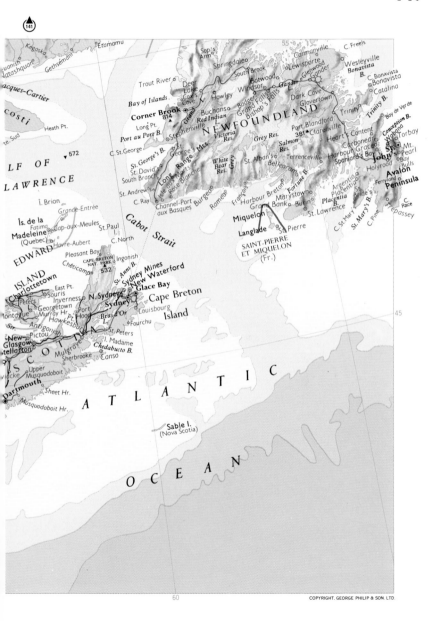

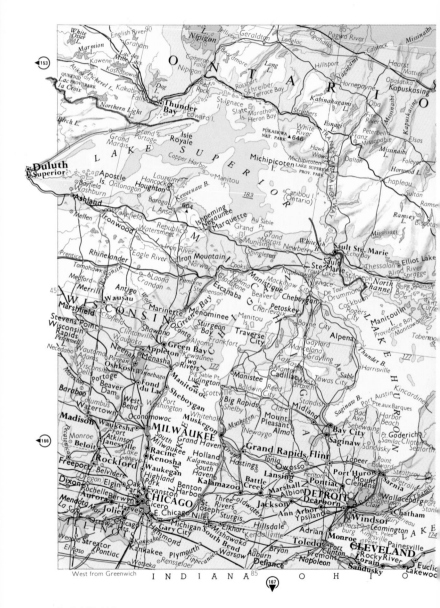

1 : 7 000 000

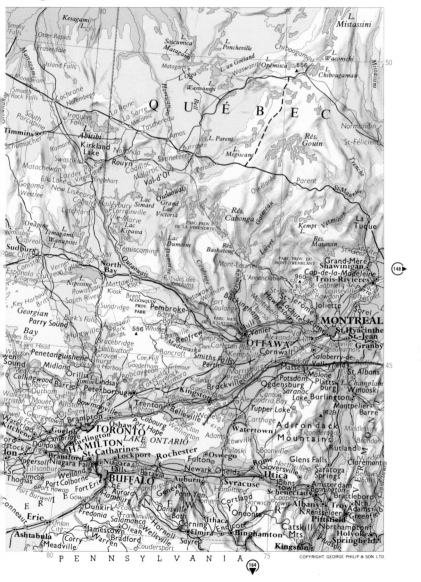

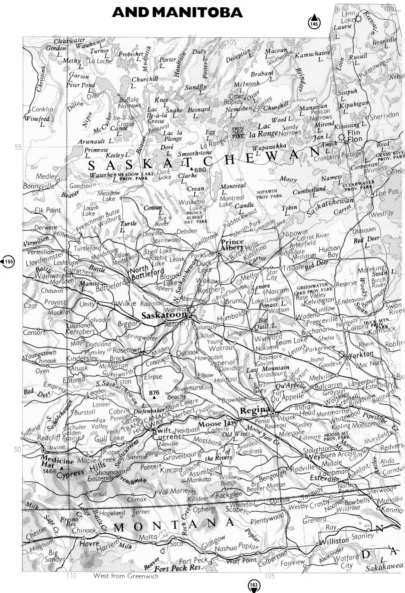

1 : 7 000 000

West from Greenwich

1 : 7 000 000

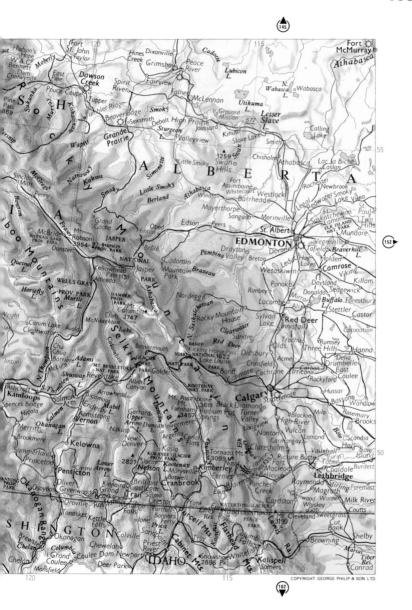

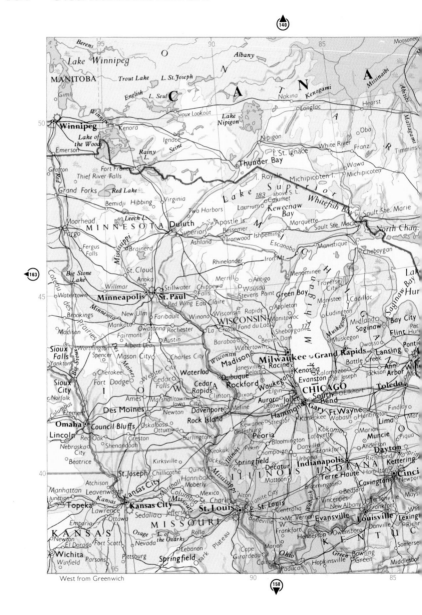

1 : 12 000 000

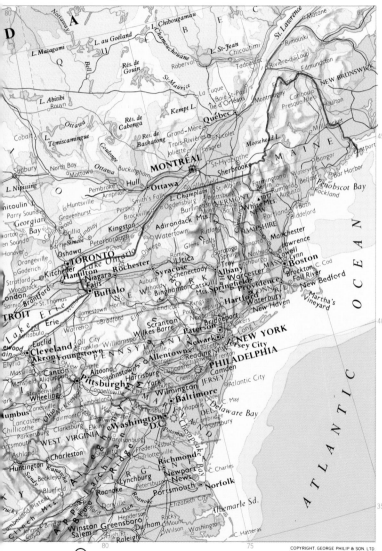

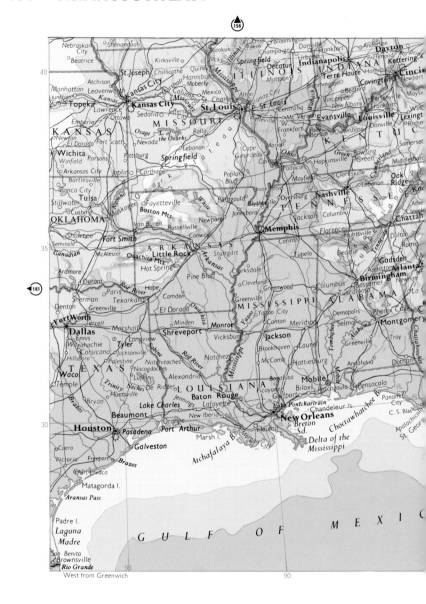

West from Greenwich

1 : 12 000 000

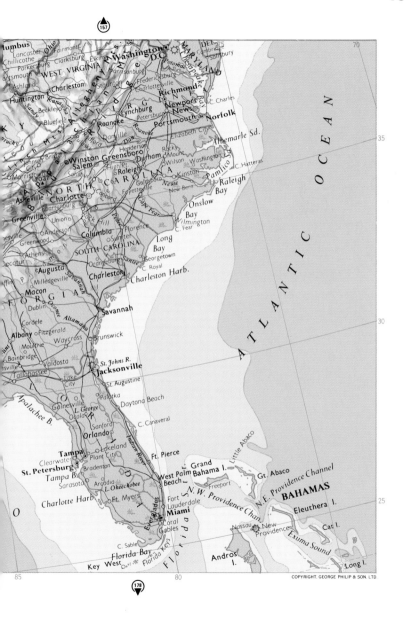

70

Ohio Lancaster Fairmont
Chillicothe Parkersburg Clarksburg Elkins Harrisonburg
Portsmouth **WEST VIRGINIA** Washington
Ashland **Charleston** Kanawha Staunton Fredericksburg Charlottesville
Huntington Beckley **Richmond**
Sandy Bluefield Lynchburg Petersburg Newport News
Johnson Bristol Roanoke Portsmouth **Norfolk**
Morristown 2037 Danville Roanoke Elizabeth City
Asheville Winston Greensboro High Pt. Durham Rocky Mount Washington C. Hatteras
Salem Raleigh Wilson
NORTH CAROLINA Neuse Goldsboro Kinston Pamlico
Charlotte Concord New Bern Raleigh
Greenville Union Rock Hill Fayetteville Bay
Greenwood Anderson Cape Fear Onslow
Athens **Columbia** Sumter Florence Bay
Decatur **SOUTH CAROLINA** Long C. Fear Wilmington
Augusta Orangeburg Santee Georgetown Bay
Milledgeville Savannah Royal
Macon **Charleston** Charleston Harb.
GEORGIA Dublin Oconee
Cordele Altamaha Savannah
Albany Fitzgerald
Moultrie Waycross Brunswick
Bainbridge Valdosta
Tallahassee St. Johns R. **Jacksonville**
Lake City St. Augustine
Gainesville Palatka Daytona Beach
L. George Ocala
Orlando C. Canaveral
Sanford
Tampa Lakeland Ft. Pierce
Clearwater Plant City Indian River
St. Petersburg Bradenton West Palm **Grand**
Tampa B. Sarasota Beach **Bahama I.** Little Abaco
Arcadia L. Okeechobee Freeport Gt. Abaco
Charlotte Harb. Fort N.W. Providence Chan. N.E. Providence Channel
Ft. Myers Lauderdale **BAHAMAS**
Miami New Eleuthera I.
Coral Gables Nassau Providence
C. Sable Exuma Sound Cat I.
Florida Bay Andros
Key West Florida Keys I. Long I.

ATLANTIC OCEAN

35

30

25

85

80

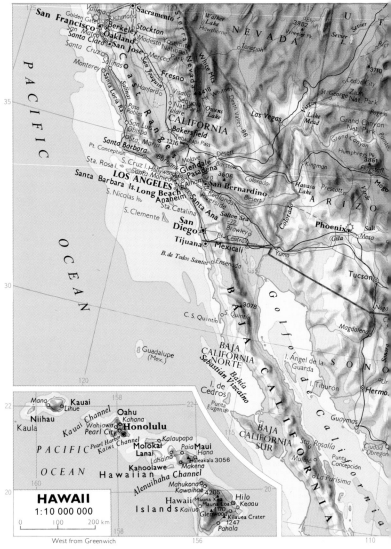

HAWAII

1:10 000 000

0   100   200 km

West from Greenwich

1 : 12 000 000

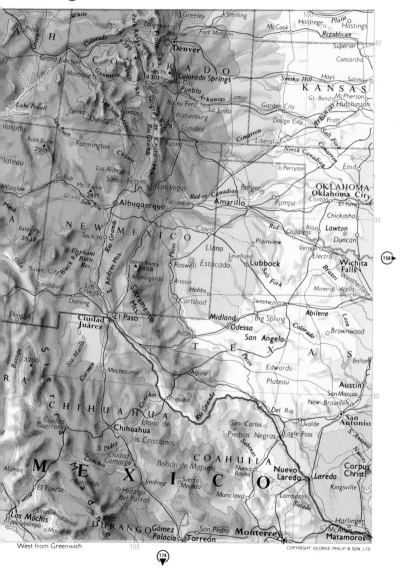

COPYRIGHT GEORGE PHILIP & SON LTD.

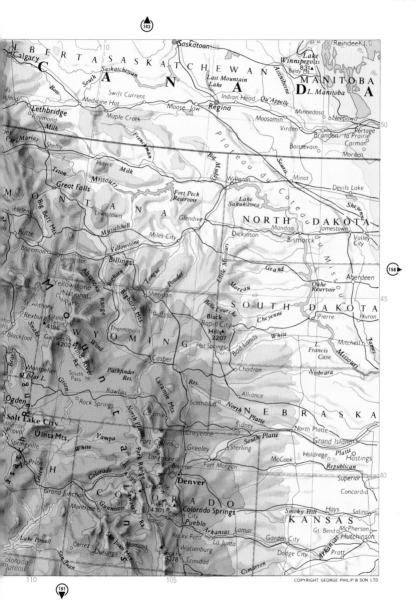

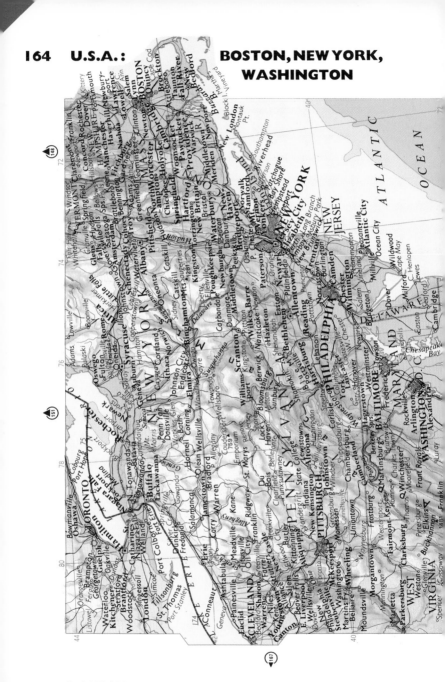

1 : 6 000 000

West from Greenwich

1 : 6 000 000

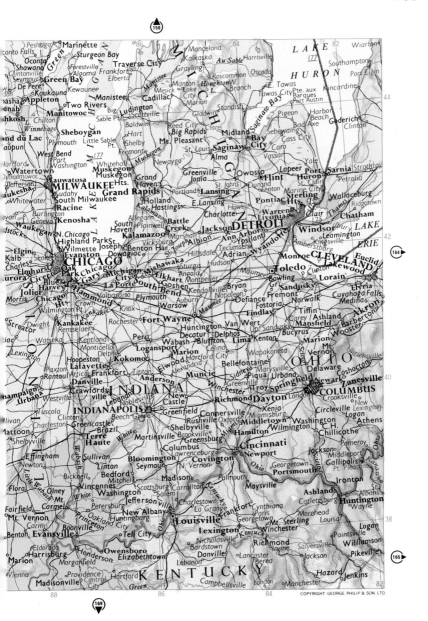

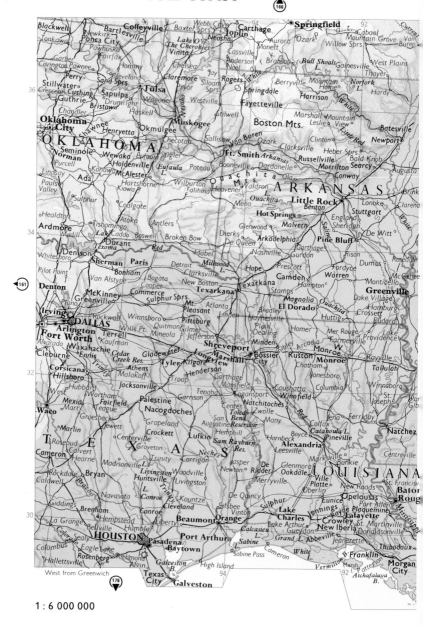

West from Greenwich

1 : 6 000 000

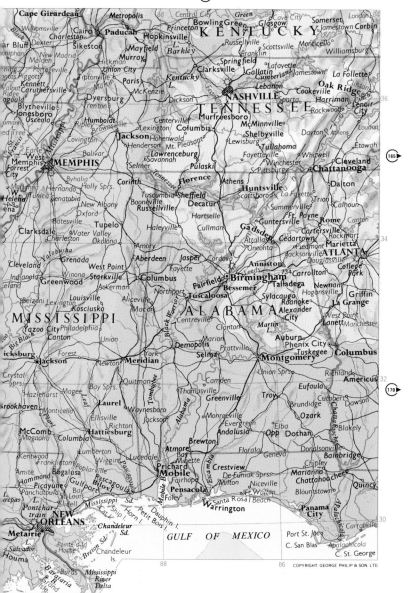

COPYRIGHT. GEORGE PHILIP & SON. LTD.

ATLANTA Decatur
Douglasville East Point
College Covington Greensboro Augusta Aiken Orangeburg L. Andrews Georgetown
Park Eatonton Sparta Bamberg Marion Moultrie
Carrollton Newnan Griffin Summerville St. George Walterboro Charleston Mt. Pleasant
La Grange GEORGIA Wrens Hampton
Barnesville Milledgeville Tennille Waynesboro Ridgeland Beaufort
West Point Thomaston Millen Sylvania Parris I.
Lanett Manchester Macon Warner Dublin Pembroke Savannah
Phenix Fort Valley Robins Statesboro
City Columbus Perry Cochran Hawkinsville Vidalia Ossabaw I.
Richland Eastman Lyons St. Catherines I.
Americus Cordele Sapelo I.
Eufaula Hazlehurst Altamaha Baxley St. Simons I.
Cuthbert Dawson Ashburn Fitzgerald Jesup Brunswick Jekyll I.
Albany Sylvester Ocilla Alma
Blakely Tifton Douglas Cumberland I.
Donalsonville Pelham Nashville Adel Waycross Folkston Fernandina Beach
Bainbridge Cairo Moultrie Okefenokee
Thomasville Quitman Valdosta Swamp
Chattahoochee Monticello Jasper
Quincy Madison
Tallahassee Live Oak FLORIDA JACKSONVILLE Jacksonville
Lake Baldwin St. Johns Beach
Perry City
Starke Green ATLANTIC
High Sprs. Cove Sprs. St. Augustine
Apalachee Williston Palatka
Carrabelle B. Cross City Gainesville Bunnell
Apalachicola Ocala Ormond OCEAN
C. St. George Cedar Key Dunnellon De Land Beach Holly Hill
Crystal River Eustis Sanford New
Inverness Mt. Smyrna
GULF Leesburg Dora Titusville Beach
Brooksville Winter Winter C. Canaveral
Garden Park Cocoa
Dade City Kissimmee Orlando St. Cloud
Tarpon Sprs. Auburndale Melbourne
Dunedin Lakeland Winter Haven
Clearwater Plant City Lake Wales Vero Beach
St. Petersburg Tampa Bartow Ft. Pierce
OF Palmetto Ft. Meade Wauchula Okeechobee Stuart
Bradenton Sebring
Sarasota Istokpoga L. Pahokee Palm Beach
Arcadia Okeechobee Belle West Palm
MEXICO Punta Gorda La Belle Glade Beach
Charlotte Hbr. Clewiston Lake Worth Boynton Beach
Ft. Pompano Delray Beach
Myers Immokalee Boca Raton Pompano Beach
Naples Big Cypress Swamp Everglades Ft. Lauderdale
Carol City Hollywood
West from Greenwich Everglades Hialeah Miami Beach
City EVERGLADES Miami
NAT. PARK Biscayne
Coral Gables B.
Homestead

1 : 6 000 000

COPYRIGHT. GEORGE PHILIP & SON LTD

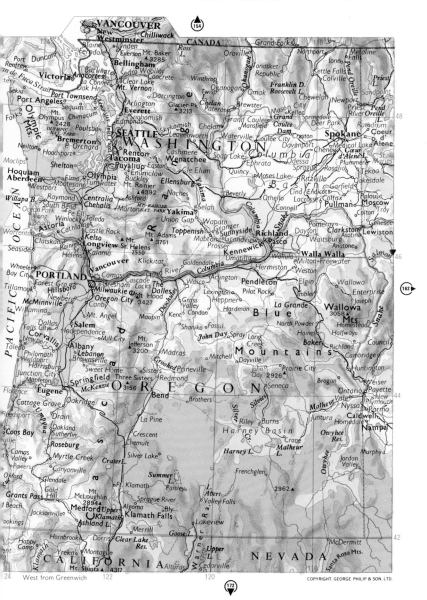

West from Greenwich

1 : 6 000 000

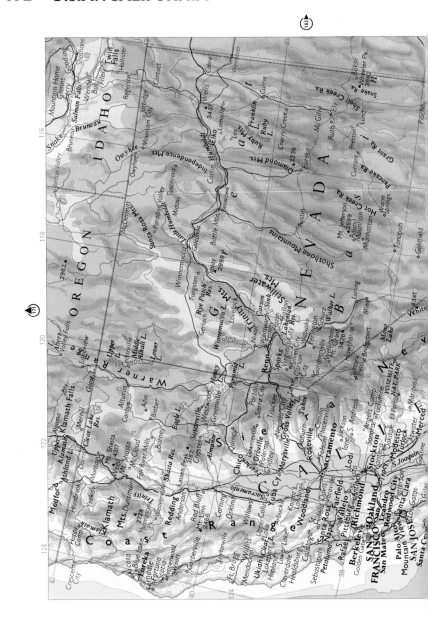

1 : 6 000 000

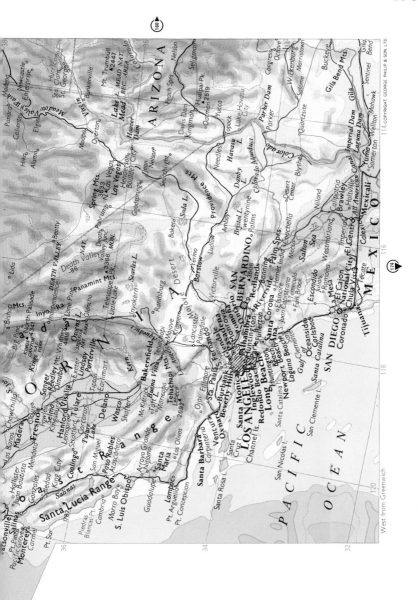

West from Greenwich

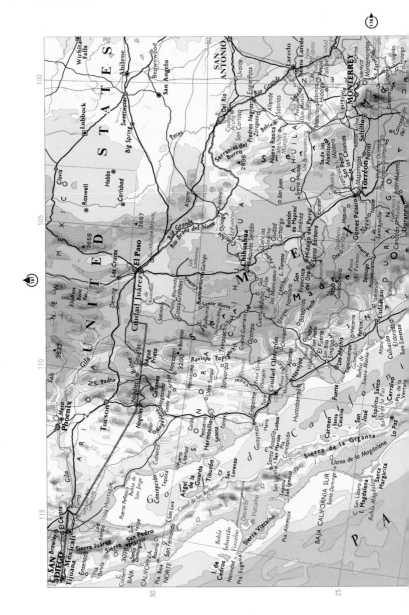

1 : 12 000 000

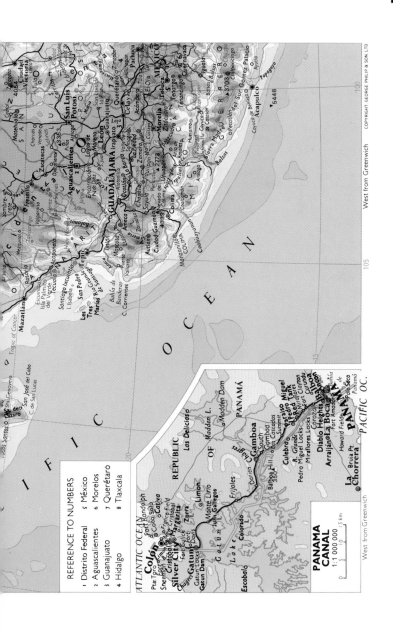

REFERENCE TO NUMBERS

1 Distrito Federal   5 México
2 Aguascalientes   6 Morelos
3 Guanajuato   7 Querétaro
4 Hidalgo   8 Tlaxcala

PANAMÁ CANAL
1:1 000 000

West from Greenwich

West from Greenwich

105

110

COPYRIGHT GEORGE PHILIP & SON LTD

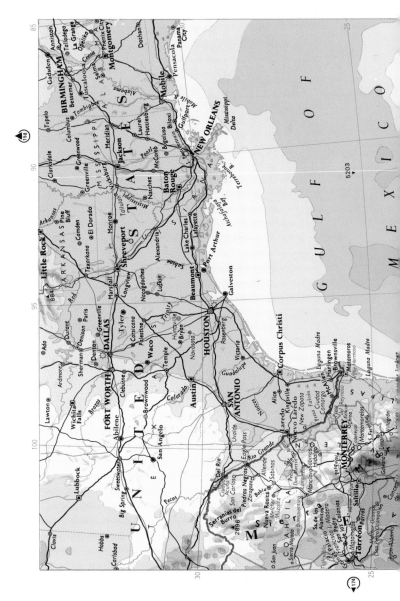

1 : 12 000 000

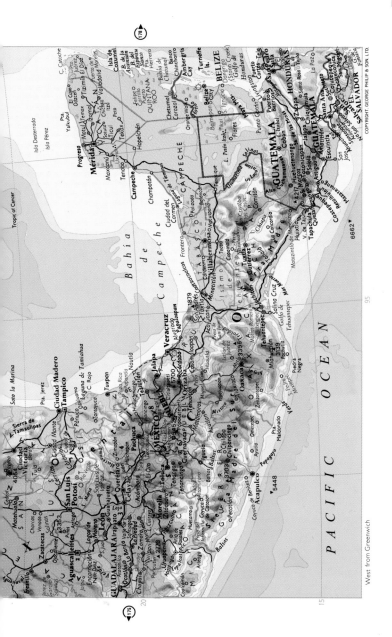

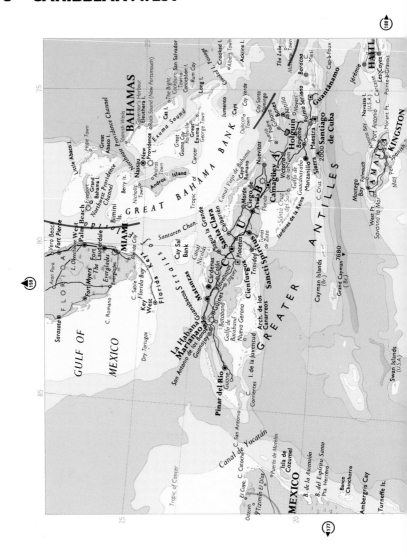

1 : 12 000 000

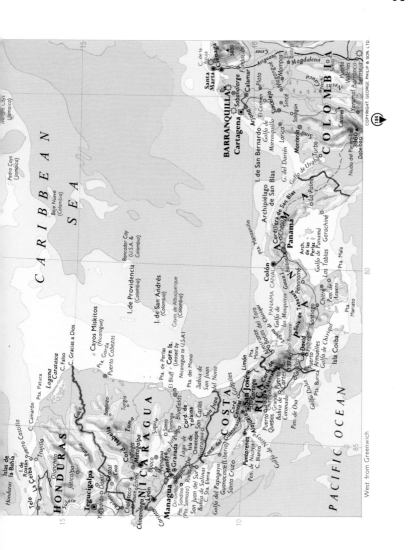

CARIBBEAN SEA

COLOMBIA

PANAMA

COSTA RICA

NICARAGUA

HONDURAS

PACIFIC OCEAN

West from Greenwich

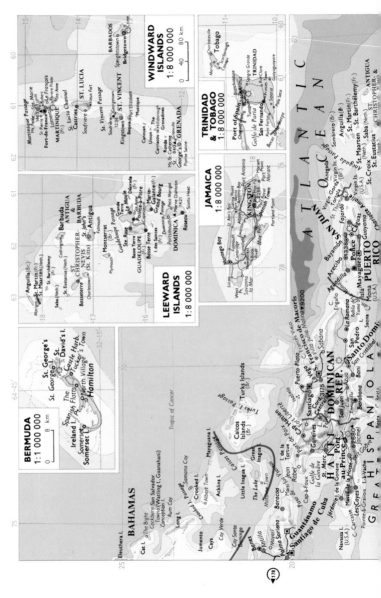

1 : 12 000 000

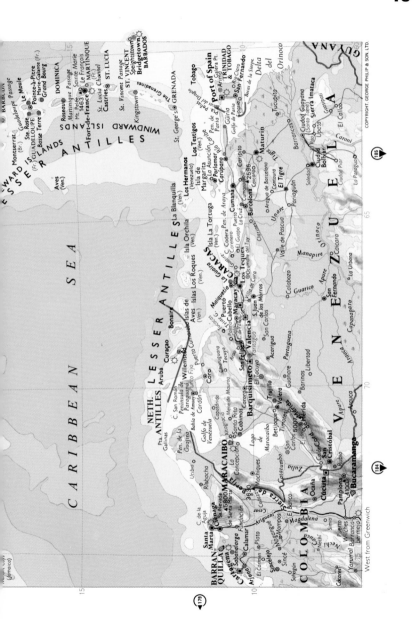

SOUTH AMERICA :
PHYSICAL

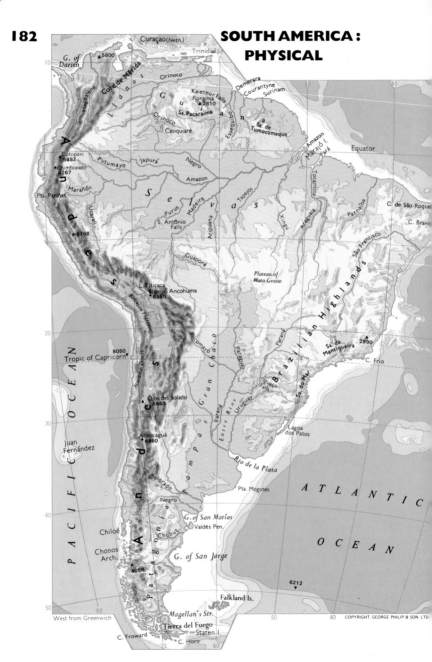

Curaçao (Neth.)
Trinidad
G. of Darien
▲ 5800
10
Cord. de Mérida
L l a n o s
Orinoco
Kaieteur Falls
Demerara
Courantyne
Surinam
Roraima
▲ 2810
G u a y a n a
Ses.
Sa. Pacaraima
Magdalena
Orinoco
Casiquiare
S.a de
Tumucumaque
Essequibo
Amazon
Marajó I.
Pará
Equator
Putumayo
Japurá
Negro
Cotopaxi
▲ 5897
▲ Chimborazo
6267
Amazon
Marañón
Tocantins
Parnaiba
C. de São Roque
C. Branc
S e l v a s
Purus
Madeira
Tapajós
Xingu
Araguaia
Ucayali
▲ 6768
S. Antônio
Falls
Aripuanã
P e r u
Guaporé
P t a . Parinas
Plateau of
Mato Grosso
São Francisco
L. Titicaca
Illampu Ancohuma
6550
B r a z i l i a n   H i g h l a n d s
Bolivian Plateau
20
A n d e s
Pilcomayo
Paraná
Sa. da
Mantiqueira
▲ 2890
8050
▼
Tropic of Capricorn
Atacama Desert
Gran Chaco
Paraguay
Serra do Mar
C. Frio
Ojos del Solado
▲ 6863
Paraná
Iguaçu
Falls
Uruguay
Entre Rios
P A C I F I C   O C E A N
30
Aconcagua
▲ 6960
Lagoa
dos Patos
P a m p a s
Juan
Fernández
Colorado
Rio de la Plata
A T L A N T I C
Negro
Pta. Mogotes
G. of San Matías
Valdés Pen.
40
Chiloé
P a t a g o n i a
Chubut
O C E A N
Chonos
Arch.
▲ 4058
G. of San Jorge
A n d e s
6212
▼
West from Greenwich
50
Falkland Is.
Magellan's Str.
Tierra del Fuego
Staten I.
C. Froward
C. Horn

COPYRIGHT GEORGE PHILIP & SON LTD.

1 : 50 000 000

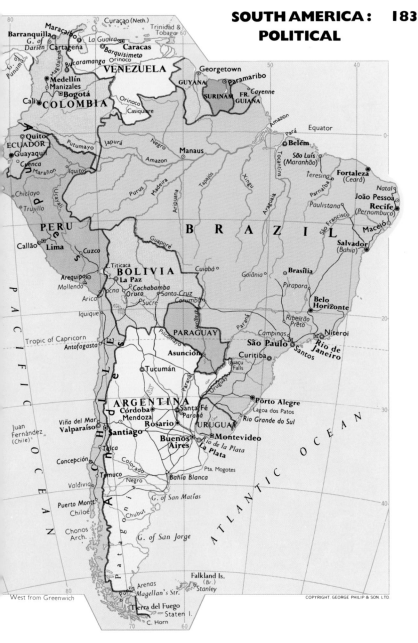

West from Greenwich

COPYRIGHT. GEORGE PHILIP & SON LTD.

1 : 50 000 000

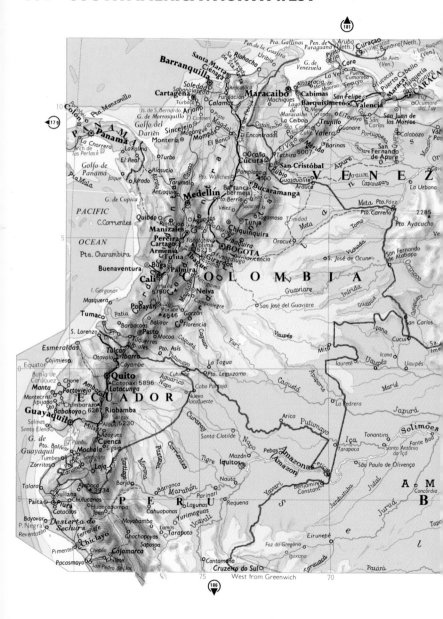

1 : 16 000 000

Salinas
Santa Elena
Guayaquil
G. de Guayaquil
Machala
Pto. Bolivar
I. Puná
Milagro ECUADOR
Azogues
Cuenca
Sigsig
Alausi 230
Santa Clotilde
Napo
Pebas
Iquitos
Mazán
Nauta
Requena
Taura
Tumbes
Zorritos
Zaruma
Saraguro
Loja
Macara
Santiago
Morona
Pastaza
Corrientes
Tigre
Yavari
Talara
Sullana
Piura
Catacaos
Bayovar
Pta. Negra
Reventazón
Ayabaca
Chulucanas
Huancabamba
Jaen
Chachapoyas
Saposoa
Lamas
Tarapoto
Moyobamba
Cahuapanas
Lagunas
Yurimaguas
Ucayali
Borja
Barranca
Marañón
Parinari
Contamana
Cruzeiro do Sul
Porto V
3934
Desierto de
Sechura
Ferreñafe
Chiclayo
Pimentel
Chepén
Cajamarca
Chilete
Pacasmayo
San Pedro de Lloc
Pto. Chicama
Ascope
Trujillo
Salaverry
Huallaga
Huamachuco
Tayabamba
Pucallpa
Masisea
Taumatu
Chimbote
Casma
Aija
Huarmey
Carás
Huascarán
6768
Huaraz
Chiquián
Goylarisquisga
Huánuco
Ambo
Tingo
Maria
Panáo
Cerro de Pasco
Pto. Bermúdez
Atalaya
Uruhua
PERU
Barranca
Sayán
Huacho
Huaral
Chancay
Ancón
Callao
I. San Lorenzo
LIMA
6369
La Oroya
Morococha
Marcapomacocha
Huancayo
Tarma
Jauja
Pampas
Apurimac
Motucana
Yauyos
Huancavelica
Cañete
Chincha Alta
Pisco
Tambo de Mora
Huancapi
Ayacucho
Cuzco
Abancay
Andahuaylas
Urubamba
Ica
Chalhuanca
Puquio
Rufino
Antabamba
Coracora
San Juan
Chala
Caravelí
Atica
Aplao
Camaná
Matarani
6425
Nudo Coropy
6866
Krümmer
Trench

PACIFIC OCEAN

Milne Edwards Trench

Peru Trench

Chile Trench

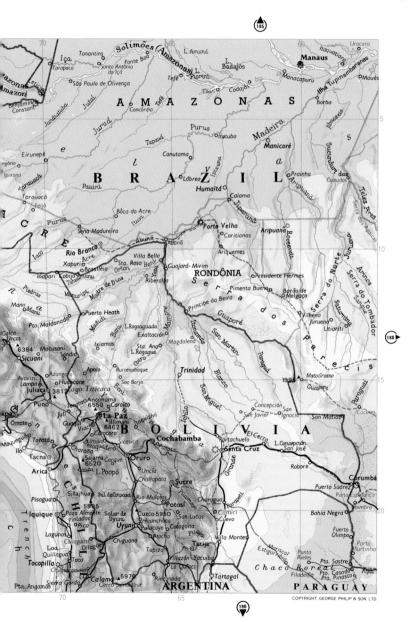

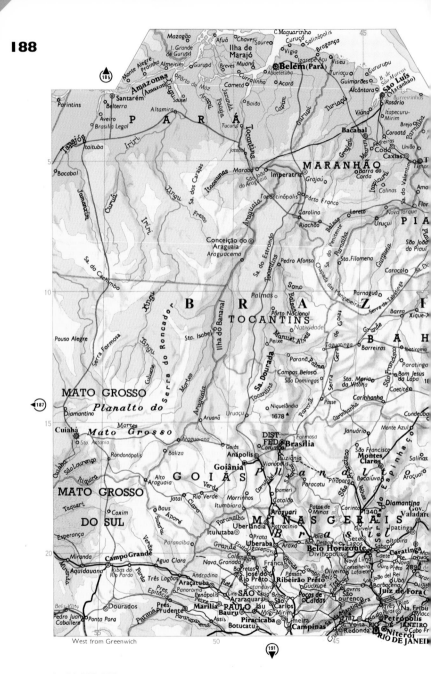

West from Greenwich

1 : 16 000 000

Tutóia
Luís Correia
Camocim
áiba
Granja
Itapipoca
racurucá
Sobral
Maranguape
Fortaleza (Ceará)
Rocas
Fernando de Noronha
(Braz.)
piri
Barros
npoMaior
Ipu
Baturité
Aracati
Branca
Cascavel
Quixadá
Russas
Areia
Macau
Qiticica
Limoeiro
do Norte
Crateús
Mossoró
Ceará Mirim
5
Senador Pompeu
CEARÁ
RIO GRANDE
C. de São Roque
Valença do
Piauí
Oros
Caraúbas
DO NORTE
Natal
Iguatú
Sout
Caicó
Currais
Novos
Cruz
Oeiras
Cedro
Pombal
Alagoa
Grande
Conguaretamu
UI
Crato
Cajazeiras
Patos
Momanguape
Cabedelo
Chap. do Araripe
Juàzeiro
PARAÍBA
João Pessoa
Norte
Campina Grande
(Paraíba)
Paulistana
Ouricuri
Sertânia
Limoeiro
Caruaru
Olinda
PERNAMBUCO
Arcoverde
1234
Pesqueira
RECIFE
(Pernambuco)
Irmãos
Garanhuns
Boatao
Petrolina
Petrolândia
Palmares
R. de Santa
osa Nova
Juàzeiro
Delmiro
Gouveia
Viçosa
Rio Largo
Remansa
Paulo Afonso
Pal das Indias
Maceió
Vaza-Barris
ALAGOAS
Arapiraca
L
Senhor do
Bonfim
Proprió
Penedo
6059
10
Campo
Formosó
SERGIPE
Jacobina
Queimadas
Itapicuru
Capela
A
Aracaju
Serrinha
São Cristóvão
I
Jacuípe
Feira de
Santana
Estância
Mundo
Novo
Cachoeira
Castro
Alves
Alagoinhas
Itaberaba
Santo Amaro
Itaeté
Amargosa
Sincorá
Valença
Salvador (Bahia)
Jequié
B. de Todos os Santos
Ubaitaba
Vitória da
Conquista
Itacaré
Itabuna
Ilhéus
Pedra Azul
Canavieiras
Belmonte
Pôrto Seguro
Jequitinhonha
Teófilo
Otoni
Prado
Nanuque
Caravelas
Banka
Mucuri
Abrolhos
Nova
Venécia
Conceição da Barra
São Mateus
SANTO
Doce
Linhares
Cariacica
Vitória
da
Bandeira
Vila Velha
Cachoeiro de Itapemirim
Trindade
(Braz.)
20

ATLANTIC OCEAN

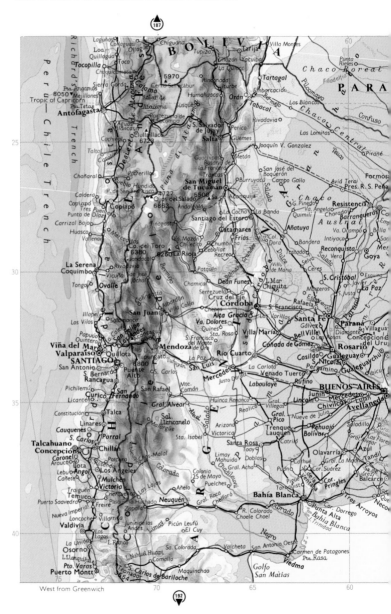

West from Greenwich

1 : 16 000 000

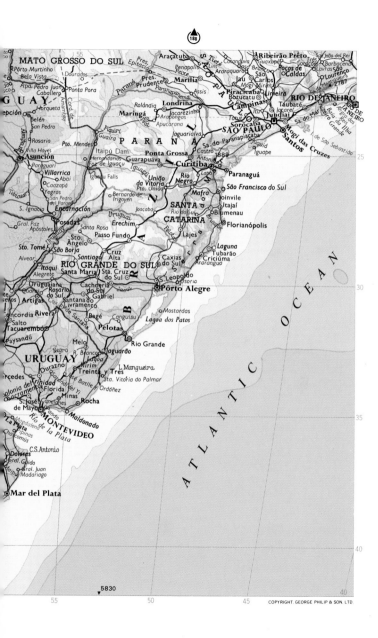

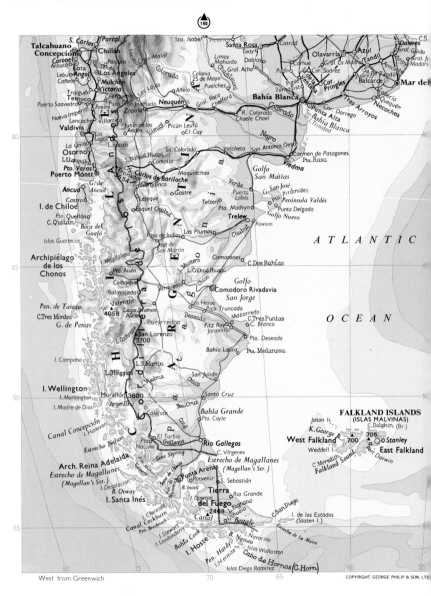

S. Carlos / Porral
Talcahuano
Concepción
Chillán
Coronel
Lebu
Angol
Cañete
Traiguén
Temuco
Freire
Puerto Saavedra
Nueva Imperial
Loncoche
Valdivia
La Unión
Osorno
L.Llanquihue
Pto. Varas
Puerto Montt
Ancud
G. de Ancud
I. de Chiloé
Castro
Pto. Quellón
C. Quilán
Boca del Guafó
Islas Guaitecas

Sta. Isabel
Santa Rosa
Malal
Limay Mahuida
Gral. Acha
Colonia 25 de Mayo
Puelches
Añelo
Neuquén
Paso Plño Hachado
Picún Leufú
El Cuy

Victoria
Olavarría
Azul
Catriló
Doblas
Toay
Dolores
Gral. Guido
Gral. Ju
Madari
Gral. La Madrid
Tandil
Puán
Cor. Suárez
Balcarce
Mar del
Cor. Pringles
Quequén
Necochea
Tres Arroyos

Bahía Blanca
Bahía Alta
Bahía Blanca
Pta. Trinidad

Negro
Valcheta
San Antonio Oeste
Carmen de Patagones
Pta. Rasa
Viedma
Golfo San Matías
Verde
G. San José
Pirámides
Península Valdés
Puerto Lobos
Pto. Madryn
Punta Delgada
Golfo Nuevo
Trelew
Rawson
Chubut

ATLANTIC

Moquinchao
Maquinchao
Comallo
Gastre
Telsen
Pto. de Indios
José de San Martín
Las Plumas
Camarones
C. Dos Bahías

Paso de Indios
L. Musters
L. Colhué Huapi
Golfo San Jorge
Comodoro Rivadavia
Las Heras
Pico Truncado
Mazarredo
C. Tres Puntas
Fitz Roy
Jaramillo
C. Blanco
Pto. Deseado
Deseado
Bahía Laura
Pto. Medanosa

OCEAN

Pen. de Taitao
C. Tres Montes
G. de Penas
I. Campana
I. Wellington
I. Morninton
I. Madre de Dios

San Lorenzo 3700
L. S. Martín
L. O'Higgins
L. Viedma
Murallón 3600
Argentino
Calafate
El Turbio
Puerto Natales
Bahía Grande
Pto. Cayle
Santa Cruz
Sta. Cruz
Coig
San Julián
Chico

FALKLAND ISLANDS
(ISLAS MALVINAS)
Jason Is.
K. George
C. Dolphin (Br.)
West Falkland
700
705
Stanley
Weddell I.
East Falkland
C. Meredith
Falkland Sound
Darwin

Arch. Reina Adelaida
Estrecho de Magallanes
(Magellan's Str.)
I. Desalación
B. Otway
I. Santa Inés
C. Vírgenes
Estrecho de Magallanes
(Magellan's Str.)
Porvenir
Punta Arenas
S. Sebastián
Tierra
del Fuego
Río Grande
2469
C. San Diego
I. de los Estados
(Staten I.)

I. Clarence
Canal Cockburn
Pen. Brecknock
I. Stewart
I. Londonderry
Bahía Cook
I. Hoste
Pen. Hardy
I. Hermite
Islas Diego Ramírez
B. Nassau
Islas Wollaston
Cabo de Hornos (C. Horn)
Canal Beagle
I. Navarino
Ushuaia
Estrecho de Le Maire

West from Greenwich

1 : 16 000 000

INDEX

Abbreviations used

Ala. – *Alabama*
Arch. – *Archipelago*
Ark. – *Arkansas*
Austral. – *Australia*
B. – *Baie, Bahia, Bay, Boca, Bucht, Bugt*
B.C. – *British Columbia*
Bangla. – *Bangladesh*
Br. – *British*
C. – *Cabo, Cap, Cape, Coast, Costa*
C. Rica – *Costa Rica*
Calif. – *California*
Cap. Terr. – *Capital Territory*
Cat. – *Cataract*
Cent. – *Central*
Chan. – *Channel*
Colo. – *Colorado*
Conn. – *Connecticut*
Cord. – *Cordillera*
D.C. – *District of Columbia*
Del. – *Delaware*
Dét. – *Détroit*
Dom. Rep. – *Dominican Republic*
Domin. – *Dominica*
E. – *East, Eastern*
Est. – *Estrecho*
Falk. Is. – *Falkland Islands*
Fla. – *Florida*
Fr. Gui. – *French Guiana*
G. – *Golfe, Golfo, Gulf, Guba, Gebel*
Ga. – *Georgia*
Gt. – *Great*
Guat. – *Guatemala*
Hants. – *Hampshire*
Hd. – *Head*
Hond. – *Honduras*
Hts. – *Heights*
I. (s) – *Ile, Ilha, Insel, Isla, Island(s)*
I. of W. – *Isle of Wight*
Ill. – *Illinois*
Ind. – *Indiana*
Ind. Oc. – *Indian Ocean*
J. – *Jabal, Jazira*
K. – *Kap, Kapp*
Kans. – *Kansas*
Ky. – *Kentucky*

L. – *Lac, Lacul, Lago, Lagoa, Lake, Limni, Loch, Lough*
La. – *Louisiana*
Lag. – *Laguna*
Lancs. – *Lancashire*
Man. – *Manitoba*
Mass. – *Massachusetts*
Md. – *Maryland*
Mich. – *Michigan*
Minn. – *Minnesota*
Miss. – *Mississippi*
Mo. – *Missouri*
Mont. – *Montana*
Mt.(s) – *Mont, Monta, Monti, Muntii, Montaña, Mount, Mountain(s)*
N. – *North, Northern*
N.B. – *New Brunswick*
M.C. – *North Carolina*
N. Dak. – *North Dakota*
N.H. – *New Hampshire*
N.J. – *New Jersey*
N. Mex. – *New Mexico*
N.S.W. – *New South Wales*
N.W.T. – *North West Territories*
N.Y. – *New York*
N.Z. – *New Zealand*
Nebr. – *Nebraska*
Neth. – *Netherlands*
Nev. – *Nevada*
Nfld. – *Newfoundland*
Nic. – *Nicaragua*
Okla. – *Oklahoma*
Ont. – *Ontario*
Oreg. – *Oregon*
Os. – *Ostrov*
Oz. – *Ozero*
P. – *Pass, Passo, Pasul, Pulau*
P.E.I. – *Prince Edward Island*
Pa. – *Pennsylvania*
Pac. Oc. – *Pacific Ocean*
Papua N.G. – *Papua New Guinea*
Pen. – *Peninsula*
Pk. – *Peak*
Plat. – *Plateau*

P-ov. – *Poluostrov*
Pt. – *Point*
Pta. – *Ponta, Punta*
Queens. – *Queensland*
R. – *Rio, River, Rivière*
R.I. – *Rhode Island*
Ra.(s) – *Range(s)*
Raj. – *Rajasthan*
Rep. – *Republic*
Res. – *Reserve, Reservoir*
S. – *South, Southern, Sea, Sur*
S.C. – *South Carolina*
S. Africa – *South Africa*
S. Dak. – *South Dakota*
Sa. – *Serra, Sierra*
Salop. – *Shropshire*
Sard. – *Sardinia*
Sask. – *Saskatchewan*
Sd. – *Sound*
Sev. – *Severnaya*
Si. Arabia – *Saudi Arabia*
St. – *Saint*
Sta. – *Santa*
Ste. – *Sainte*
Str. – *Strait, Stretto*
Switz. – *Switzerland*
Tas. – *Tasmania*
Tenn. – *Tennessee*
Terr. – *Territory*
Tex. – *Texas*
Tipp. – *Tipperary*
Trin. & Tob. – *Trinidad and Tobago*
U.K. – *United Kingdom*
U.S.A. – *United States of America*
Ut. P. – *Uttar Pradesh*
Va. – *Virginia*
Vic. – *Victoria*
Vol. – *Volcano*
Vt. – *Vermont*
Wash. – *Washington*
W. – *West, Western, Wadi*
W. Va. – *West Virginia*
Wis. – *Wisconsin*
Worcs. – *Worcestershire*
Yorks. – *Yorkshire*

Introduction to Index

The number printed in bold type against each entry indicates the map page where the feature can be found. This is followed by its geographical coordinates. The first coordinate indicates latitude, i.e. distance north or south of the Equator. The second coordinate indicates longitude, i.e. distance east or west of the meridian of Greenwich in England (shown as 0° longitude). Both latitude and longitude are measured in degrees and minutes (with 60 minutes in a degree), and appear on the map as horizontal and vertical gridlines respectively. Thus the entry for Paris in France reads:

Paris, France . . . . **39**   48 50N   2 20 E

This entry indicates that Paris is on page **39**, at latitude 48 degrees 50 minutes north (approximately five-sixths of the distance between horizontal gridlines 48 and 49, marked on either side of the page) and at longitude 2 degrees 20 minutes east (approximately one-third of the distance between vertical gridlines 2 and 3, marked at top and bottom of the page). Paris can be found where lines extended from these two points cross on the page. The geographical coordinates are sometimes only approximate but are close enough for the place to be located. Rivers have been indexed to their mouth or confluence.

An open square □ signifies that the name refers to an administrative subdivision of a country while a solid square ■ follows the name of a country. An arrow → follows the name of a river.

The alphabetical order of names composed of two or more words is governed primarily by the first word and then by the second. This rule applies even if the second word is a description or its abbreviation, R., L., I., for example:

> North Walsham
> Northallerton
> Northampton
> Northern Circars
> Northumberland Is.
> Northumberland Str.

Names composed of a proper name (Gibraltar) and a description (Strait of) are positioned alphabetically by the proper name. This is the case where the definite article follows a proper name (Mans, Le). If the same word occurs in the name of a town and a geographical feature, the town name is listed first followed by the name or names of the geographical features.

Names beginning with M', Mc are all indexed as if they were spelt Mac. All names beginning St. are alphabetised under Saint, but Sankt, Sint, Santa and San are all spelt in full and are alphabetised accordingly.

If the same place name occurs twice or more times in the index and all are in the same country, each is followed by the name of the administrative subdivision in which it is located. The names are placed in the alphabetical order of the subdivisions. If the same place name occurs twice or more in the index and the places are in different countries they will be followed by their country names, the latter governing the alphabetical order. In a mixture of these situations the primary order is fixed by the alphabetical sequence of the countries and the secondary order by that of the country subdivisions.

The index shows Welsh and Scottish administrative names prior to April 1996. The maps on pages 24 to 33 show the new administrative areas and names.

A

Name	Page	Lat °	Lat ′	N/S	Lon °	Lon ′	E/W
Aachen	42	50	47	N	6	4	E
Aalborg = Ålborg	61	57	2	N	9	54	E
Aalsmeer	40	52	17	N	4	43	E
Aalst	42	50	56	N	4	2	E
Aalten	41	51	56	N	6	35	E
Aarhus = Århus	61	56	8	N	10	11	E
Aba	131	5	10	N	7	19	E
Ābādān	84	30	22	N	48	20	E
Ābādeh	85	31	8	N	52	40	E
Abadla	126	31	2	N	2	45	W
Abai	191	25	58	S	55	54	W
Abakan	74	53	40	N	91	10	E
Abancay	186	13	35	S	72	55	W
Abariringa I.	122	2	50	S	171	40	W
Abashiri	103	44	0	N	144	15	E
Abashiri-Wan	103	44	0	N	144	30	E
Abaya, L.	133	6	30	N	37	50	E
Abbay = Nîl el Azraq →	129	15	38	N	32	31	E
Abbeville, France	38	50	6	N	1	49	E
Abbeville, U.S.A.	165	34	12	N	82	21	W
Abéché	129	13	50	N	20	35	E
Abeokuta	131	7	3	N	3	19	E
Aberaeron	26	52	15	N	4	16	W
Aberayron = Aberaeron	26	52	15	N	4	16	W
Aberdare	27	51	43	N	3	27	W
Aberdeen, U.K.	33	57	9	N	2	6	W
Aberdeen, S. Dak., U.S.A.	163	45	30	N	98	30	W
Aberdeen, Wash., U.S.A.	171	47	0	N	123	50	W
Aberdovey	26	52	33	N	4	3	W
Aberfeldy	33	56	37	N	3	50	W
Abergavenny	26	51	49	N	3	1	W
Aberystwyth	26	52	25	N	4	6	W
Abha	82	18	0	N	42	34	E
Abidjan	130	5	26	N	3	58	W
Abilene	161	32	22	N	99	40	W
Abington	25	55	30	N	3	42	W
Abkhazia □	70	43	12	N	41	5	E
Abohar	89	30	10	N	74	10	E
Abomey	131	7	10	N	2	5	E
Abong-Mbang	131	4	0	N	13	8	E
Abrud	56	46	19	N	23	5	E
Abruzzi □	47	42	15	N	14	0	E
Absaroka Ra.	163	44	40	N	110	0	W
Abū al Khaşīb	84	30	25	N	48	0	E
Abū 'Alī	84	27	20	N	49	27	E
Abū 'Arīsh	82	16	58	N	45	20	E
Abu Dhabi = Abū Ẓāby	85	24	28	N	54	22	E
Abu Hamed	129	19	32	N	33	13	E
Abū Ẓāby	85	24	28	N	54	22	E
Abunã	187	9	40	S	65	20	W
Abunã →	187	9	41	S	65	20	W
Abut Hd.	123	43	7	S	170	15	E
Acámbaro	177	20	2	N	100	44	W
Acaponeta	175	22	30	N	105	22	W
Acapulco	177	16	51	N	99	56	W
Acatlán	177	18	10	N	98	3	W
Acayucan	177	17	57	N	94	55	W
Accra	130	5	35	N	0	6	W
Accrington	28	53	46	N	2	22	W
Achill I.	34	53	58	N	10	5	W
Achinsk	74	56	20	N	90	20	E
Aconcagua, Cerro	190	32	39	S	70	0	W
Aconquija, Mt.	190	27	0	S	66	0	W
Açores, Is. dos = Azores	126	38	44	N	29	0	W
Acre = 'Akko	80	32	55	N	35	4	E
Acre □	187	9	1	S	71	0	W
Ad Dawhah	85	25	15	N	51	35	E
Ada	168	34	50	N	96	45	W
Adamaoua, Massif de l'	131	7	20	N	12	20	E
Adamawa Highlands = Adamaoua, Massif de l'	131	7	20	N	12	20	E
Adaminaby	117	36	0	S	148	45	E
Adams, Mt.	171	46	10	N	121	28	W
Adam's Bridge	90	9	15	N	79	40	E
Adana	80	37	0	N	35	16	E
Adapazarı	80	40	48	N	30	25	E
Adare, C.	15	71	0	S	171	0	E
Addis Ababa = Addis Abeba	133	9	2	N	38	42	E
Addis Abeba	133	9	2	N	38	42	E
Adelaide	119	34	52	S	138	30	E
Adelaide Pen.	145	68	15	N	97	30	W
Adélie, Terre	15	68	0	S	140	0	E
Aden = Al 'Adan	83	12	45	N	45	0	E
Aden, G. of	133	13	0	N	50	0	E
Adige →	47	45	9	N	12	20	E
Adirondack Mts.	151	44	0	N	74	15	W
Admiralty Is.	115	2	0	S	147	0	E
Adoni	90	15	33	N	77	18	W
Adrian	167	41	55	N	84	0	W
Adriatic Sea	52	43	0	N	16	0	E
Adwa	132	14	15	N	38	52	E
Ægean Sea	55	37	0	N	25	0	E
Æolian Is. = Éolie, I.	49	38	30	N	14	50	E
Aerht'ai Shan	100	46	40	N	92	45	E
Afars & Issas, Terr. of = Djibouti ■	133	12	0	N	43	0	E
Afghanistan ■	87	33	0	N	65	0	E
Afuá	188	0	15	S	50	20	W
Afyonkarahisar	80	38	45	N	30	33	E
Agadir	126	30	28	N	9	35	W
Agano →	103	37	57	N	139	8	E
Agartala	93	23	50	N	91	23	E
Agen	36	44	12	N	0	38	E
Ageo	107	35	58	N	139	36	E
Aghil Pass	89	36	15	N	76	35	E
Agra	89	27	17	N	77	58	E
Ağri Daği	81	39	50	N	44	15	E
Água Clara	188	20	25	S	52	45	W
Agua Prieta	174	31	18	N	109	34	W
Aguadas	184	5	40	N	75	38	W
Aguadilla	180	18	27	N	67	10	W
Aguas Blancas	190	24	15	S	69	55	W
Aguascalientes	175	21	53	N	102	18	W
Aguascalientes □	175	22	0	N	102	30	W
Agulhas, Kaap	136	34	52	S	20	0	E
Ahaggar	127	23	0	N	6	30	E
Ahaura →	123	42	21	S	171	34	E
Ahmadabad	91	23	0	N	72	40	E
Ahmadnagar	91	19	7	N	74	46	E
Ahmedabad = Ahmadabad	91	23	0	N	72	40	E
Ahmednagar = Ahmadnagar	91	19	7	N	74	46	E
Ahvāz	84	31	20	N	48	40	E
Ahvenanmaa = Åland	66	60	15	N	20	0	E
Ahwar	83	13	30	N	46	40	E
Aigle, L'	39	48	46	N	0	38	E
Aigues-Mortes	37	43	35	N	4	12	E
Aiken	170	33	34	N	81	50	W
Ailsa Craig	30	55	15	N	5	7	W
Aimorés	189	19	30	S	41	4	W
Aïn Ben Tili	126	25	59	N	9	27	W
Aioi	109	34	48	N	134	28	E
Aïr	127	18	30	N	8	0	E
Airdrie	31	55	53	N	3	57	W
Aire →	29	53	42	N	0	55	W
Airlie Beach	121	20	16	S	148	43	E
Aisne →	37	49	26	N	2	50	E
Aix-en-Provence	37	43	32	N	5	27	E
Aix-la-Chapelle = Aachen	42	50	47	N	6	4	E
Aix-les-Bains	37	45	41	N	5	53	E
Aizuwakamatsu	105	37	30	N	139	56	E
Ajaccio	36	41	55	N	8	40	E
Ajanta Ra.	91	20	28	N	75	50	E
Ajaria □	70	41	30	N	42	0	E
Ajmer	91	26	28	N	74	37	E
Akaishi-Dake	107	35	27	N	138	9	E
Akaishi-Sammyaku	107	35	25	N	138	10	E
Akashi	109	34	45	N	135	0	E
Akershus fylke □	60	60	0	N	11	10	E
Akhelóös →	54	38	36	N	21	14	E
Akhisar	80	38	56	N	27	48	E
Aki	109	33	30	N	133	54	E
Aki-Nada	109	34	5	N	132	40	E
Akita	103	39	45	N	140	7	E
'Akko	80	32	55	N	35	4	E
Aklavik	144	68	12	N	135	0	W
Akö	109	34	45	N	134	24	E
Akola	91	20	42	N	77	2	E
Akranes	64	64	19	N	21	58	W
Akron	167	41	7	N	81	31	W

Name	Page	Lat			Long		
Aksaray	80	38	25N	34	2	E	
Aksarka	69	66	31N	67	50	E	
Akşehir	80	38	18N	31	30	E	
Aksum	132	14	5N	38	40	E	
Aktyubinsk = Aqtöbe	70	50	17N	57	10	E	
Akune	108	32	1N	130	12	E	
Akureyri	64	65	40N	18	6W		
Al 'Adan	83	12	45N	45	0	E	
Al Amādīyah	81	37	5N	43	30	E	
Al Amārah	84	31	55N	47	15	E	
Al 'Aqabah	80	29	31N	35	0	E	
Al Başrah	84	30	30N	47	50	E	
Al Ḥadīthah	81	31	28N	37	8	E	
Al Ḥāmad	80	31	30N	39	30	E	
Al Ḥasakah	81	36	35N	40	45	E	
Al Ḥawrah	83	13	50N	47	35	E	
Al Ḥayy	84	32	5N	46	5	E	
Al Ḥillah, Iraq	84	32	30N	44	25	E	
Al Ḥillah, Si. Arabia	83	23	35N	46	50	E	
Al Hindīyah	84	32	30N	44	10	E	
Al Ḥudaydah	82	14	50N	43	0	E	
Al Ḥūfuf	84	25	25N	49	45	E	
Al Jāfūrah	84	25	0N	50	15	E	
Al Jawf, Libya	128	24	10N	23	24	E	
Al Jawf, Si. Arabia	82	29	55N	39	40	E	
Al Jazirah	81	33	30N	44	0	E	
Al Khalīl	80	31	32N	35	6	E	
Al Kūt	84	32	30N	46	0	E	
Al Kuwayt	84	29	30N	47	30	E	
Al Lādhiqīyah	80	35	30N	35	45	E	
Al Lidām	82	20	33N	44	45	E	
Al Luḥayyah	82	15	45N	42	40	E	
Al Madīnah	82	24	35N	39	52	E	
Al Manāmāh	85	26	10N	50	30	E	
Al Marj	128	32	25N	20	30	E	
Al Mawşil	81	36	15N	43	5	E	
Al Mubarraz	84	25	30N	49	40	E	
Al Muḥarraq	85	26	15N	50	40	E	
Al Mukallā	83	14	33N	49	2	E	
Al Qaţīf	84	26	35N	50	0	E	
Al Quds = Jerusalem	80	31	47N	35	10	E	
Al Qunfudhah	82	19	3N	41	4	E	
Al Qurnah	84	31	1N	47	25	E	
Al 'Ubaylah	83	21	59N	50	57	E	
Al 'Uthmānīyah	84	25	5N	49	22	E	
Al Wajh	82	26	10N	36	30	E	
Alabama □	169	33	0N	87	0W		
Alabama ⟶	169	31	8N	87	57W		
Alagoas □	189	9	0S	36	0W		
Alagoinhas	189	12	7S	38	20W		
Alajuela	179	10	2N	84	8W		
Alamogordo	161	32	59N	106	0W		
Álamos	174	27	1N	108	56W		
Alamosa	163	37	30N	106	0W		
Åland	66	60	15N	20	0	E	
Alaska □	142	65	0N	150	0W		
Alaska, G. of	142	58	0N	145	0W		
Alaska Pen.	142	56	0N	160	0W		
Alaska Range	142	62	50N	151	0W		
Alba Iulia	56	46	8N	23	39	E	
Albacete	51	39	0N	1	50W		
Albania ■	52	41	0N	20	0	E	
Albany, Australia	120	35	1S	117	58	E	
Albany, Ga., U.S.A.	170	31	40N	84	10W		
Albany, N.Y., U.S.A.	164	42	35N	73	47W		
Albany, Oreg., U.S.A.	171	44	41N	123	0W		
Albany ⟶	140	52	17N	81	31W		
Albemarle	165	35	27N	80	15W		
Albemarle Sd.	165	36	0N	76	30W		
Albert	38	50	0N	2	38	E	
Albert, L. = Mobutu Sese Seko, L.	132	1	30N	31	0	E	
Albert Lea	166	43	32N	93	20W		
Alberta □	155	54	40N	115	0W		
Albertville = Kalemie	135	5	55S	29	9	E	
Albi	37	43	56N	2	9	E	
Albion	167	42	15N	84	45W		
Ålborg	61	57	2N	9	54	E	
Alborz, Reshteh-ye Kūhhā-ye	86	36	0N	52	0	E	
Albuquerque	161	35	5N	106	47W		
Alburquerque	50	39	15N	6	59W		
Albury	117	36	3S	146	56	E	
Alcântara	188	2	20S	44	30W		
Alcázar de San Juan	50	39	24N	3	12W		
Alcira	51	39	9N	0	30W		
Aldan ⟶	75	63	28N	129	35	E	
Aldeburgh	25	52	9N	1	35	E	
Alderney	36	49	42N	2	12W		
Aldershot	25	51	15N	0	43W		
Alençon	39	48	27N	0	4	E	
Aleppo = Ḥalab	80	36	10N	37	15	E	
Alès	37	44	9N	4	5	E	
Alessándria	46	44	54N	8	37	E	
Ålesund	65	62	28N	6	12	E	
Aleutian Is.	142	52	0N	175	0W		
Alexander Arch.	143	57	0N	135	0W		
Alexander City	169	32	58N	85	57W		
Alexandra, Australia	117	37	8S	145	40	E	
Alexandra, N.Z.	123	45	14S	169	25	E	
Alexandretta = İskenderun	80	36	32N	36	10	E	
Alexandria = El Iskandarîya	128	31	0N	30	0	E	
Alexandria, La., U.S.A.	168	31	20N	92	30W		
Alexandria, Va., U.S.A.	164	38	47N	77	1W		
Alexandrina, L.	119	35	25S	139	10	E	
Alexandroúpolis	55	40	50N	25	54	E	
Alexis Creek	154	52	10N	123	20W		
Alfreton	29	53	6N	1	22W		
Algarve	50	36	58N	8	20W		
Alger	127	36	42N	3	8	E	
Algeria ■	127	35	10N	3	11	E	
Algiers = Alger	127	36	42N	3	8	E	
Algoa B.	136	33	50S	25	45	E	
Alhambra	173	34	2N	118	10W		
Alicante	51	38	23N	0	30W		
Alice Springs	114	23	40S	133	50	E	
Aligarh	89	27	55N	78	10	E	
Alipur Duar	92	26	30N	89	35	E	
Aliquippa	164	40	38N	80	18W		
Alkmaar	40	52	37N	4	45	E	
Allahabad	92	25	25N	81	58	E	
Allegheny Mts.	165	38	0N	80	0W		
Allen, Bog of	35	53	15N	7	0W		
Allende	174	28	20N	100	51W		
Allentown	164	40	36N	75	30W		
Alleppey	90	9	30N	76	28	E	
Aller ⟶	42	52	57N	9	10	E	
Allier ⟶	37	46	57N	3	4	E	
Alloa	31	56	7N	3	49W		
Alma, Canada	148	48	35N	71	40W		
Alma, U.S.A.	167	43	25N	84	40W		
Alma Ata	71	43	15N	76	57	E	
Almada	50	38	40N	9	9W		
Almelo	41	52	22N	6	42	E	
Almería	51	36	52N	2	27W		
Almirante	179	9	10N	82	30W		
Alor	113	8	15S	124	30	E	
Alor Setar	96	6	7N	100	22	E	
Alpena	150	45	6N	83	24W		
Alphen	40	51	29N	4	58	E	
Alpine	161	30	25N	103	35W		
Alps	16	47	0N	8	0	E	
Alsace	37	48	15N	7	25	E	
Alsask	152	51	21N	109	59W		
Alston	28	54	48N	2	26W		
Alta Gracia	190	31	40S	64	30W		
Altagracia	184	10	45N	71	30W		
Altai = Aerht'ai Shan	100	46	40N	92	45	E	
Altamaha ⟶	170	31	19N	81	17W		
Altamira	188	3	12S	52	10W		
Alto Adige = Trentino-Alto Adige □	47	46	30N	11	0	E	
Alton	166	38	55N	90	5W		
Altoona	164	40	32N	78	24W		
Altun Shan	100	38	30N	88	0	E	
Alvarado	177	18	46N	95	46W		
Älvsborgs län □	60	58	30N	12	30	E	
Alwar	89	27	38N	76	34	E	
Alxa Zuoqi	98	38	50N	105	40	E	
Am-Timan	129	11	0N	20	10	E	
Amadjuak	146	64	0N	72	39W		
Amadjuak L.	146	65	0N	71	8W		

Name	Page	Lat °	Lat ′	N/S	Lon °	Lon ′	E/W
Amagasaki	106	34	42N		135	20	E
Amagi	108	33	25N		130	39	E
Amakusa-Nada	108	32	35N		130	5	E
Amalner	91	21	5N		75	5	E
Amapá	185	2	5N		50	50W	
Amapá □	185	1	40N		52	0W	
Amarillo	161	35	14N		101	46W	
Amasya	80	40	40N		35	50	E
Amatitlán	177	14	29N		90	38W	
Amazon = Amazonas →	185	0	5S		50	0W	
Amazonas □	185	4	0S		62	0W	
Amazonas →	185	0	5S		50	0W	
Ambala	89	30	23N		76	56	E
Ambato	184	1	5S		78	42W	
Ambikapur	92	23	15N		83	15	E
Ambleside	28	54	26N		2	58W	
Ambo	186	10	5S		76	10W	
Ambon	113	3	35S		128	20	E
Amboyna I.	112	7	50N		112	50	E
Amderma	69	69	45N		61	30	E
Ameca	175	20	33N		104	2W	
Ameca, R. →	175	20	41N		105	18W	
Ameland	41	53	27N		5	45	E
American Highland	14	73	0S		75	0	E
American Samoa ■	123	14	20S		170	40W	
Americus	170	32	0N		84	10W	
Amersfoort	40	52	9N		5	23	E
Amery	143	56	34N		94	3W	
Ames	166	42	0N		93	40W	
Amga →	75	62	38N		134	32	E
Amgu	75	45	45N		137	15	E
Amgun →	75	52	56N		139	38	E
Amherst	148	45	48N		64	8W	
Amherstburg	150	42	6N		83	6W	
Amiens	38	49	54N		2	16	E
Amlwch	26	53	24N		4	21W	
'Ammān	80	31	57N		35	52	E
Amorgós	55	36	50N		25	57	E
Amos	151	48	35N		78	5W	
Amoy = Xiamen	99	24	25N		118	4	E
Amravati	91	20	55N		77	45	E
Amreli	91	21	35N		71	17	E
Amritsar	89	31	35N		74	57	E
Amsterdam, Neths.	40	52	23N		4	54	E
Amsterdam, U.S.A.	164	42	58N		74	10W	
Amudarya →	70	43	40N		59	0	E
Amundsen Gulf	145	71	0N		124	0W	
Amundsen Sea	15	72	0S		115	0W	
Amur →	75	52	56N		141	10	E
An Nafūd	82	28	15N		41	0	E
An Najaf	84	32	3N		44	15	E
An Nāşirīyah	84	31	0N		46	15	E
An Nhon	95	13	55N		109	7	E
An Nu'ayrīyah	84	27	30N		48	30	E
An Uaimh	34	53	39N		6	40W	
Anabar →	72	73	8N		113	36	E
Anaconda	163	46	7N		113	0W	
Anacortes	171	48	30N		122	40W	
Anadolu	80	38	0N		30	0	E
Anadyr →	73	64	55N		176	5	E
Anadyrskiy Zaliv	73	64	0N		180	0	E
Anaheim	173	33	50N		118	0W	
Anambas Is.	111	3	20N		106	30	E
Anamur	80	36	8N		32	58	E
Anan	109	33	54N		134	40	E
Anápolis	188	16	15S		48	50W	
Anārak	85	33	25N		53	40	E
Anatolia = Anadolu	80	38	0N		30	0	E
Añatuya	190	28	20S		62	50W	
Anchorage	142	61	10N		149	50W	
Anchuma, Nevada	187	16	0S		68	50W	
Ancona	47	43	37N		13	30	E
Ancud	192	42	0S		73	50W	
Ancud, G. de	192	42	0S		73	0W	
Åndalsnes	65	62	35N		7	43	E
Andalucía □	50	37	35N		5	0W	
Andalusia	169	31	19N		86	30W	
Andalusia □ = Andalucía □	50	37	35N		5	0W	
Andaman Is.	94	12	30N		92	30	E
Andaman Sea	94	13	0N		96	0	E
Andaman Str.	94	12	15N		92	20	E
Andelys, Les	39	49	15N		1	25	E
Anderson, Ind., U.S.A.	167	40	5N		85	40W	
Anderson, S.C., U.S.A.	165	34	32N		82	40W	
Andes, Cord. de los	182	20	0S		68	0W	
Andhra Pradesh □	91	16	0N		79	0	E
Andikíthira	55	35	52N		23	15	E
Andizhan	71	41	10N		72	0	E
Andorra ■	36	42	30N		1	30	E
Andover	24	51	13N		1	29W	
Andreanof Is.	142	52	0N		178	0W	
Andrewilla	118	26	31S		139	17	E
Ándria	49	41	13N		16	17	E
Andropov = Rybinsk	68	58	5N		38	50	E
Ándros	55	37	50N		24	57	E
Andros I.	178	24	30N		78	0W	
Angara →	74	58	30N		97	0	E
Angarsk	74	52	30N		104	0	E
Angaston	119	34	30S		139	8	E
Ånge	66	62	31N		15	35	E
Ängelholm	61	56	15N		12	58	E
Angels Camp	172	38	8N		120	30W	
Ångerman →	66	64	0N		17	20	E
Angers	36	47	30N		0	35W	
Angkor	95	13	22N		103	50	E
Anglesey	26	53	17N		4	20W	
Angmagssalik	147	65	40N		37	20W	
Angol	190	37	56S		72	45W	
Angola ■	134	12	0S		18	0	E
Angoulême	36	45	39N		0	10	E
Angoumois	36	45	50N		0	25	E
Anguilla	180	18	14N		63	-5W	
Angus, Braes of	33	56	51N		3	10W	
Anhui □	99	32	0N		117	0	E
Anhwei □ = Anhui □	99	32	0N		117	0	E
Anin	94	15	36N		97	50	E
Anjō	106	34	57N		137	5	E
Anjou	36	47	20N		0	15W	
Anju	98	39	36N		125	40	E
Ankang	99	32	40N		109	1	E
Ankara	80	40	0N		32	54	E
Ann Arbor	167	42	17N		83	45W	
Annaba	127	36	50N		7	46	E
Annam = Trung-Phan	95	16	0N		108	0	E
Annamitique, Chaîne	95	17	0N		106	0	E
Annan	31	55	0N		3	17W	
Annapolis	164	39	0N		76	30W	
Annecy	37	45	55N		6	8	E
Anniston	169	33	45N		85	50W	
Annobón	131	1	25S		5	36	E
Annonay	37	45	15N		4	40	E
Annotto Bay	180	18	17N		77	3W	
Anqing	99	30	30N		117	3	E
Anse, L'	150	46	47N		88	28W	
Anshan	98	41	3N		122	58	E
Anshun	99	26	18N		105	57	E
Anstruther	31	56	14N		2	40W	
Antabamba	186	14	40S		73	0W	
Antakya	80	36	14N		36	10	E
Antalya	80	36	52N		30	45	E
Antalya Körfezi	80	36	15N		31	30	E
Antananarivo	137	18	55S		47	31	E
Antarctic Pen.	14	67	0S		60	0W	
Antarctica	14	90	0S		0	0	E
Anti Atlas	126	30	0N		8	30W	
Antibes	37	43	34N		7	6	E
Anticosti, Î. d'	148	49	30N		63	0W	
Antigo	150	45	8N		89	5W	
Antigua, Guatemala	177	14	34N		90	41W	
Antigua, W. Indies	180	17	0N		61	50W	
Antigua and Barbuda ■	180	17	20N		61	48W	
Antilla	178	20	40N		75	50W	
Antioch	172	38	7N		121	45W	
Antioquia	184	6	40N		75	55W	
Antipodes Is.	11	49	45S		178	40	E
Antofagasta	190	23	50S		70	30W	
Antrim	34	54	43N		6	13W	
Antrim, Mts. of	34	54	57N		6	8W	
Antsiranana	137	12	25S		49	20	E
Antwerp = Antwerpen	42	51	13N		4	25	E
Antwerpen	42	51	13N		4	25	E
Anvers = Antwerpen	42	51	13N		4	25	E

Name	Map	Lat °	Lat ′	Long °	Long ′
Anvik	142	62	37N	160	20W
Anxious B.	119	33	24S	134	45 E
Anyang	98	36	5N	114	21 E
Anzhero-Sudzhensk	71	56	10N	86	0 E
Ánzio	46	41	28N	12	37 E
Aoga-Shima	105	32	28N	139	46 E
Aomori	103	40	45N	140	45 E
Apalachee B.	170	30	0N	84	0W
Apalachicola	170	29	40N	85	0W
Apalachicola →	170	29	40N	85	0W
Aparri	112	18	22N	121	38 E
Apeldoorn	41	52	13N	5	57 E
Apennines	16	44	20N	10	20 E
Apizaco	177	19	25N	98	9W
Aplao	186	16	0S	72	40W
Apolo	187	14	30S	68	30W
Apostle Is.	150	47	0N	90	30W
Apostolos Andreas, C.	80	35	42N	34	35 E
Appalachian Mts.	138	38	0N	80	0W
Appingedam	41	53	19N	6	51 E
Appleby	28	54	35N	2	29W
Appleton	167	44	17N	88	25W
Apulia = Púglia □	49	41	0N	16	30 E
Apure →	184	7	37N	66	25W
Aqabah = Al 'Aqabah	80	29	31N	35	0 E
Aqtöbe	70	50	17N	57	10 E
Aquidauana	188	20	30S	55	50W
Áquila, L'	47	42	21N	13	24 E
Aquiles Serdán	174	28	36N	105	53W
Ar Riyāḍ	83	24	41N	46	42 E
Ar Ruṭbah	81	33	0N	40	15 E
Ara	92	25	35N	84	32 E
Arab, Bahr el →	129	9	50N	29	0 E
Arab, Shatt al	84	30	0N	48	31 E
Arabia	76	25	0N	45	0 E
Arabian Gulf = Gulf, The	85	27	0N	50	0 E
Arabian Sea	76	16	0N	65	0 E
Aracaju	189	10	55S	37	4W
Aracati	189	4	30S	37	44W
Araçatuba	188	21	10S	50	30W
Arad	56	46	10N	21	20 E
Arafura Sea	113	9	0S	135	0 E
Aragón □	51	41	25N	1	0W
Araguacema	188	8	50S	49	20W
Araguaia →	188	5	21S	48	41W
Araguari	188	18	38S	48	11W
Arāk	84	34	0N	49	40 E
Arakan Coast	93	19	0N	94	0 E
Arakan Yoma	93	20	0N	94	40 E
Araks = Aras, Rūd-e →	81	39	10N	47	10 E
Aral Sea = Aralskoye More	70	44	30N	60	0 E
Aralsk	70	46	50N	61	20 E
Aralskoye More	70	44	30N	60	0 E
Aran I.	34	55	0N	8	30W
Aran Is.	35	53	5N	9	42W
Aranjuez	50	40	1N	3	40W
Aransas Pass	158	27	55N	97	9W
Arao	108	32	59N	130	25 E
Araraquara	188	21	50S	48	0W
Ararat	119	37	16S	143	0 E
Ararat, Mt. = Ağri Daği	81	39	50N	44	15 E
Aras, Rūd-e →	81	39	10N	47	10 E
Araya, Pen. de	185	10	40N	64	0W
Arbīl	81	36	15N	44	5 E
Arbroath	31	56	34N	2	35W
Arcachon	36	44	40N	1	10W
Arcadia	170	27	20N	81	50W
Archangel = Arkhangelsk	69	64	40N	41	0 E
Arcot	90	12	53N	79	20 E
Arctic Bay	146	73	1N	85	7W
Arctic Ocean	12	78	0N	160	0W
Arctic Red River	144	67	15N	134	0W
Ardabīl	81	38	15N	48	18 E
Ardennes	42	50	0N	5	10 E
Ardgour	32	56	45N	5	25W
Ardlethan	117	34	22S	146	53 E
Ardmore	168	34	10N	97	5W
Ardnacrusha	35	52	43N	8	38W
Ardnamurchan, Pt. of	32	56	44N	6	14W
Ards Pen.	34	54	30N	5	25W
Arecibo	180	18	29N	66	42W
Arequipa	187	16	20S	71	30W
Arezzo	46	43	28N	11	50 E
Argentan	39	48	45N	0	1W
Argentário, Mte.	46	42	23N	11	11 E
Argentina ■	190	35	0S	66	0W
Argentino, L.	192	50	10S	73	0W
Árgos	54	37	40N	22	43 E
Argostólion	54	38	12N	20	33 E
Argun →	74	53	20N	121	28 E
Århus	61	56	8N	10	11 E
Arica, Chile	187	18	32S	70	20W
Arica, Colombia	184	2	0S	71	50W
Arida	106	34	5N	135	8 E
Arima	180	10	38N	61	17W
Ario de Rosales	175	19	12N	101	43W
Aripuanã	187	9	25S	60	30W
Aripuanã →	187	5	7S	60	25W
Ariquemes	187	9	55S	63	6W
Arisaig	32	56	55N	5	50W
Aristazabal I.	154	52	40N	129	10W
Arizona □	160	34	20N	111	30W
Arjona	184	10	14N	75	22W
Arkadelphia	168	34	5N	93	0W
Arkansas □	168	35	0N	92	30W
Arkansas →	168	33	48N	91	4W
Arkansas City	158	37	4N	97	3W
Arkhangelsk	69	64	40N	41	0 E
Arklow	35	52	48N	6	10W
Arkticheskiy, Mys	72	81	10N	95	0 E
Arles	37	43	41N	4	40 E
Arlington	164	38	52N	77	5W
Armagh	34	54	22N	6	40W
Armavir	70	45	2N	41	7 E
Armenia	184	4	35N	75	45W
Armenia ■	70	40	0N	41	0 E
Armentières	38	50	40N	2	50 E
Armidale	116	30	30S	151	40 E
Armstrong	155	50	25N	119	10W
Arnaouti, C.	80	35	6N	32	17 E
Arnaud →	146	59	59N	69	46W
Arnhem	41	51	58N	5	55 E
Arnhem, C.	115	12	20S	137	30 E
Arnhem Land	114	13	10S	134	30 E
Arnprior	151	45	26N	76	21W
Arran	30	55	34N	5	12W
Arras	38	50	17N	2	46 E
Arriaga	177	16	14N	93	54W
Árta	54	39	8N	21	2 E
Artigas	191	30	20S	56	30W
Artois	38	50	20N	2	30 E
Aru, Kepulauan	113	6	0S	134	30 E
Arua	132	3	1N	30	58 E
Aruanã	188	14	54S	51	10W
Aruba	181	12	30N	70	0W
Arusha	135	3	20S	36	40 E
Arvida	148	48	25N	71	14W
Arys	71	42	26N	68	48 E
'As Saffānīyah	84	28	5N	48	50 E
As Samāwah	84	31	15N	45	15 E
As Sulaymānīyah	83	24	9N	47	18 E
As Sumaymānīyah	81	35	35N	45	29 E
As Suwaydā'	80	32	40N	36	30 E
As Şuwayrah	84	32	55N	45	0 E
Asahi	107	35	43N	140	39 E
Asahi-Gawa →	109	34	36N	133	58 E
Asahigawa	103	43	46N	142	22 E
Asama-Yama	107	36	24N	138	31 E
Asamankese	130	5	50N	0	40W
Asansol	92	23	40N	87	1 E
Asbestos	148	45	47N	71	58W
Ascension I.	125	8	0S	14	15W
Áscoli Piceno	47	42	51N	13	34 E
Aseb	133	13	0N	42	40 E
Ash Shām, Bādiyat	80	32	0N	40	0 E
Ash Shāmīyah	84	31	55N	44	35 E
Ash Shāriqah	85	25	23N	55	26 E
Ash Shaṭrah	84	31	30N	46	10 E
Ashburton	123	43	53S	171	48 E
Ashby-de-la-Zouch	28	52	45N	1	29W
Ashcroft	155	50	40N	121	20W
Asheboro	165	35	43N	79	46W

Place	Ref	Lat	Long
Asheville	165	35 39N	82 30W
Ashford, Australia	116	29 15S	151 3 E
Ashford, U.K.	25	51 8N	0 53 E
Ashikaga	107	36 28N	139 29 E
Ashizuri-Zaki	109	32 44N	133 0 E
Ashkhabad	70	38 0N	57 50 E
Ashland, Kans., U.S.A.	156	37 13N	99 43W
Ashland, Ky., U.S.A.	165	38 25N	82 40W
Ashland, Oreg., U.S.A.	171	42 10N	122 38W
Ashland, Wis., U.S.A.	150	46 40N	90 52W
Ashq'elon	80	31 42N	34 35 E
Ashtabula	164	41 52N	80 50W
Ashton-under-Lyne	28	53 30N	2 8W
Ashuanipi, L.	147	52 45N	66 15W
Asinara I.	48	41 5N	8 15 E
'Asīr □	82	18 40N	42 30 E
Asir, Ras	133	11 55N	51 10 E
Asmara = Asmera	132	15 19N	38 55 E
Asmera	132	15 19N	38 55 E
Aso	108	33 0N	131 5 E
Aso-Zan	108	32 53N	131 6 E
Aspiring, Mt.	123	44 23S	168 46 E
Assam □	93	26 0N	93 0 E
Assen	41	53 0N	6 35 E
Assiniboia	152	49 40N	105 59W
Assiniboine →	153	49 53N	97 8W
Assisi	46	43 4N	12 36 E
Asti	46	44 54N	8 11 E
Astipálaia	55	36 32N	26 22 E
Astoria	171	46 16N	123 50W
Astrakhan	70	46 25N	48 5 E
Asturias □	50	43 15N	6 0W
Asunción	191	25 10S	57 30W
Aswân	128	24 4N	32 57 E
Asyût	128	27 11N	31 4 E
At Ţafīlah	80	30 45N	35 30 E
At Ta'if	82	21 5N	40 27 E
Atacama, Desierto de	190	24 0S	69 20W
Atalaya	186	10 45S	73 50W
Atami	107	35 5N	139 4 E
Atbara	129	17 42N	33 59 E
'Atbara →	129	17 40N	33 56 E
Atchafalaya B.	168	29 30N	91 20W
Atchison	166	39 40N	95 10W
Athabasca	155	54 45N	113 20W
Athabasca →	145	58 40N	110 50W
Athabasca, L.	145	59 15N	109 15W
Athenry	35	53 18N	8 45W
Athens = Athínai	55	37 58N	23 46 E
Athens, Ala., U.S.A.	169	34 49N	86 58W
Athens, Ga., U.S.A.	165	33 56N	83 24W
Athens, Ohio, U.S.A.	167	39 25N	82 6W
Athens, Tenn., U.S.A.	169	35 45N	84 38W
Athens, Tex., U.S.A.	168	32 11N	95 48W
Atherton	121	17 17S	145 30 E
Athínai	55	37 58N	23 46 E
Athlone	34	53 26N	7 57W
Atholl, Forest of	33	56 51N	3 50W
Áthos	55	40 9N	24 22 E
Athy	35	53 0N	7 0W
Atico	186	16 14S	73 40W
Atlanta	170	33 50N	84 24W
Atlantic	166	41 25N	95 0W
Atlantic City	164	39 25N	74 25W
Atlantic Ocean	9	0 0	20 0W
Atlas Mts. = Haut Atlas	126	32 30N	5 0W
Atmore	169	31 2N	87 30W
Atsugi	107	35 25N	139 21 E
Atsumi	106	34 35N	137 4 E
Atsumi-Wan	106	34 44N	137 13 E
Attawapiskat →	140	52 57N	82 18W
Attleboro	164	41 56N	71 18W
Atyraū	70	47 5N	52 0 E
Aubagne	37	43 17N	5 37 E
Aube →	37	48 34N	3 43 E
Aubenas	37	44 37N	4 24 E
Auburn, Ala., U.S.A.	169	32 37N	85 30W
Auburn, N.Y., U.S.A.	164	42 57N	76 39W
Auckland	122	36 52S	174 46 E
Auckland Is.	15	50 40S	166 5 E
Aude →	37	43 13N	3 14 E
Augsburg	43	48 22N	10 54 E
Augusta, Ga., U.S.A.	170	33 29N	81 59W
Augusta, Maine, U.S.A.	148	44 20N	69 46W
Aunis	36	46 5N	0 50W
Aurangabad	91	19 50N	75 23 E
Aurillac	37	44 55N	2 26 E
Aurora	167	41 42N	88 12W
Aust-Agder fylke □	60	58 55N	7 40 E
Austin, Minn., U.S.A.	166	43 37N	92 59W
Austin, Tex., U.S.A.	161	30 20N	97 45W
Austral Is. = Tubuai Is.	123	25 0S	150 0W
Australia ■	114	23 0S	135 0 E
Australian Alps	117	36 30S	148 30 E
Australian Cap. Terr. □	117	35 30S	149 0 E
Austria ■	45	47 0N	14 0 E
Autlán	175	19 40N	104 30W
Auvergne	37	45 20N	3 15 E
Auxerre	39	47 48N	3 32 E
Avalon Pen.	149	47 30N	53 20W
Aveiro	185	3 10S	55 5W
Avellaneda	190	34 50S	58 10W
Aves, I. de	181	15 45N	63 55W
Avesnes-sur-Helpe	38	50 8N	3 55 E
Aveyron →	36	44 7N	1 5 E
Aviemore	33	57 11N	3 50W
Avignon	37	43 57N	4 50 E
Ávila	50	40 39N	4 43W
Avon □	27	51 30N	2 40W
Avon →, Avon, U.K.	24	51 30N	2 43W
Avon →, Hants., U.K.	24	50 44N	1 45W
Avonmouth	27	51 30N	2 42W
Avranches	36	48 40N	1 20W
Awaji-Shima	109	34 30N	134 50 E
Aweil	129	8 42N	27 20 E
Axel Heiberg I.	12	80 0N	90 0W
Axminster	27	50 47N	3 1W
Ayabe	106	35 20N	135 20 E
Ayacucho	186	13 0S	74 0W
Ayios Evstrátios	55	39 34N	24 58 E
Ayon, Ostrov	73	69 50N	169 0 E
Ayr, Australia	121	19 35S	147 25 E
Ayr, U.K.	31	55 28N	4 37W
Ayre, Pt. of	28	54 27N	4 21W
Aytos	53	42 42N	27 16 E
Ayutla	177	16 58N	99 17W
Az Zahrān	84	26 10N	50 7 E
Az Zubayr	84	30 20N	47 50 E
Azamgarh	92	26 5N	83 13 E
Azbine = Aïr	127	18 30N	8 0 E
Azerbaijan ■	70	40 20N	48 0 E
Azores	126	38 44N	29 0W
Azov Sea = Azovskoye More	68	46 0N	36 30 E
Azovskoye More	68	46 0N	36 30 E
Azúa de Compostela	180	18 25N	70 44W
Azuero, Pen. de	179	7 30N	80 30W
Azul	190	36 42S	59 43W

B

Place	Ref	Lat	Long
Ba Ngoi = Cam Lam	95	11 54N	109 10 E
Baarn	40	52 12N	5 17 E
Bāb el Mândeb	133	12 35N	43 25 E
Babahoyo	184	1 40S	79 30W
Babinda	121	17 20S	145 56 E
Babine L.	154	54 48N	126 0W
Bābol	86	36 40N	52 50 E
Babuyan Is.	112	19 10N	121 40 E
Babylon	84	32 40N	44 30 E
Bac Ninh	95	21 13N	106 4 E
Bac Phan	95	22 0N	105 0 E
Bac Quang	95	22 30N	104 48 E
Bacabal	188	4 15S	44 45W
Bacău	57	46 35N	26 55 E
Back →	145	65 10N	104 0W
Bacolod	112	10 40N	122 57 E
Bad Lands	163	43 40N	102 10W
Badajoz	50	38 50N	6 59W
Badakhshān □	87	36 30N	71 0 E

Name	Page	Lat°	Lat′	N/S	Long°	Long′	E/W
Badalona	51	41	26N		2	15	E
Badanah	82	30	58N		41	30	E
Baden-Baden	42	48	45N		8	15	E
Baden-Württemberg □	42	48	40N		9	0	E
Bādghīsāt □	87	35	0N		63	0	E
Badin	88	24	38N		68	54	E
Baffin □	146	70	0N		80	0	W
Baffin B.	13	72	0N		64	0	W
Baffin I.	146	68	0N		75	0	W
Bafra	80	41	34N		35	54	E
Bäft	85	29	15N		56	38	E
Bagé	191	31	20S		54	15	W
Baghdād	84	33	20N		44	30	E
Baghlan	87	36	12N		69	0	E
Baghlān □	87	36	0N		68	30	E
Bahamas ■	178	24	0N		75	0	W
Baharampur	92	24	2N		88	27	E
Bahawalpur	89	29	24N		71	40	E
Bahía = Salvador	189	13	0S		38	30	W
Bahía □	189	12	0S		42	0	W
Bahía Blanca	190	38	35S		62	13	W
Bahr el Jebel →	129	7	30N		30	30	E
Bahraich	92	27	38N		81	37	E
Bahrain ■	85	26	0N		50	35	E
Baia Mare	56	47	40N		23	35	E
Baie Comeau	148	49	12N		68	10	W
Baie-St-Paul	148	47	28N		70	32	W
Ba'iji	81	35	0N		43	30	E
Baikal, L. = Baykal, Oz.	74	53	0N		108	0	E
Baile Atha Cliath = Dublin	35	53	20N		6	18	W
Bailleul	38	50	44N		2	41	E
Bainbridge	170	30	53N		84	34	W
Baird Mts.	142	67	10N		160	15	W
Bairnsdale	117	37	48S		147	36	E
Baiyin	98	36	45N		104	14	E
Baja	59	46	12N		18	59	E
Baja California	174	31	10N		115	12	W
Baja California Norte □	174	30	0N		115	0	W
Baja California Sur □	174	25	50N		111	50	W
Bajimba, Mt.	116	29	17S		152	6	E
Baker	171	44	50N		117	55	W
Baker I.	122	0	10N		176	35	W
Baker Lake	145	64	20N		96	3	W
Bakersfield	173	35	25N		119	0	W
Bākhtarān	84	34	23N		47	0	E
Bakony Forest = Bakony Hegység	59	47	10N		17	30	E
Bakony Hegység	59	47	10N		17	30	E
Baku	70	40	25N		49	45	E
Bala	26	52	54N		3	36	W
Balabac, Str.	112	7	53N		117	5	E
Balabakk	80	34	0N		36	10	E
Balaghat	91	21	49N		80	12	E
Balaghat Ra.	91	18	50N		76	30	E
Balaklava	119	34	7S		138	22	E
Balakovo	68	52	4N		47	55	E
Balaton	59	46	50N		17	40	E
Balboa	179	9	0N		79	30	W
Balbriggan	34	53	35N		6	10	W
Balcarce	190	38	0S		58	10	W
Balclutha	123	46	15S		169	45	E
Baldy Peak	161	33	50N		109	30	W
Baleares, Islas	51	39	30N		3	0	E
Balearic Is. = Baleares, Islas	51	39	30N		3	0	E
Bali	111	8	20S		115	0	E
Balikesir	80	39	35N		27	58	E
Balikpapan	111	1	10S		116	55	E
Balkan Mts. = Stara Planina	53	43	15N		23	0	E
Balkan Pen.	17	42	0N		22	0	E
Balkh □	87	36	30N		67	0	E
Balkhash	71	46	50N		74	50	E
Balkhash, Ozero	71	46	0N		74	50	E
Ballachulish	32	56	40N		5	10	W
Ballarat	117	37	33S		143	50	E
Ballard, L.	120	29	20S		120	10	E
Ballater	33	57	2N		3	2	W
Ballina, Australia	116	28	50S		153	31	E
Ballina, Mayo, Ireland	34	54	7N		9	10	W
Ballina, Tipp., Ireland	35	52	49N		8	27	W
Ballinasloe	35	53	20N		8	12	W
Ballinrobe	34	53	36N		9	13	W
Ballycastle	34	55	12N		6	15	W
Ballymena	34	54	53N		6	18	W
Ballymoney	34	55	5N		6	30	W
Ballyshannon	34	54	30N		8	10	W
Balmaceda	192	46	0S		71	50	W
Balmoral	33	57	3N		3	13	W
Balrampur	92	27	30N		82	20	E
Balranald	117	34	38S		143	33	E
Balsas, R. →	177	17	55N		102	10	W
Baltic Sea	16	56	0N		20	0	E
Baltimore	164	39	18N		76	37	W
Baluchistan □	88	27	30N		65	0	E
Bamako	130	12	34N		7	55	W
Bambari	129	5	40N		20	35	E
Bamberg	43	49	54N		10	53	E
Bāmiān □	87	35	0N		67	0	E
Ban Aranyaprathet	95	13	41N		102	30	E
Ban Don = Surat Thani	96	9	6N		99	20	E
Ban Houei Sai	95	20	22N		100	32	E
Ban Khe Bo	95	19	10N		104	39	E
Ban Khun Yuam	94	18	49N		97	57	E
Ban Nong Pling	94	15	40N		100	10	E
Ban Phai	95	16	4N		102	44	E
Banaras = Varanasi	92	25	22N		83	0	E
Banbridge	34	54	21N		6	17	W
Banbury	25	52	4N		1	21	W
Bancroft	151	45	3N		77	51	W
Banda	91	25	30N		80	26	E
Banda, Kepulauan	113	4	37S		129	50	E
Banda Aceh	111	5	35N		95	20	E
Banda Banda, Mt.	116	31	10S		152	28	E
Banda Sea	113	6	0S		130	0	E
Bandar = Machilipatnam	92	16	12N		81	8	E
Bandār 'Abbās	85	27	15N		56	15	E
Bandar-e Anzalī	81	37	30N		49	30	E
Bandar-e Khomeyni	84	30	30N		49	5	E
Bandar-e Lengeh	85	26	35N		54	58	E
Bandar-e Nakhīlū	85	26	58N		53	30	E
Bandar-e Torkeman	86	37	0N		54	10	E
Bandar Seri Begawan	112	' 4	52N		115	0	E
Bandeira, Pico da	188	20	26S		41	47	W
Bandırma	80	40	20N		28	0	E
Bandon	35	51	44N		8	45	W
Bandung	111	6	54S		107	36	E
Banes	178	21	0N		75	42	W
Banff, Canada	155	51	10N		115	34	W
Banff, U.K.	33	57	40N		2	32	W
Bangalore	90	12	59N		77	40	E
Bangassou	129	4	55N		23	7	E
Banggai	113	1	40S		123	30	E
Banghāzī	128	32	11N		20	3	E
Bangka, Selat	111	2	30S		105	30	E
Bangkok	94	13	45N		100	35	E
Bangladesh ■	92	24	0N		90	0	E
Bangor, N. Ireland, U.K.	34	54	40N		5	40	W
Bangor, Wales, U.K.	26	53	13N		4	9	W
Bangor, U.S.A.	148	44	48N		68	42	W
Bangui	131	4	23N		18	35	E
Bangweulu, L.	135	11	0S		30	0	E
Bani	180	18	16N		70	22	W
Banja Luka	52	44	49N		17	11	E
Banjarmasin	111	3	20S		114	35	E
Banjul	130	13	28N		16	40	W
Bankipore	92	25	35N		85	10	E
Banks I., B.C., Canada	154	53	20N		130	0	W
Banks I., N.W.T., Canada	145	73	15N		121	30	W
Banks Pen.	123	43	45S		173	15	E
Banks Str.	119	40	40S		148	10	E
Bann →	34	54	30N		6	31	W
Banning	173	33	58N		116	52	W
Bannockburn	31	56	5N		3	55	W
Bannu	89	33	0N		70	18	E
Bantry	35	51	40N		9	28	W
Baoding	98	38	50N		115	28	E
Baoji	99	34	20N		107	5	E
Baotou	98	40	32N		110	2	E
Ba'qūbah	81	33	45N		44	50	E
Bar	52	42	8N		19	8	E
Bar Harbor	148	44	15N		68	20	W
Baraboo	166	43	28N		89	46	W
Baracoa	178	20	20N		74	30	W

Name					
Barahona	180	18	13N	71	7W
Barail Range	93	25	15N	93	20 E
Baramula	89	34	15N	74	20 E
Baran	91	25	9N	76	40 E
Baranof I.	143	57	0N	135	10W
Baranovichi	68	53	10N	26	0 E
Barbacoas	184	1	45N	78	0W
Barbados ■	180	13	0N	59	30W
Barbuda I.	180	17	30N	61	40W
Barca, La	175	20	17N	102	34W
Barcaldine	121	23	43S	145	6 E
Barcelona, Spain	51	41	21N	2	10 E
Barcelona, Venezuela	185	10	10N	64	40W
Barcelos	185	1	0S	63	0W
Barddhaman	92	23	14N	87	39 E
Bardera	133	2	20N	42	27 E
Bardsey I.	26	52	46N	4	47W
Bareilly	89	28	22N	79	27 E
Barentin	38	49	33N	0	58 E
Barents Sea	13	73	0N	39	0 E
Bargara	121	24	50S	152	25 E
Bari	49	41	6N	16	52 E
Bari Doab	89	30	20N	73	0 E
Barīm	82	12	39N	43	25 E
Barinas	184	8	36N	70	15W
Barisal	92	22	45N	90	20 E
Barito →	111	4	0S	114	50 E
Barlee, L.	120	29	15S	119	30 E
Barletta	49	41	20N	16	17 E
Barmer	91	25	45N	71	20 E
Barmera	119	34	15S	140	28 E
Barmouth	26	52	44N	4	3W
Barnard Castle	28	54	33N	1	55W
Barnaul	71	53	20N	83	40 E
Barneveld	41	52	7N	5	36 E
Barnsley	28	53	33N	1	29W
Barnstaple	27	51	5N	4	3W
Baro	131	8	35N	6	18 E
Baroda = Vadodara	91	22	20N	73	10 E
Barpeta	93	26	20N	91	10 E
Barquísimeto	184	10	4N	69	19W
Barra	32	57	0N	7	30W
Barra Hd.	32	56	47N	7	40W
Barraba	116	30	21S	150	35 E
Barranca	186	10	45S	77	50W
Barrancabermeja	184	7	0N	73	50W
Barrancas	185	8	55N	62	5W
Barranqueras	190	27	30S	59	0W
Barranquilla	184	11	0N	74	50W
Barre	151	44	15N	72	30W
Barreiros	188	8	49S	35	12W
Barrhead	155	54	10N	114	24W
Barrie	151	44	24N	79	40W
Barrier Ra.	118	31	0S	141	30 E
Barrington Tops	116	32	6S	151	28 E
Barrow →	35	52	10N	6	57W
Barrow, Pt.	138	71	22N	156	30W
Barrow-in-Furness	28	54	8N	3	15W
Barry	27	51	23N	3	19W
Barry's Bay	151	45	29N	77	41W
Barsi	91	18	10N	75	50 E
Barstow	173	34	58N	117	2W
Bartica	185	6	25N	58	40W
Bartow	170	27	53N	81	49W
Basel	44	47	35N	7	35 E
Bashi Channel	99	21	15N	122	0 E
Bashkortostan □	69	54	0N	57	0 E
Basilan	112	6	35N	122	0 E
Basildon	25	51	34N	0	29 E
Basilicata □	49	40	30N	16	0 E
Basim = Washim	91	20	3N	77	0 E
Basle = Basel	44	47	35N	7	35 E
Basoka	134	1	16N	23	40 E
Basque Provinces = Vascongadas	50	42	50N	2	45W
Basra = Al Baṣrah	84	30	30N	47	50 E
Bass Rock	31	56	5N	2	40W
Bass Str.	117	39	15S	146	30 E
Bassano	155	50	48N	112	20W
Basse-Terre	180	16	0N	61	40W
Bassein	93	16	45N	94	30 E
Basseterre	180	17	17N	62	43W
Basti	92	26	52N	82	55 E
Bastia	36	42	40N	9	30 E
Batabanó	178	22	40N	82	20W
Batamay	74	63	30N	129	15 E
Batan Is.	112	20	25N	121	59 E
Batang	101	30	1N	99	0 E
Batavia	164	43	0N	78	10W
Batemans Bay	117	35	44S	150	11 E
Batesville	168	35	48N	91	40W
Bath, U.K.	27	51	22N	2	22W
Bath, Maine, U.S.A.	148	43	50N	69	49W
Bath, N.Y., U.S.A.	164	42	20N	77	17W
Bathurst = Banjul	130	13	28N	16	40W
Bathurst, Australia	117	33	25S	149	31 E
Bathurst, Canada	148	47	37N	65	43W
Bathurst, C.	145	70	34N	128	0W
Bathurst Inlet	145	66	50N	108	1W
Batlow	117	35	31S	148	9 E
Batman	81	37	55N	41	5 E
Batna	127	35	34N	6	15 E
Baton Rouge	168	30	30N	91	5W
Batopilas	174	27	1N	107	44W
Battambang	95	13	7N	103	12 E
Batticaloa	90	7	43N	81	45 E
Battle	25	50	55N	0	30 E
Battle Creek	167	42	20N	85	6W
Battle Harbour	147	52	16N	55	35W
Battleford	152	52	45N	108	15W
Batu Gajah	96	4	28N	101	3 E
Batu Is.	111	0	30S	98	25 E
Batumi	70	41	30N	41	30 E
Bauchi	131	10	22N	9	48 E
Bauru	188	22	10S	49	0W
Bavaria = Bayern □	43	49	7N	11	30 E
Bawdwin	93	23	5N	97	20 E
Bawean	111	5	46S	112	35 E
Bawku	130	11	3N	0	19W
Bay City	167	43	35N	83	51W
Bay Shore	164	40	44N	73	15W
Bayamo	178	20	20N	76	40W
Bayamón	180	18	24N	66	10W
Bayan Har Shan	101	34	0N	98	0 E
Bayan Hot = Alxa Zuoqi	98	38	50N	105	40 E
Bayern □	43	49	7N	11	30 E
Bayeux	36	49	17N	0	42W
Bayfield	150	43	34N	81	42W
Baykal, Oz.	74	53	0N	108	0 E
Baykonur	71	47	48N	65	50 E
Bayonne	36	43	30N	1	28W
Bayreuth	43	49	56N	11	35 E
Bayrūt	80	33	53N	35	31 E
Baytown	168	29	42N	94	57W
Beachy Head	25	50	44N	0	16 E
Beagle, Canal	192	55	0S	68	30W
Béarn	36	43	8N	0	36W
Beauce, Plaine de la	37	48	10N	1	45 E
Beaudesert	116	27	59S	153	0 E
Beaufort	170	32	25N	80	40W
Beaufort Sea	12	72	0N	140	0W
Beaugency	39	47	47N	1	38 E
Beauharnois	151	45	20N	73	52W
Beauly	33	57	29N	4	27W
Beaumaris	26	53	16N	4	7W
Beaumont	168	30	5N	94	8W
Beaumont-sur-Oise	39	49	9N	2	17 E
Beauséjour	153	50	5N	96	35W
Beauvais	38	49	25N	2	8 E
Beauval	142	55	9N	107	37W
Beaver →	142	66	20N	147	30W
Beaver →	152	55	26N	107	45W
Beaver Falls	164	40	44N	80	20W
Beaverlodge	155	55	11N	119	29W
Beawar	91	26	3N	74	18 E
Bečej	52	45	36N	20	3 E
Béchar	127	31	38N	2	18W
Beckley	165	37	50N	81	8W
Bedford, U.K.	25	52	8N	0	28W
Bedford, U.S.A.	167	38	50N	86	30W
Bedford □	25	52	4N	0	28W
Beenleigh	116	27	43S	153	10 E

Name						
Be'er Sheva'	80	31	15N	34	48	E
Beersheba = Be'er Sheva'	80	31	15N	34	48	E
Beeston	29	52	55N	1	11	W
Bega	117	36	41S	149	51	E
Behbehän	84	30	30N	50	15	E
Beibei	99	29	47N	106	22	E
Beihai	99	21	28N	109	6	E
Beijing	98	39	55N	116	20	E
Beira	137	19	50S	34	52	E
Beira-Alta	50	40	35N	7	35	W
Beira-Baixa	50	40	2N	7	30	W
Beira-Litoral	50	40	5N	8	30	W
Beirut = Bayrūt	80	33	53N	35	31	E
Bejaia	127	36	42N	5	2	E
Békéscsaba	59	46	40N	21	5	E
Bela	92	25	50N	82	0	E
Bela Crkva	52	44	55N	21	27	E
Belarus ■	68	53	30N	27	0	E
Belaya Tserkov	68	49	45N	30	10	E
Belcher Is.	140	56	15N	78	45	W
Belém	188	1	20S	48	30	W
Belfast, U.K.	34	54	35N	5	56	W
Belfast, U.S.A.	148	44	30N	69	0	W
Belfort	37	47	38N	6	50	E
Belgaum	91	15	55N	74	35	E
Belgium ■	42	50	30N	5	0	E
Belgorod	68	50	35N	36	35	E
Belgrade = Beograd	52	44	50N	20	37	E
Belitung	111	3	10S	107	50	E
Belize ■	177	17	0N	88	30	W
Belize City	177	17	25N	88	0	W
Bell Peninsula	146	63	50N	82	0	W
Bell Ville	190	32	40S	62	40	W
Bella Coola	154	52	25N	126	40	W
Bellaire	164	40	1N	80	46	W
Bellary	90	15	10N	76	56	E
Belle Fourche →	163	44	25N	102	19	W
Belle Glade	170	26	43N	80	38	W
Belle Isle	147	51	57N	55	25	W
Belle Isle, Str. of	141	51	30N	56	30	W
Bellefontaine	167	40	20N	83	45	W
Belleville, Canada	151	44	10N	77	23	W
Belleville, U.S.A.	166	38	30N	90	0	W
Bellevue	155	49	35N	114	22	W
Bellin	146	60	0N	70	0	W
Bellingham	171	48	45N	122	27	W
Bellingshausen Sea	14	66	0S	80	0	W
Belmont	117	33	4S	151	42	E
Belmopan	177	17	18N	88	30	W
Belo Horizonte	188	19	55S	43	56	W
Belogorsk	75	51	0N	128	20	E
Beloit	166	42	35N	89	0	W
Belomorsk	68	64	35N	34	30	E
Belovo	71	54	30N	86	0	E
Beloye More	69	66	30N	38	0	E
Beloye Ozero	68	45	15N	46	50	E
Belper	28	53	2N	1	29	W
Belukha	71	49	50N	86	50	E
Belyy, Ostrov	69	73	30N	71	0	E
Bemidji	156	47	30N	94	50	W
Ben Lomond, N.S.W., Australia	116	30	1S	151	40	E
Ben Lomond, Tas., Australia	119	41	38S	147	42	E
Ben Macdhui	33	57	4N	3	40	W
Ben More, Central, U.K.	32	56	23N	4	31	W
Ben More, Strath., U.K.	30	56	26N	6	2	W
Ben More Assynt	32	58	7N	4	51	W
Ben Nevis	32	56	48N	5	0	W
Benalla	117	36	30S	146	0	E
Benares = Varanasi	92	25	22N	83	0	E
Benbecula	32	57	26N	7	21	W
Benbonyathe, Mt.	118	30	25S	139	11	E
Bencubbin	120	30	48S	117	52	E
Bend	171	44	2N	121	15	W
Bendemeer	116	30	53S	151	8	E
Bender Beila	133	9	30N	50	48	E
Bendigo	117	36	40S	144	15	E
Benevento	49	41	7N	14	45	E
Bengal, Bay of	92	15	0N	90	0	E
Bengbu	99	32	58N	117	20	E
Benghazi = Banghāzī	128	32	11N	20	3	E
Benguela	134	12	37S	13	25	E
Beni →	187	10	23S	65	24	W
Beni Suef	128	29	5N	31	6	E
Benidorm	51	38	33N	0	9	W
Benin ■	131	10	0N	2	0	E
Benin, Bight of	131	5	0N	3	0	E
Benin City	131	6	20N	5	31	E
Benjamin Constant	187	4	40S	70	15	W
Bennett	144	59	56N	134	53	W
Bennettsville	165	34	38N	79	39	W
Benton	168	34	30N	92	35	W
Benue →	131	7	48N	6	46	E
Benxi	98	41	20N	123	48	E
Beograd	52	44	50N	20	37	E
Beppu	108	33	15N	131	30	E
Berau, Teluk	113	2	30S	132	30	E
Berber	129	18	0N	34	0	E
Berbera	133	10	30N	45	2	E
Berck-sur-Mer	38	50	25N	1	36	E
Berezniki	69	59	24N	56	46	E
Bérgamo	46	45	42N	9	40	E
Bergen, Neths.	40	52	40N	4	43	E
Bergen, Norway	60	60	23N	5	20	E
Bergen-op-Zoom	40	51	30N	4	18	E
Bergerac	36	44	51N	0	30	E
Berhala, Selat	111	1	0S	104	15	E
Berhampore = Baharampur	92	24	2N	88	27	E
Berhampur	92	19	15N	84	54	E
Bering Sea	142	58	0N	167	0	E
Bering Str.	142	66	0N	170	0	W
Berkeley	172	37	52N	122	20	W
Berkshire □	25	51	30N	1	20	W
Berkshire Downs	24	51	30N	1	30	W
Berlin, Germany	43	52	32N	13	24	E
Berlin, U.S.A.	148	44	29N	71	10	W
Bermuda ■	180	32	45N	65	0	W
Bern	44	46	57N	7	28	E
Bernay	39	49	5N	0	35	E
Berne = Bern	44	46	57N	7	28	E
Berri	119	34	14S	140	35	E
Berry	37	47	0N	2	0	E
Bertoua	131	4	30N	13	45	E
Berwick-upon-Tweed	31	55	47N	2	0	W
Berwyn Mts.	26	52	54N	3	26	W
Besançon	37	47	15N	6	0	E
Bessemer, Ala., U.S.A.	169	33	25N	86	57	W
Bessemer, Mich., U.S.A.	156	46	27N	90	0	W
Bethel	142	60	50N	161	50	W
Bethlehem	164	40	39N	75	24	W
Béthune	38	50	30N	2	38	E
Betsiboka →	137	16	3S	46	36	E
Beverley	29	53	52N	0	26	W
Beverly Hills	173	34	4N	118	29	W
Beverwijk	40	52	28N	4	38	E
Bexhill	24	50	51N	0	29	E
Beyneu	70	45	10N	55	3	E
Beyşehir Gölü	80	37	40N	31	45	E
Béziers	37	43	20N	3	12	E
Bezwada = Vijayawada	92	16	31N	80	39	E
Bhadravati	90	13	49N	75	40	E
Bhagalpur	92	25	10N	87	0	E
Bhakra Dam	89	31	30N	76	45	E
Bhandara	91	21	5N	79	42	E
Bhanrer Ra.	91	23	40N	79	45	E
Bharat = India ■	78	20	0N	78	0	E
Bharatpur	89	27	15N	77	30	E
Bharuch	91	21	47N	73	0	E
Bhatpara	92	22	50N	88	25	E
Bhaunagar = Bhavnagar	91	21	45N	72	10	E
Bhavnagar	91	21	45N	72	10	E
Bhilwara	91	25	25N	74	38	E
Bhima →	91	16	25N	77	17	E
Bhiwandi	91	19	20N	73	0	E
Bhiwani	89	28	50N	76	9	E
Bhopal	91	23	20N	77	30	E
Bhubaneshwar	92	20	15N	85	50	E
Bhusaval	91	21	3N	75	46	E
Bhutan ■	92	27	25N	90	30	E
Biafra, B. of = Bonny, Bight of	131	3	30N	9	20	E
Biała Podlaska	58	52	4N	23	6	E

Name	Page	Lat.	Long.
Białystok	58	53 10N	23 10 E
Biarritz	36	43 29N	1 33W
Bibai	103	43 19N	141 52 E
Bicester	25	51 53N	1 9W
Biche, L. la	155	54 50N	112 3W
Bidar	91	17 55N	77 35 E
Biddeford	148	43 30N	70 28W
Bideford	27	51 1N	4 13W
Bié, Planalto de	136	12 0S	16 0 E
Bieber	172	41 4N	121 6W
Biel	44	47 8N	7 14 E
Bielé Karpaty	59	49 5N	18 0 E
Bielefeld	42	52 2N	8 31 E
Bielsko-Biała	59	49 50N	19 2 E
Bien Hoa	95	10 57N	106 49 E
Bienne = Biel	44	47 8N	7 14 E
Bienville, L.	146	55 5N	72 40W
Big Belt Mts.	163	46 50N	111 30W
Big Cypress Swamp	170	26 12N	81 10W
Big Horn Mts. = Bighorn Mts.	163	44 30N	107 30W
Big Rapids	167	43 42N	85 27W
Big Sioux →	156	42 30N	96 25W
Big Spring	161	32 10N	101 25W
Big Stone Gap	165	36 52N	82 45W
Big Trout L.	153	53 40N	90 0W
Biggar, Canada	152	52 4N	108 0W
Biggar, U.K.	31	55 38N	3 31W
Bighorn →	163	46 9N	107 28W
Bighorn Mts.	163	44 30N	107 30W
Bihar	92	25 5N	85 40 E
Bihar □	92	25 0N	86 0 E
Bijagós, Arquipélago dos	130	11 15N	16 10W
Bijapur	91	16 50N	75 55 E
Bijeljina	52	44 46N	19 17 E
Bikaner	89	28 2N	73 18 E
Bikin	75	46 50N	134 20 E
Bilaspur	92	22 2N	82 15 E
Bilauk Taungdan	94	13 0N	99 0 E
Bilbao	50	43 16N	2 56W
Billingham	29	54 36N	1 18W
Billings	163	45 43N	108 29W
Billiton Is. = Belitung	111	3 10S	107 50 E
Bilma	127	18 50N	13 30 E
Biloela	121	24 24S	150 31 E
Biloxi	169	30 24N	88 53W
Bina-Etawah	91	24 13N	78 14 E
Bīnālūd, Kūh-e	86	36 30N	58 30 E
Bindi Bindi	120	30 37S	116 22 E
Bingara	116	29 52S	150 36 E
Bingerville	130	5 18N	3 49W
Bingham	148	45 5N	69 50W
Binghamton	164	42 9N	75 54W
Binh Dinh = An Nhon	95	13 55N	109 7 E
Binnaway	116	31 28S	149 24 E
Binzert = Bizerte	127	37 15N	9 50 E
Bioko	131	3 30N	8 40 E
Bir Mogrein	126	25 10N	11 25W
Birchip	119	35 56S	142 55 E
Bird I. = Aves, I. de	181	15 45N	63 55W
Birdum	114	15 39S	133 13 E
Birkenhead	28	53 24N	3 1W
Birmingham, U.K.	24	52 30N	1 55W
Birmingham, U.S.A.	169	33 31N	86 50W
Birobidzhan	75	48 50N	132 50 E
Birr	35	53 7N	7 55W
Bisai	106	35 16N	136 44 E
Biscay, B. of	36	45 0N	2 0W
Biscostasing	150	47 18N	82 9W
Bishkek	71	42 54N	74 46 E
Bishop Auckland	28	54 40N	1 40W
Bishop's Stortford	25	51 52N	0 11 E
Bismarck	163	46 49N	100 49W
Bismarck Arch.	115	2 30S	150 0 E
Bissagos = Bijagós, Arquipélago dos	130	11 15N	16 10W
Bissau	130	11 45N	15 45W
Bitola	52	41 5N	21 10 E
Bitolj = Bitola	52	41 5N	21 10 E
Bitterroot Range	162	46 0N	114 20W
Biu	131	10 40N	12 3 E
Biwa-Ko	106	35 15N	136 10 E
Biysk	71	52 40N	85 0 E
Bizen	109	34 43N	134 8 E
Bizerte	127	37 15N	9 50 E
Bjørnøya	13	74 30N	19 0 E
Black → = Da →	95	21 15N	105 20 E
Black Diamond	155	50 45N	114 14W
Black Forest = Schwarzwald	42	48 0N	8 0 E
Black Hills	163	44 0N	103 50W
Black Mts.	26	51 52N	3 5W
Black Sea	17	43 30N	35 0 E
Blackall	121	24 25S	145 45 E
Blackburn	28	53 44N	2 30W
Blackpool	28	53 48N	3 3W
Blackwater	121	23 35S	148 53 E
Blackwater →, Meath, Ireland	34	53 46N	7 0W
Blackwater →, Munster, Ireland	35	51 55N	7 50W
Blackwater →, U.K.	34	54 31N	6 35W
Blackwell	168	36 55N	97 20W
Blaenau Ffestiniog	26	53 0N	3 57W
Blagoveshchensk	75	50 20N	127 30 E
Blair Atholl	33	56 46N	3 50W
Blairmore	155	49 40N	114 25W
Blanc, Mont	37	45 48N	6 50 E
Blanca Peak	163	37 35N	105 29W
Blanche L.	118	29 15S	139 40 E
Blanco, C.	171	42 50N	124 40W
Blandford Forum	24	50 52N	2 10W
Blantyre	137	15 45S	35 0 E
Blarney	35	51 57N	8 35W
Blaydon	28	54 56N	1 47W
Blayney	117	33 32S	149 14 E
Blekinge län □	61	56 20N	15 20 E
Blenheim	123	41 38S	173 57 E
Bletchley	25	51 59N	0 44W
Blida	127	36 30N	2 49 E
Blind River	150	46 10N	82 58W
Blitar	111	8 5S	112 11 E
Bloemfontein	137	29 6S	26 14 E
Blois	36	47 35N	1 20 E
Bloody Foreland	34	55 10N	8 18W
Bloomington, Ill., U.S.A.	166	40 27N	89 0W
Bloomington, Ind., U.S.A.	167	39 10N	86 30W
Bloomsburg	164	41 0N	76 30W
Blue Mts., Oreg., U.S.A.	171	45 15N	119 0W
Blue Mts., Pa., U.S.A.	164	40 30N	76 30W
Blue Nile = Nîl el Azraq →	129	15 38N	32 31 E
Blue Ridge Mts.	165	36 30N	80 15W
Bluefield	165	37 18N	81 14W
Bluefields	179	12 20N	83 50W
Bluestack, mt.	34	54 46N	8 5W
Bluff	123	46 37S	168 20 E
Blumenau	191	27 0S	49 0W
Blyth	28	55 8N	1 32W
Bo	130	7 55N	11 50W
Bo Hai	98	39 0N	120 0 E
Boa Vista	185	2 48N	60 30W
Boaco	179	12 29N	85 35W
Bobadah	116	32 19S	146 41 E
Bobcaygeon	151	44 33N	78 33W
Bobo-Dioulasso	130	11 8N	4 13W
Bobraomby, Tanjon' i	137	12 40S	49 10 E
Bobruysk	68	53 10N	29 15 E
Bôca do Acre	187	8 50S	67 27W
Boca Raton	170	26 21N	80 5W
Bocas del Toro	179	9 15N	82 20W
Bocholt	42	51 50N	6 35 E
Bochum	42	51 28N	7 12 E
Boden	67	65 50N	21 42 E
Bodensee	44	47 35N	9 25 E
Bodhan	91	18 40N	77 44 E
Bodmin	27	50 28N	4 44W
Bodmin Moor	27	50 33N	4 36W
Bodø	64	67 17N	14 24 E
Bogalusa	169	30 50N	89 55W
Boggabilla	116	28 36S	150 24 E
Boggabri	116	30 45S	150 0 E
Boggeragh Mts.	35	52 2N	8 55W
Bognor Regis	25	50 47N	0 40W
Bogong, Mt.	117	36 47S	147 17 E

Bogor	111	6	36S	106	48 E
Bogota	184	4	34N	74	0W
Boguchany	74	58	40N	97	30 E
Bohain	38	49	59N	3	28 E
Bohemian Forest =					
Böhmerwald	43	49	30N	12	40 E
Böhmerwald	43	49	30N	12	40 E
Bohol	112	9	50N	124	10 E
Bohol Sea	112	9	0N	124	0 E
Bohotleh	133	8	20N	46	25 E
Boise	162	43	43N	116	9W
Boissevain	153	49	15N	100	5W
Boké	130	10	56N	14	17W
Bolan Pass	88	29	50N	67	20 E
Bolaños, R. →	175	21	12N	104	5W
Bolbec	38	49	30N	0	30 E
Bolgatanga	130	10	44N	0	53W
Bolívar	190	36	15S	60	53W
Bolivia ■	187	17	6S	64	0W
Bollnäs	60	61	21N	16	24 E
Bollon	116	28	2S	147	29 E
Bologna	47	44	30N	11	20 E
Boloven, Cao Nguyen	95	15	10N	106	30 E
Bolsena, L. di	46	42	35N	11	55 E
Bolshevik, Ostrov	72	78	30N	102	0 E
Bolshoi Kavkas	70	42	50N	44	0 E
Bolshoy Begichev, Ostrov	72	74	20N	112	30 E
Bolsward	41	53	3N	5	32 E
Bolton	28	53	35N	2	26W
Bolzano	47	46	30N	11	20 E
Boma	134	5	50S	13	4 E
Bombala	117	36	56S	149	15 E
Bombay	91	18	55N	72	50 E
Bomu →	129	4	40N	23	30 E
Bon, C.	127	37	1N	11	2 E
Bonaire	181	12	10N	68	15W
Bonavista	149	48	40N	53	5W
Bonifacio, Bouches de	48	41	12N	9	15 E
Bonn	42	50	43N	7	6 E
Bonneval	39	48	11N	1	24 E
Bonnie Rock	120	30	29S	118	22 E
Bonny, Bight of	131	3	30N	9	20 E
Bonnyville	152	54	20N	110	45W
Bonthe	130	7	30N	12	33W
Boonah	116	27	58S	152	41 E
Boone	166	42	5N	93	53W
Boonville	167	38	3N	87	13W
Boorowa	117	34	28S	148	44 E
Boothia, Gulf of	146	71	0N	90	0W
Boothia Pen.	145	71	0N	94	0W
Bootle	28	53	28N	3	1W
Bör	129	6	10N	31	40 E
Borås	60	57	43N	12	56 E
Borãzjãn	85	29	22N	51	10 E
Bordeaux	36	44	50N	0	36W
Borders □	31	55	35N	2	50W
Bordertown	119	36	19S	140	45 E
Bordj Omar Driss	127	28	10N	6	40 E
Borger	161	35	40N	101	20W
Borja	186	4	20S	77	40W
Borlänge	60	60	29N	15	26 E
Borneo	111	1	0N	115	0 E
Bornholm	61	55	10N	15	0 E
Borujerd	84	33	55N	48	50 E
Borzya	74	50	24N	116	31 E
Boscastle	27	50	42N	4	42W
Boshan	98	36	28N	117	49 E
Bosna →	52	45	4N	18	29 E
Bosnia-Herzegovina ■	52	44	0N	18	0 E
Bōsō-Hantō	107	35	20N	140	20 E
Bosporus = Karadeniz					
Boğazı	80	41	10N	29	10 E
Bossangoa	131	6	35N	17	30 E
Bossembélé	131	5	25N	17	40 E
Bossier City	168	32	28N	93	48W
Bosten Hu	100	41	55N	87	40 E
Boston, U.K.	29	52	59N	0	2W
Boston, U.S.A.	164	42	20N	71	0W
Bothnia, G. of	67	63	0N	20	0 E
Botletle →	136	20	10S	23	15 E
Botoşani	57	47	42N	26	41 E

Botswana ■	136	22	0S	24	0 E
Botucatu	188	22	55S	48	30W
Bou Djébéha	126	18	25N	2	45W
Bouaké	130	7	40N	5	2W
Bougie = Bejaia	127	36	42N	5	2 E
Boulogne-sur-Mer	38	50	42N	1	36 E
Bourbonnais	37	46	28N	3	0 E
Bourem	130	17	0N	0	24W
Bourg-en-Bresse	37	46	13N	5	12 E
Bourges	37	47	9N	2	25 E
Bourgogne	37	47	0N	4	30 E
Bourke	116	30	8S	145	55 E
Bournemouth	24	50	43N	1	53W
Bousso	131	10	34N	16	52 E
Bouvet I. = Bouvetøya	14	54	26S	3	24 E
Bouvetøya	14	54	26S	3	24 E
Bowen	121	20	0S	148	16 E
Bowland, Forest of	28	54	0N	2	30W
Bowling Green, Ky., U.S.A.	169	37	0N	86	25W
Bowling Green, Ohio, U.S.A.	167	41	22N	83	40W
Bowling Green, C.	121	19	19S	147	25 E
Bowmanville	151	43	55N	78	41W
Bowral	117	34	26S	150	27 E
Boyle	34	53	58N	8	19W
Boyne →	34	53	43N	6	15W
Boyne City	150	45	13N	85	1W
Boyup Brook	120	33	50S	116	23 E
Bozeman	163	45	40N	111	0W
Bozen = Bolzano	47	46	30N	11	20 E
Brač	52	43	20N	16	40 E
Bracciano, L. di	46	42	8N	12	11 E
Bracebridge	151	45	2N	79	19W
Bräcke	66	62	45N	15	26 E
Brad	56	46	10N	22	50 E
Bradenton	170	27	25N	82	35W
Bradford, U.K.	28	53	47N	1	45W
Bradford, U.S.A.	164	41	58N	78	41W
Braemar	33	57	2N	3	20W
Braga	50	41	35N	8	25W
Bragança, Brazil	188	1	0S	47	2W
Bragança, Portugal	50	41	48N	6	50W
Brahmanbaria	93	23	58N	91	15 E
Brahmani →	92	20	39N	86	46 E
Brahmaputra →	93	24	2N	90	59 E
Braidwood	117	35	27S	149	49 E
Bràila	57	45	19N	27	59 E
Brainerd	156	46	20N	94	10W
Braintree	25	51	53N	0	34 E
Brampton	151	43	45N	79	45W
Branco →	185	1	20S	61	50W
Branco, Cabo	182	7	9S	34	47W
Brandenburg	43	52	24N	12	33 E
Brandon	153	49	50N	99	57W
Brantford	151	43	10N	80	15W
Brasil, Planalto	188	18	0S	46	30W
Brasília	188	15	47S	47	55W
Braşov	57	45	38N	25	35 E
Brassey, Banjaran	111	5	0N	117	15 E
Brasstown Bald, Mt.	165	34	54N	83	45W
Bratislava	59	48	10N	17	7 E
Bratsk	74	56	10N	101	30 E
Brattleboro	164	42	53N	72	37W
Braunschweig	43	52	17N	10	28 E
Brava	133	1	20N	44	8 E
Bravo del Norte →	174	25	57N	97	9W
Brawley	173	32	58N	115	30W
Bray	35	53	12N	6	6W
Brazil	167	39	32N	87	8W
Brazil ■	188	10	0S	50	0W
Brazilian Highlands = Brasil,					
Planalto	188	18	0S	46	30W
Brazos →	168	28	53N	95	23W
Brazzaville	134	4	9S	15	12 E
Brčko	52	44	54N	18	46 E
Breadalbane	31	56	30N	4	15W
Bream Bay	122	35	56S	174	28 E
Brecon	26	51	57N	3	23W
Brecon Beacons	26	51	53N	3	27W
Breda	40	51	35N	4	45 E
Breiðafjörður	64	65	15N	23	15W
Bremen	42	53	4N	8	47 E

Name	Page	Lat	Long
Bremerhaven	**42**	53 34N	8 35 E
Bremerton	**171**	47 30N	122 38W
Brenham	**168**	30 5N	96 27W
Brentwood	**25**	51 37N	0 19 E
Bréscia	**46**	45 33N	10 13 E
Breslau = Wrocław	**58**	51 5N	17 5 E
Brest, France	**36**	48 24N	4 31W
Brest, U.S.S.R.	**68**	52 10N	23 40 E
Bretagne	**36**	48 0N	3 0W
Bretçu	**57**	46 7N	26 18 E
Breton Sd.	**169**	29 40N	89 12W
Brett, C.	**122**	35 10S	174 20 E
Brewer	**148**	44 43N	68 50W
Brewster	**171**	48 10N	119 51W
Brewton	**169**	31 9N	87 2W
Brezhnev = Naberezhnyye			
Chelny	**68**	55 42N	52 19 E
Briançon	**37**	44 54N	6 39 E
Bridgend	**27**	51 30N	3 35W
Bridgeport	**164**	41 12N	73 12W
Bridgeton	**164**	39 29N	75 10W
Bridgetown, Australia	**120**	33 58S	116 7 E
Bridgetown, Barbados	**180**	13 0N	59 30W
Bridgnorth	**24**	52 33N	2 25W
Bridgwater	**27**	51 7N	3 0W
Bridlington	**29**	54 6N	0 11W
Bridport	**27**	50 43N	2 45W
Brigham City	**163**	41 30N	112 1W
Bright	**117**	36 42S	146 56 E
Brighton, Australia	**119**	42 42S	147 16 E
Brighton, U.K.	**25**	50 50N	0 9W
Brindisi	**49**	40 39N	17 55 E
Brisbane	**116**	27 25S	153 2 E
Bristol, U.K.	**27**	51 26N	2 35W
Bristol, Conn., U.S.A.	**164**	41 44N	72 57W
Bristol, Tenn., U.S.A.	**165**	36 36N	82 11W
Bristol B.	**142**	58 0N	160 0W
Bristol Channel	**27**	51 18N	4 30W
Bristow	**168**	35 55N	96 28W
British Columbia □	**154**	55 0N	125 15W
British Guiana = Guyana ■	**185**	5 0N	59 0W
British Honduras = Belize ■	**177**	17 0N	88 30W
British Isles	**18**	55 0N	4 0W
Brittany = Bretagne	**36**	48 0N	3 0W
Brive-la-Gaillarde	**36**	45 10N	1 32 E
Brlik	**71**	44 0N	74 5 E
Brno	**59**	49 10N	16 35 E
Broach = Bharuch	**91**	21 47N	73 0 E
Broad Law	**31**	55 30N	3 22W
Broad Sd.	**121**	22 0S	149 45 E
Brochet	**145**	57 53N	101 40W
Brockton	**164**	42 8N	71 2W
Brockville	**151**	44 35N	75 41W
Brod	**52**	41 35N	21 17 E
Brodeur Pen.	**146**	72 30N	88 10W
Broken Hill = Kabwe	**135**	14 30S	28 29 E
Broken Hill	**118**	31 58S	141 29 E
Bromley	**25**	51 20N	0 5 E
Brookhaven	**169**	31 40N	90 25W
Brooks	**155**	50 35N	111 55W
Brooks Ra.	**142**	68 40N	147 0W
Brosna →	**35**	53 8N	8 0W
Brough	**28**	54 32N	2 19W
Broughty Ferry	**31**	56 29N	2 50W
Brouwershaven	**40**	51 45N	3 55 E
Brownsville	**158**	25 56N	97 25W
Brownwood	**161**	31 45N	99 0W
Bruay-en-Artois	**38**	50 29N	2 33 E
Bruce, Mt.	**114**	22 37S	118 8 E
Bruce Rock	**120**	31 52S	118 8 E
Bruck an der Leitha	**45**	48 1N	16 47 E
Bruges = Brugge	**42**	51 13N	3 13 E
Brugge	**42**	51 13N	3 13 E
Brunei = Bandar Seri			
Begawan	**112**	4 52N	115 0 E
Brunei ■	**111**	4 50N	115 0 E
Bruno	**152**	52 20N	105 30W
Brunswick = Braunschweig	**43**	52 17N	10 28 E
Brunswick, Ga., U.S.A.	**170**	31 10N	81 30W
Brunswick, Maine, U.S.A.	**148**	43 53N	69 50W
Bruny I.	**119**	43 20S	147 15 E
Brussel	**42**	50 51N	4 21 E
Bruthen	**117**	37 42S	147 50 E
Bruton	**27**	51 6N	2 28W
Bryan, Ohio, U.S.A.	**167**	41 30N	84 30W
Bryan, Tex., U.S.A.	**168**	30 40N	96 27W
Bryan, Mt.	**119**	33 30S	139 0 E
Bryansk	**68**	53 13N	34 25 E
Brzeg	**58**	50 52N	17 30 E
Bucaramanga	**184**	7 0N	73 0W
Buchan	**33**	57 32N	2 8W
Buchan Ness	**33**	57 29N	1 48W
Buchanan	**130**	5 57N	10 2W
Buchans	**149**	48 50N	56 52W
Bucharest = Bucureşti	**57**	44 27N	26 10 E
Buckhannon	**165**	39 2N	80 10W
Buckhaven	**31**	56 10N	3 2W
Buckingham, Canada	**151**	45 37N	75 24W
Buckingham, U.K.	**25**	52 0N	0 59W
Buckingham □	**25**	51 50N	0 55W
Buckleboo	**118**	32 54S	136 12 E
Bucureşti	**57**	44 27N	26 10 E
Bucyrus	**167**	40 48N	83 0W
Budalin	**93**	22 20N	95 10 E
Budapest	**59**	47 29N	19 5 E
Budaun	**89**	28 5N	79 10 E
Bude	**27**	50 49N	4 33W
Budgewoi Lake	**117**	33 13S	151 34 E
Buenaventura, Colombia	**184**	3 53N	77 4W
Buenaventura, Mexico	**174**	29 51N	107 29W
Buenos Aires	**190**	34 30S	58 20W
Buffalo	**164**	42 55N	78 50W
Bug →	**58**	52 31N	21 5 E
Buga	**184**	4 0N	76 15W
Bugun Shara	**100**	49 0N	104 0 E
Builth Wells	**26**	52 10N	3 26W
Buir Nur	**98**	47 50N	117 42 E
Bujumbura	**135**	3 16S	29 18 E
Bukachacha	**74**	52 55N	116 50 E
Bukavu	**23**	2 20S	28 52 E
Bukhara	**70**	39 48N	64 25 E
Bukit Mertajam	**96**	5 22N	100 28 E
Bukittinggi	**111**	0 20S	100 20 E
Bukoba	**135**	1 20S	31 49 E
Bukuru	**131**	9 42N	8 48 E
Bulahdelah	**117**	32 23S	152 13 E
Bulandshahr	**89**	28 28N	77 51 E
Bulawayo	**137**	20 7S	28 32 E
Bulgaria ■	**53**	42 35N	25 30 E
Bull Shoals L.	**168**	36 40N	93 5W
Bully-les-Mines	**38**	50 27N	2 44 E
Bulsar = Valsad	**91**	20 40N	72 58 E
Bulun	**72**	70 37N	127 30 E
Bunbury	**120**	33 20S	115 35 E
Buncrana	**34**	55 8N	7 28W
Bundaberg	**116**	24 54S	152 22 E
Bundi	**91**	25 30N	75 35 E
Bundoran	**34**	54 24N	8 17W
Bungo-Suidō	**109**	33 0N	132 15 E
Buorkhaya, Mys	**72**	71 50N	132 40 E
Bûr Sa'îd	**128**	31 16N	32 18 E
Bûr Sûdân	**129**	19 32N	37 9 E
Buraymī, Al Wāhāt al	**83**	24 10N	55 43 E
Burbank	**173**	34 9N	118 23W
Burdur	**80**	37 45N	30 22 E
Burdwan = Barddhaman	**92**	23 14N	87 39 E
Burgas	**53**	42 33N	27 29 E
Burgenland □	**45**	47 20N	16 20 E
Burgos	**50**	42 21N	3 41W
Burgundy = Bourgogne	**37**	47 0N	4 30 E
Burin	**149**	47 1N	55 14W
Burkina Faso ■	**130**	12 0N	1 0W
Burlington, Canada	**151**	43 18N	79 45W
Burlington, Iowa, U.S.A.	**166**	40 50N	91 5W
Burlington, N.C., U.S.A.	**165**	36 7N	79 27W
Burlington, N.J., U.S.A.	**164**	40 5N	74 50W
Burlington, Vt., U.S.A.	**151**	44 27N	73 14W
Burma ■	**93**	21 0N	96 30 E
Burnie	**119**	41 4S	145 56 E
Burnley	**28**	53 47N	2 15W
Burns	**171**	43 40N	119 4W

Burns Lake	**154**	54	20N	125	45W	
Burra	**119**	33	40S	138	55 E	
Bursa	**80**	40	15N	29	5 E	
Burton-upon-Trent	**28**	52	48N	1	39W	
Buru	**113**	3	30S	126	30 E	
Burundi ■	**135**	3	15S	30	0 E	
Bury	**28**	53	36N	2	19W	
Bury St. Edmunds	**25**	52	15N	0	42 E	
Buryat Rep. □	**74**	53	0N	110	0 E	
Buskerud fylke □	**60**	60	13N	9	0 E	
Busselton	**120**	33	42S	115	15 E	
Bussum	**40**	52	16N	5	10 E	
Bute	**30**	55	48N	5	2W	
Butiaba	**132**	1	50N	31	20 E	
Butler	**164**	40	52N	79	52W	
Butte	**163**	46	0N	112	31W	
Butterworth	**96**	5	24N	100	23 E	
Butuan	**112**	8	57N	125	33 E	
Butung	**113**	5	0S	122	45 E	
Buxton	**28**	53	16N	1	54W	
Buyaga	**74**	59	50N	127	0 E	
Buzău	**57**	45	10N	26	50 E	
Buzen	**108**	33	35N	131	5 E	
Buzzards Bay	**164**	41	45N	70	38W	
Bydgoszcz	**58**	53	10N	18	0 E	
Byelorussia = Belorussia ■	**68**	53	30N	27	0 E	
Bylot I.	**146**	73	13N	78	34W	
Byrd Land	**15**	79	30S	125	0W	
Byron Bay	**116**	28	43S	153	37 E	
Byrranga, Gory	**72**	75	0N	100	0 E	
Bytom	**58**	50	25N	18	54 E	

C

Cabimas	**184**	10	23N	71	25W	
Cabinda	**134**	5	33S	12	11 E	
Cabinda □	**134**	5	0S	12	30 E	
Cabo Pantoja	**184**	1	0S	75	10W	
Cabonga, Réservoir	**151**	47	20N	76	40W	
Caboolture	**116**	27	5S	152	58 E	
Cabora Bassa Dam	**137**	15	20S	32	50 E	
Caborca	**174**	30	40N	112	10W	
Cabot Strait	**149**	47	15N	59	40W	
Cabrera, I.	**51**	39	8N	2	57 E	
Cabri	**152**	50	35N	108	25W	
Čačak	**52**	43	54N	20	20 E	
Cáceres	**50**	39	26N	6	23W	
Cache Bay	**151**	46	22N	80	0W	
Cachoeira	**189**	12	30S	39	0W	
Cachoeira de Itapemirim	**189**	20	51S	41	7W	
Cachoeira do Sul	**191**	30	3S	52	53W	
Cader Idris	**26**	52	43N	3	56W	
Cadibarrawirracanna, L.	**118**	28	52S	135	27 E	
Cadillac, Canada	**151**	48	14N	78	23W	
Cadillac, U.S.A.	**167**	44	16N	85	25W	
Cádiz	**50**	36	30N	6	20W	
Cádiz, G. de	**50**	36	40N	7	0W	
Caen	**36**	49	10N	0	22W	
Caernarfon	**26**	53	8N	4	17W	
Caernarfon B.	**26**	53	4N	4	40W	
Caernarvon = Caernarfon	**26**	53	8N	4	17W	
Caerphilly	**27**	51	34N	3	13W	
Cagayan de Oro	**112**	8	30N	124	40 E	
Cágliari	**48**	39	15N	9	6 E	
Caguas	**180**	18	14N	66	4W	
Caha Mts.	**35**	51	45N	9	40W	
Caher	**35**	52	23N	7	56W	
Cahors	**36**	44	27N	1	27 E	
Cahuapanas	**186**	5	15S	77	0W	
Caibarién	**178**	22	30N	79	30W	
Caicos Is.	**180**	21	40N	71	40W	
Cairngorm Mts.	**33**	57	6N	3	42W	
Cairns	**121**	16	57S	145	45 E	
Cairo = El Qâhira	**128**	30	1N	31	14 E	
Cairo	**169**	37	0N	89	10W	
Cajamarca	**186**	7	5S	78	28W	
Calabar	**131**	4	57N	8	20 E	
Calabozo	**184**	9	0N	67	28W	
Calábria □	**49**	39	24N	16	30 E	
Calais, France	**38**	50	57N	1	56 E	
Calais, U.S.A.	**148**	45	11N	67	20W	
Calama, Brazil	**187**	8	0S	62	50W	
Calama, Chile	**190**	22	30S	68	55W	
Calamar	**184**	10	15N	74	55W	
Calamian Group	**112**	11	50N	119	55 E	
Calca	**187**	13	22S	72	0W	
Calcutta	**92**	22	36N	88	24 E	
Caldwell	**171**	43	45N	116	42W	
Calgary	**155**	51	0N	114	10W	
Cali	**184**	3	25N	76	35W	
Calicut	**90**	11	15N	75	43 E	
California □	**172**	37	25N	120	0W	
California, Golfo de	**174**	28	0N	112	0W	
Callander	**31**	56	15N	4	14W	
Callao	**186**	12	0S	77	0W	
Caloundra	**116**	26	45S	153	10 E	
Caltanissetta	**49**	37	30N	14	3 E	
Cam Lam	**95**	11	54N	109	10 E	
Cam Ranh	**95**	11	54N	109	12 E	
Camagüey	**178**	21	20N	78	0W	
Camaná	**186**	16	30S	72	50W	
Camargue	**37**	43	34N	4	34 E	
Camarones	**192**	44	50S	65	40W	
Cambay = Khambhat	**91**	22	23N	72	33 E	
Cambodia ■	**95**	12	15N	105	0 E	
Camborne	**27**	50	13N	5	18W	
Cambrai	**38**	50	11N	3	14 E	
Cambrian Mts.	**26**	52	25N	3	52W	
Cambridge, Canada	**151**	43	23N	80	15W	
Cambridge, N.Z.	**122**	37	54S	175	29 E	
Cambridge, U.K.	**25**	52	13N	0	8 E	
Cambridge, Mass., U.S.A.	**164**	42	20N	71	8W	
Cambridge, Md., U.S.A.	**164**	38	33N	76	2W	
Cambridge, Ohio, U.S.A.	**167**	40	1N	81	35W	
Cambridge Bay	**145**	69	10N	105	0W	
Cambridge Gulf	**114**	14	55S	128	15 E	
Cambridgeshire □	**25**	52	12N	0	7 E	
Camden, Ark., U.S.A.	**168**	33	40N	92	50W	
Camden, N.J., U.S.A.	**164**	39	57N	75	7W	
Camden, S.C., U.S.A.	**165**	34	17N	80	34W	
Cameroon ■	**131**	6	0N	12	30 E	
Cameroun, Mt.	**131**	4	13N	9	10 E	
Cametá	**188**	2	12S	49	30W	
Camiri	**187**	20	3S	63	31W	
Camocim	**189**	2	55S	40	50W	
Campagna	**46**	40	40N	15	5 E	
Campania □	**49**	40	50N	14	45 E	
Campbell I.	**15**	52	30S	169	0 E	
Campbell River	**154**	50	5N	125	20W	
Campbellton	**148**	47	57N	66	43W	
Campbelltown, Australia	**117**	34	4S	150	49 E	
Campbeltown, U.K.	**30**	57	34N	4	2W	
Campeche	**177**	19	51N	90	32W	
Campeche □	**177**	19	0N	90	30W	
Campeche, B. de	**177**	20	0N	94	0W	
Camperdown	**119**	38	14S	143	9 E	
Camperville	**153**	51	59N	100	9W	
Campina Grande	**189**	7	20S	35	47W	
Campinas	**188**	22	50S	47	0W	
Campo Grande	**188**	20	25S	54	40W	
Campos	**188**	21	50S	41	20W	
Camrose	**155**	53	0N	112	50W	
Can Tho	**95**	10	2N	105	46 E	
Canada ■	**139**	60	0N	100	0W	
Cañada de Gómez	**190**	32	40S	61	30W	
Canadian →	**158**	35	27N	95	3W	
Çanakkale Boğazı	**80**	40	0N	26	0 E	
Cananea	**174**	30	57N	110	18W	
Canarias, Islas	**126**	28	30N	16	0W	
Canary Is. = Canarias, Islas	**126**	28	30N	16	0W	
Canaveral, C.	**170**	28	28N	80	31W	
Canberra	**117**	35	15S	149	8 E	
Candala	**133**	11	30N	49	58 E	
Candia = Iráklion	**55**	35	20N	25	12 E	
Canea = Khaniá	**55**	35	30N	24	4 E	
Çankırı	**80**	40	40N	33	37 E	
Canmore	**155**	51	7N	115	18W	
Canna	**32**	57	3N	6	33W	
Cannanore	**90**	11	53N	75	27 E	

Name	Page	Lat		Long	
Cannes	37	43	32N	7	0 E
Cannock	28	52	42N	2	2W
Canora	152	51	40N	102	30W
Canowindra	117	33	35S	148	38 E
Canso	149	45	20N	61	0W
Cantabrian Mts. =					
Cantábrica, Cordillera	50	43	0N	5	10W
Cantábrica, Cordillera	50	43	0N	5	10W
Canterbury	25	51	17N	1	5 E
Canterbury □	123	43	45S	171	19 E
Canterbury Bight	123	44	16S	171	55 E
Canterbury Plains	123	43	55S	171	22 E
Canton = Guangzhou	99	23	5N	113	10 E
Canton, Ill., U.S.A.	166	40	32N	90	0W
Canton, Miss., U.S.A.	169	32	40N	90	1W
Canton, Ohio, U.S.A.	167	40	47N	81	22W
Canutama	185	6	30S	64	20W
Cap-Chat	148	49	6N	66	40W
Cap-de-la-Madeleine	151	46	22N	72	31W
Cap-Haïtien	180	19	40N	72	20W
Cape Barren I.	119	40	25S	148	15 E
Cape Breton I.	149	46	0N	60	30W
Cape Coast	130	5	5N	1	15W
Cape Dorset	146	64	14N	76	32W
Cape Fear →	165	34	30N	78	25W
Cape Girardeau	169	37	20N	89	30W
Cape May	164	39	1N	74	53W
Cape Montague	149	46	5N	62	25W
Cape Town	136	33	55S	18	22 E
Cape Verde Is. ■	9	17	10N	25	20W
Cape York Peninsula	115	12	0S	142	30 E
Caquetá →	184	1	15S	69	15W
Caracal	57	44	8N	24	22 E
Caracas	184	10	30N	66	55W
Caratinga	188	19	50S	42	10W
Carberry	153	49	50N	99	25W
Carbonara, C.	48	39	8N	9	30 E
Carbondale	166	37	45N	89	10W
Carbonear	149	47	42N	53	13W
Carcassonne	37	43	13N	2	20 E
Carcross	144	60	13N	134	45W
Cárdenas, Cuba	178	23	0N	81	30W
Cárdenas, Mexico	177	21	0N	99	40W
Cardiff	27	51	28N	3	11W
Cardigan	26	52	6N	4	41W
Cardigan B.	26	52	30N	4	30W
Cardston	155	49	15N	113	20W
Cardwell	121	18	14S	146	2 E
Caribbean Sea	181	15	0N	75	0W
Cariboo Mts.	155	53	0N	121	0W
Caribou	148	46	55N	68	0W
Caribou Mts.	145	59	12N	115	40W
Carinhanha	188	14	15S	44	46W
Carinthia = Kärnten □	45	46	52N	13	30 E
Carlisle, U.K.	28	54	54N	2	55W
Carlisle, U.S.A.	164	40	12N	77	10W
Carlow	35	52	50N	6	58W
Carlow □	35	52	43N	6	50W
Carlsbad, Calif., U.S.A.	173	33	11N	117	25W
Carlsbad, N. Mex., U.S.A.	161	32	20N	104	14W
Carlyle	152	49	40N	102	20W
Carmacks	144	62	5N	136	16W
Carman	153	49	30N	98	0W
Carmarthen	26	51	52N	4	20W
Carmarthen B.	27	51	40N	4	30W
Carnarvon	120	24	51S	113	42 E
Carnegie, L.	114	26	5S	122	30 E
Carniche, Alpi	47	46	36N	13	0 E
Carnsore Pt.	35	52	10N	6	20W
Caroline Is.	122	8	0N	150	0 E
Caroona	116	31	24S	150	26 E
Carpathians, Mts.	17	49	50N	21	0 E
Carpaţii Meridionali	57	45	30N	25	0 E
Carpentaria, G. of	115	14	0S	139	0 E
Carrara	46	44	5N	10	7 E
Carrick-on-Shannon	34	53	57N	8	7W
Carrick-on-Suir	35	52	22N	7	30W
Carrickfergus	34	54	43N	5	50W
Carrickmacross	34	54	0N	6	43W
Carroll	166	42	2N	94	55W
Carrollton	170	33	36N	85	5W
Carse of Gowrie	31	56	30N	3	10W
Carson City	172	39	12N	119	46W
Carstairs	31	55	42N	3	41W
Cartagena, Colombia	184	10	25N	75	33W
Cartagena, Spain	51	37	38N	0	59W
Cartago, Colombia	184	4	45N	75	55W
Cartago, Costa Rica	179	9	50N	85	52W
Cartersville	169	34	11N	84	48W
Carthage	168	37	10N	94	20W
Cartwright	147	53	41N	56	58W
Caruaru	189	8	15S	35	55W
Carúpano	185	10	39N	63	15W
Caruthersville	169	36	10N	89	40W
Carvin	38	50	30N	2	57 E
Casablanca	126	33	36N	7	36W
Casas Grandes	174	30	22N	107	57W
Cascade Ra.	171	47	0N	121	30W
Casilda	190	33	10S	61	10W
Casino	116	28	52S	153	3 E
Casiquiare →	184	2	1N	67	7W
Casma	186	9	30S	78	20W
Casper	163	42	52N	106	20W
Caspian Sea	70	43	0N	50	0 E
Cassiar Mts.	144	59	30N	130	30W
Castellón de la Plana	51	39	58N	0	3W
Castelsarrasin	36	44	2N	1	7 E
Casterton	119	37	30S	141	30 E
Castilla La Nueva	50	39	45N	3	20W
Castilla La Vieja	50	41	55N	4	0W
Castle Douglas	31	54	57N	3	57W
Castlebar	34	53	52N	9	17W
Castleblaney	34	54	7N	6	44W
Castlegar	155	49	20N	117	40W
Castlemaine	117	37	2S	144	12 E
Castlereagh	34	53	47N	8	30W
Castletown	28	58	35N	3	22W
Castletown Bearhaven	35	51	40N	9	54W
Castor	155	52	15N	111	50W
Castres	37	43	37N	2	13 E
Castricum	40	52	33N	4	40 E
Castries	180	14	0N	60	50W
Castro	192	42	30S	73	50W
Cat I.	178	24	30N	75	30W
Catacáos	186	5	20S	80	45W
Catalonia = Cataluña □	51	41	40N	1	15 E
Cataluña □	51	41	40N	1	15 E
Catamarca	190	28	30S	65	50W
Catanduanes	112	13	50N	124	20 E
Catánia	49	37	31N	15	4 E
Catanzaro	49	38	54N	16	38 E
Catoche, C.	177	21	35N	87	5W
Catskill Mts.	164	42	15N	74	15W
Cauca →	184	8	54N	74	28W
Caucasus Mts. = Bolshoi					
Kavkas	70	42	50N	44	0 E
Caudry	38	50	7N	3	22 E
Cauquenes	190	36	0S	72	22W
Cavaillon	37	43	50N	5	2 E
Cavan	34	54	0N	7	22W
Cawnpore = Kanpur	91	26	28N	80	20 E
Caxias	188	4	55S	43	20W
Caxias do Sul	191	29	10S	51	10W
Cayenne	185	5	0N	52	18W
Cayes, Les	180	18	15N	73	46W
Cayman Is.	178	19	40N	80	30W
Ceanannus Mor	34	53	42N	6	53W
Ceará = Fortaleza	189	3	45S	38	35W
Ceará □	189	5	0S	40	0W
Cebu	112	10	18N	123	54 E
Cedar →	166	41	17N	91	21W
Cedar City	162	37	41N	113	3W
Cedar Falls	166	42	39N	92	29W
Cedar L.	152	53	10N	100	0W
Cedar Rapids	166	42	0N	91	38W
Cedartown	169	34	1N	85	15W
Ceduna	118	32	7S	133	46 E
Cegléd	21	47	11N	19	47 E
Ceiba, La	179	15	40N	86	50W
Celaya	177	20	31N	100	37W
Celebes = Sulawesi □	113	2	0S	120	0 E

Celebes Sea .... 113 3 0N 123 0 E
Center 168 31 50N 94 10W
Centerville 166 40 45N 92 57W
Central □ 31 56 10N 4 30W
Central, Cordillera 184 5 0N 75 0W
Central African Republic ■ . 129 7 0N 20 0 E
Central Makran Range ..... 88 26 30N 64 15 E
Central Russian Uplands ... 17 54 0N 36 0 E
Central Siberian Plateau ... 77 65 0N 105 0 E
Centralia 166 38 32N 89 5W
Cephalonia = Kefallinía ... 54 38 20N 20 30 E
Ceram = Seram .... 113 3 10S 129 0 E
Ceram Sea = Seram Sea .. 113 2 30S 128 30 E
Cerignola .... 49 41 17N 15 53 E
Cerigo = Kíthira .... 55 36 9N 23 0 E
Cerritos 177 22 26N 100 17W
Cesena .... 47 44 9N 12 14 E
Českomoravská Vrchovina .. 59 49 30N 15 40 E
Český Těšín .... 59 49 45N 18 39 E
Cessnock .... 117 32 50S 151 21 E
Cetinje .... 52 42 23N 18 59 E
Ceuta 126 35 52N 5 18W
Cévennes .... 37 44 10N 3 50 E
Ceylon = Sri Lanka ■ .... 90 7 30N 80 50 E
Chachapoyas 186 6 15S 77 50W
Chachoengsao .... 95 13 42N 101 5 E
Chad ■ .... 131 15 0N 17 15 E
Chad, L. = Tchad, L. ...... 131 13 30N 14 30 E
Chadron 163 42 50N 103 0W
Chagos Arch. .... 76 6 0S 72 0 E
Cháh Bahár .... 85 25 20N 60 40 E
Chakradharpur .... 92 22 45N 85 40 E
Chala 186 15 48S 74 20W
Chalcis = Khalkís .... 55 38 27N 23 42 E
Chalhuanca 186 14 15S 73 15W
Chalisgaon .... 91 20 30N 75 10 E
Challapata 187 18 53S 66 50W
Chalon-sur-Saône .... 37 46 48N 4 50 E
Châlons-sur-Marne .... 37 48 58N 4 20 E
Chambal —► .... 91 26 29N 79 15 E
Chambersburg 164 39 53N 77 41W
Chambéry .... 37 45 34N 5 55 E
Chamonix .... 37 45 55N 6 51 E
Champagne .... 37 49 0N 4 40 E
Champaign 167 40 8N 88 14W
Champlain, L. 151 44 30N 73 20W
Chañaral 190 26 23S 70 40W
Chandigarh .... 89 30 43N 76 47 E
Chandler .... 118 27 0S 133 19 E
Chang Jiang —► .... 99 31 48N 121 10 E
Changchiak'ou =
  Zhangjiakou .... 98 40 48N 114 55 E
Ch'angchou = Changzhou . 99 31 47N 119 58 E
Changchun .... 98 43 57N 125 17 E
Changde .... 99 29 4N 111 35 E
Changhai = Shanghai .... 99 31 15N 121 26 E
Changsha .... 99 28 12N 113 0 E
Changzhi .... 98 36 10N 113 6 E
Changzhou .... 99 31 47N 119 58 E
Channel Is. 36 49 30N 2 40W
Channel-Port aux Basques . 149 47 30N 59 9W
Chanthaburi .... 95 12 38N 102 12 E
Chantilly .... 39 49 12N 2 29 E
Chanute 166 37 45N 95 25W
Chao Phraya —► .... 94 13 32N 100 36 E
Ch'aoan .... 99 23 41N 116 33 E
Chapala, L. de 175 20 15N 103 0W
Chapayevsk .... 68 53 0N 49 40 E
Chapel Hill 165 35 53N 79 3W
Chapleau 150 47 50N 83 24W
Charagua 187 19 45S 63 10W
Charaña 187 17 30S 69 25W
Chard 27 50 52N 2 59W
Chardzhou .... 70 39 6N 63 34 E
Chari —► .... 131 12 58N 14 31 E
Chārīkār .... 87 35 0N 69 10 E
Charleroi .... 42 50 24N 4 27 E
Charles, C. 165 37 10N 75 59W
Charles City 166 43 2N 92 41W
Charleston, S.C., U.S.A. ... 170 32 47N 79 56W
Charleston, W. Va., U.S.A. .. 165 38 24N 81 36W
Charleville = Rath Luirc 35 52 21N 8 40W
Charleville .... 116 26 24S 146 15 E
Charleville-Mézières .... 37 49 44N 4 40 E
Charlotte, Mich., U.S.A. 167 42 36N 84 48W
Charlotte, N.C., U.S.A. 165 35 16N 80 46W
Charlotte Amalie 180 18 22N 64 56W
Charlotte Harbor 170 26 58N 82 4W
Charlottenburg .... 43 52 31N 13 15 E
Charlottesville 165 38 1N 78 30W
Charlottetown 149 46 14N 63 8W
Charlton, Australia .... 117 36 16S 143 24 E
Charlton, U.S.A. 166 40 59N 93 20W
Charters Towers .... 121 20 5S 146 13 E
Chartres .... 39 48 29N 1 30 E
Chascomús 191 35 30S 58 0W
Château-du-Loir .... 39 47 40N 0 25 E
Château-Thierry .... 39 49 3N 3 20 E
Châteaubriant 36 47 43N 1 23W
Châteaudun .... 39 48 3N 1 20 E
Châteauroux .... 37 46 50N 1 40 E
Châtellerault .... 36 46 50N 0 30 E
Chatham, N.B., Canada ... 148 47 2N 65 28W
Chatham, Ont., Canada ... 141 42 24N 82 11W
Chatham, U.K. .... 25 51 22N 0 32 E
Chatta-Hantō .... 106 34 45N 136 55 E
Chattahoochee —► 170 30 43N 84 51W
Chattanooga 169 35 2N 85 17W
Chaumont .... 37 48 7N 5 8 E
Chauny .... 38 49 37N 3 12 E
Cheboksary .... 68 56 8N 47 12 E
Cheboygan 150 45 38N 84 29W
Chechenia □ .... 70 43 30N 45 29 E
Chegdomyn .... 75 51 7N 133 1 E
Chegga 126 25 27N 5 40W
Chehalis 171 46 44N 122 59W
Cheju Do .... 99 33 29N 126 34 E
Chekiang = Zhejiang □ .... 99 29 0N 120 0 E
Chelforó 190 39 0S 66 33W
Chelkar Tengiz, Solonchak . 70 48 0N 62 30 E
Chełm .... 58 51 8N 23 30 E
Chełmża .... 58 53 10N 18 39 E
Cheltenham 24 51 55N 2 5W
Chelyabinsk .... 71 55 10N 61 24 E
Chemainus 154 48 55N 123 42W
Chemnitz .... 43 50 50N 12 55 E
Chemult 171 43 14N 121 47W
Chen, Gora .... 73 65 16N 141 50 E
Chencha .... 132 6 15N 37 32 E
Chenchiang = Zhenjiang ... 99 32 11N 119 26 E
Chengchou = Zhengzhou .. 99 34 45N 113 34 E
Chengde .... 98 40 59N 117 58 E
Chengdu .... 99 30 38N 104 2 E
Ch'engtu = Chengdu ...... 99 30 38N 104 2 E
Cheo Reo .... 95 13 25N 108 28 E
Chepstow 27 51 38N 2 40W
Cher —► .... 36 47 21N 0 29 E
Cherbourg 36 49 39N 1 40W
Cheremkhovo .... 74 53 8N 103 1 E
Cherepovets .... 68 59 5N 37 55 E
Cherkassy .... 68 49 27N 32 4 E
Chernigov .... 68 51 28N 31 20 E
Chernovtsy .... 68 48 15N 25 52 E
Chernoye .... 72 70 30N 89 10 E
Cherokee 166 42 40N 95 30W
Cherrapunji .... 93 25 17N 91 47 E
Cherskiy .... 73 68 45N 161 18 E
Cherskogo Khrebet ...... 73 65 0N 143 0 E
Cherwell —► 25 51 46N 1 18W
Chesapeake 165 36 43N 76 15W
Chesapeake Bay 165 38 0N 76 12W
Cheshire □ 28 53 14N 2 30W
Cheshskaya Guba .... 69 67 20N 47 0 E
Chester, U.K. 28 53 12N 2 53W
Chester, Pa., U.S.A. 164 39 54N 75 20W
Chester, S.C., U.S.A. 165 34 44N 81 13W
Chesterfield 28 53 14N 1 26W
Chesterfield Inlet 145 63 30N 90 45W
Chetumal 177 18 30N 88 18W
Cheviot, The 31 55 29N 2 8W
Cheviot Hills 31 55 20N 2 30W
Chew Bahir .... 132 4 40N 36 50 E

Place	Page	Lat	Long
Cheyenne	163	41 9N	104 49W
Cheyenne ~►	163	44 40N	101 15W
Chhapra	92	25 48N	84 44 E
Chiamussu = Jiamusi	98	46 40N	130 26 E
Chiang Mai	94	18 47N	98 59 E
Chiapa ~►	177	16 42N	93 0W
Chiapas □	177	16 30N	92 30W
Chiba	107	35 30N	140 7 E
Chibougamau	151	49 56N	74 24W
Chicago	167	41 53N	87 40W
Chicago Heights	167	41 29N	87 37W
Chichagof I.	143	58 0N	136 0W
Chichester	25	50 50N	0 47W
Chichibu	107	36 5N	139 10 E
Ch'ich'ihaerh = Qiqihar	98	47 26N	124 0 E
Chiclayo	186	6 42S	79 50W
Chico	172	39 45N	121 54W
Chicopee	164	42 6N	72 37W
Chicoutimi	148	48 28N	71 5W
Chidambaram	90	11 20N	79 45 E
Chidley C.	146	60 23N	64 26W
Chigasaki	107	35 19N	139 24 E
Chihli, G. of = Bo Hai	98	39 0N	120 0 E
Chihuahua	174	28 38N	106 5W
Chihuahua □	174	28 30N	106 0W
Chikugo	108	33 14N	130 28 E
Chilapa	177	17 40N	99 11W
Childress	161	34 30N	100 15W
Chile ■	190	35 0S	72 0W
Chilin = Jilin	98	43 44N	126 30 E
Chilka L.	92	19 40N	85 25 E
Chillán	190	36 40S	72 10W
Chillicothe, Mo., U.S.A.	166	39 45N	93 30W
Chillicothe, Ohio, U.S.A.	167	39 20N	82 58W
Chilliwack	154	49 10N	121 54W
Chiloé, I. de	192	42 30S	73 50W
Chilpancingo	177	17 30N	99 30W
Chiltern Hills	25	51 44N	0 42W
Chimborazo	184	1 29S	78 55W
Chimbote	186	9 0S	78 35W
Chimkent	71	42 18N	69 36 E
Chin □	93	22 0N	93 0 E
China ■	79	30 0N	110 0 E
Chinan = Jinan	98	36 38N	117 1 E
Chinandega	179	12 35N	87 12W
Chincha Alta	186	13 25S	76 7W
Chinchilla	116	26 45S	150 38 E
Chinchou = Jinzhou	98	41 5N	121 3 E
Chindwin ~►	93	21 26N	95 15 E
Ch'ingtao = Qingdao	98	36 5N	120 20 E
Chinju	98	35 12N	128 2 E
Chinnampo	98	38 52N	125 10 E
Chino	107	35 59N	138 9 E
Chinon	36	47 10N	0 15 E
Chippenham	24	51 27N	2 7W
Chippewa Falls	166	44 55N	91 22W
Chiquián	186	10 10S	77 0W
Chiquimula	177	14 51N	89 37W
Chiquinquira	184	5 37N	73 50W
Chirala	90	15 50N	80 26 E
Chirchik	71	41 29N	69 35 E
Chita	74	52 0N	113 35 E
Chitral	89	35 50N	71 56 E
Chitré	179	7 59N	80 27W
Chittagong	93	22 19N	91 48 E
Chittagong □	93	24 5N	91 0 E
Chivilcoy	190	34 55S	60 0W
Chkalov = Orenburg	70	51 45N	55 6 E
Chōfu	107	35 39N	139 33 E
Choix	174	26 43N	108 17W
Chojnice	58	53 42N	17 32 E
Cholet	36	47 4N	0 52W
Choluteca	179	13 20N	87 14W
Chon Buri	95	13 21N	101 1 E
Chongjin	98	41 47N	129 50 E
Chŏngju	98	36 39N	127 27 E
Chongqing	99	29 35N	106 25 E
Chŏnju	98	35 50N	127 4 E
Chonos, Arch. de los	192	45 0S	75 0W
Chorley	28	53 39N	2 39W
Chorzów	58	50 18N	18 57 E
Chōshi	107	35 45N	140 51 E
Christchurch, N.Z.	123	43 33S	172 47 E
Christchurch, U.K.	24	50 44N	1 33W
Christianshåb	147	68 50N	51 18W
Christmas I. = Kiritimati	123	1 58N	157 27W
Christmas I.	111	10 30S	105 40 E
Ch'uanchou = Quanzhou	99	24 55N	118 34 E
Chūbu □	106	36 45N	137 30 E
Chubut ~►	192	43 20S	65 5W
Chūgoku □	109	35 0N	133 0 E
Chūgoku-Sanchi	109	35 0N	133 0 E
Chukotskiy Khrebet	73	68 0N	175 0 E
Chukotskoye More	73	68 0N	175 0W
Chula Vista	173	32 39N	117 8W
Chulman	74	56 52N	124 52 E
Chulucanas	186	5 8S	80 10W
Chumikan	75	54 40N	135 10 E
Chumphon	94	10 35N	99 14 E
Chunchŏn	98	37 58N	127 44 E
Chungking = Chongqing	99	29 35N	106 25 E
Chuquibamba	186	15 47S	72 44W
Chur	44	46 52N	9 32 E
Churchill ~►, Man., Canada	143	58 47N	94 12W
Churchill ~►, Nfld., Canada	147	53 19N	60 10W
Churchill, C.	143	58 46N	93 12W
Churchill Falls	147	53 36N	64 19W
Churchill Pk.	144	58 10N	125 10W
Churu	89	28 20N	74 50 E
Chuvashia □	68	55 30N	47 0 E
Chuxiong	101	25 2N	101 28 E
Cicero	167	41 48N	87 48W
Ciego de Avila	178	21 50N	78 50W
Ciénaga	184	11 1N	74 15W
Cienfuegos	178	22 10N	80 30W
Cimarron ~►	161	36 10N	96 17W
Cincinnati	167	39 10N	84 26W
Cinto, Mt.	36	42 24N	8 54 E
Ciotat, La	37	43 12N	5 36 E
Circle	142	65 50N	144 10W
Circleville	167	39 35N	82 57W
Cirebon	111	6 45S	108 32 E
Cirencester	24	51 43N	1 59W
Citlaltépetl, Volcán	177	19 1N	97 16W
Ciudad Acuña	174	29 20N	100 58W
Ciudad Bolívar	185	8 5N	63 36W
Ciudad Camargo, Chihuahua, Mexico	174	27 40N	105 10W
Ciudad Camargo, Tamaulipas, Mexico	176	26 19N	98 50W
Ciudad de Valles	177	21 59N	99 1W
Ciudad del Carmen	177	18 38N	91 50W
Ciudad Guayana	185	8 0N	62 30W
Ciudad Guzmán	175	19 41N	103 29W
Ciudad Juárez	174	31 44N	106 29W
Ciudad Madero	177	22 16N	97 50W
Ciudad Mante	177	22 44N	98 57W
Ciudad Obregón	174	27 29N	109 56W
Ciudad Real	50	38 59N	3 55W
Ciudad Rodrigo	50	40 35N	6 32W
Ciudad Trujillo = Santo Domingo	180	18 30N	64 54W
Ciudad Victoria	177	23 44N	99 8W
Çivril	80	38 20N	29 43 E
Cizre	81	37 19N	42 10 E
Clare	119	33 50S	138 37 E
Clare □	35	52 20N	9 0W
Clare ~►	35	53 22N	9 5W
Clare I.	34	53 48N	10 0W
Claremont	164	43 23N	72 20W
Claremore	168	36 40N	95 37W
Claremorris	34	53 45N	9 0W
Claresholm	155	50 0N	113 33W
Clark Fork ~►	162	48 9N	116 15W
Clarksburg	164	39 18N	80 21W
Clarksdale	169	34 12N	90 33W
Clarkston	171	46 28N	117 2W
Clarksville	169	36 32N	87 20W
Clear, C.	20	51 26N	9 30W
Clearwater, Canada	155	51 38N	120 2W
Clearwater, U.S.A.	170	27 58N	82 45W
Cleburne	168	32 18N	97 25W

Clee Hills	24	52	26N	2	35W
Cleethorpes	29	53	33N	0	2W
Cleeve Hill	24	51	54N	2	0W
Clermont, Australia	121	22	49S	147	39 E
Clermont, France	39	49	23N	2	24 E
Clermont-Ferrand	37	45	46N	3	4 E
Clevedon	27	51	26N	2	52W
Cleveland, Miss., U.S.A.	169	33	43N	90	43W
Cleveland, Ohio, U.S.A.	167	41	28N	81	43W
Cleveland, Tenn., U.S.A.	169	35	9N	84	52W
Cleveland, Tex., U.S.A.	169	30	18N	95	0W
Cleveland □	29	54	35N	1	8 E
Cleveleys	28	53	52N	3	3W
Clew B.	34	53	54N	9	50W
Clifton Beach	121	16	46S	145	39 E
Clifton Forge	165	37	49N	79	51W
Clinton, Canada	150	43	37N	81	32W
Clinton, Iowa, U.S.A.	166	41	50N	90	12W
Clinton, Mass., U.S.A.	164	42	26N	71	40W
Clinton, Mo., U.S.A.	166	38	20N	93	46W
Clinton, Okla., U.S.A.	161	35	30N	99	0W
Clinton, S.C., U.S.A.	165	34	30N	81	54W
Clinton Colden L.	145	63	58N	107	27W
Clonakilty	35	51	37N	8	53W
Cloncurry	115	20	40S	140	28 E
Clones	34	54	10N	7	13W
Clonmel	35	52	22N	7	42W
Clovis	161	34	20N	103	10W
Cluj-Napoca	56	46	47N	23	38 E
Clunes	117	37	20S	143	45 E
Clwyd □	26	53	5N	3	20W
Clyde →	31	55	56N	4	29W
Clyde, Firth of	30	55	20N	5	0W
Clydebank	31	55	54N	4	25W
Coahuila □	174	27	20N	102	0W
Coaldale	155	49	45N	112	35W
Coalinga	173	36	10N	120	21W
Coalville	29	52	43N	1	21W
Coast Mts.	144	55	0N	129	0W
Coast Ranges	173	41	0N	123	0W
Coatbridge	31	55	52N	4	2W
Coatepeque	177	14	46N	91	55W
Coats I.	146	62	30N	83	0W
Coats Land	14	77	0S	25	0W
Coatzacoalcos	177	18	9N	94	25W
Cobalt	151	47	25N	79	42W
Cobán	177	15	30N	90	21W
Cobar	116	31	27S	145	48 E
Cóbh	35	51	50N	8	18W
Cobham	118	30	18S	142	7 E
Cobourg	151	43	58N	78	10W
Cobram	117	35	54S	145	40 E
Cocanada = Kakinada	92	16	57N	82	11 E
Cochabamba	187	17	26S	66	10W
Cochin China = Nam-Phan	95	10	30N	106	0 E
Cochran	170	32	25N	83	23W
Cochrane	151	49	0N	81	0W
Cockburn, Canal	192	54	30S	72	0W
Coco →	179	15	0N	83	8W
Coco Chan.	94	13	50N	93	25 E
Cocos Is.	111	12	10S	96	55 E
Cod, C.	164	42	8N	70	10W
Codajás	185	3	55S	62	0W
Codó	185	4	30S	43	55W
Cœur d'Alene	171	47	45N	116	51W
Coffs Harbour	116	30	16S	153	5 E
Cohoes	164	42	47N	73	42W
Cohuna	117	35	45S	144	15 E
Coiba, I.	179	7	30N	81	40W
Coihaique	192	45	30S	71	45W
Coimbatore	90	11	2N	76	59 E
Coimbra	50	40	15N	8	27W
Cojimies	184	0	20N	80	0W
Cojutepequé	177	13	41N	88	54W
Colac	117	38	21S	143	35 E
Colchester	25	51	54N	0	55 E
Coldstream	31	55	39N	2	14W
Coleman	155	49	40N	114	30W
Coleraine, Australia	119	37	36S	141	40 E
Coleraine, U.K.	34	55	8N	6	40W
Colima	175	19	14N	103	43W
Colima □	175	19	10N	104	0W
Coll	30	56	40N	6	35W
College Park	170	33	42N	84	27W
Collie	120	33	22S	116	8 E
Collingwood	151	44	29N	80	13W
Collinsville	121	20	30S	147	56 E
Collooney	34	54	11N	8	28W
Colmar	37	48	5N	7	20 E
Colne	28	53	51N	2	11W
Cologne = Köln	42	50	56N	6	58 E
Colomb-Béchar = Béchar	127	31	38N	2	18W
Colômbia	188	20	10S	48	40W
Colombia ■	184	3	45N	73	0W
Colombo	90	6	56N	79	58 E
Colón, Cuba	178	22	42N	80	54W
Colón, Panama	179	9	20N	79	54W
Colonia	191	34	25S	57	50W
Colorado □	163	37	40N	106	0W
Colorado →, Argentina	190	39	50S	62	8W
Colorado →, Calif., U.S.A.	173	34	45N	114	40W
Colorado →, Tex., U.S.A.	161	28	36N	95	58W
Colorado Desert	160	34	20N	116	0W
Colorado Plateau	161	36	40N	110	30W
Colorado Springs	163	38	55N	104	50W
Columbia, Miss., U.S.A.	169	31	16N	89	50W
Columbia, Mo., U.S.A.	166	38	58N	92	20W
Columbia, S.C., U.S.A.	165	34	0N	81	0W
Columbia, Tenn., U.S.A.	169	35	40N	87	0W
Columbia →	171	46	15N	124	5W
Columbia, District of □	164	38	55N	77	0W
Columbia Basin	171	47	30N	118	30W
Columbretes, Is.	51	39	50N	0	50 E
Columbus, Ga., U.S.A.	170	32	30N	84	58W
Columbus, Ind., U.S.A.	167	39	14N	85	55W
Columbus, Miss., U.S.A.	169	33	30N	88	26W
Columbus, Ohio, U.S.A.	167	39	57N	83	1W
Colwyn Bay	26	53	17N	3	44W
Comeragh Mts.	35	52	17N	7	35W
Comilla	93	23	28N	91	10 E
Comitán	177	16	18N	92	9W
Committee B.	146	68	30N	86	30W
Communism Pk. = Kommunizma, Pik	71	39	0N	72	2 E
Como	46	45	48N	9	5 E
Como, L. di	46	46	5N	9	17 E
Comodoro Rivadavia	192	45	50S	67	40W
Comorin, C.	90	8	3N	77	40 E
Comoro Is. ■	125	12	10S	44	15 E
Comox	154	49	42N	124	55W
Compiègne	38	49	24N	2	50 E
Côn Dao	95	8	45N	106	45 E
Conakry	130	9	29N	13	49W
Conceição da Barra	189	18	35S	39	45W
Concepción, Argentina	191	27	20S	65	35W
Concepción, Chile	190	36	50S	73	0W
Concepción, Est. de	192	50	30S	74	55W
Concepción del Oro	174	24	38N	101	25W
Concepción del Uruguay	190	32	35S	58	20W
Conchos, R. →	174	29	35N	104	25W
Concord, Calif., U.S.A.	172	37	59N	122	2W
Concord, N.C., U.S.A.	165	35	28N	80	35W
Concord, N.H., U.S.A.	164	43	12N	71	30W
Concordia, Argentina	190	31	20S	58	2W
Concordia, U.S.A.	161	39	35N	97	40W
Condamine	155	26	56S	150	9 E
Condé	38	50	26N	3	34 E
Condobolin	117	33	4S	147	6 E
Congleton	28	53	10N	2	12W
Congo = Zaïre →	134	6	4S	12	24 E
Congo (Kinshasa) = Zaïre ■	134	3	0S	23	0 E
Congo ■	134	1	0S	16	0 E
Congo Basin	124	0	10S	24	30 E
Conjeeveram = Kanchipuram	90	12	52N	79	45 E
Connacht	34	53	23N	8	40W
Conneaut	164	41	55N	80	32W
Connecticut □	164	41	40N	72	40W
Connecticut →	157	41	17N	72	21W
Connemara	34	53	29N	9	45W
Connors Ra.	121	21	40S	149	10 E
Consett	28	54	52N	1	50W

Constance = Konstanz .... **44** 47 39N 9 10 E
Constance, L. = Bodensee . **44** 47 35N 9 25 E
Constanţa .... **57** 44 14N 28 38 E
Constantine .... **127** 36 25N 6 42 E
Contamana **186** 7 19S 74 55W
Conway = Conwy **26** 53 17N 3 50W
Conway = Conwy ~► **26** 53 18N 3 50W
Conway, N.H., U.S.A. **148** 43 58N 71 8W
Conway, S.C., U.S.A. **165** 33 49N 79 2W
Conwy **26** 53 17N 3 50W
Conwy ~► **26** 53 18N 3 50W
Cook, Mt. .... **123** 43 36S 170 9 E
Cook Inlet **142** 59 0N 151 0W
Cook Is. **123** 17 0S 160 0W
Cook Strait .... **123** 41 15S 174 29 E
Cookeville **169** 36 12N 85 30W
Cookstown **34** 54 40N 6 43W
Coolah .... **116** 31 48S 149 41 E
Coolamon .... **117** 34 46S 147 8 E
Coolangatta .... **116** 28 11S 153 29 E
Coolgardie .... **120** 30 55S 121 8 E
Cooma .... **117** 36 12S 149 8 E
Coonabarabran .... **116** 31 14S 149 18 E
Coonamble .... **116** 30 56S 148 27 E
Cooper Cr. ~► .... **118** 12 7S 132 41 E
Coorong, The .... **119** 35 50S 139 20 E
Coorow .... **120** 29 53S 116 2 E
Coos Bay **171** 43 26N 124 7W
Cootamundra .... **117** 34 36S 148 1 E
Copenhagen = København . **61** 55 41N 12 34 E
Copiapó **190** 27 30S 70 20W
Copper Center **142** 62 10N 145 25W
Coppermine **145** 67 50N 115 5W
Coppermine ~► **145** 67 49N 116 4W
Coquilhatville = Mbandaka . **134** 0 1N 18 18 E
Coquimbo **190** 30 0S 71 20W
Coracora **186** 15 5S 73 45W
Coral Gables **170** 25 45N 80 16W
Coral Harbour **146** 64 8N 83 10W
Coral Sea .... **121** 15 0S 150 0 E
Corbeil-Essonnes .... **39** 48 36N 2 26 E
Corbin **165** 37 0N 84 3W
Corby **25** 52 29N 0 41W
Cordele **170** 31 55N 83 49W
Córdoba, Argentina **190** 31 20S 64 10W
Córdoba, México **177** 18 53N 96 56W
Córdoba, Spain **50** 37 50N 4 50W
Córdoba, Sierra de **190** 31 10S 64 25W
Cordova **142** 60 36N 145 45W
Corfu = Kérkira .... **54** 39 38N 19 50 E
Corinth = Kórinthos ...... **54** 37 56N 22 55 E
Corinth **169** 34 54N 88 30W
Corinth, G. of = Korinthiakós
Kólpos .... **54** 38 16N 22 30 E
Corinto, Brazil **188** 18 20S 44 30W
Corinto, Nic. **179** 12 30N 87 10W
Cork **35** 51 54N 8 30W
Cork □ **35** 51 50N 8 50W
Çorlu .... **80** 41 11N 27 49 E
Corn Is. = Maíz, Islas del .. **179** 12 15N 83 4W
Corner Brook **140** 48 57N 57 58W
Cornwall **151** 45 2N 74 44W
Cornwall □ **27** 50 26N 4 40W
Coro **184** 11 25N 69 41W
Coroatá **188** 4 8S 44 0W
Corocoro **187** 17 15S 68 28W
Coroico **187** 16 0S 67 50W
Coromandel Coast .... **90** 12 30N 81 0 E
Corona **173** 33 49N 117 36W
Coronado **173** 32 45N 117 9W
Coronation Gulf **145** 68 25N 110 0W
Coronel **190** 37 0S 73 10W
Coronel Pringles **190** 38 0S 61 30W
Corowa .... **117** 35 58S 146 21 E
Corozal **177** 9 19N 75 18W
Corpus Christi **161** 27 50N 97 28W
Corrib, L. **34** 53 5N 9 10W
Corrientes **190** 27 30S 58 45W
Corrientes, C., Colombia ... **184** 5 30N 77 34W
Corrientes, C., Cuba **178** 21 43N 84 30W
Corrientes, C., Mexico **175** 20 25N 105 42W

Corrigin .... **120** 32 20S 117 53 E
Corse .... **36** 42 0N 9 0 E
Corsica = Corse .... **36** 42 0N 9 0 E
Corsicana **168** 32 5N 96 30W
Cortez **163** 37 24N 108 35W
Cortland **164** 42 35N 76 11W
Çorum .... **80** 40 30N 34 57 E
Corumbá **187** 19 0S 57 30W
Coruña, La **50** 43 20N 8 25W
Corunna = Coruña, La **50** 43 20N 8 25W
Corvallis **171** 44 36N 123 15W
Cosamaloapan **177** 18 23N 95 50W
Cosenza .... **49** 39 17N 16 14 E
Coshocton **167** 40 17N 81 51W
Costa Blanca **51** 38 25N 0 10W
Costa Brava .... **51** 41 30N 3 0 E
Costa del Sol **50** 36 30N 4 30W
Costa Dorada .... **51** 40 45N 1 15 E
Costa Rica ■ **179** 10 0N 84 0W
Cotagaita **187** 20 45S 65 40W
Côte d'Or .... **37** 47 10N 4 50 E
Coteau des Prairies **156** 44 30N 97 0W
Cotonou .... **131** 6 20N 2 25 E
Cotopaxi, Vol. **184** 0 40S 78 30W
Cotswold Hills **24** 51 42N 2 10W
Cottbus .... **43** 51 44N 14 20 E
Coulommiers .... **39** 48 50N 3 3 E
Council **142** 64 55N 163 45W
Council Bluffs **166** 41 20N 95 50W
Courantyne ~► **185** 5 55N 57 5W
Courtrai = Kortrijk ...... **42** 50 50N 3 17 E
Coventry **24** 52 25N 1 31W
Covington, Ga., U.S.A. ... **170** 33 36N 83 50W
Covington, Ky., U.S.A. **167** 39 5N 84 30W
Cowdenbeath **31** 56 7N 3 20W
Cowes **25** 50 45N 1 18W
Cowra .... **117** 33 49S 148 42 E
Coxim **188** 18 30S 54 55W
Cracow = Kraków .... **58** 50 4N 19 57 E
Craigavon = Lurgan **34** 54 28N 6 20W
Craiova .... **57** 44 21N 23 48 E
Cranbrook, Australia ..... **120** 34 18S 117 33 E
Cranbrook, Canada **155** 49 30N 115 46W
Crateús **189** 5 10S 40 39W
Crato **189** 7 10S 39 25W
Crawfordsville **167** 40 2N 86 51W
Crawley **24** 51 7N 0 10W
Creil .... **39** 49 15N 2 34 E
Cremona .... **46** 45 8N 10 2 E
Crépy-en-Valois .... **39** 49 14N 2 54 E
Cres .... **52** 44 58N 14 25 E
Crescent City **172** 41 45N 124 12W
Creston, Canada **155** 49 10N 116 31W
Creston, U.S.A. **166** 41 0N 94 20W
Crestview **169** 30 45N 86 35W
Crete = Kríti .... **55** 35 15N 25 0 E
Creuse ~► .... **36** 47 0N 0 34 E
Creusot, Le .... **37** 46 50N 4 24 E
Crewe **28** 53 6N 2 28W
Criciúma **191** 28 40S 49 23W
Crieff **31** 56 22N 3 50W
Crimea □ .... **70** 45 30N 33 10 E
Crişul Alb ~► .... **56** 46 42N 21 17 E
Crişul Negru ~► .... **56** 46 38N 22 26 E
Crna Gora = Montenegro □ **52** 42 40N 19 20 E
Crna Gora .... **52** 42 10N 21 30 E
Croatia ■ .... **52** 45 20N 18 0 E
Crockett **168** 31 20N 95 30W
Cromarty **33** 57 40N 4 2W
Cromer .... **29** 52 56N 1 18 E
Crooked I. **180** 22 50N 74 10W
Crookwell .... **117** 34 28S 149 24 E
Cross Fell **28** 54 44N 2 29W
Cross L. **153** 54 45N 97 30W
Crosse, La **166** 43 48N 91 13W
Crowley **168** 30 15N 92 20W
Crowsnest Pass **155** 49 40N 114 40W
Cruz, C. **178** 19 50N 77 50W
Cruz Alta **191** 28 45S 53 40W
Cruz del Eje **190** 30 45S 64 50W
Cruzeiro do Sul **186** 7 35S 72 35W

Name	Page	Lat	Long
Crystal Brook	119	33 21S	138 12 E
Cu Lao Hon	95	10 54N	108 18 E
Cuando →	134	14 0S	19 30 E
Cuanza →	134	9 2S	13 30 E
Cuba ■	178	22 0N	79 0W
Cubango →	134	18 50S	22 25 E
Cucuí	184	1 12N	66 50W
Cúcuta	184	7 54N	72 31W
Cuddalore	90	11 46N	79 45 E
Cuddapah	90	14 30N	78 47 E
Cue →	120	27 25S	117 54 E
Cuenca, Ecuador	184	2 50S	79 9W
Cuenca, Spain	51	40 5N	2 10W
Cuenca, Serranía de	51	39 55N	1 50W
Cuernavaca	177	18 55N	99 15W
Cuevo	187	20 15S	63 30W
Cuiabá	188	15 30S	56 0W
Cuillin Hills	32	57 14N	6 15W
Cuitzeo, L. de	175	19 55N	101 5W
Culcairn	117	35 41S	147 3 E
Culiacán	174	24 48N	107 24W
Cullarin Range	117	34 30S	149 30 E
Culloden Moor	33	57 29N	4 7W
Culverden	123	42 47S	172 49 E
Cumaná	185	10 30N	64 5W
Cumberland	164	39 40N	78 43W
Cumberland →	169	36 15N	87 0W
Cumberland Is.	121	20 35S	149 10 E
Cumberland Pen.	146	67 0N	64 0W
Cumberland Plat.	169	36 0N	84 30W
Cumberland Sd.	146	65 30N	66 0W
Cumbria □	28	54 35N	2 55W
Cumbrian Mts.	28	54 30N	3 0W
Cumbum	90	15 40N	79 10 E
Cummins	119	34 16S	135 43 E
Cumnock	31	55 27N	4 18W
Cunene →	134	17 20S	11 50 E
Cunnamulla	116	28 2S	145 38 E
Curaçao	181	12 10N	69 0W
Curaray →	184	2 20S	74 5W
Curiapo	185	8 33N	61 5W
Curicó	190	34 55S	71 20W
Curitiba	191	25 20S	49 10W
Curtis Group	117	39 30S	146 37 E
Curuá →	188	5 23S	54 22W
Curuçá	188	0 43S	47 50W
Curuzú Cuatiá	191	29 50S	58 5W
Cushing	168	35 59N	96 46W
Cusihuiriáchic	174	28 14N	106 50W
Cuthbert	170	31 47N	84 47W
Cuttack	92	20 25N	85 57 E
Cuxhaven	42	53 51N	8 41 E
Cuyahoga Falls	167	41 8N	81 30W
Cuzco, Bolivia	187	20 0S	66 50W
Cuzco, Peru	186	13 32S	72 0W
Cwmbran	27	51 39N	3 0W
Cypress Hills	152	49 40N	109 30W
Cyprus ■	80	35 0N	33 0 E
Cyrenaica	124	27 0N	23 0 E
Czech Republic ■	59	49 0N	15 0 E
Czeremcha	58	52 31N	23 21 E
Częstochowa	58	50 49N	19 7 E

D

Name	Page	Lat	Long
Da →	95	21 15N	105 20 E
Da Hinggan Ling	98	48 0N	121 0 E
Da Nang	95	16 4N	108 13 E
Da Yunhe →	99	34 25S	120 5 E
Daba Shan	99	32 0N	109 0 E
Dacca = Dhaka	92	23 43N	90 26 E
Dacca □ = Dhaka □	93	24 25N	90 25 E
Dadanawa	185	2 50N	59 30W
Dadra and Nagar Haveli □	91	20 5N	73 0 E
Daghestan □	70	42 30N	47 0 E
Dahomey = Benin ■	131	10 0N	2 0 E
Dai-Sen	109	35 22N	133 32 E
Daiō-Misaki	106	34 15N	136 45 E
Daisetsu-Zan	103	43 30N	142 57 E
Daito	109	35 19N	132 58 E
Dajarra	115	21 42S	139 30 E
Dakar	130	14 34N	17 29W
Dakhla	126	23 50N	15 53W
Dakhla, El Wâhât el-	128	25 30N	28 50 E
Ðakovica	52	42 22N	20 26 E
Dalandzadgad	98	43 27N	104 30 E
Dalbeattie	31	54 55N	3 50W
Dalby	116	27 10S	151 17 E
Dalhousie	148	48 5N	66 26W
Dalí	99	25 40N	100 10 E
Dalian	98	38 50N	121 40 E
Daliang Shan	99	28 0N	102 45 E
Dallas, Oreg., U.S.A.	171	45 0N	123 15W
Dallas, Tex., U.S.A.	168	32 50N	96 50W
Dalmacija	52	43 20N	17 0 E
Dalmatia = Dalmacija	52	43 20N	17 0 E
Daloa	130	7 0N	6 30W
Dalton	169	34 47N	84 58W
Daly Waters	114	16 15S	133 24 E
Daman	91	20 25N	72 57 E
Damaraland	136	21 0S	17 0 E
Damascus = Dimashq	80	33 30N	36 18 E
Damãvand	86	35 47N	52 0 E
Damãvand, Qolleh-ye	86	35 56N	52 10 E
Dampier	114	20 41S	116 42 E
Dampier Arch.	114	20 38S	116 32 E
Danbury	164	41 23N	73 29W
Dandenong	117	38 0S	145 15 E
Dandong	98	40 10N	124 20 E
Dangriga	177	17 0N	88 13W
Dannevirke	122	40 12S	176 8 E
Dansville	164	42 32N	77 41W
Danville, Ill., U.S.A.	167	40 10N	87 40W
Danville, Ky., U.S.A.	167	37 40N	84 45W
Danville, Va., U.S.A.	165	36 40N	79 20W
Danzig = Gdańsk	58	54 22N	18 40 E
Dar es Salaam	135	6 50S	39 12 E
Darbhanga	92	26 15N	85 55 E
Dardanelles = Çanakkale Boğazı	80	40 0N	26 0 E
Dârfûr	129	13 40N	24 0 E
Dargan Ata	70	40 29N	62 10 E
Dargaville	122	35 57S	173 52 E
Darién, G. del	184	9 0N	77 0W
Darjeeling = Darjiling	92	27 3N	88 18 E
Darjiling	92	27 3N	88 18 E
Darling →	119	34 4S	141 54 E
Darling Downs	116	27 30S	150 30 E
Darling Ra.	120	32 30S	116 0 E
Darlington	28	54 33N	1 33W
Darmstadt	42	49 51N	8 40 E
Darnley, C.	14	68 0S	69 0 E
Dart →	27	50 24N	3 36W
Dartmoor	27	50 36N	4 0W
Dartmouth, Canada	149	44 40N	63 30W
Dartmouth, U.K.	27	50 21N	3 35W
Darwin	114	12 25S	130 51 E
Dasht-e Kavïr	86	34 30N	55 0 E
Dasht-e Lût	85	31 30N	58 0 E
Dasht-e Mãrgow	87	30 40N	62 30 E
Datia	91	25 39N	78 27 E
Datong	98	40 6N	113 18 E
Daugavpils	68	55 53N	26 32 E
Dauphin	153	51 9N	100 5W
Dauphiné	37	45 15N	5 25 E
Davangere	90	14 25N	75 55 E
Davao	112	7 0N	125 40 E
Davenport	166	41 30N	90 40W
Daventry	24	52 16N	1 10W
David	179	8 30N	82 30W
Davis Sea	15	66 0S	92 0 E
Davis Str.	146	65 0N	58 0W
Davos	44	46 48N	9 49 E
Dawson	144	64 10N	139 30W
Dawson Creek	155	55 45N	120 15W
Dawson Range	121	24 30S	149 48 E
Daylesford	117	37 21S	144 9 E
Dayr az Zawr	81	35 20N	40 5 E
Dayton, Ohio, U.S.A.	167	39 45N	84 10W

Name	Ref	Lat	Long
Dayton, Wash., U.S.A.	171	46 20N	118 10W
Daytona Beach	170	29 14N	81 0W
De Aar	136	30 39S	24 0 E
De Land	170	29 1N	81 19W
De Ridder	168	30 48N	93 15W
De Soto	166	38 7N	90 33W
Deakin	114	30 46S	128 0 E
Deal	25	51 13N	1 25 E
Dean, Forest of	24	51 50N	2 35W
Deán Funes	190	30 20S	64 20W
Dease →	144	59 56N	128 32W
Dease Lake	144	58 25N	130 6W
Death Valley	173	36 19N	116 52W
Deauville	38	49 23N	0 2 E
Debar	52	41 31N	20 30 E
Debre Markos	132	10 20N	37 40 E
Debre Tabor	132	11 50N	38 26 E
Debrecen	59	47 33N	21 42 E
Decatur, Ala., U.S.A.	169	34 35N	87 0W
Decatur, Ga., U.S.A.	170	33 47N	84 17W
Decatur, Ill., U.S.A.	166	39 50N	89 0W
Deccan	76	18 0N	79 0 E
Dedéagach = Alexandroúpolis	55	40 50N	25 54 E
Dee →, Scotland, U.K.	33	57 4N	2 7W
Dee →, Wales, U.K.	26	53 15N	3 7W
Deepwater	116	29 25S	151 51 E
Deer Lake	149	49 11N	57 27W
Defiance	167	41 20N	84 20W
Deh Bïd	85	30 39N	53 11 E
Dehra Dun	89	30 20N	78 4 E
Dej	56	47 10N	23 52 E
Del Rio	161	29 23N	100 50W
Delano	173	35 48N	119 13W
Delaware □	164	39 0N	75 40W
Delaware →	164	39 20N	75 25W
Delaware B.	157	38 50N	75 0W
Delft	40	52 1N	4 22 E
Delfzijl	41	53 20N	6 55 E
Delgado, C.	137	10 45S	40 40 E
Delgo	129	20 6N	30 40 E
Delhi	89	28 38N	77 17 E
Delice →	80	39 45N	34 15 E
Delicias	174	28 13N	105 28W
Delong, Ostrova	72	76 40N	149 20 E
Deloraine	119	41 30S	146 40 E
Delray Beach	170	26 27N	80 4W
Demanda, Sierra de la	50	42 15N	3 0W
Dembidolo	132	8 34N	34 50 E
Deming	161	32 10N	107 50W
Demopolis	169	32 30N	87 48W
Den Burg	40	53 3N	4 47 E
Den Haag = 's-Gravenhage	40	52 7N	4 17 E
Den Helder	40	52 57N	4 45 E
Den Oever	40	52 56N	5 2 E
Denain	38	50 20N	3 22 E
Denbigh	26	53 12N	3 26W
Denham	120	25 56S	113 31 E
Deniliquin	117	35 30S	144 58 E
Denison	168	33 50N	96 40W
Denizli	80	37 42N	29 2 E
Denmark	120	34 59S	117 25 E
Denmark ■	61	55 30N	9 0 E
Denmark Str.	13	66 0N	30 0W
Denton	168	33 12N	97 10W
D'Entrecasteaux Is.	115	9 0S	151 0 E
Denver	163	39 45N	105 0W
Deolali	91	19 58N	73 50 E
Deoria	92	26 31N	83 48 E
Deosai Mts.	89	35 40N	75 0 E
Dera Ghazi Khan	89	30 5N	70 43 E
Dera Ismail Khan	89	31 50N	70 50 E
Derby	28	52 55N	1 28W
Derby □	28	52 55N	1 28W
Derg, L.	35	53 0N	8 20W
Derry = Londonderry	34	55 0N	7 20W
Derryveagh Mts.	34	55 0N	8 40W
Derwent →, Cumb., U.K.	28	54 42N	3 22W
Derwent →, Derby, U.K.	29	52 53N	1 17W
Derwent →, N. Yorks., U.K.	29	53 45N	0 57W
Derwent Water, L.	28	54 35N	3 9W
Des Moines	166	41 35N	93 37W
Des Moines →	166	40 23N	91 25W
Deschutes →	171	45 30N	121 0W
Dese	133	11 5N	39 40 E
Despeñaperros, Paso	50	38 24N	3 30W
Dessau	43	51 49N	12 15 E
Dessye = Dese	133	11 5N	39 40 E
Desvrès	38	50 40N	1 48 E
Detroit	167	42 23N	83 5W
Deurne	41	51 27N	5 49 E
Deutsche Bucht	42	54 10N	7 51 E
Devakottai	90	9 55N	78 45 E
Deventer	41	52 15N	6 10 E
Devizes	24	51 21N	2 0W
Devon I.	13	75 10N	85 0W
Devonport, Australia	119	41 10S	146 22 E
Devonport, N.Z.	122	36 49S	174 49 E
Devonport, U.K.	27	50 23N	4 11W
Devonshire □	27	50 50N	3 40W
Dewsbury	28	53 42N	1 38W
Dezfül	84	32 20N	48 30 E
Dezhneva, Mys	73	66 5N	169 40W
Dhahran = Az Zahrän	84	26 10N	50 7 E
Dhaka	92	23 43N	90 26 E
Dhaka □	93	24 25N	90 25 E
Dhamar	83	14 30N	44 20 E
Dhar	91	22 35N	75 26 E
Dharmapuri	90	12 10N	78 10 E
Dharwad	90	15 22N	75 15 E
Dhidhimótikhon	55	41 22N	26 29 E
Dhikti	55	35 8N	25 22 E
Dhodhekánisos	55	36 35N	27 0 E
Dhuburi	92	26 2N	89 59 E
Dhule	91	20 58N	74 50 E
Di Linh, Cao Nguyen	95	11 30N	108 0 E
Diamantina	188	18 17S	43 40W
Diamantina →	115	26 45S	139 10 E
Diamantino	188	14 30S	56 30W
Dibrugarh	93	27 29N	94 55 E
Dickinson	163	46 50N	102 48W
Didsbury	155	51 35N	114 10W
Diefenbaker L.	152	51 0N	106 55W
Dieppe	38	49 54N	1 4 E
Dieren	41	52 3N	6 6 E
Digby	148	44 38N	65 50W
Digne	37	44 5N	6 12 E
Dijlah, Nahr →	81	31 0N	47 25 E
Dijon	37	47 20N	5 0 E
Díla	133	6 21N	38 22 E
Dillon	165	34 26N	79 20W
Dimashq	80	33 30N	36 18 E
Dimboola	119	36 28S	142 7 E
Dîmbovita →	57	44 14N	26 13 E
Dimitrovgrad	53	42 5N	25 35 E
Dimitrovo = Pernik	53	42 35N	23 2 E
Dinan	36	48 28N	2 2W
Dinara Planina	52	44 0N	16 30 E
Dinaric Alps = Dinara Planina	52	44 0N	16 30 E
Dindigul	90	10 25N	78 0 E
Dingle	35	52 9N	10 17W
Dingle B.	35	52 3N	10 20W
Dingwall	33	57 36N	4 26W
Dinuba	173	36 31N	119 22W
Dire Dawa	133	9 35N	41 45 E
Diriamba	179	11 51N	86 19W
Dirranbandi	116	28 33S	148 17 E
Disappointment L.	114	23 20S	122 40 E
Discovery B.	119	38 10S	140 40 E
Disko	146	69 45N	53 30W
Diss	25	52 23N	1 6 E
Diu	91	20 45N	70 58 E
Dives-sur-Mer	39	49 18N	0 8W
Dixon	166	41 50N	89 30W
Dixon Entrance	154	54 30N	132 0W
Diyarbakir	81	37 55N	40 18 E
Djakarta = Jakarta	111	6 9S	106 49 E
Djelfa	130	34 40N	3 15 E
Djerid, Chott	127	33 42N	8 30 E
Djibouti	133	11 30N	43 5 E
Djibouti ■	133	12 0N	43 0 E
Djoum	131	2 41N	12 35 E

Dmitriya Lapteva, Proliv	72	73	0N	140	0 E
Dnepr →	68	46	30N	32	18 E
Dnepropetrovsk	68	48	30N	35	0 E
Dnestr →	68	46	18N	30	17 E
Dnestrovski = Belgorod -	68	50	35N	36	35 E
Dnieper = Dnepr →	68	46	30N	32	18 E
Dniester = Dnestr → ..	68	46	18N	30	17 E
Dobrich	53	43	37N	27	49 E
Dobruja	57	44	30N	28	15 E
Dodecanese =					
Dhodhekánisos	55	36	35N	27	0 E
Dodge City	161	37	42N	100	0W
Dodoma	135	6	8S	35	45 E
Doesburg	41	52	1N	6	9 E
Doetinchem	41	51	59N	6	18 E
Dogger Bank	124	54	50N	2	0 E
Doi Luang	95	18	30N	101	0 E
Dojran	54	41	10N	22	45 E
Dokkum	41	53	20N	5	59 E
Dolbeau	148	48	53N	72	18W
Dole	37	47	7N	5	31 E
Dolgellau	26	52	44N	3	53W
Dolgelley = Dolgellau	26	52	44N	3	53W
Dolomites = Dolomiti	47	46	30N	11	40 E
Dolomiti	47	46	30N	11	40 E
Dolores	191	36	20S	57	40W
Dolphin and Union Str.	145	69	5N	114	45W
Domel I. = Letsôk-aw Kyun	94	11	30N	98	25 E
Dominica ■	180	15	20N	61	20W
Dominican Rep. ■	180	19	0N	70	30W
Don →, Russia	68	47	4N	39	18 E
Don →, U.K.	33	57	14N	2	5W
Donaghadee	34	54	38N	5	32W
Donau →	42	48	10N	17	0 E
Doncaster	29	53	31N	1	9W
Dondra Head	90	5	55N	80	40 E
Donegal	34	54	39N	8	8W
Donegal □	34	54	53N	8	0W
Donegal B.	34	54	30N	8	35W
Donetsk	68	48	0N	37	45 E
Dongara	120	29	14S	114	57 E
Dongen	40	51	38N	4	56 E
Dongting Hu	99	29	18N	112	45 E
Donnelly's Crossing	122	35	42S	173	38 E
Donnybrook	120	33	34S	115	48 E
Doon →	31	55	26N	4	41W
Dorada, La	184	5	30N	74	40W
Dorchester	27	50	42N	2	28W
Dorchester, C.	146	65	27N	77	27W
Dordogne □	36	45	5N	0	40 E
Dordrecht	40	51	48N	4	39 E
Dornoch	33	57	52N	4	0W
Dorrigo	116	30	20S	152	44 E
Dorris	172	41	59N	121	58W
Dorset □	27	50	48N	2	25W
Dortmund	42	51	32N	7	28 E
Dothan	169	31	10N	85	25W
Douai	38	50	21N	3	4 E
Douala	131	4	0N	9	45 E
Douarnenez	36	48	6N	4	21W
Douglas, U.K.	28	54	9N	4	29W
Douglas, U.S.A.	170	31	32N	82	52W
Doullens	38	50	10N	2	20 E
Dounreay	33	58	34N	3	44W
Dourados	188	22	9S	54	50W
Douro →	50	41	8N	8	40W
Douro Litoral □	50	41	10N	8	20W
Dove →	28	52	51N	1	36W
Dover, U.K.	25	51	7N	1	19 E
Dover, Del., U.S.A.	164	39	10N	75	31W
Dover, N.H., U.S.A.	164	43	12N	70	51W
Dover, Str. of	38	51	0N	1	30 E
Dovey →	26	52	32N	4	0W
Downham Market	25	52	36N	0	22 E
Downpatrick	34	54	20N	5	43W
Drachten	41	53	7N	6	5 E
Dragoman, Prokhod	53	43	0N	22	53 E
Draguignan	37	43	30N	6	27 E
Drakensberg	137	31	0S	28	0 E
Dráma	55	41	9N	24	10 E
Drammen	60	59	42N	10	12 E
Drau = Drava →	59	45	33N	18	55 E
Drava →	59	45	33N	18	55 E
Drayton Valley	155	53	12N	114	58W
Drenthe □	41	52	52N	6	40 E
Dresden	43	51	2N	13	45 E
Dreux	39	48	44N	1	23 E
Driffield	29	54	0N	0	25W
Drin i zi →	52	41	37N	20	28 E
Drina →	52	44	53N	19	21 E
Drogheda	34	53	45N	6	20W
Droitwich	24	52	16N	2	10W
Dronne →	36	45	2N	0	9W
Dronning Maud Land	14	72	30S	12	0 E
Drumheller	155	51	25N	112	40W
Drummond Ra.	121	23	45S	147	10 E
Drummondville	151	45	55N	72	25W
Dryden	153	49	47N	92	50W
Du Bois	164	41	8N	78	46W
Du Quoin	166	38	0N	89	10W
Dubai = Dubayy	85	25	18N	55	20 E
Dubawnt →	145	64	33N	100	6W
Dubawnt, L.	143	63	4N	101	42W
Dubayy	85	25	18N	55	20 E
Dubbo	116	32	11S	148	35 E
Dublin, Ireland	35	53	20N	6	18W
Dublin, U.S.A.	170	32	30N	82	34W
Dublin □	34	53	24N	6	20W
Dubrovnik	52	42	39N	18	6 E
Dubuque	166	42	30N	90	41W
Dudley	24	52	30N	2	5W
Dugi Otok	52	44	0N	15	0 E
Duisburg	42	51	27N	6	42 E
Duluth	150	46	48N	92	10W
Dumbarton	31	55	58N	4	35W
Dumfries	31	55	4N	3	37W
Dumfries & Galloway □ ...	31	55	0N	4	0W
Dun Laoghaire	35	53	17N	6	9W
Dunărea →	57	45	30N	8	15 E
Dunaújváros	59	47	0N	18	57 E
Dunbar	31	56	0N	2	32W
Dunblane	31	56	10N	3	58W
Duncan, Canada	154	48	45N	123	40W
Duncan, U.S.A.	161	34	25N	98	0W
Duncan Pass.	94	11	0N	92	30 E
Dundalk	34	54	1N	6	25W
Dundas, Canada	151	43	17N	79	59W
Dundas, Greenland	13	77	0N	69	0W
Dundee	31	56	29N	3	0W
Dundrum	34	54	17N	5	50W
Dunedin	123	45	50S	170	33 E
Dunedoo	116	32	0S	149	25 E
Dunfermline	31	56	5N	3	28W
Dungannon	34	54	30N	6	47W
Dungarvan	35	52	6N	7	40W
Dungeness	25	50	54N	0	59 E
Dungog	117	32	22S	151	46 E
Dunhuang	100	40	8N	94	36 E
Dunkeld	33	56	34N	3	36W
Dunkerque	38	51	2N	2	20 E
Dunkery Beacon	27	51	15N	3	37W
Dunkirk = Dunkerque	38	51	2N	2	20 E
Dunkirk	164	42	30N	79	18W
Dúnleary = Dun Laoghaire .	35	53	17N	6	9W
Dunmore	164	41	27N	75	38W
Dunn	165	35	18N	78	36W
Dunnet Hd.	33	58	38N	3	22W
Duns	31	55	47N	2	20W
Dunsmuir	172	41	10N	122	18W
Dunstan Mts.	123	44	53S	169	35 E
Durance →	37	43	55N	4	45 E
Durango, Mexico	174	24	3N	104	39W
Durango, U.S.A.	163	37	16N	107	50W
Durango □	174	24	50N	104	50W
Durant	168	34	0N	96	25W
Durazno	191	33	25S	56	31W
Durban	137	29	49S	31	1 E
Durg	92	21	15N	81	22 E
Durham, U.K.	28	54	47N	1	34W
Durham, U.S.A.	165	36	0N	78	55W
Durham □	28	54	42N	1	45W
Durmitor	52	43	10N	19	0 E

Durness	32	58	34N	4	45W
D'Urville I.	122	40	50S	173	55 E
Dushanbe	71	38	33N	68	48 E
Düsseldorf	42	51	15N	6	46 E
Duwādimi	82	24	35N	44	15 E
Duyun	99	26	18N	107	29 E
Duzce	80	40	50N	31	10 E
Duzdab = Zāhedān	86	29	30N	60	50 E
Dvina, Sev. →	69	64	32N	40	30 E
Dvinsk = Daugavpils	68	55	53N	26	32 E
Dyer, C.	146	66	40N	61	0W
Dyersburg	169	36	2N	89	20W
Dyfed □	26	52	0N	4	30W
Dysart	121	22	32S	148	23 E
Dzamin Üüd	98	43	50N	111	58 E
Dzerzhinsk	68	53	40N	27	1 E
Dzhalal-Abad	71	40	56N	73	0 E
Dzhalinda	75	53	26N	124	0 E
Dzhambul	71	42	54N	71	22 E
Dzhardzhan	72	68	10N	124	10 E
Dzhetygara	71	52	11N	61	12 E
Dzhezkazgan	71	47	44N	67	40 E
Dzhugdzur, Khrebet	75	57	30N	138	0 E
Dzuumod	98	47	45N	106	58 E

E

Eagle	142	64	44N	141	7W
Eagle Pass	161	28	45N	100	35W
Eagle River	150	45	55N	89	17W
Ealing	25	51	30N	0	19W
Earn →	31	56	20N	3	19W
Easley	165	34	52N	82	35W
East Angus	148	45	30N	71	40W
East Bengal	92	24	0N	90	0 E
East Beskids = Vychodné					
Beskydy	59	49	30N	22	0 E
East C.	122	37	42S	178	35 E
East Chicago	167	41	40N	87	30W
East China Sea	99	30	5N	126	0 E
East Falkland	192	51	30S	58	30W
East Indies	77	0	0	120	0 E
East Kilbride	31	55	46N	4	10W
East Liverpool	164	40	39N	80	35W
East London	137	33	0S	27	55 E
East Main = Eastmain	140	52	10N	78	30W
East Pakistan =					
Bangladesh ■	92	24	0N	90	0 E
East Point	170	33	40N	84	28W
East St. Louis	166	38	37N	90	4W
East Schelde → =					
Oosterschelde	40	51	33N	4	0 E
East Siberian Sea	73	73	0N	160	0 E
East Sussex □	25	51	0N	0	20 E
Eastbourne, N.Z.	123	41	19S	174	55 E
Eastbourne, U.K.	25	50	46N	0	18 E
Eastern Ghats	90	14	0N	78	50 E
Eastleigh	25	50	58N	1	21W
Eastmain	140	52	10N	78	30W
Eastmain →	140	52	27N	78	26W
Easton	164	40	41N	75	15W
Eau Claire	166	44	46N	91	30W
Eau Claire, L. à l'	146	56	10N	74	25W
Ebbw Vale	26	51	47N	3	12W
Eboli	49	40	39N	15	2 E
Ebro →	51	40	43N	0	54 E
Echizen-Misaki	106	35	59N	135	57 E
Echo Bay	145	46	29N	84	4W
Echuca	117	36	10S	144	20 E
Ecuador ■	184	2	0S	78	0W
Ed Dämer	129	17	27N	34	0 E
Edam	40	52	31N	5	3 E
Eddystone	27	50	11N	4	16W
Ede	41	52	4N	5	40 E
Eden	117	37	3S	149	55 E
Eden →	28	54	57N	3	2W
Edenhope	119	37	4S	141	19 E
Edge Hill	24	52	7N	1	28W
Edhessa	54	40	48N	22	5 E
Edinburgh	31	55	57N	3	12W
Edirne	80	41	40N	26	34 E
Edmonton, Australia	121	17	2S	145	46 E
Edmonton, Canada	155	53	30N	113	30W
Edmundston	148	47	23N	68	20W
Edson	155	53	35N	116	28W
Edward, L.	132	0	25S	29	40 E
Edward VII Land	15	80	0S	150	0W
Edwards Plat.	161	30	30N	101	5W
Effingham	167	39	8N	88	30W
Égadi, Ísole	48	37	55N	12	16 E
Eger	59	47	53N	20	27 E
Egmont, Mt.	122	39	17S	174	5 E
Eğridir Gölü	80	37	53N	30	50 E
Egypt ■	128	28	0N	31	0 E
Eifel	42	50	10N	6	45 E
Eigg	32	56	54N	6	10W
Eil	133	8	0N	49	50 E
Eindhoven	41	51	26N	5	30 E
Eirunepé	187	6	35S	69	53W
El Aaiún	126	27	9N	13	12W
El Cajon	173	32	49N	117	0W
El Callao	185	7	18N	61	50W
El Centro	173	32	50N	115	40W
El Cerro	187	17	30S	61	40W
El Dere	133	3	50N	47	8 E
El Djouf	126	20	0N	11	30 E
El Dorado	168	33	10N	92	40W
El Escorial	50	40	35N	4	7W
El Faiyûm	128	29	19N	30	50 E
El Fâsher	129	13	33N	25	26 E
El Ferrol	50	43	29N	8	15W
El Fuerte	174	26	25N	108	39W
El Geteina	129	14	50N	32	27 E
El Iskandarîya	128	31	0N	30	0 E
El Jadida	126	33	11N	8	17W
El Khârga	128	25	30N	30	33 E
El Khartûm	129	15	31N	32	35 E
El Mahalla el Kubra	128	31	0N	31	0 E
El Minyâ	128	28	7N	30	33 E
El Obeid	129	13	8N	30	10 E
El Oro	177	27	15N	103	30W
El Paso	161	31	50N	106	30W
El Progreso	177	15	26N	87	51W
El Qâhira	128	30	1N	31	14 E
El Qasr	128	25	44N	28	42 E
El Salvador ■	177	13	50N	89	0W
El Suweis	128	29	58N	32	31 E
El Tigre	185	8	44N	64	15W
El Turbio	192	51	45S	72	5W
Elat	80	29	30N	34	56 E
Elâzığ	81	38	37N	39	14 E
Elba	46	42	48N	10	15 E
Elbasani	52	41	9N	20	9 E
Elbe →	42	53	50N	9	0 E
Elbert, Mt.	163	39	5N	106	27W
Elberton	165	34	7N	82	51W
Elbeuf	39	49	17N	1	2 E
Elbing = Elbląg	58	54	10N	19	25 E
Elbląg	58	54	10N	19	25 E
Elbrus	70	43	21N	42	30 E
Elburg	41	52	26N	5	50 E
Elburz Mts. = Alborz,					
Reshteh-ye Kühhä-ye	86	36	0N	52	0 E
Elche	51	38	15N	0	42W
Eldorado	174	24	20N	107	22W
Eldorado Springs	166	37	54N	93	59W
Eldoret	132	0	30N	35	17 E
Eleanora, Peak	120	32	57S	121	9 E
Electra	161	34	0N	99	0W
Elephant Butte Res.	161	33	45N	107	30W
Eleuthera	178	25	0N	76	20W
Elgin, U.K.	33	57	39N	3	20W
Elgin, Ill., U.S.A.	167	42	0N	88	20W
Elgin, Oreg., U.S.A.	171	45	37N	118	0W
Elgon, Mt.	132	1	10N	34	30 E
Elisabethville = Lubumbashi	135	11	40S	27	28 E
Elizabeth, Australia	119	34	42S	138	41 E
Elizabeth, U.S.A.	164	40	37N	74	12W
Elizabeth City	165	36	18N	76	16W

Name	Page	Lat			Long		
Elizabethton	165	36	20N		82	13W	
Elizabethtown	167	37	40N		85	54W	
Elk Point	152	53	54N		110	55W	
Elkhart	167	41	42N		85	55W	
Elkins	165	38	53N		79	53W	
Elko	172	40	50N		115	50W	
Ellensburg	171	47	0N		120	30W	
Ellery, Mt.	117	37	28S		148	47 E	
Ellesmere I.	13	79	30N		80	0W	
Ellesmere Port	28	53	17N		2	55W	
Ellice Is. = Tuvalu ■	122	8	0S		178	0 E	
Elliot Lake	150	46	25N		82	35W	
Ellore = Eluru	92	16	48N		81	8 E	
Ellsworth Land	14	76	0S		89	0W	
Ellsworth Mts.	14	78	30S		85	0W	
Elmhurst	167	41	52N		87	58W	
Elmira	164	42	8N		76	49W	
Elrose	152	51	12N		108	0W	
Eluru	92	16	48N		81	8 E	
Elvas	50	38	50N		7	10W	
Elwood	167	40	20N		85	50W	
Ely	172	39	10N		114	50W	
Elyria	167	41	22N		82	8W	
Emämrüd	86	36	30N		55	0 E	
Emba ➝	70	46	38N		53	14 E	
Emden	42	53	22N		7	12 E	
Emerald	121	23	32S		148	10 E	
Emilia-Romagna □	46	44	33N		10	40 E	
Emmeloord	41	52	44N		5	46 E	
Emmen	41	52	48N		6	57 E	
Empalme	174	27	58N		110	51W	
Emporia, Kans., U.S.A.	158	38	25N		96	10W	
Emporia, Va., U.S.A.	165	36	41N		77	32W	
Ems ➝	42	52	37N		9	26 E	
En Nahud	129	12	45N		28	25 E	
Ena	106	35	25N		137	25 E	
Ena-San	106	35	26N		137	36 E	
Encarnación	191	27	15S		55	50W	
Encarnación de Díaz	175	21	31N		102	14W	
Encontrados	184	9	3N		72	14W	
Enderby	155	50	35N		119	10W	
Enderby Land	14	66	0S		53	0 E	
Endicott	164	42	6N		76	2W	
Engaño, C.	180	18	30N		68	20W	
Engels	68	51	28N		46	6 E	
Enggano	111	5	20S		102	40 E	
England □	21	53	0N		2	0W	
English Bazar = Ingraj Bazar	92	24	58N		88	10 E	
English Channel	16	50	0N		2	0W	
Enid	161	36	26N		97	52W	
Enkhuizen	40	52	42N		5	17 E	
Ennedi	129	17	15N		22	0 E	
Ennis	35	52	51N		8	59W	
Enniscorthy	35	52	30N		6	35W	
Enniskillen	34	54	20N		7	40W	
Enriquillo, L.	180	18	20N		72	5W	
Enschede	41	52	13N		6	53 E	
Ensenada	174	31	52N		116	37W	
Enshū-Nada	106	34	27N		137	38 E	
Entebbe	132	0	4N		32	28 E	
Enterprise	171	45	30N		117	18W	
Entre Ríos □	190	30	30S		58	30W	
Enugu	131	6	20N		7	30 E	
Enzan	107	35	42N		138	44 E	
Eólie, I.	49	38	30N		14	50 E	
Epe	41	52	21N		5	59 E	
Épernay	39	49	3N		3	56 E	
Ephesus	80	37	50N		27	33 E	
Épinal	37	48	10N		6	27 E	
Epping	25	51	42N		0	8 E	
Equatorial Guinea ■	134	2	0S		8	0 E	
Er Rif	126	35	1N		4	1W	
Erāwadī Myit ➝ = Irrawaddy ➝	93	15	50N		95	6 E	
Ercha = Shamanovo	73	69	45N		147	20 E	
Erciyaş Daği	80	38	30N		35	30 E	
Erebus, Mt.	15	77	35S		167	0 E	
Erechim	191	27	35S		52	15W	
Ereğli	80	41	15N		31	30 E	
Erfurt	43	50	58N		11	2 E	
Erg Chech	126	50	59N		11	0 E	
Erie	164	42	10N		80	7W	
Erie, L.	151	42	15N		81	0W	
Erimanthos	54	37	57N		21	50 E	
Erimo-misaki	103	41	50N		143	15 E	
Eritrea ■	132	14	0N		41	0 E	
Ermoúpolis = Síros	55	37	28N		24	57 E	
Erne, Lough	34	54	26N		7	46W	
Erode	90	11	24N		77	45 E	
Erramala Hills	90	15	30N		78	15 E	
Erris Hd.	34	54	19N		10	0W	
Erzgebirge	43	50	25N		13	0 E	
Erzincan	81	39	46N		39	30 E	
Erzurum	81	39	57N		41	15 E	
Es Sînâ'	128	29	0N		34	0 E	
Esan-Misaki	103	41	40N		141	10 E	
Esashi	103	41	52N		140	7 E	
Esbjerg	61	55	29N		8	29 E	
Escanaba	150	45	44N		87	5W	
Escondido	173	33	9N		117	4W	
Escuintla	177	14	20N		90	48W	
Eşfahān	85	33	0N		53	0 E	
Esh Sham = Dimashq	80	33	30N		36	18 E	
Esk ➝	29	54	27N		0	36W	
Eskilstuna	60	59	22N		16	32 E	
Eskimo Pt.	145	61	10N		94	15W	
Eskişehir	80	39	50N		30	35 E	
Eslāmābād-e Gharb	84	34	10N		46	30 E	
Esmeraldas	184	1	0N		79	40W	
Espanola	151	46	15N		81	46W	
Esperance	114	33	45S		121	55 E	
Espinazo, Sierra del = Espinhaço, Serra do	188	17	30S		43	30W	
Espinhaço, Serra do	188	17	30S		43	30W	
Espírito Santo □	189	20	0S		40	45W	
Essaouira	126	31	32N		9	42W	
Essen	42	51	28N		6	59 E	
Essequibo ➝	185	6	50N		58	30W	
Essex □	25	51	48N		0	30 E	
Estados, I. de los	192	54	40S		64	30W	
Estelí	179	13	9N		86	22W	
Estevan	152	49	10N		102	59W	
Estherville	166	43	25N		94	50W	
Estonia ■	68	58	30N		25	30 E	
Estoril	50	38	42N		9	23W	
Estrêla, Serra da	50	40	10N		7	45W	
Estremadura	50	39	0N		9	0W	
Étampes	39	48	26N		2	10 E	
Étaples	38	50	30N		1	39 E	
Etawah	91	26	48N		79	6 E	
Ethiopia ■	133	8	0N		40	0 E	
Ethiopian Highlands	132	10	0N		37	0 E	
Etna	49	37	45N		15	0 E	
Etosha Pan	136	18	40S		16	30 E	
Etzatlán	175	20	46N		104	5W	
Euboea = Évvoia	55	38	30N		24	0 E	
Euclid	167	41	32N		81	31W	
Eucumbene, L.	117	36	2S		148	40 E	
Eufaula	169	35	20N		95	33W	
Eugene	171	44	0N		123	8W	
Eupen	42	50	37N		6	3 E	
Euphrates = Furāt, Nahr al ➝	84	31	0N		47	25 E	
Eureka, Calif., U.S.A.	172	40	50N		124	0W	
Eureka, Nev., U.S.A.	172	39	32N		116	2W	
Euroa	117	36	44S		145	35 E	
Europa, Pta. de	50	36	3N		5	21W	
Europa Pt. = Europa, Pta. de	50	36	3N		5	21W	
Europoort	40	51	57N		4	10 E	
Euston	119	34	30S		142	46 E	
Eutsuk L.	154	53	20N		126	45W	
Evans Head	116	29	7S		153	27 E	
Everard, L.	118	31	30S		135	0 E	
Everest, Mt.	92	28	5N		86	58 E	
Everett	171	48	0N		122	10W	
Everglades	170	26	0N		80	30W	
Evesham	24	52	6N		1	57W	
Évora	50	38	33N		7	57W	
Évreux	39	49	0N		1	8 E	
Évvoia	55	38	30N		24	0 E	

Name	Page	°	′	N/S	°	′	E/W
Excelsior Springs	166	39	20	N	94	10	W
Exe →	27	50	38	N	3	27	W
Exeter	27	50	43	N	3	31	W
Exmoor	27	51	10	N	3	59	W
Exmouth	27	50	37	N	3	26	W
Extremadura □	50	39	30	N	6	5	W
Eyasi, L.	135	3	30	S	35	0	E
Eye Pen.	32	58	13	N	6	10	W
Eyre, L.	118	29	30	S	137	26	E
Eyre Mts.	123	45	25	S	168	25	E
Eyre Pen.	119	33	30	S	137	17	E

F

Name	Page	°	′	N/S	°	′	E/W
Facatativá	184	4	49	N	74	22	W
Faddeyevskiy, Ostrov	72	76	0	N	150	0	E
Fair Hd.	34	55	14	N	6	10	W
Fairbanks	142	64	50	N	147	50	W
Fairfield, N.Z.	123	45	54	S	170	24	E
Fairfield, Ala., U.S.A.	169	33	30	N	87	0	W
Fairfield, Calif., U.S.A.	172	38	14	N	122	1	W
Fairfield, Tex., U.S.A.	168	31	40	N	96	0	W
Fairmont, Minn., U.S.A.	166	43	37	N	94	30	W
Fairmont, W. Va., U.S.A.	164	39	29	N	80	10	W
Fairview	155	56	5	N	118	25	W
Fairweather, Mt.	143	58	55	N	137	45	W
Faisalabad	89	31	30	N	73	5	E
Faizabad	92	26	45	N	82	10	E
Fajardo	180	18	20	N	65	39	W
Fakenham	29	52	50	N	0	51	E
Falam	93	23	0	N	93	45	E
Falkirk	31	56	0	N	3	47	W
Falkland Is.	192	51	30	S	59	0	W
Falköping	60	58	12	N	13	33	E
Fall River	164	41	45	N	71	5	W
Falls City	166	40	0	N	95	40	W
Falmouth, Jamaica	180	18	30	N	77	40	W
Falmouth, U.K.	27	50	9	N	5	5	W
Famagusta	80	35	8	N	33	55	E
Farāh	87	32	20	N	62	7	E
Farāh □	87	32	25	N	62	10	E
Fareham	25	50	52	N	1	11	W
Farewell, C.	122	40	29	S	172	43	E
Farewell C. = Farvel, Kap	147	59	48	N	43	55	W
Fargo	156	46	52	N	96	40	W
Farmington, N.H., U.S.A.	157	43	25	N	71	3	W
Farmington, N. Mex., U.S.A.	161	36	45	N	108	28	W
Farnborough	25	51	17	N	0	46	W
Faro	50	37	2	N	7	55	W
Faroe Is.	16	62	0	N	7	0	W
Fars □	85	29	30	N	55	0	E
Fársala	54	39	17	N	22	23	E
Farvel, Kap	147	59	48	N	43	55	W
Fāryāb □	87	36	0	N	65	0	E
Fatehgarh	89	27	25	N	79	35	E
Fatehpur, Raj., India	92	28	0	N	74	40	E
Fatehpur, Ut. P., India	89	25	56	N	81	13	E
Faxaflói	64	64	29	N	23	0	W
Fayetteville, Ark., U.S.A.	168	36	0	N	94	5	W
Fayetteville, N.C., U.S.A.	165	35	0	N	78	58	W
Fazilka	89	30	27	N	74	2	E
Fdérik	126	22	40	N	12	45	W
Fear, C.	165	33	51	N	78	0	W
Fécamp	38	49	45	N	0	22	E
Feilding	122	40	13	S	175	35	E
Feira de Santana	189	12	15	S	38	57	W
Felixstowe	25	51	58	N	1	22	E
Fengjie	99	31	5	N	109	36	E
Fens, The	29	52	45	N	0	2	E
Fenyang	98	37	19	N	111	46	E
Ferfer	133	5	4	N	45	9	E
Fergana	71	40	23	N	71	19	E
Fergus Falls	156	46	18	N	96	7	W
Fermoy	35	52	4	N	8	18	W
Fernando de Noronha	189	4	0	S	33	10	W
Fernando Póo = Bioko	131	3	30	N	8	40	E
Fernie	155	49	30	N	115	5	W
Ferrara	47	44	50	N	11	36	E
Ferté-Bernard, La	39	48	10	N	0	40	E
Fès	126	34	0	N	5	0	W
Feuilles →	146	58	47	N	70	4	W
Feyzābād	87	37	7	N	70	33	E
Fezzan	124	27	0	N	15	0	E
Fianarantsoa	137	21	26	S	47	5	E
Fichtelgebirge	43	50	10	N	12	0	E
Fife □	31	56	13	N	3	2	W
Fife Ness	31	56	17	N	2	35	W
Fiji ■	122	17	20	S	179	0	E
Filey	29	54	13	N	0	18	W
Findlay	167	41	0	N	83	41	W
Finisterre, C.	50	42	50	N	9	19	W
Finland ■	67	63	0	N	27	0	E
Finland, G. of	67	60	0	N	26	0	E
Finlay →	144	57	0	N	125	10	W
Finley	117	35	38	S	145	35	E
Firenze	47	43	47	N	11	15	E
Firozabad	89	27	10	N	78	25	E
Fishguard	26	51	59	N	4	59	W
Fiskenæsset	147	63	5	N	50	45	W
Fitchburg	164	42	35	N	71	47	W
Fitzgerald	170	31	45	N	83	16	W
Fitzroy →	121	23	32	S	150	52	E
Fiume = Rijeka	52	45	20	N	14	21	E
Flagstaff	160	35	10	N	111	40	W
Flamborough Hd.	29	54	8	N	0	4	W
Flannan Is.	32	58	9	N	7	52	W
Flattery, C.	171	48	21	N	124	43	W
Flèche, La	39	47	42	N	0	4	W
Fleetwood	28	53	55	N	3	1	W
Flekkefjord	60	58	18	N	6	39	E
Flensburg	43	54	46	N	9	28	E
Flers	36	48	47	N	0	33	W
Flin Flon	152	54	46	N	101	53	W
Flinders I.	117	40	0	S	148	0	E
Flinders Ranges	118	31	30	S	138	30	E
Flinders Reefs	121	17	37	S	148	31	E
Flint, U.K.	26	53	15	N	3	7	W
Flint, U.S.A.	167	43	5	N	83	40	W
Flint →	170	30	52	N	84	38	W
Flodden	31	55	37	N	2	8	W
Flora	167	38	40	N	88	30	W
Florence = Firenze	47	43	47	N	11	15	E
Florence, Ala., U.S.A.	169	34	50	N	87	40	W
Florence, S.C., U.S.A.	165	34	12	N	79	44	W
Flores, Guatemala	177	16	59	N	89	50	W
Flores, Indonesia	113	8	35	S	121	0	E
Flores Sea	113	6	30	S	124	0	E
Floriano	188	6	50	S	43	0	W
Florianópolis	191	27	30	S	48	30	W
Florida	191	34	7	S	56	10	W
Florida □	170	28	30	N	82	0	W
Florida, Straits of	159	25	0	N	80	0	W
Florida B.	159	25	0	N	81	20	W
Florida Keys	159	25	0	N	80	40	W
Flórina	54	40	48	N	21	26	E
Flushing = Vlissingen	40	51	26	N	3	34	E
Fly →	115	8	25	S	143	0	E
Foam Lake	152	51	40	N	103	32	W
Fóggia	49	41	28	N	15	31	E
Foix	36	42	58	N	1	38	E
Folda	64	64	41	N	10	50	E
Folkestone	25	51	5	N	1	11	E
Follette, La	169	36	23	N	84	9	W
Fond-du-Lac, Canada	145	59	19	N	107	12	W
Fond du Lac, U.S.A.	167	43	46	N	88	26	W
Fontainebleau	39	48	24	N	2	40	E
Fonte Boa	184	2	33	S	66	0	W
Foochow = Fuzhou	99	26	5	N	119	16	E
Forbes	117	33	22	S	148	0	E
Forestburg	155	52	35	N	112	1	W
Forestville	148	48	48	N	69	2	W
Forfar	33	56	40	N	2	53	W
Forli	47	44	14	N	12	2	E
Formby Pt.	28	53	33	N	3	7	W
Formentera	51	38	43	N	1	27	E
Formosa = Taiwan ■	99	23	30	N	121	0	E
Formosa	191	26	15	S	58	10	W
Forrest City	169	35	0	N	90	50	W
Fort Albany	140	52	15	N	81	35	W

Fort Augustus	32	57	9N	4	40W
Fort Chipewyan	145	58	42N	111	8W
Fort Collins	163	40	30N	105	4W
Fort-Coulonge	151	45	50N	76	45W
Fort-de-France	180	14	36N	61	2W
Fort Dodge	166	42	29N	94	10W
Fort Frances	153	48	36N	93	24W
Fort Franklin	145	65	10N	123	30W
Fort George	140	53	50N	79	0W
Fort Good-Hope	144	66	14N	128	40W
Fort Hertz = Putao	93	27	28N	97	30 E
Fort Kent	148	47	12N	68	30W
Fort-Lamy = Ndjamena	131	12	10N	14	59 E
Fort Lauderdale	170	26	10N	80	5W
Fort Liard	144	60	14N	123	30W
Fort Mackay	143	57	12N	111	41W
Fort Macleod	155	49	45N	113	30W
Fort McMurray	155	56	44N	111	7W
Fort McPherson	144	67	30N	134	55W
Fort Madison	166	40	39N	91	20W
Fort Morgan	163	40	10N	103	50W
Fort Myers	170	26	39N	81	51W
Fort Nelson	144	58	50N	122	44W
Fort Nelson →	144	59	32N	124	0W
Fort Payne	169	34	25N	85	44W
Fort Peck L.	163	47	40N	107	0W
Fort Pierce	170	27	29N	80	19W
Fort Providence	145	61	3N	117	40W
Fort Qu'Appelle	152	50	45N	103	50W
Fort Resolution	145	61	10N	113	40W
Fort Rupert	140	51	30N	78	40W
Fort St. James	154	54	30N	124	10W
Fort St. John	155	56	15N	120	50W
Fort Sandeman	88	31	20N	69	31 E
Fort Saskatchewan	155	53	40N	113	15W
Fort Scott	166	37	50N	94	40W
Fort Severn	140	56	0N	87	40W
Fort Shevchenko	70	43	40N	51	20 E
Fort Simpson	144	61	45N	121	15W
Fort Smith, Canada	145	60	0N	111	51W
Fort Smith, U.S.A.	168	35	25N	94	25W
Fort Smith Region □	145	63	0N	120	0W
Fort Trinquet = Bir Mogrein	126	25	10N	11	25W
Fort Valley	170	32	33N	83	52W
Fort Vermilion	145	58	24N	116	0W
Fort Wayne	167	41	5N	85	10W
Fort William	32	56	48N	5	8W
Fort Worth	168	32	45N	97	25W
Fort Yukon	142	66	35N	145	20W
Fortaleza	189	3	45S	38	35W
Forth →	31	56	9N	4	18W
Forth, Firth of	31	56	5N	2	55W
Fortuna	172	40	38N	124	8W
Foshan	99	23	4N	113	5 E
Foster	117	38	40S	146	15 E
Fougères	36	48	21N	1	14W
Foula, I.	30	60	10N	2	5W
Foulness I.	24	51	36N	0	55 E
Fourmies	38	50	1N	4	2 E
Foúrnoi	55	37	36N	26	32 E
Fouta Djalon	130	11	20N	12	10W
Foveaux Str.	123	46	42S	168	10 E
Fowey	27	50	20N	4	39W
Foxe Basin	146	66	0N	77	0W
Foxe Chan.	146	65	0N	80	0W
Foxe Pen.	146	65	0N	76	0W
Foxton	122	40	29S	175	18 E
Foyle, Lough	34	55	6N	7	8W
Foynes	35	52	37N	9	5W
Franca	188	20	33S	47	30W
France ■	37	47	0N	3	0 E
Franche-Comté	37	46	30N	5	50 E
François	180	14	38N	60	57W
Franeker	41	53	12N	5	33 E
Frankfort, Ind., U.S.A.	167	40	20N	86	33W
Frankfort, Ky., U.S.A.	165	38	12N	84	52W
Frankfurt am Main	42	50	7N	8	40 E
Frankfurt an der Oder	43	52	50N	14	31 E
Fränkische Alb	43	49	20N	11	30 E
Franklin, La., U.S.A.	168	29	45N	91	30W
Franklin, N.H., U.S.A.	164	43	28N	71	39W
Franklin, W. Va., U.S.A.	165	38	38N	79	21W
Franklin D. Roosevelt L.	162	48	30N	118	16W
Franklin Mts.	145	65	0N	125	0W
Franklin Str.	145	72	0N	96	0W
Frankston	117	38	8S	145	8 E
Franz	150	48	25N	84	30W
Fraser →	154	49	7N	123	11W
Fraser, Mt.	120	25	35S	118	20 E
Fraser I.	116	25	15S	153	10 E
Fraserburgh	33	57	41N	2	0W
Fray Bentos	190	33	10S	58	15W
Frederick	164	39	25N	77	23W
Fredericksburg	165	38	16N	77	29W
Fredericton	148	45	57N	66	40W
Frederikshavn	61	57	28N	10	31 E
Fredrikstad	60	59	13N	10	57 E
Freeport, Bahamas	178	26	30N	78	47W
Freeport, Ill., U.S.A.	166	42	18N	89	40W
Freeport, N.Y., U.S.A.	164	40	39N	73	35W
Freeport, Tex., U.S.A.	158	28	55N	95	22W
Freetown	130	8	30N	13	17W
Freiberg	42	50	55N	13	20 E
Freibourg = Fribourg	44	46	49N	7	9 E
Fréjus	37	43	25N	6	44 E
Fremantle	120	32	7S	115	47 E
Fremont, Calif., U.S.A.	172	37	32N	122	1W
Fremont, Nebr., U.S.A.	166	41	30N	96	30W
French Guiana ■	185	4	0N	53	0W
French Pass	123	40	55S	173	55 E
French Terr. of Afars & Issas = Djibouti ■	133	12	0N	43	0 E
Fresnillo	175	23	10N	102	53W
Fresno	173	36	47N	119	50W
Fria, C.	136	18	0S	12	0 E
Frias	190	28	40S	65	5W
Fribourg	44	46	49N	7	9 E
Friendly, Is. = Tonga ■	123	19	50S	174	30W
Friesland □	41	53	5N	5	50 E
Frio, C.	182	22	50S	41	50W
Friuli-Venezia Giulia □	47	46	0N	13	0 E
Frobisher B.	146	62	30N	66	0W
Frobisher Bay	146	63	44N	68	31W
Frobisher L.	152	56	20N	108	15W
Frome	27	51	16N	2	17W
Frome, L.	118	30	45S	139	45 E
Frome Downs	118	31	13S	139	45 E
Front Range	163	40	0N	105	40W
Front Royal	164	38	55N	78	10W
Frontera	177	18	32N	92	38W
Frostburg	164	39	43N	78	57W
Frunze = Bishkek	71	42	54N	74	46 E
Frutal	188	20	0S	49	0W
Fuchou = Fuzhou	99	26	5N	119	16 E
Fuchū, Hiroshima, Japan	109	34	34N	133	14 E
Fūchū, Tōkyō, Japan	107	35	40N	139	29 E
Fuerte, R. →	174	25	54N	109	22W
Fuji	107	35	9N	138	39 E
Fuji-no-miya	107	35	10N	138	40 E
Fuji-San	107	35	22N	138	44 E
Fuji-yoshida	107	35	30N	138	46 E
Fujian □	99	26	0N	118	0 E
Fujieda	107	34	52N	138	16 E
Fujisawa	107	35	22N	139	29 E
Fukaya	107	36	12N	139	12 E
Fukien = Fujian □	99	26	0N	118	0 E
Fukuchiyama	106	35	19N	135	9 E
Fukue-Shima	104	32	40N	128	45 E
Fukui	106	36	0N	136	10 E
Fukuoka	108	33	39N	130	21 E
Fukushima	103	37	44N	140	28 E
Fukuyama	109	34	35N	133	20 E
Fulton, Mo., U.S.A.	166	38	50N	91	55W
Fulton, N.Y., U.S.A.	164	43	20N	76	22W
Funabashi	107	35	45N	140	0 E
Funchal	126	32	38N	16	54W
Fundación	184	10	31N	74	11W
Fundy, B. of	148	45	0N	66	0W
Furāt, Nahr al →	84	31	0N	47	25 E
Furneaux Group	119	40	10S	147	50 E
Furness	28	54	14N	3	8W
Fürth	43	49	29N	11	0 E

Name	Page	Lat	Long
Fury and Hecla Str.	146	69 56N	84 0W
Fushun	98	41 50N	123 55 E
Fuxin	98	42 5N	121 48 E
Fuzhou	99	26 5N	119 16 E
Fylde	28	53 50N	2 58W
Fyn	61	55 20N	10 30 E
Fyne, L.	30	56 0N	5 20W

G

Name	Page	Lat	Long
Gabès, Golfe de	127	34 0N	10 30 E
Gabon ■	134	0 10S	10 0 E
Gaborone	137	24 45S	25 57 E
Gachsārān	85	30 15N	50 45 E
Gadag	90	15 30N	75 45 E
Gadsden	169	34 1N	86 0W
Gaeta	49	41 12N	13 35 E
Gaffney	165	35 3N	81 40W
Gagnon	141	51 50N	68 5W
Gainesville, Fla., U.S.A.	170	29 38N	82 20W
Gainesville, Ga., U.S.A.	165	34 17N	83 47W
Gainesville, Tex., U.S.A.	168	33 40N	97 10W
Gainsborough	29	53 23N	0 46W
Gairdner L.	118	31 30S	136 0 E
Galápagos	10	0 0	89 0W
Galas ~►	96	4 55N	101 57 E
Galashiels	31	55 37N	2 50W
Galați	57	45 27N	28 2 E
Galatina	49	40 10N	18 10 E
Galdhøpiggen	60	61 38N	8 18 E
Galesburg	166	40 57N	90 23W
Galicia □	50	42 43N	7 45W
Galilee, L.	121	22 20S	145 50 E
Gallatin	169	36 24N	86 27W
Galle	90	6 5N	80 10 E
Gallinas, Pta.	184	12 28N	71 40W
Gallipoli = Gelibolu	80	40 28N	26 43 E
Gallípoli	49	40 8N	18 0 E
Gällivare	66	67 9N	20 40 E
Galloway	31	55 0N	4 25W
Galloway, Mull of	30	54 38N	4 50W
Gallup	161	35 30N	108 45W
Galty Mts.	35	52 22N	8 10W
Galveston	168	29 15N	94 48W
Galveston B.	168	29 30N	94 50W
Galway	35	53 16N	9 4W
Galway □	34	53 16N	9 3W
Gamagori	106	34 50N	137 14 E
Gambia ■	130	13 25N	16 0W
Gambia ~►	130	13 28N	16 34W
Gand = Gent	42	51 2N	3 42 E
Gander	149	48 58N	54 35W
Gandhi Sagar	91	24 40N	75 40 E
Gandi	131	12 55N	5 49 E
Ganga ~►	92	23 20N	90 30 E
Ganges = Ganga ~►	92	23 20N	90 30 E
Gangtok	92	27 20N	88 37 E
Gannett Pk.	163	43 15N	109 38W
Gansu □	98	36 0N	104 0 E
Ganzhou	99	25 51N	114 56 E
Gao	130	16 15N	0 5W
Gaoxiong	99	22 38N	120 18 E
Garachiné	179	8 0N	78 12W
Garanhuns	189	8 50S	36 30W
Garberville	172	40 11N	123 50W
Garda, L. di	46	45 40N	10 40 E
Garden City	161	38 0N	100 45W
Garden Grove	173	33 47N	117 55W
Gardēz	87	33 37N	69 9 E
Garmsār	86	35 20N	52 25 E
Garonne ~►	36	45 2N	0 36W
Garoua	131	9 19N	13 21 E
Garrison Res. = Sakakawea, L.	163	47 30N	102 0W
Garry L.	145	65 58N	100 18W
Garvie Mts.	123	45 30S	168 50 E
Garwa = Garoua	131	9 19N	13 21 E
Gary	167	41 35N	87 20W
Garzón	184	2 10N	75 40W
Gascogne	36	43 45N	0 20 E
Gascony = Gascogne	36	43 45N	0 20 E
Gaspé	148	48 52N	64 30W
Gaspé, C. de	148	48 48N	64 7W
Gaspé, Pén. de	148	48 45N	65 40W
Gastonia	165	35 17N	81 10W
Gastre	192	42 20S	69 15W
Gata, C. de	51	36 41N	2 13W
Gateshead	28	54 57N	1 37W
Gauhati	93	26 10N	91 45 E
Gävle	60	60 40N	17 9 E
Gävleborgs län □	60	61 30N	16 15 E
Gawilgarh Hills	91	21 15N	76 45 E
Gawler	119	34 30S	138 42 E
Gawler Ranges	114	32 30S	135 45 E
Gaxun Nur	100	42 22N	100 30 E
Gaya	92	24 47N	85 4 E
Gaylord	150	45 1N	84 41W
Gayndah	116	25 35S	151 32 E
Gaza	80	31 30N	34 28 E
Gaziantep	80	37 6N	37 23 E
Gdańsk	58	54 22N	18 40 E
Gdańska, Zatoka	58	54 30N	19 20 E
Gdynia	58	54 35N	18 33 E
Gedaref	129	14 2N	35 28 E
Geelong	117	38 10S	144 22 E
Gejiu	99	23 20N	103 10 E
Gelderland □	41	52 5N	6 10 E
Geldermalsen	40	51 53N	5 17 E
Geldrop	41	51 25N	5 32 E
Geleen	41	50 57N	5 49 E
Gelibolu	80	40 28N	26 43 E
Gelsenkirchen	42	51 30N	7 5 E
Gemert	41	51 33N	5 41 E
General Alvear	190	35 0S	67 40W
General Pico	190	35 45S	63 50W
Geneva = Genève	44	46 12N	6 9 E
Geneva	164	42 53N	77 0W
Geneva, L. = Léman, Lac	44	46 26N	6 30 E
Genève	44	46 12N	6 9 E
Genk	41	50 58N	5 32 E
Genkai-Nada	108	34 0N	130 0 E
Gennargentu, Mti. del	48	40 0N	9 10 E
Genoa = Génova	46	44 24N	8 56 E
Génova	46	44 24N	8 56 E
Génova, Golfo di	46	44 0N	9 0 E
Gent	42	51 2N	3 42 E
George, L.	132	0 5N	30 10 E
George River = Port Nouveau-Québec	146	58 30N	65 59W
George Town	96	5 25N	100 15 E
Georgetown, Australia	119	18 17S	143 33 E
Georgetown, Canada	151	43 40N	79 56W
Georgetown, Guyana	185	6 50N	58 12W
Georgetown, U.S.A.	170	33 22N	79 15W
Georgia □	170	32 0N	82 0W
Georgia ■	70	42 0N	43 0 E
Georgian B.	151	45 15N	81 0W
Gera	43	50 53N	12 11 E
Geraldton, Australia	120	28 48S	114 32 E
Geraldton, Canada	150	49 44N	86 59W
Gereshk	87	31 47N	64 35 E
Germany ■	18	52 0N	12 0 E
Germiston	137	26 15S	28 10 E
Gerona	51	41 58N	2 46 E
Ghana ■	130	6 0N	1 0W
Ghat	127	24 59N	10 11 E
Ghawdex = Gozo	49	36 0N	14 13 E
Ghaziabad	89	28 42N	77 26 E
Ghazipur	92	25 38N	83 35 E
Ghaznī	87	33 30N	68 28 E
Ghaznī □	87	32 10N	68 20 E
Ghent = Gent	42	51 2N	3 42 E
Ghowr □	87	34 0N	64 20 E
Ghulam Mohammad Barrage	88	25 30N	68 20 E
Giant's Causeway	34	55 15N	6 30W
Gibara	178	21 9N	76 11W
Gibraltar	50	36 7N	5 22W
Gibraltar, Str. of	50	35 55N	5 40W
Gien	39	47 40N	2 36 E

Place	Page	Lat			Long		
Gifu	106	35	30N		136	45	E
Gigha	30	55	42N		5	45	W
Gijón	50	43	32N		5	42	W
Gila →	173	32	43N		114	33	W
Gīlān □	81	37	0N		50	0	E
Gilbert Is. = Kiribati ■	122	1	0N		176	0	E
Gilford I.	154	50	40N		126	30	W
Gilgandra	116	31	43S		148	39	E
Gilgit	89	35	50N		74	15	E
Gillingham	25	51	23N		0	34	E
Gingin	120	31	22S		115	54	E
Gippsland	117	37	45S		147	15	E
Girardot	184	4	18N		74	48	W
Giresun	81	40	55N		38	30	E
Gironde →	36	45	32N		1	7	W
Girvan	30	55	15N		4	50	W
Gisborne	122	38	39S		178	5	E
Gisors	39	49	15N		1	47	E
Gizhiga	73	62	3N		160	30	E
Gizhiginskaya, Guba	73	61	0N		158	0	E
Giżycko	58	54	2N		21	48	E
Gjoa Haven	145	68	20N		96	8	W
Glace Bay	149	46	11N		59	58	W
Gladstone, Queens., Australia	121	23	52S		151	16	E
Gladstone, S. Austral., Australia	118	33	15S		138	22	E
Gláma	64	65	48N		23	0	W
Glasgow, U.K.	31	55	52N		4	14	W
Glasgow, U.S.A.	169	37	2N		85	55	W
Glastonbury	27	51	9N		2	42	W
Gleiwitz = Gliwice	58	50	22N		18	41	E
Glen Coe	32	56	40N		5	0	W
Glen Innes	116	29	44S		151	44	E
Glen Mor	33	57	12N		4	37	E
Glenburgh	120	25	26S		116	6	E
Glendale	173	34	7N		118	18	W
Glendive	163	47	7N		104	40	W
Glenelg	119	34	58S		138	31	E
Glenns Ferry	172	43	0N		115	15	W
Glenorchy	119	42	49S		147	18	E
Glenrothes	31	56	12N		3	11	W
Glens Falls	164	43	20N		73	40	W
Gliwice	58	50	22N		18	41	E
Głogów	58	51	37N		16	5	E
Glossop	28	53	27N		1	56	W
Gloucester	24	51	52N		2	15	W
Gloucestershire □	24	51	44N		2	10	W
Gloversville	164	43	5N		74	18	W
Gniezno	58	52	30N		17	35	E
Go Cong	95	10	22N		106	40	E
Goa	91	15	33N		73	59	E
Goa □	90	15	33N		73	59	E
Goat Fell	30	55	37N		5	11	W
Goba	133	7	1N		39	59	E
Gobi	98	44	0N		111	0	E
Gobō	106	33	53N		135	10	E
Godavari →	91	16	25N		82	18	E
Godbout	148	49	20N		67	38	W
Goderich	150	43	45N		81	41	W
Godhra	91	22	49N		73	40	E
Gods L.	153	54	40N		94	15	W
Godthåb	147	64	10N		51	35	W
Goeie Hoop, Kaap die	136	34	24S		18	30	E
Goeree	40	51	50N		4	0	E
Goes	40	51	30N		3	55	E
Gogama	151	47	35N		81	43	W
Goiânia	188	16	43S		49	20	W
Goiás □	188	12	10S		48	0	W
Goirle	40	51	31N		5	4	E
Gojō	106	34	21N		135	42	E
Gökçeada	55	40	10N		25	50	E
Gold Coast, Australia	116	28	0S		153	25	E
Gold Coast, W. Afr.	124	4	0N		1	40	W
Golden Bay	122	40	40S		172	50	E
Golden Gate	172	37	54N		122	30	W
Golden Hinde	154	49	40N		125	44	W
Golden Vale	35	52	33N		8	17	W
Goldfield	172	37	45N		117	13	W
Goldsboro	165	35	24N		77	59	W
Goldsworthy	114	20	21S		119	30	E
Golfo Aranci	48	41	0N		9	35	E
Gomel	68	52	28N		31	0	E
Gómez Palacio	174	25	34N		103	30	W
Gonābād	86	34	15N		58	45	E
Gonaïves	180	19	20N		72	42	W
Gonda	92	27	9N		81	58	E
Gonder	132	12	39N		37	30	E
Good Hope, C. of = Goeie Hoop, Kaap die	136	34	24S		18	30	E
Goole	29	53	42N		0	52	W
Goondiwindi	116	28	30S		150	21	E
Goose Bay	147	53	15N		60	20	W
Gorakhpur	92	26	47N		83	23	E
Gordonvale	121	17	5S		145	50	E
Gore, Ethiopia	132	8	12N		35	32	E
Gore, N.Z.	123	46	5S		168	58	E
Gorey	35	52	41N		6	18	W
Gorinchem	40	51	50N		4	59	E
Gorkiy = Nizhniy Novgorod	68	56	20N		44	0	E
Görlitz	43	51	10N		14	59	E
Gorna Oryakhovitsa	53	43	7N		25	40	E
Gorno-Altay □	71	51	0N		86	0	E
Gorzów Wielkopolski	58	52	43N		15	15	E
Gosford	117	33	23S		151	18	E
Gospič	52	44	35N		15	23	E
Gosport	25	50	48N		1	8	W
Göteborg	60	57	43N		11	59	E
Göteborgs och Bohus län □	60	58	30N		11	30	E
Gotemba	107	35	18N		138	56	E
Gotha	43	50	56N		10	42	E
Gotland	60	57	30N		18	33	E
Gōtsu	109	35	0N		132	14	E
Gottwaldov = Zlin	59	49	14N		17	40	E
Gouda	40	52	1N		4	42	E
Gouin, Rés.	151	48	35N		74	40	W
Goulburn	117	34	44S		149	44	E
Goundam	130	16	25N		3	45	W
Gournay-en-Bray	38	49	29N		1	44	E
Governador Valadares	188	18	15S		41	57	W
Governor's Harbour	178	25	10N		76	14	W
Gower, The	27	51	35N		4	10	W
Goya	190	29	10S		59	10	W
Gozo	49	36	0N		14	13	E
Graaff-Reinet	136	32	13S		24	32	E
Gracias a Dios, C.	179	15	0N		83	10	W
Grafton	116	29	38S		152	58	E
Graham	165	36	5N		79	22	W
Graham I.	154	53	40N		132	30	W
Graham Land	14	65	0S		64	0	W
Grahamstown	137	33	19S		26	31	E
Grain Coast	124	4	20N		10	0	W
Grampian □	33	57	0N		3	0	W
Grampian Mts.	33	56	50N		4	0	W
Grampians, The	119	37	0S		142	20	E
Gran Chaco	190	25	0S		61	0	W
Gran Sasso d'Italia	47	42	25N		13	30	E
Granada, Nic.	179	11	58N		86	0	W
Granada, Spain	50	37	10N		3	35	W
Granby	151	45	25N		72	45	W
Grand Bank	149	47	6N		55	48	W
Grand Bassam	130	5	10N		3	49	W
Grand Canyon	160	36	3N		112	9	W
Grand Cayman	178	19	20N		81	20	W
Grand Cess	130	4	40N		8	12	W
Grand Falls	149	48	56N		55	40	W
Grand Forks, Canada	155	49	0N		118	30	W
Grand Forks, U.S.A.	156	48	0N		97	3	W
Grand Island	163	40	59N		98	25	W
Grand Junction	163	39	0N		108	30	W
Grand Mère	151	46	36N		72	40	W
Grand Portage	150	47	58N		89	41	W
Grand Rapids, Canada	153	53	12N		99	19	W
Grand Rapids, U.S.A.	167	42	57N		86	40	W
Grand St.-Bernard, Col. du	44	45	53N		7	11	E
Grand Teton	163	43	54N		111	50	W
Grand View	153	51	10N		100	42	W
Grande →, Bolivia	187	15	51S		64	39	W
Grande →, Brazil	188	20	6S		51	4	W
Grande, B.	192	50	30S		68	20	W
Grande, La	171	45	15N		118	0	W
Grande, La →	140	53	50N		79	0	W
Grande Baleine, R. de la →	140	55	16N		77	47	W

Name						
Grande de Santiago, R. →	175	21	36N	105	26W
Grande Prairie	155	55	10N	118	50W
Grande-Rivière	148	48	26N	64	30W
Grange, La	170	33	4N	85	0W
Grangemouth	31	56	1N	3	43W
Grangeville	162	45	57N	116	4W
Granite City	166	38	45N	90	3W
Grant, Mt.	172	38	34N	118	48W
Grantham	29	52	55N	0	39W
Grantown-on-Spey	33	57	19N	3	36W
Grants Pass	171	42	30N	123	22W
Grass Valley	172	39	18N	121	0W
Grasse	37	43	38N	6	56 E
Gravelbourg	152	49	50N	106	35W
Gravelines	38	51	0N	2	10 E
's-Gravenhage	40	52	7N	4	17 E
Gravesend	25	51	25N	0	22 E
Grayling	167	44	40N	84	42W
Graz	45	47	4N	15	27 E
Great Abaco I.	178	26	25N	77	10W
Great Australian Bight	114	33	30S	130	0 E
Great Bahama Bank	178	23	15N	78	0W
Great Barrier I.	122	36	11S	175	25 E
Great Barrier Reef	121	18	0S	146	50 E
Great Basin	172	40	0N	116	30W
Great Bear L.	145	65	30N	120	0W
Great Britain	16	54	0N	2	15W
Great Divide, The	117	35	0S	149	17 E
Great Dividing Ra.	121	23	0S	146	0 E
Great Exuma I.	178	23	30N	75	50W
Great Falls	163	47	27N	111	12W
Great Inagua I.	180	21	0N	73	20W
Great Indian Desert = Thar Desert	89	28	0N	72	0 E
Great Orme's Head	26	53	20N	3	52W
Great Ouse →	29	52	47N	0	22 E
Great Plains	138	47	0N	105	0W
Great Salt Lake	162	41	0N	112	30W
Great Salt Lake Desert	162	40	20N	113	50W
Great Slave L.	145	61	23N	115	38W
Great Wall	98	38	30N	109	30 E
Great Whernside	28	54	9N	1	59W
Great Yarmouth	29	52	40N	1	45 E
Greater Antilles	181	17	40N	74	0W
Greater Manchester □	28	53	30N	2	15W
Greater Sunda Is.	111	2	30S	110	0 E
Gredos, Sierra de	50	40	20N	5	0W
Greece ■	54	40	0N	23	0 E
Greeley	163	40	30N	104	40W
Green →, Ky., U.S.A.	167	37	54N	87	30W
Green →, Utah, U.S.A.	163	38	11N	109	53W
Green Bay	167	44	30N	88	0W
Greenfield	164	42	38N	72	38W
Greenland □	147	66	0N	45	0W
Greenland Sea	13	73	0N	10	0W
Greenock	30	55	57N	4	46W
Greensboro	165	36	7N	79	46W
Greenville, Ala., U.S.A.	169	31	50N	86	37W
Greenville, Mich., U.S.A.	167	43	12N	85	14W
Greenville, Miss., U.S.A.	168	33	25N	91	0W
Greenville, N.C., U.S.A.	165	35	37N	77	26W
Greenville, S.C., U.S.A.	165	34	54N	82	24W
Greenville, Tenn., U.S.A.	165	36	13N	82	51W
Greenwood, Miss., U.S.A.	169	33	30N	90	4W
Greenwood, S.C., U.S.A.	165	34	13N	82	13W
Grenada	169	33	45N	89	50W
Grenada ■	180	12	10N	61	40W
Grenoble	37	45	12N	5	42 E
Grenville	117	37	46S	143	52 E
Gretna Green	31	55	0N	3	3W
Grey Range	116	27	0S	143	30 E
Grey Res.	149	48	20N	56	30W
Greymouth	123	42	29S	171	13 E
Griffin	170	33	17N	84	14W
Griffith	117	34	18S	146	2 E
Grimsby	29	53	35N	0	5W
Grimshaw	155	56	10N	117	40W
Grinnell	166	41	45N	92	43W
Grodno	68	53	42N	23	52 E
Groningen	41	53	15N	6	35 E
Groningen □	41	53	16N	6	40 E
Grootfontein	136	19	31S	18	6 E
Groznyy	70	43	20N	45	45 E
Grudziądz	58	53	30N	18	47 E
Grytviken	14	53	50S	37	10W
Gt. Stour = Stour →	25	51	15N	1	20 E
Guadalajara, Mexico	175	20	40N	103	20W
Guadalajara, Spain	50	40	37N	3	12W
Guadalquivir →	50	36	47N	6	22W
Guadalupe = Guadeloupe ■	180	16	20N	61	40W
Guadalupe Bravos	174	31	23N	106	7W
Guadarrama, Sierra de	50	41	0N	4	0W
Guadeloupe ■	180	16	20N	61	40W
Guadiana →	50	37	14N	7	22W
Guadix	50	37	18N	3	11W
Guaira	191	24	5S	54	10W
Guajará-Mirim	187	10	50S	65	20W
Gualeguay	190	33	10S	59	14W
Gualeguaychú	190	33	3S	59	31W
Guam	10	13	27N	144	45 E
Guanabacoa	178	23	8N	82	18W
Guanacaste, Cordillera del	179	10	40N	85	4W
Guanahani = San Salvador	178	24	0N	74	40W
Guanajay	178	22	56N	82	42W
Guanajuato	177	21	1N	101	15W
Guanajuato □	177	21	0N	101	0W
Guanare	184	8	42N	69	12W
Guangdong □	99	23	0N	113	0 E
Guangxi Zhuangzu Zizhiqu □	99	24	0N	109	0 E
Guangzhou	99	23	5N	113	10 E
Guantánamo	178	20	10N	75	14W
Guaporé →	187	11	55S	65	4W
Guaqui	187	16	41S	68	54W
Guarapuava	191	25	20S	51	30W
Guarda	50	40	32N	7	20W
Guardafui, C. = Asir, Ras	133	11	55N	51	10 E
Guatemala	177	14	40N	90	22W
Guatemala ■	177	15	40N	90	30W
Guaviare →	184	4	3N	67	44W
Guayama	180	17	59N	66	7W
Guayaquil	184	2	15S	79	52W
Guayaquil, G. de	186	3	10S	81	0W
Guaymas	174	27	56N	110	54W
Guddu Barrage	89	28	30N	69	50 E
Gudur	90	14	12N	79	55 E
Guelph	151	43	35N	80	20W
Guernica	50	43	19N	2	40W
Guernsey	36	49	30N	2	35W
Guerrero □	177	17	40N	100	0W
Guilin	99	25	18N	110	15 E
Guimarães	188	2	9S	44	42W
Guinea ■	130	10	20N	10	0W
Guinea, Gulf of	130	3	0N	2	30 E
Guinea-Bissau ■	130	12	0N	15	0W
Güines	178	22	50N	82	0W
Guiyang	99	26	32N	106	40 E
Guizhou □	99	27	0N	107	0 E
Gujarat □	91	23	20N	71	0 E
Gujranwala	89	32	10N	74	12 E
Gujrat	89	32	40N	74	2 E
Gulbarga	91	17	20N	76	50 E
Gulf, The	85	27	0N	50	0 E
Gulfport	169	30	21N	89	3W
Gulgong	116	32	20S	149	49 E
Gull Lake	152	50	10N	108	29W
Gümüsane	81	40	30N	39	30 E
Guna	91	24	40N	77	19 E
Gundagai	117	35	3S	148	6 E
Gunnedah	116	30	59S	150	15 E
Gunningbar Cr. →	116	31	14S	147	6 E
Guntakal	90	15	11N	77	27 E
Guntersville	169	34	18N	86	16W
Guntur	92	16	23N	80	30 E
Gurdaspur	89	32	5N	75	31 E
Gurgaon	89	28	27N	77	1 E
Gurkha	92	28	5N	84	40 E
Gurupi →	188	1	13S	46	6W
Guryev = Atyraū	70	47	5N	52	0 E
Gusau	131	12	12N	6	40 E
Guthrie	168	35	55N	97	30W
Guyana ■	185	5	0N	59	0W
Guyenne	36	44	30N	0	40 E

Name	Page	Latitude	Longitude
Guyra	116	30 15S	151 40 E
Gwalior	91	26 12N	78 10 E
Gwent □	27	51 45N	2 55W
Gweru	137	19 28S	29 45 E
Gwynedd □	26	53 0N	4 0W
Gyandzha	70	40 45N	46 20 E
Gyaring Hu	101	34 50N	97 40 E
Gydanskiy P-ov.	69	70 0N	78 0 E
Gympie	116	26 11S	152 38 E
Gyoda	107	36 10N	139 30 E
Gyöngyös	59	47 48N	20 0 E
Györ	59	47 41N	17 40 E
Gypsumville	153	51 45N	98 40W

H

Name	Page	Latitude	Longitude
Ha 'Arava	80	30 50N	35 20 E
Ha Giang	95	22 50N	104 59 E
Haarlem	40	52 23N	4 39 E
Habana, La	178	23 8N	82 22W
Hachijō-Jima	105	33 5N	139 45 E
Hachinohe	103	40 30N	141 29 E
Hachiōji	107	35 40N	139 20 E
Hadera	80	32 27N	34 55 E
Hadhramaut = Hadramawt	83	15 30N	49 30 E
Hadiya	82	25 30N	36 56 E
Hadramawt	83	15 30N	49 30 E
Hadrians Wall	28	55 0N	2 30W
Haeju	98	38 3N	125 45 E
Haerhpin = Harbin	98	45 48N	126 40 E
Hafar al Bāṭin	82	28 25N	46 0 E
Hafnarfjörður	64	64 4N	21 57W
Haft-Gel	84	31 30N	49 32 E
Hagen	42	51 21N	7 29 E
Hagerstown	164	39 39N	77 46W
Hagi	108	34 30N	131 22 E
Hags Hd.	35	52 57N	9 30W
Hague, The = 's-Gravenhage	40	52 7N	4 17 E
Hai'an	99	32 37N	120 27 E
Haifa = Hefa	80	32 46N	35 0 E
Haikou	99	20 1N	110 16 E
Hā'il	82	27 28N	41 45 E
Hailar	98	49 10N	119 38 E
Hailey	162	43 30N	114 15W
Haileybury	151	47 30N	79 38W
Hainan	99	19 0N	110 0 E
Hainan Dao	99	19 0N	109 30 E
Haiphong	95	20 47N	106 41 E
Haiti ■	180	19 0N	72 30W
Hakken-Zan	106	34 10N	135 54 E
Hakodate	103	41 45N	140 44 E
Halab	80	36 10N	37 15 E
Halaib	129	22 12N	36 30 E
Halberstadt	43	51 53N	11 2 E
Halfmoon Bay	123	46 50S	168 5 E
Halifax, Canada	148	44 38N	63 35W
Halifax, U.K.	28	53 43N	1 51W
Halifax B.	121	18 50S	147 0 E
Hallands län □	61	56 50N	12 50 E
Halle	43	51 29N	12 0 E
Halls Creek	114	18 16S	127 38 E
Halmahera	113	0 40N	128 0 E
Halmstad	61	56 41N	12 52 E
Hälsingborg = Helsingborg	61	56 3N	12 42 E
Hamada	109	34 56N	132 4 E
Hamadān	81	34 52N	48 32 E
Hamadān □	81	35 0N	49 0 E
Hamāh	80	35 5N	36 40 E
Hamakita	107	34 45N	137 47 E
Hamamatsu	106	34 45N	137 45 E
Hamar	60	60 48N	11 7 E
Hamburg	43	53 32N	9 59 E
Hämeenlinna	67	61 0N	24 28 E
Hamelin Pool	120	26 22S	114 20 E
Hameln	42	52 7N	9 24 E
Hamhung	98	39 54N	127 30 E
Hamilton, Australia	119	37 45S	142 2 E
Hamilton, Bermuda	180	32 15N	64 45W
Hamilton, Canada	151	43 15N	79 50W
Hamilton, N.Z.	122	37 47S	175 19 E
Hamilton, U.K.	31	55 47N	4 2W
Hamilton, U.S.A.	167	39 20N	84 35W
Hamm	42	51 40N	7 49 E
Hammerfest	67	70 39N	23 41 E
Hammond, Ind., U.S.A.	167	41 40N	87 30W
Hammond, La., U.S.A.	169	30 32N	90 30W
Hampshire □	25	51 3N	1 20W
Hampshire Downs	25	51 10N	1 10W
Hampton	165	37 4N	76 18W
Hanamaki	103	39 23N	141 7 E
Hancock	150	47 10N	88 40W
Handa	106	34 53N	137 0 E
Handan	98	36 35N	114 28 E
Haney	154	49 12N	122 40W
Hanford	173	36 23N	119 39W
Hangayn Nuruu	100	47 30N	100 0 E
Hangchou = Hangzhou	99	30 18N	120 11 E
Hangö	67	59 50N	22 57 E
Hangu	98	39 18N	117 53 E
Hangzhou	99	30 18N	120 11 E
Hanna	155	51 40N	111 54W
Hannibal	166	39 42N	91 22W
Hannover	42	52 23N	9 43 E
Hanoi	95	21 5N	105 55 E
Hanover = Hannover	42	52 23N	9 43 E
Hanover, N.H., U.S.A.	148	43 43N	72 17W
Hanover, Pa., U.S.A.	164	39 46N	76 59W
Hansi	89	29 10N	75 57 E
Hanyü	107	36 10N	139 32 E
Hanzhong	99	33 10N	107 1 E
Haora	92	22 37N	88 20 E
Haparanda	67	65 52N	24 8 E
Harad, Si. Arabia	83	24 22N	49 0 E
Harad, Yemen	83	16 26N	43 5 E
Harare	137	17 43S	31 2 E
Harbin	98	45 48N	126 40 E
Harbour Breton	149	47 29N	55 50W
Harbour Grace	149	47 40N	53 22W
Hardap Dam	136	24 32S	17 50 E
Hardenberg	41	52 34N	6 37 E
Harderwijk	41	52 21N	5 38 E
Hardinxveld	40	51 49N	4 53 E
Hardwar = Haridwar	89	29 58N	78 9 E
Harer	133	9 20N	42 8 E
Harfleur	38	49 30N	0 10 E
Hargeisa	133	9 30N	44 2 E
Hari →	111	1 16S	104 5 E
Haridwar	89	29 58N	78 9 E
Harima-Nada	109	34 30N	134 35 E
Harīrūd →	86	34 20N	62 30 E
Harlech	26	52 52N	4 7W
Harlingen, Neths.	41	53 11N	5 25 E
Harlingen, U.S.A.	161	26 20N	97 50W
Harlow	25	51 47N	0 9 E
Harney Basin	171	43 30N	119 0W
Härnösand	66	62 38N	18 0 E
Harriman	169	36 0N	84 35W
Harris	32	57 50N	6 55W
Harris L.	118	31 10S	135 10 E
Harrisburg, Ill., U.S.A.	167	37 42N	88 30W
Harrisburg, Pa., U.S.A.	164	40 18N	76 52W
Harrison	168	36 10N	93 4W
Harrison, C.	147	54 55N	57 55W
Harrison B.	142	70 25N	151 30W
Harrisonburg	165	38 28N	78 52W
Harrogate	28	53 59N	1 32W
Harrow	25	51 35N	0 15W
Hartford	164	41 47N	72 41W
Hartland Pt.	27	51 2N	4 32W
Hartlepool	29	54 42N	1 11W
Hartsville	165	34 23N	80 2W
Harvey, Australia	120	33 5S	115 54 E
Harvey, U.S.A.	167	41 40N	87 40W
Harwich	25	51 56N	1 18 E
Haryana □	89	29 0N	76 10 E
Hashima	106	35 20N	136 40 E
Hashimoto	106	34 19N	135 37 E
Hastings, N.Z.	122	39 39S	176 52 E
Hastings, U.K.	25	50 51N	0 36 E

Name	Map	°	′		°	′	
Hastings, U.S.A.	163	40	34N		98	22W	
Hastings Ra.	116	31	15S		152	14 E	
Hatano	107	35	22N		139	14 E	
Hathras	89	27	36N		78	6 E	
Hatteras, C.	165	35	10N		75	30W	
Hattiesburg	169	31	20N		89	20W	
Hatvan	59	47	40N		19	45 E	
Hau Bon = Cheo Reo	95	13	25N		108	28 E	
Hauraki Gulf	122	36	35S		175	5 E	
Haut Atlas	126	32	30N		5	0W	
Havana = Habana, La	178	23	8N		82	22W	
Havant	25	50	51N		0	59W	
Havelock	151	44	26N		77	53W	
Haverfordwest	26	51	48N		4	59W	
Haverhill	164	42	50N		71	2W	
Havre	163	48	34N		109	40W	
Havre, Le	38	49	30N		0	5 E	
Hawaii □	160	20	30N		157	0W	
Hawaiian Is.	160	20	30N		156	0W	
Hawea Lake	123	44	28S		169	19 E	
Hawera	122	39	35S		174	19 E	
Hawick	31	55	25N		2	48W	
Hawke B.	122	39	25S		177	20 E	
Hawkesbury	151	45	37N		74	37W	
Hawthorne	172	38	31N		118	37W	
Hay, Australia	117	34	30S		144	51 E	
Hay, U.K.	26	52	4N		3	9W	
Hay River	145	60	51N		115	44W	
Hayward's Heath	25	51	0N		0	5W	
Hazard	165	37	18N		83	10W	
Hazaribag	92	23	58N		85	26 E	
Hazebrouck	38	50	42N		2	31 E	
Hazelton	154	55	20N		127	42W	
Hazleton	164	40	58N		76	0W	
Healdsburg	172	38	33N		122	51W	
Healesville	117	37	35S		145	30 E	
Heanor	29	53	1N		1	20W	
Hearst	150	49	40N		83	41W	
Hebei □	98	39	0N		116	0 E	
Hebel	116	28	58S		147	47 E	
Hebrides	16	57	30N		7	0W	
Hebron = Al Khalīl	80	31	32N		35	6 E	
Hebron	147	58	5N		62	30W	
Hecate Str.	154	53	10N		130	30W	
Hechuan	99	30	2N		106	12 E	
Hedmark fylke □	60	61	17N		11	40 E	
Heemstede	40	52	22N		4	37 E	
Heerenveen	41	52	57N		5	55 E	
Heerlen	41	50	55N		6	0 E	
Hefa	80	32	46N		35	0 E	
Hefei	99	31	52N		117	18 E	
Hegang	98	47	20N		130	19 E	
Heidelberg	42	49	23N		8	41 E	
Heilbronn	42	49	8N		9	13 E	
Heilongjiang □	98	48	0N		126	0 E	
Heilunkiang = Heilongjiang □	98	48	0N		126	0 E	
Heinze Is.	94	14	25N		97	45 E	
Hekimhan	81	38	50N		38	0 E	
Hekinan	106	34	52N		137	0 E	
Hekla	16	63	56N		19	35W	
Helena, Ark., U.S.A.	169	34	30N		90	35W	
Helena, Mont., U.S.A.	163	46	40N		112	0W	
Helensburgh	30	56	0N		4	44W	
Helmand →	87	31	12N		61	34 E	
Helmond	41	51	29N		5	41 E	
Helmsdale	33	58	7N		3	40W	
Helsingborg	61	56	3N		12	42 E	
Helsinki	67	60	15N		25	3 E	
Helston	27	50	7N		5	17W	
Helvellyn	28	54	31N		3	1W	
Hemel Hempstead	25	51	45N		0	28W	
Hempstead	164	30	5N		96	5W	
Henan □	99	34	0N		114	0 E	
Henderson	165	36	20N		78	25W	
Hendersonville	165	35	21N		82	28W	
Hengelo	41	52	16N		6	48 E	
Hengyang	99	26	51N		112	30 E	
Hénin-Beaumont	38	50	25N		2	58 E	
Hennebont	36	47	49N		3	19W	
Henrietta Maria C.	140	55	9N		82	20W	
Henty	117	35	30S		147	0 E	
Henzada	93	17	38N		95	26 E	
Herāt	87	34	20N		62	7 E	
Herāt □	87	35	0N		62	0 E	
Herbert →	121	18	31S		146	17 E	
Herbiers, Les	36	46	52N		1	0W	
Hercegnovi	52	42	30N		18	33 E	
Hercegovina = Bosnia &							
Herzegovina □	52	44	0N		18	0 E	
Hereford	24	52	4N		2	42W	
Hereford and Worcester □	24	52	10N		2	30W	
Herford	42	52	7N		8	40 E	
Hermosillo	174	29	4N		110	58W	
Heroica = Caborca	174	30	40N		112	10W	
Heroica Nogales = Nogales	174	31	20N		110	56W	
Heron Bay	150	48	40N		86	25W	
Herrin	166	37	50N		89	0W	
Hertford □	25	51	51N		0	5W	
's-Hertogenbosch	40	51	42N		5	17 E	
Hesse = Hessen □	42	50	40N		9	20 E	
Hessen □	42	50	40N		9	20 E	
Hewett, C.	146	70	16N		67	45W	
Hexham	28	54	58N		2	7W	
Heysham	28	54	5N		2	53W	
Heywood	119	38	8S		141	37 E	
Hi-no-Misaki	109	35	26N		132	38 E	
Hialeach	170	25	49N		80	17W	
Hibiki-Nada	108	34	0N		130	0 E	
Hickory	165	35	46N		81	17W	
Hida-Gawa →	106	35	26N		137	3 E	
Hida-Sammyaku	106	36	30N		137	40 E	
Hida-Sanchi	106	36	10N		137	0 E	
Hidaka	109	35	30N		134	44 E	
Hidalgo □	177	20	30N		99	0W	
Hidalgo del Parral	174	26	56N		105	40W	
Higashi-matsuyama	107	36	2N		139	25 E	
Higashiōsaka	106	34	40N		135	37 E	
Higasi-Suidō	108	34	0N		129	30 E	
High Atlas = Haut Atlas	126	32	30N		5	0W	
High Point	165	35	57N		79	58W	
High Prairie	155	55	30N		116	30W	
Highland □	32	57	30N		5	0W	
Highland Park	167	42	10N		87	50W	
Ḥijārah, Ṣaḥrā' al	84	30	25N		44	30 E	
Hikari	108	33	58N		131	58 E	
Hikone	106	35	15N		136	10 E	
Hildesheim	43	52	9N		9	55 E	
Hillegom	40	52	18N		4	35 E	
Hillsboro	171	45	31N		123	0W	
Hillston	117	33	30S		145	31 E	
Hilo	160	19	44N		155	5W	
Hilversum	40	52	14N		5	10 E	
Himachal Pradesh □	89	31	30N		77	0 E	
Himalaya, Mts.	101	29	0N		84	0 E	
Hime-Jima	108	33	43N		131	40 E	
Himeji	109	34	50N		134	40 E	
Himi	106	36	50N		137	0 E	
Ḥimş	80	34	40N		36	45 E	
Hinchinbrook I.	121	18	20S		146	15 E	
Hinckley	25	52	33N		1	21W	
Hindmarsh	119	34	54S		138	34 E	
Hindu Kush	89	36	0N		71	0 E	
Hindupur	90	13	49N		77	32 E	
Hines Creek	155	56	20N		118	40W	
Hingoli	91	19	41N		77	15 E	
Hinton	165	37	40N		80	51W	
Hirado	108	33	22N		129	33 E	
Hirakata	106	34	48N		135	40 E	
Hirakud Dam	92	21	32N		83	45 E	
Hirata	109	35	24N		132	49 E	
Hiratsuka	107	35	19N		139	21 E	
Hirosaki	103	40	34N		140	28 E	
Hiroshima	109	34	24N		132	30 E	
Hirson	38	49	55N		4	4 E	
Hispaniola	180	19	0N		71	0W	
Hita	108	33	20N		130	58 E	
Hitachi	107	36	36N		140	39 E	
Hitachiota	107	36	30N		140	30 E	
Hitchin	25	51	57N		0	16W	
Hitoyoshi	108	32	13N		130	45 E	
Hitra	65	63	30N		8	45 E	
Hiuchi-Nada	109	34	5N		133	20 E	

Ho Chi Minh City = Thanh
  Pho Ho Chi Minh .... **95** 10 58N 106 40 E
Hoa Binh .... **95** 20 50N 105 20 E
Hobart .... **119** 42 50S 147 21 E
Hobbs **161** 32 40N 103 3W
Hodaka-Dake .... **106** 36 17N 137 39 E
Hódmezővásárhely .... **59** 46 28N 20 22 E
Hoek van Holland .... **40** 52 0N 4 7 E
Hofsjökull **64** 64 49N 18 48W
Höfu .... **108** 34 3N 131 34 E
Hogan Group .... **117** 39 13S 147 1 E
Hoh Xil Shan .... **101** 35 0N 89 0 E
Hohhot .... **98** 40 52N 111 40 E
Hōjō .... **109** 33 58N 132 46 E
Hokitika .... **123** 42 42S 171 0 E
Hokkaidō □ .... **103** 43 30N 143 0 E
Holbrook .... **117** 35 42S 147 18 E
Holderness **29** 53 45N 0 5W
Holdrege **163** 40 26N 99 22W
Holguín **178** 20 50N 76 20W
Holland **167** 42 47N 86 7W
Holly Springs **169** 34 45N 89 25W
Hollywood, Calif., U.S.A. ... **173** 34 7N 118 25W
Hollywood, Fla., U.S.A. **170** 26 0N 80 9W
Holsteinsborg **147** 66 40N 53 30W
Holsworthy **27** 50 48N 4 21W
Holt **64** 63 33N 19 48W
Holy I., Scotland, U.K. **31** 55 31N 5 4W
Holy I., Wales, U.K. **26** 53 17N 4 37W
Holyhead **26** 53 18N 4 38W
Holyoke **164** 42 14N 72 37W
Hombori **130** 15 20N 1 38W
Home Hill .... **121** 19 43S 147 25 E
Homer **142** 59 40N 151 35W
Homs = Ḥimṣ .... **80** 34 40N 36 45 E
Honan = Henan □ .... **99** 34 0N 114 0 E
Hondo .... **108** 32 27N 130 12 E
Honduras ■ **179** 14 40N 86 30W
Honduras, Golfo de **177** 16 50N 87 0W
Hong Kong ■ .... **99** 22 11N 114 14 E
Hongha --► .... **95** 22 0N 104 0 E
Hongshui He --► .... **99** 23 48N 109 30 E
Honiton **27** 50 48N 3 11W
Honolulu **160** 21 19N 157 52W
Honshū .... **106** 36 0N 138 0 E
Hoogeveen .... **41** 52 44N 6 30 E
Hook Hd. **35** 52 8N 6 57W
Hook of Holland = Hoek van
  Holland .... **40** 52 0N 4 7 E
Hoorn .... **40** 52 38N 5 4 E
Hope, Canada .... **154** 49 25N 121 25 E
Hope, U.S.A. **168** 33 40N 93 36W
Hope Town **178** 26 35N 76 57W
Hopedale **147** 55 28N 60 13W
Hopei = Hebei □ .... **98** 39 0N 116 0 E
Hopelchén **177** 19 46N 89 51W
Hopetoun, Vic., Australia ... **119** 35 42S 142 22 E
Hopetoun, W. Austral.,
  Australia .... **120** 33 57S 120 7 E
Hopkinsville **169** 36 52N 87 26W
Hoquiam **171** 46 50N 123 55W
Hordaland fylke □ .... **60** 60 25N 6 15 E
Hormoz .... **85** 27 35N 55 0 E
Hormuz Str. .... **85** 26 30N 56 30 E
Horn, Cape = Hornos, Cabo
  de **192** 55 50S 67 30W
Hornavan .... **66** 66 15N 17 30 E
Hornell **164** 42 23N 77 41W
Hornos, Cabo de **192** 55 50S 67 30W
Hornsby .... **117** 33 42S 151 2 E
Hornsea **29** 53 55N 0 10W
Horqin Youyi Qianqi ...... **98** 46 5N 122 3 E
Horsens .... **61** 55 52N 9 51 E
Horsham .... **119** 36 44S 142 13 E
Horton --► **145** 69 56N 126 52W
Hoshiarpur .... **89** 31 30N 75 58 E
Hospet .... **90** 15 15N 76 20 E
Hospitalet de Llobregat .... **51** 41 21N 2 6 E
Hoste, I. **192** 55 0S 69 0W
Hot Springs **168** 34 30N 93 0W
Houghton **150** 47 9N 88 39W

Houghton-le-Spring **28** 54 51N 1 28W
Houhora .... **122** 34 49S 173 9 E
Houlton **148** 46 5N 67 50W
Houma **169** 29 35N 90 44W
Houston, Canada **154** 54 25N 126 39W
Houston, U.S.A. **168** 29 50N 95 20W
Houtman Abrolhos .... **120** 28 43S 113 48 E
Hovd .... **100** 48 2N 91 37 E
Hove **25** 50 50N 0 10W
Howe, C. .... **117** 37 30S 150 0 E
Howrah = Haora .... **92** 22 37N 88 20 E
Hoy I. **33** 58 50N 3 15W
Hrádec Králové .... **58** 50 15N 15 50 E
Hrvatska = Croatia ■ .... **52** 45 20N 18 0 E
Hsiamen = Xiamen ...... **99** 24 25N 118 4 E
Hsian = Xi'an .... **99** 34 15N 109 0 E
Hsinhailien = Lianyungang . **99** 34 40N 119 11 E
Hsüchou = Xuzhou ...... **99** 34 18N 117 10 E
Hua Hin .... **94** 12 34N 99 58 E
Huacho **186** 11 10S 77 35W
Huainan .... **99** 32 38N 116 58 E
Huallaga --► **186** 5 0S 75 30W
Huambo .... **134** 12 42S 15 54 E
Huancane **187** 15 10S 69 44W
Huancavelica **186** 12 50S 75 5W
Huancayo **186** 12 5S 75 12W
Huanchaca **187** 20 15S 66 40W
Huang Hai = Yellow Sea ... **99** 35 0N 123 0 E
Huang Ho --► .... **98** 37 30N 118 50 E
Huangshi .... **99** 30 10N 115 3 E
Huánuco **186** 9 55S 76 15W
Huaraz **186** 9 30S 77 32W
Huascarán **186** 9 8S 77 36W
Huasco **190** 28 30S 71 15W
Huatabampo **174** 26 50N 109 38W
Huautla **177** 17 51N 100 5W
Hubei □ .... **99** 31 0N 112 0 E
Hubli-Dharwad = Dharwad . **90** 15 22N 75 15 E
Huddersfield **28** 53 38N 1 49W
Hudiksvall .... **66** 61 43N 17 10 E
Hudson **164** 42 15N 73 46W
Hudson --► **164** 40 42N 74 2W
Hudson Bay **146** 52 51N 102 23W
Hudson Str. **146** 62 0N 70 0W
Hudson's Hope **155** 56 0N 121 54W
Hue .... **95** 16 30N 107 35 E
Huehuetenango **177** 15 20N 91 28W
Huelva **50** 37 18N 6 57W
Huesca **51** 42 8N 0 25W
Hughenden .... **121** 20 52S 144 10 E
Huila, Nevado del **184** 3 0N 76 0W
Huinca Renancó **190** 34 51S 64 22W
Huixtla **177** 15 9N 92 28W
Huizen .... **40** 52 18N 5 14 E
Hukawng Valley .... **93** 26 30N 96 30 E
Hull, Canada **151** 45 25N 75 44W
Hull, U.K. **29** 53 45N 0 20W
Hulst .... **40** 51 17N 4 2 E
Hulun Nur .... **98** 49 0N 117 30 E
Humaitá **187** 27 2S 58 31W
Humber --► **29** 53 40N 0 10W
Humberside □ **29** 53 50N 0 30W
Humboldt, Canada **152** 52 15N 105 9W
Humboldt, U.S.A. **169** 35 50N 88 55W
Humboldt --► **172** 40 2N 118 31W
Hume, L. .... **117** 36 0S 147 0 E
Húnaflói **64** 65 50N 20 50W
Hunan □ .... **99** 27 30N 111 30 E
Hunedoara .... **56** 45 40N 22 50 E
Hungary ■ .... **59** 47 20N 19 20 E
Hungary, Plain of ...... **17** 47 0N 20 0 E
Hüngnam .... **98** 39 49N 127 45 E
Hunsrück .... **42** 49 30N 7 0 E
Hunstanton .... **29** 52 57N 0 30 E
Hunter Ra. .... **117** 32 45S 150 15 E
Huntingdon **25** 52 20N 0 11W
Huntington, Ind., U.S.A. .. **167** 40 52N 85 30W
Huntington, W. Va., U.S.A. . **165** 38 20N 82 30W
Huntington Beach **173** 33 40N 118 0W
Huntly .... **122** 37 34S 175 11 E
Huntsville, Canada **151** 45 20N 79 14W

Huntsville, Ala., U.S.A.	169	34 45N	86 35W
Huntsville, Tex., U.S.A.	168	30 45N	95 35W
Huonville	119	43 0S	147 5 E
Hupeh = Hubei □	99	31 0N	112 0 E
Huron, L.	150	45 0N	83 0W
Hurricane	173	37 10N	113 12W
Húsavík	64	66 3N	17 21W
Hutchinson	161	38 3N	97 59W
Hvar	52	43 11N	16 28 E
Hwang Ho = Huang Ho →	98	37 30N	118 50 E
Hwange	137	18 18S	26 30 E
Hyden	120	32 24S	118 53 E
Hyderabad, India	91	17 22N	78 29 E
Hyderabad, Pakistan	88	25 23N	68 24 E
Hyères	37	43 8N	6 9 E
Hyndman Pk.	162	43 50N	114 10W
Hythe	24	51 4N	1 5 E
Hyūga	108	32 25N	131 35 E

I

Iaşi	57	47 10N	27 40 E
Ibadan	131	7 22N	3 58 E
Ibagué	184	4 20N	75 20W
Ibara	109	34 36N	133 28 E
Ibaraki	106	34 49N	135 34 E
Ibarra	184	0 21N	78 7W
Iberian Peninsula	16	40 0N	5 0W
Ibiza	51	38 54N	1 26 E
Ibuki-Sanchi	106	35 25N	136 18 E
Ibusuki	108	31 12N	130 40 E
Icá	186	14 0S	75 48W
Iça →	184	2 55S	67 58W
Iceland ■	64	65 0N	19 0W
Icha	73	55 30N	156 0 E
Ich'ang = Yichang	99	30 40N	111 20 E
Ichchapuram	92	19 10N	84 40 E
Ichihara	107	35 28N	140 5 E
Ichikawa	107	35 44N	139 55 E
Ichinomiya	106	35 18N	136 48 E
Ichinoseki	103	38 55N	141 8 E
Idaho □	162	44 10N	114 0W
Idaho Falls	163	43 30N	112 1W
Ídhi Óros	55	35 15N	24 45 E
Ídhra	55	37 20N	23 28 E
Ierápetra	55	35 0N	25 44 E
Ife	131	7 30N	4 31 E
Igloolik	146	69 20N	81 49W
Iguaçu →	191	25 36S	54 36W
Iguaçu, Cat. del	191	25 41S	54 26W
Iguaçu Falls = Iguaçu, Cat. del	191	25 41S	54 26W
Iguala de la Independencia	177	18 21N	99 32W
Iguassu = Iguaçu →	191	25 36S	54 36W
Iida	107	35 35N	137 50 E
Iisalmi	67	63 32N	27 10 E
Iizuka	108	33 38N	130 42 E
IJmuiden	40	52 28N	4 35 E
IJsselmeer	40	52 45N	5 20 E
IJsselstein	40	52 1N	5 2 E
Ikaría	55	37 35N	26 10 E
Ikeda	109	34 1N	133 48 E
Iki	108	33 45N	129 42 E
Iki-Kaikyō	108	33 40N	129 45 E
Île-de-France	37	49 0N	2 20 E
Ilebo	134	4 17S	20 55 E
Ilfracombe	27	51 13N	4 8W
Ilhéus	189	14 49S	39 2W
Ili →	71	45 53N	77 10 E
Iliamna L.	142	59 35N	155 30W
Iliodhrómia	55	39 12N	23 50 E
Ilkeston	29	52 59N	1 19W
Illampu = Ancohuma, Nevada	187	16 0S	68 50W
Illinois □	166	40 15N	89 30W
Illinois →	166	38 55N	90 28W
Ilo	187	17 40S	71 20W
Iloilo	112	10 45N	122 33 E
Ilorin	131	8 30N	4 35 E

Imabari	109	34 4N	133 0 E
Imari	108	33 15N	129 52 E
Imatra	67	61 12N	28 48 E
Immingham	29	53 37N	0 12W
Imperial	152	51 21N	105 28W
Imphal	92	24 48N	93 56 E
Imroz = Gökçeada	55	40 10N	25 50 E
Ina	107	35 50N	138 0 E
Iñapari	187	11 0S	69 40W
Inari	67	68 54N	27 5 E
Inarijärvi	67	69 0N	28 0 E
Inazawa	106	35 15N	136 47 E
Inchon	98	37 27N	126 40 E
Indalsälven →	66	62 36N	17 30 E
Independence, Kans., U.S.A.	166	37 10N	95 43W
Independence, Mo., U.S.A.	166	39 3N	94 25W
India ■	78	20 0N	78 0 E
Indian Head	152	50 30N	103 41W
Indiana	164	40 38N	79 9W
Indiana □	167	40 0N	86 0W
Indianapolis	167	39 42N	86 10W
Indigirka →	73	70 48N	148 54 E
Indonesia ■	111	5 0S	115 0 E
Indore	91	22 42N	75 53 E
Indre →	36	47 16N	0 19 E
Indus →	88	24 20N	67 47 E
Indus, Mouth of the	88	24 0N	68 0 E
Inebolu	80	41 55N	33 40 E
İnegöl	80	40 5N	29 31 E
Ingersoll	151	43 4N	80 55W
Ingham	121	18 43S	146 10 E
Ingleborough	28	54 11N	2 23W
Inglewood, N.Z.	122	39 9S	174 14 E
Inglewood, U.S.A.	173	33 58N	118 21W
Ingolstadt	43	48 45N	11 26 E
Ingushetia □	70	43 20N	44 50 E
Inhambane	137	23 54S	35 30 E
Ining = Yining	100	43 58N	81 10 E
Inishmore	35	53 8N	9 45W
Inishowen	34	55 14N	7 15W
Inn →	43	48 35N	13 28 E
Innamincka	118	27 44S	140 46 E
Inner Hebrides	32	57 0N	6 30W
Inner Mongolia = Nei Monggol Zizhiqu □	98	42 0N	112 0 E
Innisfail, Australia	121	17 33S	146 5 E
Innisfail, Canada	155	52 0N	113 57W
In'no-shima	109	34 19N	133 10 E
Innsbruck	45	47 16N	11 23 E
Inoucdjouac	146	58 25N	78 15W
Inowrocław	58	52 50N	18 12 E
Inquisivi	187	16 50S	67 10W
Insein	93	16 50N	96 5 E
Interlaken	44	46 41N	7 50 E
Inuvik	144	68 16N	133 40W
Inuvik □	144	70 0N	130 0W
Inuyama	106	35 23N	136 56 E
Inveraray	30	56 13N	5 5W
Invercargill	123	46 24S	168 24 E
Inverell	116	29 45S	151 8 E
Invergordon	33	57 41N	4 10W
Inverness	33	57 29N	4 12W
Investigator Group	119	34 45S	134 20 E
Investigator Str.	119	35 30S	137 0 E
Ioánnina	54	39 42N	20 47 E
Iola	166	38 0N	95 20W
Iona	30	56 20N	6 25W
Ionian Is. = Iónioi Nísoi	54	38 40N	20 0 E
Ionian Sea	54	37 30N	17 30 E
Iónioi Nísoi	54	38 40N	20 0 E
Íos	55	36 41N	25 20 E
Iowa □	166	42 18N	93 30W
Iowa City	166	41 40N	91 35W
Iowa Falls	166	42 30N	93 15W
Ipiales	184	0 50N	77 37W
Ipin = Yibin	99	28 45N	104 32 E
Ípiros □	54	39 30N	20 30 E
Ipoh	96	4 35N	101 5 E
Ipswich, Australia	116	27 35S	152 40 E
Ipswich, U.K.	25	52 4N	1 9 E
Iquique	187	20 19S	70 5W

Iquitos	**186**	3	45S	73	10W
Iracoubo	**185**	5	30N	53	10W
Iráklion	**55**	35	20N	25	12 E
Iran ■	**86**	33	0N	53	0 E
Iran Ra.	**111**	2	20N	114	50 E
Irapuato	**177**	20	41N	101	28W
Iraq ■	**81**	33	0N	44	0 E
Irbid	**80**	32	35N	35	48 E
Ireland ■	**34**	53	0N	8	0W
Irian Jaya □	**113**	4	0S	137	0 E
Iriri →	**188**	3	52S	52	37W
Irish Republic ■	**20**	53	0N	8	0W
Irish Sea	**20**	54	0N	5	0W
Irkutsk	**74**	52	18N	104	20 E
Irõ-Zaki	**107**	34	36N	138	51 E
Iron Gate = Portile de Fier	**56**	44	42N	22	30 E
Iron Knob	**118**	32	46S	137	8 E
Iron Mountain	**150**	45	49N	88	4W
Ironbridge	**24**	52	38N	2	29W
Ironton	**167**	38	35N	82	40W
Ironwood	**150**	46	30N	90	10W
Iroquois Falls	**151**	48	46N	80	41W
Irrawaddy →	**93**	15	50N	95	6 E
Irtysh →	**69**	61	4N	68	52 E
Irumu	**135**	1	32N	29	53 E
Irún	**51**	43	20N	1	52W
Irvine	**31**	55	37N	4	40W
Irvinestown	**34**	54	28N	7	38W
Ísafjörður	**64**	66	5N	23	9W
Isahaya	**108**	32	52N	130	2 E
Ischia	**49**	40	45N	13	51 E
Ise	**106**	34	25N	136	45 E
Ise-Wan	**106**	34	43N	136	43 E
Isère →	**37**	44	59N	4	51 E
Isesaki	**107**	36	19N	139	12 E
Ishikari-Wan	**103**	43	25N	141	1 E
Ishinomaki	**103**	38	32N	141	20 E
Ishioka	**107**	36	11N	140	16 E
Ishkuman	**89**	36	30N	73	50 E
Ishpeming	**150**	46	30N	87	40W
İskenderun	**80**	36	32N	36	10 E
Islamabad	**89**	33	40N	73	10 E
Island L.	**153**	53	47N	94	25W
Island Pond	**148**	48	25N	56	23W
Islay	**30**	55	46N	6	10W
Isle-Adam, L'	**39**	49	6N	2	14 E
Isle Royale	**150**	48	0N	88	50W
Ísparta	**80**	37	47N	30	30 E
Israel ■	**80**	32	0N	34	50 E
Issoire	**37**	45	32N	3	15 E
Issyk-Kul, Ozero	**71**	42	25N	77	15 E
İstanbul	**80**	41	0N	29	0 E
Istra	**52**	45	10N	14	0 E
Istria = Istra	**52**	45	10N	14	0 E
Itabuna	**189**	14	48S	39	16W
Itaituba	**185**	4	10S	55	50W
Itajaí	**191**	27	50S	48	39W
Italy ■	**19**	42	0N	13	0 E
Itaquatiara	**185**	2	58S	58	30W
Itaquí	**191**	29	8S	56	30W
Itchen →	**24**	50	57N	1	20W
Ithaca = Itháki	**54**	38	25N	20	40 E
Ithaca	**164**	42	25N	76	30W
Itháki	**54**	38	25N	20	40 E
Ito	**107**	34	58N	139	5 E
Ituaçu	**189**	13	50S	41	18W
Ituiutaba	**188**	19	0S	49	25W
Iturup, Ostrov	**75**	45	0N	148	0 E
Ivano-Frankovsk	**68**	48	40N	24	40 E
Ivanovo, Belorussia	**68**	52	7N	25	29 E
Ivanovo, Russia	**68**	57	5N	41	0 E
Ivigtut	**147**	61	14N	48	12W
Iviza = Ibiza	**51**	38	54N	1	26 E
Ivory Coast ■	**130**	7	30N	5	0W
Iwai-Jima	**108**	33	47N	131	58 E
Iwaki	**105**	37	3N	140	55 E
Iwakuni	**109**	34	15N	132	8 E
Iwami	**109**	35	32N	134	15 E
Iwamizawa	**103**	43	12N	141	46 E
Iwanuma	**103**	38	7N	140	51 E
Iwata	**107**	34	42N	137	51 E
Iwo	**131**	7	39N	4	9 E
Ixiamas	**187**	13	50S	68	5W
Ixtepec	**177**	16	34N	95	6W
Ixtlán	**175**	20	11N	102	24W
Ixtlán de Juárez	**177**	17	23N	96	28W
Iyo	**109**	33	45N	132	45 E
Iyo-mishima	**109**	33	58N	133	30 E
Iyo-Nada	**109**	33	40N	132	20 E
Izamal	**177**	20	56N	89	1W
Izhevsk	**69**	56	51N	53	14 E
İzmir	**80**	38	25N	27	8 E
İzmit	**80**	40	45N	29	50 E
Izu-Hantõ	**107**	34	45N	139	0 E
Izumi	**108**	32	5N	130	22 E
Izumi-sano	**106**	34	23N	135	18 E
Izumiotsu	**106**	34	30N	135	24 E
Izumo	**109**	35	20N	132	46 E

J

Jabalpur	**91**	23	9N	79	58 E
Jacarèzinho	**191**	23	5S	50	0W
Jackson, Mich., U.S.A.	**167**	42	18N	84	25W
Jackson, Miss., U.S.A.	**169**	32	20N	90	10W
Jackson, Tenn., U.S.A.	**169**	35	40N	88	50W
Jacksonville, Fla., U.S.A.	**170**	30	15N	81	38W
Jacksonville, Ill., U.S.A.	**166**	39	42N	90	15W
Jacksonville, N.C., U.S.A.	**165**	34	50N	77	29W
Jacksonville, Tex., U.S.A.	**168**	31	58N	95	19W
Jacmel	**180**	18	14N	72	32W
Jacobabad	**88**	28	20N	68	29 E
Jacques Cartier, Dét. de	**149**	50	0N	63	30W
Jadotville = Likasi	**135**	10	55S	26	48 E
Jaén, Peru	**186**	5	25S	78	40W
Jaén, Spain	**50**	37	44N	3	43W
Jaffa = Tel Aviv-Yafo	**80**	32	4N	34	48 E
Jaffna	**90**	9	45N	80	2 E
Jagdalpur	**92**	19	3N	82	0 E
Jaguariaíva	**191**	24	10S	49	50W
Jagüey Grande	**178**	22	35N	81	7W
Jahrom	**85**	28	30N	53	31 E
Jaipur	**91**	27	0N	75	50 E
Jakarta	**111**	6	9S	106	49 E
Jalalabad	**87**	34	30N	70	29 E
Jalapa, Guatemala	**177**	14	39N	89	59W
Jalapa, Mexico	**177**	17	43N	92	49W
Jalgaon	**91**	21	0N	75	42 E
Jalisco □	**175**	20	20N	103	40W
Jalna	**91**	19	48N	75	38 E
Jalón →	**51**	41	47N	1	4W
Jalpaiguri	**92**	26	32N	88	46 E
Jamaica ■	**180**	18	10N	77	30W
Jamalpur, Bangla.	**92**	24	52N	89	56 E
Jamalpur, India	**92**	25	18N	86	28 E
Jambi	**111**	1	38S	103	30 E
James →	**163**	42	52N	97	18W
James B.	**140**	51	30N	80	0W
Jamestown, Australia	**118**	33	10S	138	32 E
Jamestown, N. Dak., U.S.A.	**163**	46	54N	98	42W
Jamestown, N.Y., U.S.A.	**164**	42	5N	79	18W
Jamkhandi	**91**	16	30N	75	15 E
Jammu	**89**	32	43N	74	54 E
Jammu & Kashmir □	**89**	34	25N	77	0 E
Jamnagar	**90**	22	30N	70	6 E
Jamshedpur	**92**	22	44N	86	12 E
Jan Mayen Is.	**13**	71	0N	9	0W
Janesville	**166**	42	39N	89	1W
Januária	**188**	15	25S	44	25W
Jaora	**91**	23	40N	75	10 E
Japan ■	**79**	36	0N	136	0 E
Japan, Sea of	**102**	40	0N	135	0 E
Japurá →	**185**	3	8S	64	46W
Jargalant = Hovd	**100**	48	2N	91	37 E
Jargeau	**39**	47	50N	2	1 E
Jarosław	**58**	50	2N	22	42 E
Jāsk	**85**	25	38N	57	45 E
Jasło	**59**	49	45N	21	30 E
Jasper, Canada	**155**	52	55N	118	5W

228 Jasper

Jasper, U.S.A.	**169**	33 48N	87	16W
Jassy = Iaşi	**57**	47 10N	27	40 E
Jataí	**188**	17 58S	51	48W
Jaú	**188**	22 10S	48	30W
Jaunpur	**92**	25 46N	82	44 E
Java, I.	**111**	7 0S	110	0 E
Java Sea	**111**	4 35S	107	15 E
Javhlant = Ulyasutay	**100**	47 56N	97	28 E
Jean Marie River	**144**	61 32N	120	38W
Jean Rabel	**180**	19 50N	73	5W
Jedburgh	**31**	55 28N	2	33W
Jędrzejów	**58**	50 35N	20	15 E
Jefferson, Mt.	**171**	44 45N	121	50W
Jefferson City	**166**	38 34N	92	10W
Jeffersonville	**167**	38 20N	85	42W
Jelenia Góra	**58**	50 50N	15	45 E
Jena	**43**	50 56N	11	33 E
Jenkins	**165**	37 13N	82	41W
Jennings	**168**	30 10N	92	45W
Jeparit	**119**	36 8S	142	1 E
Jequié	**189**	13 51S	40	5W
Jequitinhonha	**189**	16 30S	41	0W
Jérémie	**180**	18 40N	74	10W
Jerez de García Salinas	**175**	22 39N	103	0W
Jerez de la Frontera	**50**	36 41N	6	7W
Jerez de los Caballeros	**50**	38 20N	6	45W
Jericho	**121**	23 38S	146	6 E
Jerilderie	**117**	35 20S	145	41 E
Jerome	**148**	47 37N	82	14W
Jersey, I.	**36**	49 13N	2	7W
Jersey City	**164**	40 41N	74	8W
Jerseyville	**166**	39 5N	90	20W
Jerusalem	**80**	31 47N	35	10 E
Jesselton = Kota Kinabalu	**112**	6 0N	116	4 E
Jhang Maghiana	**89**	31 15N	72	22 E
Jhansi	**91**	25 30N	78	36 E
Jharsuguda	**92**	21 56N	84	5 E
Jhelum →	**89**	31 20N	72	10 E
Jhunjhunu	**89**	28 10N	75	30 E
Jiamusi	**98**	46 40N	130	26 E
Ji'an	**99**	27 6N	114	59 E
Jiangmen	**99**	22 32N	113	0 E
Jiangsu □	**99**	33 0N	120	0 E
Jiangxi □	**99**	27 30N	116	0 E
Jian'ou	**99**	27 3N	118	17 E
Jiao Xian	**98**	36 18N	120	1 E
Jiaozuo	**99**	35 16N	113	12 E
Jiaxing	**99**	30 49N	120	45 E
Jiayi	**99**	23 30N	120	24 E
Jibuti = Djibouti ■	**133**	12 0N	43	0 E
Jiddah	**82**	21 29N	39	10 E
Jido	**93**	29 2N	94	58 E
Jihlava	**59**	49 28N	15	35 E
Jilin	**98**	43 44N	126	30 E
Jilong	**99**	25 8N	121	42 E
Jima	**132**	7 40N	36	47 E
Jiménez	**174**	27 8N	104	54W
Jinan	**98**	36 38N	117	1 E
Jingdezhen	**99**	29 20N	117	11 E
Jining, Nei Mongol Zizhiqu, China	**98**	41 5N	113	0 E
Jining, Shandong, China	**99**	35 22N	116	34 E
Jinja	**132**	0 25N	33	12 E
Jinnah Barrage	**89**	32 58N	71	33 E
Jinotega	**179**	13 6N	85	59W
Jinotepe	**179**	11 50N	86	10W
Jinshi	**99**	29 40N	111	50 E
Jinzhou	**98**	41 5N	121	3 E
Jipijapa	**184**	1 0S	80	40W
Jiquilpan de Juárez	**175**	19 59N	102	43W
Jisr ash Shughūr	**80**	35 49N	36	18 E
Jiujiang	**99**	29 42N	115	58 E
Jixi	**98**	45 20N	130	50 E
João Pessoa	**189**	7 10S	34	52W
Jodhpur	**91**	26 23N	73	8 E
Joensuu	**67**	62 37N	29	49 E
Jogjakarta = Yogyakarta	**111**	7 49S	110	22 E
Jōhana	**106**	36 30N	136	57 E
Johannesburg	**137**	26 10S	28	2 E
John o' Groats	**33**	58 39N	3	3W
Johnson City, N.Y., U.S.A.	**164**	42 7N	75	57W
Johnson City, Tenn., U.S.A.	**165**	36 18N	82	21W
Johnston	**31**	51 45N	5	5W
Johnstown, N.Y., U.S.A.	**164**	43 1N	74	20W
Johnstown, Pa., U.S.A.	**164**	40 19N	78	53W
Johor □	**96**	2 5N	103	20 E
Johor Baharu	**96**	1 28N	103	46 E
Joigny	**39**	48 0N	3	20 E
Joinvile	**191**	26 15S	48	55 E
Joliet	**167**	41 30N	88	0W
Joliette	**151**	46 3N	73	24W
Jolo	**112**	6 0N	121	0 E
Jonesboro	**169**	35 50N	90	45W
Jönköping	**60**	57 45N	14	10 E
Jönköpings län □	**61**	57 30N	14	30 E
Jonquière	**148**	48 27N	71	14W
Joplin	**168**	37 0N	94	31W
Jordan ■	**80**	31 0N	36	0 E
Jordan →	**80**	31 48N	35	32 E
Jorhat	**93**	26 45N	94	12 E
José de San Martín	**192**	44 4S	70	26W
Jowzjān □	**87**	36 10N	66	0 E
Juan de Fuca Str.	**142**	48 15N	124	0W
Juan Fernández, Arch. de	**183**	33 50S	80	0W
Juàzeiro	**189**	9 30S	40	30W
Juàzeiro do Norte	**189**	7 10S	39	18W
Jubbulpore = Jabalpur	**91**	23 9N	79	58 E
Júcar →	**51**	39 5N	0	10W
Juchitán de Zaragoza	**177**	16 26N	95	1W
Jugoslavia = Yugoslavia ■	**52**	44 0N	21	0 E
Juiz de Fora	**188**	21 43S	43	19W
Juli	**187**	16 10S	69	25W
Juliaca	**187**	15 25S	70	10W
Julianehåb	**147**	60 43N	46	0W
Jullundur	**89**	31 20N	75	40 E
Jumla	**92**	29 15N	82	13 E
Jumna = Yamuna →	**92**	25 30N	81	53 E
Junagadh	**91**	21 30N	70	30 E
Jundiaí	**191**	24 30S	47	0W
Juneau	**143**	58 20N	134	20W
Junee	**117**	34 53S	147	35 E
Junggar Pendi	**100**	44 30N	86	0 E
Junín	**190**	34 33S	60	57W
Jura, Europe	**37**	46 35N	6	5 E
Jura, U.K.	**30**	56 0N	5	50W
Jurado	**184**	7 7N	77	46W
Juruá →	**184**	2 37S	65	44W
Juruena	**187**	13 0S	58	10W
Juruena →	**187**	7 20S	58	3W
Juticalpa	**179**	14 40N	86	12W
Jutland = Jylland	**61**	56 25N	9	30 E
Juventud, I. de la	**178**	21 40N	82	40W
Jylland	**61**	56 25N	9	30 E
Jyväskylä	**67**	62 14N	25	50 E

K

Kaapstad = Cape Town	**136**	33 55S	18	22 E
Kabala	**130**	9 38N	11	37W
Kabardino-Balkaria □	**70**	43 30N	43	30 E
Kabarega Falls	**132**	2 15N	31	30 E
Kabīr Kūh	**84**	33 0N	47	30 E
Kābul	**87**	34 28N	69	11 E
Kābul □	**87**	34 30N	69	0 E
Kabwe	**135**	14 30S	28	29 E
Kachin □	**93**	26 0N	97	30 E
Kadan Kyun	**94**	12 30N	98	20 E
Kadina	**119**	34 0S	137	43 E
Kaduna	**131**	10 30N	7	21 E
Kaédi	**126**	16 9N	13	28W
Kāf	**80**	31 25N	37	29 E
Kafirévs, Ákra	**55**	38 9N	24	38 E
Kafue →	**135**	15 30S	26	0 E
Kaga	**106**	36 16N	136	15 E
Kagoshima	**108**	31 35N	130	33 E
Kagoshima-Wan	**108**	31 25N	130	40 E
Kai, Kepulauan	**113**	5 55S	132	45W
Kaieteur Falls	**185**	5 1N	59	10W
Kaifeng	**99**	34 49N	114	30 E

Name	Ref	Lat °	Lat ′	Long °	Long ′
Kaikoura Ra.	123	41	59S	173	41 E
Kailua	160	19	39N	156	0W
Kaimanawa Mts.	122	39	15S	175	56 E
Kainan	106	34	9N	135	12 E
Kainji Res.	131	10	1N	4	40 E
Kaipara Harbour	122	36	25S	174	14 E
Kaiserslautern	42	49	30N	7	43 E
Kaitaia	122	35	8S	173	17 E
Kajaani	67	64	17N	27	46 E
Kajana = Kajaani	67	64	17N	27	46 E
Kakabeka Falls	150	48	24N	89	37W
Kakamigahara	106	35	28N	136	48 E
Kakanui Mts.	123	45	10S	170	30 E
Kakegawa	107	34	45N	138	1 E
Kakinada	92	16	57N	82	11 E
Kakogawa	109	34	46N	134	51 E
Kalabáka	54	39	42N	21	39 E
Kalahari	136	24	0S	21	30 E
Kalamata	54	37	3N	22	10 E
Kalamazoo	167	42	20N	85	35W
Kalamazoo →	167	42	40N	86	12W
Kalat	88	29	8N	66	31 E
Kalaupapa	160	21	12N	156	59W
Kalemie	135	5	55S	29	9 E
Kalgan = Zhangjiakou	98	40	48N	114	55 E
Kalgoorlie-Boulder	120	30	40S	121	22 E
Kálimnos	55	37	0N	27	0 E
Kalinin = Tver	68	56	55N	35	55 E
Kaliningrad	68	54	42N	20	32 E
Kalispell	162	48	10N	114	22W
Kalisz	58	51	45N	18	8 E
Kalmar	61	56	40N	16	20 E
Kalmar län □	61	57	25N	16	0 E
Kalmykia □	70	46	5N	46	1 E
Kalocsa	59	46	32N	19	0 E
Kaluga	68	54	35N	36	10 E
Kama →	68	55	45N	52	0 E
Kamaishi	103	39	16N	141	53 E
Kamakura	107	35	19N	139	33 E
Kamaran	82	15	21N	42	35 E
Kamchatka, P-ov.	73	57	0N	160	0 E
Kamenka	69	53	10N	44	5 E
Kamensk Uralskiy	69	56	25N	62	2 E
Kamenskoye	73	62	45N	165	30 E
Kameoka	106	35	0N	135	35 E
Kameyama	106	34	51N	136	27 E
Kami-koshiki-Jima	108	31	50N	129	52 E
Kamioka	106	36	25N	137	15 E
Kamloops	155	50	40N	120	20W
Kampala	132	0	20N	32	30 E
Kampar	96	4	18N	101	9 E
Kampen	41	52	33N	5	53 E
Kampot	95	10	36N	104	10 E
Kampuchea = Cambodia ■	95	12	15N	105	0 E
Kamsack	152	51	34N	101	54W
Kamui-Misaki	103	43	20N	140	21 E
Kamyshin	68	50	10N	45	24 E
Kananga	134	5	55S	22	18 E
Kanawha →	165	38	50N	82	8W
Kanazawa	106	36	30N	136	38 E
Kanchenjunga	92	27	50N	88	10 E
Kanchipuram	90	12	52N	79	45 E
Kandahar = Qandahār	87	31	32N	65	30 E
Kandalaksha	69	67	9N	32	30 E
Kandi	131	11	7N	2	55 E
Kandos	117	32	45S	149	58 E
Kandy	90	7	18N	80	43 E
Kangar	97	6	27N	100	12 E
Kangaroo I.	119	35	45S	137	0 E
Kangean Is.	113	6	55S	115	23 E
Kangnüng	98	37	45N	128	54 E
Kangto	93	27	50N	92	35 E
Kaniapiskau →	146	56	40N	69	30W
Kanin, P-ov.	69	68	0N	45	0 E
Kaniva	119	36	22S	141	18 E
Kankakee	167	41	6N	87	50W
Kankakee →	167	41	23N	88	16W
Kankan	130	10	23N	9	15W
Kanmuri-Yama	109	34	30N	132	4 E
Kannapolis	165	35	32N	80	37W
Kano	131	12	2N	8	30 E
Kan'onji	109	34	7N	133	39 E
Kanoya	108	31	25N	130	50 E
Kanpur	91	26	28N	80	20 E
Kansas □	161	38	40N	98	0W
Kansas →	158	39	7N	94	36W
Kansas City, Kans., U.S.A.	166	39	0N	94	40W
Kansas City, Mo., U.S.A.	166	39	3N	94	30W
Kansk	74	56	20N	95	37 E
Kansu = Gansu □	98	36	0N	104	0 E
Kantō □	107	36	15N	139	30 E
Kantō-Sanchi	107	35	59N	138	50 E
Kanuma	107	36	34N	139	42 E
Kaohsiung = Gaoxiong	99	22	38N	120	18 E
Kaolack	130	14	5N	16	8W
Kāpīsā □	87	35	0N	69	20 E
Kapoeta	129	4	50N	33	35 E
Kapuas →	111	0	25S	109	20 E
Kapunda	119	34	20S	138	56 E
Kapuskasing	150	49	25N	82	30W
Kaputar, Mt.	116	30	15S	150	10 E
Kara Bogaz Gol, Zaliv	70	41	0N	53	30 E
Kara Kum = Karakum, Peski	70	39	30N	60	0 E
Kara Sea	69	75	0N	70	0 E
Karabük	80	41	12N	32	37 E
Karachi	88	24	53N	67	0 E
Karad	91	17	15N	74	10 E
Karadeniz Boğazı	80	41	10N	29	10 E
Karaganda	71	49	50N	73	10 E
Karaj	86	35	48N	51	0 E
Karakalpakstan □	70	43	0N	58	0 E
Karakoram Pass	89	35	33N	77	50 E
Karakoram Ra.	89	35	30N	77	0 E
Karakum, Peski	70	39	30N	60	0 E
Karaman	80	37	14N	33	13 E
Karamea Bight	123	41	22S	171	40 E
Karasuk	71	53	44N	78	2 E
Karatau, Khrebet	71	43	30N	69	30 E
Karbalā	84	32	36N	44	3 E
Karelian Rep. □	68	65	30N	32	0 E
Karen	94	12	49N	92	53 E
Kariba Lake	137	16	40S	28	25 E
Karimata I.	111	1	40S	109	0 E
Karimnagar	91	18	26N	79	10 E
Karimunjawa, Kepulauan	111	5	50S	110	30 E
Kariya	106	34	58N	137	1 E
Karl-Marx-Stadt = Chemnitz	43	50	50N	12	55 E
Karlskrona	61	56	10N	15	35 E
Karlsruhe	42	49	3N	8	23 E
Karlstad	60	59	23N	13	30 E
Karnal	89	29	42N	77	2 E
Karnaphuli Res.	93	22	40N	92	20 E
Karnataka □	90	13	15N	77	0 E
Kärnten □	45	46	52N	13	30 E
Kárpathos	55	35	37N	27	10 E
Kars	81	40	40N	43	5 E
Karshi	70	38	53N	65	48 E
Kasai →	134	3	30S	16	10 E
Kasaoka	109	34	30N	133	30 E
Kaseda	108	31	25N	130	19 E
Kāshān	86	34	5N	51	30 E
Kashi	100	39	30N	76	2 E
Kashihara	106	34	27N	135	46 E
Kashima	108	33	7N	130	6 E
Kashima-Nada	107	36	0N	140	45 E
Kashiwa	107	35	52N	139	59 E
Kāshmar	86	35	16N	58	26 E
Kashmir	78	34	0N	76	0 E
Kashun Noerh = Gaxun Nur	100	42	22N	100	30 E
Kásos	55	35	20N	26	55 E
Kassala	129	16	0N	36	0 E
Kassel	42	51	19N	9	32 E
Kastoria	54	40	30N	21	19 E
Kasugai	106	35	12N	136	59 E
Kasukabe	107	35	58N	139	49 E
Kasumiga-Ura	107	36	0N	140	25 E
Kasur	89	31	5N	74	25 E
Katanning	120	33	40S	117	33 E
Katha	93	24	10N	96	30 E
Katherîna, Gebel	128	28	30N	33	57 E
Katherine	114	14	27S	132	20 E
Kathiawar	91	22	20N	71	0 E

Name	Pg	Lat	Long
Katihar	92	25 34N	87 36 E
Katmandu	92	27 45N	85 20 E
Katoomba	117	33 41S	150 19 E
Katowice	58	50 17N	19 5 E
Katsuta	107	36 25N	140 31 E
Katsuura	107	35 10N	140 20 E
Katsuyama	106	36 3N	136 30 E
Kattegatt	61	57 0N	11 20 E
Katwijk-aan-Zee	40	52 12N	4 24 E
Kauai	160	22 0N	159 30W
Kaukauna	167	44 20N	88 13W
Kaunas	68	54 54N	23 54 E
Kawachi-Nagano	106	34 28N	135 31 E
Kawagoe	107	35 55N	139 29 E
Kawaguchi	107	35 52N	139 45 E
Kawanoe	109	34 1N	133 34 E
Kawarau	122	45 3S	168 45 E
Kawasaki	107	35 35N	139 42 E
Kayah □	93	19 15N	97 15 E
Kayes	130	14 25N	11 30W
Kayseri	80	38 45N	35 30 E
Kazachye	72	70 52N	135 58 E
Kazakstan ■	71	50 0N	70 0 E
Kazan	68	55 48N	49 3 E
Kazanlŭk	53	42 38N	25 20 E
Kāzerūn	85	29 38N	51 40 E
Kazo	107	36 7N	139 36 E
Kéa	55	37 35N	24 22 E
Keaau	160	19 37N	155 3W
Kebnekaise	66	67 53N	18 33 E
Kecskemét	59	46 57N	19 42 E
Kedah □	96	5 50N	100 40 E
Kediri	111	7 51S	112 1 E
Keeling Is. = Cocos Is.	111	12 10S	96 55 E
Keene	164	42 57N	72 17W
Keetmanshoop	136	26 35S	18 8 E
Keewatin	153	49 46N	94 34W
Keewatin □	145	63 20N	95 0W
Kefallinía	54	38 20N	20 30 E
Keflavík	64	64 2N	22 35W
Keighley	28	53 52N	1 54W
Keith, Australia	119	36 6S	140 20 E
Keith, U.K.	33	57 33N	2 58W
Kelang	96	3 2N	101 26 E
Kelantan □	96	5 10N	102 0 E
Kelantan →	96	6 13N	102 14 E
Kellerberrin	120	31 36S	117 38 E
Kellogg	162	47 30N	116 5W
Kells = Ceanannus Mor	34	53 42N	6 53W
Kelowna	155	49 50N	119 25W
Kelso, U.K.	31	55 36N	2 27W
Kelso, U.S.A.	171	46 10N	122 57W
Keluang	96	2 3N	103 18 E
Kelvington	152	52 10N	103 30W
Kemerovo	71	55 20N	86 5 E
Kemi	67	65 44N	24 34 E
Kemi →	67	67 30N	28 30 E
Kempsey	116	31 1S	152 50 E
Kendal	28	54 19N	2 44W
Keng Tung	93	21 0N	99 30 E
Kenitra	126	34 15N	6 40W
Kenmare	35	51 52N	9 35W
Kennewick	171	46 11N	119 2W
Keno Hill	144	63 57N	135 18W
Kenora	153	49 47N	94 29W
Kenosha	167	42 33N	87 48W
Kent	164	41 8N	81 20W
Kent □	25	51 12N	0 40 E
Kent Group	117	39 30S	147 20 E
Kent Pen.	145	68 30N	107 0W
Kentucky □	167	37 20N	85 0W
Kentucky →	167	38 41N	85 11W
Kenya ■	133	1 0N	38 0 E
Kenya, Mt.	132	0 10S	37 18 E
Keokuk	166	40 25N	91 24W
Kepsut	80	39 40N	28 9 E
Kerala □	90	11 0N	76 15 E
Kerang	117	35 40S	143 55 E
Kerch	68	45 20N	36 20 E
Kerki	70	37 50N	65 12 E
Kérkira	54	39 38N	19 50 E
Kerkrade	41	50 53N	6 4 E
Kermadec Is.	122	30 0S	178 15W
Kermān	85	30 15N	57 1 E
Kermān □	85	30 0N	57 0 E
Kermānshāh = Bākhtarān	84	34 23N	47 0 E
Kerrobert	152	52 0N	109 11W
Kerry □	35	52 7N	9 35W
Kerulen →	98	48 48N	117 0 E
Kestenga	68	66 0N	31 50 E
Keswick	28	54 35N	3 9W
Ketchikan	143	55 25N	131 40W
Kettering	156	39 41N	84 10W
Kewanee	166	41 18N	89 55W
Keweenaw B.	150	46 56N	88 23W
Key West	159	24 33N	82 0W
Keyser	164	39 26N	79 0W
Khabarovsk	75	48 30N	135 5 E
Khalkhāl	81	37 37N	48 32 E
Khalkis	55	38 27N	23 42 E
Khalmer Yu	69	67 58N	65 1 E
Khambhat	91	22 23N	72 33 E
Khambhat, G. of	91	20 45N	72 30 E
Khamir	82	16 0N	44 0 E
Khānābād	87	36 45N	69 5 E
Khānaqīn	81	34 23N	45 25 E
Khandwa	91	21 49N	76 22 E
Khanewal	89	30 20N	71 55 E
Khaniá	55	35 30N	24 4 E
Khanka, Ozero	75	45 0N	132 24 E
Kharagpur	92	22 20N	87 25 E
Kharkov	68	49 58N	36 20 E
Khartoum = El Khartûm	129	15 31N	32 35 E
Khashm el Girba	129	14 59N	35 58 E
Khaskovo	53	41 56N	25 30 E
Khatanga	72	72 0N	102 20 E
Khatanga →	72	72 55N	106 0 E
Khenchela	127	35 28N	7 11 E
Kherson	68	46 35N	32 35 E
Kheta →	72	71 54N	102 6 E
Khíos, I.	55	38 20N	26 0 E
Khmer Rep. = Cambodia ■	95	12 15N	105 0 E
Khodzhent	71	40 17N	69 37 E
Khojak P.	88	30 55N	66 30 E
Kholm	87	36 45N	67 40 E
Khon Kaen	95	16 30N	102 47 E
Khoper →	68	49 30N	42 20 E
Khorāsān □	86	34 0N	58 0 E
Khorat = Nakhon Ratchasima	95	14 59N	102 12 E
Khorat, Cao Nguyen	95	15 30N	102 50 E
Khorog	71	37 30N	71 36 E
Khorramābād	84	33 30N	48 25 E
Khorrāmshahr	84	30 29N	48 15 E
Khulna	92	22 45N	89 34 E
Khulna □	92	22 25N	89 35 E
Khushab	89	32 20N	72 20 E
Khūzestān □	84	31 0N	49 0 E
Khvor	86	33 45N	55 0 E
Khvoy	81	38 35N	45 0 E
Khyber Pass	89	34 10N	71 8 E
Kiama	117	34 40S	150 50 E
Kiangsi = Jiangxi □	99	27 30N	116 0 E
Kiangsu = Jiangsu □	99	33 0N	120 0 E
Kichiga	73	59 50N	163 5 E
Kicking Horse Pass	155	51 28N	116 16W
Kidderminster	24	52 24N	2 13W
Kidnappers, C.	122	39 38S	177 5 E
Kiel	43	54 16N	10 8 E
Kielce	58	50 52N	20 42 E
Kieler Bucht	42	54 30N	10 30 E
Kiev = Kiyev	68	50 30N	30 28 E
Kigali	135	1 59S	30 4 E
Kii-Hantō	106	34 0N	135 45 E
Kii-Sanchi	106	34 20N	136 0 E
Kii-Suidō	109	33 40N	135 0 E
Kikládhes □	55	37 0N	25 0 E
Kikuchi	108	32 59N	130 47 E
Kilcoy	116	26 59S	152 30 E
Kildare □	35	53 10N	6 50W
Kilimanjaro	132	3 7S	37 20 E
Kilis	80	36 50N	37 10 E

Kilkenny	35	52 40N	7	17W
Kilkenny □	35	52 35N	7	15W
Killala B.	34	54 20N	9	12W
Killarney, Canada	153	49 10N	99	40W
Killarney, Ireland	35	52 2N	9	30W
Killary Harbour	34	53 38N	9	52W
Killiecrankie, Pass of	33	56 44N	3	46W
Kilmarnock	31	55 36N	4	30W
Kilmore	117	37 25S	144	53 E
Kilrush	35	52 39N	9	30W
Kimba	118	33 8S	136	23 E
Kimberley, Australia	114	16 20S	127	0 E
Kimberley, Canada	155	49 40N	115	59W
Kimberley, S. Africa	136	28 43S	24	46 E
Kinabalu	112	6 3N	116	14 E
Kincardine	150	44 10N	81	40W
Kindersley	152	51 30N	109	10W
Kindia	130	10 0N	12	52W
King Frederick VI Land =				
Kong Frederik VI.s Kyst ..	147	63 0N	43	0W
King George Is.	140	57 20N	80	30W
King I. = Kadan Kyun	94	12 30N	98	20 E
King I., Australia	119	39 50S	144	0 E
King I., Canada	154	52 10N	127	40W
King Sd.	114	16 50S	123	20 E
King William I.	145	69 10N	97	25W
Kingaroy	116	26 32S	151	51 E
Kingman	173	35 12N	114	2W
King's Lynn	29	52 45N	0	25 E
Kingscote	119	35 40S	137	38 E
Kingsport	165	36 33N	82	36W
Kingston, Canada	151	44 14N	76	30W
Kingston, Jamaica	180	18 0N	76	50W
Kingston, N.Z.	123	45 20S	168	43 E
Kingston, U.S.A.	164	41 55N	74	0W
Kingston South East	119	36 51S	139	55 E
Kingstown	180	13 10N	61	10W
Kingsville	150	42 2N	82	45W
Kingussie	33	57 5N	4	2W
Kinistino	152	52 57N	105	2W
Kinki □	106	33 30N	136	0 E
Kinnairds Hd.	33	57 40N	2	0W
Kinsale, Old Hd. of	35	51 37N	8	32W
Kinshasa	134	4 20S	15	15 E
Kinston	165	35 18N	77	35W
Kintyre	30	55 30N	5	35W
Kintyre, Mull of	30	55 17N	5	55W
Kinu-Gawa →	107	35 36N	139	57 E
Kiparissía	54	37 15N	21	40 E
Kirensk	74	57 50N	107	55 E
Kirghizia = Kyrgyzstan ■ ..	71	42 0N	75	0 E
Kiribati ■	122	1 0N	176	0 E
Kınkkale	80	39 51N	33	32 E
Kirin = Jilin	98	43 44N	126	30 E
Kiritimati	123	1 58N	157	27W
Kirkcaldy	31	56 7N	3	10W
Kirkcudbright	31	54 50N	4	3W
Kirkee	91	18 34N	73	56 E
Kirkintilloch	31	55 57N	4	10W
Kirkland Lake	151	48 9N	80	2W
Kirksville	166	40 8N	92	35W
Kirkūk	81	35 30N	44	21 E
Kirkwall	33	58 59N	2	59W
Kirov	69	58 35N	49	40 E
Kirovabad = Gyandzha	70	40 45N	46	20 E
Kirovograd	68	48 35N	32	20 E
Kirthar Range	88	27 0N	67	0 E
Kiruna	66	67 52N	20	15 E
Kiryū	107	36 24N	139	20 E
Kisangani	135	0 35N	25	15 E
Kisarazu	107	35 23N	139	55 E
Kiselevsk	71	54 5N	86	39 E
Kishangarh	89	27 50N	70	30 E
Kishinev	68	47 0N	28	50 E
Kishiwada	106	34 28N	135	22 E
Kiskunfélégyháza	59	46 42N	19	53 E
Kiso-Gawa →	106	35 20N	136	45 E
Kisumu	132	0 3S	34	45 E
Kita	130	13 5N	9	25W
Kita-Ura	107	36 0N	140	34 E
Kitakami-Gawa →	103	38 25N	141	19 E
Kitakyūshū	108	33 50N	130	50 E
Kitale	132	1 0N	35	0 E
Kitami	103	43 48N	143	54 E
Kitchener	151	43 27N	80	29W
Kíthira	55	36 9N	23	0 E
Kíthnos	55	37 26N	24	27 E
Kitikmeot □	145	70 0N	110	0W
Kitimat	154	54 3N	128	38W
Kitsuki	108	33 25N	131	37 E
Kittakittaooloo, L.	118	28 3S	138	14 E
Kitwe	135	12 54S	28	13 E
Kiyev	68	50 30N	30	28 E
Klagenfurt	45	46 38N	14	20 E
Klaipeda	68	55 43N	21	10 E
Klamath →	172	41 40N	124	4W
Klamath Falls	171	42 20N	121	50W
Klamath Mts.	172	41 20N	123	0W
Kleena Kleene	154	52 0N	124	59W
Klondike	144	64 0N	139	26W
Kluane L.	144	61 15N	138	40W
Klyuchevsk	73	55 50N	160	30 E
Knaresborough	28	54 1N	1	29W
Knockmealdown Mts.	35	52 16N	8	0W
Knossos	55	35 16N	25	10 E
Knoxville, Iowa, U.S.A.	166	41 20N	93	5W
Knoxville, Tenn., U.S.A.	165	35 58N	83	57W
Ko Chang	95	12 0N	102	20 E
Ko Kut	95	11 40N	102	32 E
Koartac	146	60 55N	69	40W
Kobarid	52	46 15N	13	30 E
Kobayashi	108	31 56N	130	59 E
Kobdo = Hovd	100	48 2N	91	37 E
Kōbe	106	34 45N	135	10 E
København	61	55 41N	12	34 E
Koblenz	42	50 21N	7	36 E
Kobroor, Kepulauan	113	6 10S	134	30 E
Kočani	53	41 55N	22	25 E
Kōchi	109	33 30N	133	35 E
Kochiu = Gejiu	99	23 20N	103	10 E
Kodaira	107	35 44N	139	29 E
Kodiak I.	142	57 30N	152	45W
Kōfu	107	35 40N	138	30 E
Koga	107	36 11N	139	43 E
Kogota	103	38 33N	141	3 E
Koh-i-Bābā	87	34 30N	67	0 E
Kohat	89	33 40N	71	29 E
Kokand	71	40 30N	70	57 E
Kokchetav	71	53 20N	69	25 E
Koko Kyunzu	94	14 10N	93	25 E
Kokomo	167	40 30N	86	6W
Kokopo	115	4 22S	152	19 E
Koksoak →	146	58 30N	68	10W
Kokubu	108	31 44N	130	46 E
Kola Pen. = Kolskiy				
Poluostrov	69	67 30N	38	0 E
Kolar	90	13 12N	78	15 E
Kolar Gold Fields	90	12 58N	78	16 E
Kolarovgrad	53	43 18N	26	55 E
Kolding	61	55 30N	9	29 E
Kolguyev, Ostrov	69	69 20N	48	30 E
Kolhapur	91	16 43N	74	15 E
Köln	42	50 56N	6	58 E
Koło	58	52 14N	18	40 E
Kolomna	68	55 8N	38	45 E
Kolskiy Poluostrov	69	67 30N	38	0 E
Kolyma →	73	69 30N	161	0 E
Komagene	107	35 44N	137	58 E
Komaki	106	35 17N	136	55 E
Komandorskiye, Is.	73	55 0N	167	0 E
Komárno	59	47 49N	18	5 E
Komatsu	106	36 25N	136	30 E
Komatsujima	109	34 0N	134	35 E
Komi □	69	64 0N	55	0 E
Kommunizma, Pik	71	39 0N	72	2 E
Komoro	107	36 19N	138	26 E
Kompong Cham	95	12 0N	105	30 E
Kompong Chhnang	95	12 20N	104	35 E
Kompong Som	95	10 38N	103	30 E
Komsomolets, Ostrov	72	80 30N	95	0 E
Komsomolsk	75	50 30N	137	0 E
Konarhá □	87	35 30N	71	3 E

Name	Map	Lat	Long
Kong	130	8 54N	4 36W
Kong, Koh	95	11 20N	103 0 E
Kong Christian X.s Land	13	74 0N	29 0W
Kong Frederik VI.s Kyst	147	63 0N	43 0W
Kong Frederik VIII.s Land	13	78 30N	26 0W
Kongor	129	7 1N	31 27 E
Königsberg = Kaliningrad	68	54 42N	20 32 E
Konin	58	52 12N	18 15 E
Konjic	52	43 42N	17 58 E
Konosha	68	61 0N	40 5 E
Konstanz	44	47 39N	9 10 E
Kontagora	131	10 23N	5 27 E
Konya	80	37 52N	32 35 E
Konya Ovasi	80	38 30N	33 0 E
Koolyanobbing	120	30 48S	119 36 E
Kopaonik Planina	52	43 10N	21 50 E
Kopeysk	71	55 7N	61 37 E
Kopparberg	60	59 52N	15 0 E
Koppeh Dägh	86	38 0N	58 0 E
Korab	52	41 44N	20 40 E
Korça	52	40 37N	20 50 E
Korčula	52	42 57N	17 8 E
Kordestän □	81	36 0N	47 0 E
Korea Bay	98	39 0N	124 0 E
Korea Strait	104	34 0N	129 30 E
Korhogo	130	9 29N	5 28W
Korinthiakós Kólpos	54	38 16N	22 30 E
Kórinthos	54	37 56N	22 55 E
Kōriyama	105	37 24N	140 23 E
Koroit	119	38 18S	142 24 E
Kortrijk	42	50 50N	3 17 E
Koryakskiy Khrebet	73	61 0N	171 0 E
Kos	55	36 50N	27 15 E
Kosciusko	169	33 3N	89 34W
Kosciusko, Mt.	117	36 27S	148 16 E
Koshigaya	107	35 54N	139 48 E
K'oshih = Kashi	100	39 30N	76 2 E
Koshiki-Rettō	108	31 45N	129 49 E
Kōshoku	107	36 38N	138 6 E
Košice	59	48 42N	21 15 E
Kosovska-Mitrovica	52	42 54N	20 52 E
Kôstî	129	13 8N	32 43 E
Kostroma	68	57 50N	40 58 E
Koszalin	58	53 50N	16 8 E
Kota	91	25 14N	75 49 E
Kota Baharu	96	6 7N	102 14 E
Kota Kinabalu	112	6 0N	116 4 E
Kotelnich	68	58 20N	48 10 E
Kotka	67	60 28N	26 58 E
Kotlas	69	61 15N	47 0 E
Kotor	52	42 25N	18 47 E
Kotuy ~►	77	71 54N	102 6 E
Kotzebue	142	66 50N	162 40W
Kowloon	99	22 20N	114 15 E
Kōyama	108	31 20N	130 56 E
Koyukuk ~►	142	64 56N	157 30W
Kozáni	55	40 19N	21 47 E
Kozhikode = Calicut	90	11 15N	75 43 E
Kōzu-Shima	107	34 13N	139 10 E
Kra, Isthmus of = Kra, Kho Khot	94	10 15N	99 30 E
Kra, Kho Khot	94	10 15N	99 30 E
Kragujevac	52	44 2N	20 56 E
Kraków	58	50 4N	19 57 E
Kraljevo	52	43 44N	20 41 E
Krasnodar	68	45 5N	39 0 E
Krasnovodsk	70	40 0N	52 52 E
Krasnoyarsk	74	56 8N	93 0 E
Krasnyy Kut	68	50 50N	47 0 E
Kratie	95	12 32N	106 10 E
Kravanh, Chuor Phnum	95	12 0N	103 32 E
Krefeld	42	51 20N	6 32 E
Kremenchug	68	49 5N	33 25 E
Krishna ~►	91	15 57N	80 59 E
Krishnanagar	92	23 24N	88 33 E
Kristiansand	60	58 9N	8 1 E
Kristianstad	61	56 2N	14 9 E
Kristianstads län □	61	56 15N	14 0 E
Kristiansund	65	63 7N	7 45 E
Kriti	55	35 15N	25 0 E
Krivoy Rog	68	47 51N	33 20 E
Krk	52	45 8N	14 40 E
Kronobergs län □	61	56 45N	14 30 E
Kronshtadt	68	60 5N	29 45 E
Krotoszyn	58	51 42N	17 23 E
Krugersdorp	137	26 5S	27 46 E
Krung Thep = Bangkok	94	13 45N	100 35 E
Kruševac	52	43 35N	21 28 E
Krymskiy P-ov.	68	45 0N	34 0 E
Kuala Dungun	96	4 45N	103 25 E
Kuala Kangsar	96	4 46N	100 56 E
Kuala Lipis	96	4 10N	102 3 E
Kuala Lumpur	96	3 9N	101 41 E
Kuala Pilah	96	2 45N	102 15 E
Kuala Trengganu	96	5 20N	103 8 E
Kuangchou = Guangzhou	99	23 5N	113 10 E
Kuantan	96	3 49N	103 20 E
Kubak	88	27 10N	63 10 E
Kuban ~►	68	45 20N	37 30 E
Kubokawa	109	33 12N	133 8 E
Kuchinoerabu-Jima	104	30 28N	130 11 E
Kucing	111	1 33N	110 25 E
Kudamatsu	108	34 0N	131 52 E
Kueiyang = Guiyang	99	26 32N	106 40 E
Kūh-e-Jebāl Bārez	85	29 0N	58 0 E
Kūh-e Sorkh	86	35 30N	58 45 E
Kūhhā-ye-Bashākerd	85	26 45N	59 0 E
Kūhhā-ye Sabalān	81	38 15N	47 45 E
Kuji	103	40 11N	141 46 E
Kuldja = Yining	100	43 58N	81 10 E
Kulunda	71	52 35N	78 57 E
Kumagaya	107	36 9N	139 22 E
Kumamoto	108	32 45N	130 45 E
Kumano	106	33 54N	136 5 E
Kumano-Nada	106	33 47N	136 20 E
Kumasi	130	6 41N	1 38W
Kumayri	70	40 47N	43 50 E
Kumon Bum	93	26 30N	97 15 E
Kunashir, Ostrov	75	44 0N	146 0 E
Kunimi-Dake	109	32 33N	131 1 E
Kunlun Shan	100	36 0N	86 30 E
Kunming	101	25 1N	102 41 E
Kunsan	98	35 59N	126 45 E
Kuopio	67	62 53N	27 35 E
Kupang	113	10 19S	123 39 E
Kurashiki	109	34 40N	133 50 E
Kurayoshi	109	35 26N	133 50 E
Kure	109	34 14N	132 32 E
Kurgan	71	55 26N	65 18 E
Kuril Is. = Kurilskiye Ostrova	75	45 0N	150 0 E
Kurilskiye Ostrova	75	45 0N	150 0 E
Kurnool	90	15 45N	78 0 E
Kurobe-Gawe ~►	106	36 55N	137 25 E
Kurri Kurri	117	32 50S	151 28 E
Kursk	68	51 42N	36 11 E
Kuršumlija	52	43 9N	21 19 E
Kurume	108	33 15N	130 30 E
Kurunegala	90	7 30N	80 23 E
Kusatsu	106	34 58N	135 57 E
Kushikino	108	31 44N	130 16 E
Kushima	108	31 29N	131 14 E
Kushimoto	106	33 28N	135 47 E
Kushiro	103	43 0N	144 25 E
Kushka	70	35 20N	62 18 E
Kushtia	92	23 55N	89 5 E
Kuskokwim Bay	142	59 50N	162 56W
Kustanay	71	53 10N	63 35 E
Kusu	108	33 16N	131 9 E
Kütahya	80	39 30N	30 2 E
Kutaisi	70	42 19N	42 40 E
Kutaraja = Banda Aceh	111	5 35N	95 20 E
Kutno	58	52 15N	19 23 E
Kuujjuaq	146	58 6N	68 15W
Kuwait = Al Kuwayt	84	29 30N	47 30 E
Kuwait ■	84	29 30N	47 30 E
Kuwana	106	35 0N	136 43 E
Kuybyshev = Samara	68	53 8N	50 6 E
Kwakoegron	185	5 12N	55 25W
Kwangju	98	35 9N	126 54 E
Kwangsi-Chuang = Guangxi Zhuangzu Zizhiqu □	99	24 0N	109 0 E
Kwangtung = Guangdong □	99	23 0N	113 0 E

Name	Page	Lat	Lat dir	Long	Long dir
Kweichow = Guizhou □ ...	99	27	0N	107	0 E
Kwinana New Town	120	32	15S	115	47 E
Kyabram	117	36	19S	145	4 E
Kyaukpadaung	93	20	52N	95	8 E
Kyle of Lochalsh	32	57	17N	5	43W
Kyneton	117	37	10S	144	29 E
Kyō-ga-Saki	106	35	45N	135	15 E
Kyoga, L.	132	1	35N	33	0 E
Kyogle	116	28	40S	153	0 E
Kyōto	106	35	0N	135	45 E
Kyrenia	80	35	20N	33	20 E
Kyrgyzstan ■	71	42	0N	75	0 E
Kyūshū	108	33	0N	131	0 E
Kyūshū □	108	33	0N	131	0 E
Kyūshū-Sanchi	108	32	35N	131	17 E
Kyustendil	53	42	16N	22	41 E
Kyzyl	74	51	50N	94	30 E
Kyzylkum, Peski	70	42	30N	65	0 E
Kzyl-Orda	71	44	48N	65	28 E

L

Name	Page	Lat	Lat dir	Long	Long dir
Labe = Elbe ➜	42	53	50N	9	0 E
Laboulaye	190	34	10S	63	30W
Labrador, Coast of □	147	53	20N	61	0W
Lábrea	187	7	15S	64	51W
Lac la Martre	145	63	8N	117	16W
Laccadive Is. =					
Lakshadweep Is.	78	10	0N	72	30 E
Lachine	151	45	30N	73	40W
Lachute	151	45	39N	74	21W
Lackawanna	164	42	49N	78	50W
Lacombe	155	52	30N	113	44W
Laconia	148	43	32N	71	30W
Ladakh Ra.	89	34	0N	78	0 E
Ladoga, L. = Ladozhskoye					
Ozero	68	61	15N	30	30 E
Ladozhskoye Ozero	68	61	15N	30	30 E
Ladysmith	154	49	0N	123	49W
Lae	115	6	40S	147	2 E
Lafayette, Ind., U.S.A.	167	40	25N	86	54W
Lafayette, La., U.S.A.	168	30	18N	92	0W
Laghmān □	87	34	20N	70	0 E
Laghouat	127	33	50N	2	59 E
Lagny	39	48	52N	2	40 E
Lagos, Nigeria	131	6	25N	3	27 E
Lagos, Portugal	50	37	5N	8	41W
Lagos de Moreno	175	21	21N	101	55W
Laguna	191	28	30S	48	50W
Laguna Beach	173	33	31N	117	52W
Laguna Madre	158	27	0N	97	20W
Lagunas, Chile	187	21	0S	69	45W
Lagunas, Peru	186	5	10S	75	35W
Lahore	89	31	32N	74	22 E
Lahti	67	60	58N	25	40 E
Lahtis = Lahti	67	60	58N	25	40 E
Laï	131	9	25N	16	18 E
Laidley	116	27	39S	152	20 E
Lairg	33	58	1N	4	24W
Laja, R. de la ➜	177	20	55N	100	46W
Lajes	191	27	48S	50	20W
Lake Cargelligo	117	33	15S	146	22 E
Lake Charles	168	30	15N	93	10W
Lake City, Fla., U.S.A.	170	30	10N	82	40W
Lake City, S.C., U.S.A.	165	33	51N	79	44W
Lake Grace	120	33	7S	118	28 E
Lake Harbour	146	62	50N	69	50W
Lake Worth	170	26	36N	80	3W
Lakeland	170	28	0N	82	0W
Lakes Entrance	117	37	50S	148	0 E
Lakewood	167	41	28N	81	50W
Lakshadweep Is.	78	10	0N	72	30 E
Lala Ghat	93	24	30N	92	40 E
Lalitpur	91	24	42N	78	28 E
Lamar	163	38	9N	102	35W
Lambi Kyun	96	10	50N	98	20 E
Lameroo	119	35	19S	140	33 E
Lamia	54	38	55N	22	26 E
Lammermuir Hills	31	55	50N	2	40W
Lamon Bay	112	14	30N	122	20 E
Lampa	187	15	22S	70	22W
Lampang	94	18	16N	99	32 E
Lampeter	26	52	6N	4	6W
Lamu	133	2	16S	40	55 E
Lanark	31	55	40N	3	48W
Lancang Jiang ➜	101	21	40N	101	10 E
Lancashire □	28	53	40N	2	30W
Lancaster, U.K.	28	54	3N	2	48W
Lancaster, U.S.A.	164	40	4N	76	19W
Lancaster Sd.	146	74	13N	84	0W
Lanchow = Lanzhou	99	36	1N	103	52 E
Landes, Les	36	44	20N	1	0W
Land's End	27	50	4N	5	43W
Landskrona	61	55	53N	12	50 E
Lanett	169	33	0N	85	15W
Langjökull	64	64	39N	20	12W
Langlade	149	46	50N	56	20W
Langøya	64	68	45N	14	50 E
Langres, Plateau de	37	47	45N	5	3 E
Languedoc	37	43	58N	4	0 E
Lannion	36	48	46N	3	29W
Lansing	167	42	47N	84	40W
Lanzhou	99	36	1N	103	52 E
Laois □	35	53	0N	7	20W
Laon	38	49	33N	3	35 E
Laona	150	45	32N	88	41W
Laos ■	95	17	45N	105	0 E
Lapeer	167	43	3N	83	20W
Lapland = Lappland	67	68	7N	24	0 E
Lappland	67	68	7N	24	0 E
Laptev Sea	72	76	0N	125	0 E
Laramie	163	41	20N	105	38W
Laramie Mts.	163	42	0N	105	30W
Laredo	161	27	34N	99	29W
Laren	40	52	16N	5	14 E
Largs	30	55	48N	4	51W
Lárisa	54	39	49N	22	28 E
Larkana	88	27	32N	68	18 E
Larnaca	80	35	0N	33	35 E
Larne	34	54	52N	5	50W
Laryak	69	61	15N	80	0 E
Las Cruces	161	32	18N	106	50W
Las Lajas	190	38	30S	70	25W
Las Palmas	126	28	7N	15	26W
Las Vegas, N. Mex., U.S.A.	161	35	35N	105	10W
Las Vegas, Nev., U.S.A.	173	36	10N	115	5W
Lashio	93	22	56N	97	45 E
Latacunga	184	0	50S	78	35W
Latakia = Al Lādhiqīyah	80	35	30N	35	45 E
Latium = Lazio □	46	42	10N	12	30 E
Latrobe	119	41	14S	146	30 E
Latur	91	18	25N	76	40 E
Latvia ■	68	56	50N	24	0 E
Lauchhammer	43	51	35N	13	48 E
Launceston, Australia	119	41	24S	147	8 E
Launceston, U.K.	27	50	38N	4	21W
Launglon Bok	94	13	50N	97	54 E
Laurel	169	31	41N	89	9W
Laurens	165	34	32N	82	2W
Laurentian Plat.	138	52	0N	70	0W
Laurinburg	165	34	50N	79	25W
Lausanne	44	46	32N	6	38 E
Laut, Pulau	111	3	40S	116	10 E
Laut Ketil, Kepulauan	113	4	45S	115	40 E
Lauzon	148	46	48N	71	10W
Laval	36	48	4N	0	48W
Lávrion	55	37	40N	24	4 E
Lawrence, Kans., U.S.A.	166	39	0N	95	10W
Lawrence, Mass., U.S.A.	164	42	40N	71	9W
Lawrenceburg	169	35	12N	87	19W
Lawton	161	34	33N	98	25W
Lazio □	46	42	10N	12	30 E
Lea ➜	25	51	30N	0	10W
Leader	152	50	50N	109	30W
Leadhills	31	55	25N	3	47W
Leadville	163	39	17N	106	23W
Leamington, Canada	150	42	3N	82	36W
Leamington, U.K.	24	52	18N	1	32W
Leavenworth	166	39	25N	95	0W
Lebanon, Mo., U.S.A.	166	37	40N	92	40W

Lebanon, Orég., U.S.A.	**171**	44	31N	122 57W
Lebanon, Pa., U.S.A.	**164**	40	20N	76 28W
Lebanon, Tenn., U.S.A.	**169**	36	15N	86 20W
Lebanon ■	**80**	34	0N	36 0 E
Lecce	**49**	40	20N	18 10 E
Ledbury	**24**	52	3N	2 25W
Leduc	**155**	53	15N	113 30W
Leeds	**28**	53	48N	1 34W
Leek	**28**	53	7N	2 2W
Leerdam	**40**	51	54N	5 6 E
Leesburg	**170**	28	47N	81 52W
Leeton	**117**	34	33S	146 23 E
Leeuwarden	**41**	53	15N	5 48 E
Leeuwin, C.	**120**	34	20S	115 9 E
Leeward Is.	**181**	16	30N	63 30W
Leghorn = Livorno	**46**	43	32N	10 18 E
Legnica	**58**	51	12N	16 10 E
Leicester	**25**	52	39N	1 9W
Leicester □	**25**	52	40N	1 10W
Leichhardt	**121**	33	53S	151 9 E
Leiden	**40**	52	9N	4 30 E
Leigh Creek South	**118**	30	38S	138 26 E
Leinster	**120**	27	51S	120 36 E
Leinster □	**35**	53	0N	7 10W
Leinster, Mt.	**35**	52	38N	6 47W
Leipzig	**43**	51	20N	12 23 E
Leith	**31**	55	59N	3 10W
Leith Hill	**24**	51	10N	0 23W
Leitrim	**34**	54	0N	8 5W
Lek ↝	**40**	51	54N	4 35 E
Leleque	**192**	42	28S	71 0W
Léman, Lac	**44**	46	26N	6 30 E
Lemmer	**41**	52	51N	5 43 E
Lena ↝	**72**	72	52N	126 40 E
Leninabad = Khodzhent	**71**	40	17N	69 37 E
Leninakan = Kumayri	**70**	40	47N	43 50 E
Leningrad = Sankt-Peterburg	**68**	59	55N	30 20 E
Leninsk-Kuznetskiy	**71**	54	44N	86 10 E
Leninskoye	**75**	47	56N	132 38 E
Lenoir City	**165**	35	40N	84 20W
Lens, Belgium	**38**	50	33N	3 54 E
Lens, France	**37**	50	26N	2 50 E
Lensk	**74**	60	48N	114 55 E
Leominster, U.K.	**24**	52	15N	2 43W
Leominster, U.S.A.	**164**	42	32N	71 45W
León, Mexico	**177**	21	7N	101 40W
León, Nic.	**179**	12	20N	86 51W
León, Spain	**50**	42	38N	5 34W
León □	**50**	42	40N	5 55W
Leongatha	**117**	38	30S	145 58 E
Léopold II, Lac = Mai-				
Ndombe, L.	**134**	2	0S	18 20 E
Léopoldville = Kinshasa	**134**	4	20S	15 15 E
Lérida	**51**	41	37N	0 39 E
Lerwick	**30**	60	10N	1 10W
Lesbos, I. = Lésvos	**55**	39	10N	26 20 E
Lesotho ■	**137**	29	40S	28 0 E
Lesozavodsk	**75**	45	30N	133 29 E
Lesser Antilles	**181**	15	0N	61 0W
Lesser Slave L.	**155**	55	30N	115 25W
Lésvos	**55**	39	10N	26 20 E
Letchworth	**25**	51	58N	0 13W
Lethbridge	**155**	49	45N	112 45W
Leti, Kepulauan	**113**	8	10S	128 0 E
Leticia	**184**	4	9S	70 0W
Letsôk-aw Kyun	**94**	11	30N	98 25 E
Letterkenny	**34**	54	57N	7 42W
Leuven	**42**	50	52N	4 42 E
Levanger	**65**	63	45N	11 19 E
Levin	**122**	40	37S	175 18 E
Lévis	**148**	46	48N	71 9W
Levkás	**54**	38	40N	20 43 E
Levkôsia = Nicosia	**80**	35	10N	33 25 E
Lewes	**25**	50	53N	0 2 E
Lewis	**32**	58	10N	6 40W
Lewis, Butt of	**32**	58	30N	6 12W
Lewis Ra.	**162**	48	0N	113 15W
Lewisporte	**149**	49	15N	55 3W
Lewiston	**148**	44	3N	70 10 E
Lexington, Ky., U.S.A.	**165**	38	6N	84 30W
Lexington, Mo., U.S.A.	**166**	39	7N	93 55W
Lexington, N.C., U.S.A.	**165**	35	50N	80 13W
Lexington, Oreg., U.S.A.	**171**	45	29N	119 46W
Lexington Park	**165**	38	16N	76 27W
Leyte	**112**	11	0N	125 0 E
Lhasa	**101**	29	50N	91 3 E
Lhazê	**101**	29	5N	87 38 E
Lianyungang	**99**	34	40N	119 11 E
Liaoning □	**98**	41	40N	122 30 E
Liaoyuan	**98**	42	58N	125 2 E
Liard ↝	**144**	61	51N	121 18W
Libau = Liepāja	**68**	56	30N	21 0 E
Liberec	**58**	50	47N	15 7 E
Liberia ■	**130**	6	30N	9 30W
Lĭbĭya, Sahrâ'	**128**	27	35N	25 0 E
Libreville	**134**	0	25N	9 26 E
Libya ■	**127**	27	0N	17 0 E
Lichfield	**28**	52	40N	1 50W
Liechtenstein ■	**44**	47	8N	9 35 E
Liège	**42**	50	38N	5 35 E
Liegnitz = Legnica	**58**	51	12N	16 10 E
Lienyünchiangshih =				
Lianyungang	**99**	34	40N	119 11 E
Liepāja	**68**	56	30N	21 0 E
Liévin	**38**	50	24N	2 47 E
Liffey ↝	**35**	53	21N	6 20W
Lifford	**34**	54	50N	7 30W
Liguria □	**46**	44	30N	9 0 E
Ligurian Sea	**46**	43	20N	9 0 E
Lihou Reefs and Cays	**121**	17	25S	151 40 E
Lihue	**160**	21	59N	159 24W
Likasi	**135**	10	55S	26 48 E
Lille, Belgium	**38**	51	15N	4 50 E
Lille, France	**37**	50	38N	3 3 E
Lille Bælt	**61**	55	20N	9 45 E
Lillehammer	**60**	61	8N	10 30 E
Lillers	**38**	50	35N	2 28 E
Lillooet	**154**	50	44N	121 57W
Lilongwe	**137**	14	0S	33 48 E
Lima, Peru	**186**	12	0S	77 0W
Lima, U.S.A.	**167**	40	42N	84 5W
Limassol	**80**	34	42N	33 1 E
Limavady	**34**	55	3N	6 58W
Limbe	**137**	15	55S	35 2 E
Limburg □	**41**	51	20N	5 55 E
Limeira	**188**	22	35S	47 28W
Limerick	**35**	52	40N	8 38W
Limerick □	**35**	52	30N	8 50W
Limfjorden	**61**	56	55N	9 0 E
Límnos	**55**	39	50N	25 5 E
Limoges	**36**	45	50N	1 15 E
Limón	**179**	10	0N	83 2W
Limousin	**36**	46	0N	1 0 E
Limpopo ↝	**137**	25	15S	33 30 E
Linares, Chile	**190**	35	50S	71 40W
Linares, Mexico	**176**	24	50N	99 40W
Linares, Spain	**50**	38	10N	3 40W
Lincoln, Argentina	**190**	34	55S	61 30W
Lincoln, U.K.	**29**	53	14N	0 32W
Lincoln, Ill., U.S.A.	**166**	40	10N	89 20W
Lincoln, Maine, U.S.A.	**148**	45	27N	68 29W
Lincoln, Nebr., U.S.A.	**156**	40	50N	96 42W
Lincoln □	**29**	53	14N	0 32W
Lincoln Sea	**12**	84	0N	55 0W
Lincoln Wolds	**29**	53	20N	0 5W
Lindsay, Canada	**151**	44	22N	78 43W
Lindsay, U.S.A.	**173**	36	14N	119 6W
Linea de la Concepción, La	**50**	36	15N	5 23W
Lingga, Kepulauan	**111**	0	10S	104 30 E
Linguéré	**130**	15	25N	15 5W
Linköping	**60**	58	28N	15 36 E
Linlithgow	**31**	55	58N	3 38W
Linxia	**99**	35	36N	103 10 E
Linz	**45**	48	18N	14 18 E
Lion, G. du	**37**	43	0N	4 0 E
Lípari, Is.	**49**	38	30N	14 50 E
Lipetsk	**68**	52	37N	39 35 E
Lippe ↝	**42**	51	39N	6 38 E
Lisboa	**50**	38	42N	9 10W
Lisbon = Lisboa	**50**	38	42N	9 10W
Lisburn	**34**	54	30N	6 9W
Lisburne, C.	**142**	68	50N	166 0W

Lisieux	**39**	49	10N	0	12 E
Lismore	**116**	28	44S	153	21 E
Lister, Mt.	**15**	78	0S	162	0 E
Listowel	**35**	52	27N	9	30W
Litchfield	**166**	39	10N	89	40W
Lithgow	**117**	33	25S	150	8 E
Lithuania ■	**68**	55	30N	24	0 E
Little Andaman I.	**94**	10	40N	92	15 E
Little Barrier I.	**122**	36	12S	175	8 E
Little Current	**150**	45	55N	82	0W
Little Falls	**164**	43	3N	74	50W
Little Minch	**32**	57	35N	6	45W
Little Rann	**91**	23	25N	71	25 E
Little Rock	**168**	34	41N	92	10W
Littlehampton	**25**	50	48N	0	32W
Liuzhou	**99**	24	22N	109	22 E
Liverpool, Australia	**117**	33	54S	150	58 E
Liverpool, Canada	**148**	44	5N	64	41W
Liverpool, U.K.	**28**	53	25N	3	0W
Liverpool Plains	**116**	31	15S	150	15 E
Livingston, Guatemala	**177**	15	50N	88	50W
Livingston, U.K.	**31**	55	52N	3	33W
Livingston, Mont., U.S.A.	**163**	45	40N	110	40W
Livingston, Tex., U.S.A.	**168**	30	44N	94	54W
Livingstone	**135**	17	46S	25	52 E
Livonia	**167**	42	25N	83	23W
Livorno	**46**	43	32N	10	18 E
Lizard Pt.	**27**	49	57N	5	11W
Ljubljana	**52**	46	4N	14	33 E
Ljusnan ~►	**66**	61	12N	17	8 E
Llandeilo	**26**	51	53N	4	0W
Llandovery	**26**	51	59N	3	49W
Llandrindod Wells	**26**	52	15N	3	23W
Llandudno	**26**	53	19N	3	51W
Llanelli	**27**	51	41N	4	11W
Llanes	**50**	43	25N	4	50W
Llangollen	**26**	52	58N	3	10W
Llanidloes	**26**	52	28N	3	31W
Llano Estacado	**161**	34	0N	103	0W
Llanos	**184**	5	0N	71	35W
Lloydminster	**152**	53	17N	110	0W
Loc Ninh	**95**	11	50N	106	34 E
Lochaber	**32**	56	55N	5	0W
Lochboisdale	**32**	57	10N	7	20W
Lochem	**41**	52	9N	6	26 E
Lochgilphead	**30**	56	2N	5	37W
Lochinver	**32**	58	9N	5	15W
Lochmaddy	**32**	57	36N	7	10W
Lochy, L.	**32**	56	58N	4	55W
Lock Haven	**164**	41	7N	77	31W
Lockhart	**117**	35	14S	146	40 E
Lockport	**164**	43	12N	78	42W
Lodi	**172**	38	12N	121	16W
Łódź	**58**	51	45N	19	27 E
Lofoten	**64**	68	30N	15	0 E
Logan, Utah, U.S.A.	**163**	41	45N	111	50W
Logan, W. Va., U.S.A.	**165**	37	51N	81	59W
Logan, Mt .	**144**	60	31N	140	22W
Logansport	**167**	40	45N	86	21W
Logroño	**51**	42	28N	2	27W
Loire ~►	**36**	47	16N	2	10W
Loja	**184**	3	59S	79	16W
Lokka	**67**	67	55N	27	35 E
Lolland	**61**	54	45N	11	30 E
Lom	**53**	43	48N	23	12 E
Lomami ~►	**134**	0	46N	24	16 E
Lombardia □	**46**	45	35N	9	45 E
Lombardy = Lombardia □ .	**46**	45	35N	9	45 E
Lombok	**113**	8	45S	116	30 E
Lomé	**130**	6	9N	1	20 E
Lomond, L.	**31**	56	8N	4	38W
Lompoc	**173**	34	41N	120	32W
Łomza	**58**	53	10N	22	2 E
London, Canada	**150**	42	59N	81	15W
London, U.K.	**25**	51	30N	0	5W
Londonderry	**34**	55	0N	7	20W
Londrina	**191**	23	18S	51	10W
Long Beach	**173**	33	46N	118	12W
Long I., Bahamas	**178**	23	20N	75	10W
Long I., U.S.A.	**164**	40	50N	73	20W
Long Range Mts.	**149**	49	30N	57	30W
Long Xuyen	**95**	10	19N	105	28 E
Longford, Australia	**119**	41	32S	147	3 E
Longford, Ireland	**34**	53	43N	7	50W
Longford □	**34**	53	42N	7	45W
Longlac	**150**	49	45N	86	25W
Longmont	**163**	40	10N	105	4W
Longreach	**121**	23	28S	144	14 E
Longview, Tex., U.S.A.	**168**	32	30N	94	45W
Longview, Wash., U.S.A.	**171**	46	9N	122	58W
Looe	**27**	50	24N	4	25W
Loop Hd.	**35**	52	34N	9	55W
Lop Nor	**100**	40	20N	90	10 E
Lopez, C.	**134**	0	47S	8	40 E
Lorain	**167**	41	28N	82	55W
Lorca	**51**	37	41N	1	42W
Lord Howe I.	**122**	31	33S	159	6 E
Lordsburg	**161**	32	22N	108	45W
Lorient	**36**	47	45N	3	23W
Lorn	**30**	56	26N	5	10W
Lorn, Firth of	**30**	56	20N	5	40W
Lorraine	**37**	49	0N	6	0 E
Los Alamos	**161**	35	57N	106	17W
Los Andes	**190**	32	50S	70	40W
Los Angeles, Chile	**190**	37	28S	72	23W
Los Angeles, U.S.A.	**173**	34	0N	118	10W
Los Angeles Aqueduct	**173**	35	25N	118	0W
Los Hermanos	**181**	11	45N	84	25W
Los Mochis	**174**	25	45N	108	57W
Los Testigos	**181**	11	23N	63	6W
Lošinj	**52**	44	30N	14	30 E
Lossiemouth	**33**	57	43N	3	17W
Lot ~►	**36**	44	18N	0	20 E
Lota	**190**	37	5S	73	10W
Lothian □	**31**	55	50N	3	0W
Loughborough	**29**	52	46N	1	11W
Loughrea	**35**	53	11N	8	33W
Louisbourg	**149**	45	55N	60	0W
Louise I.	**154**	52	55N	131	50W
Louisiana □	**168**	30	50N	92	0W
Louisville, Ky., U.S.A.	**167**	38	15N	85	45W
Louisville, Miss., U.S.A.	**169**	33	7N	89	3W
Lourdes	**36**	43	6N	0	3W
Lourenço-Marques = Maputo	**137**	25	58S	32	32 E
Louth	**29**	53	23N	0	0 E
Louth □	**34**	53	55N	6	30W
Louvain = Leuven	**42**	50	52N	4	42 E
Louviers	**39**	49	12N	1	10 E
Lowell	**164**	42	38N	71	19W
Lower Austria = Niederösterreich □	**45**	48	25N	15	40 E
Lower California = Baja California	**174**	31	10N	115	12W
Lower Hutt	**123**	41	10S	174	55 E
Lower Saxony = Niedersachsen □	**42**	52	45N	9	0 E
Lowestoft	**25**	52	29N	1	44 E
Łowicz	**58**	52	6N	19	55 E
Loxton	**119**	34	28S	140	31 E
Loyalty Is. = Loyauté, Is.	**122**	21	0S	167	30 E
Loyang = Luoyang	**99**	34	40N	112	26 E
Loyauté, Is.	**122**	21	0S	167	30 E
Lualaba ~►	**135**	0	26N	25	20 E
Luan Chau	**95**	21	38N	103	24 E
Luanda	**134**	8	50S	13	15 E
Luang Prabang	**95**	19	52N	102	10 E
Luarca	**50**	43	32N	6	32W
Lubbock	**161**	33	40N	101	53W
Lübeck	**43**	53	52N	10	41 E
Lublin	**58**	51	12N	22	38 E
Lubnān, J.	**80**	33	50N	35	45 E
Lubumbashi	**135**	11	40S	27	28 E
Lucca	**46**	43	50N	10	30 E
Luce Bay	**30**	54	45N	4	48W
Lučenec	**59**	48	18N	19	42 E
Lucerne = Luzern	**44**	47	3N	8	18 E
Lucknow	**92**	26	50N	81	0 E
Lüda = Dalian	**98**	38	50N	121	40 E
Lüderitz	**136**	26	41S	15	8 E
Ludhiana	**89**	30	57N	75	56 E
Ludington	**167**	43	58N	86	27W
Ludlow	**24**	52	23N	2	42W

Name	Page	Lat		Long	
Ludwigshafen	42	49 27N		8 27 E	
Lufkin	168	31 25N		94 40W	
Lugano	44	46 0N		8 57 E	
Lugansk	68	48 38N		39 15 E	
Lugo	50	43 2N		7 35W	
Lugovoye	71	42 55N		72 43 E	
Luján	190	34 45S		59 5W	
Łuków	58	51 55N		22 23 E	
Lule älv →	67	65 35N		22 10 E	
Luleå	67	65 35N		22 10 E	
Lüleburgaz	80	41 23N		27 22 E	
Lulua →	134	6 30S		22 50 E	
Luluabourg = Kananga	134	5 55S		22 18 E	
Lumberton	165	34 37N		78 59W	
Lundy	27	51 10N		4 41W	
Lune →	28	54 0N		2 51W	
Lüneburg	43	53 15N		10 23 E	
Lüneburg Heath = Lüneburger Heide	43	53 0N		10 0 E	
Lüneburger Heide	43	53 0N		10 0 E	
Lüni →	91	24 41N		71 14 E	
Luoyang	99	34 40N		112 26 E	
Lurgan	34	54 28N		6 20W	
Lusaka	135	15 28S		28 16 E	
Luta = Dalian	98	38 50N		121 40 E	
Luton	25	51 53N		0 24W	
Lutsk	68	50 50N		25 15 E	
Luvua →	135	6 50S		27 30 E	
Luxembourg	42	49 37N		6 9 E	
Luxembourg ■	42	50 0N		6 0 E	
Luzern	44	47 3N		8 18 E	
Luzhou	99	28 52N		105 20 E	
Luziânia	188	16 20S		48 0W	
Luzon	112	16 0N		121 0 E	
Lvov	68	49 50N		24 0 E	
Lyakhovskiye, Ostrova	73	73 40N		141 0 E	
Lyallpur = Faisalabad	89	31 30N		73 5 E	
Lyell I.	154	52 40N		131 35W	
Lyell Range	123	41 38S		172 20 E	
Lyme Regis	27	50 44N		2 57W	
Lymington	24	50 46N		1 32W	
Lynchburg	165	37 23N		79 10W	
Lynn	164	42 28N		70 57W	
Lynn Lake	152	56 51N		101 3W	
Lynton	27	51 14N		3 50W	
Lyon	37	45 46N		4 50 E	
Lyons = Lyon	37	45 46N		4 50 E	
Lytham St. Anne's	28	53 45N		2 58W	
Lyttelton	122	43 35S		172 44 E	

M

Name	Page	Lat		Long	
Ma'än	80	30 12N		35 44 E	
Ma'anshan	99	31 44N		118 29 E	
Ma'arrat an Nu'mān	80	35 43N		36 43 E	
Maas →	40	51 45N		4 32 E	
Maaseik	41	51 6N		5 45 E	
Maastricht	41	50 50N		5 40 E	
Mablethorpe	29	53 21N		0 14 E	
McAlester	168	34 57N		95 46W	
Macao = Macau ■	99	22 16N		113 35 E	
Macapá	185	0 5N		51 4W	
Macau	189	5 0S		36 40W	
Macau ■	99	22 16N		113 35 E	
McBride	155	53 20N		120 19W	
Macclesfield	28	53 16N		2 9W	
McClure Str.	12	75 0N		119 0W	
McComb	169	31 13N		90 30W	
McCook	163	40 15N		100 35W	
McDermitt	172	42 0N		117 45W	
Macdonald L.	114	23 30S		129 0 E	
Macdonnell Ranges	114	23 40S		133 0 E	
McDouall Peak	118	29 51S		134 55 E	
Macduff	33	57 40N		2 30W	
Macedonia ■	55	41 39N		22 0 E	
Maceió	189	9 40S		35 41W	
Macfarlane, L.	118	32 0S		136 40 E	
Macgillycuddy's Reeks	35	52 2N		9 45W	

Name	Page	Lat		Long	
Machala	184	3 20S		79 57W	
Machida	107	35 28N		139 23 E	
Machilipatnam	92	16 12N		81 8 E	
Machiques	184	10 4N		72 34W	
Machynlleth	26	52 36N		3 51W	
Mackay	121	21 8S		149 11 E	
Mackay, L.	114	22 30S		129 0 E	
McKeesport	164	40 21N		79 50W	
Mackenzie →	144	69 10N		134 20W	
Mackenzie Bay	12	69 0N		137 30W	
Mackenzie Mts.	144	64 0N		130 0W	
McKinley, Mt.	142	63 2N		151 0W	
McKinley Sea	13	84 0N		10 0W	
McKinney	168	33 10N		96 40W	
Macksville	116	30 40S		152 56 E	
Maclean	116	29 26S		153 16 E	
McLennan	155	55 42N		116 50W	
MacLeod Lake	154	54 58N		123 0W	
M'Clintock Chan.	145	72 0N		102 0W	
McMinnville, Oreg., U.S.A.	171	45 16N		123 11W	
McMinnville, Tenn., U.S.A.	169	35 43N		85 45W	
McMurdo Sd.	15	77 0S		170 0 E	
McMurray = Fort McMurray	155	56 44N		111 7W	
McNaughton L.	155	52 0N		118 10W	
Macomb	166	40 25N		90 40W	
Mâcon, France	37	46 19N		4 50 E	
Macon, U.S.A.	170	32 50N		83 37W	
McPherson	161	38 25N		97 40W	
Macpherson Ra.	116	28 15S		153 15 E	
Macquarie →	116	30 5S		147 30 E	
Macquarie Is.	15	54 36S		158 55 E	
MacRobertson Land	14	71 0S		64 0 E	
Macroom	35	51 54N		8 57W	
Madagascar ■	137	20 0S		47 0 E	
Madang	115	5 12S		145 49 E	
Madaripur	93	23 19N		90 15 E	
Made	40	51 41N		4 49 E	
Madeira	126	32 50N		17 0W	
Madeira →	185	3 22S		58 45W	
Madeleine, Îs. de la	149	47 30N		61 40W	
Madera	173	37 0N		120 1W	
Madhya Pradesh □	91	21 50N		81 0 E	
Madison, Fla., U.S.A.	170	30 29N		83 39W	
Madison, Ind., U.S.A.	167	38 42N		85 20W	
Madison, Wis., U.S.A.	166	43 5N		89 25W	
Madisonville	167	37 20N		87 30W	
Madiun	111	7 38S		111 32 E	
Madras = Tamil Nadu □	90	11 0N		77 0 E	
Madras, India	90	13 8N		80 19 E	
Madras, U.S.A.	171	44 40N		121 10W	
Madre, Laguna	176	25 0N		97 30W	
Madre de Dios →	187	10 59S		66 8W	
Madre del Sur, Sa.	177	17 0N		100 0W	
Madre Occidental, Sa.	174	25 0N		105 0W	
Madre Oriental, Sa.	177	22 0N		99 30W	
Madrid	50	40 25N		3 45W	
Madura, Selat	111	7 30S		113 20 E	
Madurai	90	9 55N		78 10 E	
Madurantakam	90	12 30N		79 50 E	
Mae Rim	94	18 54N		98 57 E	
Maebashi	107	36 24N		139 4 E	
Maesteg	27	51 36N		3 40W	
Maestra, Sierra	178	20 15N		77 0W	
Mafeking	152	52 40N		101 10W	
Maffra	117	37 53S		146 58 E	
Mafia	135	7 45S		39 50 E	
Mafikeng	136	25 50S		25 38 E	
Mafra	191	26 10S		50 0W	
Magadan	73	59 38N		150 50 E	
Magallanes, Estrecho de	192	52 30S		75 0W	
Magangué	184	9 14N		74 45W	
Magdalena, Bolivia	187	13 13S		63 57W	
Magdalena, Mexico	174	30 38N		110 57W	
Magdalena →	184	11 6N		74 51W	
Magdeburg	43	52 8N		11 36 E	
Magelang	111	7 29S		110 13 E	
Magellan's Str. = Magallanes, Estrecho de	192	52 30S		75 0W	
Magherafelt	34	54 44N		6 37W	
Magnitogorsk	71	53 27N		59 4 E	
Magog	148	45 18N		72 9W	

Name	Page	Lat °	Lat ′ N/S	Long °	Long ′ E/W
Magosa = Famagusta	80	35	8N	33	55 E
Magrath	155	49	25N	112	50W
Mahābād	81	36	50N	45	45 E
Mahajanga □	137	17	0S	47	0 E
Mahakam →	111	0	35S	117	17 E
Maḥallāt	86	33	55N	50	30 E
Mahanadi →	92	20	20N	86	25 E
Maharashtra □	91	20	30N	75	30 E
Mahbubnagar	91	16	45N	77	59 E
Mahia Pen.	122	39	9S	177	55 E
Mahón	51	39	53N	4	16 E
Mahone Bay	148	44	30N	64	20W
Mahukona	160	20	11N	155	52W
Mai-Ndombe, L.	134	2	0S	18	20 E
Maidenhead	25	51	31N	0	42W
Maiduguri	131	12	0N	13	20 E
Maikala Ra.	92	22	0N	81	0 E
Main →	42	50	0N	8	18 E
Maine	36	48	0N	0	0 E
Maine □	148	45	20N	69	0W
Mainland, Orkney, U.K.	33	59	0N	3	10W
Mainland, Shet., U.K.	30	60	15N	1	22W
Mainpuri	89	27	18N	79	4 E
Mainz	42	50	0N	8	17 E
Maiquetia	184	10	36N	66	57W
Maisi, Pta. de	178	20	10N	74	10W
Maitland, N.S.W., Australia	117	32	33S	151	36 E
Maitland, S. Austral., Australia	119	34	23S	137	40 E
Maiz, Islas del	179	12	15N	83	4W
Maizuru	106	35	25N	135	22 E
Majorca, I. = Mallorca	51	39	30N	3	0 E
Makarikari = Makgadikgadi Salt Pans	136	20	40S	25	45 E
Makasar = Ujung Pandang	113	5	10S	119	20 E
Makasar, Selat	113	1	0S	118	20 E
Makedhonía = Macedonia □	55	41	39N	22	0 E
Makena	160	20	39N	156	27W
Makeyevka	68	48	0N	38	0 E
Makgadikgadi Salt Pans	136	20	40S	25	45 E
Makhachkala	70	43	0N	47	30 E
Makkah	82	21	30N	39	54 E
Makó	59	46	14N	20	33 E
Makran Coast Range	88	25	40N	64	0 E
Makurazaki	108	31	15N	130	20 E
Makurdi	131	7	43N	8	35 E
Malabar Coast	90	11	0N	75	0 E
Malacca, Str. of	111	3	0N	101	0 E
Malad City	162	42	10N	112	20 E
Málaga	50	36	43N	4	23W
Malakal	129	9	33N	31	50 E
Malang	111	7	59S	112	45 E
Mälaren	60	59	30N	17	10 E
Malatya	81	38	25N	38	20 E
Malawi ■	137	13	0S	34	0 E
Malawi, L.	137	12	30S	34	30 E
Malay Pen.	97	7	25N	100	0 E
Malãyer	84	34	19N	48	51 E
Malaysia ■	111	5	0N	110	0 E
Malbaie, La	148	47	40N	70	10W
Malbork	58	54	3N	19	1 E
Malcolm	120	28	51S	121	25 E
Maldives ■	78	7	0N	73	0 E
Maldonado	191	35	0S	55	0W
Malebo, Pool	134	4	17S	15	20 E
Malegaon	91	20	30N	74	38 E
Mali ■	130	15	0N	2	0W
Mali Kyun	94	13	0N	98	20 E
Malin Hd.	34	55	18N	7	24W
Malindi	133	3	12S	40	5 E
Malines = Mechelen	42	51	2N	4	29 E
Mallaig	32	57	0N	5	50W
Mallorca	51	39	30N	3	0 E
Mallow	35	52	8N	8	40W
Malmédy	42	50	25N	6	2 E
Malmö	61	55	36N	12	59 E
Malmöhus län □	61	55	45N	13	30 E
Malone	151	44	50N	74	19W
Malta ■	49	35	50N	14	30 E
Malton	29	54	9N	0	48W
Maluku	113	1	0S	127	0 E
Malvern, U.K.	24	52	7N	2	19W
Malvern, U.S.A.	168	34	22N	92	50W
Malvern Hills	24	52	0N	2	19W
Malvinas, Is. = Falkland Is.	192	51	30S	59	0W
Mamers	39	48	21N	0	22 E
Mamoré →	187	10	23S	65	53W
Mamou	130	10	15N	12	0W
Man	130	7	30N	7	40W
Man, I. of	28	54	15N	4	30W
Mana, Fr. Guiana	185	5	45N	53	55W
Mana, U.S.A.	160	22	3N	159	45W
Manaar, Gulf of = Mannar, G. of	90	8	30N	79	0 E
Manacapuru	185	3	16S	60	37W
Manado	113	1	29N	124	51 E
Managua	179	12	6N	86	20W
Manaos = Manaus	185	3	0S	60	0W
Manapouri	123	45	34S	167	39 E
Manaung	93	18	45N	93	40 E
Manaus	185	3	0S	60	0W
Mancha, La	50	39	10N	2	54W
Manchester, U.K.	28	53	30N	2	15W
Manchester, U.S.A.	164	42	58N	71	29W
Mandalay	93	22	0N	96	4 E
Mandale = Mandalay	93	22	0N	96	4 E
Mandurah	120	32	36S	115	48 E
Manfredónia, G. di	49	41	30N	16	10 E
Mangalore	90	12	55N	74	47 E
Mangla Dam	89	33	9N	73	44 E
Mangole	113	1	50S	125	55 E
Mangonui	122	35	1S	173	32 E
Mangyshlak P-ov.	70	44	30N	52	30 E
Manhattan	158	39	10N	96	40W
Manicoré	185	5	48S	61	16W
Manicouagan →	148	49	30N	68	30W
Manila	112	14	40N	121	3 E
Manilla	116	30	45S	150	43 E
Manipur □	93	25	0N	94	0 E
Manisa	80	38	38N	27	30 E
Manistee	167	44	15N	86	20W
Manistique	150	45	59N	86	18W
Manitoba □	153	55	30N	97	0W
Manitoba, L.	153	51	0N	98	45W
Manitoulin I.	150	45	40N	82	30W
Manitowoc	167	44	8N	87	40W
Manizales	184	5	5N	75	32W
Manjil	81	36	46N	49	30 E
Manjimup	120	34	15S	116	6 E
Mankato	166	44	8N	93	59W
Manly	117	33	48S	151	17 E
Mannar, G. of	90	8	30N	79	0 E
Mannar I.	90	9	5N	79	45 E
Mannheim	42	49	28N	8	29 E
Mannum	119	34	50S	139	20 E
Manosque	37	43	49N	5	47 E
Manouane, L.	148	50	45N	70	45W
Mans, Le	39	48	0N	0	10 E
Mansel I.	146	62	0N	80	0W
Mansfield, Australia	117	37	4S	146	6 E
Mansfield, U.K.	29	53	8N	1	12W
Mansfield, U.S.A.	167	40	45N	82	30W
Manta	184	1	0S	80	40W
Mantes-la-Jolie	39	49	0N	1	41 E
Mantiqueira, Serra da	188	22	0S	44	0W
Mántova	46	45	20N	10	42 E
Mantua = Mántova	46	45	20N	10	42 E
Manu	187	12	10S	70	51W
Manukau	122	35	14S	173	13 E
Manyara, L.	135	3	40S	35	50 E
Manzanillo, Cuba	178	20	20N	77	31W
Manzanillo, Mexico	175	19	3N	104	20W
Manzhouli	98	49	35N	117	25 E
Mapimí	174	25	49N	103	51W
Maple	152	43	51N	79	31W
Maputo	137	25	58S	32	32 E
Maquinchao	192	41	15S	68	50W
Mar, Serra do	191	25	30S	49	0W
Mar Chiquita, L.	190	30	40S	62	50W
Mar del Plata	191	38	0S	57	30W
Mar Menor, L.	51	37	40N	0	45W
Marabá	188	5	20S	49	5W
Maracaibo	184	10	40N	71	37W

Maracaibo, Lago de **184** 9 40N 71 30W
Maracay **184** 10 15N 67 28W
Marajó, Ilha de **188** 1 0S 49 30W
Maranhão = São Luís **188** 2 39S 44 15W
Maranhão □ **188** 5 0S 46 0W
Marañón ──► **186** 4 30S 73 35W
Maraş .... **80** 37 37N 36 53 E
Marathón .... **55** 38 11N 23 58 E
Marbella **50** 36 30N 4 57W
Marble Bar .... **114** 21 9S 119 44 E
March .... **25** 52 33N 0 5 E
Marché .... **36** 46 0N 1 20 E
Marche □ .... **47** 43 22N 13 10 E
Marchena **50** 37 18N 5 23W
Marches = Marche □ .... **47** 43 22N 13 10 E
Mardan .... **89** 34 20N 72 0 E
Mardin .... **81** 37 20N 40 43 E
Mareeba .... **121** 16 59S 145 28 E
Margarita **175** 9 20N 79 55W
Margarita I. **185** 11 0N 64 0W
Margate .... **25** 51 23N 1 24 E
Mari El □ .... **68** 56 30N 48 0 E
Maria van Diemen, C. .... **122** 34 29S 172 40 E
Marianao **178** 23 8N 82 24W
Marianna **169** 30 45N 85 15W
Maribor .... **52** 46 36N 15 40 E
Maricourt **146** 61 30N 72 0W
Marie-Galante **180** 15 56N 61 16W
Marienberg .... **41** 52 30N 6 35 E
Marietta, Ga., U.S.A. **169** 34 0N 84 30W
Marietta, Ohio, U.S.A. ... **164** 39 27N 81 27W
Marília **188** 22 13S 50 0W
Marín **50** 42 23N 8 42W
Marinette **167** 45 4N 87 40W
Maringá **191** 23 26S 52 2W
Marion, Ill., U.S.A. **166** 37 45N 88 55W
Marion, Ind., U.S.A. **167** 40 35N 85 40W
Marion, Ohio, U.S.A. **167** 40 38N 83 8W
Mariupol .... **68** 47 5N 37 31 E
Marken .... **40** 52 26N 5 12 E
Market Drayton **28** 52 55N 2 30W
Market Harborough **25** 52 29N 0 55W
Market Rasen **29** 53 24N 0 20W
Markham, Mt. .... **15** 83 0S 164 0 E
Marlborough **24** 51 26N 1 44W
Marlborough □ .... **123** 41 45S 173 33 E
Marlborough Downs **24** 51 25N 1 55W
Marlin **168** 31 25N 96 50W
Marmagao .... **91** 15 25N 73 56 E
Marmara, Sea of = Marmara
   Denizi .... **80** 40 45N 28 15 E
Marmara Denizi .... **80** 40 45N 28 15 E
Marmaris .... **80** 36 50N 28 14 E
Marne ──► .... **39** 8 23N 18 36 E
Maroochydore .... **116** 26 29S 153 5 E
Marquesas Is. **123** 9 30S 140 0W
Marquette **150** 46 30N 87 21W
Marrakech **126** 31 9N 8 0W
Marree .... **118** 29 39S 138 1 E
Marsabit .... **133** 2 18N 38 0 E
Marseille .... **37** 43 18N 5 23 E
Marseilles = Marseille ... **37** 43 18N 5 23 E
Marshall, Minn., U.S.A. .. **166** 44 25N 95 45W
Marshall, Mo., U.S.A. **166** 39 8N 93 15W
Marshall, Tex., U.S.A. ... **168** 32 29N 94 20W
Marshalltown **166** 42 5N 92 56W
Marshfield **166** 44 42N 90 10W
Martaban, G. of .... **93** 16 5N 96 30 E
Martha's Vineyard **164** 41 25N 70 35W
Martigues .... **37** 43 24N 5 4 E
Martinique **180** 14 40N 61 0W
Martinsburg **164** 39 30N 77 57W
Martinsville, Ind., U.S.A. . **167** 39 29N 86 23W
Martinsville, Va., U.S.A. .. **165** 36 41N 79 52W
Marton .... **122** 40 4S 175 23 E
Marugame .... **109** 34 15N 133 40 E
Maruoka .... **106** 36 9N 136 16 E
Marwar .... **91** 25 43N 73 45 E
Mary .... **70** 37 40N 61 50 E
Maryborough = Port Laoise **35** 53 2N 7 20W
Maryborough, Queens.,
   Australia .... **116** 25 31S 152 37 E
Maryborough, Vic., Australia **117** 37 0S 143 44 E
Maryland □ **164** 39 10N 76 40W
Maryport **28** 54 43N 3 30W
Marysville **172** 39 14N 121 40W
Maryville **165** 35 50N 84 0W
Marzūq .... **127** 25 53N 13 57 E
Masan .... **98** 35 11N 128 32 E
Masaya **179** 12 0N 86 7W
Masbate, I. .... **112** 12 21N 123 36 E
Mascota **175** 20 32N 104 49W
Maseru .... **137** 29 18S 27 30 E
Mashhad .... **86** 36 20N 59 35 E
Masisea **186** 8 35S 74 22W
Masjed Soleyman .... **84** 31 55N 49 18 E
Mask, L. **34** 53 36N 9 24W
Mason City **166** 43 9N 93 12W
Masqat .... **83** 23 37N 58 36 E
Massachusetts □ **164** 42 25N 72 0W
Massawa = Mitsiwa ..... **132** 15 35N 39 25 E
Massena **151** 44 52N 74 55W
Massif Central .... **37** 45 30N 2 21 E
Massillon **167** 40 47N 81 30W
Mastanli = Momchilgrad .. **53** 41 33N 25 23 E
Masterton .... **123** 40 56S 175 39 E
Mastūrah .... **82** 23 7N 38 52 E
Masuda .... **108** 34 40N 131 51 E
Matachewan **151** 47 56N 80 39W
Matadi .... **134** 5 52S 13 31 E
Matagalpa **179** 13 0N 85 58W
Matamoros, Coahuila, Mexico **174** 25 32N 103 15W
Matamoros, Puebla, Mexico **177** 18 2N 98 17W
Matane **148** 48 50N 67 33W
Matanzas **178** 23 0N 81 40W
Matapan, C. = Taínaron, Ákra **54** 36 22N 22 27 E
Matarani **186** 77 0S 72 10W
Matehuala **177** 23 39N 100 39W
Mathura .... **89** 27 30N 77 40 E
Matlock **28** 53 8N 1 32W
Mato Grosso □ **188** 14 0S 55 0W
Mato Grosso, Planalto do . **188** 15 0S 59 57W
Matopo Hills .... **137** 20 36S 28 20 E
Matrah .... **83** 23 37N 58 30 E
Matsubara .... **106** 34 33N 135 34 E
Matsudo .... **107** 35 47N 139 54 E
Matsue .... **109** 35 25N 133 10 E
Matsumoto .... **107** 36 15N 138 0 E
Matsusaka .... **106** 34 34N 136 32 E
Matsutō .... **106** 36 31N 136 34 E
Matsuura .... **108** 33 20N 129 49 E
Matsuyama .... **109** 33 45N 132 45 E
Mattancheri .... **90** 9 50N 76 15 E
Mattawa **151** 46 20N 78 45W
Matterhorn .... **44** 45 58N 7 39 E
Matucana **186** 11 55S 76 25W
Maturín **185** 9 45N 63 11W
Mau Ranipur .... **91** 25 16N 79 8 E
Maubeuge .... **38** 50 17N 3 57 E
Maudin Sun .... **93** 16 0N 94 30 E
Maui .... **160** 20 45N 156 20 E
Maulamyaing .... **93** 16 30N 97 40 E
Mauna Kea **160** 19 50N 155 28W
Mauna Loa **160** 21 8N 157 10W
Maungmagan Kyunzu .... **94** 14 0N 97 48 E
Mauritania ■ **126** 20 50N 10 0W
Mauritius ■ .... **9** 20 0S 57 0 E
Mawlaik .... **93** 23 40N 94 26 E
May Pen **180** 17 58N 77 15W
Maya ──► .... **75** 54 31N 134 41 E
Mayagüez **180** 18 12N 67 9W
Mayerthorpe **155** 53 57N 115 8W
Mayfield **169** 36 45N 88 40W
Maykop .... **70** 44 35N 40 25 E
Maynooth **34** 53 22N 6 38W
Mayo **144** 63 38N 135 57W
Mayo □ **34** 53 47N 9 7W
Mayor I. .... **122** 37 16S 176 17 E
Maysville **167** 38 39N 83 46W
Mazagán = El Jadida **126** 33 11N 8 17W
Mazán **186** 3 30S 73 0W
Mazar-e Sharīf .... **87** 36 41N 67 0 E
Mazarredo **192** 47 10S 66 50W

Mazatenango	177	14	35N	91	30W
Mazatlán	175	23	13N	106	25W
Mbandaka	134	0	1N	18	18 E
Mdina	49	35	51N	14	25 E
Mead, L.	173	36	1N	114	44W
Meadville	164	41	39N	80	9W
Meander River	145	59	2N	117	42W
Meath □	34	53	32N	6	40W
Meaux	39	48	58N	2	50 E
Mecca = Makkah	82	21	30N	39	54 E
Mechelen	42	51	2N	4	29 E
Mecklenburger Bucht	42	54	20N	11	40 E
Medan	111	3	40N	98	38 E
Medellín	184	6	15N	75	35W
Medford	171	42	20N	122	52W
Mediaş	57	46	9N	24	22 E
Medicine Hat	152	50	0N	110	45W
Medina = Al Madïnah	82	24	35N	39	52 E
Medina	167	41	9N	81	50W
Medina del Campo	50	41	18N	4	55W
Mediterranean Sea	124	35	0N	15	0 E
Medley	152	54	25N	110	16W
Médoc	36	45	10N	0	56W
Medvezhi, Ostrava	73	71	0N	161	0 E
Medway →	25	51	28N	0	45 E
Meekatharra	120	26	32S	118	29 E
Meerut	89	29	1N	77	42 E
Mega	133	3	57N	38	19 E
Mégantic, L.	148	45	32N	70	53W
Mégara	55	37	58N	23	22 E
Meghalaya □	93	25	50N	91	0 E
Mei Xian	99	24	16N	116	6 E
Meknès	126	33	57N	5	33W
Mekong →	95	9	30N	106	15 E
Melaka	96	2	15N	102	15 E
Melaka □	96	2	15N	102	15 E
Melanesia	122	4	0S	155	0 E
Melbourne	117	37	50S	145	0 E
Melchor Muzquiz	174	27	53N	101	31W
Melfort	152	52	50N	104	37W
Melilla	126	35	21N	2	57W
Melitopol	68	46	50N	35	22 E
Melo	191	32	20S	54	10W
Melrose	31	53	35N	2	44W
Melton Mowbray	29	52	46N	0	52W
Melun	39	48	32N	2	39 E
Melville	152	50	55N	102	50W
Melville, L.	147	53	30N	60	0W
Melville I., Australia	114	11	30S	131	0 E
Melville I., Canada	12	75	30N	112	0W
Melville Pen.	146	68	0N	84	0W
Memel = Klaipeda	68	55	43N	21	10 E
Memphis	169	35	7N	90	0W
Menai Strait	26	53	14N	4	10W
Ménaka	131	15	59N	2	18 E
Menan = Chao Phraya → .	94	13	32N	100	36 E
Menasha	167	44	13N	88	27W
Mende	37	44	31N	3	30 E
Mendip Hills	27	51	17N	2	40W
Mendocino	172	39	26N	123	50W
Mendoza	190	32	50S	68	52W
Menindee	118	32	20S	142	25 E
Menindee, L.	118	32	20S	142	25 E
Menominee	150	45	9N	87	39W
Menorca	51	40	0N	4	0 E
Mentawai, Kepulauan	111	2	0S	99	0 E
Menzies	120	29	40S	120	58 E
Meppel	41	52	42N	6	12 E
Merbein	119	34	10S	142	2 E
Merca	133	1	48N	44	50 E
Merced	172	37	18N	120	30W
Mercedes, Buenos Aires, Argentina	190	34	40S	59	30W
Mercedes, Corrientes, Argentina	191	29	10S	58	5W
Mercedes, San Luis, Argentina	190	33	40S	65	21W
Mercedes, Uruguay	191	33	12S	58	0W
Mere	24	51	5N	2	16W
Mergui Arch. = Myeik Kyunzu	94	11	30N	97	30 E
Mérida, Mexico	177	20	58N	89	37W
Mérida, Spain	50	38	55N	6	25W
Mérida, Venezuela	184	8	24N	71	8W
Mérida, Cord. de	182	9	0N	71	0W
Meriden	164	41	33N	72	47W
Meridian	169	32	20N	88	42W
Merowe	129	18	29N	31	46 E
Merredin	120	31	28S	118	18 E
Merrill	156	45	11N	89	41W
Merritt	155	50	10N	120	45W
Merriwa	116	32	6S	150	22 E
Mersey →	28	53	20N	2	56W
Merseyside □	28	53	25N	2	55W
Mersin	80	36	51N	34	36 E
Merthyr Tydfil	27	51	45N	3	23W
Méru	39	49	13N	2	8 E
Merville	38	50	38N	2	38 E
Mesa	160	33	20N	111	56W
Mesa, La	173	32	48N	117	5W
Meshed = Mashhad	86	36	20N	59	35 E
Mesolóngion	54	38	21N	21	28 E
Mesopotamia = Al Jazirah .	81	33	30N	44	0 E
Mesquite	173	36	47N	114	6W
Messina, Italy	49	38	10N	15	32 E
Messina, S. Africa	137	22	20S	30	0 E
Messina, Str. di	49	38	5N	15	35 E
Messíni	54	37	4N	22	1 E
Meta →	184	6	12N	67	28W
Metairie	169	29	59N	90	9W
Metán	190	25	30S	65	0W
Metropolis	169	37	10N	88	47W
Metz	37	49	8N	6	10 E
Meuse →	42	50	45N	5	41 E
Mexia	168	31	38N	96	32W
Mexicali	174	32	40N	115	29W
México, Mexico	177	19	20N	99	10W
Mexico, U.S.A.	166	39	10N	91	55W
México □	177	19	20N	99	30W
Mexico ■	174	20	0N	100	0W
Mexico, G. of	138	25	0N	90	0W
Mezen →	69	66	11N	43	59 E
Mhow	91	22	33N	75	50 E
Miahuatlán	177	16	21N	96	36W
Miami	170	25	45N	80	15W
Miami Beach	170	25	49N	80	6W
Miāneh	81	37	30N	47	40 E
Mianwali	89	32	38N	71	28 E
Miaoli	99	24	37N	120	49 E
Miass	69	54	59N	60	6 E
Michigan □	167	44	40N	85	40W
Michigan, L.	150	44	0N	87	0W
Michigan City	167	41	42N	86	56W
Michikamau L.	147	54	20N	63	10W
Michipicoten	150	47	55N	84	55W
Michoacán □	175	19	10N	101	50W
Michurinsk	68	52	58N	40	27 E
Micronesia	122	11	0N	160	0 E
Mid Glamorgan □	27	51	40N	3	25W
Middelburg	40	51	30N	3	36 E
Middle Andaman I.	94	12	30N	92	30 E
Middlesboro	165	36	36N	83	43W
Middlesbrough	29	54	35N	1	14W
Middleton	148	44	57N	65	4W
Middletown, Conn., U.S.A.	164	41	37N	72	40W
Middletown, N.Y., U.S.A.	164	41	28N	74	28W
Middletown, Ohio, U.S.A.	167	39	29N	84	25W
Midland, Canada	151	44	45N	79	50W
Midland, Mich., U.S.A.	167	43	37N	84	17W
Midland, Tex., U.S.A.	161	32	0N	102	3W
Międzyrzec Podlaski	58	51	58N	22	45 E
Miercurea Ciuc	57	46	21N	25	48 E
Mieres	50	43	18N	5	48W
Migennes	39	47	58N	3	31 E
Mihara	109	34	24N	133	5 E
Miki	109	34	48N	134	59 E
Míkonos	55	37	30N	25	25 E
Mikuni-Tōge	107	36	50N	138	50 E
Mikura-Jima	107	33	52N	139	36 E
Milagro	184	2	11S	79	36W
Milan = Milano	46	45	28N	9	10 E
Milano	46	45	28N	9	10 E
Milâs	80	37	20N	27	50 E

Name	Page	Lat°	Lat′	Lat	Long°	Long′	Long
Mildura	119	34	13S		142	9	E
Miles	116	26	40S		150	9	E
Miles City	163	46	24N		105	50W	
Milford	164	38	52N		75	27W	
Milford Haven	27	51	43N		5	2W	
Milk →	163	48	5N		106	15W	
Millau	37	44	8N		3	4	E
Millicent	119	37	34S		140	21	E
Millinocket	148	45	45N		68	45W	
Millmerran	116	27	53S		151	16	E
Millom	28	54	13N		3	16W	
Millville	164	39	22N		75	0W	
Milne Inlet	146	72	30N		80	0W	
Milos	55	36	44N		24	25	E
Milton Keynes	25	52	3N		0	42W	
Milwaukee	167	43	9N		87	58W	
Milwaukie	171	45	27N		122	39W	
Minamata	108	32	10N		130	30	E
Minas	191	34	20S		55	10W	
Minas Gerais □	188	18	50S		46	0W	
Minatitlán	177	17	59N		94	31W	
Mindanao	112	8	0N		125	0	E
Mindanao Sea = Bohol Sea	112	9	0N		124	0	E
Minden	168	32	40N		93	20W	
Mindoro	112	13	0N		121	0	E
Mindoro Strait	112	12	30N		120	30	E
Mine	108	34	12N		131	7	E
Minehead	27	51	12N		3	29W	
Mineral Wells	161	32	50N		98	5W	
Mingan	148	50	20N		64	0W	
Mingenew	120	29	12S		115	21	E
Minho □	50	41	25N		8	20W	
Minneapolis	166	44	58N		93	20W	
Minnedosa	153	50	14N		99	50W	
Minnesota □	156	46	40N		94	0W	
Mino	106	35	32N		136	55	E
Mino-Kamo	106	35	23N		137	2	E
Mino-Mikawa-Kōgen	106	35	10N		137	23	E
Minorca = Menorca	51	40	0N		4	0	E
Minot	163	48	10N		101	15W	
Minsk	68	53	52N		27	30	E
Mintaka Pass	89	37	0N		74	58	E
Miquelon, I.	149	47	2N		56	20W	
Miraj	91	16	50N		74	45	E
Miranda do Douro	50	41	30N		6	16W	
Mirpur Khas	88	25	30N		69	0	E
Mirzapur	92	25	10N		82	34	E
Mirzapur-cum-Vindhyachal = Mirzapur	92	25	10N		82	34	E
Miscou I.	148	47	57N		64	31W	
Mishawaka	167	41	40N		86	8W	
Mishima	107	35	10N		138	52	E
Miskitos, Cayos	179	14	26N		82	50W	
Miskolc	59	48	7N		20	50	E
Misool	113	1	52S		130	10	E
Misrātah	127	32	24N		15	3	E
Mission City	154	49	10N		122	15W	
Mississippi □	169	33	0N		90	0W	
Mississippi →	169	29	0N		89	15W	
Mississippi, Delta of the	169	29	15N		90	30W	
Missoula	162	46	52N		114	0W	
Missouri □	166	38	25N		92	30W	
Missouri →	166	38	50N		90	8W	
Mistassini L.	151	51	0N		73	30W	
Mitaka	107	35	40N		139	33	E
Mitchell, Australia	116	26	29S		147	58	E
Mitchell, U.S.A.	163	43	40N		98	0W	
Mitchell →	115	15	12S		141	35	E
Mitilíni	55	39	6N		26	35	E
Mito	107	36	20N		140	30	E
Mitsiwa	132	15	35N		39	25	E
Mitsukaidō	107	36	1N		139	59	E
Mittagong	117	34	28S		150	29	E
Mitú	184	1	8N		70	3W	
Miura	107	35	12N		139	40	E
Miyake-Jima	107	34	0N		139	30	E
Miyako	103	39	40N		141	59	E
Miyakonojō	108	31	40N		131	5	E
Miyanojō	108	31	54N		130	27	E
Miyazaki	108	31	56N		131	30	E
Miyazu	106	35	35N		135	10	E
Miyoshi	109	34	48N		132	51	E
Mizamis = Ozamis	112	8	15N		123	50	E
Mizen Hd.	35	51	27N		9	50W	
Mizoram □	93	23	30N		92	40	E
Mizunami	106	35	22N		137	15	E
Mława	58	53	9N		20	25	E
Mobara	107	35	25N		140	18	E
Moberley	166	39	25N		92	25W	
Mobile	169	30	41N		88	3W	
Mobutu Sese Seko, L.	132	1	30N		31	0	E
Moçâmedes = Namibe	134	15	7S		12	11	E
Moctezuma, R. →	177	21	59N		98	34W	
Módena	46	44	39N		10	55	E
Modesto	172	37	43N		121	0W	
Moe	117	38	12S		146	19	E
Moei →	94	17	25N		98	10	E
Moengo	185	5	45N		54	20W	
Moffat	31	55	20N		3	27W	
Mogadishu = Muqdisho	133	2	2N		45	25	E
Mogador = Essaouira	126	31	32N		9	42W	
Mogami →	103	38	45N		140	0	E
Mogi das Cruzes	191	23	31S		46	11W	
Mogilev	68	53	55N		30	18	E
Mointy	71	47	10N		73	18	E
Moisie	148	50	12N		66	1W	
Mojave Desert	173	35	0N		116	30W	
Mold	26	53	10N		3	10W	
Molde	65	62	45N		7	9	E
Moldova ■	68	47	0N		28	0	E
Molfetta	49	41	12N		16	35	E
Moline	166	41	30N		90	30W	
Molise □	49	41	45N		14	30	E
Mollendo	187	17	0S		72	0W	
Mölndal	60	57	40N		12	3	E
Molong	117	33	5S		148	54	E
Molopo →	136	28	30S		20	13	E
Molotov = Perm	69	58	0N		57	10	E
Molucca Sea	113	4	0S		124	0	E
Moluccas = Maluku	113	1	0S		127	0	E
Mombasa	135	4	2S		39	43	E
Mombetsu	103	42	27N		142	4	E
Momchilgrad	53	41	33N		25	23	E
Mompós	184	9	14N		74	26W	
Møn	61	54	57N		12	15	E
Mona, Canal de la	180	18	30N		67	45W	
Monach Is.	32	57	32N		7	40W	
Monaco ■	37	43	46N		7	23	E
Monaghan	34	54	15N		6	58W	
Monaghan □	34	54	10N		7	0W	
Monastir = Bitola	52	41	5N		21	10	E
Mönchengladbach	42	51	12N		6	23	E
Monchique	50	37	19N		8	38W	
Monclova	174	26	50N		101	30W	
Mohcton	148	46	7N		64	51W	
Monessen	164	40	9N		79	50W	
Monforte	50	39	6N		7	25W	
Mongalla	129	5	8N		31	42	E
Monghyr = Munger	92	25	23N		86	30	E
Mongolia ■	98	47	0N		103	0	E
Monmouth, U.K.	26	51	48N		2	43W	
Monmouth, U.S.A.	166	40	50N		90	40W	
Monroe, La., U.S.A.	168	32	32N		92	4W	
Monroe, Mich., U.S.A.	167	41	55N		83	26W	
Monroe, N.C., U.S.A.	165	35	2N		80	37W	
Monrovia, Liberia	130	6	18N		10	47W	
Monrovia, U.S.A.	173	34	7N		118	1W	
Mons	42	50	27N		3	58	E
Mont-de-Marsan	36	43	54N		0	31W	
Mont Laurier	151	46	35N		75	30W	
Montague	172	41	47N		122	30W	
Montana □	163	47	0N		110	0W	
Montargis	39	48	0N		2	43	E
Montauban	36	44	0N		1	21	E
Montbéliard	37	47	31N		6	48	E
Montceau-les-Mines	37	46	40N		4	23	E
Montdidier	38	49	38N		2	35	E
Monte-Carlo	37	43	46N		7	23	E
Monte Caseros	191	30	10S		57	50W	
Montego Bay	180	18	30N		78	0W	
Montélimar	37	44	33N		4	45	E
Montemorelos	176	25	11N		99	42W	

Name	Page	Lat °	'	N/S	Long °	'	E/W
Montenegro □	52	42	40N		19	20 E	
Monterey	173	36	35N		121	57W	
Monteria	184	8	46N		75	53W	
Monterrey	176	25	40N		100	30W	
Montes Claros	188	16	30S		43	50W	
Montevideo, Uruguay	191	34	50S		56	11W	
Montevideo, U.S.A.	166	44	55N		95	40W	
Montgomery = Sahiwal	89	30	45N		73	8 E	
Montgomery, U.K.	26	52	34N		3	9W	
Montgomery, U.S.A.	169	32	20N		86	20W	
Montluçon	37	46	22N		2	36 E	
Montmagny	148	46	58N		70	34W	
Montmorency	148	46	53N		71	11W	
Montpelier, Idaho, U.S.A.	163	42	15N		111	20W	
Montpelier, Vt., U.S.A.	151	44	15N		72	38W	
Montpellier	37	43	37N		3	52 E	
Montréal	151	45	31N		73	34W	
Montrose, U.K.	33	56	43N		2	28W	
Montrose, U.S.A.	163	38	30N		107	52W	
Montserrat	180	16	40N		62	10W	
Monywa	93	22	7N		95	11 E	
Monze, C.	88	24	47N		66	37 E	
Mo'oka	107	36	26N		140	1 E	
Moonta	119	34	6S		137	32 E	
Moora	120	30	37S		115	58 E	
Moorfoot Hills	31	55	44N		3	8W	
Moorhead	156	46	51N		96	44W	
Mooroopna	117	36	25S		145	22 E	
Moose Jaw	152	50	24N		105	30W	
Moosehead L.	148	45	34N		69	40W	
Moosomin	152	50	9N		101	40W	
Moosonee	140	51	17N		80	39W	
Mopti	130	14	30N		4	0W	
Moradabad	89	28	50N		78	50 E	
Moranbah	121	22	1S		148	6 E	
Moratuwa	90	6	45N		79	55 E	
Morava →	59	48	10N		16	59 E	
Moravian Hts. = Ceskomoravská Vrchovina	59	49	30N		15	40 E	
Morawa	120	29	13S		116	0 E	
Morawhanna	185	8	30N		59	40W	
Moray Firth	33	57	50N		3	30W	
Morden	153	49	15N		98	10W	
Mordvinia □	68	54	20N		44	30 E	
Møre og Romsdal fylke □	65	62	30N		8	0 E	
Morecambe	28	54	5N		2	52W	
Morecambe B.	28	54	7N		3	0W	
Moree	116	29	28S		149	54 E	
Morehead City	165	34	46N		76	44W	
Morelia	175	19	42N		101	7W	
Morelos □	177	18	45N		99	0W	
Morena, Sierra	50	38	20N		4	0W	
Moresby I.	154	52	30N		131	40W	
Morgan City	168	29	40N		91	15W	
Morganton	165	35	46N		81	48W	
Morgantown	164	39	39N		79	58W	
Moriguchi	106	34	44N		135	34 E	
Morlaix	36	48	36N		3	52W	
Mornington	117	38	15S		145	5 E	
Moro G.	112	6	30N		123	0 E	
Morocco ■	126	32	0N		5	50W	
Moroleón	177	20	8N		101	12W	
Morón	178	22	8N		78	39W	
Morotai	113	2	10N		128	30 E	
Morrilton	168	35	10N		92	45W	
Morrinhos	188	17	45S		49	10W	
Morris	153	49	25N		97	22W	
Morristown	165	36	18N		83	20W	
Mortes, R. das →	188	11	45S		50	44W	
Mortlake	119	38	5S		142	50 E	
Moruya	117	35	58S		150	3 E	
Morvern	30	56	38N		5	44W	
Morwell	117	38	10S		146	22 E	
Moscos Is.	94	14	0N		97	30 E	
Moscow = Moskva	68	55	45N		37	35 E	
Moscow	171	46	45N		116	59W	
Mosel →	42	50	22N		7	36 E	
Moselle = Mosel →	42	50	22N		7	36 E	
Mosgiel	123	45	53S		170	21 E	
Mosjøen	65	65	51N		13	12 E	
Moskva	68	55	45N		37	35 E	
Mosquera	184	2	35N		78	24W	
Mosquitos, Golfo de los	179	9	15N		81	10W	
Moss Vale	117	34	32S		150	25 E	
Mosselbaai	136	34	11S		22	8 E	
Mossman	121	16	21S		145	15 E	
Mossoró	189	5	10S		37	15W	
Mostaganem	127	35	54N		0	5 E	
Mostar	52	43	22N		17	50 E	
Mosul = Al Mawşil	81	36	15N		43	5 E	
Motala	60	58	32N		15	1 E	
Motherwell	31	55	48N		4	0W	
Motihari	92	26	30N		84	55 E	
Motueka	123	41	7S		173	1 E	
Motul	177	21	6N		89	17W	
Moúdhros	55	39	50N		25	18 E	
Moule	180	16	20N		61	22W	
Moulins	37	46	35N		3	19 E	
Moultrie	170	31	11N		83	47W	
Moundsville	164	39	53N		80	43W	
Mount Airy	165	36	31N		80	37W	
Mount Barker, S. Austral., Australia	119	35	5S		138	52 E	
Mount Barker, W. Austral., Australia	120	34	38S		117	40 E	
Mount Carmel	167	38	20N		87	48W	
Mount Forest	151	43	59N		80	43W	
Mount Gambier	119	37	50S		140	46 E	
Mount Isa	115	20	42S		139	26 E	
Mount Lofty Ra.	119	34	35S		139	5 E	
Mount Magnet	120	28	2S		117	47 E	
Mount Maunganui	122	37	40S		176	14 E	
Mount Morgan	121	23	40S		150	25 E	
Mount Pearl	149	47	31N		52	47W	
Mount Pleasant, Mich., U.S.A.	167	43	35N		84	47W	
Mount Pleasant, Tex., U.S.A.	168	33	5N		95	0W	
Mount Sterling	165	38	0N		84	0W	
Mount Vernon, Ill., U.S.A.	166	38	17N		88	57W	
Mount Vernon, N.Y., U.S.A.	164	40	57N		73	49W	
Mount Vernon, Wash., U.S.A.	171	48	25N		122	20W	
Mount Whaleback	114	23	18S		119	44 E	
Mountain City	172	41	54N		116	0W	
Mountain View	172	37	26N		122	5W	
Moura, Australia	121	24	35S		149	58 E	
Moura, Brazil	185	1	32S		61	38W	
Mourne →	34	54	45N		7	39W	
Mourne Mts.	34	54	10N		6	0W	
Moyale	133	3	30N		39	0 E	
Mozambique ■	137	19	0S		35	0 E	
Mozambique Chan.	137	20	0S		39	0 E	
Mu Us Shamo	98	39	0N		109	0 E	
Muaná	188	1	25S		49	15W	
Muang Chiang Rai	94	19	52N		99	50 E	
Muck	32	56	50N		6	15W	
Mucuri	189	18	0S		39	36W	
Mudanjiang	98	44	38N		129	30 E	
Mudgee	117	32	32S		149	31 E	
Muğla	80	37	15N		28	22 E	
Mukden = Shenyang	98	41	50N		123	25 E	
Mukhtuya = Lensk	74	60	48N		114	55 E	
Mukinbudin	120	30	55S		118	5 E	
Muktsar	89	30	30N		74	30 E	
Mulchén	190	37	45S		72	20W	
Mulgrave	149	45	38N		61	31W	
Mulhacén	50	37	4N		3	20W	
Mülheim	42	51	26N		6	53 E	
Mulhouse	37	47	40N		7	20 E	
Mull	30	56	27N		6	0W	
Muller, Pegunungan	111	0	30N		113	30 E	
Mullet Pen.	34	54	10N		10	2W	
Mullewa	120	28	29S		115	30 E	
Mullingar	34	53	31N		7	20W	
Mullumbimby	116	28	30S		153	30 E	
Multan	89	30	15N		71	36 E	
Muna	113	5	0S		122	30 E	
München	43	48	8N		11	33 E	
München-Gladbach = Mönchengladbach	42	51	12N		6	23 E	
Muncie	167	40	10N		85	20W	
Mundo Novo	189	11	50S		40	29W	
Mungana	121	17	8S		144	27 E	
Munger	92	25	23N		86	30 E	

Munich = München	43	48	8N	11 33 E
Munising	150	46	25N	86 39W
Munku-Sardyk	74	51	45N	100 20 E
Münster	42	51	58N	7 37 E
Munster □	35	52	20N	8 40W
Muqdisho	133	2	2N	45 25 E
Murallón, Cuerro	192	49	48S	73 30W
Murchison →	120	27	45S	114 0 E
Murchison Falls = Kabarega				
Falls	132	2	15N	31 30 E
Murcia	51	38	20N	1 10W
Murcia □	51	37	50N	1 30W
Mureş →	56	46	15N	20 13 E
Mureşul = Mureş →	56	46	15N	20 13 E
Murfreesboro	169	35	50N	86 21W
Murgon	116	26	15S	151 54 E
Müritz See	43	53	25N	12 40 E
Murmansk	69	68	57N	33 10 E
Muroran	103	42	25N	141 0 E
Muroto	109	33	18N	134 9 E
Muroto-Misaki	109	33	15N	134 10 E
Murphysboro	166	37	50N	89 20W
Murray	169	36	40N	88 20W
Murray →	119	35	20S	139 22 E
Murray Bridge	119	35	6S	139 14 E
Murrumbidgee →	117	34	43S	143 12 E
Murrurundi	116	31	42S	150 51 E
Murtoa	119	36	35S	142 28 E
Murupara	122	38	28S	176 42 E
Murwillumbah	116	28	18S	153 27 E
Muş	81	38	45N	41 30 E
Musashino	107	35	42N	139 34 E
Muscat = Masqat	83	23	37N	58 36 E
Muscat & Oman = Oman ■	83	23	0N	58 0 E
Muscatine	166	41	25N	91 5W
Musgrave Ras.	114	26	0S	132 0 E
Musi →	111	2	20S	104 56 E
Muskegon	167	43	15N	86 17W
Muskegon →	167	43	25N	86 0W
Muskegon Hts.	167	43	12N	86 17W
Muskogee	168	35	50N	95 25W
Musselburgh	31	55	57N	3 3W
Muswellbrook	116	32	16S	150 56 E
Mutare	137	18	58S	32 38 E
Mutsu	103	41	5N	140 55 E
Mutsu-Wan	103	41	5N	140 55 E
Muzaffargarh	89	30	5N	71 14 E
Muzaffarnagar	89	29	26N	77 40 E
Muzaffarpur	92	26	7N	85 23 E
Mwanza	135	2	30S	32 58 E
Mweru, L.	135	9	0S	28 40 E
My Tho	95	10	29N	106 23 E
Myanaung	93	18	18N	95 22 E
Myeik Kyunzu	94	11	30N	97 30 E
Myingyan	93	21	30N	95 20 E
Myitkyina	93	25	24N	97 26 E
Mýrdalsjökull	64	63	40N	19 6W
Myrtle Point	171	43	0N	124 4W
Mysore = Karnataka □ ..	90	13	15N	77 0 E
Mysore	90	12	17N	76 41 E

N

Naaldwijk	40	51	59N	4 13 E
Nabari	106	34	37N	136 5 E
Naberezhnyye Chelny	68	55	42N	52 19 E
Nablus = Nābulus	80	32	14N	35 15 E
Nābulus	80	32	14N	35 15 E
Nacogdoches	168	31	33N	94 39W
Nacozari	174	30	24N	109 39W
Nadiad	91	22	41N	72 56 E
Nadym	69	65	35N	72 42 E
Nagahama	106	35	23N	136 16 E
Nagaland □	93	26	0N	94 30 E
Nagano	107	36	40N	138 10 E
Nagaoka	105	37	27N	138 51 E
Nagappattinam	90	10	46N	79 51 E
Nagasaki	108	32	47N	129 50 E

Nagato	108	34	19N	131 5 E
Nagercoil	90	8	12N	77 26 E
Nagornyy	75	55	58N	124 57 E
Nagoya	106	35	10N	136 50 E
Nagpur	91	21	8N	79 10 E
Nahanni Butte	144	61	2N	123 31W
Nahāvand	84	34	10N	48 22 E
Naicam	152	52	30N	104 30W
Nain	147	56	34N	61 40W
Nainpur	91	22	30N	80 10 E
Nairn	33	57	35N	3 54W
Nairobi	132	1	17S	36 48 E
Naivasha	132	0	40S	36 30 E
Najafābād	85	32	40N	51 15 E
Najibabad	89	29	40N	78 20 E
Naka →	107	36	20N	140 36 E
Naka-no-Shima	104	29	51N	129 46 E
Nakama	108	33	56N	130 43 E
Nakamura	109	33	0N	133 0 E
Nakano	107	36	45N	138 22 E
Nakanojō	107	36	35N	138 51 E
Nakatsu	108	33	34N	131 15 E
Nakatsugawa	106	35	29N	137 30 E
Nakhichevan □	70	39	25N	45 26 E
Nakhodka	75	42	53N	132 54 E
Nakhon Phanom	95	17	23N	104 43 E
Nakhon Ratchasima	95	14	59N	102 12 E
Nakhon Sawan	94	15	35N	100 10 E
Nakhon Si Thammarat ...	96	8	29N	100 0 E
Nakina	140	50	10N	86 40W
Nakskov	61	54	50N	11 8 E
Nakuru	132	0	15S	36 4 E
Nalchik	70	43	30N	43 33 E
Nalgonda	91	17	6N	79 15 E
Nam Co	101	30	30N	90 45 E
Nam Dinh	95	20	25N	106 5 E
Nam-Phan	95	10	30N	106 0 E
Nam Tha	95	20	58N	101 30 E
Nam Tok	94	14	21N	99 4 E
Namaland	136	24	30S	17 0 E
Namangan	71	41	0N	71 40 E
Namaqualand	136	30	0S	17 25 E
Nambour	116	26	32S	152 58 E
Nambucca Heads	116	30	37S	153 0 E
Namerikawa	106	36	46N	137 20 E
Namib Desert = Namib-				
Woestyn	124	22	30S	15 0 E
Namib-Woestyn	124	22	30S	15 0 E
Namibe	134	15	7S	12 11 E
Namibia ■	136	22	0S	18 9 E
Nampa	171	43	34N	116 34W
Namsos	65	64	29N	11 30 E
Namur	42	50	27N	4 52 E
Nanaimo	154	49	10N	124 0W
Nanango	116	26	40S	152 0 E
Nanao	105	37	0N	137 0 E
Nanchang	99	28	42N	115 55 E
Nanching = Nanjing	99	32	2N	118 47 E
Nanching	99	32	3N	118 47 E
Nancy	37	48	42N	6 12 E
Nanda Devi	101	30	23N	79 59 E
Nandan	109	34	10N	134 42 E
Nanded	91	19	10N	77 20 E
Nandurbar	91	21	20N	74 15 E
Nanga Parbat	89	35	10N	74 35 E
Nangarhár □	87	34	20N	70 0 E
Nanjing	99	32	2N	118 47 E
Nanking = Nanching	99	32	3N	118 47 E
Nanking = Nanjing	99	32	2N	118 47 E
Nankoku	109	33	39N	133 44 E
Nanning	99	22	48N	108 20 E
Nanping	99	26	38N	118 10 E
Nantes	36	47	12N	1 33W
Nanticoke	164	41	12N	76 1W
Nanton	155	50	21N	113 46W
Nanuque	189	17	50S	40 21W
Napa	172	38	18N	122 17W
Napier	122	39	30S	176 56 E
Naples = Nápoli	49	40	50N	14 17 E
Napo →	186	3	20S	72 40W
Nápoli	49	40	50N	14 17 E

Name	No.	Lat °	Lat ′ Dir	Long °	Long ′ Dir
Nara, Japan	106	34	40N	135	49 E
Nara, Mali	130	15	10N	7	20W
Naracoorte	119	36	58S	140	45 E
Narasapur	92	16	26N	81	40 E
Narayanganj	92	23	40N	90	33 E
Narayanpet	91	16	45N	77	30 E
Narbonne	37	43	11N	3	0 E
Narita	107	35	47N	140	19 E
Narmada →	91	21	38N	72	36 E
Narooma	117	36	14S	150	4 E
Narrabri	116	30	19S	149	46 E
Narrandera	117	34	42S	146	31 E
Narrogin	120	32	58S	117	14 E
Narromine	116	32	12S	148	12 E
Naruto	109	34	11N	134	37 E
Narvik	64	68	28N	17	26 E
Narym	71	59	0N	81	30 E
Naser, Buheirat en	128	23	0N	32	30 E
Nashua	164	42	50N	71	25W
Nashville	169	36	12N	86	46W
Nasik	91	19	58N	73	50 E
Nasirabad	91	26	15N	74	45 E
Nassau	178	25	0N	77	20W
Nasser, L. = Naser, Buheirat en	128	23	0N	32	30 E
Nässjö	60	57	39N	14	42 E
Natal	189	5	47S	35	13W
Natashquan	149	50	14N	61	46W
Natchez	168	31	35N	91	25W
Natchitoches	168	31	47N	93	4W
Nathalia	117	36	1S	145	13 E
National City	173	32	39N	117	7W
Natuna Besar, Kepulauan	111	4	0N	108	15 E
Natuna Selatan, Kepulauan	111	2	45N	109	0 E
Nauru ■	122	1	0S	166	0 E
Nauta	186	4	31S	73	35W
Nautanwa	92	27	20N	83	25 E
Nautla	177	20	20N	96	50W
Navarra □	51	42	40N	1	40W
Navojoa	174	27	0N	109	30W
Navsari	91	20	57N	72	59 E
Nawabshah	88	26	15N	68	25 E
Nawalgarh	89	27	50N	75	15 E
Náxos	55	37	8N	25	25 E
Nāy Band	87	27	20N	52	40 E
Nayakhan	73	61	56N	159	0 E
Nayarit □	175	22	0N	105	0W
Ndélé	129	8	25N	20	36 E
Ndjamena	131	12	10N	14	59 E
Ndola	135	13	0S	28	34 E
Neagh, Lough	34	54	35N	6	25W
Near Is.	142	53	0N	172	0 E
Neath	27	51	39N	3	49W
Nebraska □	163	41	30N	100	0W
Nebraska City	166	40	40N	95	52W
Nebrodi Mts.	49	37	55N	14	45 E
Neches →	168	29	55N	93	52W
Neckar →	42	49	31N	8	26 E
Necochea	190	38	30S	58	50W
Needles, The	24	50	39N	1	35W
Neenah	167	44	10N	88	30W
Neepawa	153	50	15N	99	30W
Negapatam = Nagappattinam	90	10	46N	79	51 E
Negeri Sembilan □	96	2	45N	102	10 E
Negotin	53	44	16N	22	37 E
Negra, Pta.	186	6	6S	81	10W
Negro →, Argentina	190	41	2S	62	47W
Negro →, Brazil	185	3	0S	60	0W
Negros	112	9	30N	122	40 E
Nehbandān	85	31	35N	60	5 E
Nei Monggol Zizhiqu □	98	42	0N	112	0 E
Neijiang	99	29	35N	104	55 E
Neiva	184	2	56N	75	18W
Nellore	90	14	27N	79	59 E
Nelson, Canada	155	49	30N	117	20W
Nelson, N.Z.	123	41	18S	173	16 E
Nelson, U.K.	28	53	50N	2	14W
Nelson →	153	54	33N	98	2W
Néma	126	16	40N	7	15W
Neman →	68	55	25N	21	10 E
Nemours	39	48	16N	2	40 E
Nemunas = Neman → ...	68	55	25N	21	10 E
Nemuro	103	43	20N	145	35 E
Nemuro-Kaikyō	103	43	30N	145	30 E
Nenagh	35	52	52N	8	11W
Nenana	142	64	30N	149	20W
Nene →	29	52	38N	0	13 E
Neosho	168	36	56N	94	28W
Neosho →	168	35	59N	95	10W
Nepal ■	92	28	0N	84	30 E
Nephi	162	39	43N	111	52W
Ness, Loch	33	57	15N	4	30W
Netanya	80	32	20N	34	51 E
Netherlands ■	41	52	0N	5	30 E
Netherlands Antilles ■	181	12	15N	69	0W
Netherlands Guiana = Surinam ■	185	4	0N	56	0W
Nettilling L.	146	66	30N	71	0W
Netzahualcoyotl, Presa	177	17	10N	93	30W
Neuchâtel	44	47	0N	6	55 E
Neuchâtel, Lac de	44	46	53N	6	50 E
Neuquén	190	38	55S	68	0 E
Neuse →	165	35	5N	76	30W
Neusiedler See	45	47	50N	16	47 E
Nevada	166	37	51N	94	22W
Nevada □	172	39	20N	117	0W
Nevada, Sierra, Spain	50	37	3N	3	15W
Nevada, Sierra, U.S.A.	172	39	0N	120	30W
Nevada City	172	39	20N	121	0W
Nevada de Sta. Marta, Sa.	184	10	55N	73	50W
Nevers	37	47	0N	3	9 E
New Albany	167	38	20N	85	50W
New Amsterdam	185	6	15N	57	36W
New Bedford	164	41	40N	70	52W
New Bern	165	35	8N	77	3W
New Braunfels	161	29	43N	98	9W
New Brighton	123	43	29S	172	43 E
New Britain, Papua N. G.	115	5	50S	150	20 E
New Britain, U.S.A.	164	41	41N	72	47W
New Brunswick	164	40	30N	74	28W
New Brunswick □	148	46	50N	66	30W
New Caledonia = Nouvelle Calédonie	122	21	0S	165	0 E
New Castile = Castilla La Nueva	50	39	45N	3	20W
New Castle, Ind., U.S.A.	164	39	55N	85	23W
New Castle, Pa., U.S.A.	164	41	0N	80	20W
New England Ra.	116	30	20S	151	45 E
New Forest	24	50	53N	1	40W
New Glasgow	149	45	35N	62	36W
New Hampshire □	164	43	40N	71	40W
New Haven	164	41	20N	72	54W
New Hebrides = Vanuatu ■	122	15	0S	168	0 E
New Iberia	168	30	2N	91	54W
New Ireland	115	3	20S	151	50 E
New Jersey □	164	40	30N	74	10W
New Kensington	164	40	36N	79	43W
New London	164	41	23N	72	8W
New Mexico □	161	34	30N	106	0W
New Norfolk	119	42	46S	147	2 E
New Orleans	169	30	0N	90	5W
New Philadelphia	164	40	29N	81	25W
New Plymouth	122	39	4S	174	5 E
New Providence	178	25	25N	78	35W
New Radnor	26	52	15N	3	10W
New Siberian Is. = Novosibirskiye Ostrova	72	75	0N	142	0 E
New South Wales □	116	33	0S	146	0 E
New Ulm	166	44	15N	94	30W
New Waterford	149	46	13N	60	4W
New Westminster	154	49	13N	122	55W
New York □	164	42	40N	76	0W
New York City	164	40	45N	74	0W
New Zealand ■	122	40	0S	176	0 E
Newark, N.J., U.S.A.	164	40	41N	74	12W
Newark, N.Y., U.S.A.	164	43	2N	77	10W
Newark, Ohio, U.S.A.	167	40	5N	82	24W
Newark-on-Trent	29	53	6N	0	48W
Newberry, Mich., U.S.A.	150	46	20N	85	32W
Newberry, S.C., U.S.A.	165	34	17N	81	37W
Newburgh	164	41	30N	74	1W
Newburyport	164	42	48N	70	50W

Place	Page	Lat	Long
Newcastle, Australia	117	33 0S	151 46 E
Newcastle, Canada	148	47 1N	65 38W
Newcastle, U.K.	34	54 13N	5 54W
Newcastle Emlyn	26	52 2N	4 29W
Newcastle-under-Lyme	28	53 2N	2 15W
Newcastle-upon-Tyne	28	54 59N	1 37W
Newfoundland □	149	53 0N	58 0W
Newhaven	25	50 47N	0 4 E
Newmarket	25	52 15N	0 23 E
Newnan	170	33 22N	84 48W
Newport, Gwent, U.K.	27	51 35N	3 0W
Newport, I. of W., U.K.	25	50 42N	1 18W
Newport, Ark., U.S.A.	168	35 38N	91 15W
Newport, Ky., U.S.A.	167	39 5N	84 23W
Newport, Oreg., U.S.A.	171	44 41N	124 2W
Newport, R.I., U.S.A.	164	41 13N	71 19W
Newport, Vt., U.S.A.	148	44 57N	72 17W
Newport Beach	173	33 40N	117 58W
Newport News	165	37 2N	76 30W
Newquay	27	50 24N	5 6W
Newry	34	54 10N	6 20W
Newton, Iowa, U.S.A.	166	41 40N	93 3W
Newton, Mass., U.S.A.	164	42 21N	71 10W
Newton Abbot	27	50 32N	3 37W
Newton Stewart	31	54 57N	4 30W
Newtonmore	33	57 4N	4 7W
Newtown	26	52 31N	3 19W
Newtownards	34	54 37N	5 40W
Ngaoundéré	131	7 15N	13 35 E
Ngoring Hu	101	34 55N	97 5 E
Nguru	131	12 56N	10 29 E
Nha Trang	95	12 16N	109 10 E
Nhill	119	36 18S	141 40 E
Niagara Falls, Canada	151	43 7N	79 5W
Niagara Falls, U.S.A.	164	43 5N	79 0W
Niamey	131	13 27N	2 6 E
Nias	111	1 0N	97 30 E
Nicaragua ■	179	11 40N	85 30W
Nicaragua, Lago de	179	12 0N	85 30W
Nice	37	43 42N	7 14 E
Nichinan	108	31 38N	131 23 E
Nicobar Is.	8	9 0N	93 0 E
Nicosia	80	35 10N	33 25 E
Nicoya, Pen. de	179	9 45N	85 40W
Nidd →	28	54 1N	1 32W
Niederösterreich □	45	48 25N	15 40 E
Niedersachsen □	42	52 45N	9 0 E
Nieuw Nickerie	185	6 0N	56 59W
Niger ■	131	13 30N	10 0 E
Niger →	131	5 33N	6 33 E
Nigeria ■	131	8 30N	8 0 E
Nii-Jima	107	34 20N	139 15 E
Niigata	103	37 58N	139 0 E
Niihama	109	33 55N	133 16 E
Niimi	109	34 59N	133 28 E
Nijkerk	41	52 13N	5 30 E
Nijmegen	41	51 50N	5 52 E
Nikki	131	9 58N	3 12 E
Nikkō	107	36 45N	139 35 E
Nikolayev	68	46 58N	32 0 E
Nikolayevsk-na-Amur	75	53 8N	140 44 E
Nikolskoye	73	55 12N	166 0 E
Nikšić	52	42 50N	18 57 E
Nîl, Nahr en →	128	30 10N	31 6 E
Nîl el Abyad →	129	15 38N	32 31 E
Nîl el Azraq →	129	15 38N	32 31 E
Nile = Nîl, Nahr en →	128	30 10N	31 6 E
Niles	164	41 8N	80 40W
Nîmes	37	43 50N	4 23 E
Nimule	129	3 32N	32 3 E
Nīnawá	81	36 25N	43 10 E
Nineveh = Nînawá	81	36 25N	43 10 E
Ningbo	99	29 51N	121 28 E
Ningde	99	26 38N	119 23 E
Ningpo = Ningbo	99	29 51N	121 28 E
Ningsia Hui A.R. = Ningxia Huizu Zizhiqu □	98	38 0N	106 0 E
Ningxia Huizu Zizhiqu □	98	38 0N	106 0 E
Niobrara →	163	42 45N	98 0W
Nioro du Sahel	130	15 15N	9 30W
Niort	36	46 19N	0 29W
Nipawin	152	53 20N	104 0W
Nipigon	150	49 0N	88 17W
Nipigon, L.	150	49 50N	88 30W
Niš	53	43 19N	21 58 E
Nişāb	83	14 25N	46 29 E
Nishinomiya	106	34 45N	135 20 E
Nishio	106	34 52N	137 3 E
Nishiwaki	109	34 59N	134 58 E
Niterói	188	22 52S	43 0W
Nith →	31	55 20N	3 5W
Nitra	59	48 19N	18 4 E
Nivernais	37	47 0N	3 40 E
Nizamabad	91	18 45N	78 7 E
Nizhne Kolymsk	73	68 34N	160 55 E
Nizhneudinsk	74	54 54N	99 3 E
Nizhnevartovsk	69	60 56N	76 38 E
Nizhniy Novgorod	68	56 20N	44 0 E
Nizhniy Tagil	69	57 55N	59 57 E
Nizhnyaya Tunguska →	74	64 20N	93 0 E
Nizké Tatry	59	48 55N	20 0 E
Nkongsamba	131	4 55N	9 55 E
Noatak	142	67 32N	162 59W
Nobeoka	108	32 36N	131 41 E
Noda	107	35 56N	139 52 E
Nogales	174	31 20N	110 56W
Nōgata	108	33 48N	130 44 E
Nogent-le-Rotrou	39	48 20N	0 50 E
Noi →	94	14 50N	100 15 E
Noirmoutier, Î. de	36	46 58N	2 10W
Nojima-Zaki	107	34 54N	139 53 E
Nok Kundi	88	28 50N	62 45 E
Nome	142	64 30N	165 24W
Nong Khae	95	14 29N	100 53 E
Nong Khai	95	17 50N	102 46 E
Nonoava	174	27 28N	106 44W
Noord Brabant □	40	51 40N	5 0 E
Noord Holland □	40	52 30N	4 45 E
Noordbeveland	40	51 35N	3 50 E
Noordoostpolder	41	52 45N	5 45 E
Noordwijk aan Zee	40	52 14N	4 26 E
Nootka I.	154	49 32N	126 42W
Nord-Trøndelag fylke □	65	64 20N	12 0 E
Nordaustlandet	13	79 14N	23 0 E
Nordegg	155	52 29N	116 5W
Nordkapp	67	71 10N	25 44 E
Nordkinn	67	71 8N	27 40 E
Nordland fylke □	65	65 40N	13 0 E
Nordrhein-Westfalen □	42	51 45N	7 30 E
Nordvik	72	74 2N	111 32 E
Nore →	35	52 40N	7 20W
Norfolk	165	36 40N	76 15W
Norfolk □	29	52 39N	1 0 E
Norfolk I.	122	28 58S	168 3 E
Norilsk	72	69 20N	88 6 E
Norman	168	35 12N	97 30W
Norman Wells	144	65 17N	126 51W
Normandie	39	48 45N	0 10 E
Normandin	151	48 49N	72 31W
Normandy = Normandie	39	48 45N	0 10 E
Normanton	115	17 40S	141 10 E
Norquinco	192	41 51S	70 55W
Norristown	164	40 9N	75 21W
Norrköping	60	58 37N	16 11 E
Norrland □	66	66 50N	18 0 E
Norseman	114	32 8S	121 43 E
Norsk	75	52 30N	130 0 E
North Andaman I.	94	13 15N	92 40 E
North Battleford	152	52 50N	108 17W
North Bay	151	46 20N	79 30W
North Bend	171	43 28N	124 14W
North Berwick	31	56 4N	2 44W
North C.	122	34 23S	173 4 E
North Carolina □	165	35 30N	80 0W
North Channel, Br. Is.	30	55 0N	5 30W
North Channel, Canada	150	46 0N	83 0W
North Dakota □	163	47 30N	100 0W
North Downs	25	51 17N	0 30 E
North European Plain	17	55 0N	20 0 E
North I.	122	38 0S	175 0 E
North Korea ■	98	40 0N	127 0 E
North Minch	32	58 5N	5 55W

Name	Page	Lat °	′	N/S	Long °	′	E/W
North Ossetia □	70	43	30	N	44	30	E
North Platte	163	41	10	N	100	50	W
North Platte ~➤	163	41	15	N	100	45	W
North Pole	12	90	0	N	0	0	E
North Ronaldsay	33	59	20	N	2	30	W
North Saskatchewan ~➤	143	53	15	N	105	5	W
North Sea	16	56	0	N	4	0	E
North Sentinel I.	94	11	35	N	92	15	E
North Sporades = Voriai Sporádhes	55	39	15	N	23	30	E
North Sydney	149	46	12	N	60	15	W
North Tonawanda	164	43	5	N	78	50	W
North Uist	32	57	40	N	7	15	W
North Vancouver	154	49	25	N	123		3W
North Walsham	29	52	49	N	1	22	E
North West Frontier □	89	34	0	N	71	0	E
North West Highlands	32	57	35	N	5		2W
North West River	147	53	30	N	60	10	W
North West Territories □	145	67	0	N	110	0	W
North York Moors	29	54	25	N	0	50	W
North Yorkshire □	28	54	15	N	1	25	W
Northallerton	28	54	20	N	1	26	W
Northam	120	31	35	S	116	42	E
Northampton, Australia	120	28	27	S	114	33	E
Northampton, U.K.	25	52	14	N	0	54	W
Northampton, U.S.A.	164	42	22	N	72	31	W
Northampton □	25	52	16	N	0	55	W
Northcliffe	120	34	39	S	116	7	E
Northern Circars	92	17	30	N	82	30	E
Northern Ireland □	34	54	45	N	7	0	W
Northern Territory □	114	16	0	S	133	0	E
Northfield	166	44	30	N	93	10	W
Northumberland □	28	55	12	N	2	0	W
Northumberland Is.	121	21	30	S	149	50	E
Northumberland Str.	148	46	20	N	64	0	W
Northwich	28	53	16	N	2	30	W
Norton Sd.	142	64	0	N	164	0	W
Norwalk	164	41	9	N	73	25	W
Norway ■	18	63	0	N	11	0	E
Norwegian Sea	16	66	0	N	1	0	E
Norwich	29	52	38	N	1	17	E
Nos Kaliakra	53	43	21	N	28	30	E
Noshiro	103	40	12	N	140	0	E
Noss Hd.	33	58	29	N	3		4W
Nossob ~➤	136	26	55	S	20	37	E
Noteć ~➤	58	52	44	N	15	26	E
Notre Dame de Koartac = Koartac	146	60	55	N	69	40	W
Nottaway ~➤	140	51	22	N	78	55	W
Nottingham	29	52	57	N	1	10	W
Nottingham □	29	53	10	N	1	0	W
Nouâdhibou	126	20	54	N	17	0	W
Nouâdhibou, Ras	126	20	50	N	17	0	W
Nouakchott	126	18	9	N	15	58	W
Noumea	122	22	17	S	166	30	E
Nouveau Comptoir	140	53	0	N	78	49	W
Nouvelle Calédonie	122	21	0	S	165	0	E
Nova Friburgo	188	22	16	S	42	30	W
Nova Granada	188	20	30	S	49	20	W
Nova Lisboa = Huambo	134	12	42	S	15	54	E
Nova Scotia □	149	45	10	N	63	0	W
Novara	46	45	27	N	8	36	E
Novaya Sibir, Ostrov	72	75	10	N	150	0	E
Novaya Zemlya	69	75	0	N	56	0	E
Novgorod	68	58	30	N	31	25	E
Novi Pazar	52	43	12	N	20	28	E
Novi Sad	52	45	18	N	19	52	E
Novocherkassk	68	47	27	N	40	5	E
Novokuznetsk	71	53	45	N	87	10	E
Novomoskovsk	68	54	5	N	38	15	E
Novorossiysk	68	44	43	N	37	46	E
Novosibirsk	71	55	0	N	83	5	E
Novosibirskiye Ostrova	72	75	0	N	142	0	E
Nowgong	93	26	20	N	92	50	E
Nowra	117	34	53	S	150	35	E
Nowy Sącz	59	49	40	N	20	41	E
Noyon	38	49	34	N	3	0	E
Nûbîya, Es Sahrâ En	129	21	30	N	33	30	E
Nueces ~➤	161	27	50	N	97	30	W
Nueltin L.	145	60	30	N	99	30	W
Nueva Gerona	178	21	53	N	82	49	W
Nueva Rosita	174	27	57	N	101	13	W
Nuevitas	178	21	30	N	77	20	W
Nuevo Laredo	176	27	30	N	99	30	W
Nuevo Leon □	176	25	40	N	100	0	W
Nuhaka	122	39	3	S	177	45	E
Nukey Bluff, Mt.	118	32	26	S	135	29	E
Nukus	70	42	20	N	59	7	E
Nulato	142	64	40	N	158	10	W
Nullarbor Plain	114	30	45	S	129	0	E
Numan	131	9	29	N	12	3	E
Numazu	107	35	7	N	138	51	E
Numurkah	117	36	5	S	145	26	E
Nuneaton	25	52	32	N	1	29	W
Nunivak	142	60	0	N	166	0	W
Nunspeet	41	52	21	N	5	45	E
Nuoro	48	40	20	N	9	20	E
Nuremburg = Nürnberg	43	49	26	N	11	5	E
Nuriootpa	119	34	27	S	139	0	E
Nürnberg	43	49	26	N	11	5	E
Nurran, L. = Terewah, L.	116	29	52	S	147	35	E
Nutak	147	57	28	N	61	59	W
Nuweveldberge	136	32	10	S	21	45	E
Nuyts Arch.	118	32	35	S	133	20	E
Nyaake	130	4	52	N	7	37	W
Nyainqentanglha Shan	101	30	0	N	90	0	E
Nyasa, L. = Malawi, L.	137	12	30	S	34	30	E
Nyíregyháza	59	47	58	N	21	47	E
Nyngan	116	31	30	S	147	8	E
Nysa	58	50	30	N	17	22	E

O

Name	Page	Lat °	′	N/S	Long °	′	E/W
Oahe L.	163	45	30	N	100	25	W
Oahu	160	21	30	N	158	0	W
Oak Hill	165	38	0	N	81	7	W
Oak Park	167	41	55	N	87	45	W
Oak Ridge	169	36	1	N	84	12	W
Oakengates	28	52	42	N	2	29	W
Oakey	116	27	25	S	151	43	E
Oakham	29	52	40	N	0	43	W
Oakland	172	37	50	N	122	18	W
Oakridge	171	43	47	N	122	31	W
Oamaru	123	45	5	S	170	59	E
Oaxaca	177	17	2	N	96	40	W
Oaxaca □	177	17	0	N	96	30	W
Ob ~➤	69	66	45	N	69	30	E
Oba	150	49	4	N	84	7	W
Obama	106	35	30	N	135	45	E
Oban	30	56	25	N	5	30	W
Obbia	133	5	25	N	48	30	E
Oberhausen	42	51	28	N	6	50	E
Oberon	117	33	45	S	149	52	E
Oberösterreich □	45	48	10	N	14	0	E
Obi, Is.	113	1	30	S	127	30	E
Obihiro	103	42	56	N	143	12	E
Obskaya Guba	69	69	0	N	73	0	E
Ocala	170	29	11	N	82	5	W
Ocampo	174	28	11	N	108	23	W
Ocaña	184	8	15	N	73	20	W
Occidental, Cordillera	184	5	0	N	76	0	W
Ocean City	164	39	18	N	74	34	W
Oceanside	173	33	13	N	117	26	W
Ochil Hills	31	56	14	N	3	40	W
Oconee ~➤	170	31	58	N	82	32	W
Oconto	167	44	52	N	87	53	W
Ocotlán	175	20	21	N	102	46	W
Ōda	109	35	11	N	132	30	E
Ódáðahraun	64	65	5	N	17	0	W
Odate	103	40	16	N	140	34	E
Odawara	107	35	20	N	139	6	E
Ödemiş	80	38	15	N	28	0	E
Odense	61	55	22	N	10	23	E
Oder ~➤	58	53	33	N	14	38	E
Odessa, Ukraine	68	46	30	N	30	45	E
Odessa, U.S.A.	161	31	51	N	102	23	W
Odra ~➤	58	53	33	N	14	38	E
Odžak	52	45	3	N	18	18	E
Offaly □	35	53	15	N	7	30	W

Name	Page	°	′		°	′	
Offenbach	42	50	6N		8	46	E
Oga-Hantō	103	39	58N		139	47	E
Ogaden	133	7	30N		45	30	E
Ōgaki	106	35	21N		136	37	E
Ogbomosho	131	8	1N		4	11	E
Ogden	163	41	13N		112	1	W
Ogdensburg	151	44	40N		75	27	W
Ohio □	167	40	20N		14	10	E
Ohio ⟶	167	38	0N		86	0	W
Ohrid	52	41	8N		20	52	E
Ohridsko, Jezero	52	41	8N		20	52	E
Oil City	164	41	26N		79	40	W
Oise ⟶	38	49	0N		2	4	E
Oisterwijk	40	51	35N		5	12	E
Ōita	108	33	14N		131	36	E
Ojos del Salado, Cerro	190	27	0S		68	40	W
Oka ⟶	68	56	20N		43	59	E
Okawa	108	33	9N		130	21	E
Okaya	107	36	0N		138	10	E
Okayama	109	34	40N		133	54	E
Okazaki	106	34	57N		137	10	E
Okeechobee, L.	170	27	0N		80	50	W
Okehampton	27	50	44N		4	1	W
Okha	75	53	40N		143	0	E
Okhotsk	75	59	20N		143	10	E
Okhotsk, Sea of	77	55	0N		145	0	E
Okhotsko Kolymskoye	73	63	0N		157	0	E
Oki-no-Shima	109	32	44N		132	33	E
Oki-Shotō	109	36	5N		133	15	E
Okinawa-Jima	99	26	32N		128	0	E
Oklahoma □	161	35	20N		97	30	W
Oklahoma City	161	35	25N		97	30	W
Okmulgee	168	35	38N		96	0	W
Oktabrsk	70	49	28N		57	25	E
Oktyabrskoy Revolyutsii, Os.	72	79	30N		97	0	E
Oktyabrskoye	69	62	28N		66	3	E
Ōkuchi	108	32	4N		130	37	E
Okuru	123	43	55S		168	55	E
Okushiri-Tō	103	42	15N		139	30	E
Olanchito	179	15	30N		86	30	W
Öland	61	56	45N		16	38	E
Olary	118	32	18S		140	19	E
Olavarría	190	36	55S		60	20	W
Old Castile = Castilla La Vieja	50	41	55N		4	0	W
Old Town	148	45	0N		68	41	W
Oldenburg	42	53	10N		8	10	E
Oldenzaal	41	52	19N		6	53	E
Oldham	28	53	33N		2	8	W
Olds	155	51	50N		114	10	W
Olekma ⟶	74	60	22N		120	42	E
Olekminsk	74	60	25N		120	30	E
Olenek	72	68	28N		112	18	E
Olenek ⟶	72	73	0N		120	10	E
Oléron, Île d'	36	45	55N		1	15	W
Oleśnica	58	51	13N		17	22	E
Olifants ⟶	137	24	5S		31	20	E
Ólimbos, Óros	54	40	6N		22	23	E
Oliveira	188	20	39S		44	50	W
Oliver	155	49	13N		119	37	W
Ollagüe	187	21	15S		68	10	W
Olney	167	38	40N		88	0	W
Olomouc	59	49	38N		17	12	E
Olsztyn	58	53	48N		20	29	E
Olt ⟶	57	43	50N		24	40	E
Olympia, Greece	54	37	39N		21	39	E
Olympia, U.S.A.	171	47	0N		122	58	W
Olympic Mts.	171	47	50N		123	45	W
Olympus, Mt. = Ólimbos, Óros	54	40	6N		22	23	E
Olympus, Mt.	171	47	52N		123	40	W
Ōmachi	107	36	30N		137	50	E
Omae-Zaki	107	34	36N		138	14	E
Omagh	34	54	36N		7	20	W
Omaha	166	41	15N		96	0	W
Omak	171	48	24N		119	31	W
Oman ■	83	23	0N		58	0	E
Oman, G. of	83	24	30N		58	30	E
Omdurmân	129	15	40N		32	28	E
Ōme	107	35	47N		139	15	E
Omeo	117	37	6S		147	36	E
Omihachiman	106	35	7N		136	3	E
Ōmiya	107	35	54N		139	38	E
Omo ⟶	132	6	25N		36	10	E
Omolon ⟶	73	68	42N		158	36	E
Omono-Gawa ⟶	103	39	46N		140	3	E
Omsk	71	55	0N		73	12	E
Ōmura	108	32	56N		130	0	E
Ōmuta	108	33	0N		130	26	E
Onega	68	64	0N		38	10	E
Onega, L. = Onezhskoye Ozero	68	62	0N		35	30	E
Onehunga	122	36	55S		174	48	E
Oneida	164	43	5N		75	40	W
Onekotan, Ostrov	75	49	25N		154	45	E
Onezhskoye Ozero	68	62	0N		35	30	E
Ongerup	120	33	58S		118	28	E
Ongole	90	15	33N		80	2	E
Onguren	74	53	38N		107	36	E
Onitsha	131	6	6N		6	42	E
Ono, Fukui, Japan	106	35	59N		136	29	E
Ono, Hyōgo, Japan	109	34	51N		134	56	E
Onoda	108	34	2N		131	25	E
Onomichi	109	34	25N		133	12	E
Onslow	114	21	40S		115	12	E
Onslow B.	165	34	20N		77	20	W
Ontake-San	106	35	53N		137	29	E
Ontario	173	34	2N		117	40	W
Ontario □	140	52	0N		88	10	W
Ontario, L.	151	43	40N		78	0	W
Oodnadatta	118	27	33S		135	30	E
Ooldea	114	30	27S		131	50	E
Oostende	42	51	15N		2	50	E
Oosterhout	40	51	39N		4	47	E
Oosterschelde	40	51	33N		4	0	E
Opala	73	51	58N		156	30	E
Opava	58	49	57N		17	58	E
Opelousas	168	30	35N		92	7	W
Ophir	142	63	10N		156	40	W
Opole	58	50	42N		17	58	E
Oporto = Porto	50	41	8N		8	40	W
Opp	169	31	19N		86	13	W
Oppland fylke □	60	61	15N		9	40	E
Opua	122	35	19S		174	9	E
Oradea	56	47	2N		21	58	E
Öræfajökull	64	64	2N		16	39	W
Orai	91	25	58N		79	30	E
Oran, Algeria	127	35	45N		0	39	W
Oran, Argentina	190	23	10S		64	20	W
Orange, Australia	117	33	15S		149	7	E
Orange, France	37	44	8N		4	47	E
Orange, U.S.A.	168	30	10N		93	50	W
Orange ⟶ = Oranje ⟶	136	28	41S		16	28	E
Orange, C.	185	4	20N		51	30	W
Orangeburg	170	33	35N		80	53	W
Oranje ⟶	136	28	41S		16	28	E
Oraşul Stalin = Braşov	57	45	38N		25	35	E
Orbost	117	37	40S		148	29	E
Orchies	38	50	28N		3	14	E
Ordos = Mu Us Shamo	98	39	0N		109	0	E
Ordu	81	40	55N		37	53	E
Ordzhonikidze = Vladikavkaz	70	43	0N		44	35	E
Ore Mts. = Erzgebirge	43	50	25N		13	0	E
Örebro	60	59	20N		15	18	E
Oregon □	171	44	0N		121	0	W
Oregon City	171	45	21N		122	35	W
Orel	68	52	57N		36	3	E
Orenburg	70	51	45N		55	6	E
Orense	50	42	19N		7	55	W
Orepuki	123	46	19S		167	46	E
Orford Ness	24	52	6N		1	31	E
Oriental, Cordillera	184	6	0N		73	0	W
Orillia	151	44	40N		79	24	W
Orinoco ⟶	185	9	15N		61	30	W
Orissa □	92	20	0N		84	0	E
Oristano	48	39	54N		8	35	E
Oristano, Golfo di	48	39	50N		8	22	E
Orizaba	177	18	51N		97	6	W
Orkney Is.	33	59	0N		3	0	W
Orland	172	39	46N		122	12	W
Orlando	170	28	30N		81	25	W
Orléanais	39	48	0N		2	0	E
Orléans	39	47	54N		1	52	E

Name					
Ormara	88	25	16N	64	33 E
Ormskirk	28	53	35N	2	53W
Örnsköldsvik	66	63	17N	18	40 E
Orocué	184	4	48N	71	20W
Oroville	172	39	31N	121	30W
Orsha	68	54	30N	30	25 E
Orsk	70	51	12N	58	34 E
Ortegal, C.	50	43	43N	7	52W
Orūmīyeh	81	37	40N	45	0 E
Orūmīyeh, Daryācheh-ye ...	81	37	50N	45	30 E
Oruro	187	18	0S	67	9W
Oruzgān □	87	33	30N	66	0 E
Oryakhovo	53	43	40N	23	57 E
Osage ➤	166	38	35N	91	57W
Ōsaka	106	34	40N	135	30 E
Osceola	169	35	40N	90	0W
Ösel = Saaremaa	68	58	30N	22	30 E
Osh	71	40	37N	72	49 E
Oshawa	151	43	50N	78	50W
Oshima	107	33	55N	132	14 E
Oshkosh	167	44	3N	88	35W
Oshogbo	131	7	48N	4	37 E
Osijek	52	45	34N	18	41 E
Oskaloosa	166	41	18N	92	40W
Oslo	60	59	55N	10	45 E
Osmaniye	80	37	5N	36	10 E
Osnabrück	42	52	16N	8	2 E
Osorno	190	40	25S	73	0W
Oss	41	51	46N	5	32 E
Ossa, Mt.	119	41	52S	146	3 E
Ostend = Oostende	42	51	15N	2	50 E
Östergötlands län □	60	58	35N	15	45 E
Östersund	66	63	10N	14	38 E
Østfold fylke □	60	59	25N	11	25 E
Ostfriesische Inseln	42	53	45N	7	15 E
Ostia	46	41	40N	12	20 E
Ostrava	59	49	51N	18	18 E
Ostróda	58	53	42N	19	58 E
Ostrołeka	58	53	4N	21	32 E
Ostrów Mazowiecka	58	52	50N	21	51 E
Ostrów Wielkopolski	58	51	36N	17	44 E
Ōsumi-Kaikyō	104	30	55N	131	0 E
Ōsumi-Shotō	104	30	30N	130	0 E
Oswego	164	43	29N	76	30W
Oswestry	28	52	52N	3	3W
Ōta	107	36	18N	139	22 E
Otago □	123	44	44S	169	10 E
Ōtake	109	34	12N	132	13 E
Otaki	122	40	45S	175	10 E
Otaru	103	43	10N	141	0 E
Otaru-Wan = Ishikari-Wan ..	103	43	25N	141	1 E
Otira Gorge	123	42	53S	171	33 E
Otoineppu	103	44	44N	142	16 E
Otranto	49	40	9N	18	28 E
Otranto, C. d'	49	40	7N	18	30 E
Otranto, Str. of	52	40	15N	18	40 E
Ōtsu	106	35	0N	135	50 E
Ottawa, Canada	151	45	27N	75	42W
Ottawa, U.S.A.	166	38	40N	95	6W
Ottawa ➤ = Outaouais ➤	140	45	27N	74	8W
Ottawa Is.	146	59	35N	80	10W
Otter Rapids, Ont., Canada .	151	50	11N	81	39W
Otter Rapids, Sask., Canada	152	55	38N	104	44W
Ottumwa	166	41	0N	92	25W
Otwock	58	52	5N	21	20 E
Ouachita ➤	168	31	38N	91	49W
Ouachita Mts.	168	34	50N	94	30W
Ouagadougou	130	12	25N	1	30W
Ouahran = Oran	127	35	45N	0	39W
Ouargla	127	31	59N	5	16 E
Oubangi ➤	131	1	0N	17	50 E
Oudenbosch	40	51	35N	4	32 E
Oudtshoorn	136	33	35S	22	14 E
Ouessant, Île d'	36	48	28N	5	6W
Oujda	127	34	41N	1	55W
Oulu	67	65	1N	25	29 E
Oulujärvi	67	64	25N	27	15 E
Oulujoki ➤	67	65	1N	25	30 E
Ouse ➤	29	54	3N	0	7 E
Outaouais ➤	140	45	27N	74	8W
Outer Hebrides	32	57	30N	7	40W
Outlook	152	51	30N	107	0W
Outreau	38	50	40N	1	36 E
Ouyen	119	35	1S	142	22 E
Ovalle	190	30	33S	71	18W
Overflakkee	40	51	44N	4	10 E
Overijssel □	41	52	25N	6	35 E
Oviedo	50	43	25N	5	50W
Owaka	123	46	27S	169	40 E
Owase	106	34	7N	136	12 E
Owatonna	166	44	3N	93	10W
Owen Sound	151	44	35N	80	55W
Owen Stanley Range	115	8	30S	147	0 E
Owensboro	167	37	40N	87	5W
Owosso	167	43	0N	84	10W
Owyhee ➤	171	43	46N	117	2W
Oxford, U.K.	25	51	45N	1	15W
Oxford, U.S.A.	165	36	19N	78	36W
Oxford □	25	51	45N	1	15W
Oxford L.	153	54	51N	95	37W
Oxnard	173	34	10N	119	14W
Oyabe	106	36	47N	136	56 E
Oyama	107	36	18N	139	48 E
Oyana	108	32	32N	130	30 E
Oyo	131	7	46N	3	56 E
Oyonnax	37	46	16N	5	40 E
Ozamis	112	8	15N	123	50 E
Ozark	169	31	29N	85	39W
Ozark Plateau	168	37	20N	91	40W
Ozarks, L. of	166	38	10N	92	40W
Ozu, Ehime, Japan	109	33	30N	132	33 E
Ozu, Kumamoto, Japan	108	32	52N	130	52 E

P

Name					
Paarl	136	33	45S	18	56 E
Pabna	92	24	1N	89	18 E
Pacaraima, Sierra	185	4	0N	62	30W
Pacasmayo	186	7	20S	79	35W
Pachuca	177	20	10N	98	40W
Padang	111	1	0S	100	20 E
Pádova	47	45	24N	11	52 E
Padstow	27	50	33N	4	57W
Padua = Pádova	47	45	24N	11	52 E
Paducah	169	37	0N	88	40W
Pag	52	44	30N	14	50 E
Pagalu = Annobón	131	1	25S	5	36 E
Pagastikós Kólpos	54	39	15N	23	0 E
Page	160	36	57N	111	27W
Pahala	160	19	12N	155	25W
Pahang □	96	3	30N	102	45 E
Pahiatua	122	40	27S	175	50 E
Paignton	27	50	26N	3	33W
Painesville	167	41	42N	81	18W
Paint Hills = Nouveau Comptoir	140	53	0N	78	49W
Painted Desert	160	36	0N	111	30W
Paisley	31	55	51N	4	27W
Paita	186	5	11S	81	9W
Pak Sane	95	18	22N	103	39 E
Pakistan ■	78	30	0N	70	0 E
Pakistan, East = Bangladesh ■	92	24	0N	90	0 E
Pakokku	93	21	20N	95	0 E
Pakse	95	15	5N	105	52 E
Paktiā □	87	33	0N	69	15 E
Palanpur	91	24	10N	72	25 E
Palatka	170	29	40N	81	40W
Palawan	112	9	30N	118	30 E
Palembang	111	3	0S	104	50 E
Palencia	50	42	1N	4	34W
Palermo	48	38	8N	13	20 E
Palestine	168	31	42N	95	35W
Palghat	90	10	46N	76	42 E
Pali	91	25	50N	73	20 E
Palizada	177	18	15N	92	5W
Palk Bay	90	9	30N	79	15 E
Palk Strait	90	10	0N	79	45 E
Palm Is.	121	18	40S	146	35 E
Palm Springs	173	33	51N	116	35W

248 Palma, La

Name	Map	Lat °	Lat ′ N/S	Long °	Long ′ E/W
Palma, La	179	8	15N	78	0W
Palma de Mallorca	51	39	35N	2	39 E
Palma Soriano	178	20	15N	76	0W
Palmas, C.	130	4	27N	7	46W
Palmer Land	14	73	0S	60	0W
Palmerston North	122	40	21S	175	39 E
Palmi	49	38	21N	15	51 E
Palmira	184	3	32N	76	16W
Palmyra = Tudmur	80	34	36N	38	15 E
Palo Alto	172	37	25N	122	8W
Pamirs	71	37	40N	73	0 E
Pamlico Sd.	165	35	20N	76	0W
Pampa	161	35	35N	100	58W
Pampas	190	35	0S	63	0W
Pamplona	51	42	48N	1	38W
Panaca	173	37	51N	114	23W
Panaji	91	15	25N	73	50 E
Panamá	179	9	0N	79	25W
Panama ■	179	8	48N	79	55W
Panamá, Golfo de	179	8	4N	79	20W
Panama Canal	175	9	10N	79	37W
Panama City	169	30	10N	85	41W
Panay	112	11	10N	122	30 E
Pančevo	52	44	52N	20	41 E
Pandharpur	91	17	41N	75	20 E
Pangfou = Bengbu	99	32	58N	117	20 E
Pangkalpinang	111	2	0S	106	0 E
Pangnirtung	146	66	8N	65	54W
Panjim = Panaji	91	15	25N	73	50 E
Panjnad Barrage	89	29	22N	71	15 E
Pantelleria	48	36	52N	12	0 E
Pánuco	177	22	3N	98	10W
Paoting = Baoding	98	38	50N	115	28 E
Paot'ou = Baotou	98	40	32N	110	2 E
Papien Chiang = Da ⟶	95	21	15N	105	20 E
Papua, Gulf of	115	9	0S	144	50 E
Papua New Guinea ■	115	8	0S	145	0 E
Pará = Belém	188	1	20S	48	30W
Pará □	188	3	20S	52	0W
Paracatu	188	17	10S	46	50W
Paragua, La	185	6	50N	63	20W
Paraguay ■	191	23	0S	57	0W
Paraguay ⟶	191	27	18S	58	38W
Paraíba = João Pessoa	189	7	10S	34	52W
Paraíba □	189	7	0S	36	0W
Parakou	131	9	25N	2	40 E
Paramaribo	185	5	50N	55	10W
Paraná	190	31	45S	60	30W
Paraná □	191	24	30S	51	0W
Paraná ⟶	190	33	43S	59	15W
Paranaguá	191	25	30S	48	30W
Paranaíba ⟶	188	20	6S	51	4W
Parbhani	91	19	8N	76	52 E
Parecis, Serra dos	187	13	0S	60	0W
Parent	151	47	55N	74	35W
Paria, Golfo de	180	10	20N	62	0W
Parika	185	6	50N	58	20W
Parintins	185	2	40S	56	50W
Pariparit Kyun	94	14	55S	93	45 E
Paris, France	39	48	50N	2	20 E
Paris, Tenn., U.S.A.	169	36	20N	88	20W
Paris, Tex., U.S.A.	168	33	40N	95	30W
Park Range	163	40	0N	106	30W
Parker	173	34	8N	114	16W
Parkersburg	164	39	18N	81	31W
Parkes	117	33	9S	148	11 E
Parma	46	44	50N	10	20 E
Parnaguá	188	10	10S	44	38W
Parnaíba	189	2	54S	41	47W
Parnaíba ⟶	188	3	0S	41	50W
Parnassós	54	38	35N	22	30 E
Pärnu	68	58	28N	24	33 E
Páros	55	37	5N	25	12 E
Parral	190	36	10S	71	52W
Parramatta	117	33	48S	151	1 E
Parras	174	25	30N	102	20W
Parrett ⟶	27	51	7N	2	58W
Parry Is.	12	77	0N	110	0W
Parry Sound	151	45	20N	80	0W
Parsons	166	37	20N	95	17W
Paruro	187	13	45S	71	50W
Parvān □	87	35	0N	69	0 E
Pasadena, Calif., U.S.A.	173	34	5N	118	9W
Pasadena, Tex., U.S.A.	168	29	45N	95	14W
Pasaje	184	3	23S	79	50W
Pascagoula	169	30	21N	88	30W
Pasco	171	46	10N	119	0W
Pasco, Cerro de	186	10	45S	76	10W
Paso Robles	173	35	40N	120	45W
Passero, C.	49	36	42N	15	8 E
Passo Fundo	191	28	10S	52	20W
Pasto	184	1	13N	77	17W
Patagonia	192	45	0S	69	0W
Patan	91	23	54N	72	14 E
Patchogue	164	40	46N	73	1W
Paterson	164	40	55N	74	10W
Pathankot	89	32	18N	75	45 E
Patiala	89	30	23N	76	26 E
Patkai Bum	93	27	0N	95	30 E
Pátmos	55	37	21N	26	36 E
Patna	92	25	35N	85	12 E
Patos, Lag. dos	191	31	20S	51	0 E
Patos de Minas	188	18	35S	46	32W
Pátrai	54	38	14N	21	47 E
Patuca ⟶	179	15	50N	84	18W
Pátzcuaro	175	19	32N	101	36W
Pau	36	43	19N	0	25W
Paulistana	189	8	9S	41	9W
Paulo Afonso	189	9	21S	38	15W
Pavia	46	45	10N	9	10 E
Pavlodar	71	52	33N	77	0 E
Pavlovo	74	63	5N	115	25 E
Pawtucket	164	41	51N	71	22W
Payette	171	44	0N	117	0W
Payne Bay = Bellin	146	60	0N	70	0W
Payne L.	146	59	30N	74	30W
Paynes Find	120	29	15S	117	42 E
Paysandú	191	32	19S	58	8W
Paz, La, Argentina	190	30	50S	59	45W
Paz, La, Bolivia	187	16	20S	68	10W
Paz, La, Mexico	174	24	10N	110	18W
Pazardzhik	53	42	12N	24	20 E
Peace ⟶	145	59	0N	111	25W
Peace River	155	56	15N	117	18W
Peak, The	28	53	24N	1	53W
Peak Hill	116	32	47S	148	11 E
Pearl City	160	21	24N	158	0W
Pearl Harbor	160	21	20N	158	0W
Peary Land	13	82	40N	33	0W
Pebas	186	3	10S	71	46W
Pechenga	69	69	30N	31	25 E
Pechora ⟶	69	68	13N	54	15 E
Pechorskaya Guba	69	68	40N	54	0 E
Pecos	161	31	25N	103	35W
Pecos ⟶	161	29	42N	102	30W
Pécs	59	46	5N	18	15 E
Pedro Afonso	188	9	0S	48	10W
Pedro Juan Caballero	191	22	30S	55	40W
Peebles	31	55	40N	3	12W
Peekskill	164	41	18N	73	57W
Peel	28	54	14N	4	40W
Peel ⟶	144	67	0N	135	0W
Pegasus Bay	123	43	20S	173	10 E
Pegu	93	17	20N	96	29 E
Pegu Yoma	93	19	0N	96	0 E
Pehuajó	190	35	45S	62	0W
Peip'ing = Beijing	98	39	55N	116	20 E
Pekalongan	111	6	53S	109	40 E
Pekan	96	3	30N	103	25 E
Pekanbaru	111	0	30N	101	15 E
Pekin	166	40	35N	89	40W
Peking = Beijing	98	39	55N	116	20 E
Peleng	113	1	20S	123	30 E
Pelly ⟶	144	62	47N	137	19W
Pelly Bay	146	68	38N	89	50W
Peloponnes = Pelopónnisos □	54	37	10N	22	0 E
Pelopónnisos □	54	37	10N	22	0 E
Peloro, C.	49	38	15N	15	40 E
Pelorus Sound	123	40	59S	173	59 E
Pelotas	191	31	42S	52	23W
Pelvoux, Massif de	37	44	52N	6	20 E
Pematangsiantar	111	2	57N	99	5 E
Pemba	135	5	0S	39	45 E

Place	Page	Lat°	Lat′	N/S	Long°	Long′	E/W
Pembroke, Canada	151	45	50N		77	7W	
Pembroke, U.K.	27	51	41N		4	57W	
Pen-y-Ghent	28	54	10N		2	15W	
Penas, G. de	192	47	0S		75	0W	
Pench'i = Benxi	98	41	20N		123	48 E	
Pendembu	130	9	7N		12	14W	
Pendleton	171	45	35N		118	50W	
Penetanguishene	151	44	50N		79	55W	
Penguin	119	41	8S		146	6 E	
Penicuik	31	55	50N		3	14W	
Peninsular Malaysia □	96	4	0N		102	0 E	
Pennines	28	54	50N		2	20W	
Pennsylvania □	164	40	50N		78	0W	
Penola	119	37	25S		140	21 E	
Penonomé	179	8	31N		80	21W	
Penrith, Australia	117	33	43S		150	38 E	
Penrith, U.K.	28	54	40N		2	45W	
Pensacola	169	30	30N		87	10W	
Pensacola Mts.	14	84	0S		40	0W	
Penshurst	119	37	49S		142	20 E	
Penticton	155	49	30N		119	38W	
Pentland Firth	33	58	43N		3	10W	
Pentland Hills	31	55	48N		3	25W	
Penza	68	53	15N		45	5 E	
Penzance	27	50	7N		5	32W	
Penzhinskaya Guba	73	61	30N		163	0 E	
Peoria	166	40	40N		89	40W	
Perak □	96	5	0N		101	0 E	
Perche	36	48	31N		1	1 E	
Pereira	184	4	49N		75	43W	
Perenjori	120	29	26S		116	16 E	
Pergamino	190	33	52S		60	30W	
Périgueux	36	45	10N		0	42 E	
Perlis □	96	6	30N		100	15 E	
Perm	69	58	0N		57	10 E	
Pernambuco = Recife	189	8	0S		35	0W	
Pernambuco □	189	8	0S		37	0W	
Pernatty Lagoon	118	31	30S		137	12 E	
Pernik	53	42	35N		23	2 E	
Peron Pen.	120	26	0S		113	10 E	
Péronne	38	49	55N		2	57 E	
Perouse Str., La	77	45	40N		142	0 E	
Perpignan	37	42	42N		2	53 E	
Perry, Iowa, U.S.A.	166	41	48N		94	5W	
Perry, Okla., U.S.A.	168	36	20N		97	20W	
Persepolis	85	29	55N		52	50 E	
Persia = Iran ■	86	33	0N		53	0 E	
Persian Gulf = Gulf, The	85	27	0N		50	0 E	
Perth, Australia	120	31	57S		115	52 E	
Perth, Canada	151	44	55N		76	15W	
Perth, U.K.	31	56	24N		3	27W	
Perth Amboy	164	40	31N		74	16W	
Peru	167	40	42N		86	0W	
Peru ■	186	8	0S		75	0W	
Perúgia	46	43	6N		12	24 E	
Pervouralsk	69	56	55N		60	0 E	
Pésaro	47	43	55N		12	53 E	
Pescara	47	42	28N		14	13 E	
Peshawar	89	34	2N		71	37 E	
Pesqueria →	176	25	54N		99	11W	
Petah Tiqwa	80	32	6N		34	53 E	
Petaling Jaya	96	3	4N		101	42 E	
Petaluma	172	38	13N		122	39W	
Petatlán	177	17	31N		101	16W	
Peterborough, Australia	118	32	58S		138	51 E	
Peterborough, Canada	151	44	20N		78	20W	
Peterborough, U.K.	25	52	35N		0	14W	
Peterhead	33	57	30N		1	49W	
Peterlee	29	54	45N		1	18W	
Petersburg, Alaska, U.S.A.	143	56	50N		133	0W	
Petersburg, Va., U.S.A.	164	37	17N		77	26W	
Petit Goâve	180	18	27N		72	51W	
Petitsikapau, L.	147	54	37N		66	25W	
Petlad	91	22	30N		72	45 E	
Petone	123	41	13S		174	53 E	
Petoskey	150	45	22N		84	57W	
Petrich	53	41	24N		23	13 E	
Petrolia	150	42	54N		82	9W	
Petrolina	189	9	24S		40	30W	
Petropavlovsk	71	54	53N		69	13 E	
Petropavlovsk-Kamchatskiy	73	53	3N		158	43 E	
Petrópolis	188	22	33S		43	9W	
Petrovaradin	52	45	16N		19	55 E	
Petrozavodsk	68	61	41N		34	20 E	
Pevek	73	69	41N		171	19 E	
Pforzheim	42	48	53N		8	43 E	
Phan Rang	95	11	34N		109	0 E	
Phangan, Ko	96	9	45N		100	0 E	
Phenix City	169	32	30N		85	0W	
Philadelphia	164	40	0N		75	10W	
Philippi	55	41	1N		24	16 E	
Philippines ■	112	12	0N		123	0 E	
Philippopolis = Plovdiv	53	42	8N		24	44 E	
Phitsanulok	94	16	50N		100	12 E	
Phnom Penh	95	11	33N		104	55 E	
Phoenix	160	33	30N		112	10W	
Phoenix Is.	123	3	30S		172	0W	
Phra Chedi Sam Ong	94	15	16N		98	23 E	
Phuket	96	7	52N		98	22 E	
Piacenza	46	45	2N		9	42 E	
Piauí □	188	7	0S		43	0W	
Picardie	38	50	0N		2	15 E	
Picardie, Plaine de	37	50	0N		2	0 E	
Picardy = Picardie	38	50	0N		2	15 E	
Picayune	169	30	31N		89	40W	
Pickering	29	54	15N		0	46W	
Picton, Australia	117	34	12S		150	34 E	
Picton, N.Z.	123	41	18S		174	3 E	
Pictou	149	45	41N		62	42W	
Pidurutalagala	90	7	10N		80	50 E	
Piedad, La	175	20	20N		102	1W	
Piedmont = Piemonte □	46	45	0N		7	30 E	
Piedmont Plat.	165	34	0N		81	30W	
Piedras Negras	174	28	42N		100	31W	
Piemonte □	46	45	0N		7	30 E	
Pierre	163	44	23N		100	20W	
Pietermaritzburg	137	29	35S		30	25 E	
Pietrosul	57	47	35N		24	43 E	
Pikeville	165	37	30N		82	30W	
Pilcomayo →	190	25	21S		57	42W	
Pilsen = Plzen	43	49	45N		13	22 E	
Pimenta Bueno	187	11	35S		61	10W	
Pinang □	96	5	20N		100	20 E	
Pinar del Río	178	22	26N		83	40W	
Pinaroo	119	35	17S		140	53 E	
Pinawa	153	50	9N		95	50W	
Pincher Creek	155	49	30N		113	57W	
Pinczów	58	50	30N		20	35 E	
Pindos Óros	54	40	0N		21	0 E	
Pindus Mts. = Pindos Óros	54	40	0N		21	0 E	
Pine Bluff	168	34	10N		92	0W	
Pine Pass	155	55	25N		122	42W	
Pineville	168	31	22N		92	30W	
Ping →	94	15	42N		100	9 E	
Pingdong	99	22	39N		120	30 E	
Pingliang	99	35	35N		106	31 E	
Pingxiang	99	22	6N		106	46 E	
Piniós	54	37	48N		21	20 E	
Pinjarra	120	32	37S		115	52 E	
Piombino	46	42	54N		10	30 E	
Piotrków Trybunalski	58	51	23N		19	43 E	
Piqua	167	40	10N		84	10W	
Piracicaba	188	22	45S		47	40W	
Piraeus = Piraiévs	55	37	57N		23	42 E	
Piraiévs	55	37	57N		23	42 E	
Pirapora	188	17	20S		44	56W	
Pírgos	54	37	40N		21	27 E	
Pirin Planina	53	41	40N		23	30 E	
Pirineos	51	42	40N		1	0 E	
Pisa	46	43	43N		10	23 E	
Pisagua	187	19	40S		70	15W	
Pisco	186	13	50S		76	12W	
Pistóia	46	43	57N		10	53 E	
Pitcairn I.	10	25	5S		130	5W	
Piteå	67	65	20N		21	25 E	
Pitești	57	44	52N		24	54 E	
Pithiviers	39	48	10N		2	13 E	
Pitlochry	33	56	43N		3	43W	
Pitt I.	154	53	30N		129	50W	
Pittsburg, Kans., U.S.A.	166	37	21N		94	43W	
Pittsburg, Tex., U.S.A.	168	32	59N		94	58W	
Pittsburgh	164	40	25N		79	55W	
Pittsfield	164	42	28N		73	17W	
Pittsworth	116	27	41S		151	37 E	

250 Piura

Place	Page	Lat		Long	
Piura	186	5 15S		80	38W
Placentia	149	47 20N		54	0W
Placerville	172	38 47N		120	51W
Placetas	178	22 15N		79	44W
Plainfield	164	40 37N		74	28W
Plainview	161	34 10N		101	40W
Plaster Rock	148	46 53N		67	22W
Plata, La	191	35 0S		57	55W
Plata, Río de la	191	34 45S		57	30W
Platte →	163	39 16N		94	50W
Plattsburg	151	44 41N		73	30W
Plauen	43	50 29N		12	9 E
Pleasantville	164	39 25N		74	30W
Plenty, Bay of	122	37 45S		177	0 E
Plessisville	148	46 14N		71	47W
Pleven	53	43 26N		24	37 E
Płock	58	52 32N		19	40 E
Ploieşti	57	44 57N		26	5 E
Plovdiv	53	42 8N		24	44 E
Plymouth	27	50 23N		4	9W
Plzen	43	49 45N		13	22 E
Po →	47	44 57N		12	4 E
Po Hai = Bo Hai	98	39 0N		120	0 E
Pobeda	73	65 12N		146	12 E
Pobedy Pik	71	40 45N		79	58 E
Pocatello	163	42 50N		112	25W
Pochutla	177	15 50N		96	31W
Poços de Caldas	188	21 50S		46	33W
Podgorica	52	42 30N		19	19 E
Podkamennaya Tunguska →	74	61 50N		90	13 E
Point Edward	150	43 0N		82	30W
Pointe-à-Pitre	180	16 10N		61	30W
Pointe Noire	134	4 48S		11	53 E
Poissy	39	48 55N		2	0 E
Poitiers	36	46 35N		0	20 E
Poitou, Plaines et Seuil du	36	46 30N		0	1W
Pokaran	91	27 0N		71	50 E
Pokrovsk = Engels	68	51 28N		46	6 E
Pola = Pula	52	44 54N		13	57 E
Poland ■	58	52 0N		20	0 E
Polden Hills	27	51 7N		2	50W
Polesye	17	52 0N		28	10 E
Polillo Is.	112	14 56N		122	0 E
Polyíros	55	40 23N		23	25 E
Pollachi	90	10 35N		77	0 E
Polotsk	68	55 30N		28	50 E
Poltava	68	49 35N		34	35 E
Polynesia	123	10 0S		162	0W
Pomona	173	34 2N		117	49W
Pompano Beach	170	26 12N		80	6W
Ponca City	168	36 40N		97	5W
Ponce	180	18 1N		66	37W
Pond Inlet	146	72 40N		77	0W
Pondicherry	90	11 59N		79	50 E
Ponnyadaung	93	22 0N		94	10 E
Ponoka	155	52 42N		113	40W
Pont-Audemer	39	49 21N		0	30 E
Ponta Grossa	191	25 7S		50	10W
Ponta Pora	188	22 20S		55	35W
Pontchartrain, L.	169	30 12N		90	0W
Pontefract	29	53 42N		1	19W
Pontevedra	50	42 26N		8	40W
Pontiac	167	42 40N		83	20W
Pontianak	111	0 3S		109	15 E
Pontine Is. = Ponziane, Isole	48	40 55N		13	0 E
Pontoise	39	49 3N		2	5 E
Pontypool	27	51 42N		3	1W
Pontypridd	27	51 36N		3	21W
Ponziane, Isole	48	40 55N		13	0 E
Poochera	118	32 43S		134	51 E
Poole	24	50 42N		1	58W
Pooley I.	154	52 45N		128	15W
Poona = Pune	91	18 29N		73	57 E
Poopó, Lago de	187	18 30S		67	35W
Popayán	184	2 27N		76	36W
Poplar Bluff	169	36 45N		90	22W
Popocatépetl, Volcán	177	19 2N		98	38W
Porcher I.	154	53 50N		130	30W
Porcupine →	142	66 35N		145	15W
Pori	67	61 29N		21	48 E
Porkkala	67	59 59N		24	26 E
Port Adelaide	119	34 46S		138	30 E
Port Alberni	154	49 40N		124	50W
Port Albert	115	38 42S		146	42 E
Port Alfred	148	48 18N		70	53W
Port Angeles	171	48 7N		123	30W
Port Antonio	180	18 10N		76	30W
Port Arthur	168	30 0N		94	0W
Port-au-Prince	180	18 40N		72	20W
Port Augusta	118	32 30S		137	50 E
Port Blair	94	11 40N		92	30 E
Port-Cartier	148	50 2N		66	50W
Port Chalmers	123	45 49S		170	30 E
Port Colborne	151	42 50N		79	10W
Port Coquitlam	154	49 15N		122	45W
Port Darwin	192	51 50S		59	0W
Port-de-Paix	180	19 50N		72	50W
Port Elgin	150	44 25N		81	25W
Port Elizabeth	136	33 58S		25	40 E
Port Erin	28	54 5N		4	45W
Port Etienne = Nouâdhibou .	126	20 54N		17	0W
Port Fairy	119	38 22S		142	12 E
Port Glasgow	30	55 57N		4	40W
Port Harcourt	131	4 40N		7	10 E
Port Harrison = Inoucdjouac	146	58 25N		78	15W
Port Hawkesbury	149	45 36N		61	22W
Port Hope	151	43 56N		78	20W
Port Huron	167	43 0N		82	28W
Port Kembla	117	34 52S		150	49 E
Port Laoise	35	53 2N		7	20W
Port Lavaca	158	28 38N		96	38W
Port Lincoln	119	34 42S		135	52 E
Port Lyautey = Kenitra	126	34 15N		6	40W
Port Macquarie	116	31 25S		152	25 E
Port Morant	180	17 54N		76	19W
Port Moresby	115	9 24S		147	8 E
Port Nelson	143	57 3N		92	36W
Port Nolloth	136	29 17S		16	52 E
Port Nouveau-Québec	146	58 30N		65	59W
Port of Spain	180	10 40N		61	31W
Port Phillip B.	117	38 10S		144	50 E
Port Pirie	118	33 10S		138	1 E
Port Said = Bûr Sa'îd	128	31 16N		32	18 E
Port Simpson	154	54 30N		130	20W
Port Stanley	150	42 40N		81	10W
Port Sudan = Bûr Sûdân	129	19 32N		37	9 E
Port Talbot	27	51 35N		3	48W
Port Townsend	171	48 7N		122	50W
Portadown	34	54 27N		6	26W
Portage La Prairie	153	49 58N		98	18W
Portarlington	35	53 10N		7	10W
Porte, La	167	41 36N		86	43W
Porterville	173	36 5N		119	0W
Porthcawl	27	51 28N		3	42W
Porthmadog	26	52 55N		4	13W
Portile de Fier	56	44 42N		22	30 E
Portland, Australia	119	38 20S		141	35 E
Portland, Maine, U.S.A.	148	43 40N		70	15W
Portland, Oreg., U.S.A.	171	45 35N		122	40W
Portland, Bill of	24	50 31N		2	27W
Portland Prom.	146	58 40N		78	33W
Porto	50	41 8N		8	40W
Pôrto Alegre	191	30 5S		51	10W
Porto Empédocle	48	37 18N		13	30 E
Porto Mendes	191	24 30S		54	15W
Porto Novo	131	6 23N		2	42 E
Pôrto Seguro	189	16 26S		39	5W
Pôrto Velho	187	8 46S		63	54W
Portoferráio	46	42 50N		10	20 E
Portoscuso	48	39 12N		8	22 E
Portoviejo	184	1 7S		80	28W
Portpatrick	30	54 50N		5	7W
Portree	32	57 25N		6	11W
Portrush	34	55 13N		6	40W
Portsmouth, Domin.	180	15 34N		61	27W
Portsmouth, U.K.	25	50 48N		1	6W
Portsmouth, N.H., U.S.A.	164	43 5N		70	45W
Portsmouth, Ohio, U.S.A.	167	38 45N		83	0W
Portsmouth, Va., U.S.A.	165	36 50N		76	20W
Porttipahta	67	68 5N		26	40 E
Portugal ■	50	40 0N		7	0W
Portuguese-Guinea = Guinea-Bissau ■	130	12 0N		15	0W

Portuguese Timor ■ = Timor 113 9 0S 125 0 E
Portumna 35 53 5N 8 12W
Porvenir 192 53 10S 70 16W
Posadas 191 27 30S 55 50W
Poshan = Boshan 98 36 28N 117 49 E
Poste-de-la-Baleine 140 55 17N 77 45W
Potchefstroom 137 26 41S 27 7 E
Potenza 49 40 40N 15 50 E
Potomac → 165 38 0N 76 23W
Potosí 187 19 38S 65 50W
Potsdam, Germany 43 52 23N 13 4 E
Potsdam, U.S.A. 151 44 40N 74 59W
Pottsville 164 40 39N 76 12W
Pouce Coupé 155 55 40N 120 10W
Poughkeepsie 164 41 40N 73 57W
Poulaphouca Res. 35 53 8N 6 30W
Póvoa de Varzim 50 41 25N 8 46W
Powell, L. 163 37 25N 110 45W
Powell River 154 49 50N 124 35W
Powys □ 26 52 20N 3 20W
Poyang Hu 99 29 10N 116 10 E
Poyarkovo 75 49 36N 128 41 E
Poznań 58 52 25N 16 55 E
Prachuap Khiri Khan 94 11 49N 99 48 E
Prague = Praha 58 50 5N 14 22 E
Praha 58 50 5N 14 22 E
Prainha, Amazonas, Brazil 187 7 10S 60 30W
Prainha, Pará, Brazil 185 1 45S 53 30W
Prairie du Chien 166 43 1N 91 9W
Prato 46 43 53N 11 5 E
Pratt 161 37 40N 98 45W
Prepansko Jezero 52 40 55N 21 0 E
Preparis North Channel 94 15 12N 93 40 E
Preparis South Channel 94 14 36N 93 40 E
Prescott 160 34 35N 112 30W
Preservation Inlet 123 46 8S 166 35 E
Presidencia Roque Saenz
  Peña 190 26 45S 60 30W
Presidente Prudente 188 22 5S 51 25W
Presidio 161 29 30N 104 20W
Prespa, L. = Prepansko
  Jezero 52 40 55N 21 0 E
Presque Isle 148 46 40N 68 0W
Preston, Borders, U.K. 28 55 48N 2 18W
Preston, Lancs., U.K. 21 53 46N 2 42W
Prestonpans 31 55 58N 3 0W
Prestwick 31 55 30N 4 38W
Pretoria 137 25 44S 28 12 E
Préveza 55 38 57N 20 47 E
Prichard 169 30 47N 88 5W
Prilep 52 41 21N 21 37 E
Prince Albert 152 53 15N 105 50W
Prince Albert Pen. 145 72 30N 116 0W
Prince Albert Sd. 145 70 25N 115 0W
Prince Charles I. 146 67 47N 76 12W
Prince Edward I. □ 148 46 20N 63 20W
Prince George 154 53 55N 122 50W
Prince of Wales I., Canada 145 73 0N 99 0W
Prince of Wales I., U.S.A. 143 55 30N 133 0W
Prince Patrick I. 12 77 0N 120 0W
Prince Rupert 154 54 20N 130 20W
Princess Royal I. 154 53 0N 128 40W
Princeton 155 49 27N 120 30W
Principe, I. de 131 1 37N 7 27 E
Principe da Beira 187 12 20S 64 30W
Pripet = Pripyat → 68 51 20N 30 9 E
Pripet Marshes = Polesye 17 52 0N 28 10 E
Pripyat → 68 51 20N 30 9 E
Pripyat Marshes = Polesye 17 52 0N 28 10 E
Priština 52 42 40N 21 13 E
Privolzhskaya Vozvyshennost 17 51 0N 46 0 E
Prizren 52 42 13N 20 45 E
Proddatur 90 14 45N 78 30 E
Progreso 177 21 17N 89 40W
Prokopyevsk 71 54 0N 86 45 E
Proserpine 121 20 21S 148 36 E
Provence 37 43 40N 5 46 E
Providence 164 41 50N 71 28W
Provo 163 40 16N 111 37W
Prudhoe Bay 142 70 20N 148 20W
Pruszków 58 52 9N 20 49 E
Prut → 57 46 3N 28 10 E

Przemyśl 58 49 50N 22 45 E
Przeworsk 58 50 6N 22 32 E
Pskov 68 57 50N 28 25 E
Pucallpa 186 8 25S 74 30W
Puebla 177 19 3N 98 12W
Puebla □ 177 18 50N 98 0W
Pueblo 163 38 20N 104 40W
Puelches 190 38 5S 65 51W
Puente Alto 190 33 32S 70 35W
Puerto Armuelles 179 8 20N 82 51W
Puerto Ayacucho 184 5 40N 67 35W
Puerto Barrios 177 15 40N 88 32W
Puerto Cabello 184 10 28N 68 1W
Puerto Cabezas 179 14 0N 83 30W
Puerto Castilla 179 16 0N 86 0W
Puerto Cortes, Costa Rica 179 8 55N 84 0W
Puerto Cortés, Honduras 177 15 51N 88 0W
Puerto Heath 187 12 34S 68 39W
Puerto La Cruz 185 10 13N 64 38W
Puerto Libertad 174 29 55N 112 41W
Puerto Lobos 192 42 0S 65 3W
Puerto Maldonado 187 12 30S 69 10W
Puerto Montt 190 41 28S 73 0W
Puerto Padre 178 21 13N 76 35W
Puerto Pinasco 191 22 36S 57 50W
Puerto Plata 180 19 48N 70 45W
Puerto Quepos 179 9 29N 84 6W
Puerto Rico ■ 180 18 15N 66 45W
Puerto Vallarta 175 20 37N 105 15W
Puertollano 50 38 43N 4 7W
Puget Sd. 171 47 15N 122 30W
Púglia □ 49 41 0N 16 30 E
Pula 52 44 54N 13 57 E
Pulaski, Tenn., U.S.A. 169 35 10N 87 0W
Pulaski, Va., U.S.A. 165 37 4N 80 49W
Pulicat, L. 90 13 40N 80 15 E
Pullman 171 46 49N 117 10W
Punakha 92 27 42N 89 52 E
Punata 187 17 32S 65 50W
Pune 91 18 29N 73 57 E
Punjab □, India 89 31 0N 76 0 E
Punjab □, Pakistan 89 30 0N 72 0 E
Puno 187 15 55S 70 3W
Punta Alta 190 38 53S 62 4W
Punta Arenas 192 53 10S 71 0W
Punta Gorda 177 16 10N 88 45W
Puntabie 118 32 12S 134 13 E
Puntarenas 179 10 0N 84 50W
Punto Fijo 184 11 50N 70 13W
Puquio 186 14 45S 74 10W
Pur → 69 67 31N 77 55 E
Purbeck, Isle of 24 50 40N 2 5W
Purmerend 40 52 30N 4 58 E
Purnia 92 25 45N 87 31 E
Pursat 95 12 34N 103 50 E
Purus → 185 3 42S 61 28W
Pusan 98 35 5N 129 0 E
Putao 93 27 28N 97 30 E
Putorana, Gory 72 69 0N 95 0 E
Putumayo → 184 3 7S 67 58W
Puy, Le 37 45 2N 3 53 E
Puy-de-Dôme 37 45 46N 2 57 E
Puyallup 171 47 10N 122 22W
Pwllheli 26 52 54N 4 26W
Pyasina → 72 73 30N 87 0 E
Pyatigorsk 70 44 2N 43 6 E
Pyinmana 93 19 45N 96 12 E
Pyŏngyang 98 39 0N 125 30 E
Pyramid L. 172 40 0N 119 30W
Pyrénées 124 42 45N 0 18 E

Q

Qã'emshahr 86 36 30N 52 55 E
Qahremānshahr = Bākhtarān 84 34 23N 47 0 E
Qaidam Pendi 100 37 0N 95 0 E
Qal'at al Akhḍar 82 28 0N 37 10 E
Qamar, Ghubbat al 83 16 20N 52 30 E
Qamdo 101 31 15N 97 6 E

252 Qandahār

Name	Page	Lat °	Lat ′	N/S	Lon °	Lon ′	E/W
Qandahār	87	31	32	N	65	30	E
Qaṣr-e Qand	85	26	15	N	60	45	E
Qatar ■	85	25	30	N	51	15	E
Qāyen	86	33	40	N	59	10	E
Qazvin	81	36	15	N	50	0	E
Qena	128	26	10	N	32	43	E
Qeshm	85	26	55	N	56	10	E
Qilian Shan	100	38	30	N	96	0	E
Qingdao	98	36	5	N	120	20	E
Qinghai □	101	36	0	N	98	0	E
Qinghai Hu	100	36	40	N	100	10	E
Qinhuangdao	98	39	56	N	119	30	E
Qiqihar	98	47	26	N	124	0	E
Qom	86	34	40	N	51	0	E
Qomsheh	85	32	0	N	51	55	E
Qondūz □	87	36	50	N	68	50	E
Qu Xian	99	30	48	N	106	58	E
Quang Ngai	95	15	13	N	108	58	E
Quantock Hills	27	51	8	N	3	10	W
Quanzhou	99	24	55	N	118	34	E
Quatsino	154	50	30	N	127	40	W
Queanbeyan	117	35	17	S	149	14	E
Québec	148	46	52	N	71	13	W
Québec □	140	50	0	N	70	0	W
Queen Alexandra Ra.	15	85	0	S	170	0	E
Queen Charlotte	154	53	15	N	132	2	W
Queen Charlotte Is.	154	53	20	N	132	10	W
Queen Charlotte Str.	154	51	0	N	128	0	W
Queen Elizabeth Is.	138	76	0	N	95	0	W
Queen Mary Land	15	70	0	S	95	0	E
Queen Maud G.	145	68	15	N	102	30	W
Queen Maud Mts.	15	86	0	S	160	0	W
Queenscliff	117	38	16	S	144	39	E
Queensland □	115	22	0	S	142	0	E
Queenstown, Australia	119	42	4	S	145	35	E
Queenstown, N.Z.	123	45	1	S	168	40	E
Quelimane	137	17	53	S	36	58	E
Quelpart = Cheju Do	99	33	29	N	126	34	E
Querétaro	177	20	36	N	100	23	W
Querétaro □	177	21	0	N	99	55	W
Quesnel	154	53	0	N	122	30	W
Quetta	88	30	15	N	66	55	E
Quezaltenango	177	14	50	N	91	30	W
Quezon City	112	14	38	N	121	0	E
Qui Nhon	95	13	40	N	109	13	E
Quibdo	184	5	42	N	76	40	W
Quillabamba	186	12	50	S	72	50	W
Quilon	90	8	50	N	76	38	E
Quilpie	116	26	35	S	144	11	E
Quimper	36	48	0	N	4	9	W
Quincy, Calif., U.S.A.	172	39	56	N	121	0	W
Quincy, Fla., U.S.A.	170	30	34	N	84	34	W
Quincy, Ill., U.S.A.	166	39	55	N	91	20	W
Quincy, Mass., U.S.A.	164	42	14	N	71	0	W
Quintana Roo □	177	19	40	N	88	30	W
Quirindi	116	31	28	S	150	40	E
Quitman	170	30	49	N	83	35	W
Quito	184	0	15	S	78	35	W
Quixadá	189	4	55	S	39	0	W
Quorn	118	32	25	S	138	0	E
Quseir	128	26	7	N	34	16	E

R

Name	Page	Lat °	Lat ′	N/S	Lon °	Lon ′	E/W
Raahe	67	64	40	N	24	28	E
Raasay	32	57	25	N	6	4	W
Rabat	126	34	2	N	6	48	W
Rabaul	115	4	24	S	152	18	E
Rābigh	82	22	50	N	39	5	E
Race, C.	149	46	40	N	53	5	W
Rach Gia	95	10	5	N	105	5	E
Racibórz	58	50	7	N	18	18	E
Racine	167	42	41	N	87	51	W
Radium Hot Springs	155	50	35	N	116	2	W
Radnor Forest	26	52	17	N	3	10	W
Radom	58	51	23	N	21	12	E
Radomir	53	42	37	N	23	4	E
Radstock	27	51	17	N	2	25	W
Radville	152	49	30	N	104	15	W
Rae	145	62	50	N	116	3	W
Rae Bareli	92	26	18	N	81	20	E
Raetihi	122	39	25	S	175	17	E
Rafaela	190	31	10	S	61	30	W
Rafḥā	82	29	35	N	43	35	E
Rafsanjān	85	30	30	N	56	5	E
Ragama	90	7	0	N	79	50	E
Raglan	122	37	55	S	174	55	E
Ragusa	49	36	56	N	14	42	E
Rahaeng = Tak	94	16	52	N	99	8	E
Raichur	91	16	10	N	77	20	E
Rainier, Mt.	171	46	50	N	121	50	W
Rainy L.	153	48	42	N	93	10	W
Rainy River	153	48	43	N	94	29	W
Raipur	92	21	17	N	81	45	E
Rajahmundry	92	17	1	N	81	48	E
Rajapalaiyam	90	9	25	N	77	35	E
Rajasthan □	91	26	45	N	73	30	E
Rajasthan Canal	89	28	0	N	72	0	E
Rajkot	91	22	15	N	70	56	E
Rajshahi □	92	25	0	N	89	0	E
Raleigh	165	35	47	N	78	39	W
Raleigh B.	165	34	50	N	76	15	W
Rambouillet	39	48	40	N	1	48	E
Rampur	89	28	50	N	79	5	E
Ramsey	28	54	20	N	4	21	W
Rancagua	190	34	10	S	70	50	W
Ranchi	92	23	19	N	85	27	E
Rangiora	123	43	19	S	172	36	E
Rangoon	93	16	45	N	96	20	E
Rangpur	92	25	42	N	89	22	E
Raniwara	91	24	50	N	72	10	E
Rankin Inlet	145	62	30	N	93	0	W
Rankins Springs	117	33	49	S	146	14	E
Rannoch, L.	33	56	41	N	4	20	W
Rannoch Moor	33	56	38	N	4	48	W
Rapid City	163	44	0	N	103	0	W
Ras Dashen	132	13	8	N	38	26	E
Rasa, Punta	192	40	50	S	62	15	W
Rasht	81	37	20	N	49	40	E
Rat Is.	142	51	50	N	178	15	E
Ratangarh	89	28	5	N	74	35	E
Rath Luirc	35	52	21	N	8	40	W
Rathlin I.	34	55	18	N	6	14	W
Ratibor = Racibórz	58	50	7	N	18	18	E
Ratlam	91	23	20	N	75	0	E
Ratnagiri	91	16	57	N	73	18	E
Rattray Hd.	33	57	38	N	1	50	W
Raub	96	3	47	N	101	52	E
Raukumara Ra.	122	38	5	S	177	55	E
Ravenna	47	44	28	N	12	15	E
Ravenshoe	121	17	37	S	145	29	E
Ravensthorpe	120	33	35	S	120	2	E
Rawalpindi	89	33	38	N	73	8	E
Rawlins	163	41	50	N	107	20	W
Ray, C.	149	47	33	N	59	15	W
Raymond	155	49	30	N	112	35	W
Razgrad	53	43	33	N	26	34	E
Ré, Île de	36	46	12	N	1	30	W
Reading, U.K.	25	51	27	N	0	57	W
Reading, U.S.A.	164	40	20	N	75	53	W
Reay Forest	32	58	20	N	4	55	W
Rebun-Tō	103	45	23	N	141	2	E
Recife	189	8	0	S	35	0	W
Reconquista	190	29	10	S	59	45	W
Recreo	190	29	25	S	65	10	W
Red →	168	31	0	N	91	40	W
Red Bluff	172	40	11	N	122	11	W
Red Cliffs	119	34	19	S	142	11	E
Red Deer	155	52	20	N	113	50	W
Red Lake	153	51	3	N	93	49	W
Red Oak	166	41	0	N	95	10	W
Red Sea	128	25	0	N	36	0	E
Red Tower Pass = Turnu Rosu Pasul	57	45	33	N	24	17	E
Red Wing	166	44	32	N	92	35	W
Redcar	29	54	37	N	1	4	W
Redcliff	152	50	10	N	110	50	W
Redcliffe	116	27	12	S	153	0	E
Redding	172	40	30	N	122	25	W
Redditch	24	52	18	N	1	57	W
Redlands	173	34	0	N	117	11	W

Redruth	27	50	14N	5	14W
Redwater	155	53	55N	113	6W
Redwood City	172	37	30N	122	15W
Ree, L.	34	53	35N	8	0W
Reedley	173	36	36N	119	27W
Regensburg	43	49	1N	12	7 E
Réggio di Calábria	49	38	7N	15	38 E
Réggio nell' Emilia	46	44	42N	10	38 E
Regina	152	50	27N	104	35W
Rehovot	80	31	54N	34	48 E
Reichenbach	43	50	36N	12	19 E
Reidsville	165	36	21N	79	40W
Reims	39	49	15N	4	0 E
Reina Adelaida, Arch.	192	52	20S	74	0W
Reindeer L.	143	57	15N	102	15W
Reliance	145	63	0N	109	20W
Remanso	189	9	41S	42	4W
Remarkable, Mt.	118	32	48S	138	10 E
Remscheid	42	51	11N	7	12 E
Rendsburg	42	54	18N	9	41 E
Renfrew, Canada	151	45	30N	76	40W
Renfrew, U.K.	31	55	52N	4	24W
Renkum	41	51	58N	5	43 E
Renmark	119	34	11S	140	43 E
Rennes	36	48	7N	1	41W
Reno	172	39	30N	119	50W
Republic	150	46	25N	87	59W
Republican ~►	163	39	3N	96	48W
Repulse Bay	146	66	30N	86	30W
Requena	186	5	5S	73	52W
Resht = Rasht	81	37	20N	49	40 E
Resistencia	190	27	30S	59	0W
Resolution I., Canada	146	61	30N	65	0W
Resolution I., N.Z.	123	45	40S	166	40 E
Retalhuleu	177	14	33N	91	46W
Réthímnon	55	35	18N	24	30 E
Réunion	9	22	0S	56	0 E
Reval = Tallinn	68	59	22N	24	48 E
Revelstoke	155	51	0N	118	10W
Revilla Gigedo, Is.	139	18	40N	112	0W
Rewa	92	24	33N	81	25 E
Rewari	89	28	15N	76	40 E
Rexburg	163	43	55N	111	50W
Rey Malabo	131	3	45N	8	50 E
Reykjavik	64	64	10N	21	57 E
Reynosa	176	26	5N	98	18W
Rhayader	26	52	19N	3	30W
Rhein ~►	42	51	52N	6	20 E
Rheinland-Pfalz □	42	50	0N	7	0 E
Rhin = Rhein ~►	42	51	52N	6	20 E
Rhine = Rhein ~►	42	51	52N	6	20 E
Rhineland-Palatinate = Rheinland-Pfalz □	42	50	0N	7	0 E
Rhinelander	150	45	38N	89	29W
Rhode Island □	164	41	38N	71	37W
Rhodes = Ródhos	55	36	15N	28	10 E
Rhodesia = Zimbabwe ■	137	20	0S	30	0 E
Rhodope Mts. = Rhodopi Planina	53	41	40N	24	20 E
Rhodopi Planina	53	41	40N	24	20 E
Rhön	42	50	24N	9	58 E
Rhondda	27	51	39N	3	30W
Rhône ~►	37	43	28N	4	42 E
Rhum	32	57	0N	6	20W
Rhyl	26	53	19N	3	29W
Rhymney	27	51	45N	3	17W
Riachão	188	7	20S	46	37W
Riau, Kepulauan	111	0	30N	104	20 E
Ribatejo □	50	39	15N	8	30W
Ribble ~►	28	54	13N	2	20W
Ribeirão Prêto	188	21	10S	47	50W
Riberalta	187	11	0S	66	0W
Riccarton	123	43	32S	172	37 E
Richland	171	46	15N	119	15W
Richmond, Australia	116	20	43S	143	8 E
Richmond, N.Z.	123	41	20S	173	12 E
Richmond, N. Yorks., U.K.	28	54	24N	1	43W
Richmond, Surrey, U.K.	25	51	28N	0	18W
Richmond, Calif., U.S.A.	172	37	58N	122	21W
Richmond, Ind., U.S.A.	167	39	50N	84	50W
Richmond, Ky., U.S.A.	165	37	40N	84	20W
Richmond, Va., U.S.A.	165	37	33N	77	27W
Richwood	165	38	17N	80	32W
Ridgeway	164	42	56S	147	16 E
Riga	68	56	53N	24	8 E
Rigestān □	87	30	15N	65	0 E
Rigolet	147	54	10N	58	23W
Rijeka	52	45	20N	14	21 E
Rijssen	41	52	19N	6	30 E
Rijswijk	40	52	4N	4	22 E
Rímini	47	44	3N	12	33 E
Rîmnicu Vîlcea	57	45	9N	24	21 E
Rimouski	148	48	27N	68	30W
Rinía	55	37	23N	25	13 E
Rio Branco	187	9	58S	67	49W
Rio Claro	180	10	20N	61	25W
Rio Cuarto	190	33	10S	64	25W
Rio de Janeiro	188	23	0S	43	12W
Rio de Janeiro □	188	22	50S	43	0W
Río Gallegos	192	51	35S	69	15W
Rio Grande	191	32	0S	52	20W
Río Grande ~►	161	25	57N	97	9W
Rio Grande do Norte □	189	5	40S	36	0W
Rio Grande do Sul □	191	30	0S	53	0W
Río Mulatos	187	19	40S	66	50W
Rio Negro	191	26	0S	50	0W
Rio Verde	188	17	50S	51	0W
Ríobamba	184	1	50S	78	45W
Ríohacha	184	11	33N	72	55W
Rioja, La	190	29	20S	67	0W
Rioja, La □	50	42	20N	2	20W
Ríosucio	184	7	27N	77	7W
Ripon	28	54	8N	1	31W
Rishiri-Tō	103	45	11N	141	15 E
Ritchies Archipelago	94	12	5N	94	0 E
Rivas	179	11	30N	85	50W
Riverhead	164	40	53N	72	40W
Riverside	173	34	0N	117	22W
Riverton	153	51	1N	97	0W
Riviera di Levante	46	44	23N	9	15 E
Riviera di Ponente	46	43	50N	7	58 E
Rivière-du-Loup	148	47	50N	69	30W
Riyadh = Ar Riyāḍ	83	24	41N	46	42 E
Roanne	37	46	3N	4	4 E
Roanoke, Ala., U.S.A.	169	33	9N	85	23W
Roanoke, Va., U.S.A.	165	37	19N	79	55W
Roanoke ~►	165	35	56N	76	43W
Roanoke Rapids	165	36	28N	77	42W
Robinvale	119	34	40S	142	45 E
Roblin	152	51	14N	101	21W
Roboré	187	18	10S	59	45W
Robson, Mt.	155	53	10N	119	10W
Roca, C. da	50	38	40N	9	31W
Rocha	191	34	30S	54	25W
Rochdale	28	53	36N	2	10W
Roche-sur-Yon, La	36	46	40N	1	25W
Rochefort	36	45	56N	0	57W
Rochelle, La	36	46	10N	1	9W
Rochester, Minn., U.S.A.	166	44	1N	92	28W
Rochester, N.H., U.S.A.	164	43	19N	70	57W
Rochester, N.Y., U.S.A.	164	43	10N	77	40W
Rock Hill	165	34	55N	81	2W
Rock Island	166	41	30N	90	35W
Rock Sprs.	163	41	40N	109	10W
Rockall	16	57	37N	13	42W
Rockford	166	42	20N	89	0W
Rockglen	152	49	11N	105	57W
Rockhampton	119	23	22S	150	32 E
Rockingham	120	32	15S	115	38 E
Rockland	148	44	6N	69	6W
Rocky Mount	165	35	55N	77	48W
Rocky Mountain House	155	52	22N	114	55W
Rocky Mts.	138	55	0N	121	0W
Ródhos	55	36	15N	28	10 E
Roebourne	114	20	44S	117	9 E
Roermond	41	51	12N	6	0 E
Roes Welcome Sd.	146	65	0N	87	0W
Rogaland fylke □	60	59	12N	6	20 E
Rogers	168	36	20N	94	5W
Rohri	88	27	45N	68	51 E
Rohtak	89	28	55N	76	43 E
Rojo, C.	177	21	33N	97	20W
Rolla	166	37	56N	91	42W
Roma, Australia	116	26	32S	148	49 E

Roma, Italy .... **46** 41 54N 12 30 E
Romaine → **141** 50 18N 63 47W
Roman .... **57** 46 57N 26 55 E
Romana, La **180** 18 27N 68 57W
Romania ■ .... **57** 46 0N 25 0 E
Romans .... **37** 45 3N 5 3 E
Romanzof, C. **142** 62 0N 165 50W
Rome = Roma .... **46** 41 54N 12 30 E
Rome, Ga., U.S.A. **169** 34 20N 85 0W
Rome, N.Y., U.S.A. **164** 43 14N 75 29W
Romilly .... **39** 48 31N 3 44 E
Romney Marsh .... **25** 51 0N 1 0 E
Rona **32** 57 33N 6 0W
Rondônia □ **187** 11 0S 63 0W
Rong, Koh .... **95** 10 45N 103 15 E
Ronge, L. la **152** 55 6N 105 17W
Roosendaal .... **40** 51 32N 4 29 E
Roraima □ **185** 2 0N 61 30W
Roraima, Mt. **185** 5 10N 60 40W
Rosario, Argentina **190** 33 0S 60 40W
Rosário, Brazil **188** 3 0S 44 15W
Rosario, Mexico **175** 22 58N 105 53W
Rosario, Paraguay **191** 24 30S 57 35W
Rosário do Sul **191** 30 15S 54 55W
Roscommon **34** 53 38N 8 11W
Roscommon □ **34** 53 40N 8 15W
Roscrea **35** 52 58N 7 50W
Roseau **180** 15 20N 61 24W
Roseburg **171** 43 10N 123 20W
Rosenberg **168** 29 30N 95 48W
Rosendaël .... **38** 51 3N 2 24 E
Rosetown **152** 51 35N 107 59W
Roseville **172** 38 46N 121 17W
Rosewood .... **116** 27 38S 152 36 E
Roskilde .... **61** 55 38N 12 3 E
Ross on Wye **24** 51 55N 2 34W
Ross Sea .... **15** 74 0S 178 0 E
Rossan Pt. **34** 54 42N 8 47W
Rossland **155** 49 6N 117 50W
Rosslare **35** 52 17N 6 23W
Rossvatnet .... **65** 65 45N 14 5 E
Rosthern **152** 52 40N 106 20W
Rostock .... **43** 54 4N 12 9 E
Rostov .... **68** 47 15N 39 45 E
Roswell **161** 33 26N 104 32W
Rosyth **31** 56 2N 3 26W
Rother → .... **25** 50 59N 0 40 E
Rotherham **29** 53 26N 1 21W
Rothesay **30** 55 50N 5 3W
Roto .... **117** 33 0S 145 30 E
Rotorua .... **122** 38 9S 176 16 E
Rotorua, L. .... **122** 38 5S 176 18 E
Rotterdam .... **40** 51 55N 4 30 E
Rotuma .... **122** 12 25S 177 5 E
Roubaix .... **37** 50 40N 3 10 E
Rouen .... **38** 49 27N 1 4 E
Round Mt. .... **116** 30 26S 152 16 E
Roussillon .... **37** 42 30N 2 35 E
Rouyn **151** 48 20N 79 0W
Rovaniemi .... **67** 66 29N 25 41 E
Rovno .... **68** 50 40N 26 10 E
Ruahine Ra. .... **122** 39 55S 176 2 E
Ruapehu .... **122** 39 17S 175 35 E
Rub' al Khali .... **83** 18 0N 48 0 E
Rubh a' Mhail **30** 55 55N 6 10W
Rubio **184** 7 43N 72 22W
Rubtsovsk .... **71** 51 30N 81 10 E
Rudnyy .... **71** 52 57N 63 7 E
Rudolf, Ostrov .... **69** 81 45N 58 30 E
Rufiji → .... **135** 7 50S 39 15 E
Rufino **190** 34 20S 62 50W
Rugby **25** 52 23N 1 16W
Rügen .... **43** 54 22N 13 25 E
Ruhr → .... **42** 51 25N 6 44 E
Rukwa L. .... **135** 8 0S 32 20 E
Rumania = Romania ■ .... **57** 46 0N 25 0 E
Rumford **148** 44 30N 70 30W
Rumoi **103** 43 56N 141 39W
Runcorn **28** 53 20N 2 44W
Rupat .... **111** 1 45N 101 40 E
Rupert → **140** 51 29N 78 45W
Rupert House = Fort Rupert **140** 51 30N 78 40W

Ruschuk = Ruse .... **53** 43 48N 25 59 E
Ruse .... **53** 43 48N 25 59 E
Russell **152** 50 50N 101 20W
Russellville, Ala., U.S.A. **169** 34 30N 87 44W
Russellville, Ark., U.S.A. **168** 35 15N 93 8W
Russia ■ .... **78** 60 0N 100 0 E
Ruston **168** 32 30N 92 58W
Rutherglen **31** 55 50N 4 11W
Rutland I. .... **94** 11 25N 92 40 E
Ruwenzori .... **132** 0 30N 29 55 E
Rwanda ■ .... **135** 2 0S 30 0 E
Ryan, L. **30** 55 0N 5 2W
Ryazan .... **68** 54 40N 39 40 E
Rybache .... **71** 46 40N 81 20 E
Rybinsk .... **68** 58 5N 38 50 E
Ryde **25** 50 44N 1 9W
Rye .... **25** 50 57N 0 46 E
Rylstone .... **117** 32 46S 149 58 E
Ryōhaku-Sanchi .... **106** 36 9N 136 49 E
Ryūgasaki .... **107** 35 54N 140 11 E
Rzeszów .... **58** 50 5N 21 58 E

S

Sa Dec .... **95** 10 20N 105 46 E
Saar → .... **42** 49 41N 6 32 E
Saarbrücken .... **42** 49 15N 6 58 E
Saaremaa .... **68** 58 30N 22 30 E
Saarland □ .... **42** 49 15N 7 0 E
Sabadell .... **51** 41 28N 2 7 E
Sabae .... **106** 35 57N 136 11 E
Sabah □ .... **112** 6 0N 117 0 E
Sábana de la Mar **180** 19 7N 69 24W
Sabhah .... **127** 27 9N 14 29 E
Sabi → .... **137** 18 50S 31 40 E
Sabinas **174** 27 51N 101 7W
Sabinas Hidalgo, R. → ... **176** 26 50N 99 35W
Sabine → **158** 30 0N 93 35W
Sable, C., Canada **148** 43 29N 65 38W
Sable, C., U.S.A. **159** 25 13N 81 0W
Sable I. **149** 44 0N 60 0W
Sabrina Coast .... **15** 68 0S 120 0 E
Sabzevär .... **86** 36 15N 57 40 E
Saco **148** 43 30N 70 27W
Sacramento .... **172** 38 33N 121 30 E
Sacramento → **172** 38 3N 121 56W
Sacramento Mts. **161** 32 30N 105 30W
Sado, Shima .... **103** 38 15N 138 30 E
Safed Koh .... **87** 34 0N 70 0 E
Saffron Walden .... **25** 52 2N 0 15 E
Safi **126** 32 18N 9 20W
Saga .... **108** 33 15N 130 16 E
Sagami-Nada .... **107** 34 58N 139 30 E
Sagami-Wan .... **107** 35 15N 139 25 E
Sagamihara .... **107** 35 33N 139 25 E
Sagar .... **91** 14 14N 75 6 E
Sagara .... **107** 34 41N 138 12 E
Saginaw **167** 43 26N 83 55W
Saginaw B. **167** 43 50N 83 40W
Saglouc **146** 62 14N 75 38W
Sagres **50** 37 0N 8 58W
Sagua la Grande **178** 22 50N 80 10W
Saguenay → **148** 48 22N 71 0W
Sahara .... **126** 23 0N 5 0 E
Saharanpur .... **89** 29 58N 77 33 E
Saharien, Atlas .... **127** 33 30N 1 0 E
Sahiwal .... **89** 30 45N 73 8 E
Sahuaripa **174** 29 3N 109 14W
Saïgô .... **109** 36 12N 133 20 E
Saigon = Thanh Pho Ho Chi
  Minh .... **95** 10 58N 106 40 E
Saijō, Ehime, Japan .... **109** 33 55N 133 11 E
Saijō, Hiroshima, Japan .... **109** 34 25N 132 45 E
Saikhoa Ghat .... **93** 27 50N 95 40 E
Saiki .... **108** 32 58N 131 51 E
Saimaa .... **67** 61 15N 28 15 E
Şa'in Dezh .... **81** 36 40N 46 25 E
St. Abb's Head **31** 55 55N 2 10W
St. Albans, U.K. **25** 51 44N 0 19W

Name	No.	Lat °	′	N/S	Long °	′	E/W
St. Albans, U.S.A.	151	44	49	N	73	7	W
St. Alban's Head	24	50	34	N	2	3	W
St. Albert	155	53	37	N	113	32	W
St. Andrews	31	56	20	N	2	48	W
St. Arnaud	119	36	40	S	143	16	E
St. Asaph	26	53	15	N	3	27	W
St-Augustin-Saguenay	141	51	13	N	58	38	W
St. Augustine	170	29	52	N	81	20	W
St. Austell	27	50	20	N	4	48	W
St. Bee's Hd.	28	54	30	N	3	38	E
St. Boniface	153	49	53	N	97	5	W
St. Bride's B.	26	51	48	N	5	15	W
St-Brieuc	36	48	30	N	2	46	W
St. Catharines	151	43	10	N	79	15	W
St. Charles	166	38	46	N	90	30	W
St. Christopher-Nevis ■	180	17	20	N	62	40	W
St. Cloud	156	45	30	N	94	11	W
St. Croix	180	17	45	N	64	45	W
St. David's	26	51	54	N	5	16	W
St. David's Head	26	51	55	N	5	16	W
St-Denis	39	48	56	N	2	22	E
St-Dizier	37	48	40	N	5	0	E
St. Elias, Mt.	144	60	14	N	140	50	W
St. Elias Mts.	144	60	33	N	139	28	W
St-Étienne	37	45	27	N	4	22	E
St-Félicien	151	48	40	N	72	25	W
St. Gallen	44	47	25	N	9	20	E
St. George, Australia	116	28	1	S	148	30	E
St. George, Bermuda	180	32	24	N	64	42	W
St. Georges, Fr. Guiana	185	4	0	N	52	0	W
St. George's, Grenada	180	12	5	N	61	43	W
St. George's Channel	20	52	0	N	6	0	W
St. Gotthard P. = San Gottardo, Paso del	44	46	33	N	8	33	E
St. Helena	125	15	55	S	5	44	W
St. Helena B.	136	32	40	S	18	10	E
St. Helens, Australia	119	41	20	S	148	15	E
St. Helens, U.K.	28	53	28	N	2	44	W
St. Helens, U.S.A.	171	45	55	N	122	50	W
St. Helier	36	49	11	N	2	6	W
St-Hyacinthe	151	45	40	N	72	58	W
St. Ives, Cambs., U.K.	25	52	20	N	0	5	W
St. Ives, Corn., U.K.	27	50	13	N	5	29	W
St-Jean	151	45	20	N	73	20	W
St-Jérôme	151	45	47	N	74	0	W
St. John	148	45	20	N	66	8	W
St. John's	149	47	35	N	52	40	W
St. John's ─►	170	30	20	N	81	30	W
St. Johnsbury	148	44	25	N	72	1	W
St. Joseph, Mich., U.S.A.	167	42	5	N	86	30	W
St. Joseph, Mo., U.S.A.	166	39	46	N	94	50	W
St. Kilda, N.Z.	123	45	53	S	170	31	E
St. Kilda, U.K.	22	57	9	N	8	34	W
St. Lawrence	149	46	54	N	55	23	W
St. Lawrence ─►	148	49	30	N	66	0	W
St. Lawrence, Gulf of	149	48	25	N	62	0	W
St. Lawrence I.	142	63	0	N	170	0	W
St. Leonard	148	47	12	N	67	58	W
St-Louis	130	16	8	N	16	27	W
St. Louis	166	38	40	N	90	12	W
St. Lucia ■	180	14	0	N	60	50	W
St. Maarten	180	18	0	N	63	5	W
St-Malo	36	48	39	N	2	1	W
St-Marc	180	19	10	N	72	41	W
St-Martin, I.	180	18	0	N	63	0	W
St. Mary Pk.	118	31	32	S	138	34	E
St. Marys	164	41	27	N	78	33	W
St. Matthews, I. = Zadetkyi Kyun	94	10	0	N	98	25	E
St. Michael's Mt.	27	50	7	N	5	30	W
St. Moritz	44	46	30	N	9	51	E
St-Nazaire	36	47	17	N	2	12	W
St. Neots	25	52	14	N	0	16	W
St-Omer	38	50	45	N	2	15	E
St. Pascal	148	47	32	N	69	48	W
St. Paul	166	44	54	N	93	5	W
St. Paul, I.	149	47	12	N	60	9	W
St-Petersburg = Sankt-Peterburg	68	59	55	N	30	20	E
St. Petersburg	170	27	45	N	82	40	W
St-Pierre et Miquelon □	149	46	55	N	56	10	W
St-Quentin	38	49	50	N	3	16	E
St-Raphaël	37	43	25	N	6	46	E
St-Servan-sur-Mer	36	48	38	N	2	0	W
St. Thomas, Canada	151	42	45	N	81	10	W
St. Thomas, W. Indies	180	18	21	N	64	55	W
St-Tropez	37	43	17	N	6	38	E
St. Vincent and the Grenadines ■	180	13	0	N	61	10	W
Ste-Adresse	38	49	31	N	0	5	E
Ste. Anne de Beaupré	148	47	2	N	70	58	W
Ste. Marie	180	14	48	N	61	1	W
Ste-Rose	180	16	20	N	61	45	W
Ste. Rose du lac	153	51	4	N	99	30	W
Saintes	36	45	45	N	0	37	W
Saintonge	36	45	40	N	0	50	W
Sajama	187	18	7	S	69	0	W
Sakai	106	34	30	N	135	30	E
Sakaide	109	34	15	N	133	50	E
Sakaiminato	109	35	38	N	133	11	E
Sakakawea, L.	163	47	30	N	102	0	W
Sakata	103	38	55	N	139	50	E
Sakha □	72	62	0	N	130	0	E
Sakhalin	79	51	0	N	143	0	E
Sakhalinskiy Zaliv	75	54	0	N	141	0	E
Saku	107	36	17	N	138	31	E
Sakura	107	35	43	N	140	14	E
Sakurai	106	34	30	N	135	51	E
Salaberry-de-Valleyfield	151	45	15	N	74	8	W
Salado ─►	190	31	40	S	60	41	W
Salado, R. ─►	176	26	52	N	99	19	W
Salamanca, Spain	50	40	58	N	5	39	W
Salamanca, U.S.A.	164	42	10	N	78	42	W
Salamis	55	37	56	N	23	30	E
Salcombe	27	50	14	N	3	47	W
Sale	117	38	6	S	147	6	E
Salem, India	90	11	40	N	78	11	E
Salem, Mass., U.S.A.	164	42	29	N	70	53	W
Salem, Oreg., U.S.A.	171	45	0	N	123	0	W
Salem, Va., U.S.A.	165	37	19	N	80	8	W
Salerno	49	40	40	N	14	44	E
Salford	28	53	30	N	2	17	W
Salida	163	38	35	N	106	0	W
Salina, Italy	49	38	35	N	14	50	E
Salina, U.S.A.	163	38	50	N	97	40	W
Salina Cruz	177	16	10	N	95	12	W
Salinas, Ecuador	184	2	10	S	80	58	W
Salinas, U.S.A.	173	36	40	N	121	41	W
Salinas ─►	173	36	45	N	121	48	W
Salinas Grandes	190	30	0	S	65	0	W
Salisbury = Harare	137	17	43	S	31	2	E
Salisbury, U.K.	24	51	4	N	1	48	W
Salisbury, Md., U.S.A.	165	38	20	N	75	38	W
Salisbury, N.C., U.S.A.	165	35	20	N	80	29	W
Salisbury Plain	24	51	13	N	1	50	W
Salle, La	166	41	20	N	89	6	W
Salmon	162	45	12	N	113	56	W
Salmon ─►	171	45	51	N	116	46	W
Salmon Arm	155	50	40	N	119	15	W
Salmon River Mts.	162	45	0	N	114	30	W
Salon-de-Provence	37	43	39	N	5	6	E
Salonica = Thessaloníki	54	40	38	N	22	58	E
Salop = Shropshire □	24	52	36	N	2	45	W
Salt Fork ─►	161	36	37	N	97	7	W
Salt Lake City	163	40	45	N	111	58	W
Salta	190	24	57	S	65	25	W
Saltcoats	30	55	38	N	4	47	W
Saltillo	174	25	25	N	101	0	W
Salto	191	31	27	S	57	50	W
Salton Sea	173	33	20	N	115	50	W
Salûm	128	31	31	N	25	7	E
Salvador	189	13	0	S	38	30	W
Salween ─►	93	16	31	N	97	37	E
Salzburg	45	47	48	N	13	2	E
Salzburg □	45	47	15	N	13	0	E
Salzgitter	43	52	13	N	10	22	E
Sam Neua	95	20	29	N	104	0	E
Sama	69	60	12	N	60	22	E
Samangán □	87	36	15	N	68	3	E
Samar	112	12	0	N	125	0	E
Samara	68	53	8	N	50	6	E
Samarkand	70	39	40	N	66	55	E
Sâmarrä	81	34	12	N	43	52	E
Sambalpur	92	21	28	N	84	4	E

Name	Page	°	′	N/S	°	′	E/W
Sambhal	89	28	35N		78	37	E
Sámos	55	37	45N		26	50	E
Samothráki	55	40	28N		25	28	E
Samsun	80	41	15N		36	22	E
Samut Prakan	95	13	32N		100	40	E
Samut Sakhon	94	13	31N		100	13	E
Samut Songkhram →	94	13	24N		100	1	E
San Andreas	172	38	0N		120	39	W
San Andres Mts.	161	33	0N		106	45	W
San Andrés Tuxtla	177	18	27N		95	13	W
San Angelo	161	31	30N		100	30	W
San Antonio, Chile	190	33	40S		71	40	W
San Antonio, U.S.A.	161	29	30N		98	30	W
San Antonio, C., Argentina	191	36	15S		56	40	W
San Antonio, C., Cuba	178	21	50N		84	57	W
San Antonio de los Baños	178	22	54N		82	31	W
San Antônio Falls	182	9	30S		65	0	W
San Antonio Oeste	192	40	40S		65	0	W
San Bernardino	173	34	7N		117	18	W
San Bernardino Str.	112	13	0N		125	0	E
San Bernardo	190	33	40S		70	50	W
San Blas, C.	169	29	40N		85	12	W
San Carlos, Chile	190	36	10S		72	0	W
San Carlos, Mexico	174	29	1N		100	51	W
San Carlos, Nic.	179	11	12N		84	50	W
San Carlos de Bariloche	192	41	10S		71	25	W
San Clemente I.	173	32	53N		118	30	W
San Cristóbal, Argentina	190	30	20S		61	10	W
San Cristóbal, Dom. Rep.	180	18	25N		70	6	W
San Cristóbal, Venezuela	184	16	50N		92	40	W
San Cristóbal de las Casas	177	16	45N		92	38	W
San Diego	173	32	43N		117	10	W
San Felipe, Chile	190	32	43S		70	42	W
San Felipe, Colombia	184	1	55N		67	6	W
San Fernando, Chile	190	34	30S		71	0	W
San Fernando, Mexico	174	30	0N		115	10	W
San Fernando, Trin. & Tob.	180	10	20N		61	30	W
San Fernando, U.S.A.	173	34	15N		118	29	W
San Fernando de Apure	184	7	54N		67	15	W
San Francisco	172	37	47N		122	30	W
San Francisco de Macorís	180	19	19N		70	15	W
San Francisco del Oro	174	26	52N		105	51	W
San Gabriel	191	0	36N		77	49	W
San Gottardo, Paso del	44	46	33N		8	33	E
San Ignacio	187	16	20S		60	55	W
San Joaquin →	172	37	4N		121	51	W
San Jorge, Golfo	192	46	0S		66	0	W
San Jorge, G. de	51	40	50N		0	55	W
San José, Bolivia	187	17	53S		60	50	W
San José, Costa Rica	179	10	0N		84	2	W
San Jose, U.S.A.	172	37	20N		121	53	W
San José de Mayo	191	34	27S		56	40	W
San José del Cabo	175	23	3N		109	41	W
San José del Guaviare	184	2	35N		72	38	W
San Juan, Argentina	190	31	30S		68	30	W
San Juan, Dom. Rep.	180	18	49N		71	12	W
San Juan, Puerto Rico	180	18	28N		66	8	W
San Juan →	179	10	56N		83	42	W
San Juan de los Morros	184	9	55N		67	21	W
San Juan Mts.	163	38	30N		108	30	W
San Julián	192	49	15S		67	45	W
San Leandro	172	37	40N		122	6	W
San Lorenzo	184	1	15N		78	50	W
San Lucas, C. de	175	22	50N		110	0	W
San Luis	190	33	20S		66	20	W
San Luis de la Paz	177	21	18N		100	31	W
San Luis Obispo	173	35	21N		120	38	W
San Luis Potosí	177	22	9N		100	59	W
San Luis Potosí □	177	22	30N		100	30	W
San Marcos	177	14	59N		91	52	W
San Marino ■	47	43	56N		12	25	E
San Mateo	172	37	32N		122	19	W
San Matías	187	16	25S		58	20	W
San Matías, Golfo	192	41	30S		64	0	W
San Miguel	177	13	30N		88	12	W
San Miguel de Tucumán	190	26	50S		65	20	W
San Pedro →	175	21	45N		105	30	W
San Pedro de las Colonias	174	25	45N		102	59	W
San Pedro de Macorís	180	18	30N		69	18	W
San Pedro Sula	177	15	30N		88	0	W
San Rafael, Argentina	190	34	40S		68	21	W
San Rafael, U.S.A.	172	37	59N		122	32	W
San Roque	190	28	25S		58	45	W
San Salvador, Bahamas	178	24	0N		74	40	W
San Salvador, El Salv.	177	13	40N		89	10	W
San Salvador de Jujuy	190	24	10S		64	48	W
San Sebastián	51	43	17N		1	58	W
San Valentin, Mte.	192	46	30S		73	30	W
Sana'	82	15	27N		44	12	E
Sanandaj	81	35	18N		47	1	E
Sancti-Spíritus	178	21	52N		79	33	W
Sanda	106	34	53N		135	14	E
Sandgate	116	27	18S		153	3	E
Sandomierz	58	50	40N		21	43	E
Sandpoint	171	48	20N		116	34	W
Sandringham	29	52	50N		0	30	E
Sandstone	120	27	59S		119	16	E
Sandusky	167	41	25N		82	40	W
Sandwip Chan.	93	22	35N		91	35	E
Sandy C.	119	41	25S		144	45	E
Sandy Lake	153	53	0N		93	15	W
Sanford, Fla., U.S.A.	170	28	45N		81	20	W
Sanford, Maine, U.S.A.	148	43	28N		70	47	W
Sanford, N.C., U.S.A.	165	35	30N		79	10	W
Sangay	184	2	0S		78	20	W
Sangihe, P.	113	3	45N		125	30	E
Sangli	91	16	55N		74	33	E
Sangre de Cristo Mts.	161	37	0N		105	0	W
Sankt-Peterburg	68	59	55N		30	20	E
Sankuru →	134	4	17S		20	25	E
Sanliurfa	81	37	12N		38	50	E
Sano	107	36	19N		139	35	E
Sanok	59	49	35N		22	10	E
Sanquhar	31	55	21N		3	56	W
Sanshui	99	23	10N		112	56	E
Santa Ana, Bolivia	187	13	50S		65	40	W
Santa Ana, Mexico	174	30	33N		111	7	W
Santa Ana, U.S.A.	173	33	48N		117	55	W
Santa Bárbara, Mexico	174	26	48N		105	49	W
Santa Barbara, U.S.A.	173	34	25N		119	40	W
Santa Barbara I.	160	33	29N		119	2	W
Santa Catarina □	191	27	25S		48	30	W
Santa Clara, Cuba	178	22	20N		80	0	W
Santa Clara, U.S.A.	162	37	21N		122	0	W
Santa Clotilde	186	2	33S		73	45	W
Santa Cruz, Bolivia	187	17	43S		63	10	W
Santa Cruz, U.S.A.	172	36	55N		122	1	W
Santa Cruz, Is.	122	10	30S		166	0	E
Santa Cruz de Tenerife	126	28	28N		16	15	W
Santa Cruz del Sur	178	20	44N		78	0	W
Santa Cruz do Sul	191	29	42S		52	25	W
Santa Fe, Argentina	190	31	35S		60	41	W
Santa Fe, U.S.A.	161	35	40N		106	0	W
Santa Inés, I.	192	54	0S		73	0	W
Santa Isabel = Rey Malabo	131	3	45N		8	50	E
Santa Lucia Range	173	36	0N		121	20	W
Santa Maria, Brazil	191	29	40S		53	48	W
Santa Maria, U.S.A.	173	34	58N		120	29	W
Santa Maria da Vitória	188	13	24S		44	12	W
Santa Maria di Leuca, C.	49	39	48N		18	20	E
Santa Maura = Levkás	54	38	40N		20	43	E
Santa Monica	173	34	0N		118	30	W
Santa Rosa, Argentina	190	36	40S		64	17	W
Santa Rosa, U.S.A.	172	38	26N		122	43	W
Santa Rosa I., Calif., U.S.A.	173	34	0N		120	6	W
Santa Rosa I., Fla., U.S.A.	169	30	23N		87	0	W
Santa Rosalía	174	27	19N		112	17	W
Santana do Livramento	191	30	55S		55	30	W
Santander	50	43	27N		3	51	W
Santander Jiménez	176	24	13N		98	28	W
Santarém, Brazil	185	2	25S		54	42	W
Santarém, Portugal	50	39	12N		8	42	W
Santiago, Brazil	191	29	11S		54	52	W
Santiago, Chile	190	33	24S		70	40	W
Santiago, Panama	179	8	0N		81	0	W
Santiago de Compostela	50	42	52N		8	37	W
Santiago de Cuba	178	20	0N		75	49	W
Santiago de los Caballeros	180	19	30N		70	40	W
Santiago del Estero	190	27	50S		64	15	W
Santiago Ixcuintla	175	21	50N		105	11	W
Santo Amaro	189	12	30S		38	43	W
Santo Ângelo	191	28	15S		54	15	W
Santo Domingo	180	18	30N		64	54	W

Santo Tomé **191** 28 40S 56 5W
Santoña **50** 43 29N 3 27W
Santos **191** 24 0S 46 20W
São Borja **191** 28 39S 56 0W
São Carlos **188** 22 0S 47 50W
São Francisco ─► **189** 10 30S 36 24W
São Francisco do Sul **191** 26 15S 48 36W
São João del Rei **188** 21 8S 44 15W
São José do Rio Prêto ... **188** 20 50S 49 20W
São Leopoldo **191** 29 50S 51 10W
São Lourenço **188** 22 7S 45 3W
São Luís **188** 2 39S 44 15W
São Paulo **191** 23 32S 46 37W
São Paulo □ **188** 22 0S 49 0W
São Paulo de Olivença ... **184** 3 27S 68 48W
São Roque, C. de **189** 5 30S 35 16W
São Tomé .... **131** 0 10N 6 39 E
São Tomé & Principe ■ .... **131** 0 12N 6 39 E
São Vicente, Cabo de ... **50** 37 0N 9 0W
Saône ─► .... **37** 45 44N 4 50 E
Sapporo .... **103** 43 0N 141 21 E
Sapulpa **168** 36 0N 96 0W
Saqqez .... **81** 36 15N 46 20 E
Sar Planina .... **52** 42 10N 21 0 E
Saragossa = Zaragoza ... **51** 41 39N 0 53W
Sarajevo .... **52** 43 52N 18 26 E
Saranac Lake **151** 44 20N 74 10W
Sarangani B. .... **112** 6 0N 125 13 E
Saransk .... **68** 54 10N 45 10 E
Sarapul .... **69** 56 28N 53 48 E
Sarasota **165** 27 20N 82 30W
Saratoga Springs **164** 43 5N 73 47W
Saratov .... **68** 51 30N 46 2 E
Sarawak □ .... **111** 2 0N 113 0 E
Sardegna .... **48** 39 57N 9 0 E
Sardinia = Sardegna .... **48** 39 57N 9 0 E
Sargodha .... **89** 32 10N 72 40 E
Sarh .... **131** 9 5N 18 23 E
Sārī .... **86** 36 30N 53 4 E
Sarina .... **121** 21 22S 149 13 E
Sarmiento **192** 45 35S 69 5W
Sarnia **150** 42 58N 82 23W
Saronikós Kólpos ...... **55** 37 45N 23 45 E
Sarre = Saar ─► .... **42** 49 41N 6 32 E
Sarre, La **151** 48 45N 79 15W
Sarthe ─► **36** 47 33N 0 31W
Sasaram .... **92** 24 57N 84 5 E
Sasebo .... **108** 33 10N 129 43 E
Saskatchewan □ **152** 54 40N 106 0W
Saskatchewan ─► **152** 53 37N 100 40W
Saskatoon **152** 52 10N 106 38W
Sassandra **130** 5 0N 6 8W
Sássari .... **48** 40 44N 8 33 E
Sata-Misaki .... **108** 30 59N 130 40 E
Satara .... **91** 17 44N 73 58 E
Satmala Hills .... **91** 20 15N 74 40 E
Satna .... **92** 24 35N 80 50 E
Satpura Ra. .... **91** 21 25N 76 10 E
Sattahip .... **95** 12 41N 100 54 E
Satu Mare .... **56** 47 46N 22 55 E
Sauðarkrókur **64** 65 45N 19 40W
Saudi Arabia ■ .... **82** 26 0N 44 0 E
Sault Ste. Marie, Canada .. **150** 46 30N 84 20W
Sault Ste. Marie, U.S.A. .. **150** 46 27N 84 22W
Saumur **36** 47 15N 0 5W
Sava ─► .... **52** 44 50N 20 26 E
Savanna la Mar **180** 18 10N 78 10W
Savannah **170** 32 4N 81 4W
Savannah ─► **170** 32 2N 80 53W
Savannakhet .... **95** 16 30N 104 49 E
Savoie □ .... **37** 45 26N 6 35 E
Savona .... **46** 44 19N 8 29 E
Sawankhalok .... **94** 17 19N 99 50 E
Sawara .... **107** 35 55N 140 30 E
Sawatch Mts. **163** 38 30N 106 30W
Sawu, I. .... **113** 10 35S 121 50 E
Sawu Sea .... **113** 9 30S 121 50 E
Saxony, Lower =
  Niedersachsen □ ..... **42** 52 45N 9 0 E
Sayan, Zapadnyy ..... **77** 52 30N 94 0 E
Saydā .... **80** 33 35N 35 25 E
Sayḥut .... **83** 15 12N 51 10 E

Sayula **175** 19 52N 103 36W
Sazan .... **52** 40 30N 19 20 E
Scafell Pikes **28** 54 26N 3 14W
Scalloway **30** 60 9N 1 16W
Scandinavia .... **16** 64 0N 12 0 E
Scapa Flow **33** 58 52N 3 6W
Scarborough **29** 54 17N 0 24W
Schaffhausen .... **44** 47 42N 8 39 E
Schefferville **146** 54 48N 66 50W
Schelde ─► .... **42** 51 15N 4 16 E
Schenectady **164** 42 50N 73 58W
Scheveningen .... **40** 52 6N 4 16 E
Schiedam .... **40** 51 55N 4 25 E
Schiermonnikoog ..... **41** 53 30N 6 15 E
Schleswig-Holstein □ ... **42** 54 10N 9 40 E
Schouten I. .... **119** 42 20S 148 20 E
Schouten Is. .... **113** 1 0S 136 0 E
Schouwen .... **40** 51 43N 3 45 E
Schreiber **150** 48 45N 87 20W
Schwäbische Alb ..... **42** 48 30N 9 30 E
Schwarzwald .... **42** 48 0N 8 0 E
Schwerin .... **43** 53 37N 11 22 E
Schwyz .... **44** 47 2N 8 39 E
Scilly, Isles of **20** 49 55N 6 15W
Scone, Australia ...... **116** 32 5S 150 52 E
Scone, U.K. **31** 56 25N 3 26W
Scoresbysund **13** 70 20N 23 0W
Scotia Sea **14** 56 5S 56 0W
Scotland □ **23** 57 0N 4 0W
Scottsbluff **163** 41 55N 103 35W
Scottsdale .... **119** 41 9S 147 31 E
Scranton **164** 41 22N 75 41W
Scunthorpe **29** 53 35N 0 38W
Scutari = Üsküdar .... **80** 41 0N 29 5 E
Seaforth **150** 43 35N 81 25W
Searcy **168** 35 15N 91 45W
Seascale **28** 54 24N 3 29W
Seattle **171** 47 41N 122 15W
Sebastián Vizcaíno, B. .. **174** 28 0N 114 30W
Sebastopol = Sevastopol .. **68** 44 35N 33 30 E
Sebring **170** 27 30N 81 26W
Sebta = Ceuta **126** 35 52N 5 18W
Sebuku, Teluk .... **111** 4 0N 118 10 E
Sechura, Desierto de ... **186** 6 0S 80 30W
Seclin .... **38** 50 33N 3 2 E
Sedalia **166** 38 40N 93 18W
Segamat .... **96** 2 30N 102 50 E
Ségou **130** 13 30N 6 16W
Segovia = Coco ─► **179** 15 0N 83 8W
Segovia **50** 40 57N 4 10W
Séguéla **130** 7 55N 6 40W
Segura ─► **51** 38 6N 0 54W
Seine ─► .... **38** 49 26N 0 26 E
Seistan .... **85** 30 50N 61 0 E
Seki .... **106** 35 29N 136 55 E
Sekondi-Takoradi **130** 4 58N 1 45W
Selangor □ .... **96** 3 10N 101 30 E
Selby **29** 53 47N 1 5W
Sélibabi **130** 15 10N 12 15W
Selkirk, Canada **153** 50 10N 96 55W
Selkirk, U.K. **31** 55 33N 2 50W
Selkirk Mts. **155** 51 15N 117 40W
Selma, Ala., U.S.A. **169** 32 30N 87 0W
Selma, Calif., U.S.A. ... **173** 36 39N 119 39W
Selsey Bill **24** 50 44N 0 47W
Selvas **187** 6 30S 67 0W
Semarang .... **111** 7 0S 110 26 E
Semey .... **71** 50 30N 80 10 E
Semipalatinsk = Semey ... **71** 50 30N 80 10 E
Semnān .... **86** 35 55N 53 25 E
Semnān □ .... **86** 36 0N 54 0 E
Sendai, Kagoshima, Japan .. **108** 31 50N 130 20 E
Sendai, Miyagi, Japan .... **103** 38 15N 140 53 E
Senegal ■ **130** 14 30N 14 30W
Senegal ─► **126** 15 48N 16 32W
Senge Khambab = Indus ─► **88** 24 20N 67 47 E
Senhor-do-Bonfim **189** 10 30S 40 10W
Senja I. .... **64** 69 15N 17 30 E
Senlis .... **39** 49 13N 2 35 E
Sennär .... **129** 13 30N 33 35 E
Senneterre **151** 48 25N 77 15W

Name	Page	Lat °	Lat ′	N/S	Long °	Long ′	E/W
Sens	39	48	11	N	3	15	E
Senta	52	45	55	N	20	3	E
Seoul = Sŏul	98	37	31	N	126	58	E
Sept-Îles	148	50	13	N	66	22	W
Seram	113	3	10	S	129	0	E
Seram Sea	113	2	30	S	128	30	E
Seremban	96	2	43	N	101	53	E
Serena, La	190	29	55	S	71	10	W
Sereth = Siret →	57	47	58	N	26	5	E
Sergipe □	189	10	30	S	37	30	W
Sérifos	55	37	9	N	24	30	E
Serny Zavod	70	39	59	N	58	50	E
Serov	69	59	29	N	60	35	E
Serowe	137	22	25	S	26	43	E
Serpukhov	68	54	55	N	37	28	E
Serra do Navio	185	0	59	N	52	3	W
Sérrai	55	41	5	N	23	31	E
Sesheke	134	17	29	S	24	13	E
Setana	103	42	26	N	139	51	E
Sète	37	43	25	N	3	42	E
Sétif	127	36	9	N	5	26	E
Seto	106	35	14	N	137	6	E
Setonaikai	109	34	20	N	133	30	E
Settle	28	54	5	N	2	18	W
Setúbal	50	38	30	N	8	58	W
Sevastopol	68	44	35	N	33	30	E
Seven Sisters	154	54	56	N	128	10	W
Severn →, Canada	140	56	2	N	87	36	W
Severn →, U.K.	24	51	35	N	2	38	W
Severnaya Zemlya	72	79	0	N	100	0	E
Severodvinsk	69	64	27	N	39	58	E
Sevilla	50	37	23	N	6	0	W
Seville = Sevilla	50	37	23	N	6	0	W
Seward	142	60	6	N	149	26	W
Seward Pen.	142	65	0	N	164	0	W
Seychelles ■	78	5	0	S	56	0	E
Seyðisfjörður	64	65	16	N	14	0	W
Seymour	117	37	0	S	145	10	E
Seyne-sur-Mer, La	37	43	7	N	5	52	E
Sézanne	39	48	40	N	3	40	E
Sfax	127	34	49	N	10	48	E
Sfîntu Gheorghe	57	45	52	N	25	48	E
Shaanxi □	99	35	0	N	109	0	E
Shaba □	135	8	0	S	25	0	E
Shache	100	38	20	N	77	10	E
Shaftesbury	24	51	0	N	2	12	W
Shahdād	85	30	30	N	57	40	E
Shakhty	68	47	40	N	40	16	E
Shamanovo	73	69	45	N	147	20	E
Shamo = Gobi	98	44	0	N	111	0	E
Shamokin	164	40	47	N	76	33	W
Shan □	93	21	30	N	98	30	E
Shandong □	99	36	0	N	118	0	E
Shanghai	99	31	15	N	121	26	E
Shangqiu	99	34	26	N	115	36	E
Shangrao	99	28	25	N	117	59	E
Shannon →	35	52	35	N	9	30	W
Shansi = Shanxi □	98	37	0	N	112	0	E
Shantou	99	23	18	N	116	40	E
Shantung = Shandong □	99	36	0	N	118	0	E
Shanxi □	98	37	0	N	112	0	E
Shaoguan	99	24	48	N	113	35	E
Shaoxing	99	30	0	N	120	35	E
Shaoyang	99	27	14	N	111	25	E
Shap	28	54	32	N	2	40	W
Sharjah = Ash Shāriqah	85	25	23	N	55	26	E
Shark B.	120	25	55	S	113	32	E
Sharon	164	41	18	N	80	30	W
Shashi	99	30	25	N	112	14	E
Shasta, Mt.	172	41	30	N	122	12	W
Shasta L.	172	40	50	N	122	15	W
Shaunavon	152	49	35	N	108	25	W
Shawano	167	44	45	N	88	38	W
Shawinigan	151	46	35	N	72	50	W
Shawnee	168	35	15	N	97	0	W
Shcherbakov = Andropov	68	58	5	N	38	50	E
Shebele, Wabi →	133	2	0	N	44	0	E
Sheboygan	167	43	46	N	87	45	W
Sheerness	24	51	26	N	0	47	E
Sheffield	28	53	23	N	1	28	W
Shekhupura	89	31	42	N	73	58	E
Shelburne	148	43	47	N	65	20	W
Shelby, Mont., U.S.A.	163	48	30	N	111	52	W
Shelby, N.C., U.S.A.	165	35	18	N	81	34	W
Shelbyville, Ind., U.S.A.	167	39	30	N	85	42	W
Shelbyville, Tenn., U.S.A.	169	35	30	N	86	25	W
Shelikhova, Zaliv	73	59	30	N	157	0	E
Shellharbour	117	34	31	S	150	51	E
Shelton	171	47	15	N	123	6	W
Shenandoah	166	40	50	N	95	25	W
Shensi = Shaanxi □	99	35	0	N	109	0	E
Shenyang	98	41	50	N	123	25	E
Shepparton	117	36	23	S	145	26	E
Sheppey, I. of	24	51	23	N	0	50	E
Sherborne	27	50	56	N	2	31	W
Sherbrooke	148	45	28	N	71	57	W
Sheridan	163	44	50	N	107	0	W
Sherman	168	33	40	N	96	35	W
Sherridon	152	55	8	N	101	5	W
Sherwood Forest	29	53	5	N	1	5	W
Shetland Is.	30	60	30	N	1	30	W
Shibām	83	16	0	N	48	36	E
Shibata	103	37	57	N	139	20	E
Shibetsu	103	44	10	N	142	23	E
Shibukawa	107	36	29	N	139	0	E
Shibushi-Wan	108	31	24	N	131	8	E
Shiel, L.	32	56	48	N	5	32	W
Shihchiachuangi = Shijiazhuang	98	38	2	N	114	28	E
Shijiazhuang	98	38	2	N	114	28	E
Shikarpur	88	27	57	N	68	39	E
Shikine-Jima	107	34	19	N	139	13	E
Shikoku	109	33	30	N	133	30	E
Shikoku □	109	33	30	N	133	30	E
Shikoku-Sanchi	109	33	30	N	133	30	E
Shillong	93	25	35	N	91	53	E
Shimabara	108	32	48	N	130	20	E
Shimada	107	34	49	N	138	10	E
Shimizu	107	35	0	N	138	30	E
Shimo-Jima	108	32	15	N	130	7	E
Shimo-Koshiki-Jima	108	31	40	N	129	43	E
Shimoda	107	34	40	N	138	57	E
Shimodate	107	36	20	N	139	55	E
Shimoga	90	13	57	N	75	32	E
Shimonoseki	108	33	58	N	131	0	E
Shin, L.	33	58	7	N	4	30	W
Shin-Tone →	107	35	44	N	140	51	E
Shinano →	105	36	50	N	138	30	E
Shingū	106	33	40	N	135	55	E
Shinji Ko	109	35	26	N	132	57	E
Shinjō	103	38	46	N	140	18	E
Shinminato	106	36	47	N	137	4	E
Shinshiro	106	34	54	N	137	30	E
Shio-no-Misaki	106	33	25	N	135	45	E
Shiogama	103	38	19	N	141	1	E
Shiojiri	107	36	6	N	137	58	E
Shipka	53	42	46	N	25	33	E
Shirane-San, Gumma, Japan	107	36	48	N	139	22	E
Shirane-San, Yamanashi, Japan	107	35	42	N	138	9	E
Shīrāz	85	29	42	N	52	30	E
Shire →	137	17	42	S	35	19	E
Shiriya-Zaki	103	41	25	N	141	30	E
Shivpuri	91	25	26	N	77	42	E
Shizuoka	107	35	0	N	138	24	E
Shkoder = Shkodra	52	42	6	N	19	20	E
Shkodra	52	42	6	N	19	20	E
Shkumbini →	52	41	5	N	19	50	E
Shō-Gawa →	106	36	47	N	137	4	E
Shōbara	109	34	51	N	133	1	E
Shoeburyness	24	51	31	N	0	49	E
Sholapur = Solapur	91	17	43	N	75	56	E
Shoshone	172	43	0	N	114	27	W
Shreveport	168	32	30	N	93	50	W
Shrewsbury	28	52	42	N	2	45	W
Shrirampur	92	22	44	N	88	21	E
Shropshire □	24	52	36	N	2	45	W
Shuangyashan	98	46	37	N	131	22	E
Siahan Range	88	27	30	N	64	40	E
Sialkot	89	32	32	N	74	30	E
Siam = Thailand ■	95	16	0	N	102	0	E
Sian = Xi'an	99	34	15	N	109	0	E

Sololá 259

Siberia 77 60 0N 100 0 E
Siberut 111 1 30S 99 0 E
Sibi 88 29 30N 67 54 E
Sibiu 57 45 45N 24 9 E
Sichuan □ 99 31 0N 104 0 E
Sicilia 49 37 30N 14 30 E
Sicily = Sicilia 49 37 30N 14 30 E
Sicuani 187 14 21S 71 10W
Sidi-bel-Abbès 127 35 13N .0 39W
Sidlaw Hills 31 56 32N 3 10W
Sidley, Mt. 15 77 2S 126 2W
Sidmouth 27 50 40N 3 13W
Sidney 154 48 39N 123 24W
Sidon = Saydā 80 33 35N 35 25 E
Sidra, G. of = Surt, Khalīj 127 31 40N 18 30 E
Siedlce 58 52 10N 22 20 E
Siena 46 43 20N 11 20 E
Sierra Blanca Pk. 161 33 20N 105 54W
Sierra Leone ■ 130 9 0N 12 0W
Sifnos 55 37 0N 24 45 E
Siglufjörður 64 66 12N 18 55W
Sihanoukville = Kompong
Som 95 10 38N 103 30 E
Siirt 81 37 57N 41 55 E
Sikar 89 27 33N 75 10 E
Sikeston 169 36 52N 89 35W
Sikhote Alin, Khrebet 75 46 0N 136 0 E
Sikinos 55 36 40N 25 8 E
Sikkim □ 92 27 50N 88 30 E
Silchar 93 24 49N 92 48 E
Silesia = Slask 58 51 0N 16 30 E
Siling Co 101 31 50N 89 20 E
Silloth 28 54 53N 3 25W
Simbirsk 68 54 20N 48 25 E
Simcoe 151 42 50N 80 20W
Simenga 74 62 42N 108 25 E
Simeulue 111 2 45N 95 45 E
Simferopol 68 44 55N 34 3 E
Simi Valley 173 34 16N 118 47W
Simla 89 31 2N 77 9 E
Simplon Pass 44 46 15N 8 0 E
Simushir, Ostrov 75 46 50N 152 30 E
Sinai = Es Sînâ' 128 29 0N 34 0 E
Sinaloa 174 25 50N 108 20W
Sinaloa □ 174 25 0N 107 30W
Sincelejo 184 9 18N 75 24W
Sinclair Mills 155 54 5N 121 40W
Sind □ 88 26 0N 69 0 E
Sind Sagar Doab 89 32 0N 71 30 E
Singa 129 13 10N 33 57 E
Singapore ■ 96 1 17N 103 51 E
Singapore, Straits of 96 1 15N 104 0 E
Singkaling Hkamti 92 26 0N 95 39 E
Singleton 117 32 33S 151 0 E
Singora = Songkhla 97 7 13N 100 37 E
Sinkiang Uighur = Xinjiang
Uygur Zizhiqu □ 100 42 0N 86 0 E
Sioux City 166 42 32N 96 25W
Sioux Falls 166 43 35N 96 40W
Sioux Lookout 153 50 10N 91 50W
Siping 98 43 8N 124 21 E
Sipora 111 2 18S 99 40 E
Siracusa 49 37 4N 15 17 E
Sirajganj 92 24 25N 89 47 E
Siret → 57 47 58N 26 5 E
Siros 55 37 28N 24 57 E
Sitapur 92 27 38N 80 45 E
Sitka 143 57 9N 135 20W
Sittard 41 51 0N 5 52 E
Sivas 80 39 43N 36 58 E
Siverek 81 37 50N 39 19 E
Sivrihisar 80 39 30N 31 35 E
Sîwa 128 29 11N 25 31 E
Siwalik Range 92 28 0N 83 0 E
Sizewell 24 52 13N 1 38 E
Sjumen = Kolarovgrad 53 43 18N 26 55 E
Skadarsko Jezero 52 42 10N 19 20 E
Skagerrak 60 57 30N 9 0 E
Skagway 143 59 23N 135 20W
Skaraborgs län □ 60 58 20N 13 30 E
Skeena → 154 54 9N 130 5W

Skegness 29 53 9N 0 20 E
Skellefte → 66 65 30N 18 30 E
Skellefteå 67 64 45N 20 58 E
Skerries, The 26 53 27N 4 40W
Skiddaw 28 54 39N 3 9W
Skien 60 59 12N 9 35 E
Skierniewice 58 51 58N 20 10 E
Skikda 127 36 50N 6 58 E
Skipton 28 53 57N 2 1W
Skiros 55 38 55N 24 34 E
Skopje 52 42 1N 21 32 E
Skowhegan 148 44 49N 69 40W
Skull 35 51 32N 9 40W
Skye 32 57 15N 6 10W
Skyros = Skíros 55 38 55N 24 34 E
Slaney → 35 52 52N 6 45W
Slask 58 51 0N 16 30 E
Slave → 145 61 18N 113 39W
Slave Coast 124 6 0N 2 30 E
Sleaford 29 53 0N 0 22W
Sliedrecht 40 51 50N 4 45 E
Slieve Aughty 35 53 4N 8 30W
Slieve Bloom 35 53 4N 7 40W
Slieve Donard 34 54 10N 5 57W
Slieve Mish 35 52 12N 9 50W
Slievenamon 35 52 25N 7 37W
Sligo 34 54 17N 8 28W
Sligo □ 34 54 10N 8 35W
Slovak Republic ■ 59 48 30N 20 0 E
Slovakian Ore Mts. =
Slovenské Rudohorie 59 48 45N 20 0 E
Slovenia ■ 52 45 58N 14 30 E
Slovenské Rudohorie 59 48 45N 20 0 E
Słupsk 58 54 30N 17 3 E
Slyne Hd. 34 53 25N 10 10W
Smara 126 32 9N 8 16W
Smithers 154 54 45N 127 10W
Smithfield 165 35 31N 78 16W
Smiths Falls 151 44 55N 76 0W
Smithton 119 40 53S 145 6 E
Smolensk 68 54 45N 32 0 E
Smolikas, Óros 54 40 9N 20 58 E
Smyrna = İzmir 80 38 25N 27 8 E
Snæfell, Iceland 64 64 48N 15 34W
Snaefell, U.K. 28 54 18N 4 26W
Snæfellsjökull 64 64 49N 23 46W
Snake → 171 46 12N 119 2W
Sneek 41 53 2N 5 40 E
Snowdon 26 53 4N 4 8W
Snowdrift 145 62 24N 110 44W
Snowy Mts. 117 36 30S 148 20 E
Sobat → 129 8 32N 32 40 E
Sobral 177 3 50S 40 20W
Soch'e = Shache 100 38 20N 77 10 E
Sochi 70 43 35N 39 40 E
Société, Is. de la 123 17 0S 151 0W
Society Is. = Société, Is. de
la 123 17 0S 151 0W
Socorro 161 34 4N 106 54W
Socotra 78 12 30N 54 0 E
Söderhamn 60 61 18N 17 10 E
Södermanlands län □ 60 59 10N 16 30 E
Södertälje 60 59 12N 17 39 E
Sodo 132 7 0N 37 41 E
Sofala 137 33 4S 149 43 E
Sofia = Sofiya 53 42 45N 23 20 E
Sofiya 53 42 45N 23 20 E
Sogn og Fjordane fylke □ 60 61 40N 6 0 E
Soissons 39 49 25N 3 19 E
Sõja 109 34 40N 133 45 E
Söke 80 37 48N 27 28 E
Sol Iletsk 70 51 10N 55 0 E
Solapur 91 17 43N 75 56 E
Soledad, Colombia 184 10 55N 74 46W
Soledad, Venezuela 185 8 10N 63 34W
Solent, The 24 50 45N 1 25W
Solesmes 38 50 10N 3 30 E
Solikamsk 69 59 38N 56 50 E
Solimões = Amazonas → 185 0 5S 50 0W
Sóller 51 39 46N 2 43 E
Sololá 177 14 49N 91 10 E

Name	Page	Lat°	Lat′	N/S	Long°	Long′	E/W
Solomon Is. ■	122	6		0S	155	0	E
Solṭānābād	86	36	29N		58	5	E
Solway Firth	31	54	45N		3	38W	
Somali Rep. ■	133	7	0N		47	0	E
Sombor	52	45	46N		19	9	E
Sombrerete	175	23	38N		103	39W	
Somerset, Bermuda	180	32	16N		64	55W	
Somerset, U.S.A.	169	37	5N		84	40W	
Somerset □	27	51	9N		3	0W	
Somerset I.	145	73	30N		93	0W	
Somme □	36	50	0N		2	20	E
Somport, Puerto de	51	42	48N		0	31W	
Søndre Strømfjord	147	66	59N		50	40W	
Songkhla	97	7	13N		100	37	E
Sonora □	174	29	20N		110	40W	
Soochow = Suzhou	99	31	19N		120	38	E
Sop's Arm	149	49	46N		56	56W	
Sør-Rondane	14	72		0S	25	0	E
Sør-Trøndelag fylke □	65	63	0N		10	0	E
Sorata	187	15	50S		68	40W	
Sorel	151	46	0N		73	10W	
Soria	51	41	43N		2	32W	
Sorocaba	191	23	31S		47	27W	
Sørøya	67	70	40N		22	30	E
Sorsogon	112	13	0N		124	0	E
Sosnowiec	58	50	20N		19	10	E
Sotteville-lès-Rouen	38	49	24N		1	5	E
Sõul	98	37	31N		126	58	E
Souris, Man., Canada	153	49	40N		100	20W	
Souris, P.E.I., Canada	149	46	21N		62	15W	
South Africa, Rep. of ■	136	32		0S	17	0	E
South Australia □	118	32		0S	139	0	E
South Bend	167	41	38N		86	20W	
South Carolina □	165	33	45N		81	0W	
South Charleston	165	38	20N		81	40W	
South China Sea	77	10	0N		113	0	E
South Dakota □	163	45	0N		100	0W	
South Downs	25	50	53N		0	10W	
South Georgia	183	54	30S		37	0W	
South Glamorgan □	27	51	30N		3	20W	
South Haven	167	42	22N		86	20W	
South Island	123	44		0S	170	0	E
South Korea ■	98	36	0N		128	0	E
South Orkney Is.	14	63		0S	45	0W	
South Platte →	163	41	7N		100	42W	
South Pole	14	90		0S	0	0	E
South Porcupine	151	48	30N		81	12W	
South Ronaldsay	33	58	46N		2	58W	
South Sandwich Is.	14	57		0S	27	0W	
South Sentinel I.	94	11	1N		92	16	E
South Shetland Is.	14	62		0S	59	0W	
South Shields	28	54	59N		1	26W	
South Taranaki Bight	122	39	40S		174	5	E
South Uist	32	57	20N		7	15W	
South West Africa = Namibia ■	136	22		0S	18	9	E
South West Cape	123	47	16S		167	31	E
South Yorkshire □	29	53	30N		1	20W	
Southampton	25	50	54N		1	23W	
Southampton I.	146	64	30N		84	0W	
Southend-on-Sea	25	51	32N		0	42	E
Southern Alps	123	43	41S		170	11	E
Southern Cross	120	31	12S		119	15	E
Southern Indian L.	143	57	10N		98	30W	
Southern Uplands	31	55	30N		3	3W	
Southland □	123	45	51S		168	13	E
Southport, Australia	116	27	58S		153	25	E
Southport, U.K.	28	53	38N		3	1W	
Southwold	25	52	19N		1	41	E
Sovetskaya Gavan	75	48	50N		140	0	E
Sõya-Kaikyõ = Perouse Str., La	77	45	40N		142	0	E
Spain ■	50	40	0N		5	0W	
Spalding	29	52	47N		0	9W	
Spandau	43	52	35N		13	7	E
Spanish Fork	163	40	10N		111	37W	
Spanish Town	180	18	0N		76	57W	
Sparks	172	39	30N		119	45W	
Sparta = Spárti	54	37	5N		22	25	E
Sparta	166	43	55N		90	47W	
Spartanburg	165	35	0N		82	0W	
Spárti	54	37	5N		22	25	E
Spartivento, C., Calabria, Italy	49	37	56N		16	4	E
Spartivento, C., Sard., Italy	48	38	52N		8	50	E
Spassk-Dalniy	75	44	40N		132	48	E
Speightstown	180	13	15N		59	39W	
Spence Bay	145	69	32N		93	32W	
Spencer	166	43	5N		95	19W	
Spencer G.	119	34		0S	137	20	E
Spenser Mts.	123	42	15S		172	45	E
Sperrin Mts.	34	54	50N		7	0W	
Spessart	42	50	10N		9	20	E
Spey →	33	57	26N		3	25W	
Spézia, La	46	44	8N		9	50	E
Spinazzola	49	40	58N		16	5	E
Spithead	25	50	43N		1	5W	
Spitzbergen = Svalbard	13	78	0N		17	0	E
Split	52	43	31N		16	26	E
Splügenpass	44	46	30N		9	20	E
Spokane	171	47	45N		117	25W	
Sporyy Navolok, Mys	69	75	50N		68	40	E
Spratly, I.	112	8	20N		112	0	E
Spring Mts.	173	36	20N		115	43W	
Springfield, Ill., U.S.A.	166	39	48N		89	40W	
Springfield, Mass., U.S.A.	164	42	8N		72	37W	
Springfield, Mo., U.S.A.	168	37	15N		93	20W	
Springfield, Ohio, U.S.A.	167	39	58N		83	48W	
Springfield, Oreg., U.S.A.	171	44	2N		123	0W	
Springfield, Tenn., U.S.A.	169	36	35N		86	55W	
Springfield, Vt., U.S.A.	164	43	20N		72	30W	
Springhill	148	45	40N		64	4W	
Springs	137	26	13S		28	25	E
Springwood	117	33	41S		150	33	E
Spurn Hd.	29	53	34N		0	8	E
Squamish	154	49	45N		123	10W	
Sredinnyy Khrebet	73	57	0N		160	0	E
Srednekolymsk	73	67	27N		153	40	E
Sremska Mitrovica	52	44	59N		19	33	E
Srepok →	95	13	33N		106	16	E
Sretensk	74	52	10N		117	40	E
Sri Lanka ■	90	7	30N		80	50	E
Srinagar	89	34	5N		74	50	E
Stadskanaal	41	53	4N		6	55	E
Staffa	30	56	26N		6	21W	
Stafford	28	52	49N		2	9W	
Stafford □	28	52	53N		2	10W	
Staines	25	51	26N		0	30W	
Stalingrad = Volgograd	68	48	40N		44	25	E
Stalino = Donetsk	68	48	0N		37	45	E
Stalinogorsk = Novomoskovsk	68	54	5N		38	15	E
Stalybridge	28	53	29N		2	4W	
Stamford, U.K.	25	52	39N		0	29W	
Stamford, U.S.A.	164	41	5N		73	30W	
Stanislav = Ivano-Frankovsk	68	48	40N		24	40	E
Stanley, Canada	152	55	24N		104	22W	
Stanley, Falk. Is.	192	51	40S		59	51W	
Stanovoy Khrebet	75	55	0N		130	0	E
Stanthorpe	116	28	36S		151	59	E
Stara Planina	53	43	15N		23	0	E
Stara Zagora	53	42	26N		25	39	E
Starkville	169	33	26N		88	48W	
Start Pt.	27	50	13N		3	38W	
State College	164	40	47N		77	49W	
Staten, I. = Estados, I. de los	192	54	40S		64	30W	
Statesboro	170	32	26N		81	46W	
Statesville	165	35	48N		80	51W	
Staunton	165	38	7N		79	4W	
Stavanger	60	58	57N		5	40	E
Staveren	40	52	53N		5	22	E
Stavropol	70	45	5N		42	0	E
Stawell	119	37	5S		142	47	E
Steenwijk	41	52	47N		6	7	E
Stefanie L. = Chew Bahir	132	4	40N		36	50	E
Steiermark □	45	47	26N		15	0	E
Steinbach	153	49	32N		96	40W	
Steinkjer	65	63	59N		11	31	E
Stellarton	149	45	32N		62	30W	
Stephenville	149	48	31N		58	35W	
Stereá Ellas □	54	38	50N		22	0	E
Sterling, Colo., U.S.A.	163	40	40N		103	15W	
Sterling, Ill., U.S.A.	166	41	45N		89	45W	

Sterlitamak	71	53 40N	56	0 E
Stettin = Szczecin	58	53 27N	14	27 E
Stettler	155	52 19N	112	40W
Steubenville	164	40 21N	80	39W
Stevens Port	166	44 32N	89	34W
Stewart	144	63 19N	139	26W
Stewart I.	123	46 58S	167	54 E
Stikine ➤	144	56 40N	132	30W
Stillwater, Minn., U.S.A.	166	45 3N	92	47W
Stillwater, Okla., U.S.A.	168	36 5N	97	3W
Stillwater Ra.	172	39 45N	118	6W
Štip	53	41 42N	22	10 E
Stirling	31	56 7N	3	57W
Stirling Ra.	120	34 23S	118	0 E
Stockholm	60	59 20N	18	3 E
Stockholms län □	60	59 30N	18	20 E
Stockport	28	53 25N	2	11W
Stockton	172	38 0N	121	20W
Stockton-on-Tees	29	54 34N	1	20W
Stoke-on-Trent	28	53 1N	2	11W
Stonehaven	33	56 58N	2	11W
Stonehenge	24	51 9N	1	45W
Stonewall	153	50 10N	97	19W
Stora Lulevatten	66	67 10N	19	30 E
Storavan	66	65 45N	18	10 E
Store Bælt	61	55 20N	11	0 E
Storm B.	119	43 10S	147	30 E
Storm Lake	166	42 35N	95	11W
Stornoway	32	58 12N	6	23W
Storsjön	66	63 12N	14	18 E
Storuman	66	65 5N	17	10 E
Stour ➤, Here. & Worcs., U.K.	24	52 25N	2	13W
Stour ➤, Kent, U.K.	25	51 15N	1	20 E
Stour ➤, Suffolk, U.K.	25	51 55N	1	5 E
Stourbridge	24	52 28N	2	8W
Stowmarket	25	52 11N	1	0 E
Strabane	34	54 50N	7	28W
Stralsund	43	54 17N	13	5 E
Strangford, L.	34	54 30N	5	37W
Stranraer	30	54 54N	5	0W
Strasbourg	37	48 35N	7	42 E
Stratford, Canada	151	43 23N	81	0W
Stratford, N.Z.	122	39 20S	174	19 E
Stratford-on-Avon	24	52 12N	1	42W
Strath Spey	33	57 15N	3	40W
Strathalbyn	119	35 13S	138	53 E
Strathclyde □	30	56 0N	4	50W
Strathmore	33	56 40N	3	4W
Strathy Pt.	33	58 35N	4	0W
Streaky B.	118	32 51S	134	18 E
Streator	167	41 9N	88	52W
Strómboli	49	38 48N	15	12 E
Stromeferry	32	57 20N	5	33W
Stromness	33	58 58N	3	18W
Stronsay	33	59 8N	2	38W
Stroud	24	51 44N	2	12W
Strumica	53	41 28N	22	41 E
Stuart L.	154	54 30N	124	30W
Stung Treng	95	13 31N	105	58 E
Sturgeon Bay	167	44 52N	87	20W
Sturgeon Falls	151	46 25N	79	57W
Stuttgart, Germany	42	48 46N	9	10 E
Stuttgart, U.S.A.	168	34 30N	91	33W
Styria = Steiermark □	45	47 26N	15	0 E
Suakin	129	19 8N	37	20 E
Subotica	52	46 6N	19	49 E
Suchitoto	177	13 56N	89	0W
Suchou = Suzhou	99	31 19N	120	38 E
Süchow = Xuzhou	99	34 18N	117	10 E
Sucre	187	19 0S	65	15W
Sudan ■	129	15 0N	30	0 E
Sudbury, Canada	151	46 30N	81	0W
Sudbury, U.K.	25	52 2N	0	44 E
Sudetan Mts. = Sudety	58	50 20N	16	45 E
Sudety	58	50 20N	16	45 E
Suez = El Suweis	128	29 58N	32	31 E
Suez Canal = Suweis, Qanâl es	128	31 0N	32	20 E
Suffolk	165	36 47N	76	33W
Suffolk □	25	52 16N	1	0 E
Sugluk = Saglouc	146	62 14N	75	38W
Suhbaatar	98	50 17N	106	10 E
Suir ➤	35	52 15N	7	10W
Suita	106	34 45N	135	32 E
Sukhona ➤	68	60 30N	45	0 E
Sukhumi	70	43 0N	41	0 E
Sukkertoppen	147	65 26N	52	55W
Sukkur	88	27 42N	68	54 E
Sukkur Barrage	88	27 40N	68	50 E
Sukumo	109	32 56N	132	44 E
Sulaiman Range	89	30 30N	69	50 E
Sulawesi □	113	2 0S	120	0 E
Sulina	57	45 10N	29	40 E
Sulitjelma	66	67 9N	16	3 E
Sullana	186	4 52S	80	39W
Sullivan	167	39 5N	87	26W
Sullivan I. = Lambi Kyun	96	10 50N	98	20 E
Sulphur Springs	168	33 5N	95	36W
Sulu Arch.	112	6 0N	121	0 E
Sulu Sea	112	8 0N	120	0 E
Suluq	128	31 44N	20	14 E
Sumatera □	111	0 40N	100	20 E
Sumatra = Sumatera □	111	0 40N	100	20 E
Sumba	113	9 45S	119	35 E
Sumbawa	113	8 26S	117	30 E
Sumburgh Hd.	30	59 52N	1	17W
Summerland	155	49 32N	119	41W
Summerside	148	46 24N	63	47W
Sumoto	109	34 21N	134	54 E
Sumter	165	33 55N	80	22W
Sumy	68	50 57N	34	50 E
Sunbury, Australia	117	37 35S	144	44 E
Sunbury, U.S.A.	164	40 50N	76	46W
Sunda, Selat	111	6 20S	105	30 E
Sundarbans, The	92	22 0N	89	0 E
Sunderland	28	54 54N	1	22W
Sundsvall	66	62 23N	17	17 E
Sungei Patani	96	5 38N	100	29 E
Sungei Siput	96	4 51N	101	6 E
Sungurlu	80	40 12N	34	21 E
Sunnyside	171	46 24N	120	2W
Sunnyvale	172	37 23N	122	2W
Suntar	74	62 15N	117	30 E
Suō-Nada	108	33 50N	131	30 E
Superior	150	46 45N	92	5W
Superior, L.	150	47 40N	87	0W
Suphan Daği	81	38 54N	42	48 E
Sūr	80	22 34N	59	32 E
Surabaja = Surabaya	111	7 17S	112	45 E
Surabaya	111	7 17S	112	45 E
Surakarta	111	7 35S	110	48 E
Surat	91	21 12N	72	55 E
Surat Thani	96	9 6N	99	20 E
Suratgarh	89	29 18N	73	55 E
Surgut	69	61 14N	73	20 E
Surin	95	14 50N	103	34 E
Surinam ■	185	4 0N	56	0W
Surrey □	25	51 16N	0	30W
Surt	127	31 11N	16	39 E
Surt, Khalîj	127	31 40N	18	30 E
Suruga-Wan	107	34 45N	138	30 E
Susaki	109	33 22N	133	17 E
Susanville	172	40 28N	120	40W
Susquehanna ➤	164	39 33N	76	5W
Sutherland Falls	123	44 48S	167	46 E
Sutlej ➤	89	29 23N	71	3 E
Sutton-in-Ashfield	29	53 7N	1	20W
Suva	122	18 6S	178	30 E
Suwa	107	36 2N	138	8 E
Suwa-Ko	107	36 3N	138	5 E
Suwannee ➤	170	29 18N	83	9W
Suwanose-Jima	104	29 38N	129	43 E
Suweis, Qanâl es	128	31 0N	32	20 E
Suzaka	107	36 39N	138	19 E
Suzhou	99	31 19N	120	38 E
Suzu-Misaki	105	37 31N	137	21 E
Svalbard	13	78 0N	17	0 E
Svartenhuk Halvø	146	71 50N	54	30W
Svendborg	61	55 4N	10	35 E
Sverdlovsk = Yekaterinburg	69	56 50N	60	30 E
Sverdrup Is.	12	79 0N	97	0W

Name	Map	Lat	Long
Svishtov	**53**	43 36N	25 23 E
Svobodnyy	**75**	51 20N	128 0 E
Swabian Alps = Schwäbische Alb	**42**	48 30N	9 30 E
Swakopmund	**136**	22 37S	14 30 E
Swale →	**28**	54 5N	1 20W
Swan Hill	**117**	35 20S	143 33 E
Swan Hills	**155**	54 42N	115 24W
Swan Islands	**178**	17 22N	83 57W
Swan River	**152**	52 10N	101 16W
Swanage	**24**	50 36N	1 59W
Swansea	**27**	51 37N	3 57W
Swartberge	**136**	33 20S	22 0 E
Swatow = Shantou	**99**	23 18N	116 40 E
Swaziland ■	**137**	26 30S	31 30 E
Sweden ■	**66**	57 0N	15 0 E
Sweetwater	**161**	32 30N	100 28W
Swift Current	**152**	50 20N	107 45W
Swindon	**24**	51 33N	1 47W
Switzerland ■	**44**	46 30N	8 0 E
Swords	**34**	53 27N	6 15W
Sydney, Australia	**117**	33 53S	151 10 E
Sydney, Canada	**149**	46 7N	60 7W
Sydney Mines	**149**	46 18N	60 15W
Sydprøven	**147**	60 30N	45 35W
Sydra G. of = Surt, Khalīj	**127**	31 40N	18 30 E
Syktyvkar	**69**	61 45N	50 40 E
Sylacauga	**169**	33 10N	86 15W
Sylhet	**92**	24 54N	91 52 E
Sylvan Lake	**155**	52 20N	114 3W
Syracuse	**164**	43 4N	76 11W
Syrdarya →	**71**	46 3N	61 0 E
Syria ■	**80**	35 0N	38 0 E
Syrian Desert	**76**	31 0N	40 0 E
Syzran	**68**	53 12N	48 30 E
Szczecin	**58**	53 27N	14 27 E
Szechwan = Sichuan □	**99**	31 0N	104 0 E
Szeged	**59**	46 16N	20 10 E
Székesfehérvár	**59**	47 15N	18 25 E
Szolnok	**59**	47 10N	20 15 E
Szombathely	**59**	47 14N	16 38 E

T

Name	Map	Lat	Long
Tabacal	**190**	23 15S	64 15W
Ṭābah	**82**	26 55N	42 38 E
Tabasco □	**177**	18 0N	92 40W
Taber	**155**	49 47N	112 8W
Tablas	**112**	12 25N	122 2 E
Table Mt.	**136**	34 0S	18 22 E
Table Top, Mt.	**121**	23 24S	147 11 E
Tabora	**135**	5 2S	32 50 E
Tabrīz	**81**	38 7N	46 20 E
Tabūk	**82**	28 23N	36 36 E
Tachibana-Wan	**108**	32 45N	130 7 E
Tachikawa	**107**	35 42N	139 25 E
Tacna	**187**	18 0S	70 20W
Tacoma	**171**	47 15N	122 30W
Tacuarembó	**191**	31 45S	56 0W
Tademaït, Plateau du	**127**	28 30N	2 30 E
Tadoussac	**148**	48 11N	69 42W
Taegu	**98**	35 50N	128 37 E
Taejŏn	**98**	36 20N	127 28 E
Taganrog	**68**	47 12N	38 50 E
Tagish	**144**	60 19N	134 16W
Tagua, La	**184**	0 3N	74 40W
Tagus = Tajo →	**50**	38 40N	9 24W
Tahiti	**123**	17 37S	149 27W
Tahoua	**131**	14 57N	5 16 E
Taibei	**99**	25 4N	121 29 E
T'aichung = Taizhong	**99**	24 12N	120 35 E
Taidong	**99**	22 43N	121 9 E
Taihape	**122**	39 41S	175 48 E
Tailem Bend	**119**	35 12S	139 29 E
Taimyr = Taymyr, Poluostrov	**72**	75 0N	100 0 E
Tain	**33**	57 49N	4 4W
Tainan	**99**	23 17N	120 18 E
Tainaron, Ákra	**54**	36 22N	22 27 E
T'aipei = Taibei	**99**	25 4N	121 29 E
Taiping	**96**	4 51N	100 44 E
Taisha	**109**	35 24N	132 40 E
Taitao, Pen. de	**192**	46 30S	75 0W
Taiwan ■	**99**	23 30N	121 0 E
Taiyuan	**98**	37 52N	112 33 E
Taizhong	**99**	24 12N	120 35 E
Ta'izz	**83**	13 35N	44 2 E
Tajikistan ■	**71**	35 30N	70 0 E
Tajimi	**106**	35 19N	137 8 E
Tajo →	**50**	38 40N	9 24W
Tak	**94**	16 52N	99 8 E
Takachiho	**108**	32 42N	131 18 E
Takada	**105**	37 7N	138 15 E
Takahashi	**109**	34 51N	133 39 E
Takamatsu	**109**	34 20N	134 5 E
Takaoka	**106**	36 47N	137 0 E
Takapuna	**122**	36 47S	174 47 E
Takasago	**109**	34 45N	134 48 E
Takasaki	**107**	36 20N	139 0 E
Takatsuki	**106**	34 51N	135 37 E
Takawa	**108**	33 38N	130 51 E
Takayama	**106**	36 18N	137 11 E
Takayama-Bonchi	**106**	36 0N	137 18 E
Takefu	**106**	35 50N	136 10 E
Takehara	**109**	34 21N	132 55 E
Taketa	**108**	32 58N	131 24 E
Takhār □	**87**	36 40N	70 0 E
Takla Landing	**154**	55 30N	125 50W
Takla Makan	**76**	39 0N	83 0 E
Taku	**108**	33 18N	130 3 E
Talara	**186**	4 38S	81 18 E
Talaud, Kepulauan	**113**	4 30N	127 10 E
Talca	**190**	35 28S	71 40W
Talcahuano	**190**	36 40S	73 10W
Talesh, Kūhhā-ye	**81**	39 0N	48 30 E
Talguppa	**90**	14 10N	74 45 E
Taliabu	**113**	1 45S	125 0 E
Talkeetna	**142**	62 20N	150 9W
Tall 'Afar	**81**	36 22N	42 27 E
Talladega	**169**	33 28N	86 2W
Tallahassee	**170**	30 25N	84 15W
Tallangatta	**117**	36 15S	147 19 E
Tallinn	**68**	59 22N	24 48 E
Tallulah	**168**	32 25N	91 12W
Tamale	**130**	9 22N	0 50W
Tamana	**108**	32 58N	130 32 E
Tamano	**109**	34 29N	133 59 E
Tamanrasset	**127**	22 50N	5 30 E
Tamar →	**27**	50 33N	4 15W
Tamaulipas □	**176**	24 0N	98 45W
Tambellup	**120**	34 4S	117 37 E
Tambov	**68**	52 45N	41 28 E
Tamgak, Mts.	**127**	19 12N	8 35 E
Tamil Nadu □	**90**	11 0N	77 0 E
Tammerfors = Tampere	**67**	61 30N	23 50 E
Tamo Abu, Pegunungan	**111**	3 10N	115 0 E
Tampa	**170**	27 57N	82 38W
Tampa B.	**170**	27 40N	82 40W
Tampere	**67**	61 30N	23 50 E
Tampico	**177**	22 20N	97 50W
Tamrah	**83**	20 24N	45 25 E
Tamsagbulag	**98**	47 14N	117 21 E
Tamworth, Australia	**116**	31 7S	150 58 E
Tamworth, U.K.	**24**	52 38N	1 41W
Tana →, Kenya	**133**	2 32S	40 31 E
Tana →, Norway	**67**	70 30N	28 23 E
Tana, L.	**132**	13 5N	37 30 E
Tanabe	**106**	33 44N	135 22 E
Tanana	**142**	65 10N	152 15W
Tananarive = Antananarivo	**137**	18 55S	47 31 E
Tanba-Sanchi	**106**	35 7N	135 48 E
Tandil	**190**	37 15S	59 6W
Tando Adam	**88**	25 45N	68 40 E
Tane-ga-Shima	**104**	30 30N	131 0 E
Tanen Tong Dan	**93**	16 30N	98 30 E
Tanezrouft	**127**	23 9N	0 11 E
Tanga	**135**	5 5S	39 2 E
Tanganyika, L.	**135**	6 40S	30 0 E
Tanger	**126**	35 50N	5 49W
Tanggula Shan	**101**	32 40N	92 10 E

Name	Map	Lat	Long
Tangier = Tanger	126	35 50N	5 49W
Tangshan	98	39 38N	118 10 E
Tanimbar, Kepulauan	113	7 30S	131 30 E
Taniyama	108	31 31N	130 31 E
Tanjore = Thanjavur	90	10 48N	79 12 E
Tannu Ola	74	51 0N	94 0 E
Tanout	131	14 50N	8 55 E
Tanta	128	30 45N	30 57 E
Tantung = Dandong	98	40 10N	124 20 E
Tanunda	119	34 30S	139 0 E
Tanzania ■	135	6 40S	34 0 E
Tapa Shan = Daba Shan	99	32 0N	109 0 E
Tapachula	177	14 54N	92 17W
Tapajós →	185	2 24S	54 41W
Tapanui	123	45 56S	169 18 E
Tapi →	91	21 8N	72 41 E
Tara →	71	56 42N	74 36 E
Tarabagatay, Khrebet	71	48 0N	83 0 E
Tarābulus, Lebanon	80	34 31N	35 50 E
Tarābulus, Libya	127	32 49N	13 7 E
Taranaki □	122	39 5S	174 51 E
Táranto	49	40 30N	17 11 E
Táranto, G. di	49	40 0N	17 15 E
Tarapoto	186	6 30S	76 20W
Tarare	37	45 54N	4 26 E
Tararua Range	123	40 45S	175 25 E
Tarauacá	187	8 6S	70 48W
Tarbela Dam	89	34 8N	72 52 E
Tarbert	32	57 54N	6 49W
Tarbes	36	43 15N	0 3 E
Tarcoola	118	30 44S	134 36 E
Taree	116	31 50S	152 30 E
Tarfaya	126	27 55N	12 55W
Tarifa	50	36 1N	5 36W
Tarija	187	21 30S	64 40W
Tarim →	100	41 5N	86 40 E
Tarim Pendi	100	40 0N	84 0 E
Tarko Sale	69	64 55N	77 50 E
Tarn →	36	44 5N	1 6 E
Tarnobrzeg	58	50 35N	21 41 E
Tarnów	58	50 3N	21 0 E
Tarragona	51	41 5N	1 17 E
Tarrasa	51	41 34N	2 1 E
Tarsus	80	36 58N	34 55 E
Tartagal	190	22 30S	63 50W
Tartūs	80	34 55N	35 55 E
Tarumizu	108	31 29N	130 42 E
Tarutao, Ko	96	6 33N	99 40 E
Taschereau	151	48 40N	78 40W
Tashi Chho Dzong = Thimphu	92	27 31N	89 45 E
Tashkent	71	41 20N	69 10 E
Tasman B.	123	40 59S	173 25 E
Tasman Mts.	123	41 3S	172 25 E
Tasman Sea	122	36 0S	160 0 E
Tasmania □	119	42 0S	146 30 E
Tatabánya	59	47 32N	18 25 E
Tatarsk	71	55 14N	76 0 E
Tatarstan □	70	55 30N	51 30 E
Tateyama	107	35 0N	139 50 E
Tatra = Tatry	59	49 20N	20 0 E
Tatry	59	49 20N	20 0 E
Tatsuno	109	34 52N	134 33 E
Tat'ung = Datong	98	40 6N	113 18 E
Taubaté	191	23 0S	45 36W
Tauern	45	47 15N	12 40 E
Taumarunui	122	38 53S	175 15 E
Taunggyi	93	20 50N	97 0 E
Taungup Taunggya	93	18 20N	93 40 E
Taunton, U.K.	27	51 1N	3 7W
Taunton, U.S.A.	164	41 54N	71 6W
Taunus	42	50 15N	8 20 E
Taupo	122	38 41S	176 7 E
Taupo, L.	122	38 46S	175 55 E
Tauranga	122	37 42S	176 11 E
Taurus Mts. = Toros Daglari	80	37 0N	35 0 E
Taverny	39	49 2N	2 13 E
Tavistock	27	50 33N	4 9W
Tavoy	94	14 2N	98 12 E
Tawas City	167	44 16N	83 31W
Tay →	33	56 37N	3 38W
Tayabamba	186	8 15S	77 16W
Taylor Mt.	161	35 16N	107 36W
Taymä	82	27 35N	38 45 E
Taymyr, Poluostrov	72	75 0N	100 0 E
Tayshet	74	55 58N	98 1 E
Tayside □	31	56 25N	3 30W
Taz →	69	67 32N	78 40 E
Tbilisi	70	41 43N	44 50 E
Tchad = Chad ■	131	15 0N	17 15 E
Tchad, L.	131	13 30N	14 30 E
Tch'eng-tou = Chengdu	99	30 38N	104 2 E
Tch'ong-k'ing = Chongqing	99	29 35N	106 25 E
Te Anau, L.	123	45 15S	167 45 E
Te Kuiti	122	38 20S	175 11 E
Tecuala	175	22 23N	105 27W
Tefé	185	3 25S	64 50W
Tegal	111	6 52S	109 8 E
Tegucigalpa	179	14 5N	87 14W
Tehachapi Mts.	173	35 0N	118 40W
Tehrän	86	35 44N	51 30 E
Tehuacán	177	18 27N	97 23W
Tehuantepec	177	16 21N	95 13W
Tehuantepec, G. de	177	16 0N	94 50W
Tehuantepec, Istmo de	177	17 0N	94 30W
Teifi →	26	52 4N	4 14W
Teignmouth	27	50 33N	3 30W
Tejo →	50	38 40N	9 24W
Tekax	177	20 12N	89 17W
Tekeli	71	44 50N	79 0 E
Tekirdağ	80	40 58N	27 30 E
Tel Aviv-Yafo	80	32 4N	34 48 E
Tela	179	15 40N	87 28W
Telanaipura = Jambi	111	1 38S	103 30 E
Telegraph Cr. →	144	58 0N	131 10W
Telemark fylke □	60	59 25N	8 30 E
Teles Pires →	187	7 21S	58 3W
Telford	28	52 42N	2 31W
Tell City	167	38 0N	86 44W
Teme →	24	52 23N	2 15W
Temerloh	96	3 27N	102 25 E
Temirtau	71	50 5N	72 56 E
Temora	117	34 30S	147 30 E
Temosachic	174	28 57N	107 51W
Temple	158	31 5N	97 22W
Temuco	190	38 45S	72 40W
Temuka	123	44 14S	171 17 E
Tenali	91	16 15N	80 35 E
Tenancingo	177	19 0N	99 33W
Tenango	177	19 7N	99 33W
Tenby	27	51 40N	4 42W
Tenerife	126	28 15N	16 35W
Teng Xian	99	35 5N	117 10 E
Tennessee □	169	36 0N	86 30W
Tennessee →	169	37 4N	88 34W
Tenri	106	34 39N	135 49 E
Tenryü	107	34 52N	137 49 E
Tenryü-Gawa →	107	35 39N	137 48 E
Tenterfield	116	29 0S	152 0 E
Teófilo Otoni	189	17 50S	41 30W
Tepic	175	21 30N	104 54W
Terang	119	38 15S	142 55 E
Terek →	70	44 0N	47 30 E
Terengganu □	96	4 55N	103 0 E
Teresina	188	5 9S	42 45W
Terewah, L.	116	29 52S	147 35 E
Termez	70	37 15N	67 15 E
Términos, L. de	177	18 37N	91 33W
Terneuzen	40	51 20N	3 50 E
Terni	46	42 34N	12 38 E
Terrace	154	54 30N	128 35W
Terre Haute	167	39 28N	87 24W
Terrell	168	32 44N	96 19W
Terschelling	40	53 25N	5 20 E
Teruel	51	40 22N	1 8W
Teshio	103	44 53N	141 44 E
Teslin	144	60 10N	132 43W
Test →	24	51 7N	1 30W
Tete	137	16 13S	33 33 E
Teteven	53	42 58N	24 17 E
Tétouan	126	35 35N	5 21W
Tetuán = Tétouan	126	35 35N	5 21W

Name	Page	°	′ N/S	°	′ E/W
Teuco ~►	190	25	35S	60	11W
Teutoburger Wald	42	52	5N	8	20 E
Tevere ~►	46	41	44N	12	14 E
Tewkesbury	24	51	59N	2	8W
Texarkana, Ark., U.S.A.	168	33	25N	94	0W
Texarkana, Tex., U.S.A.	168	33	25N	94	3W
Texas □	161	31	40N	98	30W
Texel	40	53	5N	4	50 E
Teziutlán	177	19	49N	97	21W
Tezpur	93	26	40N	92	45 E
Thabana Ntlenyana	137	29	30S	29	16 E
Thailand ■	95	16	0N	102	0 E
Thailand, G. of	95	11	30N	101	0 E
Thal Desert	89	31	10N	71	30 E
Thame ~►	24	51	35N	1	8W
Thames	122	37	7S	175	34 E
Thames ~►	25	51	30N	0	35 E
Thane	91	19	12N	72	59 E
Thanh Hoa	95	19	48N	105	46 E
Thanh Pho Ho Chi Minh	95	10	58N	106	40 E
Thanjavur	90	10	48N	79	12 E
Thar Desert	89	28	0N	72	0 E
Thásos	55	40	40N	24	40 E
Thaungdut	93	24	30N	94	40 E
Thazi	93	21	0N	96	5 E
The Dalles	171	45	40N	121	11W
The Grenadines, Is.	180	12	40N	61	20W
The Hague = 's-Gravenhage	40	52	7N	4	17 E
The Macumba ~►	118	27	52S	137	12 E
The Neales ~►	118	28	8S	136	47 E
The Pas	152	53	45N	101	15W
The Rock	117	35	15S	147	2 E
The Warburton ~►	118	28	4S	137	28 E
Thebes = Thívai	55	38	19N	23	19 E
Thermaïkós Kólpos	54	40	15N	22	45 E
Thermopolis	163	43	35N	108	10W
Thessalía □	54	39	30N	22	0 E
Thessalon	150	46	20N	83	30W
Thessaloníki	54	40	38N	22	58 E
Thessaly = Thessalía □	54	39	30N	22	0 E
Thetford Mines	148	46	8N	71	18W
Thicket Portage	153	55	19N	97	42W
Thies	130	14	50N	16	51W
Thimphu	92	27	31N	89	45 E
Thionville	37	49	20N	6	10 E
Thíra	55	36	23N	25	27 E
Thirsk	29	54	15N	1	20W
Thisted	61	56	58N	8	40 E
Thívai	55	38	19N	23	19 E
Thomaston	170	32	54N	84	20W
Thomasville, Ga., U.S.A.	170	30	50N	84	0W
Thomasville, N.C., U.S.A.	165	35	55N	80	4W
Thon Buri	94	13	43N	100	29 E
Thornaby on Tees	29	54	36N	1	19W
Thrace = Thráki □	55	41	9N	25	30 E
Thráki □	55	41	9N	25	30 E
Three Hills	155	51	43N	113	15W
Three Hummock I.	119	40	25S	144	55 E
Thule	13	77	40N	69	0W
Thundelarra	120	28	53S	117	7 E
Thunder B.	150	45	0N	83	20W
Thunder Bay	150	48	20N	89	15W
Thüringer Wald	43	50	35N	11	0 E
Thurles	35	52	40N	7	53W
Thursday I.	115	10	30S	142	3 E
Thurso	33	58	34N	3	31W
Tian Shan	100	43	0N	84	0 E
Tianjin	98	39	8N	117	10 E
Tianshui	99	34	32N	105	40 E
Tiber = Tevere ~►	46	41	44N	12	14 E
Tibesti	127	21	0N	17	30 E
Tibet = Xizang □	101	32	0N	88	0 E
Tibooburra	118	29	26S	142	1 E
Ticul	177	20	24N	89	32W
Tiel	40	51	53N	5	26 E
Tien Shan	76	42	0N	80	0 E
Tien-tsin = Tianjin	98	39	8N	117	10 E
T'ienching = Tianjin	98	39	8N	117	10 E
Tientsin = Tianjin	98	39	8N	117	10 E
Tierra de Campos	50	42	10N	4	50W
Tierra del Fuego □	192	54	0S	67	45W
Tiffin	167	41	8N	83	10W
Tiflis = Tbilisi	70	41	43N	44	50 E
Tifton	170	31	28N	83	32W
Tignish	148	46	58N	64	2W
Tigris = Dijlah, Nahr ~►	81	31	0N	47	25 E
Tijuana	174	32	32N	117	1W
Tiksi	72	71	40N	128	45 E
Tilburg	40	51	31N	5	6 E
Tilbury	25	51	27N	0	24 E
Tillsonburg	151	42	53N	80	44W
Tílos	55	36	27N	27	27 E
Timaru	123	44	23S	171	14 E
Timbuktu = Tombouctou	130	16	50N	3	0W
Timişoara	56	45	43N	21	15 E
Timmins	151	48	28N	81	25W
Timor	113	9	0S	125	0 E
Timor Sea	113	10	0S	127	0 E
Tinaca Pt.	112	5	30N	125	25 E
Tindouf	126	27	42N	8	10W
Tinnevelly = Tirunelveli	90	8	45N	77	45 E
Tinogasta	190	28	5S	67	32W
Tinos	55	37	33N	25	8 E
Tioman, Pulau	96	2	50N	104	10 E
Tipperary	35	52	28N	8	10W
Tipperary □	35	52	37N	7	55W
Tipton	24	52	32N	2	4W
Tirana	52	41	18N	19	49 E
Tiraspol	68	46	55N	29	35 E
Tire	80	38	5N	27	50 E
Tirebolu	81	40	58N	38	45 E
Tiree	30	56	31N	6	55W
Tîrgu Mureş	57	46	31N	24	38 E
Tirol □	45	47	3N	10	43 E
Tiruchchirappalli	90	10	45N	78	45 E
Tirunelveli	90	8	45N	77	45 E
Tisa ~►	59	45	15N	20	17 E
Tisdale	152	52	50N	104	0W
Titicaca, L.	187	15	30S	69	30W
Titograd = Podgorica	52	42	30N	19	19 E
Titov Veles	53	41	46N	21	47 E
Titovo Užice	52	43	55N	19	50 E
Tiverton	27	50	54N	3	30W
Tívoli	46	41	58N	12	45 E
Tizimín	177	21	9N	88	9W
Tjirebon = Cirebon	111	6	45S	108	32 E
Tlaxcala □	177	19	25N	98	10W
Tlaxiaco	177	17	18N	97	40W
Tlemcen	127	34	52N	1	21W
To-Shima	107	34	31N	139	17 E
Toamasina	137	18	10S	49	25 E
Toba Kakar	88	31	30N	69	0 E
Tobago	180	11	10N	60	30W
Tobermory	30	56	37N	6	4W
Tobolsk	69	58	15N	68	10 E
Tobruk = Tubruq	128	32	7N	23	55 E
Tocantins ~►	188	1	45S	49	10W
Toccoa	165	34	32N	83	17W
Tochigi	107	36	25N	139	45 E
Tocopilla	190	22	5S	70	10W
Todos Santos	175	23	27N	110	13W
Tōgane	107	35	33N	140	22 E
Togliatti	68	53	32N	49	24 E
Togo ■	130	6	15N	1	35 E
Tōhoku □	103	39	50N	141	45 E
Tōjō	109	34	53N	133	16 E
Tokai	106	35	2N	136	55 E
Tokaj	58	48	8N	21	27 E
Tokara Kaikyō	104	30	0N	130	0 E
Tokat	80	40	22N	36	35 E
Tokelau Is.	123	9	0S	171	45W
Toki	106	35	18N	137	8 E
Tokoname	106	34	53N	136	51 E
Tokorozawa	107	35	47N	139	28 E
Tokushima	109	34	4N	134	34 E
Tokuyama	108	34	3N	131	50 E
Tōkyō	107	35	45N	139	45 E
Tōkyō-Wan	107	35	25N	139	47 E
Tolbukhin = Dobrich	53	43	37N	27	49 E
Toledo, Spain	50	39	50N	4	2W
Toledo, U.S.A.	167	41	37N	83	33W
Tolga	127	34	40N	5	22 E

Tolima, Vol.	184	4	40N	75 19W
Toluca	177	19	20N	99 40W
Tomakomai	103	42	38N	141 36 E
Tombigbee →	169	31	4N	87 58W
Tombouctou	130	16	50N	3 0W
Tomini, Teluk	113	0	10S	122 0 E
Tomsk	71	56	30N	85 5 E
Tonalá	177	16	4N	93 45W
Tonantins	184	2	45S	67 45W
Tonbridge	25	51	12N	0 18 E
Tong Xian	98	39	55N	116 35 E
Tonga ■	123	19	50S	174 30W
Tongchuan	99	35	6N	109 3 E
Tonghua	98	41	42N	125 58 E
Tongking, G. of	95	20	0N	108 0 E
Tongue →	33	58	29N	4 25W
Tonk	91	26	6N	75 54 E
Tonkin = Bac Phan	95	22	0N	105 0 E
Tonlé Sap	95	13	0N	104 0 E
Tonopah	172	38	4N	117 12W
Tonoshō	109	34	29N	134 11 E
Tooele	162	40	30N	112 20W
Toowoomba	116	27	32S	151 56 E
Topeka	166	39	3N	95 40W
Toppenish	171	46	27N	120 16W
Torbay	27	50	26N	3 31W
Torino	46	45	4N	7 40 E
Tormes →	50	41	18N	6 29W
Torne älv →	67	65	50N	24 12 E
Torneå = Tornio	67	65	50N	24 12 E
Torneträsk	66	68	24N	19 15 E
Tornio	67	65	50N	24 12 E
Toro, Cerro del	190	29	10S	69 50W
Toronto, Australia	117	33	0S	151 30 E
Toronto, Canada	151	43	39N	79 20W
Toros Daglari	80	37	0N	35 0 E
Torquay	27	50	27N	3 31W
Torre Annunziata	49	40	45N	14 26 E
Tôrre de Moncorvo	50	41	12N	7 8W
Torremolinos	50	36	38N	4 30W
Torrens, L.	119	31	0S	137 50 E
Torreón	174	25	33N	103 26W
Torres Vedras	50	39	5N	9 15W
Torridge →	27	50	51N	4 10W
Torrington	164	41	50N	73 9W
Tortosa	51	40	49N	0 31 E
Tortosa, C.	51	40	41N	0 52 E
Toruń	58	53	0N	18 39 E
Tory I.	34	55	17N	8 12W
Tosa-Shimizu	109	32	52N	132 58 E
Tosa-Wan	109	33	15N	133 30 E
Toscana	46	43	30N	11 5 E
Tostado	190	29	15S	61 50W
Tosu	109	33	22N	130 31 E
Totnes	27	50	26N	3 41W
Totonicapán	177	14	58N	91 12W
Tottori	109	35	30N	134 15 E
Toubkal, Djebel	126	31	0N	8 0W
Touggourt	127	33	6N	6 4 E
Toulon	37	43	10N	5 55 E
Toulouse	36	43	37N	1 27 E
Toungoo	93	19	0N	96 30 E
Touraine	36	47	20N	0 30 E
Tourane = Da Nang	95	16	4N	108 13 E
Tourcoing	38	50	42N	3 10 E
Tournai	42	50	35N	3 25 E
Tours	36	47	22N	0 40 E
Townsville	121	19	15S	146 45 E
Towson	164	39	26N	76 34W
Toyama	106	36	40N	137 15 E
Toyama-Wan	105	37	0N	137 30 E
Toyohashi	106	34	45N	137 25 E
Toyokawa	106	34	48N	137 27 E
Toyonaka	106	34	50N	135 28 E
Toyooka	109	35	35N	134 48 E
Toyota	106	35	3N	137 7 E
Tozeur	127	33	56N	8 8 E
Trabzon	81	41	0N	39 45 E
Tracy	172	37	46N	121 27W
Trafalgar, C.	50	36	10N	6 2W
Trail	155	49	5N	117 40W
Tralee	35	52	16N	9 42W
Tralee B.	35	52	17N	9 55W
Tran Ninh, Cao Nguyen	95	19	30N	103 10 E
Trangan	113	6	40S	134 20 E
Trangie	116	32	4S	148 0 E
Transantarctic Mts.	15	85	0S	170 0W
Transcona	153	49	55N	97 0W
Transilvania	57	46	19N	25 0 E
Transylvania = Transilvania	57	46	19N	25 0 E
Transylvanian Alps	17	45	30N	25 0 E
Trápani	48	38	1N	12 30 E
Traralgon	117	38	12S	146 34 E
Trasimeno, L.	46	43	10N	12 5 E
Travers, Mt.	123	42	1S	172 45 E
Traverse City	167	44	45N	85 39W
Travnik	52	44	17N	17 39 E
Tredegar	27	51	47N	3 16W
Tregaron	26	52	14N	3 56W
Treinta y Tres	191	33	16S	54 17W
Trelew	192	43	10S	65 20W
Trenque Lauquen	190	36	5S	62 45W
Trent →	29	53	33N	0 44W
Trentino-Alto Adige □	47	46	30N	11 0 E
Trento	47	46	5N	11 8 E
Trenton, Canada	151	44	10N	77 34W
Trenton, Mo., U.S.A.	166	40	5N	93 37W
Trenton, N.J., U.S.A.	164	40	15N	74 41W
Tréport, Le	38	50	3N	1 20 E
Tres Arroyos	190	38	26S	60 20W
Três Lagoas	188	20	50S	51 43W
Tres Montes, C.	192	46	50S	75 30W
Tres Puntas, C.	192	47	0S	66 0W
Treviso	47	45	40N	12 15 E
Trichinopoly = Tiruchchirappalli	90	10	45N	78 45 E
Trichur	90	10	30N	76 18 E
Trier	42	49	45N	6 37 E
Trieste	47	45	39N	13 45 E
Trikkala	54	39	34N	21 47 E
Trincomalee	90	8	38N	81 15 E
Trinidad, Bolivia	187	14	46S	64 50W
Trinidad, Colombia	184	5	25N	71 40W
Trinidad, Cuba	178	21	48N	80 0W
Trinidad, Uruguay	191	33	30S	56 50W
Trinidad, U.S.A.	163	37	15N	104 30W
Trinidad & Tobago ■	180	10	30N	61 20W
Trinity →	168	30	30N	95 0W
Trinity Mts.	172	40	20N	118 50W
Tripoli = Tarābulus, Lebanon	80	34	31N	35 50 E
Tripoli = Tarābulus, Libya	127	32	49N	13 7 E
Tripolis	54	37	31N	22 25 E
Tripura □	93	24	0N	92 0 E
Trivandrum	90	8	41N	77 0 E
Trois-Riviéres	151	46	25N	72 34W
Troitsk	71	54	10N	61 35 E
Trollhättan	60	58	17N	12 20 E
Tromsø	66	69	40N	18 56 E
Trondheim	65	63	36N	10 25 E
Trossachs, The	31	56	14N	4 24W
Trotternish	32	57	32N	6 15W
Trouville	38	49	21N	0 5 E
Trowbridge	24	51	18N	2 12W
Troy, Ala., U.S.A.	169	31	50N	85 58W
Troy, N.Y., U.S.A.	164	42	45N	73 39W
Troyes	39	48	19N	4 3 E
Trucial States = United Arab Emirates ■	85	23	50N	54 0 E
Trujillo, Honduras	179	16	0N	86 0W
Trujillo, Peru	186	8	6S	79 0W
Trujillo, Venezuela	184	9	22N	70 38W
Trundle	117	32	53S	147 35 E
Trung-Phan	95	16	0N	108 0 E
Truro, Canada	149	45	21N	63 14W
Truro, U.K.	27	50	17N	5 2W
Tselinograd	71	51	10N	71 30 E
Tsinan = Jinan	98	36	38N	117 1 E
Tsinghai = Qinghai □	101	36	0N	98 0 E
Tsingtao = Qingdao	98	36	5N	120 20 E
Tsu	106	34	45N	136 25 E

Tsuchiura	107	36	5N	140	15 E
Tsugaru-Kaikyō	103	41	35N	141	0 E
Tsukumi	108	33	4N	131	52 E
Tsukushi-Sanchi	108	33	25N	130	30 E
Tsuruga	106	35	45N	136	2 E
Tsurugi-San	109	33	51N	134	6 E
Tsuruoka	103	38	44N	139	50 E
Tsushima, Gifu, Japan	106	35	10N	136	43 E
Tsushima, Nagasaki, Japan	104	34	20N	129	20 E
Tuamotu Arch.	123	17	0S	144	0W
Tubarão	191	28	30S	49	0W
Tubruq	128	32	7N	23	55 E
Tubuai Is.	123	25	0S	150	0W
Tucacas	184	10	48N	68	19W
Tucson	160	32	14N	110	59W
Tucumcari	161	35	12N	103	45W
Tucupita	185	9	2N	62	3W
Tucuruí	188	3	42S	49	44W
Tudmur	80	34	36N	38	15 E
Tuktoyaktuk	144	69	27N	133	2W
Tula, Mexico	177	23	0N	99	43W
Tula, Russia	68	54	13N	37	38 E
Tulare	173	36	15N	119	26W
Tulcán	184	0	48N	77	43W
Tullahoma	169	35	23N	86	12W
Tullamore	35	53	17N	7	30W
Tully	121	17	56S	145	55 E
Tulsa	168	36	10N	96	0W
Tulua	184	4	6N	76	11W
Tuma ⇢	179	13	6N	84	35W
Tumaco	184	1	50N	78	45W
Tumatumari	185	5	20N	58	55W
Tumbarumba	117	35	44S	148	0 E
Túmbes	186	3	37S	80	27W
Tumkur	90	13	18N	77	6 E
Tummel, L.	33	56	43N	3	55W
Tummo	127	22	45N	14	8 E
Tump	88	26	7N	62	16 E
Tumucumaque, Serra	188	2	0N	55	0W
Tumut	117	35	16S	148	13 E
Tunbridge Wells	25	51	7N	0	16 E
Tundzha ⇢	53	41	40N	26	35 E
Tunis	127	36	50N	10	11 E
Tunisia ■	127	33	30N	9	10 E
Tunja	184	5	33N	73	25W
Tunxi	99	29	42N	118	25 E
Tupelo	169	34	15N	88	42W
Tupiza	187	21	30S	65	40W
Tupper L.	151	44	18N	74	30W
Tuque, La	151	47	30N	72	50W
Túquerres	184	1	5N	77	37W
Tura	92	25	30N	90	16 E
Turayf	82	31	41N	38	39 E
Turfan = Turpan	100	43	58N	89	10 E
Turfan Depression = Turpan					
Hami	100	42	40N	89	25 E
Türgovishte	53	43	17N	26	38 E
Turgutlu	80	38	30N	27	48 E
Turin = Torino	46	45	4N	7	40 E
Turkana, L.	132	3	30N	36	5 E
Turkestan	71	43	17N	68	16 E
Turkey ■	80	39	0N	36	0 E
Turkmenistan ■	70	39	0N	59	0 E
Turks Is.	180	21	20N	71	20W
Turku	67	60	30N	22	19 E
Turlock	172	37	30N	120	55W
Turnagain, C.	122	40	28S	176	38 E
Turnhout	42	51	19N	4	57 E
Türnovo	53	43	5N	25	41 E
Turnu Roșu Pasul	57	45	33N	24	17 E
Turnu-Severin	56	44	39N	22	41 E
Turpan	100	43	58N	89	10 E
Turpan Hami	100	42	40N	89	25 E
Turukhansk	74	65	21N	88	5 E
Tuscaloosa	169	33	13N	87	31W
Tuscany = Toscana	46	43	30N	11	5 E
Tuskegee	169	32	24N	85	39W
Tutrakan	53	44	2N	26	40 E
Tuvalu ■	122	8	0S	178	0 E
Tuxpan	177	20	57N	97	24W
Tuxtla Gutiérrez	177	16	45N	93	7W

Tuy Hoa	95	13	5N	109	10 E
Tuyen Hoa	95	17	50N	106	10 E
Tuz Gölü	80	38	45N	33	30 E
Ţūz Khurmātū	81	34	56N	44	38 E
Tuzla	52	44	34N	18	41 E
Tver	68	56	55N	35	55 E
Tweed ⇢	31	55	42N	2	10W
Tweed Heads	116	28	10S	153	31 E
Twin Falls	172	42	30N	114	30W
Two Harbors	156	47	1N	91	40W
Tyler	168	32	18N	95	18W
Tyne ⇢	28	54	58N	1	28W
Tyne & Wear □	28	54	55N	1	35W
Tynemouth	28	55	1N	1	27W
Tyrol = Tirol □	45	47	3N	10	43 E
Tyrrhenian Sea	48	40	0N	12	30 E
Tyumen	69	57	11N	65	29 E
Tzukong = Zigong	99	29	15N	104	48 E

U

Uaupés	184	0	8S	67	5W
Ubangi = Oubangi ⇢	131	1	0N	17	50 E
Ube	108	33	56N	131	15 E
Uberaba	188	19	50S	47	55W
Uberlândia	188	19	0S	48	20W
Ubon Ratchathani	95	15	15N	104	50 E
Ucayali ⇢	186	4	30S	73	30W
Uchi Lake	153	51	5N	92	35W
Uchiura-Wan	103	42	25N	140	40 E
Uchur ⇢	75	58	48N	130	35 E
Udaipur	91	24	36N	73	44 E
Uddevalla	60	58	21N	11	55 E
Údine	47	46	5N	13	10 E
Udmurtia □	69	57	30N	52	30 E
Udon Thani	95	17	29N	102	46 E
Ueda	107	36	24N	138	16 E
Uelen	73	66	10N	170	0W
Uelzen	43	53	0N	10	33 E
Ueno	106	34	45N	136	8 E
Ufa	69	54	45N	55	55 E
Uganda ■	132	2	0N	32	0 E
Uinta Mts.	163	40	45N	110	30W
Uithuizen	41	53	24N	6	41 E
Uji	106	34	53N	135	48 E
Ujjain	91	23	9N	75	43 E
Újpest	59	47	32N	19	6 E
Ujung Pandang	113	5	10S	119	20 E
Ukiah	172	39	10N	123	9W
Ukraine ■	68	49	0N	32	0 E
Ulaanbaatar	98	47	55N	106	53 E
Ulan Bator = Ulaanbaatar	98	47	55N	106	53 E
Ulan Ude	74	51	45N	107	40 E
Ulcinj	52	41	58N	19	10 E
Ulhasnagar	91	19	15N	73	10 E
Ulladulla	117	35	21S	150	29 E
Ullapool	32	57	54N	5	10W
Ullswater	28	54	35N	2	52W
Ulm	42	48	23N	10	0 E
Ulster □	34	54	35N	6	30W
Ulverston	28	54	13N	3	7W
Ulverstone	119	41	11S	146	11 E
Ulyanovsk = Simbirsk	68	54	20N	48	25 E
Ulyasutay	100	47	56N	97	28 E
Umbrella Mts.	123	45	35S	169	5 E
Umbria □	46	42	53N	12	30 E
Ume älv ⇢	66	63	45N	20	20 E
Umeå	66	63	45N	20	20 E
Umm al Qaywayn	85	25	30N	55	35 E
Umm Lajj	82	25	0N	37	23 E
Umnak	142	53	20N	168	20W
Umpang	94	16	3N	98	54 E
Umtata	137	31	36S	28	49 E
Unalaska	142	53	40N	166	40W
Ungava B.	146	59	30N	67	30W
Ungava Pen.	146	60	0N	74	0W
União da Vitória	191	26	13S	51	5W
Unimak	142	55	0N	164	0W

Place	Map	Lat	Long
Union City	**169**	36 25N	89 0W
Uniontown	**164**	39 54N	79 45W
United Arab Emirates ■	**85**	23 50N	54 0 E
United Kingdom ■	**18**	55 0N	3 0W
United States of America ■	**139**	37 0N	96 0W
Unity	**152**	52 30N	109 5W
Unnao	**92**	26 35N	80 30 E
Unst	**30**	60 50N	0 55W
Uozu	**106**	36 48N	137 24 E
Upata	**185**	8 1N	62 24W
Upper Austria = Oberösterreich □	**45**	48 10N	14 0 E
Upper Hutt	**123**	41 8S	175 5 E
Upper Taimyr ~►	**72**	74 15N	99 48 E
Upper Volta = Burkina Faso ■	**130**	12 0N	1 0W
Uppsala	**60**	59 53N	17 38 E
Uppsala län □	**60**	60 0N	17 30 E
Ur	**84**	30 55N	46 25 E
Uracara	**185**	2 20S	57 50W
Urakawa	**103**	42 9N	142 47 E
Ural ~►	**70**	47 0N	51 48 E
Ural Mts. = Uralskie Gory	**69**	60 0N	59 0 E
Uralsk	**70**	51 20N	51 20 E
Uralskie Gory	**69**	60 0N	59 0 E
Uranium City	**145**	59 34N	108 37W
Urawa	**107**	35 50N	139 40 E
Urbana, Ill., U.S.A.	**167**	40 7N	88 12W
Urbana, Ohio, U.S.A.	**167**	40 9N	83 44W
Urbana, La	**184**	7 8N	66 56W
Urcos	**187**	13 40S	71 38W
Ures	**174**	29 26N	110 24W
Urfa = Sanliurfa	**81**	37 12N	38 50 E
Urgench	**70**	41 40N	60 41 E
Uribia	**184**	11 43N	72 16W
Urk	**41**	52 39N	5 36 E
Urmia = Orūmīyeh	**81**	37 40N	45 0 E
Urmia, L. = Orūmīyeh, Daryācheh-ye	**81**	37 50N	45 30 E
Uruapan	**175**	19 30N	102 0W
Uruçuí	**188**	7 20S	44 28W
Uruguaiana	**191**	29 50S	57 0W
Uruguay ■	**191**	32 30S	56 30W
Uruguay ~►	**191**	34 12S	58 18W
Urumchi = Ürümqi	**100**	43 45N	87 45 E
Ürümqi	**100**	43 45N	87 45 E
Urup, Os.	**75**	46 0N	151 0 E
Usa	**108**	33 31N	131 21 E
Uşak	**80**	38 43N	29 28 E
Usfan	**82**	21 58N	39 27 E
Ushant = Ouessant, Île d'	**36**	48 28N	5 6W
Ushibuka	**108**	32 11N	130 1 E
Ushuaia	**192**	54 50S	68 23W
Usk ~►	**26**	51 37N	2 56W
Üsküdar	**80**	41 0N	29 5 E
Usolye Sibirskoye	**74**	52 48N	103 40 E
Uspenskiy	**71**	48 41N	72 43 E
Ussuriysk	**75**	43 48N	131 59 E
Ust-Aldan = Batamay	**74**	63 30N	129 15 E
Ust-Ilimsk	**74**	58 3N	102 39 E
Ust-Kamchatsk	**73**	56 10N	162 28 E
Ust-Kamenogorsk	**71**	50 0N	82 36 E
Ust Maya	**75**	60 30N	134 28 E
Ust Olenek	**72**	73 0N	119 48 E
Ust Port	**69**	69 40N	84 26 E
Ust Urt = Ustyurt, Plato	**70**	44 0N	55 0 E
Ust Vorkuta	**69**	67 24N	64 0 E
Ustí nad Labem	**58**	50 41N	14 3 E
Ustica	**48**	38 42N	13 10 E
Ustinov	**69**	56 51N	53 14 E
Ustyurt, Plato	**70**	44 0N	55 0 E
Usu	**100**	44 27N	84 40 E
Usuki	**108**	33 8N	131 49 E
Usumbura = Bujumbura	**135**	3 16S	29 18 E
Utah □	**163**	39 30N	111 30W
Utah, L.	**163**	40 10N	111 58W
Uthai Thani	**94**	15 22N	100 3 E
Utica	**164**	43 5N	75 18W
Uto	**108**	32 41N	130 40 E
Utrecht	**40**	52 5N	5 8 E
Utrecht □	**40**	52 6N	5 7 E
Utrera	**50**	37 12N	5 48W
Utsunomiya	**107**	36 30N	139 50 E
Uttar Pradesh □	**92**	27 0N	80 0 E
Uttoxeter	**28**	52 53N	1 50W
Uusikaupunki	**66**	60 47N	21 25 E
Uvalde	**161**	29 15N	99 48W
Uvs Nuur	**74**	50 20N	92 30 E
Uwajima	**109**	33 10N	132 35 E
Uzbekistan ■	**70**	41 30N	65 0 E

V

Place	Map	Lat	Long
Vaal ~►	**137**	29 4S	23 38 E
Vaals	**41**	50 46N	6 1 E
Vaasa	**67**	63 6N	21 38 E
Vác	**58**	47 49N	19 10 E
Vach ~►	**69**	60 45N	76 45 E
Vadodara	**91**	22 20N	73 10 E
Vadsø	**67**	70 3N	29 50 E
Váh ~►	**59**	47 55N	18 0 E
Vaigach	**69**	70 10N	59 0 E
Val d'Or	**151**	48 7N	77 47W
Valahia	**57**	44 35N	25 0 E
Valcheta	**192**	40 40S	66 8W
Valdés, Pen.	**192**	42 30S	63 45W
Valdez	**142**	61 14N	146 17W
Valdivia	**190**	39 50S	73 14W
Valdosta	**170**	30 50N	83 20W
Valence	**37**	44 57N	4 54 E
Valencia, Spain	**51**	39 27N	0 23W
Valencia, Venezuela	**184**	10 11N	68 0W
Valencia □	**51**	39 20N	0 40W
Valencia, Albufera de	**51**	39 20N	0 27W
Valencia, G. de	**51**	39 30N	0 20 E
Valencia de Alcántara	**50**	39 25N	7 14W
Valenciennes	**38**	50 20N	3 34 E
Valentia I.	**35**	51 54N	10 22W
Valera	**184**	9 19N	70 37W
Valkenswaard	**41**	51 21N	5 29 E
Valladolid, Mexico	**177**	20 41N	88 12W
Valladolid, Spain	**50**	41 38N	4 43W
Valle d'Aosta □	**46**	45 45N	7 22 E
Valle de la Pascua	**184**	9 13N	66 0W
Valle de Santiago	**177**	20 23N	101 12W
Vallecas	**50**	40 23N	3 41W
Vallejo	**172**	38 12N	122 15W
Valletta	**49**	35 54N	14 30 E
Valley City	**163**	46 57N	98 0W
Valley View	**155**	40 39N	76 33W
Valona = Vlóra	**52**	40 32N	19 28 E
Valparaíso, Chile	**190**	33 2S	71 40W
Valparaíso, Mexico	**175**	22 46N	103 34W
Valsad	**91**	20 40N	72 58 E
Van	**81**	38 30N	43 20 E
Van, L. = Van Gölü	**81**	38 30N	43 0 E
Van Buren, Canada	**148**	47 10N	67 55W
Van Buren, U.S.A.	**168**	35 28N	94 18W
Van Gölü	**81**	38 30N	43 0 E
Van Wert	**167**	40 52N	84 31W
Vancouver, Canada	**154**	49 15N	123 10W
Vancouver, U.S.A.	**171**	45 44N	122 41W
Vancouver I.	**154**	49 50N	126 0W
Vandalia	**166**	38 57N	89 4W
Vanderhoof	**154**	54 0N	124 0W
Vänern	**60**	58 47N	13 30 E
Vanier	**151**	45 27N	75 40W
Vankarem	**73**	67 51N	175 50 E
Vännäs	**66**	63 58N	19 48 E
Vannes	**36**	47 40N	2 47W
Vanua Levu	**122**	16 33S	179 15 E
Vanuatu ■	**122**	15 0S	168 0 E
Varanasi	**92**	25 22N	83 0 E
Varangerfjorden	**67**	70 3N	29 25 E
Varaždin	**52**	46 20N	16 20 E
Vardak □	**87**	34 0N	68 0 E
Vardø	**67**	70 23N	31 5 E
Värmland	**60**	60 0N	13 30 E
Varna	**53**	43 13N	27 56 E

Place	Page	Lat °	Lat ′		Long °	Long ′	
Vascongadas	50	42	50N		2	45W	
Västerås	60	59	37N		16	38	E
Västmanlands län □	60	59	45N		16	20	E
Vatnajökull	64	64	30N		16	48W	
Vatra-Dornei	57	47	22N		25	22	E
Vättern	60	58	25N		14	30	E
Vaygach, Ostrov	69	70	0N		60	0	E
Veendam	41	53	5N		6	52	E
Vega, La	180	19	20N		70	30W	
Veghel	41	51	37N		5	32	E
Vegreville	155	53	30N		112	5W	
Vela, La	184	11	27N		69	34W	
Vellore	90	12	57N		79	10	E
Venado Tuerto	190	33	50S		62	0W	
Vendôme	39	47	47N		1	3	E
Véneto □	47	45	40N		12	0	E
Venézia	47	45	27N		12	20	E
Venézia, Golfo di	47	45	20N		13	0	E
Venezuela ■	184	8	0N		65	0W	
Venezuela, Golfo de	184	11	30N		71	0W	
Vengurla	91	15	53N		73	45	E
Venice = Venézia	47	45	27N		12	20	E
Venlo	41	51	22N		6	11	E
Venraij	41	51	31N		6	0	E
Ventnor	24	50	35N		1	12W	
Ventoux	37	44	10N		5	17	E
Ventura	173	34	16N		119	18W	
Veracruz	177	19	10N		96	10W	
Veracruz □	177	19	20N		96	40W	
Verde, R. ➔	175	15	59N		97	50W	
Verdun	37	49	12N		5	24	E
Vereeniging	137	26	38S		27	57	E
Verkhoyansk	72	67	35N		133	25	E
Verkhoyanskiy Khrebet	72	66	0N		129	0	E
Vermilion	152	53	20N		110	50W	
Vermont □	164	43	40N		72	50W	
Verneuil-sur-Avre	39	48	45N		0	55	E
Vernon, Canada	155	50	20N		119	15W	
Vernon, France	39	49	5N		1	30	E
Vernon, U.S.A.	161	34	10N		99	20W	
Verona	46	45	27N		11	0	E
Versailles	39	48	48N		2	8	E
Vert, C.	130	14	45N		17	30W	
Verviers	42	50	37N		5	52	E
Vest-Agder fylke □	60	58	30N		7	15	E
Vesterålen	64	68	45N		15	0	E
Vestfjorden	64	67	55N		14	0	E
Vestfold fylke □	60	59	15N		10	0	E
Vestspitsbergen	13	78	40N		17	0	E
Vesuvio	49	40	50N		14	22	E
Vesuvius, Mt. = Vesuvio	49	40	50N		14	22	E
Viacha	187	16	39S		68	18W	
Viborg	61	56	27N		9	23	E
Vicenza	47	45	32N		11	31	E
Vichy	37	46	9N		3	26	E
Vicksburg	169	32	22N		90	56W	
Victor Harbor	119	35	30S		138	37	E
Victoria, Canada	154	48	30N		123	25W	
Victoria, Chile	190	38	13S		72	20W	
Victoria, U.S.A.	158	28	50N		97	0W	
Victoria □	117	37	0S		144	0	E
Victoria, L.	132	1	0S		33	0	E
Victoria de las Tunas	178	20	58N		76	59W	
Victoria Falls	137	17	58S		25	52	E
Victoria I.	145	71	0N		111	0W	
Victoria Ld.	15	75	0S		160	0	E
Victoriaville	148	46	4N		71	56W	
Vidalia	170	32	13N		82	25W	
Vidin	53	43	59N		22	50	E
Viedma	192	40	50S		63	0W	
Vienna = Wien	45	48	12N		16	22	E
Vienne	37	45	31N		4	53	E
Vienne ➔	36	47	13N		0	5	E
Vientiane	95	17	58N		102	36	E
Vientos, Paso de los	180	20	0N		74	0W	
Vietnam ■	95	19	0N		106	0	E
Vigo	50	42	12N		8	41W	
Vijayawada	92	16	31N		80	39	E
Vila Real de Santo António	50	37	10N		7	28W	
Vilhelmina	66	64	35N		16	39	E
Vilhena	187	12	40S		60	5W	
Villa Bella	187	10	25S		65	22W	
Villa Bens = Tarfaya	126	27	55N		12	55W	
Villa Cisneros = Dakhla	126	23	50N		15	53W	
Villa Dolores	190	31	58S		65	15W	
Villa María	190	32	20S		63	10W	
Villa Montes	187	21	10S		63	30W	
Villaguay	190	32	0S		59	0W	
Villahermosa	177	17	59N		92	55W	
Villanueva de la Serena	50	38	59N		5	50W	
Villarreal	51	39	55N		0	3W	
Villarrica	191	39	15S		72	15W	
Villazón	187	22	0S		65	35W	
Ville Platte	168	30	45N		92	17W	
Villefranche-sur-Saône	37	45	59N		4	43	E
Villers-Cotterêts	39	49	15N		3	4	E
Vilnius	68	54	38N		25	19	E
Vilskutskogo, Proliv	72	78	0N		103	0	E
Vilyuy ➔	74	64	24N		126	26	E
Vilyuysk	74	63	40N		121	35	E
Viña del Mar	190	33	0S		71	30W	
Vincennes	167	38	42N		87	29W	
Vindhya Ra.	91	22	50N		77	0	E
Vinh	95	18	45N		105	38	E
Vinita	168	36	40N		95	12W	
Vinkovci	52	45	19N		18	48	E
Vinnitsa	68	49	15N		28	30	E
Viramgam	91	23	5N		72	0	E
Virden	153	49	50N		100	56W	
Vire	36	48	50N		0	53W	
Vírgenes, C.	192	52	19S		68	21W	
Virgin ➔	173	36	50N		114	10W	
Virgin Is.	180	18	40N		64	30W	
Virginia	156	47	30N		92	32W	
Virginia □	165	37	45N		78	0W	
Virginia Beach	165	36	54N		75	58W	
Visalia	173	36	25N		119	18W	
Visby	60	57	37N		18	18	E
Viscount Melville Sd.	145	74	10N		108	0W	
Višegrad	52	43	47N		19	17	E
Vishakhapatnam	92	17	45N		83	20	E
Vistula = Wisła ➔	58	54	22N		18	55	E
Vitebsk	68	55	10N		30	15	E
Viti Levu	122	17	30S		177	30	E
Vitim ➔	74	59	26N		112	34	E
Vitória, Brazil	189	20	20S		40	22W	
Vitoria, Spain	50	42	50N		2	41W	
Vitória da Conquista	189	14	51S		40	51W	
Vizianagaram	92	18	6N		83	30	E
Vlaardingen	40	51	55N		4	21	E
Vladikavkaz	70	43	0N		44	35	E
Vladimir	68	56	15N		40	30	E
Vladivostok	75	43	10N		131	53	E
Vlieland	40	53	16N		4	55	E
Vlissingen	40	51	26N		3	34	E
Vlóra	52	40	32N		19	28	E
Vltava ➔	59	50	21N		14	30	E
Vogelkop	113	1	25S		133	0	E
Vogels Berg	42	50	37N		9	30	E
Vohimena, Tanjon' i	137	25	36S		45	8	E
Voi	133	3	25S		38	32	E
Volendam	40	52	30N		5	4	E
Volga ➔	68	48	30N		46	0	E
Volga Hts. = Privolzhskaya Vozvyshennost	17	51	0N		46	0	E
Volgograd	68	48	40N		44	25	E
Vollenhove	41	52	40N		5	58	E
Vologda	68	59	10N		40	0	E
Vólos	54	39	24N		22	59	E
Volsk	68	52	5N		47	22	E
Volta ➔	130	5	46N		0	41	E
Volta, L.	130	7	30N		0	15	E
Volta Redonda	188	22	31S		44	5W	
Voorburg	40	52	5N		4	24	E
Vopnafjörður	64	65	45N		14	40W	
Voriai Sporádhes	55	39	15N		23	30	E
Voronezh	68	51	40N		39	10	E
Voroshilovgrad = Lugansk	68	48	38N		39	15	E
Vosges	37	48	20N		7	10	E
Vostochnyy Sayan	74	54	0N		96	0	E
Vrangelya, Ostrov	73	71	0N		180	0	E
Vranje	53	42	34N		21	54	E
Vratsa	53	43	13N		23	30	E

Name				
Vršac	**52**	45	8N	21 18 E
Vught	**40**	51	38N	5 20 E
Vulcan	**155**	50	25N	113 15W
Vyatka = Kirov	**69**	58	35N	49 40 E
Vyborg	**68**	60	43N	28 47 E
Vychegda →	**69**	61	18N	46 36 E
Východné Beskydy	**59**	49	30N	22 0 E

W

Wa	**130**	10	7N	2 25W
Waal →	**41**	51	59N	4 30 E
Waalwijk	**40**	51	42N	5 4 E
Wabash	**167**	40	48N	85 46W
Wabash →	**167**	37	46N	88 2W
Wąbrzeźno	**58**	53	16N	18 57 E
Waco	**168**	31	33N	97 5W
Wād Medanī	**129**	14	28N	33 30 E
Waddenzee	**40**	53	6N	5 10 E
Waddington, Mt.	**154**	51	23N	125 15W
Waddinxveen	**40**	52	2N	4 40 E
Wadena	**152**	51	57N	103 47W
Wadi Halfa	**129**	21	53N	31 19 E
Wageningen	**41**	51	58N	5 40 E
Wager Bay	**146**	65	56N	90 49W
Wagga Wagga	**117**	35	7S	147 24 E
Wagin	**120**	33	17S	117 25 E
Waigeo	**113**	0	20S	130 40 E
Waihi	**122**	37	23S	175 52 E
Waikerie	**119**	34	9S	140 0 E
Waikokopu	**122**	39	3S	177 52 E
Waimate	**123**	44	45S	171 3 E
Wainwright, Canada	**152**	52	50N	110 50W
Wainwright, U.S.A.	**142**	70	39N	160 1W
Waipara	**123**	43	3S	172 46 E
Waipu	**122**	35	59S	174 29 E
Waipukurau	**122**	40	1S	176 33 E
Wairoa	**122**	39	3S	177 25 E
Waitara	**122**	38	59S	174 15 E
Wajima	**105**	37	30N	137 0 E
Wajir	**133**	1	42N	40 5 E
Wakasa-Wan	**106**	35	40N	135 30 E
Wakatipu, L.	**123**	45	5S	168 33 E
Wakayama	**106**	34	15N	135 15 E
Wakefield, N.Z.	**123**	41	24S	173 5 E
Wakefield, U.K.	**28**	53	41N	1 31W
Wakkanai	**103**	45	28N	141 35 E
Wałbrzych	**58**	50	45N	16 18 E
Walcha	**116**	30	55S	151 31 E
Walcheren	**40**	51	30N	3 35 E
Wales □	**26**	52	30N	3 30W
Walgett	**116**	30	0S	148 5 E
Walkerton	**151**	44	10N	81 10W
Walla Walla	**171**	46	3N	118 25W
Wallaceburg	**150**	42	34N	82 23W
Wallachia = Valahia	**57**	44	35N	25 0 E
Wallangarra	**116**	28	56S	151 58 E
Wallaroo	**119**	33	56S	137 39 E
Wallasey	**28**	53	26N	3 2W
Wallerawang	**117**	33	25S	150 4 E
Wallis & Futuna	**122**	13	18S	176 10W
Wallowa, Mts.	**171**	45	20N	117 30W
Wallsend, Australia	**117**	32	55S	151 40 E
Wallsend, U.K.	**28**	54	59N	1 30W
Walney, Isle of	**28**	54	5N	3 15W
Walpole	**120**	34	58S	116 44 E
Walsall	**24**	52	36N	1 59W
Walvis Bay	**136**	23	0S	14 28 E
Wana	**88**	32	20N	69 32 E
Wanaka L.	**123**	44	33S	169 7 E
Wang Saphung	**95**	17	18N	101 46 E
Wanganui	**122**	39	56S	175 3 E
Wangaratta	**117**	36	21S	146 19 E
Wanxian	**99**	30	42N	108 20 E
Warabi	**107**	35	49N	139 41 E
Warangal	**91**	17	58N	79 35 E
Warburton	**117**	37	47S	145 42 E
Wardha	**91**	20	45N	78 39 E
Wardha →	**91**	19	57N	79 11 E
Warialda	**116**	29	29S	150 33 E
Warley	**24**	52	30N	2 0W
Warner Mts.	**172**	41	30N	120 20W
Waroona	**120**	32	50S	115 58 E
Warracknabeal	**119**	36	9S	142 26 E
Warragul	**117**	38	10S	145 58 E
Warrego →	**116**	30	24S	145 21 E
Warrego Ra.	**121**	24	58S	146 0 E
Warren, Australia	**116**	31	42S	147 51 E
Warren, Ark., U.S.A.	**168**	33	35N	92 3W
Warren, Mich., U.S.A.	**167**	42	31N	83 2W
Warren, Ohio, U.S.A.	**164**	41	18N	80 52W
Warren, Pa., U.S.A.	**164**	41	52N	79 10W
Warrenpoint	**34**	54	7N	6 15W
Warrensburg	**166**	38	45N	93 45W
Warrington, U.K.	**28**	53	25N	2 38W
Warrington, U.S.A.	**169**	30	22N	87 16W
Warrnambool	**119**	38	25S	142 30 E
Warsaw = Warszawa	**58**	52	13N	21 0 E
Warszawa	**58**	52	13N	21 0 E
Warta →	**58**	52	35N	14 39 E
Warthe = Warta →	**58**	52	35N	14 39 E
Warwick, Australia	**116**	28	10S	152 1 E
Warwick, U.K.	**24**	52	17N	1 36W
Warwick, U.S.A.	**164**	41	43N	71 25W
Warwick □	**24**	52	20N	1 30W
Wasatch Ra.	**163**	40	30N	111 15W
Wasco	**173**	35	37N	119 16W
Wash, The	**29**	52	58N	0 20 E
Washim	**91**	20	3N	77 0 E
Washington, D.C., U.S.A.	**165**	38	52N	77 0W
Washington, Ind., U.S.A.	**167**	38	40N	87 8W
Washington, Mo., U.S.A.	**166**	38	35N	91 1W
Washington, Pa., U.S.A.	**164**	40	10N	80 20W
Washington □	**171**	47	45N	120 30W
Wassenaar	**40**	52	8N	4 24 E
Waterbury	**164**	41	32N	73 0W
Waterford	**35**	52	16N	7 8W
Waterford □	**35**	52	10N	7 40W
Waterloo, Canada	**151**	43	30N	80 32W
Waterloo, U.S.A.	**166**	42	27N	92 20W
Watertown, N.Y., U.S.A.	**151**	43	58N	75 57W
Watertown, Wis., U.S.A.	**167**	43	15N	88 45W
Waterville	**148**	44	35N	69 40W
Watling I. = San Salvador	**178**	24	0N	74 40W
Watrous	**152**	51	40N	105 25W
Watson Lake	**144**	60	6N	128 49W
Watsonville	**173**	36	55N	121 49W
Watubela, Kepulauan	**113**	4	28S	131 35 E
Wauchope	**116**	31	28S	152 45 E
Waukegan	**167**	42	22N	87 54W
Waukesha	**167**	43	0N	88 15W
Wausau	**166**	44	57N	89 40W
Wauwatosa	**167**	43	6N	87 59W
Waveney →	**25**	52	24N	1 20 E
Wâw	**129**	7	45N	28 1 E
Waxahachie	**168**	32	22N	96 53W
Waycross	**170**	31	12N	82 25W
Waynesboro, Pa., U.S.A.	**164**	39	46N	77 32W
Waynesboro, Va., U.S.A.	**165**	38	4N	78 57W
Waynesville	**165**	35	31N	83 0W
Wazirabad	**89**	32	30N	74 8 E
Weald, The	**25**	51	7N	0 9 E
Webo = Nyaake	**130**	4	52N	7 37W
Weddell Sea	**14**	72	30S	40 0W
Wedderburn	**117**	36	26S	143 33 E
Wee Waa	**116**	30	11S	149 26 E
Weert	**41**	51	15N	5 43 E
Weesp	**40**	52	18N	5 2 E
Weifang	**98**	36	47N	119 10 E
Weiser	**171**	44	10N	117 0W
Welbourn Hill	**118**	27	21S	134 6 E
Welch	**165**	37	29N	81 36W
Welland	**151**	43	0N	79 15W
Welland →	**29**	52	43N	0 10W
Wellingborough	**25**	52	18N	0 41W
Wellington, Australia	**116**	32	35S	148 59 E
Wellington, N.Z.	**123**	41	19S	174 46 E
Wellington, Shrops., U.K.	**28**	52	42N	2 31W
Wellington, Somst., U.K.	**27**	50	58N	3 13W
Wellington □	**123**	40	8S	175 36 E
Wellington, I.	**192**	49	30S	75 0W

Name	Page	Lat°	Lat′	N/S	Long°	Long′	E/W
Wells, Norfolk, U.K.	29	52	57N		0	51	E
Wells, Somst., U.K.	27	51	12N		2	39	W
Wells, U.S.A.	172	41	8N		115	0	W
Wellsville, N.Y., U.S.A.	164	42	9N		77	53	W
Wellsville, Ohio, U.S.A.	164	40	36N		80	40	W
Welshpool	26	52	40N		3	9	W
Wem	28	52	52N		2	45	W
Wenatchee	171	47	30N		120	17	W
Wenchow = Wenzhou	99	28	0N		120	38	E
Wensleydale	28	54	18N		2	0	W
Wentworth	119	34	2S		141	54	E
Wenzhou	99	28	0N		120	38	E
Werribee	117	37	54S		144	40	E
Werris Creek	116	31	18S		150	38	E
Weser →	42	53	33N		8	30	E
West Bengal □	92	23	0N		88	0	E
West Bromwich	24	52	32N		2	1	W
West Falkland	192	51	40S		60	0	W
West Frankfort	166	37	56N		89	0	W
West Glamorgan □	27	51	40N		3	55	W
West Memphis	169	35	5N		90	11	W
West Midlands □	24	52	30N		1	55	W
West Palm Beach	170	26	44N		80	3	W
West Schelde = Westerschelde →	40	51	25N		3	25	E
West Siberian Plain	76	62	0N		75	0	E
West Sussex □	25	50	55N		0	30	W
West Virginia □	165	39	0N		81	0	W
West Yorkshire □	28	53	45N		1	40	W
Western Australia □	114	25	0S		118	0	E
Western Ghats	90	14	0N		75	0	E
Western Isles □	32	57	30N		7	10	W
Western Sahara ■	126	25	0N		13	0	W
Western Samoa ■	123	14	0S		172	0	W
Westerschelde →	40	51	25N		3	25	E
Westerwald	42	50	39N		8	0	E
Westfriesche Eilanden	40	53	20N		5	10	E
Westland □	123	43	33S		169	59	E
Westland Bight	123	42	55S		170	5	E
Westlock	155	54	9N		113	55	W
Westmeath □	34	53	30N		7	30	W
Westminster	164	39	34N		77	1	W
Weston	165	39	3N		80	29	W
Weston-super-Mare	27	51	20N		2	59	W
Westport	123	41	46S		171	37	E
Westray	33	59	18N		3	0	W
Wetar	113	7	30S		126	30	E
Wetaskiwin	155	52	55N		113	24	W
Wewaka	168	35	10N		96	35	W
Wexford	35	52	20N		6	28	W
Wexford □	35	52	20N		6	25	W
Weyburn	152	49	40N		103	50	W
Weymouth	27	50	36N		2	28	W
Whakatane	122	37	57S		177	1	E
Whale Cove	145	62	11N		92	36	W
Whalsay	30	60	22N		1	0	W
Whangamomona	122	39	8S		174	44	E
Whangarei	122	35	43S		174	21	E
Wharfe →	29	53	55N		1	30	W
Wheeler Pk.	172	38	57N		114	15	W
Wheeling	164	40	2N		80	41	W
Whernside	28	54	14N		2	24	W
Whitby	29	54	29N		0	37	W
Whitchurch	28	52	58N		2	42	W
White →, Ark., U.S.A.	168	33	53N		91	3	W
White →, Ind., U.S.A.	167	38	25N		87	45	W
White →, S. Dak., U.S.A.	163	43	45N		99	30	W
White Cliffs	118	30	50S		143	10	E
White Mts.	157	44	15N		71	15	W
White Nile = Nîl el Abyad →	129	15	38N		32	31	E
White Russia = Belorussia ■	68	53	30N		27	0	E
White Sea = Beloye More	69	66	30N		38	0	E
Whitecliffs	123	43	26S		171	55	E
Whitehaven	28	54	33N		3	35	W
Whitehorse	144	60	43N		135	3	W
Whitney, Mt.	173	36	35N		118	14	W
Whitstable	25	51	21N		1	2	E
Whitsunday I.	121	20	15S		149	4	E
Whittier	142	60	46N		148	48	W
Whyalla	118	33	2S		137	30	E
Wichita	158	37	40N		97	20	W
Wichita Falls	161	33	57N		98	30	W
Wick	33	58	26N		3	5	W
Wickepin	120	32	50S		117	30	E
Wicklow	35	53	0N		6	2	W
Wicklow □	35	52	59N		6	25	W
Wicklow Mts.	35	53	0N		6	30	W
Widnes	28	53	22N		2	44	W
Wieluń	58	51	15N		18	34	E
Wien	45	48	12N		16	22	E
Wiesbaden	42	50	7N		8	17	E
Wigan	28	53	33N		2	38	W
Wight, I. of	25	50	40N		1	20	W
Wigtown	31	54	52N		4	27	W
Wigtown B.	31	54	46N		4	15	W
Wilcannia	118	31	30S		143	26	E
Wildwood	164	38	59N		74	46	W
Wilhelmshaven	42	53	30N		8	9	E
Wilkes Barre	164	41	15N		75	52	W
Wilkes Sub-Glacial Basin	15	75	0S		130	0	E
Wilkie	152	52	27N		108	42	W
Willamina	171	45	9N		123	32	W
Willemstad	181	12	5N		69	0	W
Williams L.	154	51	48N		90	45	W
Williamsburg	165	37	17N		76	44	W
Williamson	165	37	46N		82	17	W
Williamsport	164	41	18N		77	1	W
Williamstown	117	37	51S		144	52	E
Williston	163	48	10N		103	35	W
Willits	172	39	28N		123	17	W
Willmar	156	45	5N		95	0	W
Wilmette	167	42	6N		87	44	W
Wilmington, Del., U.S.A.	164	39	45N		75	32	W
Wilmington, N.C., U.S.A.	165	34	14N		77	54	W
Wilson	165	35	44N		77	54	W
Wilsons Promontory	117	38	55S		146	25	E
Wilton	24	51	5N		1	52	W
Wiltshire □	24	51	20N		2	0	W
Wiluna	120	26	36S		120	14	E
Wimereux	38	50	45N		1	37	E
Winchester, U.K.	25	51	4N		1	19	W
Winchester, Ind., U.S.A.	167	40	10N		84	56	W
Winchester, Ky., U.S.A.	165	38	0N		84	8	W
Winchester, Va., U.S.A.	164	39	14N		78	8	W
Wind River Range	163	43	0N		109	30	W
Windermere	28	54	24N		2	56	W
Windermere, L.	28	54	20N		2	57	W
Windhoek	136	22	35S		17	4	E
Windsor, Australia	117	33	37S		150	50	E
Windsor, Nfld., Canada	149	48	57N		55	40	W
Windsor, Ont., Canada	150	42	18N		83	0	W
Windsor, U.K.	25	51	28N		0	36	W
Windward Is.	181	13	0N		63	0	W
Windward Passage = Vientos, Paso de los	180	20	0N		74	0	W
Winisk →	140	55	17N		85	5	W
Winkler	153	49	10N		97	56	W
Winnemucca	172	41	0N		117	45	W
Winnfield	168	31	57N		92	38	W
Winnipeg	153	49	54N		97	9	W
Winnipeg, L.	153	52	0N		97	0	W
Winnipegosis L.	153	52	30N		100	0	W
Winona	166	44	2N		91	39	W
Winooski	151	44	31N		73	11	W
Winschoten	41	53	9N		7	3	E
Winslow	161	35	2N		110	41	W
Winston-Salem	165	36	7N		80	15	W
Winter Haven	170	28	0N		81	42	W
Winter Park	170	28	34N		81	19	W
Winterswijk	41	51	58N		6	43	E
Winterthur	44	47	30N		8	44	E
Wirral	28	53	25N		3	0	W
Wisbech	29	52	39N		0	10	E
Wisconsin □	166	44	30N		90	0	W
Wisconsin →	166	43	0N		91	15	W
Wisconsin Rapids	166	44	25N		89	50	W
Wishaw	31	55	46N		3	55	W
Wisła →	58	54	22N		18	55	E
Witham →	29	53	3N		0	8	W
Withernsea	29	53	43N		0	2	E
Witney	24	51	47N		1	29	W
Włocławek	58	52	40N		19	3	E
Wodonga	117	36	5S		146	50	E

Wokam	113	5	45S	134	28 E
Woking	25	51	18N	0	33W
Wolin	58	53	50N	14	37 E
Wollaston L.	145	58	7N	103	10W
Wollaston Pen.	145	69	30N	115	0W
Wollongong	117	34	25S	150	54 E
Wolverhampton	24	52	35N	2	6W
Wondai	116	26	20S	151	49 E
Wŏnsan	98	39	11N	127	27 E
Wonthaggi	117	38	37S	145	37 E
Woodburn	116	29	6S	153	23 E
Woodenbong	116	28	24S	152	39 E
Woodend	117	37	20S	144	33 E
Woodland	172	38	40N	121	50W
Woods, L. of the	153	49	15N	94	45W
Woodstock, N.B., Canada	148	46	11N	67	37W
Woodstock, Ont., Canada	151	43	10N	80	45W
Woolgoolga	116	30	6S	153	11 E
Woomera	118	31	30S	137	10 E
Woonsocket	164	42	0N	71	30W
Wooroloo	120	31	48S	116	18 E
Worcester, U.K.	24	52	12N	2	12W
Worcester, U.S.A.	164	42	14N	71	49W
Workington	28	54	39N	3	34W
Worksop	29	53	19N	1	9W
Wormerveer	40	52	30N	4	46 E
Worms	42	49	37N	8	21 E
Worthing	25	50	49N	0	21W
Worthington	166	43	35N	95	36W
Wou-han = Wuhan	99	30	31N	114	18 E
Woy Woy	117	33	30S	151	19 E
Wrangel I.	138	71	0N	180	0 E
Wrangell	143	56	30N	132	25W
Wrangell Mts.	142	61	40N	143	30W
Wrath, C.	32	58	38N	5	0W
Wrekin, The	28	52	41N	2	35W
Wrexham	26	53	5N	3	0W
Wrigley	144	63	16N	123	37W
Wrocław	58	51	5N	17	5 E
Września	58	52	21N	17	36 E
Wu Jiang →	99	29	40N	107	20 E
Wubin	120	30	6S	116	37 E
Wuhan	99	30	31N	114	18 E
Wuhsi = Wuxi	99	31	33N	120	18 E
Wuhu	99	31	22N	118	21 E
Wulumuchi = Ürümqi	100	43	45N	87	45 E
Wuppertal	42	51	15N	7	8 E
Würzburg	42	49	46N	9	55 E
Wutongqiao	99	29	22N	103	50 E
Wuxi	99	31	33N	120	18 E
Wuzhong	98	38	2N	106	12 E
Wuzhou	99	23	30N	111	18 E
Wyalkatchem	120	31	8S	117	22 E
Wyandotte	167	42	14N	83	13W
Wycheproof	119	36	0S	143	17 E
Wye →	27	51	36N	2	40W
Wyndham	114	15	33S	128	3 E
Wynnum	116	27	27S	153	9 E
Wynyard	152	51	45N	104	10W
Wyoming □	163	42	48N	109	0W
Wytheville	165	37	0N	81	3W

X

Xánthi	55	41	10N	24	58 E
Xapuri	187	10	35S	68	35W
Xenia	167	39	42N	83	57W
Xiamen	99	24	25N	118	4 E
Xi'an	99	34	15N	109	0 E
Xiangfan	99	32	2N	112	8 E
Xiangtan	99	27	51N	112	54 E
Xiao Hinggan Ling	98	49	0N	127	0 E
Xigazê	101	29	5N	88	45 E
Xingtai	98	37	3N	114	32 E
Xingu →	188	1	30S	51	53W
Xining	98	36	34N	101	40 E
Xinjiang Uygur Zizhiqu □	100	42	0N	86	0 E
Xinxiang	99	35	18N	113	50 E

Xinyang	99	32	6N	114	3 E
Xinzhu	99	24	49N	120	57 E
Xique-Xique	188	10	50S	42	40W
Xizang □	101	32	0N	88	0 E
Xuanhua	98	40	40N	115	2 E
Xuchang	99	34	2N	113	48 E
Xuzhou	99	34	18N	117	10 E

Y

Ya'an	99	29	58N	103	5 E
Yablonovy Khrebet	74	53	0N	114	0 E
Yablonovy Ra. = Yablonovy Khrebet	74	53	0N	114	0 E
Yacuiba	187	22	0S	63	43W
Yaizu	107	34	52N	138	20 E
Yakima	171	46	42N	120	30W
Yaku-Jima	104	30	20N	130	30 E
Yakutat	143	59	29N	139	44W
Yakutsk	75	62	5N	129	50 E
Yalgoo	120	28	16S	116	39 E
Yalinga	129	6	33N	23	10 E
Yamaga	108	33	1N	130	41 E
Yamagata	103	38	15N	140	15 E
Yamaguchi	108	34	10N	131	32 E
Yamal, Poluostrov	69	71	0N	70	0 E
Yamato	107	35	27N	139	25 E
Yamatotakada	106	34	31N	135	45 E
Yamazaki	109	35	0N	134	32 E
Yamba	116	29	26S	153	23 E
Yambol	53	42	30N	26	36 E
Yamdena	113	7	45S	131	20 E
Yame	108	33	13N	130	35 E
Yamma-Yamma, L.	118	26	16S	141	20 E
Yampa →	163	40	37N	108	59W
Yamuna →	92	25	30N	81	53 E
Yamzho Yumco	101	28	48N	90	35 E
Yana →	72	71	30N	136	0 E
Yanagawa	108	33	10N	130	24 E
Yanai	109	33	58N	132	7 E
Yanco	117	34	38S	146	27 E
Yangch'ü = Taiyuan	98	37	52N	112	33 E
Yangquan	98	37	58N	113	31 E
Yangtze Kiang = Chang Jiang →	99	31	48N	121	10 E
Yanji	98	42	59N	129	30 E
Yantai	98	37	34N	121	22 E
Yao	106	34	32N	135	36 E
Yaoundé	131	3	50N	11	35 E
Yaqui →	174	27	37N	110	39W
Yare →	25	52	36N	1	28 E
Yarensk	69	61	10N	49	8 E
Yarkand = Shache	100	38	20N	77	10 E
Yarmouth	148	43	50N	66	7W
Yaroslavl	68	57	35N	39	55 E
Yarram	117	38	29S	146	9 E
Yashiro-Jima	109	33	55N	132	15 E
Yass	117	34	49S	148	54 E
Yasugi	109	35	26N	133	15 E
Yatsushiro	108	32	30N	130	40 E
Yavari →	186	4	21S	70	2W
Yavatmal	91	20	20N	78	15 E
Yawatahama	109	33	27N	132	24 E
Yazd	85	31	55N	54	27 E
Yazoo →	169	32	35N	90	50W
Yazoo City	169	32	48N	90	28W
Ye Xian	98	37	8N	119	57 E
Yegros	191	26	20S	56	25W
Yekaterinburg	69	56	50N	60	30 E
Yelizavetgrad = Kirovograd	68	48	35N	32	20 E
Yell	30	60	35N	1	5W
Yellow Sea	99	35	0N	123	0 E
Yellowhead P.	155	52	53N	118	25W
Yellowknife	145	62	27N	114	29W
Yellowstone →	163	47	58N	103	59W
Yellowstone National Park	163	44	35N	110	0W
Yemen ■	82	15	0N	44	0 E
Yenisey →	69	71	50N	82	40 E
Yeniseyskiy Zaliv	69	72	20N	81	0 E

Name						
Yeo →	27	51	10N	3	0W	
Yeola	91	20	0N	74	30 E	
Yeovil	27	50	57N	2	38W	
Yeppoon	121	23	5S	150	47 E	
Yerevan	70	40	10N	44	31 E	
Yes Tor	27	50	41N	3	59W	
Yetman	116	28	56S	150	48 E	
Yezd = Yazd	85	31	55N	54	27 E	
Yiannitsa	54	40	46N	22	24 E	
Yibin	99	28	45N	104	32 E	
Yichang	99	30	40N	111	20 E	
Yichun	98	47	44N	128	52 E	
Yilan	99	24	51N	121	44 E	
Yinchuan	98	38	30N	106	15 E	
Yingkou	98	40	37N	122	18 E	
Yingtan	99	28	12N	117	0 E	
Yining	100	43	58N	81	10 E	
Yithion	54	36	46N	22	34 E	
Yiyang	99	28	45N	112	16 E	
Yogyakarta	111	7	49S	110	22 E	
Yōkaichiba	107	35	42N	140	33 E	
Yokkaichi	106	35	0N	136	38 E	
Yokohama	107	35	27N	139	28 E	
Yokosuka	107	35	20N	139	40 E	
Yokote	103	39	20N	140	30 E	
Yonago	109	35	25N	133	19 E	
Yoneshiro →	103	40	15N	140	15 E	
Yonezawa	103	37	57N	140	4 E	
Yongji	99	34	52N	110	28 E	
Yonkers	164	40	57N	73	51W	
York, Australia	120	31	52S	116	47 E	
York, U.K.	29	53	58N	1	7W	
York, U.S.A.	164	39	57N	76	43W	
Yorke Pen.	119	34	50S	137	40 E	
Yorkshire Wolds	29	54	0N	0	30W	
Yorkton	152	51	11N	102	28W	
Yosemite National Park	172	38	0N	119	30W	
Youghal	35	51	58N	7	51W	
Young	117	34	19S	148	18 E	
Younghusband Pen.	119	36	0S	139	25 E	
Youngstown	164	41	7N	80	41W	
Yuba City	172	39	12N	121	37W	
Yūbari	103	43	4N	141	59 E	
Yūbetsu	103	43	13N	144	5 E	
Yucatán □	177	20	50N	89	0W	
Yucatán, Canal de	178	22	0N	86	30W	
Yucatan Str. = Yucatán, Canal de	178	22	0N	86	30W	
Yuci	98	37	42N	112	46 E	
Yugoslavia ■	52	44	0N	21	0 E	
Yukon →	142	65	30N	150	0W	
Yukon Territory □	144	63	0N	135	0W	
Yuma	173	32	45N	114	37W	
Yunnan □	101	25	0N	102	30 E	
Yuribei	69	71	8N	76	58 E	
Yurimaguas	186	5	55S	76	7W	
Yushu	101	33	5N	96	55 E	
Yuzhno-Sakhalinsk	75	46	58N	142	45 E	
Yvetot	38	49	37N	0	44 E	

Z

Name						
Zaandam	40	52	26N	4	49 E	
Zabaykalskiy	74	49	40N	117	25 E	
Zabid	82	14	0N	43	10 E	
Zābol	85	31	0N	61	32 E	
Zābol □	87	32	0N	67	0 E	
Zabrze	58	50	18N	18	50 E	
Zacapa	177	14	59N	89	31W	
Zacatecas	175	22	47N	102	35W	
Zacatecas □	175	23	0N	103	0W	
Zacatecoluca	177	13	29N	88	51W	
Zadar	52	44	8N	15	14 E	
Zadetkyi Kyun	94	10	0N	98	25 E	
Zagreb	52	45	50N	16	0 E	
Zāhedān	86	29	30N	60	50 E	
Zahlah	80	33	52N	35	50 E	
Zaïre ■	134	3	0S	23	0 E	
Zaïre →	134	6	4S	12	24 E	
Zákinthos	54	37	47N	20	57 E	

Name						
Zambeze →	135	18	55S	36	4 E	
Zambezi = Zambeze →	135	18	55S	36	4 E	
Zambia ■	135	15	0S	28	0 E	
Zamboanga	112	6	59N	122	3 E	
Zamora, Mexico	175	20	0N	102	21W	
Zamora, Spain	50	41	30N	5	45W	
Zandvoort	40	52	22N	4	32 E	
Zanesville	167	39	56N	82	2W	
Zanjan	81	36	40N	48	35 E	
Zante = Zákinthos	54	37	47N	20	57 E	
Zanzibar	135	6	12S	39	12 E	
Zaouiet El-Kala = Bordj Omar Driss	127	28	10N	6	40 E	
Zaouiet Reggane	127	26	32N	0	3 E	
Zapadnaya Dvina →	68	57	4N	24	3 E	
Západné Beskydy	59	49	30N	19	0 E	
Zapala	190	39	0S	70	5W	
Zaporozhye	68	47	50N	35	10 E	
Zaragoza, Mexico	174	28	29N	100	55W	
Zaragoza, Spain	51	41	39N	0	53W	
Zaranj	87	30	55N	61	55 E	
Zaria	131	11	0N	7	40 E	
Zaruma	184	3	40S	79	38W	
Zaskar Mountains	89	33	15N	77	30 E	
Zavitinsk	75	50	10N	129	20 E	
Zaysan, Oz.	71	48	0N	83	0 E	
Zayü	101	28	48N	97	27 E	
Zduńska Wola	58	51	37N	18	59 E	
Zeebrugge	42	51	19N	3	12 E	
Zeeland □	40	51	30N	3	50 E	
Zeila	133	11	21N	43	30 E	
Zeist	40	52	5N	5	15 E	
Zemlya Frantsa Iosifa	13	81	0N	55	0 E	
Zentsüji	109	34	14N	133	47 E	
Zeya	75	53	48N	127	14 E	
Zêzere →	50	39	28N	8	20W	
Zhanghua	99	24	6N	120	29 E	
Zhangjiakou	98	40	48N	114	55 E	
Zhangzhou	99	24	30N	117	35 E	
Zhanjiang	99	21	15N	110	20 E	
Zhdanov = Mariupol	68	47	5N	37	31 E	
Zhejiang □	99	29	0N	120	0 E	
Zhengzhou	99	34	45N	113	34 E	
Zhenjiang	99	32	11N	119	26 E	
Zhenyuan	99	27	4N	108	21 E	
Zhijiang	99	27	27N	109	42 E	
Zhitomir	68	50	20N	28	40 E	
Zhumadian	99	32	59N	114	2 E	
Zhupanovo	73	53	40N	159	52 E	
Zhuzhou	99	27	49N	113	12 E	
Zibo	98	36	47N	118	3 E	
Zielona Góra	58	51	57N	15	31 E	
Zierikzee	40	51	40N	3	55 E	
Zigong	99	29	15N	104	48 E	
Zile	80	40	15N	35	52 E	
Žilina	59	49	12N	18	42 E	
Zimbabwe	137	20	16S	30	54 E	
Zimbabwe ■	137	20	0S	30	0 E	
Zinder	131	13	48N	9	0 E	
Zipaquirá	184	5	0N	74	0W	
Zitácuaro	175	19	24N	100	22W	
Zlatograd	53	41	22N	25	7 E	
Zlatoust	69	55	10N	59	40 E	
Zlín	59	49	14N	17	40 E	
Zomba	137	15	22S	35	19 E	
Zonguldak	80	41	28N	31	50 E	
Zorritos	186	3	43S	80	40W	
Zoutkamp	41	53	20N	6	18 E	
Zrenjanin	52	45	22N	20	23 E	
Zufar	83	17	40N	54	0 E	
Zug	44	47	10N	8	31 E	
Zuid-Holland □	40	52	0N	4	35 E	
Zuidhorn	41	53	15N	6	23 E	
Zungeru	131	9	48N	6	8 E	
Zunyi	99	27	42N	106	53 E	
Zürich	44	47	22N	8	32 E	
Zutphen	41	52	9N	6	12 E	
Zuwārah	127	32	58N	12	1 E	
Zvolen	59	48	33N	19	10 E	
Zwickau	43	50	43N	12	30 E	
Zwolle	41	52	31N	6	6 E	
Zyryanovsk	71	49	43N	84	20 E	